THE FASHION
BUSINESS READER

THE FASHION BUSINESS READER

EDITED BY
JOSEPH H. HANCOCK II AND ANNE PEIRSON-SMITH

BLOOMSBURY VISUAL ARTS
LONDON • NEW YORK • OXFORD • NEW DELHI • SYDNEY

BLOOMSBURY VISUAL ARTS
Bloomsbury Publishing Plc
50 Bedford Square, London, WC1B 3DP, UK
1385 Broadway, New York, NY 10018, USA

BLOOMSBURY, BLOOMSBURY VISUAL ARTS and the Diana logo are trademarks of Bloomsbury Publishing Plc

First published in Great Britain 2019

Copyright © Joseph H. Hancock II and Anne Peirson-Smith, 2019

Joseph H. Hancock II and Anne Peirson-Smith have asserted their right under the Copyright, Designs and Patents Act, 1988, to be identified as Editors of this work.

Cover design: Dani Leigh | danileighdesign.com
Cover images © Brent Luvaas

All rights reserved. No part of this publication may be reproduced or transmitted in any form or by any means, electronic or mechanical, including photocopying, recording, or any information storage or retrieval system, without prior permission in writing from the publishers.

Bloomsbury Publishing Plc does not have any control over, or responsibility for, any third-party websites referred to or in this book. All internet addresses given in this book were correct at the time of going to press. The author and publisher regret any inconvenience caused if addresses have changed or sites have ceased to exist, but can accept no responsibility for any such changes.

A catalogue record for this book is available from the British Library.

A catalog record for this book is available from the Library of Congress.

ISBN: HB: 978-1-4742-7953-6
PB: 978-1-4742-7954-3

Typeset by Deanta Global Publishing Services, Chennai, India
Printed and bound in India

To find out more about our authors and books visit www.bloomsbury.com and sign up for our newsletters.

Joseph H. Hancock II would like to dedicate this book to his mother Margaret A. Alder who encouraged him and told him he would be a success in any field if he worked hard, treated others with kindness and compassion, and above all believed in himself.

Anne Peirson-Smith would like to dedicate this book to her parents Mary and Kevin Ryder for their unconditional support and always encouraging her to question and challenge how and why things work in a particular way, which led her on the path of social and cultural enquiry.

CONTENTS

Foreword by Sean Williams — xi
Foreword by Jing Zhang — xiii
Introduction — xv
Contributors — xviii

PART I HISTORY OF FASHION AND PRODUCT DEVELOPMENT — 1

Introduction *José Blanco* — 3

1. Influence of North American Indian and First Nations dress on mainstream fashion
   Pamela C. Baker and Phyllis G. Tortora — 8
2. How New York stole modern fashion *Norma Rantisi* — 13
3. A deconstructionist perspective on menswear: A conversation with Siki Im *Joseph H. Hancock, II* — 20
4. Patrick Kelly: Fashions' great black hope *Van Dyk Lewis and Keith A. Fraley* — 26
5. Japanese conceptual fashion *Bonnie English* — 34
6. Martin Margiela: Signs of the time *Barbara Vinken* — 40

   Further reading — 46

PART II SOURCING AND MANUFACTURING — 49

Introduction *Alphonso McClendon* — 51

7. The chain store challenge *Brian Godbold* — 56
8. Connecting creativity *Luigi Maramotti* — 62
9. Buyer–supplier partnerships in the global apparel industry: A study of US buyers and Indian suppliers *Kamlesh Singh and Nancy Hodges* — 68
10. Business and industry *Colin Gale and Jasbir Kaur* — 74

    Further reading — 81

PART III SUSTAINABILITY AND SOCIAL RESPONSIBILITY 83

    Introduction *Tasha L. Lewis*   85

11 Selling whose dream? A taxonomy of aspiration in fashion imagery *Ben Barry*   93

12 Fast fashion, sustainability, and the ethical appeal of luxury brands *Annamma Joy, John F. Sherry Jr, Alladi Venkatesh, Jeff Wang, and Ricky Chan*   99

13 In Patagonia (clothing): A complicated greenness *Sharon J. Hepburn*   105

14 The sweatshop, child labor, and exploitation issues in the garment industry *Liat Smestad*   111

15 Dress and disaster: Fashioning creative responses to disaster *Valerie Rangel*   117

    Further reading   123

PART IV BRICK AND MORTAR RETAILING AND SHOPPING 125

    Introduction *Catharine Weiss*   127

16 The garment industry and retailing in Canada *Cynthia Cooper*   132

17 Creating a *Woman's Place*: The Bonwit Teller Presidency of Hortense Odlum, 1934 to 1940 *Michael Mamp and Sara Marcketti*   140

18 Stores, shoppers, and mediated images: The relational space of Uniqlo *Myles Ethan Lascity*   147

19 'Oh, honey! It's not so much the style, it's what carrying it means': Hermès bags and the transformative process *Annita Boyd*   154

    Further reading   161

PART V MEDIA AND OMNI-CHANNEL RETAILING 163

    Introduction *Nioka Wyatt*   165

20 Shooting street style in Indonesia: A photo essay *Brent Luvaas*   174

21 Co-design communities online: Turning public creativity into wearable and sellable fashions *Juanjuan Wu*   179

22 ModCloth: A case study in co-creative branding strategies *Kendra LaPolla*   186

23 A study of how small and medium-sized enterprise tailors utilize e-commerce, social media, and new 3D technological practices *Frances Ross*   193

24 Yoga, Facebook, and fandom: Examining brand devotion by lululemon customers using social media *Caroline Czajkowski and Tasha L. Lewis*   200

    Further reading   208

PART VI FASHION MERCHANDISING AND STRATEGY 211

    Introduction *Joseph H. Hancock, II* 213

25 Mappin stores: Adding an English touch to the São Paulo fashion scene *Rita Andrade* 217

26 Fashioning sports clothing as lifestyle couture *Jennifer Craik* 223

27 Co-branding strategies for luxury fashion brands: Missoni for Target
Edwina Luck, Gjoko Muratovski, and Lauren Hedley 231

28 Comme on down and choos your shoes: A study of consumer responses to the use of guest fashion designers by H&M as a co-branded fashion marketing strategy *Anne Peirson-Smith* 240

    Further reading 249

PART VII FASHION BRANDING 251

    Introduction *Veronica Manlow* 253

29 The maturation of hip-hop's menswear brands: Outfitting the urban consumer
Tasha Lewis and Natalie Gray 261

30 The habitus of Elizabeth Hurley: Celebrity, fashion, and identity branding *Lee Barron* 267

31 Creating an American mythology: A comparison of branding strategies in three fashion firms *Veronica Manlow* 278

32 Raf Simons and interdisciplinary fashion from post-punk to neo-modern *Nick Rees-Roberts* 285

33 Wishing on a star: Promoting and personifying designer collections and fashion brands
Anne Peirson-Smith 300

    Further reading 311

PART VIII FASHION COMMUNICATION 313

    Introduction *Anne Peirson-Smith* 315

34 Skivvies with the givvies: Vintage American underwear ads feature sexual innuendo between "Boys" in the brands *Bruce H. Joffe* 322

35 Magazines, the media, and Mrs Exeter *Julia Twigg* 328

36 'Nice stuff against the skin': Pleasure and spectatorship in men's underwear advertising *Paul Jobling* 336

37 The changing face(s) of the fashion magazine and the new media landscape *Pamela Church Gibson* 342

38 Production, gatekeeping, and diffusion of fashion *Yuniya Kawamura* 349

    Further reading 357

PART IX CONSUMPTION AND IDENTITY   359

    Introduction *Srikant Manchiraju*   361

39 Fashion as collective and consumer behavior *Herbert Blumer, Adam Smith, and Thorstein B. Veblen*   367

40 Fashion as cycle *Annette Lynch and Michael Strauss D.*   372

41 The high street responds: Designing for the older market *Julia Twigg*   377

42 Rebranding American men's heritage fashions through the use of visual merchandising, symbolic props and masculine iconic memes historically found in popular culture *Kevin Matthews, Joseph H. Hancock II, and Zhaohui Gu*   383

43 To have and to hold: Masculinity and the clutch bag *Benjamin L. Wild*   391

    Further reading   397

PART X GLOBAL FASHION AND REINVENTION   399

    Introduction *Brent Luvaas*   401

44 Is Australian fashion and dress distinctively Australian? *Jennifer Craik*   406

45 Secondhand clothing *Karen Tranberg Hansen*   413

46 Globalization and dress *Margaret Maynard*   419

47 Milan: The city of prêt-à-porter in a world of fast fashion *Simona Segre Reinach*   425

48 From symbols to spirit: Changing conceptions of national identity in Chinese fashion *Christine Tsui*   431

    Further reading   438

PART XI BEAUTY AND THE BODY   441

    Introduction *Myles Ethan Lascity*   443

49 Epilogue: Fashioning the body today *Susan J. Vincent*   448

50 Face value: Subversive beauty ideals in contemporary fashion marketing *Maria Mackinney-Valentin*   455

51 All ages, all races, all sexes *Joseph H. Hancock II*   463

52 Making up is masculine: The increasing cultural connections between masculinity and make-up *Janice Miller*   467

53 Hair and human identity *Sarah Cheang and Geraldine Biddle-Perry*   474

54 Outdoor pornification: Advertising heterosexuality in the streets *Leena-Maija Rossi*   480

    Further reading   487

Index   489

FOREWORD

Fashion has always been about making a statement. Each segment of fashion from the most expensive garment to the most cost conscious has the aim of speaking to a specific consumer's existence. The *Business Fashion Reader* addresses these consumer issues and more from high-end to low-end this book looks into the major issues facing the fashion industries today. Looking at all areas from an arts and humanities perspective this book takes an in-depth look at mass fashions that impact the diverse array of our daily lives. Sneakers are no different.

For over 30 years, sneakers have been a part of my life and career. They are the one consistent part of my life that has allowed me to connect with individuals from various lifestyles and in countries that I have never seen before. As a consultant, teacher, and brand/story expert who has worked for (and with) some of the biggest companies in the world, I understand how important it is to curate experiences for consumers to understand sneakers.

From the very beginning, sneakers have straddled the line between helping to enhance a person's personal performance in sport *and*, being an item we aspire to own. Over time various cultural and social movements (along with the evolution of sports) have caused sneakers to evolve in both business and fashion prominence. The divide between what I call "performance sneakers" and "lifestyle sneakers" continues to reinforce this ambiguous boundary. Performance sneakers are a part of some of the most significant moments in sports worldwide. Meanwhile, lifestyle sneakers introduce new consumers to a brand through a more "casual" lens that opens the door for someone to look further. Lifestyle sneakers have also been a part of some important moments on popular American culture. The current longstanding "athleisure" fashion trend also supports this idea as well as new sneakers at $900 US from the likes of Balenciaga.

On personal and professional observations, the sneaker industry suffers from a lack of workforce diversity. The industry is dominated by white men and lacks women and minorities. This homogenous ideology currently hinders the forward thinking and technologically advances that sneakers rely on for profits and fashion trend.

Internally, the sneaker industry has to make better efforts to find the future professionals from within their consumer base in the various cities around the world instead of hiring from outside the industry. This current hiring and talent finding method currently hinders each sneaker brand's potential to reach new heights. It also further perpetuates the myth that the sneaker industry *lacks* the viability it deserves within the greater fashion landscape.

Each day that the sneaker industry does not improve its inclusion of minorities and women in the professional ranks of its brands, is another day that it loses the opportunity to find a new way to gain new loyal customers and tell NEW stories. Those new stories and technological discoveries potentially made by minorities and women WILL lead to increased revenue and brand loyalties similar to the strides that have been made in other industries. That is why the SOLEcial Studies sneaker industry education program exists. The SOLEcial Studies mission to inspire minorities and women to consider jobs in the sneaker industry satisfies me more than obtaining any of the thousands of pairs I've owned over the years. The sneaker industry must diversify to survive. This is why *I truly enjoy the Business Fashion Reader.*

Dr. Joseph H. Hancock, II and Dr. Anne Peirson-Smith have put together a collection of essays that represent the diversity of our fashion and business world. They have search to find the diversity of scholarship that highlights what makes fashion so remarkable and I know that you will become engaged in reading this book as much as I did.

Sean Williams
Co-Founder of Obsessive Shoe Disorder/SOLEcial Studies
Consultant, Teacher and Brand/Story Expert

FOREWORD

Fashion, creativity and design do not exist in a vacuum. It is one of the most global and early to globalize industries, as well as a trillion dollar juggernaut. Fashion ties together a complex network of cultural values and heritage, personal identity, modern tribalism and rebellion. It speaks not only to the high end runways of the big four fashion weeks, but also how the white t-shirt and blue jean became the American (and soon Western) casual uniform.

Fashion has always edged and expressed major movements in society. Today it might be the streetwear and athleisure boom, decades earlier it was thigh skimming boots and miniskirts of London's swinging 60s to China's Communist Revolution and the Mao suit that became ubiquitous in its wake. Coverage of these shifts in media is an important record of changing identities being manifest.

There's always business and consumer trend analysis to give an overview of how money is flowing and through whom. But, *The Business Fashion Reader* will remind you that the human agents in fashion are not only consumers but also creators, and sometimes both. This offers a welcome antidote to the skewed view of fashion often portrayed in media.

My start in writing and journalism coincided with the sharp surge in fashion's mass cultural appeal in the late 90s and early 2000s. I think that this was in part due to fast fashion business model supported by tech and mass manufacturing, bolstered by the flush of magazines that fed public desire for new and exciting ways to dress. Fashion, runway-inspired, always changing and suddenly widely accessible to almost all.

These exciting and heady times came, suddenly bolstered by the digital boom, which of course, changed everything. Along with print media, digitalization of fashion content and later on social media would further democratize and partly demystify fashion. It's the most important conduit for the public to learn about fashion, to formulate ideas and educate on a sector of design that can be rather opaque. Though as much as there's the urge to intellectualise beyond the simple reports, most people today are more into clicking on sensational "listicles" rather than reading in-depth essays or profiles.

As the sheer volume of content grows, and the cacophony of voices gets louder, it's ever more important to cultivate a respected, distinctive voice in fashion journalism. Clever, researched opinions fortunately still count in the world of Instagram models and paid for posts/features. I've always found it important to balance the fun and frivolous with more critical and in depth coverage. After all, the sheer joy and delight, the aesthetic lure, is fundamental to fashion's powerful appeal.

In just the 12 years I've been writing about fashion, the change in how we work has been huge. I didn't study fashion but took a BSc in Psychology and then a MA in Visual and Material Culture (Anthropology), so I suppose this background informs my take – which is interdisciplinary by nature. Texts such as the *Business Fashion Reader* will be invaluable in providing people with an all round view of a complex and often mystifying industry.

Perhaps we've reached peak fashion in regards to surface level, celebrity style content – more and more readers are demanding to be let in on the good, the bad and the ugly parts of the machine.

There's also the criticism that a lot of fashion media has become too myopic, written with too many insider references and irrelevant to the lay person. That is a valid point, and I feel that fashion needs to turn back to its wider cultural roots, become again more connected to the world at large in order to gain back some authenticity. Luxury brands drive exclusivity (by their nature and price point) but also make bold statements about what's current and "now", with the ability to make fashion more inclusive of minorities.

Coverage of the diversity problem has (in some markets at least) driven more inclusive developments. Exposes of intern/employee maltreatment opened eyes towards an endemic problem under the glamorous façade. Social media helped expose copycat cultures and build rising stars. A rising eco-consciousness will further impact on how fashion is made.

So, consumption of fashion and brands can be political in its statement, as well as a projection of personal sartorial style. Just look at the rise of Punk, Rock n roll styles, 80s maximalism, vintage or how fashion evolves in post-Socialist states (this is having a particular impact on European trends).

The rise of Asia, and China in particular, can't be ignored. Power dynamic shifts as the world's manufacturing hub becomes its luxury consumption hub have a thrilling to report on as a journalist working in the region. You have front and centre seats to the unfolding show.

What about those stories of Chinese millionaires clearing out stores in one shopping trip, or the phenomenon of the South Korean K-wave in fashion? They show how fast change is in this mercurial industry. But just as interesting is analysis of India, as one of few emerging world powers that hasn't totally bought into the default Western style, instead remaining largely faithful to their traditional dress. This kind of storytelling reveals and represents a little slice of fashion as a whole, complex cultural paradigm, full of human potential, economy, creativity, desire and occasionally, also suffering.

Jing Zhang
Senior Fashion Editor Culture and Fashion
South China Morning Post

INTRODUCTION

THE BUSINESS FASHION READER

"Fashion is not necessarily about labels. It's not about brands. It's about something else that comes from within you." **Ralph Lauren**

"Retail is a customer business. You're trying to take care of the customer — solve something for the customer. And there's no way to learn that in the classroom or in the corner office, or away from the customer. You've got to be in front of the customer." **Erik Nordstrom, President, Nordstrom**

"Fashion is part of the daily air and it changes all the time, with all the events. You can even see the approaching of a revolution in clothes. You can see and feel everything in clothes." **Diana Vreeland**

"What you wear is how you present yourself to the world, especially today, when human contacts are so quick. Fashion is instant language." **Miuccia Prada**

THE RATIONALE

This text is the first reader on the subject of the fashion business from production to consumption across the supply chain. Bringing together a rich interdisciplinary and international range of writings in one volume, *The Business Fashion Reader* aims to provide scholars and students with the authoritative global and competitive anthology of both classic and cutting-edge texts.

The reader presents a range of interdisciplinary and global perspectives allowing readers to examine the business of fashion from a range of creative, theoretical and practical approaches. Studies relating to fashion design, production, consumption, merchandising, social media, branding, retailing, the body and fashion reinvention are often based exclusively on social science and positivist approaches to understanding consumers. And in the dawn of analytics and Big Data driving the fashion industry these attempts at understanding consumers may appear to be the only way to moving ahead in fashion, but we disagree. By highlighting a greater diversity of approaches, and using the arts and humanities as our conceptual base, this text demonstrates that it is just as important for understanding the qualitative meanings underlying the business of fashion and how considerations of culture and society have enabled the fashion sector to historically evolve into the giant industry that it is today. The fashion system is premised on the production of material goods both individually and collectively and symbolic representations via verbal, visual and multi-sensory modes as an instant and universal language. As such, it warrants a more nuanced investigation that can arguably only be afforded by the in-depth, articles presented by fashion writers in this reader.

This reader discusses various areas of the fashion business in a more approachable manner for those who are scholars of fashion, clothing, textiles, apparel and the body by repackaging them in a manner that is more relatable and understandable. Extracting texts from groundbreaking journal articles, book chapters, and other key writings, this reader engages with fresh methodological approaches. Each segment of the reader is comprised of approximately four to five articles that have been edited by an expert scholar with the most important passages and concepts highlighted for you. Each part is introduced by one of our experts contextualizing the articles found in each section highlighting their importance in fashion business scholarship. For those readers wanting more in a particular area a Further Readings area has been attached to each part of the text for additional study.

IMPORTANT POINTS AND HOW TO USE THIS READER

Below we have bulleted some key points of this reader and how you can either use it on your own as preparatory into the world of the business of fashion or to utilize it as an instructor of a class.

- The first reader to focus on theory and practice relating to the business of fashion, the book contains cutting-edge readings from top scholars around the globe.
- Covers all the key areas of the fashion business: design, production, sustainability, economics, supply chain, branding, retail, fashion communications, public relations, merchandising, marketing, consumption, fashion evolution and reinvention and new to this volume, issues surrounding the body and fashion.
- Contributing editors represent diversity reflecting the fashion and consumption disciplines. Each comes from various nationalities, ethnicities, genders, sexual orientations, lifestyles, and fashion experiences (both academic and practice based) allowing for this reader to become not only interdisciplinary, but also a multicultural world view to engage everyone in the complexities of the fashion system.
- The articles in this reader represent various types of colleges, universities, from land grant universities to private colleges and from urban to rural campuses across the globe.
- With introductions to every part, approachable articles, plus guides to further reading, *The Business Fashion Reader*, is the ideal course text for both undergraduate and graduate students.
- *The Business Fashion Reader* is the perfect desk reference reader for both new and advanced scholars researching all areas of the fashion industry.
- Issues concerning gender, identity, representation, diversity, sexuality, religion, age, inclusivity and other indicators of what it means to be human in the context of the fashion business will be addressed, including the emotions and memory that fashion evokes and the real lives that it encounters and impacts upon from workers to consumers along the value chain.
- Is the "go to" reader for professors, scholars and academics to understand the arts and humanities approaches to research methods in fashion from a business perspective.
- Most importantly, *The Business Fashion Reader* serves as the beginning point for all who want to know more about how the industry has been viewed from the world of academia and allows the reader to see an array of research and how they connect and are applied to the world of fashion to reveal meaningful social insights.

Both Joseph H. Hancock II and Anne Peirson-Smith would like to thank everyone at Bloomsbury who went on this long journey to create such a fantastic book. They include Frances Arnold, Anna Wright, Georgia Kennedy, Ariadne Godwin, Pari Thomson, and Lauren Crisp. We would also like to thank each and every one of our contributors who made this volume a success, because without them this book would have not been such an extraordinary composition of articles.

Enjoy!

Joseph H. Hancock II, PhD.   Anne Peirson-Smith, PhD.

CONTRIBUTORS

José Blanco F., PhD is an Associate Professor in the Department of Fashion Merchandising and Design at Dominican University in River Forest, Illinois. He is also Vice-President for Education at Costume Society of America. His research focuses on dress and popular culture in the second half of the twentieth century, with an emphasis on male fashion. He is interested in fashion and visual culture in Latin America. Jose is the general editor of the four-volume encyclopedia *Clothing and Fashion: American Fashion from Head to Toe*. He has co-authored with Raúl J. Vázquez-López several articles and book chapters on Puerto Rican dress, costume, and fashion.

Joseph "Joe" Henry Hancock, II, PhD. is an award winning professor and an international authority in the area of fashion branding as a form of storytelling. He started in academia after 20 years in the retailing industry having worked for such legendary brands as The Gap Incorporated, The Limited Corporation and Target Corporation. He released his book *Brand/Story: Ralph, Vera, Johnny, Billy and Other Adventures in Fashion Branding* (2009) and the 2nd Edition in 2016 called *Brand/Story: Explorations and Cases in Fashion Branding* both by Bloomsbury. He has completed three coedited books *Fashion in Popular Culture* (2013), *Global Fashion Brands* (2014) and *Cotton: Companies, Fashion and The Fabric of Our Lives* (2016) with Intellect Publishing through The University of Chicago Press. Dr. Hancock is the principal editor of the peer-reviewed journal *Fashion, Style and Popular Culture* (Intellect Publishers) and is the former Executive Director for Events for the Popular Culture/American Culture Associations (PCA/ACA). He has been awarded Drexel's 2008 Steinbright Cooperative Career Center's faculty of the year, the 2011 Stanley J. Gwiazda Professorship Award and the Pennoni Honors College Teaching Award in 2017.

Myles Ethan Lascity, PhD. is an Assistant Professor of Journalism and Director of the Fashion Media program at Southern Methodist University, Dallas, Texas. He earned his doctorate in Communication, Culture and Media at Drexel University and holds a Master's in Costume Studies from New York University. His research has been published in various volumes and journals, including *Fashion Practice*, *Fashion Theory*, *Fashion, Style and Popular Culture* and *Film, Fashion and Consumption*.

Tasha Lewis, PhD. is an Associate Professor in the Department of Fiber Science and Apparel Design at Cornell University where she teaches in the area of fashion design management. Her research interests include the disruptive impact of technology in the apparel industry, the behavior of fashion brands, the intersection of global and domestic apparel manufacturing issues, and the significance of social responsibility and sustainability throughout the apparel supply chain. Dr. Lewis has also worked in the apparel industry in areas of production, sourcing, and retail operations and maintains ongoing contact with industry professionals to inform her research and teaching.

Brent Luvaas, PhD. is Associate Professor of Global Studies and Modern Languages at Drexel University. A visual and cultural anthropologist, his work examines the impacts of digital technologies on fashion, music, and photography. He has published in numerous peer-reviewed journals, including *Cultural Anthropology, Visual Anthropology Review, Ethnography, Fashion Theory, Fashion Studies,* and *The International Journal of Fashion Studies*, and is the author of the books *Street Style: An Ethnography of Fashion Blogging* (Bloomsbury 2016) and *DIY Style: Fashion, Music, and Global Digital Cultures* (Berg 2012). He is the also the photographer and blogger behind Urban Fieldnotes (www.urbanfieldnotes.com).

Srikant Manchiraju, PhD is an Assistant Professor at Florida State University's Jim Moran School of Entrepreneurship. Dr. Manchiraju is also a faculty affiliate of Florida State University's Family Institute. Broadly speaking, his research and teaching interests are related to marketing and psychology. He has published several book chapters, conference proceedings, and research journal articles. He volunteers for various professional organizations on a regular basis.

Veronica Manlow, PhD is an Associate Professor in the Business Management Department of the Koppelman School of Business at Brooklyn College. The design, production and marketing of mass-marketed and luxury products is of interest to Veronica Manlow. Her research has been focused on the creative process of fashion design and branding. She has written on and studied the area of self-presentation, identity and communication from a social psychological and semiotic standpoint. Her current research involves an investigation of the work performed by luxury salespersons, and she is doing ethnographic and interview research of artisans and workers in small luxury firms and large conglomerates. She wrote *Designing Clothes* in which she explored the creative process of fashion design as it unfolds in corporate fashion brands such as Tommy Hilfiger and Ralph Lauren. She co-edited Global Fashion Brands: Style, Luxury, History with Joe Hancock, Gjoko Muratovski and Anne Peirson-Smith. She is one of the organizers of the In Pursuit of Luxury Conference.

Alphonso McClendon is an Associate Professor of Design and Merchandising at Drexel University. He has authored *Fashion and Jazz* (Bloomsbury 2015) and *Fashionable Addiction* (Intellect 2013). McClendon has developed curriculum using digital design, product lifecycle management, and enterprise resource planning software including AIMS360, ApparelMagic, PAD System, and Shima Seiki. Prior to joining Drexel University, McClendon was a Director of Product Design at Nautica. He traveled extensively in Taiwan, China, and Japan for design research, product development, and sourcing. McClendon's career has traversed accounting, design, and retail with positions at Dow Corning, 3M, Bachrach, Izod, and Phillips Van-Heusen.

Anne Peirson-Smith, PhD is Assistant Professor at City University of Hong Kong. She teaches and researches fashion communication, public relations, advertising, popular culture and the creative industries and has published widely on these topics. She has a professional background in public relations and branding and is the co-author of *Public Relations in Asia Pacific: Communicating Effectively Across Cultures,* (John Wiley, 2009), *Global Fashion Brands: Style, Luxury and History* (Intellect, 2014) and *Global Fashion: Narratives: Clothing Communication, Style Statements and Brand Storytelling* (Intellect, 2018). She is associate editor for the *Journal of Fashion, Style and Popular Culture* (Intellect) and the *Journal of Global Fashion Marketing* (Taylor and Francis).

Catharine Weiss, PhD has taught both Fashion Merchandising and Communications for Lasell College for over 10 years. She spent 15+ years working in New York and Boston for companies such as Liz Claiborne, Gucci, Ferragamo, Priscilla of Boston, and The Museum of Fine Arts. Her expertise lies in managing wholesale divisions in both sales and marketing management. She was past Vice President of Collegiate for the American Marketing

Association's Boston Chapter, and is the faculty advisor for the National Retail Federation's collegiate chapter at Lasell. Weiss' scholarship has focused on the new science of neuromarketing and has spoken at several conferences on the subject. She is also involved with several publishers as a reviewer, guest editor and writer. She continues her research in areas such as retail analytics, brand management, and new technologies such as VR and AR as vehicles for both sales and marketing delivery. She is also a part time ski instructor, avid boater, cyclist and traveler with her 14 year old daughter.

Sean Williams is a born and raised in Brooklyn, New York and fell in love with sneakers at the age of 13. By age 16, with a few years of work experience under his belt he began buying sneakers with his own money (no longer asking mom for the latest and freshest kicks). Having purchased thousands of pairs of sneakers over the years his love of sneakers has never completely died. It has simply transformed. In 2007, OSD (Obsessive Sneaker Disorder) was founded by long time friend Dee Wells and Williams was asked to become a part of the historical movement. Williams has been featured in various noteworthy television shows, publications, and websites, such as NBC's The Today Show, Maxim magazine, Slate.com, and Sneaker Freaker. In 2012, Williams and his partner Dee made the list of "50 Most Influential People in Sneakers Right Now" published by Complex magazine. Williams also teaches OSD's SOLEcial Studies, which is an education program that prepares people all over the world for potential jobs and their businesses in the athletic footwear business.

Nioka Wyatt is an Associate Professor and Program Director for the Fashion Merchandising and Management department at Jefferson University. Nioka developed the short course to China for students to tour production facilities, global retail operations, and engage in intercultural business activities. She teaches graduate and undergraduate courses throughout the supply chain. Having worked for QVC, Nioka has extensive knowledge in fashion merchandising and product development for a plethora of consumer products, such as apparel, home textiles, footwear, and accessories. Nioka serves as a consultant in product development and omni-channel retailing. Nioka's research merges culture, experiential learning, and product development. Her most recent project involved students developing product extensions for Meryl Diamond and Associates, Isaac Mizrahi, and Halston.

Jing Zhang raised in the UK, and based between Shanghai, Jing Zhang is the Editor-at-Large of Prestige HK, Senior Correspondent at the South China Morning Post (SCMP) and a Contributing Editor at NowFashion.com. Prior to this, she was the Fashion Editor at the SCMP for 7 years, covering the global fashion circuit as well as Asia's growing scene. Before that she edited the pioneering, bilingual WestEast Magazine. She's has degrees in Psychology and Anthropology, both from University College London. Her passions and interests include philosophy, visual arts, ancient architectures and politics. She is also a visual and strategy consultant for lifestyle/style companies in the China market.

PART I
History of Fashion and Product Development

Figure 1 Photo Courtesy of Brent Luvaas.
Source: Brent Luvaas

INTRODUCTION

José Blanco

THE (SOMEWHAT) UNTOLD HISTORY OF FASHION AS A BUSINESS

The essays included in this chapter present a wealth of research on the history of fashion and product development. The readings, more specifically, discuss the history of fashion as a business enterprise by looking analytically—and often critically—into the practice of those who conceive, manufacture, and sell fashion.

There are layers of meaning in a fashion product's history from concept and design to sourcing and manufacturing, promotion and retailing, and practices of consumption and disposal. Each step of that process is part of the history of every single fashion item from a pair of H&M socks to a Tom Ford suit. The truth is that we—as both researchers and consumers—know very little about manufacturers' and designers' intentions and motivations for the creation of specific products and lines; the secrets of the trade are often well kept by an industry weary of knockoffs, trademark counterfeiting, and ethical concerns regarding the impact of the fashion industry on the natural and social environment. Researchers investigating the history of fashion business practices gain access to new levels of meaning about the intentions of the creator by exploring primary sources that include designer and manufacturer interviews, business archives, extant pieces, and original reactions and interpretations from individuals involved in the creation, promotion, and retail of fashion products. The search for meaning in the history of the fashion business must, however, look beyond positivist research approaches that assume the supremacy of business data in historic contexts and ignore social and cultural historic variables that are either not fully quantifiable or difficult to quantify.

The archives of fashion businesses around the world provide a never-ending source of material about fashion business history. They can reveal the untold stories of those who participated in the process, particularly the métiers, seamstresses, tailors, fit models, and many others meant to remain hidden behind the scenes.

SWEEPING LITERATURE REVIEWS OF FASHION HISTORY

The goal of this introduction is not to include a comprehensive list of literature on the history of fashion and product development, nor a review of methods and themes. For recent sweeping reviews of the field see for instance Heike Jenss' introduction to her edited volume *Fashion Studies: Research Methods, Sites, and Practices* (2016) where she discusses evolving research interests and approaches in fashion studies including an excellent discussion of historical roots and routes. See also *The Handbook of Fashion Studies* (Black et al., 2013) particularly Section 1: Fashion/Dress and Time. In an essay there, Lou Taylor discusses literature in the field of dress history including recent material covering social and economic histories of the fashion business, dress and ethnography, and oral history and testimony. In the same volume, Regina Lee Blaszczyk reviews research on business practices that were meant to be hidden from public view but have, in recent years, become intrinsic to research in fashion history. Blaszczyk's essay also presents "several examples of behind-the-scenes business activities to demonstrate why a deeper historical understanding of processes such as design and marketing is crucial to the advancement of the discipline of fashion studies" (181). Blaszczyk insists that although fashion sociologists have begun to explore the power of the press influencing consumer choices through history, the field is still ripe for analysis. She adds: "Until the business records of editors, photographers, and publishers enter public domain, scholars need to think creatively about how to access the hidden spaces of the great publicity machine that backs the fashion industry" (193). Finally, Charlotte Nicklas and Annabella Pollen discuss terms, themes, and research tools and methodologies in the introduction to their edited volume *Dress History: New Directions in Theory and Practice* (2015), although the emphasis here is more on dress history and not on the history of fashion as a business.

E PLURIBUS UNUM? OF METHODOLOGIES AND DISCIPLINES

Fashion and dress historians traditionally approached their subject matter either by performing an analysis of specific objects, or by studying the context for the development and use of those objects. Fashion and dress scholarship in the last few decades has advocated for a variety of methods that combine both approaches, leading to critical studies that do not necessarily privilege objects over context or vice versa. Museums have been the traditional "temples" for object-based studies with a variety of collections that emphasize either local or national history, elements related to materials and construction, the impact on popular culture, or the aesthetic and artistic value of the fashion objects. Exhibitions addressing business aspects of the fashion world are rare and usually emphasize brands or stores that no longer exist, thus often imbuing the shows with a sense of nostalgia that does not pay proper attention to the actual history of the fashion enterprises themselves. Museums are often reluctant to display the work of brands and establishments that are still active due to concerns about the exhibitions appearing as promotional tools for those businesses. The Fashion and Textile Museum in London has presented several exhibitions exploring the business side of fashion including *Missoni Art Colour* (2016), *Made in Britain: Walsh Trainers* (2014) and *Tommy Nutter – Rebel on the Row* (2011). The Jewish Museum in London hosted *Moses, Mods and Mr Fish: The Menswear Revolution* tracing connections between the Jewish community and menswear design and production in Britain. Some exhibitions at the Museum at FIT in New York have incorporated content related to business practices, including *Faking It: Originals, Copies, and Counterfeits* (2015) and *Trend-ology* (2014), which examined the sources from which fashion trends have developed historically.

An ongoing debate among scholars relates to the convergence of diverse disciplines into a still nascent field of fashion and dress history. With researchers coming from a variety of disciplines such as history, art, museology, textile conservation, fashion design, retail merchandising, communications, theater, sociology, anthropology, and semiotics, the standing question is how to solidly establish an area of study that has been interdisciplinary or multidisciplinary from its inception. The convergence of these disciplines implies—or perhaps demands—more openness to a variety of methods as different scholars may look at the same historic event, moment, trend, style, or influencer in search of different information. The assumption that quantitative methods could provide a sole and objective interpretation of phenomena in the history of fashion led for decades to a plethora of studies that supported the existence of fixed and unchangeable meaning. As scholars ventured into different methods, a more complex web of meanings began to emerge, elucidating that commonly accepted interpretations of the history of the fashion business could be questioned and expanded. Qualitative research seeks to inductively develop knowledge to understand how history—in our case the history of fashion and product development—was constructed from different perspectives and angles and with a variety of meanings, and how, then, said history can be deconstructed into multiple meanings and world views by looking at it through a variety of lenses. Interpretative, non-positivist approaches allowed a new group of fashion historians to question assumptions and conclusions accepted as theoretically sound and even as normative. By moving beyond mere "objective" data, the field has opened itself to the existence of diverse approaches. The story of a retail business, for instance, is very different if told from the point of view of the customer, the retailer itself, the investor, or those actually involved in the day-to-day operations.

Jonathan Faiers (2015) discusses some pioneering work in dress history as "indisciplinary" and argues that many of these projects ignored the need of being part of one or several disciplines and simply took to task an analysis of fashion or dress that was less concerned with definitions and finding alliances to disciplines and, thus, was more flexible and indeterminate. In that sense, Faiers –albeit aware of the danger of an approach that can lead to what he calls "unspecific and inconclusive pluralism" (23)—urges researchers to carry on with their work without focusing on the need to "create" a common field or finding common methodologies and theories.

THE GLOBAL FASHION BUSINESS

Research on fashion history published in English has emphasized developments in Paris, London, New York, and Milan, the "traditional" fashion capitals central to the development of global fashion systems. For instance, Norma Rantisi, in an excerpt included in this chapter, narrates how New York became a center for fashion partly due to the physical proximity by a number of commercial and cultural institutions. The essay by Nicola White included in this chapter reviews the connection between Italian identity and a nascent fashion industry in Italy in the two decades following World War II. The analysis is based partly on descriptions of extant pieces at museums with the author exploring Italian craftsmanship and construction to observe how the "style" of such objects—made mostly for consumption of the Italian elite—ends up generating a distinct Italian look that will eventually achieve international recognition.

A pressing challenge, however, lies in tackling the exploration of geographies that expand beyond those cities and overcomes the assumption that knowledge of the history of the fashion business in Europe and North America is of higher relevance to fashion historians than a more complex understanding of global developments of the fashion business through history. Studies on colonialism, post-colonialism, and globalization, for instance, have much to gain from looking at practices of trade, distribution, and consumption of global fashion products. This urgency also expands to research addressing how groups that are otherwise under-represented in the fashion industry have developed their own products and practices. In another essay included in this chapter, Phyllis G. Tortora and Pamela C. Baker discuss influences of First Nation and North American Indian groups on mainstream fashion, including efforts by designers from these groups to create dress (and art) items that reflect their cultural identity and tell their own story. The reading also raises—but does not fully address—concerns with cultural appropriation by designers and brands that use global and minority cultural heritage for profit.

THE MATERIAL CULTURE OF THE BUSINESS OF FASHION

Fashion objects are ripe with meaning beyond their commercial value. Material culture studies analyze how fashion objects take on meaning when individuals use them to interact with their culture and society. The work of Susanne Küchler and Daniel Miller (2005) has been central to the development of material culture studies in textiles and fashion. They argue that clothes, as material culture objects, are complex and have agency themselves in what constitutes their lives, cosmologies, reasons, causes and effects. The materiality of these objects and our relationships to them is explored in terms of development, production, construction, manufacturing, textiles processing, design, and retailing, as well as in terms of consumer usage and post-usage, paying close attention to the relations between humans, objects, and their social and cultural context.

Lou Taylor (2013) explains that "material culture approaches to the study of dress focus on its design, manufacture, retailing, and consumption and on the end life of objects of clothing, in order to finally speculate on themes such as past and present social hierarchies; histories of making, manufacturing, and trading; and the cultural gendered meaning of specific garments to wearers, to communities, and indeed to nations, past and present" (29). In that sense, material culture studies also expand to research on consumption and consumer behavior that look, for instance, into historic acceptance and rejection of innovations from consumers based on prevalent notions of taste and assessments of quality and how manufactures developed products to align with consumers' perceptions of taste and quality at the time. And yet, the materiality of the business of fashion is still full of unexplored sources. What lies behind decisions made by fashion designers and retailers though history in terms of visual merchandising and store design? How is the meaning ascribed to mannequins, props, and store fixtures connected to visual culture trends of the period and how is the meaning of these objects connected to cultural and social identities?

The excerpt by Barbara Vinken included in this chapter is a perfect example of a careful material culture analysis, where the author captures Belgian designer Martin Margiela by decoding specific pieces created during the height of his practice in the 1990s. Vinken looks not only at "what is there" such as construction (or deconstruction) details but also at the empty spaces left by what Margiela omits: label, a brand name. Bonnie English also addresses material culture by discussing Japanese conceptual fashion and the cross-cultural influences at work in the creations of Issey Miyake, Rei Kawakubo, and Yohji Yamamoto. English argues that their creations offer a unique expression of creativity because they are contextualized by a stylistic philosophy that favors simplicity and naturalness. Vinken and English perform systematic examinations of primary sources and identify patterns and themes in the work of these designers that reveal how fashion creations are related to other aesthetic and social discourses.

OF CASE STUDIES, AUTO-ETHNOGRAPHIES, AND CRITICAL RESEARCH

Case studies on specific designers, manufacturers, and retailers help define patterns and connections in the history of the industry. Research into fashion businesses' archives has only on occasion explored material coming from first person accounts narrating the experiences of individuals engaged in the fashion industry. These, along with interviews and focus groups conducted with former and current employees can generate more detailed narratives of the history of fashion as a business. In this chapter, for instance, Joseph H. Hancock II interviews designer Siki Im, motivating the designer to reflect on his own career and creative process. Oral histories are essential to the effort of collecting more complex stories on how the business of fashion was impacted by issues of gender, race, ethnicity, and sexual orientation. Personal narratives from the industry could and should also make use of auto-ethnography—where a person reflects on a specific theme or issue but contextualized by self-experience. Auto-ethnography—a methodology widely embraced by feminist writers, queer researchers, and minority authors—helps turn attention from observer to observed and effectively reclassify and re-contextualize assumptions about the creation, manufacturing, retailing, and promotion of fashion and fashion-related products with "insider" information about processes and decisions, as well as day-to-day operations including the experiences of tailors, seamstresses, accessory artisans, sales representatives, store managers, etc.

Critical scholarship, when applied to fashion history, reviews information from the past to critique both the past and the present and motivate new interpretations of accepted myths connected to fashion. In this chapter, Van Dyk Lewis and Keith A. Fraley "unpack" Patrick Kelly's oeuvre, analyzing it as a political and social device placed in and from a particular position of marginalization of African Americans in the United States. Critical scholarship explores the possibility of debunking or exposing issues related to class, power, discrimination, and social justice that have been largely ignored in the history of fashion. The ultimate goal is to positively affect the human condition by understanding the maladies of the past and avoiding them in the present and future. As Susan B. Kaiser and Denise Nicole Green (2016) argue: "Critical philosophical approaches do not necessarily claim to be 'objective' in perspective: Marxist, feminist, critical race, and queer theories highlight the inequalities associated with cultural and political histories, as well as the present, and there is a stated desire to foster social justice across the categories of class, race, gender, sexuality, and other subject positions" (165).

Case studies, oral histories, auto-ethnography, and critical scholarship can further open the field to voices that are largely absent from the discourse of fashion history while also helping expand the emphasis of research beyond

Europe and North America and acknowledge the negative economic, political, and even geographic impact that the fashion industry has had through history. Qualitative approaches are essential in revising meanings assigned to the history of fashion and the business of fashion. As the essays included in this chapter suggest, the history of the business of fashion and product development is rich and intriguing. Whether it is approached from one or several disciplines, with one or more research methodologies, or perhaps from conflicting methodologies and theoretical standpoints, the field offers seemingly endless research paths into business practices within an expanding global network. Exploring the fashion business in new geographies also enriches our knowledge of other aesthetics and lifestyles, the practices of under-represented groups, and the untold stories left behind by the material culture of fashion as a business enterprise.

References

Black, Sandy, Amy de la Haye, Joanne Entwistle, Agnès Rocamora, Regina A. Root, and Helen Thomas. *The Handbook of Fashion Studies*. London: Bloomsbury, 2013.

Blaszczyk, Regina Lee. "The Hidden Spaces of Fashion Production." In *The Handbook of Fashion Studies*, edited by Sandy Black, Amy de la Haye, Joanne Entwistle, Agnès Rocamora, Regina A. Root, and Helen Thomas, 181–196. London: Bloomsbury, 2013.

Faiers, Jonathan. "Dress Thinking: Disciplines and Indisciplinarity." In *Dress History: New Directions in Theory and Practice*, edited by Charlotte Nicklas and Annebella Pollen, 15–32. London: Bloomsbury, 2015.

Jenss, Heike (ed). *Fashion Studies: Research Methods, Sites and Practices*. London: Bloomsbury, 2016.

Kaiser, Susan B. and Denise Nicole Green. "Mixing Qualitative and Quantitative Methods in Fashion Studies: Philosophical Underpinnings and Multiple Masculinities." In *Fashion Studies: Research Methods, Sites and Practices*, edited by Heike Jenss, 160–180. London: Bloomsbury, 2016.

Küchler, Susanne and Daniel Miller (eds.) *Clothing as Material Culture*. Oxford: Berg, 2005.

Nicklas, Charlotte and Annebella Pollen. *Dress History: New Directions in Theory and Practice*. London: Bloomsbury, 2015.

Taylor, Lou. "Fashion and Dress History: Theoretical and Methodological Approaches." In *The Handbook of Fashion Studies*, edited by Sandy Black, Amy de la Haye, Joanne Entwistle, Agnès Rocamora, Regina A. Root, and Helen Thomas, 17–22. London: Bloomsbury, 2013.

1

INFLUENCE OF NORTH AMERICAN INDIAN AND FIRST NATIONS DRESS ON MAINSTREAM FASHION

Pamela C. Baker and Phyllis G. Tortora[1]

Fashion designers of First Nations and North American Indian ancestry began to feel confident about being referred to as fashion designers only by the early 1970s. Fashion has not always been important to indigenous people, but telling a story has. Through their work these designers believe they are telling the story of their people; they are passionate about their work and especially passionate about how it supports their communities. The difference between North American aboriginal design and mainstream design within the fashion industry is that these designers intend to reflect their own culture, identity, and individual rights to use traditional art. Many Indian designers are knowledgeable about the meanings behind clan and tribal designs that relate to their rights and their ancestry. For example, First Nations designers from Canada speak of strong ties with their ancestors, especially their grandparents, and they say that they see it as their duty to find ways to instill pride in the younger generations by reviving the culture and traditions of their people.

Some designers describe much of their work as "wearable art." The designs that they create for customers reflect aboriginal art. It has been estimated that 90 percent of these designers create custom orders and have little or no focus on mass production. When commissioned to design a piece for a customer, these artists are not just taking directions from the customer; they are also including a touch of their culture in the piece. Sometimes they may be commissioned to replicate a fabulous traditional piece.

Designers do not ignore mainstream Western fashion and European design, because the overall trends for what is new for the next season tend to originate there. Designers do the research necessary to keep current the fashions that incorporate their art. As relative newcomers to producing fashionable items, many North American Indian and First Nations designers are only just learning to work as entrepreneurs; the Canadian and U.S. ways of doing business are new to them. Access to education was limited for most of the parents and grandparents of the present designers. The previous generations of First Nations people in Canada were allowed to go to school only until the eighth grade and could not go on to higher education. In the United States, educational policies were directed toward trying to use schools to turn Indian children into "Americans" and toward erasing their language and culture.

BORROWING INDIAN DESIGNS AND IDEAS FOR FASHIONABLE DRESS

The earliest contacts between North American Indians and Europeans led Europeans to adopt some elements of the dress they saw in native communities. The materials from which Indian dress was made or with which it was decorated were especially interesting to them. Europeans prized fur from beaver for use in making felt for hats, and in the Pacific Northwest, the Russians harvested otter skins for the China trade, nearly wiping out the otters in the process. Deerskin

---

[1] From Pamela Barker and C Phyllis Tortora, Influence of North American Indian and First Nations Dress on Mainstream Fashion, Berg Fashion Library.

garments were a practical alternative for explorers, and eventually fringed deerskin or leather became a hallmark of the stereotypical cowboy dress. European shoemakers quickly added moccasins, a style new to them, to the types of shoes they produced. These have continued to be a fashionable foot covering ever since. To this day, *blanket coats,* originally made from blankets obtained in trade by native people in the early days of European settlement, can be bought in both the United States and Canada.

Indian design motifs from both North and South America have become part of the repertory of decoration in some art movements. The *art deco style* of the 1920s and 1930s is particularly notable in this regard. Decorative elements in some art deco architecture (especially in cities in the southwestern United States), interior design, and textiles include motifs that derive from North American Indian and First Nations ornament. In the early twentieth century, U.S. fashion designers were seeking to establish something that could be seen as a truly "American" fashion, in contrast with the European and Parisian focus that predominated. Art historian Mary Donahue, in an article published on the Internet, has described how designers and museums collaborated because the museums allowed the designers access to their collections of artifacts and artworks in their North American Indian collections. She reports that in displays of dress in an exhibit at the American Museum of Natural History in 1919 called Exhibition of Industrial Art in Textiles and Costumes, designers were identified as basing designs on ornament and style from "Plains Indians," "patterns and styles associated with the Northwest Coast and Plains Indians shirts," and items described as "Pueblan." A bead company identified Woodlands traditions in displaying "Modern Uses of Beads in Dress Accessories." Donahue also notes that it is possible to find "blouses reminiscent of Plains Indians shirts and bathrobes inspired by Pueblan textiles" from 1918 to the 1920s in the Sears mail order catalog.

Sometimes an individual has been responsible for stimulating interest in North American Indian styles. Millicent Rogers, heiress to the Standard Oil fortune, spent much of her life in New Mexico. She was one of the fashion icons of the 1930s and 1940s and an individual with a highly original fashion sense. Her adoption of elements of Navajo art and dress focused attention on the styles she preferred. Her interest in Navajo garments and jewelry has continued to inspire twenty-first-century designers. Designers Jeff Mahshie and Julie Chaiken cited Rogers and the styles she wore as the "starting point" for their codesigned collection of February 2007.

Fashion designers from New York to Paris have incorporated aspects of Indian design in their couture and ready-to-wear lines. Rifat Ozbek's 1989 collection used North American Indian feathers and beads on black-velvet sheath dresses. The fashion press reported that Anna Sui showed fringed suede in 2005, as well as North American Indian embroidery and Navajo jewelry. Issac Mizrahi, in 1991, designed what he called a "totem pole dress." North American Indian designers have noted that designer Ralph Lauren's use of materials and themes related to the art of the Southwest Indian tribes has served to educate the general public about the beauty of these materials.

North American Indian–inspired elements also appeared as one of the many eclectic elements in the dress of those who were part of the hippie movement of the 1960s. Perhaps the hippies identified with another countercultural group that was struggling for its rights, or they may have been attracted to Indian spiritual connections to nature and the earth that seemed to be different from mainstream Judeo-Christian beliefs. Headbands, fringed leather garments and purses, beaded decoration, and silver jewelry were some of the many items that showed up in hippie dress. Some North American Indians became participants in the hippie movement.

JEWELRY-MAKING AND DESIGN

Archaeological excavations show that the earliest people to arrive in North America used both local materials and those that traveled over continent-wide trade routes to create jewelry. After they began to trade with Europeans and Asians, new materials, such as glass beads and silver brooches, were added. Although some limited production of jewelry for trade or sale existed earlier, it was not until the 1930s that more widespread commercial production of jewelry for sale to those outside the community began in the Southwest. Indeed, it was only in the mid-nineteenth century that Navajos began making the silver jewelry that has become so popular. Turquoise was incorporated only in the latter part of that century, and concho belts made from silver shell-shaped disks began to be made about the same time.

By the end of the twentieth century, jewelry designed by talented North American Indian and First Nation designers and inexpensive copies of the traditional designs were available from coast to coast in both the United States and Canada. Among the more popular traditional motifs in earrings are feathers, which are a metaphor for birds and for the powers of the sky, and *dream catchers,* a netted hoop design intended to catch bad dreams. *Squash-blossom necklaces* of silver or silver and turquoise are widely sold. Missionaries discouraged the use of traditional beadwork design motifs, so designers incorporated them into the ornamental jewelry. In areas such as Alaska, local designers utilize bone and fossil ivory in necklaces, bracelets, and earrings that are bought as souvenirs by tourists. Some top designers not only create traditionally based designs but also have become known nationally for their original creations.

FASHIONABLE GARMENTS AND ACCESSORIES DESIGNS

At first designing was a hobby for most of these designers; they were trying to find a way to incorporate traditional designs in a contemporary way. When they found they were passionate about their chosen field, they struggled to do what they loved in a way that would earn them a living and reach a wider audience. Some designers began by applying art to clothing they already had, and they continued their work when they realized people were interested in their designs. Some chose to go back to school to better their skills.

In the more than forty years since the first designers began to gain recognition, the number of fine artisans from Canada, the Northwest Territories, and regions of the United States has grown and continues to grow.

Some Canadians, such as Pam Baker and her T.O.C. Legends project, have become fairly well known. Tammy Beauvais is a Mohawk designer with her own fashion design company that opened in 1999. Her creations are sold in more than forty boutiques in Canada and the United States. She is especially well known for cashmere shawls she created for the wives of thirty-four heads of state when they attended a Summit of the Americas in Quebec. D'Arcy Moses is a member of the South Slave Dene nation and lives in the Northwest Territories of Canada. He gained a strong reputation for work in fur. The hallmark of the work of Dorothy Grant is designs she creates that incorporate Haida art. Sold in stores in both Canada and the United States, she includes men's and women's coats, handbags, briefcases, and wallets in her collections. Angela DeMontigny lives and works in Ontario and uses elements from Chippewa, Cree, and Metis art in hand-painted and beaded work. Her creations are sold not only in the United States and Canada but also in Europe. Ronald Green, who distributes work under the trade name Ronald Everett, is from the Tsimshian community of Lax KwaLaams in northern British Columbia, and his inspiration is drawn from his heritage. He develops ideas that he says grow out of stories, masks, powwows, and potlatches. Dene Fur Clouds, a design firm based in the Northwest Territories of Canada, has developed a line that specializes in fur. Products include fur knits made into sweaters, vests, and a wide range of accessory items.

In October 2006, the Indian Craft Shop and the Interior Museum of the U.S. Department of the Interior joined together to present a fashion show called

> "The American Indian Influence in Fashion." Among the North American Indian designers whose work was featured were Virginia Yazzie-Ballenger (Navajo) and Kathy "Elk Woman" Whitman (Mandan, Hidatsa, Artikaras). Virginia Yazzie-Ballenger has been the designer for a firm called Navajo Spirit Southwestern Wear since its founding in 1984. The firm makes both contemporary Western wear and traditional Navajo garments. Kathy Whitman is a sculptor and is also known for her jewelry. Hand-painted shawls made by Red Nations Art were also shown.

Patricia Michaels lives and works in New Mexico. Her work is known for use of unusual textures, and she stresses that it is important to her to blend tradition and contemporary style. Margaret Wood, a Navajo, creates wearable art and quilts. After working for more than twenty years, she is known for her modern adaptations of traditional garments, and she presents some of these ideas in her book *Native American Tradition*.

OBJECTIVES OF THE DESIGNERS

A similar theme runs through the statements made by and about these designers. Their objective, no matter where they are located or what their native heritage, is to express their tradition through the medium of dress. Those traditions may relate to the materials used for their creations, the vocabulary of ornament that they incorporate, or the style of dress that is intrinsic to the items produced.

Only toward the end of the twentieth century have First Nations designers begun expressing themselves through the medium of dress. When asked why she chose fashion design as their medium of expression, designer Pam Baker explains:

Dress equals identity. These designers have come a long way from the way the Residential School era had crushed our pride. Now we are working towards gaining and instilling pride back into the communities, especially our youth. We are selling our stories, and educating about where we have come from. We love the art, then we experiment with fine fabrics, traditional fabrics. On the West Coast many of the Northern tribes, upon trading in the 1800s, became familiar with wool, and utilized this fabric for traditional regalia; for button blankets with their crests appliquéd. The button blanket of my relations inspired me, the beauty, and the strength of the family crests, clan design. Many of our designers use the fabrics and designs that they view at potlatches and pow-wows.

The aforementioned designers usually utilize their tribal designs in their work or incorporate art that reflects their heritage or creates contemporary versions of these traditional ideas. The customers for their work vary. Some customers are First Nations and North American Indian people. Most items designed are for women, although native men sometimes order replicas of the traditional dress of their fathers or grandfathers or ask to have a wedding garment designed. Some buyers are collectors of wearable art. These may include celebrities and art enthusiasts. Museums take great interest in the work. On occasion nonnatives want the opportunity to enjoy the beauty of these cultures through dress.

Many designers do only custom orders, and people say that they enjoy going through the design process and fittings and having an opportunity to provide input. Designers also work on special orders and traditional wear. When designers have the opportunity to replicate something that had been worn by their ancestors, they speak of the joy of seeing a piece that may have been checked out of a museum that allows them to view and look closely at the work of their people.

Many of these designers receive a lot of attention from the media. Sometimes several designers will join to showcase their work together. Involvement in the fashion industry is difficult, often due to lack of resources. Funding is hard to obtain, and designers speak of how more training in the field of business would assist more potential designers to be financially successful. At the same time, attitudes in the mainstream fashion industry show a lack of understanding of some of the goals of native designers. One designer reported that when she met with industry representatives, she was told, "I can sell your product all day long, without the artwork." This is not the message First Nations designers want to bring to their customers. Instead, they see their objective as educating the public about who they are. They want people to know that there are First Nations people working on being self-sufficient, moving away from dependency. They believe that the next generation will have the foresight and tools to succeed more quickly, yet retain their unique identity.

North American Indian and First Nations designers are not immune to the globalization that the fashion industries have undergone. With many artists now moving toward entrepreneurship, they want to move into new products, such as accessories and footwear.

They have taken advantage of the lower production costs available in China and arrange for manufacture there or elsewhere in Asia. They expect that keeping costs lower will make their products and designs more accessible.

SOURCES OF INSPIRATION AND USE OF LOCAL MATERIALS

North American Indian and First Nations designers utilize design motifs and materials that they know from having been raised in their own particular culture. In the Northwest region, elements of clan designs play an important role. But a designer will use only designs appropriate to his or her clan and then only limited elements of the designs. Button blankets made of wool with mother-of-pearl buttons and chilkat blankets made of goat wool are another source of inspiration that might be tied into contemporary design. The ornamentation on a button blanket represents a particular clan, and the designs on them represent the thunderbird, killer whale, and the like. Chilkat blankets showcase hierarchy, chieftainship, or royalty. But care is taken not to offend members of the community by making exact reproductions.

In the Southwest, some of the designs produced have had an interesting historical journey. Both the Navajo and Apache women adapted the Victorian dress that they saw Anglo women wearing in the mid- to late nineteenth century. The Navajo style that developed had a velvet or velveteen blouse worn with a long, full-tiered cotton skirt. Present-day Navajo designers, in turn, have produced items of dress that derive from these garments. This is one of the styles associated with the aforementioned Millicent Rogers, who adopted it and helped to make it popular. During the Victorian period, Apache women wore full gathered skirts and loosely fitted overblouses. This *camp dress,* as it was called, has also served as a basis for designs by North American Indian designers.

The culture and history of the region from which the designer comes may be related to the kinds of materials that a designer favors. Several designers and design firms from Canada place special emphasis on using fur in their designs, whereas Navajo designers from the Southwest may choose velvet or velveteen and cotton. White pearl buttons on dark backgrounds appear in some of the designs from the Northwest. Patchwork designs, associated with the Seminoles of the Southeast, have been reproduced. Fringing in leather or fabric is often associated with Plains Indians and is incorporated into some designs.

However, designers do not feel themselves limited to the materials associated with North American Indians and First Nations people. Pam Baker speaks of progressing from early designs where she worked with the wool fabrics associated with her tradition to manipulating more upscale fabrics; taking velvet, for example, throwing it in the washer, applying a devore printing process, which burns out some of the fibers in a design, and then dyeing it.

The success of some designers and the notice that has come to their work will probably stimulate other designers to enter this field. But not all native people appreciate what the designers are doing; some people object to the use of cultural material in their work. The designers respond that many nonnative companies are promoting their versions of aboriginal art and making a profit. They believe it is better for them to create these styles than to have it be done by those who do not know and respect the culture. Native designers, they say, are very aware of what lines that they cannot cross.

References

Donahue, Mary. "Modern American Fashion Design American Indian Style." In *PART*, online journal of the City University of New York's Ph.D. program in art history. http://dsc.gc.cuny.edu/part/part9/identities/articles/donah.html.

Wood, Margaret. Native American Fashion: Modern Adaptations of Traditional Designs. Phoenix, AZ: Native American Fashions, 1997.

2

HOW NEW YORK STOLE MODERN FASHION

Norma Rantisi[1]

The year was 1973. The occasion was a fashion show at Versailles, an event organized by New York fashion publicist Eleanor Lambert as a benefit for the palace. Five American designers, including Bill Blass, Oscar de La Renta, Anne Klein, Stephen Burrows and Halston, were brought to France to show alongside French designers Yves Saint Laurent, Pierre Cardin, Hubert de Givenchy, Emanuel Ungaro and Marc Bohan at Christian Dior. What no one expected, however, was that the American designers would outshine the reigning stars of French (and at that time, world) fashion. But the French themselves conceded defeat. Cardin claimed the Americans were 'excellent' and Ungaro cried out 'genius'. The headlines in the New York Times read 'Fashion at Versailles: French Were Good, Americans Were Great' and several observers indicated that the Americans had stolen the show (McColl 2001).

The event marked a symbolic turning point in world fashion history. France's hegemony as a fashion centre, with Paris as its capital, was not only being challenged but slowly reversed by the ascendance of American fashion and the rise of New York as a new fashion world capital. By the late 1990s, New York-based designers Marc Jacobs and Michael Kors were given creative control at French fashion houses Louis Vuitton and Céline. As in the case of Tom Ford at Gucci, the objective was to infuse American sensibility into the European luxury market, at a time when fashion was becoming a more commercialized and global enterprise. New York always had a specialization in mass markets given its origins in ready-to-wear production. Now that fashion was becoming the 'business of commercializing art', New York's designers were well situated to ride the fashion wave.

But New York's transformation to a centre of fashion was neither an easy nor inevitable one. According to Christopher Breward, fashion represents 'clothing designed primarily for its expressive and decorative qualities, related closely to the current short-term dictates of the market, rather than for work or ceremonial functions' (1995: 15). This implies the need to strike a balance between art and industry. Yet, at the turn of the twentieth century, New York represented a manufacturing hub with little or no fashion design talent, where apparel firms were mass-producing Parisian styles for the many. How then was it able to cultivate its own design talent and to marry the commercial with the aesthetic? To be sure, part of New York's success can be attributed to 'historical accident' and to where the New York industry was situated in relation to broader socio-economic trends or to major political events, such as the Second World War. A closer examination, however, reveals that its success also lies in a set of local dynamics and in the ability of local apparel actors to anticipate or respond to new competitive pressures.

The development of a host of apparel-related institutions in the city – from design schools to buying offices to trade associations – has been critical in enabling manufacturers to acquire the knowledge, skills and resources needed to adapt and stay attuned to shifts in consumer preferences (Rantisi 2004a). The spatial concentration of these key institutions in the heart of Manhattan is also a key part of the story. Many economic geographers and sociologists have

---

[1] From Norma Rantisi, How New York Stole Modern Fashion, Berg Fashion Library.

highlighted the significance of physical proximity for the development of social networks and an open exchange of information (Storper 1997; Scott 2000). And the fact that New York's Garment District is so centrally located within the city means that manufacturers benefit from proximity to a range of cultural activities, from retail districts to museums to Broadway, not to mention the nightclubs and street culture, all of which serve as significant sources of aesthetic inspiration (Rantisi 2004b). The diverse cultural and economic fabric of the broader urban setting serves as a base for the development of major fashion houses as well as a location where 'high fashion reinvigorates and renews itself, as it bumps up against the rawness of the real city' (Gilbert 2000: 13).

The story of New York fashion is thus a story of both an industry and a place and of the dialectic between the two. In this chapter, I recount this story by tracing the evolution of the Garment District and the broader New York fashion economy. I show how the District, as a proximate network of social and economic relations (i.e. a 'cultural industry'), was able to nurture a local design community and by extension, a distinct New York aesthetic that could stand apart from – and pose a formidable challenge to – Paris. The story of New York fashion however is not just a rosy tale. At the dawn of the twenty-first century, the industry faces new challenges in retaining New York's status as a fashion world city. The chapter will conclude with some reflections on these challenges, and particularly, on the imminent decline of the Garment District as the spatial anchor for the industry.

THE RISE OF THE GARMENT DISTRICT AS INDUSTRY AND PLACE

The rise of the Garment District in its present location can be dated back to the early twentieth century and occurred in response to a number of related developments. Through much of the mid-to-late nineteenth century, the apparel industry was situated on the Lower East Side of Manhattan, which was a port of arrival for immigrants. At this location, the retailers and wholesalers who established the industry (many of whom were German Jewish immigrants) could easily tap into a readily available labour pool, often constituted by kinsfolk (Waldinger 1986). However, after later waves of immigration, the Lower East Side was no longer viable as a manufacturing and wholesaling district for a significant share of apparel producers. Due to overcrowded housing settlements and the expansion of government and financial activities there, elite and middle-class residents moved northward in search of more elegant residential locations. Retailers were quick to pursue their clients, and manufacturers, in turn, followed their market.

A new geography for the industry was also prompted by the general surge in the demand and supply for ready-to-wear apparel. Recent immigrants were feeding the apparel-making machine from the consumption as well as the production end, as US cities were undergoing a process of rapid urbanization and industrialization. The changing social and economic status of women was also integral to the rise in demand, as growing numbers were entering the workforce and had less time for custom-made fittings or making their own clothes. Due to its port and favourable location along the Hudson River, New York became the transportation hub for the US Eastern seaboard, making it a natural trading centre for the rest of the country and the main beneficiary of this heightened demand (Helfgott 1959; Green 1997).

As a consequence of these developments, wholesalers and manufacturers needed larger spaces to coordinate the production process and newer spaces in which to display their expanding commodity lines to local and out-of-town buyers. Proximity to transport nodes was also significant as the market was no longer a local one and employees were increasingly dispersed across Manhattan and the boroughs. The construction of Penn Railroad Station (in 1910) as well as the availability of spacious loft buildings made Midtown Manhattan an appealing site.

The spatial contours of the District within the Midtown area however were dictated by other political-economic factors. The northward push of retailers from Lower Manhattan resulted in the establishment of a retail district along Fifth Avenue in the eastern half of the Midtown section. In catering to the new elite residents of the area, department store and boutique owners sought to construct a centre of leisure and project an image of refinement. The merchants were concerned that an influx of manufacturers and loft-style buildings would disrupt this idyllic picture, so they formed a Fifth Avenue Merchants Association and pressured the City to pass a zoning ordinance in 1916 to restrict industrial uses in the area (Jackson 1995). In response, manufacturers congregated in the western half of the Midtown area to benefit from the Midtown amenities and remain close to the stores, creating a space of production adjacent to – though separate from – the pre-eminent space of consumption in the city.

The Garment District is usually demarcated as the area bordered by 40th street to the north, 34th to the south, Fifth Avenue to the east and Ninth Avenue to the west. Over time, as more manufacturers congregated there, support services, such as textile representatives, trim and button suppliers and lending institutions ('factors'), emerged to serve the new apparel cluster and to solidify its reputation and character as a distinct quarter. Seventh Avenue, which ran through the centre of the District, became home to fancy showrooms, signifying the power and influence that apparel would command in the local economy.

The District (or 'Seventh Avenue', as it was dubbed by industry insiders) came to represent a symbolic anchor for a broader nexus of institutions in the city to support and mediate apparel production and consumption. On the production side, for example, the International Garment Workers Union (later called UNITE) developed in response to the poor working conditions of immigrant garment workers in the early 1900s and the consequent workers' strikes. The union was instrumental in negotiating the Protocol of Peace in 1910, which led to the establishment of the Department of Labour and set the foundation for 'collective bargaining between management and labour' (Green 1997). The trade journal Women's Wear Daily (WWD), now the leading source of information on market trends, was instigated in 1910 mainly to report on the workers' strikes and played an important role in keeping industry insiders abreast of the latest developments in the trade (Waldinger 1986). Apparel design and production programmes were established at the Pratt Institute (in 1888) and the Parsons School of Design (in 1906) to qualify a new cadre of recruits for the bourgeoning industry.

On the consumption side, resident buying offices in the District marketed New York apparel to retailers, by serving as liaisons between local manufacturers and out-of-town buyers. The New-York based fashion magazines Vogue and Harper's Bazaar aroused an interest on the part of the broader population. New York's vibrant retail scene added to the excitement and buzz of consuming apparel, with trademarks such as Macy's, Lord and Taylor, Bloomingdale's and Bergdorf Goodman making shopping a pleasurable experience rather than necessity for out-of-town buyers as well as consumers (Goldman 1949).

By the early 1920s, New York's position as the centre for apparel in the country was unrivalled. The city had a particular strength in women's wear, which was more labour intensive than men's wear and relied on a fast turnaround, and for which New York constituted 80 per cent of the national share of the product value (Richards 1951, Helfgott 1959).

Despite the successes, however, a critical element of the local industry was still lacking – the conception of the product. New York mastered the manufacture, distribution and marketing of products but the inspiration for the styles was Paris. Parisian designers and fashion figured centrally in local design school instruction, in the pages of the fashion magazines and in the window displays of local department stores. Retail buyers and manufacturers would regularly send representatives to the fashion shows in Paris to purchase samples or sketch the designs (Lee 1975; De Marly 1980; Ewing 1992). For their part, the American general public endorsed this view through their consumption practices, favouring products with 'made in Paris' labels (whether real or fake), and for the wealthier clientele, by making trips to France to shop in the boutiques (Richards 1922; Roshco 1963). Guidebooks for Americans were instrumental in reinforcing the Paris-fashion link. In the symbolic ordering of world cities, Paris was clearly at the pinnacle of the fashion hierarchy (Gilbert 2000).

In New York, ready-to-wear was born in the late 1800s, in an era of industrialization, to serve the immediate, functional needs of the masses. The emphasis was on cost-efficient, volume (re)production. Consequently, the institutions that emerged in the Garment District supported the commercial imperatives of the industry. In contrast to Paris, New York lacked an infrastructure to nurture and promote artistic creation and to validate 'design' (and by extension, 'the designer') as a production strategy. By the early 1900s, apparel had already become big business for the local economy. The challenge that remained was building on the existing industrial base to attain a distinctive fashion identity by reorienting the city's 'space of production' to allow for social and cultural influences.

THE INSTITUTIONALIZATION OF NEW YORK FASHION

Economic geographers have offered critical insight into the processes that give rise to cultural products, namely, goods or services that are valued for their aesthetic or symbolic attributes relative to their utilitarian ones (e.g. Scott 1996, 2000a). In particular, these scholars have drawn attention to the urban basis of cultural production, highlighting the significance of an array of cultural and economic activities for promoting aesthetic innovation and for the development of networks among cultural institutions to facilitate the exchange of information and ideas.

New York's economic advantage would soon translate into greater demand on the part of an expanding bourgeois class for local amenities, amenities that would embody US values of 'liberal democracy' (Guilbaut 1983). While not yet on the international radar, New York did bear witness to the development of a thriving music and performing arts scene at the turn of the twentieth century. Vaudeville, Broadway and some of the major music houses (under the umbrella of Tin Pan Alley) would feed off the creative and vibrant energy that came with the rise of industry and urbanization in Manhattan. And by the 1930s, a local band of avant-garde artists, seeking to break with Parisian hegemony, started to garner attention (both negative and positive) from local press and exhibitors. The influx of European exiles, many of whom were artists and intellectuals escaping fascist regimes, added to the cultural blend by importing 'Old World' experiences and skills in ways that would mesh with 'New World' dictates (Guilbaut 1983; Scott and Rutkoff 2001).

New York's status as an arts centre was slowly coming into being and gaining legitimacy. The city's status as a cultural centre was reinforced through the establishment of landmark institutions, such as the Guggenheim Museum, Carnegie Hall and the Lincoln Center for Performing Arts. New York apparel would both benefit from and contribute to this emerging cultural matrix. Local cultural institutions and 'industries' (particularly in popular music, theatre and cinema) served as significant sources of inspiration but were also consumers of fashion. For example, the New York high-end ready-to-wear designer Norman Norell began his career designing clothes for Broadway and the movies. In the 1930s, the Costume Institute was established by a local theatre group, a testament to the links between the performing arts and fashion. It became increasingly common to see fashion publicized alongside modern art in magazines, such as Harper's Bazaar (Chase and Chase 1954, Guilbaut 1983). As Entwistle notes, a fashion system entails more than the provision of 'garments for wear', it 'endows garments with beauty and desirability, sometimes making direct contact with art' (2000: 43). New York's cultural base was a central part of the fashion system that was emerging, one that would endow apparel with aesthetic value.

Although New York fashion's coming of age could be attributed in part to the city's wider cultural transformation, it was also conditioned by industry-specific developments. As the industry was maturing, a new generation of talent was emerging from local design programmes and this generation profited from the convergence of a new supply of resources (material and economic) and new demands arising from changing social conditions. The development of fabrics (such as rayon) and the innovative uses and combinations of traditional fabrics produced materials that were not only amenable to machine production but could be used in the construction of more casual ready-to-wear styles. Such styles were in demand as increasing numbers of women were entering the workforce. These women were engaged in a broader range of activities (work and leisure), and had less time for custom-made fittings, prompting the continued rise of ready-to-wear, and within ready-to-wear, a distinctive modern fashion called 'sportswear' (Milbank 1989; Ewing 1992). Claire McCardell, who was trained at the Parsons School of Design, has been credited as one of the first sportswear designers, redefining American fashion by introducing beautiful yet comfortable garments, which were not inspired by Paris (Yohannan and Nolf 1998) These simple, wearable styles gained broad acceptance because they resonated with new social roles but also, more generally, with values of democracy and with a view of dress as a means of blurring rather than marking social distinctions (Green 1997).

However, the broader recognition and acceptance of this burgeoning New York talent demanded the support of local buyers, fashion editors and journalists, who mediated consumption trends. With the industry's continued expansion, this support came as social ties were forged between key actors in the Garment District. In February 1931, a group of leading women in the industry, including Vogue editor Edna Woolman Chase, Helena Rubinstein, Elizabeth Arden, Dorothy Shaver and Eleanor Lambert, held the first meeting of the Fashion Group (later known as Fashion Group International). This association represented all facets of the industry, including designers, textile manufacturers, retailers, fashion press and fashion educators and focused on apparel and fashion-related commodities, such as home furnishing, accessories and cosmetics.

These initial efforts to promote local talent were hastened by the onset of the Second World War and the closure of Paris as a result of the Nazi occupation in 1940. Magazines, retail buyers and Seventh Avenue manufacturers could no longer turn to Paris for inspiration or for models. Thus, the focus shifted inward. Necessity demanded that a new source of talent be nurtured to fill the void, so industry elites took on the task of bolstering this new source. On the production end, the Fashion Group's fabric division brought fabric manufacturers and designers together to develop materials that could be used to produce quality garments (Fashion Group Records, Box 73, f.8, 1940). And there was the establishment of the Fashion Institute of Technology in 1944 by industry and union leaders, which ensured a supply of specialized labour (Scranton 1998).

By the post-war period, the new institutions and networks in New York laid the foundation for a set of industry relations that could produce and endorse uniquely local designs. While the 1950s witnessed the rise of other regional apparel centres in the USA, such as Los Angeles, no other city could compete with New York's specialized fashion services and its status as publishing centre for the country. New York also had the status of cultural capital, and its museums, theatres and department stores became a favoured destination for both local and European high society after the war. As New York was becoming synonymous with style, the industry was establishing its place within the international fashion circuit.

BRANDING THE AMERICAN DESIGNER (OR 'HOW CALVIN GOT HIS GROOVE ON')

The rebirth of New York ready-to-wear as 'fashion' occurred at a unique time when the post-war economic boom had created a surge in consumer demand. The growth of a middle class with new suburban homes and disposable incomes meant that markets existed for high volume, consumer goods; and apparel manufacturers, who now had merchandising and design capabilities, were well positioned to fill such markets. But this production wave did not last. By the 1960s, mass markets were saturated. Supply exceeded demand, which had become increasingly segmented. The rise of social movements (e.g. feminism and identity politics) and the advent of subcultures such as the 'youthquake', which was grounded in both fashion and music, gave birth to alternative styles and to new sources of fashion direction. These trends, coupled with the rising incomes of the middle class, meant that the survival of ready-to-wear apparel firms would lie with their capability to cater to and manage the increasing 'individualization' of market demand, a capability that rested with their style innovators – the fashion designers.

Up until the 1960s, however, American fashion designers lacked financial and managerial independence and did not share equally in the gains that accrued to apparel manufacturers from the new-found recognition of American sportswear. Designers were the employees of apparel firms and specialty shops and were generally relegated to the backroom, with few opportunities to meet the buyers or clients. They also lacked their own identity and their own labels. In contrast to Paris, where designers were viewed as the pivotal element of the fashion system, the 'stars', New York designers were viewed as a subsidiary element. To quote Bill Blass: 'we were the help' (Gandee 1999: 537).

The new economic context of the 1960s altered this trend. Designers, such as Blass and Ralph Lauren, started opening their own operations and capitalizing on their roles as fashion originators to distinguish themselves as well as their products to cater to new markets demands.

Another significant image-maker for the industry is the Council of Fashion Designers of America (CFDA), an honorary society of high-end designers, which was established in 1962. Since its inception, the CFDA has advocated on behalf of designers and promoted their occupation as an 'art', like that of other cultural industries.

Hence, with a reorientation of New York's fashion institutions to accommodate the rise of the designer as producer and marketer of fashion, established high-end ready-to-wear lines, such as Donna Karan and Calvin Klein, have now become globally competitive brands. The demands for their minimalist styles continue to surge in Europe and Asia and have also spilled over into a demand for American talent, as European houses from Gucci to Louis Vuitton have hired US designers in the last decade to develop their ready-to-wear lines (personal interviews 1999; Hirschberg 2001).

LIVING ON THE EDGE OF THE ART–COMMERCE BALANCE: CAN NEW YORK MAINTAIN ITS STATUS AS WORLD FASHION CAPITAL?

In an era of globalization, New York fashion has fared well due to the emergence of an institutional infrastructure (or 'fashion system') that has enabled local producers to balance aesthetic attributes with commercial imperatives. Designers have been able to draw on a range of local cultural institutions for sources of inspiration and on a well-established set of production intermediaries for the commercialization of their designs (Rantisi 2004b). However, the ability of the industry to retain this edge in the face of competitive pressures proves daunting. In recent years, globalization has brought new constraints, as cost remains a significant element in capitalist competition, translating into the privileging of commercial imperatives on the part of key industry actors.

The privileging of commercial imperatives is also evident in the evolution of the Garment District as a space of production. Since the 1970s, the District has faced the loss of manufacturing jobs due to rising labour and real estate costs, as apparel firms have increasingly outsourced production needs to overseas producers. Although the union negotiated a special zoning amendment to protect manufacturing in the District, there has been limited enforcement. The activities that have remained are primarily the value-added activities of design and marketing (e.g. the showrooms), with limited production for samples and the manufacture of garments with a fast turnaround. (Much of the production that now remains in the city is centered in Lower Manhattan (particularly Chinatown) and in the outer borough of Brooklyn.) In 1993, the city established the Fashion Center Business Improvement District (BID), which has helped to clean and beautify the District and project its identity as a centre for fashion production. The revitalization of the District, however, has made it a more appealing location for new uses, such as high-tech firms or advertising agencies, from which real estate owners can extract higher rents.

At a time when 'fast fashion' is becoming the new production paradigm for apparel (Segre Reinach 2005) – a paradigm reliant on the flexible coordination and communication between retail, design, and production – the aforementioned trends which prefigure the dissolution of the District threaten to compromise the competitive advantage of New York firms. The history of New York fashion illustrates that it was the coming together of industrial and cultural activities that allowed for the dynamism, versatility and innovation of New York designs. Now more than ever, the ability to achieve a balance between art and industry demands the integrity of the District as an industry and a place.

References

Braham P. (1997) 'Fashion: Unpacking a Cultural Production', in P. DuGay (ed.) *Production of Culture/Cultures of Production*, Thousand Oaks, CA: Sage.

Breward, C. (1995) *The Culture of Fashion*, Manchester: Manchester University Press.

Chase, E. W. and I. Chase (1954) *Always in Vogue*, London: V. Gollancz.

De Marly, D. (1980) *The History of Haute Couture, 1850-1950*, New York: Holmes and Meier.

Entwistle, J. (2000) The Fashioned Body: Fashion, Dress and Modern Social Theory, Cambridge: Polity Press.

Ewing, E. (1992) A History of Twentieth Century Fashion, London: Batsford.

Gilbert, D. (2000) "Urban outfitting: The city and the spaces of fashion culture", in S. Bruzzi and P. Church Gibson (eds) *Fashion Cultures: Theories, Explorations and Analysis*, London: Routledge.

Gandee, C. (1999) "1950s: Designer Bill Blass Remembers the Years of Cocktails, Café Society and Cool American Chic (An Interview with Bill Blass)" *Vogue*, November, 470: 537–8.

Goldman, E.S. (1949) *The New York Story: A History of the New York Clothing Industry, 1924-1949*, New York: The New York Clothing Manufacturers' Exchange Inc.

Green, N. (1997) Ready-to-Wear and Ready-to-Work: A Century of Industry and Immigrants in Paris and New York, Durham: Duke University Press.

Guilbaut, S. (1983) *How New York Stole the Idea of Modern Art*, Chicago: University of Chicago Press.

Helfgott, R. (1959) "Women's and Children's Apparel", in M. Hall (ed.) *Made in New York*, Cambridge, MA: Harvard University Press.

Hirschberg, L. (2001) "Tom Ford, Ensuring a Place for Gucci in Hard Times", *The New York Times Magazine* 2, December.

Jackson, K. (1995) "Garment district" in *The Encyclopedia of New York City*, New Haven, CT: Yale University Press.

Lee, S. (ed.) (1975) American Fashion The Life and Lines of Adrian, Mainbocher, McCardell, Norell, Trigere, New York: Quadrangle/New York Times Book Co.

McColl, P. (2001) "The American Coup of Versailles", *The New York Times' Fashion of the Time Magazine*, 19 August: 138.

Milbank, C. (1989) New York Fashion: The Evolution of American Style, New York: Harry N. Abrams.

Rantisi, N. (2004a) "The Ascendance of New York Fashion" *The International Journal of Urban and Regional Affairs*, 28: 86–106.

Rantisi, N. (2004b) "The Designer in the City and the City in the Designer", in D. Power and A.J. Scott (eds) *Cultural Industries and the Production of Culture*, London: Routledge.

Richards, C. (1922) *Art in Industry*, New York: Macmillan Co.

Richards, F. (1951) *The Ready-to-Wear Industry, 1900-1950*, New York: Fairchild Publications, Inc.

Roscho, B. (1963) The Rag Race: How New York and Paris Run the Breckneck Business of Dressing American Women, New York: Funk and Wegnalls.

Scott, A. (1996) "The Craft, Fashion and Cultural Products Industries of Los Angeles: Competitive Dynamics and Policy Dilemmas in Multi-Sectoral Image-Producing Complex", *Annals of the Association of American Geographers*, 86: 306–23.

Scott, A. (2000) The Cultural Economy of Cities: Essays on the Geography of Image-Producing Industries, London: Sage Press.

Scott, W. B. and Rutkoff, P. (2001) *New York Modern: The Arts and the City*, Baltimore, MD: John Hopkins University Press.

Scranton, P. (1998) 'From Chaotic Novelty to Style Promotion: The United States Fashion Industry, 1890s-1970s' in G. Malossi (ed.) *The Style Engine*, New York: Monacelli Press.

Segre Reinach, S. (2005) "China and Italy: Fashion versus *Pret a Porter* Towards a New Culture of Fashion", *Fashion Theory*, 9(1): 43–56.

Strorper, M. (1997) *The Regional World*, New York: Guilford.

Waldinger, R. (1986). Through the Eye of the Needle: Immigrants and Enterprise in New York's Garment Trades, New York: New York University Press.

Yohannan, K. and N Nolf, (1998) *Claire McCardell: Redefining Modernism*, New York: Harry N. Abrams.

3

A DECONSTRUCTIONIST PERSPECTIVE ON MENSWEAR:
A conversation with Siki Im

Joseph H. Hancock, II

INTRODUCTION

Siki Im has been a senior designer for Karl Lagerfeld and Helmut Lang. In 2010, he received one of the highest honors for an up-and-coming fashion designer in the menswear category—the Ecco Domani Fashion Foundation Award. Deconstructionist works of art, scholarship, and non-Western styling influence his designs that explore and push the boundaries of traditional tailoring techniques with dramatic end results. Unique shapes, unusual proportions, and a sculptural attitude characterize his pieces. Perhaps as a *true* mark of success, others are now copying his approach as his fashions continue to inspire both high-end couture designers and mass merchants alike.

Just as those who mimic his creativity are varied, so are the men that purchase his collections. They cross various lifestyles, have distinctive tastes, and are international. From traditional Wall Street traders to urban hipsters in Japan, they run the gamut from the boredom of the boardroom to those with cash who live at the fringe: skateboarders, graffiti artists, gay men, and punks. His designs capture a multicultural market, with each line inspiring the future of men's fashion.

Siki Im was born and raised in Cologne, Germany (Figure 2). After completing his Baccalaureate, he studied architecture at Oxford in the UK where he graduated with first class honors. After having worked as an architect in various cities around the world, Siki landed in New York City in 2001 where he worked for Architectonics, a progressive architecture firm. Numerous projects later he decided to take a break from architecture, where after much contemplation he moved on to fashion design. After years of designing for other companies and fashion houses, he thought that it was time to fuse this knowledge with his previous experiences in architecture, furniture, graphics, art, and music by incorporating these interdisciplinary influences into fabrics and shapes. He launched his own menswear line.

In September 2010, the *New York Times Style Magazine* concluded that Siki Im's collection was ingenious, by suggesting he has blurred the lines between masculine and feminine attire. While at the same time, he has slyly subverted the ideals of Savile Row tailoring with his own sense of style and architecture. In November 2010, Siki Im was chosen to launch a "pop-up shop" as part of the "Building Fashion" at HL23 in New York City that celebrates key designers who incorporate architectural techniques into their fashion designs. This highly publicized event was sponsored by Boffo, a non-profit arts organization in New York, and Spilios Gianakopoulos, the co-founder and director. Currently, Siki Im unique menswear designs are sold at Project 8 in New York City, American Rag in Los Angeles, and Lane Crawford in Hong Kong, with more locations coming soon.

Siki Im takes a deconstructionist interdisciplinary approach to creation and design by combining the "applied" and the "academic." In 2009, William Golding's 1955 classic novel *The Lord of the Flies* inspired his first collection. But rather than focusing on the ideologies of Golding's criticism of human nature and society, Siki Im infused Golding's counter-

Moving through a series of office cubicles, the audience viewed each presentation of the latest Siki Im creations. Like expressionless mannequins, immobile models surrounded by chairs, desks, and computers in various states of disarray, displayed the

Figure 3 February 16, 2010. The setting of Siki Im's *Fall/Winter 2010—New Era* was staged like an office with the crowds moving through office cubicles to view his latest designs. Courtesy of Joseph Hancock.

Source: Joseph H. Hancock II

Figure 2 Siki Im. Photograph by Alessio Boni. © Nouveau-PR, New York.

Source: Joseph H. Hancock II

theme of the purity and sense of possibility inherent to a fresh start into his own work. As a designer, he explores both the product and process of his craft by examining how he can forward both the boundaries of institutional and conventional fashion as well as the craftsmanship of his trade. Through these interwoven means, he strives to reevaluate the existing landscape of high-end menswear. The core of his recent collection consists of hand-tailored blazers accompanied by menswear pieces across all categories of tops, bottoms, and outerwear.

Like his clothing, his fashion shows take on an unusual twist with crowds of people, loud music, and unique settings that challenge the ideas of how menswear has been traditionally presented. Harkening to site-specific performance, Siki Im's *Fall/Winter 2010—New Era* show challenged audience members to become more than passive spectators.

Figure 4 February 16, 2010. In each office cubicle, Siki Im models were featured in designs that won the Ecco Domani 2010 Menswear Award, one of the industry's highest awards for up-and-coming designers. The reader will note the use of non-traditional items such as newspapers designed to create hats for some models (foreground and background). Courtesy of Joseph Hancock.

Source: Joseph H. Hanvcock II

clothing. Siki Im not only challenged us to view his pieces as fashions, but also as cultural critique. With the anarchy of office destruction surrounded by the atmospherics of loud blaring punk acoustics, one could readily associate the actions of nearby Wall Street and its culpability in the near collapse of the economy, Golding's referents to young boys gone wild, and the call for a fresh new start (Figures 3 and 4). The cohesive message and inspired look of Siki Im menswear establishes this new designer as one to look forward to with eager anticipation.

INTERVIEW

Joseph H. Hancock II: Why did you make the switch from architecture to fashion design? What caused this change? And what were your first positions at each of the companies and design houses where you work. Why did you decide to pursue your own design interests? And how have you financed this endeavor?

Siki Im: It was more of an accidental one. I have always really enjoyed fashion and when one of my friends suggested it, I finally decided to try it. Everything literally fell into my lap. I have to admit to having turmoil over designing fashion; however, that quickly changed with my first position at Club Monaco designing men and women's. Then, I was offered a position at Karl Lagerfeld and eventually went to Helmut Lang. At both Lagerfeld and Lang, I designed both men's and women's. Although I think women's fashion offers more versatility and variety, my passion is menswear, which is why Siki Im is focused in that direction.

But after working for other design houses, I felt that it was the right time to go out on my own and live my dream of having my own company. The entire company has been self-financed, but we are currently looking for investors. Winning the Ecco Domani Award presented me with a generous stipend to continue my business. And of course, my menswear collection is sold internationally at exclusive retailers and this has also kept my business moving forward.

JH: For your *Spring/Summer Spring 2009, Black Beats White Wonder* collection, you have stated that Foucault inspired this collection. How has he inspired you? And why did you combine the Foucauldian style with Golding's (1955) *Lord of the Flies*?

SI: I was always very interested in the deconstructionist—text, media, art, architecture, music, and fashion. Foucault inspired me to be more critical and analytical of today's environment and society. Examining everything critically and looking at it in a unique and non-traditional way. This critical examination is the tool of my trade so to speak, which in my opinion is very important to having a voice in contemporary society. Designers have to use their mind as well as their visual eye to create fashions that inspire and move beyond the ordinary. Having a voice in our cultural context is important and fashion is the medium in which I express myself. In addition to the book, *Lord of the Flies,* the film was very intense, poignant, and inspiring. I used this metaphor of the island as my new world—a carte blanche for my launch of the collection. I liked the dichotomy of the story of preppy kids deconstructing not only their uniform but also society and humanism (Figure 5).

JH: For you *Fall/Winter 2010—New Era* you draw inspiration from the economist John Maynard Keynes, how did he inspire you? And why have you decided to use *American Psycho* as the form of fiction that inspired this line? Why *American Psycho* since it's so dark and almost grotesque?

SI: Well, I am not an economist. But I stumbled on to him and started reading about his work. He is quite cynical. As far as *American Psycho,* what is wrong with grotesque? It is the eye of the beholder. The reason I chose Brent Ellis Piece was that it helped me to visualize or conceptualize my ideas. The protagonist was a good analogy of the vain greedy elite quality of Wall Street, which was deconstructed last year [referring to 2009]. So, everyone outside of this arena was criticizing and attacking those who worked on Wall Street. I used this opportunity to see the beauty [of the

Figure 5 *Spring/Summer Spring 2009, Black Beats White Wonder.* Featured white dress shirt with Siki Im's signature Merino wool and cashmere "honest" blazer with translucent silk organza lining allowing the wearing to see that the coat is completely finished on the inside and hand-sewn, for quality construction. Wool shorts, leg bands, slides, and black electronic cords worn around the neck give a deconstructive appearance that moves away from the traditional. Isabel Asha Penzlien © Nouveau-PR, New York.

Source: Joseph H. Hancock II

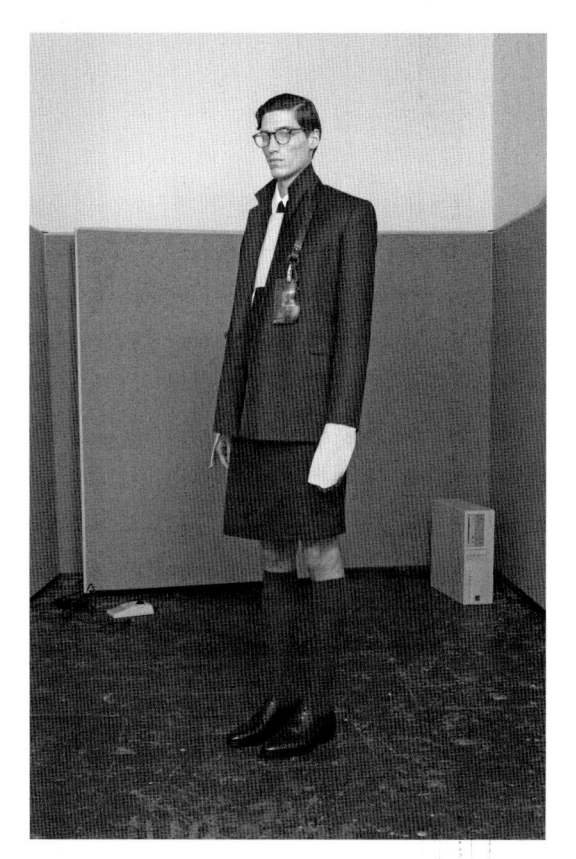

Figure 6 Ryan K. Double-breasted blazer, quilted skirt, cropped long sleeve, hidden button shirt with a boiled wool tie, black harness neck chain, and oxford shoes all by Siki Im. Glasses by Oliver Peoples. Isabel Asha Penzlien © Nouveau-PR, New York.

Source: Joseph H. Hancock II

fall and violence] and proposed a new style for Wall Street (Figures 6 and 7).

JH: It seems like most menswear collections, the blazer is the focal point of your collection. Why is that? And how is your blazer different than others? In other words, why? What particular pieces in menswear do you find the most inspiring?

SI: The blazer is maybe the most universal menswear garment. It was worn during the renaissance, the US civil war. It is worn in Afghanistan, on Wall Street, etc . . . it is also one of the most constructed and complex of all menswear garments. Especially our blazer that is fully canvassed with camel, mohair and is hand tailored in New York City. The lining is 100 percent translucent silk organza so one can experience the make [both externally and internally]. All the buttonholes are hand sewn and all the buttons are horn. I have to say while menswear is challenging, I still find women's more inspiring because there are so many choices.

JH: Did you use a fiction novel for the inspiration for your Spring 2011 line? Or have you shifted your focus?

SI: For my *Spring/Summer 2011* line, I was not inspired by a fiction novel, but by the 1995 film *La Haine*. As you know, I grew up in Germany among immigrant culture, and my parents made many

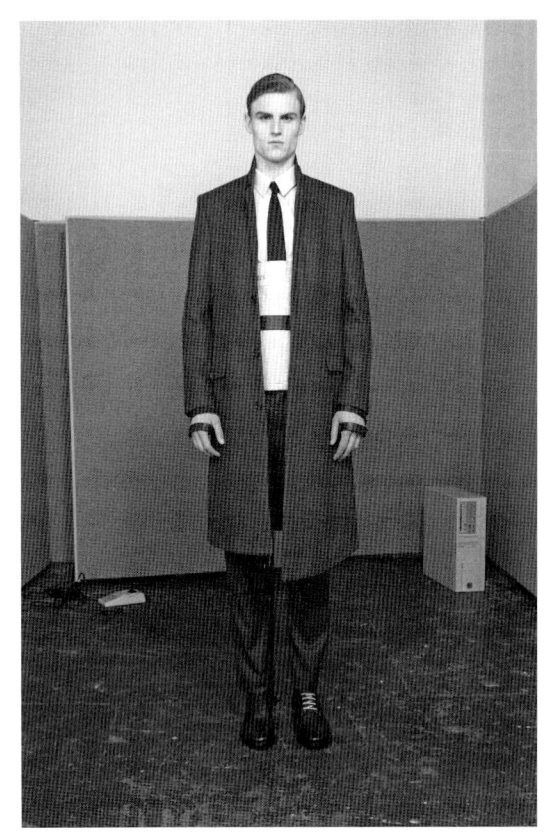

Figure 7 Reid. Cashmere coat, oxford hidden button shirt, slim trousers, flat tie, brogue shoe and oxford shoe all by Siki Im. Isabel Asha Penzlien © Nouveau-PR, New York.

Source: Joseph H. Hancock II

Figure 8 Translucent trench coat, white banded collar shirt, gray harness neck chain, shorts, and shoes all by Siki Im. Isabel Asha Penzlien © Nouveau-PR, New York.

Source: Joseph H. Hancock II

sacrifices for me. I grew up with Confucian ethics in a Western cultural context, being educated in the German school system. And as I have told you in previous conversations, my first forms of artistic expression were as a graffiti artist. The film *La Haine* was not only representative of this sort of immigrant lifestyle, but also inspiring for me in term of style, fluidity, and silhouette.

JH: It seems in your new line, you have really been inspired by non-Western ideals of menswear. Is this the case?

SI: I really like the dress of indigenous cultures, like the Middle Eastern look of wearing a long robe with a jacket over it. I think that looks amazing. I use non-Western silhouettes, but they're constructed using Western techniques, like English-style tailoring (Figures 8 and 9). It's symbolic, but it's also about me growing up in a Confucian household, having a German education, studying architecture in Britain and living in New York.

JH: Will you continue to be inspired by philosophy, fiction, and films when you design? And are you naturally drawn to what appears to be "dark themes" or has this just been by mistake.

SI: A mixture of artistic forms for design will always inspire me, but I also do not want to restrain myself to only certain types of mediums. As far as reflecting dark themes in my collections, I believe there is too much goodness around us and sometimes the dark side needs to come out!

JH: So, you are naturally drawn to dark themes and this is not by mistake?

Figure 9 Gray/white sports jacket, white tunic, and shoes all by Siki Im. Isabel Asha Penzlien © Nouveau-PR, New York.
Source: Joseph H. Hancock II

SI: Very Freud. I am not sure. I guess I appreciate the imperfect, honest, and humane existence of real people who depend on hope and grace to survive than the "bubbly makeup sheen" most people use to cover up their insecurities and fears.

JH: What does the future hold for your brand and how do you plan to expand and grow?

SI: We are sold internationally in quite a few exclusive and upscale stores. We will have our first pop-up store in New York in November [2010]. And once my menswear is more established I want to branch out and design for women . . . and hopefully some architecture as well.

CONCLUSION

Siki Im challenges our notions of what we once knew as "proper" dress and style for men. He inspires men to relook at the way we dress and view what is appropriate for the "man on the street." And while his designs are not for every man, they challenge men to think about the future of men's fashion as it moves into the next millennium. His deconstructive approach and inspiration for non-Western styles using Western tailoring techniques is representative of the multicultural and international changes that we will continue to see in the future of menswear.

4

PATRICK KELLY:
Fashions' great black hope

Van Dyk Lewis and Keith A. Fraley[1]

CONTEXT

Stuart Hall comments that, by definition, modern societies are in a state of constant, rapid and permanent change (1992: 277) as a change agent, fashion becomes a description of desire in which massive change takes place. The nature of our research started with a major contention of what is popularized and sanctioned within the fashion system. Here, fashion is unpacked as a political and social device capable of changing opinion, proffering mass acceptance, elitism, victimization, supremacy and social deviancy. We will say something about fashion in regard to creative cultures vis-à-vis the Parisian fashion system, and blackness as a pliable commodity, and the phenomenon of fashion as it is today, little different from what it has been in the past. Palpable change has come about in the degree of exposure now afforded to fashion and the idea of fashion democracy. Since the 1960s, fashion democracy has provided pivotal departures from illusions that could only be rooted in the dichotomy of opposites that tend to be understood as radicalism versus tradition, unacceptable aesthetics versus acceptable ones, and self versus myth. Such presumptions are foundationless because cultures and, indeed, societies cannot render exactitude or finality to any assemblage, material, systematic or relational human event.

Fashion is based upon multiplicities, configurations of human, object, image, natural and plastic worlds. Multiplicities according to Deleuze and Guattari (1980: 9) are flat, but increase with form when increased connection flows are made. Ultimately, Patrick Kelly's decade of the 1980s, the so-called 'designer decade', saw an explosion of accumulated reference – like most decades, fascination with change stems from a new inclusiveness born not in the neoconservative realpolitik but in the position to policies that failed to connect with youth and fashion cultures. Fashion was divided into official fashion, which remained consciously conservative, and street fashion, which reflected a wide-world perspective.

Due to the position of African-Americans within society, their creative output remains marginalized, and to some degree unobtainable. Indeed, marginalization is apparent in the heady formulas used by black youth fashion cultures; volatility, otherness, secret codes, and anger are conjoined to curiosity for luxury clothing. However in pursuit of a colonizing fervour, the fashion industry has adopted marginalization as a badge of cool.

The Parisian fashion system represents the centre of fashion where hegemony does not exist but the coercive power of a fashion system is pre-eminent. The gatekeepers of Parisian fashion are formalized in structure, consisting of the Fédération Française de la Couture du Prêt-à-Porter des Couturiers et des Créateurs de Mode, the fashion press and the trade buyers. Whatever the answers to the following questions, the contention is that gate-keepers are able to sanction fashion according to their collective idea of value and importance.

---

[1] From Van Dyk Lewis and Keith Fraley (2015), Patrick Kelly: Fashions' Great Black Hope, Fashion, Style & Popular Culture, Intellect, Volume 2, Issue 3, pp. 333–350.

- What actions does the fashion system take and what actions does the black designer reconcile in concern for heritage?
- How did this feat (the rise of Kelly in the Parisian fashion system) occur within the temple of elitist fashion production?
- Although he had to pay a cost for becoming a part of the Parisian fashion system, what is the cost of a black man becoming a celebrity designer?

Kelly's inclusion in the Paris fashion industry was a way of ensuring the fashion industry's survival by attempting one or another version of cultural integration, multiculturalism, or perhaps it was an aleatory slip. This article considers the idea that high aesthetic fashion is distinctly European in construction, and that Kelly the interloper wishes to, and does, infiltrate the Parisian fashion system. The fashion industry has an ignominious report card of how it treats dark-skinned people, whether factory workers, models, designers or consumers, and even disrespect of countries, languages, histories, faces, bodies and material culture used in the development of design themes.

A decade after Scott Barrie, Hylan Brooker, Willi Smith, Stephen Burrows and a few other black male designers became familiar, Patrick Kelly rose quickly to become a designer who seemingly did not compromise; in fact he compromised everything – heritage, legacy and respect. Kelly deserves a mention in the historical record simply for being there. Patrick Kelly made it, the thing that every student of fashion design dreams of. However, Kelly did not penetrate the American market, nor did he resonate in the global black market. Due to his heritage, Kelly is twice removed from the official structure of the French fashion system, which tended to annex innovation unless it had sanctioned movement away from traditional modes; the separation of the 'young and black designer' was palpable in his absence from the conversation. During the mid-1980s Kelly's venture as a young designer collided with the doctrine perpetrated in a mesmerizing occurrence from the gatekeepers of fashion that required them to admire and affix some kind of value to Kelly's work.

In truth, Kelly conjoined 'Americanisms' with French kitsch and became lost in utterances of urban cool. Kelly represented a gaudy kind of power-dressing based on a collection of items and forms that enabled his audience to easily consume his work. Kitsch is opposite to art; kitsch accumulates and connects the strange and unrelated, and in doing so kitsch work in fashion becomes palatable. The underlying capital of kitsch is its potential to deliver politically charged ideas that slip in under the radar.

By the late 1980s the street had interchanged with the 'catwalk' and the catwalk began to become the sidewalk. Affordable designer clothes emblazoned with graphic branding became popular and spurred wearers to consume more expensive, less obviously branded clothes in ever increasing quantities. Black fashion was simultaneously free of bourgeoisie fashion yet mimicked it in fine detail. With body movements of the fashion model, but flagrantly exaggerated to those seen on the catwalk and photographic models, one-upmanship was acted out in the show-off tactics of the vogue dancer popularized in the film *Paris is Burning* (Livingston, 1991).

Kelly was in step with the general mission of 'young designers' at that time, which was counterpoint to Parisian fashion, and particularly the question of who could practise fashion and be approved doing so. Notable young (non-black) British designers such as John Richmond and Maria Cornejo, Body Map, Rachel Auburn, Stephen Linard and the American Marc Jacobs were important, adding a new visual perspective. As a member of the unofficial young designer group, Kelly was in demand. He worked with the Italian knitwear company Benetton, practising his palette of primary colours and motifs, repetition, and cut 'n' mix.

BLACK PARIS

Paris is at once a space of freedom and restriction, in that for over a century African American exiles such as Josephine Baker, Miles Davis, Lester Young, James Baldwin and Kelly have found themselves unable to escape the brand of 'otherness'. These individuals were regarded less than human except for the certainty of their creative acts; labelled less than the *deus faber* [a creation of God], their work [homo faber] enabled their status to become that of man. Whether this status could be applied to Kelly is a question of great importance. Kelly's work embodies the unknown, and is situated culturally and aesthetically distant from commonly held expectations of what a Parisian fashion designer should be. Kelly remained characterized by another template – that of the colonized individual who has to assimilate his colonizer masters' demands if he is to establish currency. To assert himself as decolonized, Kelly had to perform, remake himself, and perform a real and mythical presentation of self. So in asking what of Patrick Kelly, what of his life, we find that Patrick Kelly's legacy, whether by informed intent or through the emotion of desires, has left the most compelling template of any black person working in the industry of fashion. By far his contribution outweighs any one past or present. In his production of self, Kelly succeeds where other black designers in their attempts to secure leading positions as creative professionals failed. Like many high-achieving blacks working in the western creative system, Kelly offered something different, but not necessarily innovative; it was a pronouncement from his culture, which clashed demonstrably with the traditional, particularly with the traditions of the fashion system, possibly because so few black individuals have risen to prominence. It is the revelations of process that make fashion so compelling, and why we might view 'Kanye West as the new Kelly', making good the narrative space by telling voyeurs what it is to be black. Kelly revolutionized Paris fashion, and by default international fashion. He did this through his presence, his images, attitude and physicality.

PATRICK KELLY

In unpacking Kelly we find him to be much more that a fashion designer; fashion for Kelly is demonstrated beyond its practical and desirable qualities of body covering made for social and functional use, to impress status and enhance any individuals passage through life. Kelly presented himself as a ready-made, a curiosity, viewed in the lens of America's tortured social conscience. Kelly purposely posed himself in the antithetical regalia of the poor boy, a specific of poverty and oppression. Wearing Converse sneakers in the hallowed temple of fashion, he presents himself as the tension breaker, the token, a contestation ensconced as the carnivalesque imposition to the fashion work. Kelly reduces his physicality to easily understood components, a veritable manual of operation, which worked to fulfil narratives of youth, urban blackness and eccentricity, all encompassed to become surface, sign and place as shown in Table 1.

Kelly's position as an influential Parisian-based fashion designer allowed him to enunciate a new kind of fashion design. His influence is detectable in the work of designers working today who utilize the visual volume of kitsch as central to their practice; Cassette Playa, Jeremy Scott and Bernhard Willhelm come to mind. Although always the astute follower of fashion, Kelly may have been overly influenced by Jean-Charles de Castelbajac who has practised fashion design since 1972 and is a fixture in the Parisian fashion scene; Castelbajac designs colourful, amusing clothes of a similar nature to Kelly. An example of accommodation rather than resistance, Kelly's work possesses a rift of formalism, which is often the case when emergent voices infiltrate closed systems that lack a representative discourse.

The experience of living as a black male member of arguably the most terrorized group of people in history provides the perspective for Patrick Kelly to create himself as a symbol maker – a creator of the liturgy of visualized inequalities reconfigured from those worn by blacks that slaved and laboured in the fields and the homes of whites and their institutions. Kelly comprehends his life as an instinctive designer, contrary to an intellectual designer moulding his work upon real life and not the jest of fantasy, although we will see that Kelly's practice is a problematic one, precisely because the reality of everyday grit is untenable within fashion (Bergerson and Mitchell 1911).

Table 1 Patrick Kelly as allegory

Surface	Place	Sign
Black skin	Mississippi	Slave
Denim	Farm	Share Cropper
Bright colour	Paris	Tourist
Signage	America	Commerce

TIME AND TRAVEL

Kelly is characterized as a postmodern creative who ignores boundaries, borders and time. His practice as interpreter of culturally sensitive topics required precisely the kind of insider knowledge that had been hardwired into his personality. Kelly seems to have been an inveterate opportunist and traveller, a vagabond in physical and in the ideological. Adept at traversing the structure of fashion's hierarchy where his doubt and surprise is both understated and is resoundingly naive. Kelly demonstrates otherness in the fashion system, and perhaps its inevitable future as it attempted to become part of the celebrity star system.

Kelly's attempt to work in the spaces of racism, race and the resultant racial is brought into clear sight by Harold Cruse in his 2005 text *The Crisis of the Negro Intellectual*. Cruse tells us that the responsibility of blacks in their professional pursuit must be to consider blackness regardless of their profession, field, discipline or activity. This is because the centre of mainstream core culture is forever altered in taking on the material culture from the periphery.

It could be argued that material interventions adopted by the mainstream core culture are commentary of what is lacking about the core, notably a lack of energy expended upon self-discovery. If, for a moment, we consider Kelly as the archetypal black fashion designer, his role has been considerable, especially in the introduction of many energies, ideas and possibilities. Kelly has provided an exemplar of the black man's attempt to discover himself internally and externally. As Quigley (1966) reminds us, 'the diffusion of material elements from one society to another has a complex effect within the importing society. In the short run it is usually benefitted by the importation, but in the long run it is frequently disorganized and weakened'.

The diaspora creator/activist, characterized by Kelly, has by necessity become skilled in reconnoitring and penetrating boundaries; by the 2000s the creation and integration of black fashion does not resemble the black fashion that Kelly once perpetrated. Fashions deemed acceptable are laden with hindrances of a non-material element such as authorship and therefore represents a clash of ideologies.

In Euro-American fashion and its insistence for expressions acculturated through filters of membership to associations, curations in magazines and museums, and journalistic criticism all conspire to effectively change and make fashion formerly viewed as outside the conversation part of Euro-American fashion.

Kelly and anyone effectively questioning the core culture are treated as antithetical, requiring them to prove that difference is understandable and important. Within the Parisian fashion system, fashion is demonstrable in its feudal pose; central control of what constitutes fashion must comply with a single vision shared by all and encapsulated by just a few nodes of distribution. The importance of fashion ideology is that all obey the comparisons and metaphors sanctioned in the official realm of the fashion systems' institutions.

As a first time visitor to Paris, Kelly's position was devoid of options except for the realization that becoming a part of the Parisian fashion system meant accepting aestheticism based upon the master's vision. Ensconced in Kelly and all other diaspora creative workers is the realization that working as far away from nature as that was lost to them in Africa, their work has become one of mitigating evil (Sartre, 1988). Kelly's purpose is to import these far from beautiful themes or maybe indigenous ones; in either case it is integrated with betrayal of his past reality and entrée to his dream. For Kelly this repositioning can only be a fantasy. Like Jean Genet, Kelly is cast as the outsider re-imagined as a prince, seeking to make the horror and evil of his culture beautiful. In his dream Kelly imagines himself belonging to an order of fashion designers whose duty is to shepherd the public towards acceptable forms of appearance beyond the traditional visual canon.

This is perhaps an impossible proposition, because in attempting to escape his past Kelly resists any casting of his aesthetic character that is not within his direct control, only in this way does he not lapse into the undesirable space of negrohood. Through assertions of self, Kelly becomes part of the core, contributing to the dominant ideology which became affixed with his brand of creative and ultimately social production. The ambition of every social-economic class is borne out in the economic interests of the ruling class (Althusser 1976).

To say the life and work of Patrick Kelly deserves 'special handling' is to acknowledge his full agency. Also this is to understand Kelly's experience and expectations as recognizably different from designers of privilege and training, with motivations of compliance to the template of the Parisian fashion system, as it has been objectified since 1858 when Englishman Charles Frederick Worth founded the first Parisian haute couture house. A cursory reading of the phases and qualities of Kelly's life shows he was devoted to a cause and chose fashion as the medium for self-expression. For Kelly, design was a catharsis, a way of conciliating his Mississippian trauma with fashion's hypermodern spectacle.

KELLY'S IMPORTANCE

Kelly adds nothing fundamental or innovative to fashion's studio practice. However, his acceptance of his trauma and a quintessential African aesthetic is sufficient to characterize difference. To the extent that fashion somewhat overshadows his potential to create nonconforming narratives that were more oppositional than the ones he offered.

After all, we are all contemporaneous narratives, adding nothing more than more contemporaneous narratives. Embedded within a vigorous work motivated by the realism the his end is close, Kelly tells us something about the actions a black designer has to make to be relevant to the broader community; the same may be said of designers coming anywhere from 'outside'. Considering Patrick Kelly's background and his position within the Parisian fashion system, it was somewhat inevitable that he would employ fashion design practice and the marketing of clothes that would (for some) appear inflammatory or even antithetical to what fashion is expected to be. Indeed Kelly's positioning of black fashion within the mainstream culture is an experiment, an attempt to claim consequences before experience. This gesture of truth requires Kelly to create work that confirms African American culture as a proclamation of equality; however, in orienting the work Kelly seeks to 'normalize' it through equal participation within the Parisian fashion system (Gramsci et al. 1972). Fashion is visualized as a coping mechanism that seized the anguish-laden protestation of Kelly. This morphogenesis may be proved mathematically, for every inequality, every missed heartbeat, every lash of the metaphorical whip, every unfounded accusation, indeed every negative has a positive contained in the inner awareness of the African diaspora. The purpose of Kelly's fashion is to do mischief with the presumption that fashion complies with a traditional form that coheres to beauty and elegance as the opening rites of fashion. Second, a conviction designer like Kelly uses 'thematics' as the basis of the exertion of his design operation; blackness is a proclamation, an iterative motivation made operational in fashion. Seemingly Kelly had to propel this idea of the black fashion designer, as if he is venturing to make a powerful proclamation of 'I am black and I am here'. Reading fashion and eventually offering criticism of fashion is beneficial to culture in many ways. Fashion is a medium of considerable social power that when made operational (indeed fashion is probably always operational, so perhaps we mean when fashion is viewed) can mobilize opinion beyond and exceeding other persuasive forms.

SELLING BLACKNESS

Black memorabilia provided a major allegorical source of inspiration to Kelly, allowing him to develop visual propaganda that delivered an ambiguous message. Apart from their racial connotations, black memorabilia such as watermelons, sambos, mammies, Aunt Jemima and golliwogs performed an important function within Kelly's work. Black memorabilia served to explain Kelly's unspoken culture to the Parisian fashion system and to transform spectators that were unfamiliar or presupposed a meaning of these 'black cultural symbols'.

Viewing Kelly's work and message through today's lens we find that he embraced and conveyed stereotypes that are now problematic, especially distortions of black memorabilia that remained important to his visual vocabulary. Kelly's trademark symbol was a little black doll that became central to his off-the-cuff marketing campaign. Bjorn Amelan, Kelly's lover and business partner, recounts that [he] Kelly would purchase 600 little black dolls a month, made of plastic, people would volunteer, and with a glue gun attach pins to the back. 'He would never leave without stuffing his pockets with them'. Kelly's immersion into collecting African-American memorabilia is not clearly understood. We know that his vast collation of over 3000 pieces of arguably problematic curiosities seems to be the motivation of an opportunist, calculated and in a similar vein to Andy Warhol's predilection for collected cookie jars, art deco, American Indian jewellery, and kitchen wares as a kind of art project with an eye on the appreciation of value; Kelly's collecting had the ambition of reconnoitering inevitable questions about race before questions emerged.

Seemingly unknowingly Kelly turned racial politics inside out and positioned fashion into the predominant view of the way that blacks are interpreted and reinterpreted, and interpreted again. Enthusiastically he embraced all of the racial platitudes for his audiences, both positive and negative. Amelan recalls that Kelly made known, 'White people are not offended by Mickey Mouse. Why should we be afraid of Aunt Jemima negro dolls?' Kelly's hubris in using African American objects that had been misunderstood and cast into stereotype did much to stem inevitable projects and questions about race before questions emerged. Indeed Kelly's prints of racialized images onto dresses could be viewed as a device where boundaries of conversation are set. In that any discussion about Kelly must be filtered through the idea that the dominant expression may be subverted by linking past and present in an attempt to elucidate ramifications of the social future. Kelly's brand of blackness is not sacred; it is a commercial product, no different from the electoral policies elucidated by political candidates. Ideas, be they surfaces or words, are contextualized through the process of interpretation. The oversized buttons, the dummy, the bows and the cycling cap, all became Kelly's armour against the dominant clique of designers and managers, the very people who allowed Kelly opportunity to work on the inside. This was a sound tactical strategy.

Facing the opportunity of success or failure once the investors had undertaken to back him Kelly may have considered his best asset and decided it to be blackness, which he then used as a theme extrapolated from the grit of everyday traumas – Kelly's mendacious use of black iconography that he rips from the collective history, the pain and sadness, joy and faith, optimism and celebration of the African American. Designers are prone to construct and animate their personal culture idyll. Kelly was not new in this, although his subject matter was truly an eclectic construction. This delimiting strategy had another purpose. It provided Kelly the opportunity to use his postmodern agency as his transitional design theme, something the Parisian couturier Christian Lacroix also did. The press seamlessly wrote about Lacriox's birthplace in France's Camargue region as being quintessential to Lacriox's operation as a fashion designer (Mauriés 1996).

As a designer in the western tradition and particularly the Parisian tradition, Kelly's aesthetic was as distinctive as Jazz and AfroPunk. Wearing bib and brace denim dungarees replete with coded meaning as a character of marginalization Kelly's persona is tensioned between the unkempt denim of the southern farmer primed to work the field and the more familiar application of denim as iconic hero wear worn by every self-respecting pop star since the mid-1950s.

How Kelly was able to rise to such a lofty level within the Parisian fashion system remains a matter of curiosity and may only be understood in the reading of the memoirs of the aforementioned gatekeepers of Parisian fashion. In this Kelly towers above all other designers, because he 'wears' the marks of ancestry, of imposition and degradation, but beyond that Kelly remains an *enfant terrible* of fashion.

WHAT WE HAVE LEARNT FROM PATRICK KELLY

Western culture aids and abets Kelly's misaligned message. The Parisian fashion system with its traditional focus on the craft of making labour-intensive clothes in its Dickensian ateliers has been eclipsed by the crafts person and by the celebrity of the designer.

Making Fashion textiles craft (making) should be recognized as the artistic theme; dissolved into the craft until all that remains is the piece of clothing. A constituent of the designer's mediation is what the foremost fashion system should allow – a bridge for the designer/artist to operate without constraint. Kelly was able to do this in Paris, first as a tourist selling his jersey dresses on the streets, free of the expectations of the usual finishes.

Patrick Kelly's exteriorizing of blackness and its traumas are especially profound in that it is rooted in the legacy of African-American culture, which from its genesis in the structural repression casted blacks as removed from the natural order and insists that blacks occupy a space outside of civility and therefore could not contribute any worth to the creative culture. The inescapable conditioning of the African-American is as product of an exploitative system of control Kelly's history will always be mysterious and surrounded by a plethora of unanswered questions; foremost is whether the African-American is capable of creating beauty that is not ladened by pain? In essence Kelly used French fashion as an opportunity to be noticed. Kelly competes not on his terms but on the terms of the Parisian fashion system. It is possible that Kelly rose to prominence because permission was granted in keeping with the Hegelian master–slave dialectic, and that Kelly's work is in fact a positive self-sabotage, a cathartic relinquishing of a painful past for the creation of clothes that might (positively) affect [inter] relations between us and them, them and us.

Patrick Kelly's unique and timely tenure at the pinnacle of global fashion articulated an idealized world system where overt racial violence ceases but the race status of individuals is present in the unspoken criticisms embroiled in questions of worth, value, rights and capabilities.

Acknowledgements

Many thanks to Dilys Blum and Laura Camerlengo from the Philadelphia Museum of Art.

References

Althusser, L. (1976), *Essays in Self-Criticism*, London and Atlantic Highlands, NJ: NLB ; Humanities Press.
Anon, A. (1990), 'Patrick Kelly Dies; made name in Paris with witty fashion', *The New York Times*, 2, http://www.nytimes.com/1990/01/02/obituaries/patrick-kelly-dies-made-name-in-paris-with-witty-fashion.html. Accessed 2 October 2014.
Bakhtin, Mikhail (1941), *Rabelais and his world*. Bloomington: Indiana University Press.
Benjamin, W. and R. Tiedemann. (1999), *The Arcades Project*, Cambridge, MA: Belknap Press.
Bergerson, H. and A. Mitchell. (1911), *Creative Evolution*, New York: Henry Holt and Company.
Blunden, A. (trans.) (1970), 'Ideology and ideological state apparatuses' (notes towards an investigation), https://www.marxists.org/reference/archive/althusser/1970/ideology.htm. Accessed 1 November 2014.
Bockris, V. (1997), *Warhol*, New York: Da Capo Press.
Buck, G. (1988), 'Fashion's clown prince – playful southerner dazzles on the seine', *Chicago Tribune*, http://articles.chicagotribune.com/1988-11-13/features/8802160193_1_fashion-show-chambre-syndicale-dressed. Accessed 7 November 2014.
Carter, L. (2014), 'How a designer from Mississippi nearly conquered Paris', 2 May, http://www.hintmag.com/post/how-a-designer-from-mississippi-nearly-conquered-paris--april-29-2014-2146. Accessed 10 November 2014.
Chiu, E. (2011), 'Adrian Joffe: The Idea of Comme des Garçons', 10 January, http://hypebeast.com/2011/1/adrian-joffe-the-idea-of-comme-desgarconsHyper Beast. Accessed 12 November 2014.
Cruse, H. (2005), *The Crisis of the Negro Intellectual: A Historical Analysis of the Failure of Black Leadership*, New York: New York Review Books.
Deleuze, G., F. Guattari. (2004), Massumi, B. (trans). (2004). *A Thousand Plateaus Capitalism and Schizophrenia*, London and New York: Continuum.
Doonan, S. (2011), *Simon Doonan Remembers Fallen Friends at FGI's 28th Annual Night of Stars*, FGI – Cipriani Wall Street – Barneys, http://thewin-dow.barneys.com/simon-doonan-remembers-friends-at-fgi/. Accessed 2 November 2014.
Ducreay, S. (n.d.), 'Fashion Is Eternal: Looking Back at Style Avant Patrick Kelly." http://www.thestarklife.com/2013/06/17/fashion-is-eternal-looking-back-at-style-avant-patrick-kelly/. Accessed November 2, 2014.
Fortuno, J., C. Whyte and J. Dressler. (2009), "Patrick Kelly (1954–1990)." July 26, https://fashionbeyondthepale.wordpress.com. Accessed 6 January 2015.
Givhan, R. (2004), 'Patrick Kelly's radical cheek', *The Washington Post*, 21 May, http://www.washingtonpost.com/wp-dyn/articles/A3561-2004May30.html. Accessed 6 October 2014.
Gramsci, A. (1972), *Selections from the Prison Notebooks of Antonio Gramsci*, trans, Q. Hoare and G. Nowell-Smith. New York: International Publishers.
Hall, S. (1992), *Culture, Media, Language: Working Papers in Cultural Studies, 1972–79*, London and

Hall, S., B. Gieben and Open University (1992), *Formations of Modernity*, Oxford: Polity in association with Open University.

Hegel, G. W. F. and J. B. Baillie. (1931), *The Phenomenology of Mind*, London and New York: G. Allen & Unwin, Ltd and Macmillan Co.

Holquist, M. (1990), *Dialogism: Bakhtin and His World*, London and New York: Routledge.

Jauss, H. R., T. Bahti and P. De Man. (1982), *Toward an Aesthetic of Reception*. Minneapolis: University of Minnesota Press.

Jennings, H. (2011), *New African Fashion*. Munich: Prestel.

Lipovetsky, G. (1994), *The Empire of Fashion: Dressing Modern Democracy*. Princeton, NJ: Princeton University Press.

Livingston, J. (1991), *Paris is Burning*. New York: Miramax.

Mauriés, P. (1996), *Christian Lacroix: The Diary of a Collection*, 1st ed. New York, NY: Simon & Schuster.

Quigley, C. (1966), *Tragedy and Hope: A History of the World in our Time*. New York and London: Macmillan and Collier-Macmillan.

Rourke, M. (1989), 'Fashion: Road to Paris paved with foreign style', *Los Angeles Times*, 6 October, http://articles.latimes.com/1989-10-06/news/vw-753_1_french-fashion/2. Accessed 2 October 2014.

Sartre, J.-P. and B. Frechtman. (2012), *Saint Genet, Actor and Martyr*, Minneapolis, MN: University of Minnesota Press.

Silva, H. (2004), 'Delta Force', *The New York Times*, 22 February, http://www.nytimes.com/2004/02/22/magazine/delta-force.html?src=pm&pagewanted=1. Accessed 2 November 2014.

Wellek, R. and A. Warren. (1949), *Theory of Literature*, New York: Harcourt, Brace.

New York: Routledge in association with the Centre for Contemporary Cultural Studies, University of Birmingham.

5

JAPANESE CONCEPTUAL FASHION

Bonnie English[1]

Cross-cultural influences, which further melded fashion design with a different form of street style, were introduced by the Japanese designers. Their Zen-based philosophy, based on a preference for simplicity and naturalness, led them to create works of art of a beauty unaffected by the shifting tides of fashion. The subtlety in their work and their distinctive stylistic philosophy have been sustained for decades on the catwalks of Paris.

ISSEY MIYAKE, YOHJI YAMAMOTO AND REI KAWAKUBO

Since the 1970s, the Japanese fashion design of Issey Miyake, Yohji Yamamoto and Rei Kawakubo of Comme des Garçons has had an unequivocal impact on Western dress. Offering a new and unique expression of creativity, they have challenged the established notions of status, display and sexuality in contemporary fashion. Ignoring stylistic trends, these Japanese designers work within a postmodernist visual arts framework, appropriating aspects of their traditional culture and embracing new technological developments and methodologies in textile design. Yet, at the same time, they infuse their work with meaning and memory. The subtleties inherent in their textiles and forms promulgate a new aesthetic in Western dress. Miyake, perhaps the most revered designer in Japan today, has consistently propagated new ideas, new materials and new design directions, which accommodate the modern lifestyle of contemporary women. While the work of Yamamoto and Kawakubo was initially framed as another form of anti-aesthetic, their contribution to the evolution of twentieth-century fashion has been more profound. Their understated work underlines the notion that culture, conceptualization and experimentation can be integral to fashion, as they are to art. By the end of the century, they had helped to change the face of fashion irrevocably.

THE AESTHETICS OF POVERTY

Postmodernist fashion relies on visual paradox—underclothing becomes outerwear, new is replaced by old, and propriety in dress is replaced by a total lack of respect for the display of status and value systems. Highly priced, slashed and torn garments symbolize an economic irrationality. A social paradigm is created and a new visual ethic is embraced. The literal deconstruction of fabric and finishing techniques seemingly reflects the deconstruction of past values.

Harold Koda, Fashion Historian of the Metropolitan Museum of Art, referred to this new concept of dress, as seen in the work of Yamamoto and Kawakubo, as the 'aesthetics of poverty'—a phrase that seemed to aptly describe the new dress code. The Japanese preference for understatement is coupled by a love of old things that imply accretions of time. In their poetry, for example, they acknowledge that perishability is a necessary element of beauty and the words exemplify their grief over the fragility of both beauty and love. In their pottery, they choose simple and irregular forms, perhaps cracked, as they represent both humility and

---

[1] From Bonnie English (2007) Japanese Conceptual Fashion. In A Cultural History of Fashion in the 20th Century: From Catwalk to the Sidewalk, 117–35, Berg.

an appreciation of the traces of the individuality of the potter. These aesthetic sensibilities are integral to the work and philosophy of these contemporary Japanese fashion designers.

In Western terms, Koda compared the 1980s trend with the 1890s, a time that also 'saw decadence as an aesthetic ideal' (Martin and Koda, 1993: 97). In ideological terms, dress design has undoubtedly responded to social, political and economic instabilities throughout history. In the 1970s, 1980s and 1990s, global events such as high rates of unemployment, youth revolutions, anti-war sentiment, global poverty and environmental catastrophes impacted greatly upon the conscience of society, and became implicit in postmodernist visual arts practice. While cultural differences existed, both punk fashion and the work of Japanese designers Yohji Yamamoto and Rei Kawakubo reflected this practice. The Japanese fashions were characterized by torn, ripped and ragged fabric, and uneven and unstitched hemlines—a disarray that was quite subversively calculated. Subsequently, due to their unprecedented influence, a new form of anti-fashion emerged as the dominant aesthetic in the early 1980s.

For centuries, Western fashion has doggedly adhered to a structured and tailored fit, which extols the virtues of sexuality, glamour and status—the mainstay of European haute couture design. Fashion historians have frequently coined the well-worn phrase 'conspicuous consumption' (first used in 1899 by Veblen, in *The Theory of the Leisure Class*), as this term underlines the key motivational role that the display of wealth in dress has played throughout history. Visual sumptuosity reflected individuals' standing in society, their status in a hierarchical order, and defined their position within a social class system. While Veblen questioned the need for this perceived pecuniary emulation, he argued that this material display of wealth reflected a 'status anxiety'. Arguably, this nineteenth-century notion of social class elitism gradually lost momentum as waves of middle-class consumerism blurred the distinctions between the classes throughout the course of the twentieth century. As history has shown, this growing 'democratization' of fashion eventually led to a contradiction of modernist ideals and practices.

What defined modernist haute couture fashion—the uniqueness of the design, fine finishing techniques, unblemished surfaces, exquisite tailoring, and hand-sewing—gave way to the predominance of mass-produced prêt-à-porter clothing. Yet this new culture of dress presented by the two Japanese designers actually appeared to mock the exclusivity of the earlier modernist fashions. In fact, according to fashion historian McDowell (1987), the Japanese designers Kawakubo and Yamamoto 'made few concessions to traditional Western ideals of dress, chic or beauty' and their clothes were 'as much a statement of philosophy as they were of design' (McDowell, 1987: 178).

These avant-garde designers produced clothes that appeared radical to Western eyes, and could almost be seen as a homage to their country's past and a challenge to the increased Western influence there (Carnegy, 1990: 20). Interestingly, both Yamamoto and Kawakubo—who are now in their sixties—grew up in post-war Japan. It is important to remember that, during and immediately after the Second World War, Japan suffered years of austerity, and this impoverishment was imprinted on the minds of many. Their early 1980s collection showings in Paris can be better understood if viewed within this context. It could also explain the media reaction to their collection in 1982, when the derisory fashion headlines screamed 'Fashion's Pearl Harbor' and Kawakubo was described as a 'rag picker'. Their models, dressed in black deconstructivist clothes, looked cadaverous, with either shaved heads or seemingly dirty, unkempt hair, with pasty white faces that were 'devoid of make-up, apart from a disturbing bruised blue on their lower lips' (Mendes and de la Haye, 1999: 234). Arguably, the fashion press saw this work as a political statement—and perhaps it was.

Yamamoto has been described as a designer who is driven by an existentialist philosophy, and whose work elicits an intellectualism that ties form with meaning and memory. In his autobiography *Talking to Myself* (Yamamoto, 2002) he asserts: 'Dirty, stained, withered, broken things seem beautiful to me'. The Japanese term *hifu* refers to a form of anti-style, and is seen as an undeniable element of Yamamoto's dressmaking. According to Yamamoto, one can actually feel *hifu* clothing—its confusion, shabbiness and disarray—as if it were reflecting a meagreness of spirit or sadness in the people wearing the clothes. In other words, the disarray of the fabric mimics the emotional fragility of the wearer. This merging of the emotional, intellectual and aesthetic encouraged many viewers to see Yamamoto's collection showings as a form of performance art.

He describes his work as being 'contradictory' to the commercialism of Western fashion. He creates clothing that has a universal appeal, a timeless quality—clothes that are meant to last a lifetime.

Authors often compare the work of Yamamoto and Kawakubo, as they were great friends and soulmates for ten years. Kawakubo also finds beauty in the unfinished, the irregular, the monochromatic and the ambiguous. Placed within the context of Zen Buddhist philosophy, this translates as an appreciation of poverty, simplicity and imperfection (Leong, 2003). Kawakubo asserts that she does not have a set definition of beauty:

> I find beauty in the unfinished and the random . . . I want to see things differently to search for beauty. I want to find something nobody has ever found . . . it is meaningless to create something predictable. (quoted in Kawamura, 2004)

Kawakubo's conceptualization is inherent in her philosophy towards design, as she is always projecting forward to the future—pushing boundaries. 'It's not good to do what others do. If you keep doing the same things without taking risks, there will be noprogress,' she said (*Undressed,* 2001). Kawakubo relies on spontaneity in her work: 'I could say that my work is about looking for accidents. Accidents are quite important for me. Something is new because it is an accident' (*Undressed,* 2001). While her work is uncompromising in its anti-fashion directions, like that of Yamamoto, it is still very personal and self-reflective. 'When I am designing, what's important to me is to express what's happening in my own life, to express my personal feelings through my designs' (*Undressed,* 2001).

A CULTURAL HERITAGE

Another strong link that ties both Yamamoto and Kawakubo to Miyake is the truth of their Japanese heritage. This embracing of their indigenous culture could be read as a backlash against a previous celebration of 'outsider' popular culture. According to a contemporary Kyoto textile artist, after the war American popular culture exerted a growing influence of on Japanese society. It seemed that the Japanese people were no longer selectively focused on their cultural heritage, instead desiring new and novel consumer items rather than cherishing traditional pieces. The kimono, for example, has always played a significant role in the culture of Japan.

All three designers insist that the underlying influence of the kimono in their work is profound. They agree that it is the space between the fabric and the body that is most important. This negates the blatant sexuality of fitted Western clothes, and introduces the possibility of layered or voluminous clothing that becomes a sculptural form of its own. Kawakubo comments on the 'gender-neutral' design of her kimono-inspired constructions: 'Fashion design is not about revealing or accentuating the shape of a woman's body, its purpose is to allow a person to be what they are' (*The Story of Fashion,* 1985). This is abundantly clear in her Spring/Summer 1997 Bump collection, where padded sections were added to the clothes to distort the back and hips of the body, thus critiquing the notion of the perfect female shape. This is very much in keeping with postmodernist practice, where self-critique and reflection challenge accepted norms of life and society. Does sexuality always have to be determined by body shape? Kate Betts (2004) argues in *Time* magazine that Kawakubo invites an open interpretation of her work, but also suggests that this collection calls for some level of self-awareness. Not surprisingly, Kawakubo commented in 1983 that she saw the New York bag lady as the 'ideal woman' to dress, and in 1984 that a woman who 'earns her own way' is her typical client. Another often-quoted statement of the 1990s refers to how she designed clothes for 'strong women who attract men with their minds rather than their bodies'. This inherent feminist critique—obvious in both her words and her work—was echoed not only in many different forms in arts practice in the 1980s and 1990s, but also in literature, media advertising, film and dramatic production.

Miyake's work comments on the recontextualization of the kimono to create a different aesthetic milieu. Miyake rejected the traditional forms of Paris collection clothing. Through the inventive use of fabric and successive layering, he developed a concept of fashion based on the use of cloth—or rather, the 'essence' of clothing: the wrapping of the body in cloth. He created anti-structural, organic clothing which takes on a sculptural quality that suggests a natural freedom, expressed through the simplicity of its cut, the abundance of new fabrics, the space between the garment and the body, and its general flexibility. Miyake stated: 'I learned about space between the body and the fabric from the traditional kimono . . . not the style, but the space' (Knafo, 1988: 108). Like Kawakubo, Miyake's designs also have parallels with architecture. His structures in bamboo recall Samurai armour, a rigid house for the body. These constructions exemplify ideas of the body moving within a space beneath an outer space (Holborn, 1988: 120).

Similarly, Yohji Yamamoto redefined male clothing forms when he introduced his Autumn/Winter 1985/1986 'unstructured' men's collection with baggy, pleated trousers—a draped look that approximated Turkish harem trousers. Suit jackets lost their tapered waists, linings and padding were removed, and the way sleeves were mounted changed the male silhouette dramatically. Different textiles were used, such as soft, elastic fabrics made of viscose and crepe yarns, and this new redefined form heralded the direction towards comfort and simplicity. Perhaps more importantly, Yamamoto saw this new aesthetic as a reflection of a new 'ideal of clothing'. He said: 'People don't "consume" these garments: they might spend their entire lives in them . . . that's what life is about. Real clothes, not fashion' (Chenoune, 1993: 305).

TEXTILE DESIGN

Another major factor that unites the postmodernist work of Yamamoto, Kawakubo and Miyake is their interest in experimentation in textile design. The Japanese fashion empire is built on the framework of its textile industry—just as, for centuries, the French industry has been. This experimentation was evident in Kawakubo's 'lace' or 'Swiss cheese' sweaters, when weaver Hiroshi Matsushita reformulated the actual fabric on the loom to create various-sized holes that appeared as rips or tears. Some textile designers believed that, with growing industrialization and complex technologies, a more humanistic approach was needed in the creation of new textiles. In Japan, when one defines imperfections in fabrics, it is called 'fabric hand', as these aberrations are considered precious (Niwa, 2002: 238). This is used as an inherent criticism of the mechanical uniformity in textile production and experimentation with new methodologies in textile design. Matsushita refers to this technique as 'loom-distressed weaves'. In postmodernist terms, it is called 'deconstruction'.

Miyake is renowned for his research in textile technology. In his ongoing series of collections using pleats, Pleats Please, which he started in 1993 and worked on for over ten years with Minagawa, Miyake has created a kaleidoscope of colour in his surface patterning, akin to the fragmentation of colour as seen on a computer screen. The interplay of pattern and colour is heightened by the technique of heat-setting pleats in the synthetic garment, resulting in an origami of pleating. As the wearer moves, the colours start to dance before your eyes. Pleating became Miyake's obsession—he would design a pure shape first, and then press it into a pleating machine. *Interview* magazine quotes Miyake as saying: 'Pleats give birth to texture and shape all at the same time. I feel I have found a new way to give individuality to today's mass-produced clothing' (Saiki, 1992: 34). The series attests to Miyake's desire to produce adaptable clothing that is both functional and reflective of modern simplicity in an egalitarian society.

Miyake's contribution to the invention of new synthetic fibres cannot be underestimated. In *Miyake Modern,* Simon (1999) remarks that one of the most remarkable aspects of his work is determined by 'an understanding of textile fibres, both natural and synthetic, and of fabrics, both hand-woven and traditionally dyed, as well as high-tech textiles that are not woven at all' (1999: 45). Mitchell, Curator of Fashion in the International Decorative Arts department of the Powerhouse Museum in Sydney, suggests that Miyake's work aims 'to rediscover the traditional beauty of a Japan which is disappearing; to emphasize the importance of industrially produced clothes by using synthetic materials' (quoted in English, 1999). It all offers fashion a focus as it walks backwards towards the twenty-first century, and offers suggestions for the future (Benaim, 1997: 7).

CONCEPTUALIZATION

All three Japanese designers rejected change for change's sake, and instead chose to work on the refinement and evolution of previous collections. This evolution of an idea was the basis of Japanese fashion. The conceptual process of serialization, revisited by many conceptual visual practitioners since the 1960s, is integral to the Japanese approach to design.

Miyake, Yamamoto and Kawakubo are often described as niche designers—designers who do not follow stylistic trends or directions. Unlike their European and American 'stylist' counterparts, they have not exclusively embraced the revivalist or popular cultural imaging that has inundated Paris catwalks for decades. The riotous and multifarious themes that we see in the repertoire collections of Alexander McQueen, Jean-Paul Gaultier and Vivienne Westwood find no place in the work of the Japanese designers. Nor is it likely that these designers will ever be nominated as possible head designers of other 'mega' fashion houses. Obviously, the uncompromising nature of the Eastern designers' work eliminates their suitability for such a role, despite the fact that the international press voted Kawakubo the leading designer in Paris in 1987.

The conceptual underpinning in their design work also explains why, in the early 1990s, their reputation as leaders in the international fashion arena was consolidated (English, 2004). It could be argued that Miyake, Kawakubo and Yamamoto all offered a meaningful alternative to the superficial, regressive and over-designed work of so many of the Western designers in the 1990s. Their work—more closely allied with postmodernist practice—did not fall neatly within the dictates of the established fashion industry, and as a result was not consumed by its self-imposed boundaries. Perhaps this is why it has appealed to noted art photographers such as Irving Penn, Nick Knight, Robert Mapplethorpe, David Sims and Inez Van Lamsweerde, whose photographs underline the notion that fashion can step beyond its immediate frame of reference. For example, the publication entitled *Issey Miyake: Photographs by Irving Penn* is a collaborative effort between the Japanese designer and the Western photographer, printed by Nissha in Kyoto (Penn, 1988). Three tons of Miyake's designs were shipped to New York, where Penn made his own choices. Penn, like Miyake, 'employs an art of reduction—his fashion photographs are emptied to allow the geometry of his clothes to be the sole uncluttered force. Penn's photographs are contextless, the subject without the surround' (Holborn, 1988: 118). In a similar way, Japanese landscape and woodblock print artists also concentrated their images by juxtaposing them with bare, unadorned elements.

Kawakubo worked collaboratively with American postmodernist artist Cindy Sherman in 1994 to promote her Comme des Garçons clothing (Glasscock, 2003). She sent Sherman garments from each of her collections to use as she wished. Sherman produced a series of unconventional photographs, which 'centred on disjointed mannequins and bizarre characters, forcing the clothing itself into the background'. Sherman presented Kawakubo's clothing in masquerade settings, but the confrontational, theatrical images are not about clothes. They are about performance art. Sherman is renowned for her interpretations of mass media stereotypes of femininity. Her critique of 'fashionable' photography is in keeping with Kawakubo's approach to the business of fashion design, which is strongly inspired by the values of the contemporary art world.

The designers Miyake, Yamamoto and Kawakubo produce work that is imbued with the history of the past, yet looks dynamically towards the future. They have become leaders in the international fashion industry. Their clothing has created a visual language that strengthens the converging line that exists between fashion and art. Miyake is amused when his work is so often referred to as an art form, stating that: 'Clothes are more important than art.'

The Japanese ability to synthesize the ideas and practices of other cultures is central to its success in the international design industry. Appropriation, pluralism and fragmentation are inherent in postmodernist practice, whether it is in the decorative, applied or fine arts. The visual anomalies or contradictions evident in Harajuku street style fashion are peculiar to the Japanese culture. More importantly, the style evolved from individual choice; it was not determined by designer trends or dictated by conglomerate ready-to-wear markets. The notion of difference, based on the adaptation of so many diverse local contexts combined in Harajuku street style fashion, suggests that this way of dressing was one of the very few which was resistant to the stereotypes of globalization.

References

Benaim, L. (1997), *Issey Miyake*, London: Thames & Hudson.

Betts, K. (2004), 'Rei Kawakubo: Comme des Garçons, Avator of the Avant-Gardé, *Time*, 16 February, p. 40.

Carnegy, V. (1990), *Fashion of the Decades: The Eighties*, London: Batsford.

Chenoune, F. (1993), *A History of Men's Fashion*, Paris: Flammarion Press.

English, B. (2004), 'Japanese Fashion as a Re-considered Form', in The Space Between: Textiles-Art-Design Conference CD, Vol. 2, Perth: Curtin University of Technology.

Glasscock, J. (2003), 'Bridging the Art/Commerce Divide: Cindy Sherman and Rei Kawakubo of Comme des Garçons', <www.nyu.edu/greyart/exhibits>.

Holborn, M. (1988), 'Image of a Second Skin', *Artforum*, Vol. 27, November, pp. 118–21.

Leong, R. (2003), 'The Zen and the Zany: Contemporary Japanese Fashion', *Visasia*, 23, March, <www.visasia.com.au>.

Kawamura, Y. (2004), 'The Japanese Revolution in Paris', *Through the Surface,* <www.throughthesurface.com/syposium/kawamura>.

Knafo, R. (1988), 'The New Japanese Standard: Issey Miyake', *Connoisseur*, March, pp. 100–109.

Martin R. and H. Koda. (1993), *Infra-Apparel*, Metropolitan Museum of Art. New York, NY: Harry Abrams.

McDowell, C. (1987), *McDowell's Directory of Twentieth-Century Fashion*. New York, NY: Prentice-Hall.

Mendes, V. and de la Haye, A. (1999), *20th Century Fashion*, London: Thames & Hudson.

Niwa, M. (2002), 'The Importance of Clothing Science and Prospects for the Future', *International Journal of Clothing Science and Technology*, Vol. 14, Nos. 3-4, p. 238.

Penn, I. (1988), *Issey Miyake, Photographs by Irving Penn*, ed. N. Calloway, A New York Graphic Society Book, Boston: Little Brown & Co.

Saiki, M. K. (1992), 'Issey Miyake – Photographs by Irving Penn', *Graphis*, July/August, Vol. 48, No. 280.

Simon, J. (1999), 'Miyake Modern', New York: Little, Brown & Co.

The Story of Fashion: The Age of Dissent (1985), video, London: RM Arts Production.

Undressed: Fashion in the 20th Century (2001)*, video. Little Bird/Tatlin Production*, London: *Beckmann Visual Productions.*

Yamamoto, Y. (2002), *Talking to Myself*, Milan: Carla Sozzani.

Veblen, T. (1965 [1899]), *The Theory of the Leisure Class (The Writings of Thornstein Veblen)*, New York: Macmillan.

6

MARTIN MARGIELA:
Signs of the time

Barbara Vinken[1]

Margiela, a member of the Antwerp school and the founder of deconstruction in fashion, is a master of reduction. In contrast to other designers, who make themselves into stars and set their face, their personality and their image to work as publicity for their fashion, Margiela does not allow himself to be photographed and makes no public appearances. He also does not sign his creations, sewing in a blank space at the place where the name would otherwise appear, a total paradox in a market completely captivated by the *griffe*. Two absences, two empty spaces, in a context in which image and name have become the dominant market strategies. Faceless, nameless.

Far from the inner-court of the Louvre, where twice a year the veil is lifted, and the secrets of the next season are displayed by the highest-paid models, Margiela's 'shows' take place in Barbès, for example, one of the poorest areas of Paris, inhabited mainly by Africans and Arabs, in empty Metro shafts, in deserted parking lots, in disused railway stations. His designs are often modeled by non-professionals who, instead of striding down the catwalk before an admiring public, mix with the audience, as in a modern theatrical staging, and only incidentally show the clothes in that they happen to be wearing them. Where the fashion industry establishment uses the image of the models to sell its clothes, Margiela models are considered, not as promotional devices, but as private people, and remain incognito. Anonymity is ostentatiously preserved by a strip printed over the eyes, or a thick veil, wrapped around the head. Instead of images, Margiela presents indexical signs – the signs of wear, among others.

Margiela applies his deconstructive talent to the subversion of the strategies of the present-day fashion scene. Perhaps more radically still than Kawakubo, his work aims at conquering a distance from the idea of fashion itself. His contribution to the exhibition, 'Le monde selon ses créateurs' is a carefully constructed allegory of this literally negative relation to fashion: presented in beaming white photographic negatives, Margiela's fashion appears as if under all-pervading x-rays that press under the surface, and let invisible elements come to light. In his work, two of the constitutive elements of fashion – perfect, invisible handicraft, and the product of this skill, the fulfilled, magical moment of the ephemeral appearance – are abandoned, unmasked, undermined. The traces of slow labor, of the production process and of the staging, all completely effaced in the blinding moment of the showing, are now exposed. In this exposure, there is more at work, however, than the disclosure of the secrets of the trade. Felix Salgado, who has spoken of 'decodification' and 'dissection' in Margiela's fashion, emphasizes the aggressive moment in Margiela's work through a scandalous comparison. It is as if Margiela lifts the skirt of Paris, and airs a terrible, frightening secret. If fashion is a process in which the feminine body is disguised as a fetish in order to conceal its alarming sexedness, then Margiela's is indeed a deconstructive work, bringing the secret of fashion to light, exposing

---

[1] From Barbara Vinken (2005). Martin Margiela: Sing of the Time, in Fashion Zeitgeist: Trends and Cycles in the Fashion System, Oxford: Berg, 127–57.

the bland perfection of the disguise, deconstructing the product of fashion, the fetishized feminine body.

Margiela, a Belgian designer – to French ears, this is almost an oxymoron – found his own style with the discovery of a peculiarly Flemish trace at the heart of French elegance. The leitmotif of his work is the *mannequin,* in low Flemish, the *mannekin*: the cloth or wooden doll in the studio of the designer. The *mannekin* is the most important tool of the dressmaker, and its influence on the design process is so far-reaching that the women who model the clothes, and who are named after it, could be said merely to bring this 'little man' to life. It is not surprising, then, that Margiela's deconstruction of fashion begins with the native *mannekin*. The standardization of the female form, accomplished by the mannequin, represents the norms of classical proportion, as canonically transmitted through Greek sculpture. But, on the other hand, this also means that the classical statue has been shrunken to the tailor's measure, has become nothing but a *mannekin*. Margiela drags the *mannekin* out of the 'obscene' beyond of the fashion show, and into the lights of the stage, showing how the uniform, ideal body of the woman is produced by the art of the dressmaker, rather than being an incarnation of nature. The body is artificial, and the art of the dressmaker consists in making this artifice appear as natural, just as the model embodies the doll's body with her own living body.

Margiela shows that the origin of the unified whole body, in its classical form, lies in the cutting up of the material. He dresses women as the 'mannekins' that they embody: his finished clothes, in which hems and dart are external and visible, look like they are pinned up on a cloth doll. The irony is not the suggestion of the woman as doll, but the doll as 'woman,' as the woman that women are not. These 'unfinished' pieces expose the fascination with the inanimate, with the statue as doll, as the hidden nexus of fashion. In postfashion, this process is laid open and reversed, turned inside out. The lifeless model appears as a living person, and conversely, the living human body appears as *mannekin,* as cloth doll. The fetishistic core of fashion, its soul or, rather, its soullessness, is no longer disguised as the veil of truth or the garment of nature. In Margiela, this soul is presented as the 'ghost in the machine,' in the term of the philosopher Gilbert Ryle for the modern Cartesian myth of man, here the ghost that haunts the machinery of dressmaking, and that fashion successfully promotes and sells as 'woman.' In his fashion, we walk around ostentatiously just as we were 'fabricated.' Turning this core of fashion outwards, Margiela's clothes no longer animate the eternal perfection of a lifeless ideal. Rather we wear this ideal, conscious of it as something fabricated and lifeless, in order that we can live ourselves as something other than this, alongside it. In a second step, Margiela wraps us up in this 'other': no longer in the normativized, immortal ideal, but in the imprint that the organic living body had left behind. His 'rag clothes' show the traces that other bodies, in the course of their life, as the way to death, have left behind and impressed upon them.

From the technical point of view, this takes place in a number of discrete steps. First the inner dimension of the dress is turned outward. The jealously guarded secrets of production, the hem, the dart, etc. come to the surface; hidden functional accessories, such as zips or press studs are emphatically visible. Then the clothes are not worked through to a finished state; the ends of the fabric, for example, are not over-edged. The individual phases of the process of production remain visible in the smallest details. It is only to a first impression that this process recalls the functionalism of the Russian avant-garde of the 1920s, which allowed no other ornament than the functional itself. 'Aesthetic aspects must be replaced by the process of sewing itself,' declared Varvara Stepanova, a Russian designer, to the members of her studio: 'Let me explain. Do not put any ornamentation on the dress: the seams which are essential for the cut give the dress form: expose how the dress is put together, the zips and so on, just as such things are visible on a machine.'[1] For Margiela, it is less a matter of the aestheticization of a form. He deconstructs this functionalism, since in his work the function without a function also becomes an ornament: he is actually more on the side of *l'art pour l'art*. The turning outward of the production process is, for him, a turning-outwards of time.

Time clings to Margiela's work. His clothes carry the traces which time leaves behind, and are themselves signs of time. Time has entered into them in two respects: 1. as the time of the production process: and 2. as traces, which time leaves behind in the fabric in the course of use. This is not a reflection of the rise of recycling as a moral and a political imperative. Rather, these works have made the signs of time into their theme in a quite literal way. There are skirts made out of the kind of scarves that can be collected at a flea market; clothes made out of old clothes which have been taken apart and then put back together again; pullovers made out of old stockings, in which the heels model the breasts and the elbows; inner-linings made out of cotton which still bears the traces of the hoof-like shoes of the models, dipped in red dye, from the last show. Even if Margiela himself designates this procedure as recycling, it is not here a matter of an ethical operation, or of a political–ecological consciousness. To the contrary, it is clear that it is not a moral, but an entirely aesthetic maneuver. Margiela does not remake the old out of new materials, he uses the old and the used, as it was. In the process, he wins for his fashion something which is *per* definition foreign to fashion, something which was exclusively reserved to the artwork: the fascination of the single piece. Every piece that is made according to this method, regardless of how many versions there may be, is a unique piece, because the materials that are used in it are unique. No scarf is like the other, no foot-imprint is identical with another. Since the piece has taken time into itself, Margiela can hope that the traces of time will complete the work: it can age like a painting.

What makes Margiela's clothes truly unique, as unique as those of the *haute couture,* even as they stand the principles of the latter on its head, is the revaluation of the act of cutting to measure on the doll. The relationship of the body to the dressmaker's dummy is reversed. For the *haute couture,* the aim was to fit a reproducible design, created on the dummy, to an individual body, and to do this in a way such as to hide its weak points and to bring it as close as possible to the perfection of the classical statue. Margiela's art no longer cuts with ideal proportions in mind, in order to cover the flaws of individuals and to set in motion our inner classical statue. On the contrary, he traces the ideal measure of the mannequin onto the individual body, which thus can only appear as divergence from ideality. In deconstructing these mechanisms and the fascination with the inorganic which keeps them in movement, he creates, on the other side of the fetishized body of the doll, the space for the individual in the imprint of the body beyond the statue – without renouncing the fetishistic attraction. The question remains open as to how successful this other side is in comparison with his impressive dismantling of the old machinery of fashion.

Nonetheless, at the high point of Margiela's career, there stands an antique statue of an altogether particular kind, figuring as a provisional and paradoxically transitory emblem of a radicalized aesthetic. With the 'new classic' we leave the realm of fashion and enter a realm of art – though an artistic realm which deconstructively crosses itself out, and which is devoted not to the eternal preservation of the museum, but rather deliberately calculates the self-destruction of the artwork. In the Boijmans Van Beuningen Museum in Rotterdam, Margiela's dressmaker's dummy was not only exposed to wind and rain but, under consultation with a microbiologist, was also subjected to yet harsher conditions through the application of a specific bacterial strain. This controlled decomposition changed over into a new, old aesthetic, an uncanny image of the classical statue,

> A doll wears a very wide dress, over which is drawn a transparent, hip-length net T-shirt made of nylon; apparently intentionally, the tight T-shirt lays the dress in graceful, lightly diagonal running folds, without pressing them flat. The whole dress is covered with a greenish mold. The effect is of a Greek statue, something that looks as classical as if Phidias himself had worked on it.[2]

A Martin Margiela jacket is made from an almost old-fashioned traditional 'Pepper and Salt' woven wool-cloth, as is classically used for men's suits. It closes off tightly around the waist, and sits closely on the upper body, as if poured on. A continuous black zip is sewed on, not hidden. That which is normally concealed between the lining and the fabric is turned outward. The hem and the dart stand on the outside, and show that they could not have been more perfectly finished. The breasts are clearly profiled, in a star-shaped pattern. The impression of the dummy, on which the material is pinned up according to the proportions of the customer, is reinforced by the untreated cotton lining, a material ordinarily used to try out a particular cut or to prepare the pattern for a dress. This inconspicuous lining is also finished, as if it were a matter of the outer side of the dress: the edges are generously pressed and the seams are covered, the zip sewed in from inside. The neck and shoulder parts are strengthened in the manner of old-fashioned men's suits, with a very fine black, ribbed, satin-like viscose material.

The arms of the jacket demonstrate the exact opposite of the careful fit: they are of an undefined excess length, and also double the necessary width. On a dummy, they would dangle down hopelessly like the arms of a marionette, underlining the point of the piece. The buttons follow the model of the old-fashioned classical suit, but are double the normal size. Although they are purely decorative, they can be opened. Their old-fashioned good-quality makes for a strange contrast with the very prosaic zips. Tending slightly towards the pompous, the sleeves are perfectly and discreetly tailored. Their lustrous white viscose lining slides on the arms, so that the material lays in heavy folds. In the all but majestic fall of the folds, these sleeves cite from afar the props of the official masculine dignity of a past era: they recall the robes of the high court, the gown of the university, the vestments of the church. It is hard to accept the connection of these sleeves with the outwards-turned mannequin-top, and indeed, one can promptly take them off. The sleeves are fastened with large press studs, attached, as if hastily and by hand, with white tacking thread. These studs, which stylistically mediate between the torso and the arm, can be undone in two different ways: one can just let them hang down behind, so that the arms have their freedom of movement; or one can have them lie completely to the side. In the latter case, all that is left is the vest-like close-fitting top, and the effect is decidedly unfinished; very short hanging sleeves, reinforced by a small round shoulder padding ring, remain behind: they are in the end not over-edged.

This creation has a double frame of reference: in the first place, it stands before the background of fashion design, in the second place before that of the traditional classical strict men's suit. The connotation of professionality implied by this latter reference is reinforced by the citation of a still more formal mode of signifying masculine professional authority, that of the judge's or professor's robe. Such relatively uniform modes of dress, with their discreet elegance and their proper finish, have the function, among others, of distracting attention from the specificity of the individual's body, of neutralizing its presence. The tailor's art here consists in bringing body and clothing to disappear before the man conscious of his responsibility. Now, however, this body becomes insistently visible, disguised as a pure body, mindless and lifeless, as a dummy.

On this background, it is the jacket which, in an initial moment, first brings the body into play. Attention is heightened by the disruption of the horizon of expectations. The body – the torso and arms – are in clothed in diametrically opposite ways: the one tight, the other wide; fullness of material is contrasted with utmost minimality, old-fashioned quality and perfection in the finish with the unfinished, merely sketched out pattern. The impression this produces is by no means harmonious: the body is not brought out as a whole, as an organic unit; rather, its divisibility, the possibility of isolating particular limbs, as utilized, for example, in jazz dance, is underlined.

In a second step, the masculine and the feminine body, and also the question of feminine authority, are brought into a new context. In the close-fitting top, in which the breasts are emphasized through the stitching, there lies clearly a physical body, whose erotic connotations are marked by the continuous zip. The sheer materiality of the physicality is emphasized, but at the same time ironized, by the fact that the outfit seems to be pinned onto a doll. Through the stitching it becomes clear that it is not a matter of a natural but of an artificial body. The classic feminine fashion, always concerned with an effective underlining of 'feminine charm,' achieved, often enough, by allowing a generous glance into the *decolleté* – the whole play, in short, along precisely defined borders of hiding, exhibiting, letting oneself be seen – is thematized and humorously commented on by the sudden and unexpected sight of an erotically uncharged zone: with certain movements, the jacket allows a glance from behind at the upper arm. The mechanism is summoned up, but it is devoid of content. In this way, it becomes clear that it is the mechanism itself, and not the question of whether or not there is anything to see, which is erotically charged.

The wearer of this jacket, then, is not dressed like a man, nor is it simply a matter of men's fashion being eroticized and feminized. Rather, the impression that there is no body underneath these garments is retrospectively denounced as a fiction: the male suit is de-sublimated, in that it is designed as women's clothing is designed, in order to reveal rather than to conceal the body. Moreover, the feminine body is exhibited as a fabricated rather than a natural body, and the mechanism of hiding and revealing by which this body is eroticized is reflected upon and ironized by the exposure of the way that it continues to operate even without any content to hide and reveal. The mythology of sexually neutral identity is shattered by the ironic staging of the feminine body. The woman can smilingly assume the inheritance of the venerable insignia of male authority, unquestionably dressed in 'professional clothing,' precisely through the fact that she undoes this myth. For all this authority comes down in the end to nothing more than a *mannekin*.

The other background before which the jacket stands, we have said, is that of fashion itself; clearly the design is highly self-reflexive. At the center of fashion lies the art of producing an effect without revealing the manner in which it is produced. Like a magician, fashion conceals its tricks. Its seduction lies not least in the surprise of this unbelievable success; it includes a moment of curiosity on the side of the spectator. The theatricality of fashion lies in its ability to create a perfect staged moment.

By contrast, postfashion, for which the jacket of Margiela stands as an exemplary instance, is not an art of the moment. Rather, it takes as its object the temporality and the historicity of fashion as a process. On the one hand, it exposes the various steps of the process by which an article of clothing is produced, and records them. It captures the truly ephemeral (as opposed to the artificial ephemerality of fashion), that which was always supposed to disappear without trace: the sheer materiality of the cloth in the unfinished support-sleeves; the dressmaker's dummy; the condition of the top as seen within, pinned up in a way such that one could now begin to sew it together; the haste and provisionality expressed by the press studs attached with the white tacking thread; the sleeve arm that, after an artful cutting out, lovingly worked out in every detail, is quickly sewn up – a perfection in the functional detail, which comes out so much the more starkly in that it is here functionless, *l'art pour l'art*. The ornament here lies in the luxurious superficiality of the function. To the perfect moment of illusion, the jacket opposes the arduous work that goes to produce the illusion.

On the other hand, the historical development of the genre 'dressmaking,' through which particular effects first became possible, also comes into the foreground. In an almost encyclopedic gesture, the work features three different modes of 'closure,' corresponding to three stages in the historical development of dressmaking: button, press stud, zip, whereby one of the decisive advantages of the last two, namely their relative invisibility, is called up *ex negativo* by their being drastically put on display. Against the extra-temporal effect of the sudden success of fashion, stands here the historical development of technical details which had made such triumphs possible in the first place.

Margiela's fashion lifts the skirt of the city of Paris. It raises the veil on a past, false ideality. From under this veil the secret of fashion steps forth: the fetishistic structure of desire. The fetish, which, according to Benjamin, underlies the sex appeal of the inorganic, is the heart of fashion. This is why fashion was the site at which the lifeless was animated, without having to bear the stigmata of life, at which the idea came to life, hard, flawless, complete and perfect like the marble of the antique statues, alive for the perfect moment of the illusion. Postfashion brings this fetishistic core to light: it exposes it. Margiela does this in a particularly drastic way; he shows how fashion brought the ideal to life, an ideal which, however, was as such located out of time, untouched, like the dummy, by the decline to which the flesh is subject. Time will not stand still, however, and the disfiguration of the ideal has inevitably to be followed by a refiguration. The rag-collecting aspect of the fashion of Margiela points to the reconstructive attempt to rethink clothes as the signs of an individual, unique life and death.

Notes

1. Varvara Stepanova, 'The dress of today is the industrial dress' (1923), cited by Isabelle Anscombe, *A Woman's Touch: Women in Design from 1860 to the Present Day*, New York 1984, p. 96.
2. Anja Seeliger, under the fine title, 'Die Pilze des Schönen,' *taz,* 4 July 1997, p. 16, in which of course the Baudelairean *Flowers of Evil* are present.

FURTHER READING

Black, Prudence. 2009. "The Detail: Setting Fashion System in Motion." *Fashion Theory* 13 (4): 499–510.

Blaszcyzk, Regina Lee (ed.) 2007. *Producing Fashion: Commerce, Culture, and Consumers*. Philadelphia: University of Pennsylvania Press.

Bugg, Jessica. 2009. "Fashion at the Interface: Designer-Wearer-Viewer." *Fashion Practice* 1 (1): 9–31.

Lemire, Beverly. 2016. "Thinking Fashion. A Historian's Reflection." *Fashion Practice* 8 (1): 10–14.

Melchior, Marie Riegels and Birgitta Svensson. 2014. *Fashion and Museums: Theory and Practice*. London: Bloomsbury.

Polese, Francesca and Regina Lee Blaszcyzk. 2012. "Fashion Forward: The Business History of Fashion." *Business History* 54 (1): 6–9.

Potvin, John (ed.). 2009. *The Places and Spaces of Fashion, 1800–2007*. London: Routledge.

Riello, Giorgio and Peter McNeil (eds.). 2010. *The Fashion History Reader: Global Perspectives*. Abingdon: Routledge.

Ruppert-Stroescu, Mary and Jana Hawley. "A Typology of Creativity in Fashion Design and Development." *Fashion Practice* 6 (1): 9–35.

Taylor, Lou. 2002. *Establishing Dress History*. Manchester and New York: Manchester University Press.

Teilmann-Lock, Stina. 2012. "The Fashion Designer as Author: The Case of the Danish T-Shirt." *Massachusetts Institute of Technology Design Issues* 28 (4): 29–41.

Figure 10 Photo Courtesy of Brent Luvaas.
Source: Brent Luvaas

PART II
Sourcing and Manufacturing

Figure 11 Steven Onoja. Photo Courtesy of Brent Luvaas.
Source: Brent Luvaas

INTRODUCTION

Alphonso McClendon

STREAMLINING PRODUCT DEVELOPMENT

Preceding an apparel product's delivery to a merchant for consumer consideration, various departments of an organization contribute to the item's lifecycle from inspiration to presentation at retail. This extensive process allows for the expertise of all parties to influence the success of the product. Identified as line, range or product development, today, the activity necessitates nimbleness to meet consumer demand for new products, equally for companies to sell these items at full retail price (Rosenau and Wilson 2014: 156). Creativity and design is paramount to the start of a collection. The amount of time permitted for this activity in the supply chain has lessened noticeably in the twenty-first century. In Part Two, Brian Godbold and Luigi Maramotti trace the traditional processes of design, sourcing, and manufacturing established in the 1970s and 1980s at Marks and Spencer and Max Mara respectively. These chapters demonstrate how various brands have responded to growth in global markets and to increasing access and consumption of fashion by the masses.

Dating back to the 1990s, line development for fashion companies, specifically in North America, involved twelve months of lead-time. Design and creative directors initiated new seasonal concepts based on travel to strategic locations that would garner fresh ideas for a collection of garments offered for sale. For instance, spring collection deliveries to retailers commenced with inspiration trips, typically January, to Catalina Island off the coast of Southern California or Cabo San Lucas in the Los Cabos Corridor of Mexico. Senior level designers would scurry local shops for apparel, textiles, thematic props, vintage goods, home décor, and photographic images to translate the aesthetic traits and character of the town's residents and their culture. Upon return to the New York design studio, these items were exhibited in similar vision to their discovery. Overview or inspiration rooms mirrored the locale with textiles draped from rusted nails, *Life* magazines spread on a rain-weathered console table, and vintage garments pinned to the wall as inspired looks. Often, music was played to complete the enticement. Assistant and Associate Designers, Merchandisers, and Buyers were given synopses of the themes, including important fabrications, signature garment details, trims, and color palettes for each delivery. Sketching followed these meetings, along with the creation of garment technical flats, the selection of fabrics and trims, an adherence to stock keeping unit (SKU) plans, and the representation of styles on computer-aided design (CAD). This six-month allowance concluded with line adoption per delivery, submission to agents and factories fully executing technical packages, fittings of prototypes, final costings, and the shipment of sales samples for market week in June.

The second half of the development calendar consisted of the original core of the supply chain that being located in overseas sourcing and proceeded by manufacturing of bulk orders written during market week. In the New York design studio, fabric, production and merchandising managers tracked and problem-solved issues for on-time spring delivery to retailers, while designers continued the development of summer and the start of fall collections. The first spring delivery (12/25) with an x-factory date by sea container shipment of September arrived at the retailer's stockroom by mid-December for post-holiday floor preview. In the 1980s and 1990s, this development process generated enormous profits for American companies such as Polo Ralph Lauren, Nautica, Tommy Hilfiger, Calvin Klein, and Liz Claiborne. Presently, this yearlong process, despite being thorough, systematic, and iterative to insure accuracy and quality, has produced a significant problem of collection staleness for retailers. Technology advances, including instant access to all fashion media via mobile phones, laptops, and tablets have resulted in consumers demanding immediate retail access to products and has shortened the period of collection storytelling, customer exhilaration, and full price selling. Prior to the 2000s, American consumers purchased large amounts of apparel and footwear usually three times a year: back-to-school (BTS), the Christmas/Holiday season, and Easter. This has yielded to seasonless clothing that is layered depending on temperatures and a tendency toward athleisure attire at school, work, and church that has reduced apparel spending for BTS and Easter. Today, the key to product design, merchandising, and sourcing success is contingent on the management of a quick response, speed to market, and speed to the consumer.

> In a speed to market environment, the product development process must be capable of reacting to subtle and rapid changes in the marketplace so that styles that are in the pipeline can be adjusted and new concepts injected into the process in time to meet production deadlines. Manufacturing and sourcing must be able to perform with low work-in-process inventories to respond quickly to change and provide a constant flow of merchandise for distribution to retail customers. (Rosenau and Wilson 2014: 305)

Design creativity, which Marmotti, described as the processes of 'origination, organisation, composition and planning' occurs in increasingly tighter intervals. These activities were responsive to the overseas sourcing timeline that has given way to obedience to the consumer's demand for newness and immediacy. Such mandates have shown fissures in the design process, where creatives express angst about the mechanization of collection development. High profile departures of creative directors, including Raf Simons from Christian Dior (2015), Alexander Wang from Balenciaga (2015), and Hedi Slimane from Yvest Saint Laurent (2016) have underscored this shift towards free agency and complex diagrams of designer movements across fashion brands.

FASHIONING PRODUCTS CHEAP AND FAST

In response to consumer behavior and marketplace changes, fast fashion companies have stepped forward to produce in shorter lead times at low cost for their customers. H&M, Uniqlo, Zara, Forever 21, and Primark are expanding their empires around the globe. Often, the products on offer are basics, such as cotton cashmere crew neck sweaters or flat front chinos, offered in a range of colors. When Irish retailer Primark opened on North American soil in 2015, Old Navy, a division of GAP, accelerated a sourcing process of applying a single fabrication to multiple garment styles that permitted the quick response of production allocations based on sell-through data (Anon 2015). The pressure on apparel gross margins, which are the profits remaining after subtracting the cost of the product from its selling price, has shifted some production from China to lower factory waged countries, including Bangladesh, Vietnam, and Indonesia.

This, in part, contributed to the tragedy of the Rana Plaza building collapse in Bangladesh that killed 1,129 people in April 2013 (Greenhouse and Julfikar 2014). A day before the disaster workers of the roughly 3,500 employee apparel factory were sent home following an electrical failure, only to return the next day without knowledge of the cracks that had been detected in support beams. In a report on the collapse, it was noted that large power generators placed on the roof due to frequent power outages had weakened the structure overall (Yardley 2013). The event recalled the devastating Triangle Shirtwaist Company fire of 1911 that killed 147 employees due to locked exit doors. Similar lapses or omissions of safety standards led American workers, mostly young women, to die from jumping out of windows, falling down elevator shafts, and succumbing to smoke inhalation. The Bangladesh disaster has drawn attention to safety inspections by American companies such as Nike, Gap, and Wal-Mart, equally raising the concern of a race to the bottom in the apparel industry, when brands and retailers sacrifice quality, service, and convenience for the lowest price and sustained profits.

As of January 2017 in the USA, total apparel and textile production workers measured a meager 240 thousand employees (Bureau of Labor Statistics 2017). This is in contrast to Bangladesh that employs 4 million plus workers in their $28 billion garment industry (Saini 2017). Since the 1990s, there has been a loss of one million apparel and textile production jobs in the USA. These manufacturing positions have moved to low wage developing countries in the Caribbean, South America, and mostly South East Asia. The earnings per hour of an apparel production employee in the USA averages $13.70, while Bangladesh's rate has shifted from a low of 21 cents per hour in 2010 to 45 cents or $68 a month (Saini 2017). Notwithstanding the recent attention on and drive for 'Made in the USA', the significant gap in labor rates and pressure on corporate gross margins have prevented the return of meaningful production to North America. Thus, coalitions, such as the Alliance for Bangladesh Worker Safety with membership by Wal-Mart Stores Inc., Target Corp. and VF Corp., have been created as watchdogs for factory abuses abroad, highlighting worker safety, training, inspections and compensation (Ellis 2016). The removal of quotas in 2005, a broadening global retail market in 2010, and the growth of ecommerce in 2015 accelerated the race to the bottom for apparel and textile production labor rates. Although developing countries benefitted from the 'footloose sourcing' with increased employment, their manufacturing employees lacked wage, safety, and union protection (Rossi, Luinstra and Pickles 2014). It is yet to be determined if the weight on the production part of the supply chain will lessen as consumers transform their discretionary spending and adopt new models of sustainable behavior regarding apparel and footwear. However, to ensure beneficial outcomes when sourcing abroad, brands must develop strategies for trust, timely deliveries, and efficient communication. Singh and Hodges, in their chapter, analyze the worth of relationship building for American companies that source in India. This country along with Bangladesh, Pakistan, and Sri Lanka represents 12 percent of global apparel exports (World Bank 2016). The strategies outlined by the authors will serve as standards for firms newly sourcing in growth countries for labor such as Nigeria, Ethiopia and Kenya.

The lean retail environment of today that competes on consumer price comparisons and accessibility has driven supply chain shifts. Rather than having production spread wide across low-wage countries, large companies are opting for sourcing in countries that have skilled and disciplined workers, as well as possessing vertical integration with textile mills and trim suppliers. For apparel firms in the USA, this became viable in 2005 following the termination of the Multi-Fibre Arrangement (MFA) that placed textile and apparel quotas on imports 'to protect domestic producers' and balance trade (Rosenau and Wilson 2014: 354). The end of the arrangement facilitated China's placement as top US importer of apparel reaching $33 billion by 2010 and 41% of all clothing imports to the USA (WTO 2010). A report published by Enlightenment Economics on the global textile and garment industry noted a preference toward concentrated sourcing, given that, 'Buyers are reducing the number of countries from which they source, especially for high-volume, basic commodity items. The biggest retailers now source in such large volumes that only big suppliers have the necessary capacity to fulfill some orders' (McNamara 2008). Fast fashion retailers are continuing this trend by providing factories with large production orders of basic items in multiple colorways.

The Uniqlo stores, owned by Fast Retailing Co., have adhered to this model of basic wear in an array of colors at affordable prices. Until 2015, the fast fashion company was pushing store expansion in the USA with a 100-store goal by 2020. Now, this plan has changed due to decreased profits, a crowded marketplace, and challenges at brick-and-mortar retail, especially in mall-based stores. Fast Retailing has a new focus on shortening its time to market (13 days from design to delivery), expansion of direct-to-consumer, and improvements of same-day delivery in certain markets. Tadashi Yanai, owner of Fast Retailing, noted urgency in being faster: 'We need to deliver products customers want quickly' (Takada and Huang 2017). Furthermore, the company is targeting investments in automation and artificial intelligence that will streamline logistics and closely forecast consumer demand. Retail disruption has positioned planning and delivering equal to that of low-cost manufacturing for Uniqlo's operational success.

SOURCING AND RETAILING GLOBALLY

'Supply chains that deliver the best value to their end use customers generate a strong demand for their products and services' (Hugos and Thomas 2006). In an environment where global sourcing is common, fast fashion companies such as Uniqlo, Zara, and others are challenged to select the best partners, utilize efficient technology, and deliver the product faster to consumers. Gale and Kaur, in their chapter on the commercial and manufacturing activities of fashion and textiles, dispute the danger of customization and supply chain nimbleness yielding dullness in product offerings. For them, advances in technology and speed can spur design variation similar to its impact on the automobile industry. Yet, the expansion of 3D printing, full garment knitting, and laser cutting are bringing apparel and footwear variation and customization in different forms than anticipated. A decade ago, customization was defined by the ability of consumers to select a graphic for a t-shirt, to vote via crowdsourcing for a garment design to go into production, or choose an athletic shoe to have a certain lace, upper or outsole color. Today, customization more fully encompasses storytelling, consumer experience, and method of delivery, as well as the manufacturing technique. The playing field has leveled in terms of the supply chain. Many brands or retailers are available globally through e-commerce or in-store purchase. Companies have to compete with an effective supply chain that manages quality, inventory, response time, technology, and global occurrences.

In addition, the product must be compelling with a memorable experience for the customer. This may involve sharing the product, posting about the product or using the product in a virtual or augmented world. For instance, Apple, Inc. has implemented a redesign of their innovative retail locations with a genius grove flanked by trees, lounge seating, and a large digital screen to foster a town square aesthetic. Consumers, while casually experiencing products, can build a sense of community with creative pros that dole out app and device based knowledge. Training classes, working hubs, and playtime are juxtaposed here with an empathetic and commercial objective. Soon to be imitated by other retailers, the store-as-product initiative by this $47 billion powerhouse emphasizes a focus on the latter part of the supply chain to propel revenues (Rao 2016).

Global retailing and the shift of sales to online platforms including mobile phones, tablets, and laptops have begun to significantly disrupt retail. Concurrently, consumers have shifted spending to technology and gaming. Industry giants like Amazon have altered consumers' interaction with products and services via online retailing, manufacturing, subscriptions, and original television programming content. While large suburban malls are finding trouble renewing leases and maintaining full occupancy, e-commerce merchants are seeking locations to deliver products quickly or same-day to consumers in their home regions. Target, Macy's, and J.C. Penney have responded by shutting underperforming stores and focusing on smaller scale and off-price units. 'The current torrent of closures comes as consumer confidence is strong and unemployment is low, suggesting that a permanent restructuring is underway, rather than a dip in the normal business cycle' (Corkery 2017). Brands and retailers will need to adjust inventories, logistics and distribution, and e-commerce initiatives to address these business shifts. The total divestment of retail as implemented by The Limited in 2017, and Sports Authority's closure in 2016 is proof of a changing landscape equally contributed by overexpansion, increased competition, and uninspiring retail. For apparel and non-apparel companies, the goal is a supply chain 'that can better adapt to business changes and deliver performance and profitability without compromising quality or service for the end users of the retail products' (Hugo and Thomas 2006).

The following four chapters assess sourcing and manufacturing and their related impact on diverse fashion firms and brands. Firsthand accounts and targeted interviews of participants by the authors accentuate an experience in product development and retailing. Regardless of the decade or retail channel, they show evidence of the importance of brands and retailers to continually innovate with design creativity, product development, strategic partnerships, and responsive supply chains that ultimately promote the all-important consumer experience.

References

Anon (2015), Primark: Faster, cheaper fashion', *The Economist*, 5 September, http://www.economist.com/news/business/21663221, accessed 8 July 2016.

Bureau of Labor Statistics-BLS (2017), Industries at a Glance: Apparel Manufacturing NAICS 315 and Textile Mills NAICS 313, https://www.bls.gov, accessed 17 March 2017.

Corkery, M. (2017), 'Is American Retail at a Historic Tipping Point?', *New York Times*, 12 April, https://www.nytimes.com, accessed 12 April 2017.

Ellis, K (2016), 'John Kerry Calls for Strengthening Worker's Rights in Bangladesh', *WWD*, 29 August, http://wwd.com, accessed 17 March 2017.

Greenhouse, S. and A. M. Julfikar, J. (2014), 'Stalemate over Safety in Bangladesh', *New York Times*, 26 June, https://www.nytimes.com, accessed 8 July 2016.

Hugos, M. and C. Thomas (2006), *Supply Chain Management in the Retail Industry*, Hoboken: John Wiley & Sons.

McNamara, K. Ed. (2008), 'The Global Textile and Garments Industry: The Role of Information and Communication Technologies (ICTs) in Exploiting the Value Chain', *Enlightened Economics*, June, www.infodev.org, accessed 8 July 2016.

Rao, L. (2016), 'Apple Retail Chief Angela Ahrendts on Turning Stores into Town Squares', *Fortune*, http://fortune.com, accessed 25 April 2017.

Rosenau, J. and D. Wilson (2014), *Apparel Merchandising: The Line Starts Here*, 3rd Edition, New York and London: Bloomsbury Publishing.

Rossi, A., A. Luinstra and J. Pickles (2014), *Advances in Labour Studies: Towards Better Work: Understanding labour in apparel global value chains*, New York: ILO with Palgrave Macmillan.

Saini, M. (2017), 'Dhaka Summit to Address Bangladesh's Safety Progress, Workers' Rights', WWD, 17 February, http://www.com, accessed 17 March 2017.

Takada, K. and G. Huang (2017), 'Uniqlo Thinks Faster Fashion Can Help it Beat Zara', https://www.bloomberg.com, accessed 17 March 2017.

World Bank (2016), China, United States: Apparel Manufacturing has potential to create 1.2 million new Jobs, says World Bank', *MENA Report*, 29 April.

Yardley, J. (2013), 'Report on Deadly Factory Collapse in Bangladesh Finds Widespread Blame', *New York Times*, 22 May, https://www.nytimes.com, accessed 8 July 2016.

7

THE CHAIN STORE CHALLENGE

Brian Godbold[1]

This chapter takes the form, initially, of an autobiography. Its story is not only that of my own life, but that of British fashion since the 1960s; I was fortunate to find myself right at the centre of the art school culture of that period, which as I hope to show, sparked off the design-conscious mass-market phenomenon by which I, as the Divisional Director of Design at Marks & Spencer was ranked as number 8 in *The Face* magazine's 100 most powerful people in fashion,[1] and at number 15 by *Elle*.[2] This chapter aims to describe the developments, challenges and opportunities for contemporary designers and retailers with reference to radical changes in consumer attitudes, redefinition of age profiles, the revolution in how and where we shop, and the advent of 'lifestyle' consumerism. But to place my analysis and projections for the future into context, I must refer to the past.

I cannot talk about my career without mentioning Walthamstow School of Art. When the Head saw my work, he immediately suggested that I join the fashion course. I must emphasize that I was embarking on a journey into the unknown; at the time there were no existing high-profile, art school trained designers whom I could regard as role models. Part of the exhilaration of those days was the feeling that we were pioneers. After my first year, Daphne Brooker left to become Head of Fashion at what was then Kingston School of Art and I continued my studies at the Royal College of Art. During vacations, I worked in the design department of Marks & Spencer, where Hans Schneider had been head since 1936 and at the end of my second year of the, then, three-year course, he offered me a permanent position. This did not appeal to me at all; like many of my contemporaries I was convinced that you had to be a star by the time you were thirty, otherwise you really had not made it. I did feel ready, though, to venture out into the world, so, with some scholarship money I had won, I bought a three-month return ticket to New York.

With little more than ten dollars a day, I had to find a job quickly, so I bought a copy of *Womenswear Daily* and answered an advertisement for a designer at a company called Jovi. I got the job and although the company was very small to begin with, it became an overnight success and I found myself designing a range of clothes bearing my name, Brian G for Jovi. The exhilarating thing about working for the newly discovered junior sportswear market was producing a completely new collection every six weeks, for clients such as Macys, the New York department store. With the success of Brian G for Jovi I felt fairly confident that my education was complete and I decided not to finish my degree at the Royal College of Art, but I did return to London and in 1967 I became head of the coat and suit design room at Wallis. Jeffrey Wallis was the great high-street entrepreneur of the late 1960s and it was a privilege to work with him.

This brings us to 1976, when, for the second time in my career, I was offered a position at Marks & Spencer, but this time as head of the Design Department, since Hans Schneider had retired. It is at this point in my story, then, that the extraordinary creativity, the appetite for innovation and originality unleashed during the 1960s feeds directly into national culture,

---

[1] From Brian Godbold, (2000) The Chain Store Challenge. In The Fashion Business: Theory, Practice, Image. Oxford: Berg, 103–117.

via Britain's biggest retailer. Not only had the 1960s created the art school culture which, I believe, revolutionized attitudes to design, they spawned a generation with levels of disposable income sufficiently high to sustain an unprecedented market for products.

However, it would be misleading to suggest that when I joined Marks & Spencer, the Design Group was poised to capture the new market. The team I inherited consisted of around a hundred pattern cutters, machinists and so-called designers, but the level of creativity and competence was modest. The practice was to promote machinists to pattern cutters and thence to designers. My first objective was to reform the department and to raise the level of design competence. In this, thankfully, I had the support of the board of directors, which was at the time telling the suppliers to improve their own design facilities in order to improve their products and meet our quality standards. The Design Group's method of working would inevitably have to change if this was to happen; we became less concerned with designing in detail on behalf of the suppliers, and more concerned with fashion prediction, colour and product coordination. The move to a more strategic role for design meant the building of a more concentrated team of higher calibre designers.

In 1985 Peter Salisbury, later Chief Executive, recommended greater concentration on research and development, separating pattern technology from design and moving it to the Technical Executive. In the same year, with the addition of menswear to my portfolio, I appointed the celebrated designer Paul Smith as a consultant. By this time, each area of the design department (Ladieswear, Childrenswear, Menswear and Lingerie) had a small but qualified team of designers, with a high level of experience in industry and forecasting. From 1986 a mode of operation was established whereby each area produced a seasonal design brief, a 'bible' to be used by the buying groups to give direction to the suppliers, covering colour fabric, print, pattern and styling.

Throughout the 1980s and most of the 1990s the success of Marks & Spencer, and the Design Group seemed unstoppable. We acquired homeware in 1990, packaging and graphics in 1995, launched the Marks & Spencer magazine in 1987, were the first chain store to shoot promotional campaigns using supermodels in 1994; we became accustomed to nominations in the British Fashion Awards and won the 'classic' section twice, in 1994 and 1995. By 1994 we had 610 stores worldwide and a group turnover of £5.9 billion. As Divisional Director of Design, my portfolio represented a business worth £3.5 billion pounds. The downturn throughout 1999 in Marks & Spencer's business has led to massive and continuing change, not just cosmetic but reaching deep into fundamental attitudes and approaches. In the second part of this chapter I will give my view of the issues challenges and opportunities, which I consider to be key to the volume retailer today and in the coming years.

AGE PROFILE

With the 'cultural flip' of the 1960s, instead of values passing from age to youth, they began to flow the other way. Although we thought at the time that you were either young and part of it or old and out of it, it seems that our generation has yet to reach its sell-by date. The post-war 'baby boomers' are now beginning to grow old, and are confounding marketeers in the process. Unlike their parents, whose lives were shaped by depression and war, this generation has in truth never had it bad. The first to enjoy significant levels of disposable income, everything throughout their adult lives has been targeted at them; the new 'third agers', as the 50–75 age group is often called, insist it should remain so, and have the financial might to ensure that it does. No longer faced with slipping into obscurity or striving to feign youthfulness, the generation of which I am part aims for continuing style and there are plenty of role models to inspire us: Calvin Klein, Paul McCartney, Catherine Deneuve and Mick Jagger are in their mid to late fifties. What will be the impact of this marketing phenomenon on product? In my opinion, the 'third-agers' will lead the demand for products which are 'modern' but will eschew ridiculousness and excess, they will prioritize ease of care, practicality and comfort appropriate to their relaxed lifestyles. In other words, they will effect a fundamental shift away from faddish or dictatorial 'fashion' towards enduring, interpretable 'style' and genuinely high-quality design.

HOW WE SHOP

We have not stopped spending our money, but it seems we are more reluctant to spend it in public. Whether it is a matter of embarrassment about appearing extravagant, or whether it is a matter of convenience I cannot say, but it is certain that home shopping is transforming the retail landscape.

The first indication of this was in the United States, during the 1980s. Industrial analysts suggest that the introduction of zip codes and toll-free telephone numbers, increasing subscription to credit cards and the development of computer networks that could cross-check individual spending habits, enabled the meteoric rise of mail order. Mail order business grew at three times the rate of store business throughout the decade and according to the Direct Marketing Association, in 1993 alone, in the United States, more than 10,000 mail order companies issued 13.5 billion catalogues and 55 per cent of the adult population bought $51.5 billion worth of goods by mail.

Moreover, as Matthew De Bord noted in his essay on the J. Crew phenomenon 'mail order used to mean dowdy, as in Sears-Roebuck stylelessness and industrial-strength presentation. It now means *reliably* stylish. It used to mean cheap; it now competes with the pricier designers for customers'.[3] The real impact of the mail order revolution is the mass dissemination of style consciousness. Most items are just like something we already own, except for some small detail, some slight improvement that makes us feel that the version we have at home is inferior; the gym shorts are in vivid colours they never come in at school, the espadrilles are in gingham, denim jackets have tartan linings. The appeal of these clothes is subtle novelty, rather than any kind of flamboyant fashion, but it is communicated with breathtaking clarity. J. Crew, Racing Green et al stimulate the desire to buy using the printed image; confident, relaxed models looking like the kind of people we would like to be or to know, idyllic locations, carefully studied styling and photography lend a kind of aspirational 'added value'. Borrowing the devices long used by fashion magazines, they have, in my view, the potential to beat the magazines at their own game. Whilst the magazines struggle to offer something to satisfy their various advertisers and disparate readers, relaying the designers' runway proclamations, they are in any case preaching to the converted. The mail order catalogues, however, insinuate themselves into the homes of the indifferent and the disaffected and they are in a position to give a distinct and coherent editorial point of view which seems to speak directly to the reader.

The next great contribution to home shopping has been the television shopping channels that, again, originated from the United States. If you had a telephone and a credit card QVC, standing for Quality, Value and Convenience, 'the-mall-you-call' allowed you to shop for everything from clothes to cookware, day or night, from your sofa or bed. In 1993, the midst of recession, 44 million Americans eagerly dialled QVC and its sister QVC Fashion Channel and parted with $1.1 billion. Its rival, the Home Shopping Network also did business of over $1 billion. QVC combined entertainment with shopping, giving viewers the opportunity to talk to programme hosts and celebrity guests on the air, participate in games show and win prizes.

After television shopping channels came virtual retail, e-commerce as it is known, which also began in the United States, where in 1994 Apple teamed up with a group of mail order companies to distribute 30,000 electronic versions of their catalogues on compact disc. With access to merchandise from retailers such as L L Bean, Landsend and Tiffany & Co., users could browse through catalogues on screen, or ask their computer to search specific items such as mens' trousers or dinner sets, they could even change the colour of garments to assess different combinations. They were also given access to supporting editorial material such as guides to fashion and financial planning supplied by publications like *Elle Décor* and the *Wall Street Journal*.

In 1999 with millions worth of goods purchased on the Internet in the UK alone it seems certain that home shopping will become a greater and greater feature of retail, and the clothing business. At Marks & Spencer we recognized this fact with the launch of Marks & Spencer Direct, our clothing catalogue in 1998, and the Marks & Spencer online shop in 1999. We offered an initial batch of 200 products, with the ambition of reaching 3,000, of which approximately one third was anticipated to be clothing, within two years of operation. This would represent the equivalent of a 5,600 square metre department store; in other words, a range of products only represented in the largest ten of the group's outlets. But I do not suggest that home shopping will wipe out the need for shops and stores. On the contrary, this is one of the greatest challenges that we currently face.

RETAIL ENVIRONMENTS

My story returns yet again to the United States, where in the 1980s and early 1990s, the department stores took quite a knock caused by the impact of home shopping. It would be naive to conclude, however, that home shopping must inevitably wipe out the stores. The pleasures of going shopping, experiencing the physical environment of the store itself, the element of social interaction, being able to touch merchandise are an important aspect of urban life that will not be eradicated by the convenience of shopping from home. I believe that department stores have a future, and that those which survive will be the ones that turn shopping into an entertaining, exciting or in some way distinctive experience, in other words, those that have the confidence to look different and separate themselves from the mainstream. In the United States, this was pioneered by Barney's, who, with Japanese finance, formulated a new concept. Rather than follow the fail-safe blanket-buying policies of other stores, Barney's dared to buy selectively from designer collections, which gave its merchandise a particular flavour enhanced by its own brand, or 'private label' collections. In the United Kingdom, first Harvey Nichols and then Selfridges reinvented themselves along similar lines. Harvey Nichols turned itself into a fashion lifestyle experience with a series of dedicated designer 'boutiques', both clothing and homewear, top-of-the-range specialist food retail in the stylishly designed food hall, ambitious private label clothing and food products and restaurants. The refurbishment of Selfridges transformed it from a 'safe' department store stocking the same kind or products in the same kind of visually uninspired or indistinctive environment as any other department store, into a fashion pantheon, where the most current collections are enticingly displayed in a showcase environment.

Alongside the innovative department stores, the generation of new specialist retailers is playing its part in the reassertion of shopping. My personal list of visionaries in this field would include Joseph Ettelgui, whose stores in London, Paris and New York carry his distinctive personal style and reflect his aim to turn shopping into a social experience, and Terence Conran, whose stores in London and Paris emphasize furniture, homewear and food as fashionable products. These retailers, as do Selma Weisser of the, sadly defunct, Chiaravari in New York, Joyce Ma of Hong Kong, Colette in Paris and Jeffrey in New York, address the concept of what I would term 'lifestyle retailing'. They have a strong point of view, their selections of merchandise have an editorial quality, which extends from clothes to food to furniture and is asserted through the interior of the store itself. The secret of their success appears to be in their refusal to attempt to be all things to all people. Maureen Doherty and Asha Sarabhai's London store, Egg, for example carries a distinctive mix of clothes and *objects* which reflect the proprietors' taste for high quality artisanal products which stand outside the usual dictates of fashion.

Egg is clearly very different from Marks & Spencer but there is no doubt in my mind that volume retailers will have to take their cue from the small-scale specialists and department stores who have restored the pleasure of the act of shopping, and have re-established it as a defining social activity. The increasing 'visual literacy' which fuelled the mass demand for well-designed or fashionable products in the first instance will, or has extended to the retail environment itself. High-street retailers must pay as much attention to the design of their stores and their visual merchandising as to the design of their products, and it is no coincidence that so many have, over the last few years, opened in-store coffee bars, créche, delivery services and home shoppers.

PRODUCT

My career bears witness to the mass-market fashion explosion of the last thirty or so years. The recent downturn in business reflects the resulting worldwide over-capacity, which I believe will be a significant factor in the industry's future. This is especially true in the area we describe as 'core casual', that is to say, the pivotal items which define generic leisure/weekend wear. In the late 1980s the American retailer Gap built a huge business on the demand, amongst all age groups and social classes, for a more relaxed and practical approach to dressing. Their hugely successful advertising campaigns offered us stylish black and white images of icons of all ages, and from all fields, wearing anonymous casual basics. The trend systematically moved performance fabrics from the active sportswear market to being an acceptable and essential part of everyone's wardrobe. At the same time, the market learned to accept casualwear classics such as chinos and jeans as staple items. For years, we at Marks & Spencer had believed that we could never move into the jeans market, that it was a business best left to the brands. But when we did introduce them in the early 1990s we discovered that the trend was so powerful that by 1994 we had developed a £60 million annual jeanswear business across mens', women's and children's wear.

Changing lifestyle dictated changing spending patterns. We found that customers were becoming less interested in carefully coordinated looks. The emerging market was motivated by the acquisition of versatile pieces, either basics or 'hot' items that would update the wardrobe. We christened the trend 'item shopping' and in terms of design we fed the demand by addressing subtle changes in core items. So, the white cotton shirt would become longer and french-cuffed, then collarless and more fitted, deconstructed then refabricated. The black polo neck would become a tunic, lose its rib, become small-shouldered and shrunken, sleek and layered, soft and felted. We discovered that customers responded to pieces that could be interpreted in a variety of ways, according to taste and allowed the gradual evolution of their wardrobes.

Item shopping is still very much part of our lives, but market saturation has taken its toll and replacement purchases of core product continue to decline. Added to this is the changing profile of the customer, who, through constant exposure, is becoming wiser, more astute, more confident in mixing products and consequently, likely to be less brand loyal. This has not only intensified the necessity to maintain demand through technological developments which provide greater comfort, functionality and practicality (supportive stretch 'footglove' shoes and non-iron shirts are just two examples) but also highlights the need for new, exciting products that stimulate the desire to buy on impulse. Alongside the 'sensible' purchases, we have discovered that the customer responds well to the aspirational, luxurious appeal of, for example, the pashminas and cashmeres that we introduced in 1999.

Predictably, the demand for anonymous basics in its turn spawned a renewed interest in conspicuous 'design'. We responded to this with the launch of our Autograph range in Spring 2000. For the first time Marks & Spencer worked directly with independent designers such as Betty Jackson, Julien MacDonald and Katherine Hamnett to produce small collections for sale in stylishly decorated dedicated areas within top stores. It seems that the demand was well met; in its first week Autograph generated £1m worth of sales. I am keenly aware that it is the interest of volume retailers to support the emergent designers and small-scale craft operations that can feed this demand. Autograph is one example of this, but the tradition stretches back to 1994, when our suppliers started, for the first time, to work with independent designers to produce ranges for Marks & Spencer. The relationship between the then small-scale niche designer operation Ghost, our supplier Coats Viyella and ourselves not only helped to raise design for the High Street to a completely new level, but enabled Ghost's Tanya Same to increase her business dramatically.

So, in reality, the beginnings of the new approach to design which I believe is the way forward were already in place before the downturn in business occurred. Our objective since 1998 has been to accelerate the rate of change. Opportunities still exist, but as I have described, the market is more knowledgeable and more fickle than it was, and we have to be more agile in order to spot and meet new demands. As a result, we now work in smaller teams with fewer people involved in developing a product. This way decisions are made by those working closest to the product, and the process is much speedier, enabling us to get the right products to the market more quickly. Marks & Spencer's designers maintain their strategic 'forecasting' role but they also work directly with suppliers on putting ranges together, ensuring high-quality definitive products which are not diluted by a drawn-out decision-making process. We have begun to assemble our products, clothes, homewears and even food, into coordinated lifestyle themes that have aspirational appeal. We have embarked on big changes in the design of our stores, the presentation of products, and the quality of supporting items such as packaging and promotional material.

I have been fortunate to be part of an influential generation, one that turned design from a minority to a mass interest. The extent of this increasing visual literacy is now so great that the way forward is without doubt greater, better and swifter design. From the art school culture of the 1960s, through the volume retail revolutions of the 1970s and 1980s to the nurturing of a new generation of art school talent in the 1990s and beyond, my story has come full circle.

Notes

1. '100 most powerful people in Fashion', *The Face* September 1994 pp. 74–80.
2. 'Elle's hottest 100 names in fashion', *Elle,* April 1998, p. 115.
3. De Bord, M., (1997) 'Texture and Taboo: The Tyranny of Texture and Ease in the J. Crew Catalogue', *Fashion Theory* vol. 1, issue 3, pp. 261–78.

8

CONNECTING CREATIVITY

Luigi Maramotti[1]

What is creativity? How are ideas generated? How do we define a creative person? Such questions have probably crossed our minds more than once, but rarely do we realise how much we depend on this very special output of human intelligence. If we look at the products around us, most of which today are manufactured industrially rather than handmade, we can appreciate how their design is related to creative thought and to the necessity for innovation and change. As the Chairman of the MaxMara group, with an annual turnover of £600 million, more than twenty separate collections and 600 stores situated around the globe, I have been confronted quite forcefully with this thought. I have devoted this chapter to discussing creativity, ideas of what it is, and how, in my experience it can be organized in order to originate some of the remarkable results that industry is capable of achieving, particularly in the world of fashion.

The first personal intuition I had about the importance of creativity was through the Disney character, Archimedes; the light bulb that appeared every time he had a good idea fascinated me. It may seem an unintellectual approach, but I have always liked the idea of invention as sudden intuition, and the magic behind it. The abstract concept of creativity can be linked to the selection, from thoughts and things, of those which lead to innovation, change or improvement. Creativity can be formatively defined as behaviour which includes such activities as origination, organisation, composition and planning. Any definition we may try will not be fully satisfying because, in order to make creativity distinguishable from mere arbitrariness, there must be a sort of legislation.

Creativity is often associated with irrationality or pure intuition, but this, in my view, is an erroneous belief. I believe that creativity has to be part of a system or structure, if we want it to be a useful instrument in helping us to understand or improve our social and physical environment. That creativity flourishes through being subjected to constraint may sound like a contradiction in terms, but I believe that it is not. Perhaps as a consequence of an overall attitude to the world based on daily experience, many today regard creativity as being linked to disorder; abstract expressionism is evidence of this. Yet as recently as the eighteenth century, Pascal asserted that order was sufficient (and necessary) to define creativity,[1] though I find myself doubting this when I find myself in the chaos of our design department.

In my opinion we tend nowadays to rarely abstract the idea of creativity. We tend instead to regard it as an attribute of certain individuals. 'That is a creative person', we are used to saying. What do we mean? Do we judge outward appearance, the image we are offered, someone's behaviour or maybe new ideas, something done in a certain way, a project or performance with a particular style? Any of these would show us to perceive creativity as 'something different'. We tend to believe that normality does not favour a creative attitude, or if you like, that human beings are not 'normally' creative.

A great and fascinating debate on creativity and genius enlivened the psychoanalytical studies of Freud and Jung. The former thought creativity to be the

---

[1] From Luigi Maramotti, (2000), Connecting Creativity. In Fashion Business: Theory, Practice, Image. Oxford: Berg, 91–103.

artist's tool, by means of which he could express the contents of his unconscious. In the writings on Leonardo and Michelangelo he analysed the two great masterpieces St Anne and Moses in which he could see turned into art, the nature and the inner secrets of the artists' souls as individuals.[2] For Jung, on the contrary, the creative person was one, who, through his or her work, is able to emancipate the self from his or her own individuality to become an interpreter of the universal themes of mankind which he, unconsciously, activates.[3] Jung's model seems to be the one which most accurately defines creativity in the context of fashion,[4] where the creative challenge is to divine unconscious collective desires, as I shall discuss.

CREATIVITY AND FASHION

It is widely agreed that clothing is a language, but a very ambiguous one. Its vocabulary changes or evolves, and can express different meanings at different times according to the wearer and the observer.[5] We might say that clothing is a dynamic language open to endless resetting. Some adhere to the view that fashion follows a 'trickle down process'[6] whereby innovative ideas are transmitted from the elite top layers of the social pyramid to the bottom. Others consider it mainly a matter of points of view, where each style creates an anti-style that defines it, and stimulates further change.[7] In reality, it is difficult to frame the rules by which creative thought gives a shape to fashion and its changes, although it appears that a good many can be linked in some way to technological innovations in textiles, and there seem to be recurrent patterns such as the relaunch of historic items in different contexts.

For as long as it has existed, fashion, being a language, has always been used as a means of communication. This very peculiar kind of communication takes place on two levels: an open one, and a hidden one. There is in fact an underlying reading we might call a creative value left to each individual, which allows the transmission of ambiguous and equivocal messages; think of the eroticism of neglected lace, the hardness of riding boots or the provocativeness of some metal details.

If we agree that fashion is a language we should emphasize that it is a very sophisticated one and in a way complementary, a tool for articulating and supporting words rather than substituting them. And if we agree that fashion is distinct from style, we must admit that its acknowledged codes are variable. These changes can occur at different levels mainly, but not only, visually, often revamping outdated meanings. The system of constantly shifting meanings, codes and values is in fact fundamental to fashion as we understand it in our culture. Designers know this well and they are the first to perceive signs of instability, the trends pervading society. The instabilities, ambiguities and ambivalences, described by Fred Davis in his excellent book on the subject drive creativity to and fro between opposites such as young/ old, male/ female, work/play, simplicity/complexity, revelation/ concealment, freedom/constraint, conformism/ rebellion, eroticism/chastity, discretion/ overstatement and so on.[8] The field where the game of change is played is framed within couples of constantly recurring antithetic meanings. Fashion delights us by playing on the tensions between these couples – we derive a frisson from the contradictions they suggest. We may tire of a look but whenever one of these themes returns, its freshness is restored; our fascination with them seems endless. Though changes in fashion correspond to macrochanges in cultures or societies, they nevertheless require human action, the work of creative people, of industry and the complicity of consumers. Fashion, after all, does not happen by accident.

The fashion industry purposefully identifies garments and accessories as indicators of social status. Historians have suggested that this has been so since the fourteenth century.[9] Nowadays, this identification has become a carefully planned and greatly accelerated activity. In the eternal ping-pong game between antithetical meanings, the motivating force for creativity within fashion is nearly always, or often, cultural. When Chanel urged her wealthy clients to dress like their maids,[10] she was playing on dialectics between rich and poor, high and low status, snobbery and inverted snobbery, but the reason for her attraction to these particular themes, and the reason for the fashion's success, was her ability to intuit the predominant social tensions of the moment (in this case ideas the uncertainties of wealth and power initiated by the economic unrest of the 1930s).

The potential of cultural models to drive creativity cannot be overemphasized. Successful designers refer to as wide a variety as possible, drawing from history and going beyond it, they focus on conceived models of an ideal future life. No matter how successful though, designers cannot create the desire to possess or acquire a particular product, but they can create products which satisfy or arouse incipient or otherwise undetected desire. This, in my opinion, is usually achieved by the 'lifestyle' associations a product has for the consumer; designers and companies like ours devote themselves increasingly to formulating our identities from visions of an ideal existence.

The stimuli for creative ideas in fashion have always originated from the widest variety of sources. Even in the last few years, we have seen influences exerted by exhibitions, films, writers, geographical areas, traditional cultures and metropolitan phenomena. It seems that fashion can appropriate practically anything and turn it into a 'look', the success of the look depending of course on its resonance with the cultural/social concerns of the day. Many enjoy the challenge of 'unpicking' fashion to reveal the influences which shaped it, but to me, what really matters is not to identify fashion's sources, but to examine how they generate innovative product ideas, the design process and the marketing of the product.

I have compared fashion to a language, and to a game, and there are sufficient similarities to justify both analogies. But where fashion differs is in its scant regard for rules. In a field which prioritizes innovation and change, practices are swept aside before they become established. Rules have a very short life indeed, and this is what I appreciate most about my work. Successful strategies inevitably become harder and harder to forecast, since the elements to be considered, from the creative and marketing point of view, have multiplied, and everything is subject to change. And yet we must attempt to devise strategies for innovation, since the successful inauguration of new fashions is increasingly likely to be the result of such planned approaches and less the result of the almost accidental fashionableness that was the case with the mini skirt in the 1960s, or Timberland shoes. In noting the necessity for a strategic approach I refute the widely held view that fashion is 'change for change's sake'; Craik has described how the current fashion acts as a determinant for the future one.[11] We who work in the industry are acutely aware that not everything is possible, and have learned by experience that new ideas must usually relate to what already exists if they are to succeed. At the same time we are conscious that the evolution of fashion is punctuated by spasmodic flashes of revolutionary genius, such as Chanel's, which radically change its course before it becomes too predictable. If we are to be successful, therefore, we must keep an ear to the ground ready to detect the first signs of such.

A company producing fashion is the utmost example of forced innovation. It is absolutely necessary to relaunch, recreate, rethink and to discuss things over and over again. Despite what one might think, this does not only apply to the design team, but the whole organization. To be successful, each element in the process of developing and marketing the product must be innovative and everybody should have a creative attitude. I must emphasize that I consider a designed garment 'fashion' only when it is marketed and worn by someone. I have a high opinion of the 'idea' but I believe we should consider it developed and embodied only when it has passed through some kind of process and become a 'product', no matter how small the market. Original ideas are only the first step of a long journey towards a desired success.

Before examining how the creative process develops in a company I should observe that companies, being human organizations, have many similarities with living organisms. Each possesses its own original 'genetic code' which is normally connected to the figure of its founder, but during its life its character may evolve in consequence of the external stimuli it is subjected to. A company possesses its own culture, which will become stronger over the years, transmitting itself through the inevitable conditioning of the individuals entering its ranks. But company culture is not necessarily positive, in fact, it is sometimes so deeply rooted that it hinders that renewal which is so critical to its survival.

If we consider the product as being at the core of a manufacturing company's culture, and all the related activities of development, production, marketing and promotion arranged around it, we can appreciate how the company's internal activities, through reciprocal flows, engender a distinctive texture in the image of the product itself. Connecting creativity means, to me, positive interaction between different functions. The designer's creativity must be linked to a project; the company itself cannot exist without one. A well-delineated project multiplies the opportunities for the application of creative ideas, just as the artists and craftspeople who symbolized creativity in the past worked freely, yet to precise briefs. At the same time, we must recognize that creativity cannot be strictly planned, and especially in such a complex organization as ours, we must be flexible and ready to modify, at least partially, our project. A simple but frequent example of that need for flexibility is evident in the process of selecting materials. We may happen, in the course of our work, to discover fabrics and colours we find interesting, and wish to include them in a project, where they had not been foreseen. This might appear straightforward but the introduction of something new in to a collection can have enormous implications for supply, production, workability and quality control. Even the smallest of variations can cause a chain reaction, which must be assimilated. The potential dangers of creativity are undoubtedly a factor in industry's ambivalence towards it, yet to cut it out of the company culture is to risk stagnation and decline.

How, then, does MaxMara handle creativity? Our firm has a singular history. It was founded by my father, Achille Maramotti, more than fifty years ago and its roofs are to be found in the tradition linking my family to dressmaking on one side and to education on the other. My great-great-grandmother was the head of a well-known local couturier in the middle of the last century, whilst my grandmother was a true pedagogue. Experimental by nature, she not only taught the techniques of design, pattern cutting and sewing, she also invented new methods, offering at the same time moral and practical guidance to the girls attending the 'Scuole Maramotti' which she established in the 1930s.

There is no doubt that this history has greatly spurred love of experimentation and innovation at every level in our company. But as I have argued, creativity is of little purpose unchecked or unsupported. We have over the years established a sequence of critical mechanisms by which creative energy is directed to the most effective ends. These are outlined in the paragraphs that follow.

MARKET RESEARCH

Despite the importance of market information, I happily confess that our group has no dedicated research department, and rarely uses the services of research consultants. We have discovered that the most effective strategy is to conduct this kind of research through those members of the group who are operative (namely the design, sales and marketing areas). We base our work on a very simple method: observation. Those who are involved with the development and marketing of the product know it well enough, and are sufficiently armed with the history of the company to know where to look for the most relevant material, and how to interpret information.

The fashion market is so segmented that it is not uncommon for a manufacturer to obtain results quite different from the ones foreseen by the macrotrend. In 1996, for instance, the sales of our coats increased by 15 per cent yet this outcome contradicted the general survey of the market that had predicted a negative trend for this item. Trends in spending, social behaviour and lifestyle, gained through macroanalysis therefore must be regarded as background information.

It is of course essential that the company applies its creativity to developing the right products for real market needs. With awareness of our capabilities, our potential and our position in the market we must be alert to new opportunities. Again, we at MaxMara believe that the most attentive and intuitive lookouts are likely to be those that work within the company.

DATA PROCESSING

This kind of work is concerned less with broad intuition and more with minutely detailed knowledge.

We are in a position to check daily precisely how the market is reacting to our products with reference to style, size and colour. This can be done thanks to a data-processing system we developed independently, to our specific requirements many years ago. Our sales information is supplemented by interviews with the managers of our stores, who can give us reasons for the success or failure of a particular model.

The importance of change in the fashion industry might tempt us to conclude that we should not be too greatly influenced by information on the market's reaction to a particular product; after all the market is bound to change and the product will be superseded. I have found that designers especially are sometimes particularly reluctant to confront this kind of information; it is unnerving to discover that the market does not affirm one's convictions. But a cumulative knowledge of how our customers' taste develops and what influences their choice, besides being deeply interesting, is an invaluable tool in predicting the chances of success for the next season's product, and in forming future strategies.

TECHNOLOGICAL AND TECHNICAL INNOVATION

I have acknowledged the role of textile developments in launching new fashions. Fabric research is of fundamental importance to MaxMara. Innovative textiles, offering for instance enhanced comfort, practicality, fluidity, lightness, stability, or which allow new techniques of construction, for example the new generation of 'double face' fabric, or can engender new modes of dressing, for example the recent 'urban sportswear' phenomenon based on luxurious interpretations of high-performance fabrics. Innovative solutions can and should extend to the entire process of the development and even the marketing of a product, and we should consider this a critical aspect of research. Innovation can be the primary reason for a product's success.

DESIGN

The market research, retail, information, fabric and technical research, the social tensions, ambivalences and ambiguities, the projections of future life, all that I have mentioned in this essay are transformed first into a drawing, then a form. This is the core of our work, and it has for me a magic and mysterious appeal. The sketches, patterns, phototypes, the styling and accessories are all equally important steps which require great investment. It is in the transition from bidimensional to tridimensional that we encounter the crucial artisanal aspect of our business. There is no substitute for the accumulated experience and craftsmanship of those pattern cutters and technicians in achieving the delicate balance that validates, authenticates or qualifies a designed garment. The designer must have an eye for these subtleties, and an appreciation of the crafts that enables his/her ideas to come into being.

COST ANALYSIS

If a seam in the back of a jacket can save 20 per cent in the fabric lay, is it worth doing? Questions of this type represent the difficult but necessary mediation between the defining characteristics of the original idea and the demands of reality. Cost analysis is a challenge to the designer since it requires him/her to devise ingenious solutions and should be regarded as a spur to the creative process, not an impediment.

PRODUCTION OPPORTUNITIES

Although most of our products are manufactured in Italy, we are conscious that in the future there will be a proliferation of opportunities for high-quality production in other parts of the world. Information on new manufacturing and finishing techniques and special processes is part of the research described above, and can stimulate new products, but we must be circumspect regarding, for example potential bottlenecks and other damaging production problems. When we embark on new projects in production, we must verify our willingness and ability to train, and the investment which that entails.

MARKETING

Creating for sale is different from creating for creation's sake. At MaxMara, the product is rigorously defined in relation to the retail concept. There are over 600 MaxMara stores and our organization regards the selling phase as integral to the project. The visual merchandizing and display of proposed products, their coordination and communication are a vital part of the design activity.

ADVERTISING

The importance of creating in this field is obvious, but more than anywhere else it must be exercised with a view to consistency since our objective is that the product should be immediately recognizable and associated with an absolute, possibly unique, identity. In my experience, the most successful advertising campaigns are those resulting from a very close collaboration between designers, photographers, and those such as stylists who, from an external perspective can add to this a story, an element of conceived reality. Advertising in the fashion field is, in my opinion, more conventional than in others. Whilst we require it to be new and innovative, conveying an important element of fantasy, imagination and feeling, fashion advertising must also be relatively representative and explicative. To the question 'do advertised garments sell better?' I simply answer: Yes, but mainly if they are original and unusual.

PROMOTION

In the field of fashion, promotion means documentation, through the press in general and through the branch of the press that serves it specifically. I recently debated with some American journalists the ideal contents of a fashion publication. Their opinions were, predictably, very different and our discussion returned to the familiar dilemma between dream and reality, between the desire to report extreme and fascinating trends and the need to give useful advice and information to the readership. Everyone agreed on one point: the apparently 'objective' documentation of a product acts as a kind of endorsement or legislation which augments its chances of commercial success. It is therefore critical that an organization such as ours invests in effective communication with the media.

When these elements are synchronized, a circle is completed where creativity can flow freely. Since the creative thought represented by Archimede's light bulb has always fascinated me, it has been a pleasure to have worked in a field where one can experiment with its deployment. Where these experiments are successful, the results are tangible and I attribute our company's success, in no small part, to the way in which creativity is embedded at the heart of its culture. Further satisfaction is to be gained from the certainty that our experiments will never reach a conclusion. The game will last forever.

Notes

1. Pascale, B., *Pensieri,* Turin: Eindaudi, 1962.
2. Freud, S., *Writing on Art and Literature,* Stanford University Press, 1997.
3. Jung, C. G. *The Spirit in Man, Art and Literature,* Princeton University Press, 1971.
4. Arieti, S., *Creativity – The Magic Synthesis,* New York: Basic Books, 1976.
5. Jullien, F., Procès ou creation, *Un Introduction á la Pensée des lettres Chinois,* Paris: Edition du Seuil, 1989.
6. After Veblen, T., *The Theory of the Leisure Class: an economic study of institutions,* London: Allen and Unwin, 1970.
7. Hollander, A., *Sex and Suits,* New York: Alfred A. Knopf, 1994.
8. Davis, F., *Fashion, Culture and Identity,* Chicago: Chicago University Press, 1992.
9. Breward, C., *The Culture of Fashion,* Manchester and New York: Manchester University Press, 1995, pp. 22–9.
10. Charlie-Roux, E. Trans Amphoux, N., *Chanel,* London: The Harrill Press, 1995.
11. Craik, J., *Cultural Studies in Fashion,* London: Routledge, 1994, p. 60.

9

BUYER–SUPPLIER PARTNERSHIPS IN THE GLOBAL APPAREL INDUSTRY:
A study of US buyers and Indian suppliers

Kamlesh Singh and Nancy Hodges[1]

INTRODUCTION

India is emerging as one of the top countries in apparel sourcing to the USA, as there has been an annual rise of approximately 13.3 percent in exports of garments from India since 2000 (Goel 2007). In 2005, India ranked third in apparel exports to the USA, increasing its total exports to 34 percent. Tariff and trade data from the US Department of Commerce and the US International Trade Commission (2007) indicate that total apparel imported into the USA from India in 1997 was US$2.9 billion, increasing to US$6.4 billion by 2006, and that the change in percentage from 2005 to 2006 increased by 18.40 percent. In 2007–8, total Indian exports saw a 2.76 percent growth, 41 percent of which consisted of ready-to-wear garments (Ministry of Textiles 2009). By 2009 India was ranked fifth among the top exporters of garments in the world (Apparel Export Promotion Council 2009).

The purpose of this study was to explore US apparel buyers' relationships with their Indian suppliers. Two primary objectives guide the study: (a) to determine what buyers believe is important when working with Indian suppliers, and (b) to augment the buyer–supplier relationship literature by focusing specifically on relationship-building between the USA and India.

BACKGROUND
Sourcing in a global context

Competition within the apparel industry has intensified as a result of the quota phase-out established by the WTO Agreement on Textile and Clothing (ATC). This has particularly been the case for US companies after the creation of several free trade agreements, including NAFTA (Taplin 1999; Teng and Jaramillo 2005). US companies have turned to Asian and Eastern European countries to meet production needs, as these countries generally have access to raw materials and offer highly skilled, low-cost labor (Cho and Kang 2001; Curran 2009; Gereffi 2001). Adoption of an aggressive devaluation policy for currency has also helped attract US companies looking to source from developing countries (Teng and Jaramillo 2005).

A focus on India

Although there was concern that the ATC would result in the complete domination of imports into the US from China, sourcing from several developing countries, including India, has continued to increase (*Apparel Sourcing from India and China* 2008; Curran 2007). According to a Confederation of Indian

---

[1] From Kamlesh Singh and Nancy Hodges, (2011) Buyer-Suppliers Partnerships in the Global Apparel Industry: A Study of US Buyers and Indian Suppliers, Fashion Practice, Volume 3, Issue 2, Taylor & Francis.

Industry/Ernst and Young Report (Textile News—India 2007), sourcing from India by global retailers is growing at an annual rate of 12 percent. This suggests a continued high growth trajectory for India's textile and apparel sector. Moreover, projections for the country's sourcing market in 2011 total US$35–37 billion, increasing from US$22–25 billion in 2007 (Textile News—India 2007).

Elements of the buyer–supplier Relationship

Selection of the right supplier is the most important stage in the buying process, in that selecting the right supplier can help reduce material purchase costs and improve the competitiveness of the buyer's company (Thomas and Jonathan 2007). An important issue for US buyers during the strategic planning process is deciding when, where, and what to outsource (Teng and Jaramillo 2005). Buyers are becoming increasingly selective and demanding in their identification of a good supplier (Wuyts 2007). Indeed, a study by Forker and Stannack (2000) revealed that buyer–supplier relationships based on cooperation may be less effective than those forged through competition. As retailing becomes more fast fashion in orientation, the primary criterion for buyers in selecting a supplier is not necessarily price, due to intense market competition and the requirement of just-in-time deliveries (Doyle et al. 2006).

Method

A total of twenty-three US apparel industry buyers (five males and eighteen females) engaged in buying apparel products from Indian suppliers participated in this study. Buyers were the focus of the sample because they generally interact with Indian suppliers on a regular basis and can therefore share their experiences with building buyer–supplier relationships. A range of large apparel companies are represented by the sample (employing greater than 1,500 people), including womenswear, menswear, and footwear companies. All operate globally, though participants work primarily within the companies' US headquarters.

Interpretation

Several themes emerged from the interview responses. Themes represent the interpretation of participants' expectations of an Indian supplier, what they look for in seeking out new suppliers in India, as well as what they have experienced when working with their Indian suppliers. These themes include: *Expertise, Convenience, Functionality, Price, Service,* and *Partnership*. Issues such as the benefits and challenges of sourcing from India are discussed relative to each theme and are important to understanding what participants look for from their suppliers. To protect participant confidentiality, pseudonyms are used throughout the interpretation.

Expertise

Expertise surfaced as an important reason why participants sought to do business with Indian suppliers. Participants frequently discussed opportunities afforded by Indian suppliers that are not offered by suppliers in other countries and noted several qualities that Indian suppliers are known for. Providing quality natural fibers and fabrics, an authentic cultural flavor and novelty, and the capacity for innovation were the key types of expertise participants associated with Indian suppliers. Several participants indicated that they moved their business to India because of its reputation for domestic production of cotton and natural yarns and because it offered a range of traditional techniques that are unique to the country.

For those participants who described being on the lookout for something new, striking, original, or unusual, India had a certain appeal. Impressed by their suppliers' presentations during the product development process, these participants explained that Indian suppliers bring more creativity and choices "to the table" as compared to suppliers in other countries. Moreover, some commented on how Indian suppliers will often take the time to collect ideas about fashion trends, indicating the extent to which, as suppliers, they are interested in providing unique services. Participants explained that they look for specialized strengths in their suppliers. However, they also said that in today's competitive apparel marketplace, they look for suppliers that not only have expertise in certain categories, but are located in places where access is easy in order to better facilitate the production process.

Convenience

According to the participants, India is known for providing the "full package." They mentioned that facilities that produce yarns, fabrics, and garments are located throughout the country and that this greatly reduces the inconveniences they may face if they choose to do more discontinuous sourcing (e.g. buying fabric from one country, cutting it in another, and sewing and finishing the garments in a third). Offering full pipeline service is an advantage, as according to participants, this reduces time, money, and effort. Despite the fact that they can get everything finished in India, some participants complained about longer lead times there as compared to other countries. However, other participants indicated that longer lead time is not necessarily a problem specific to Indian suppliers.

Participants talked about experiencing a good deal of flexibility when doing business in India, in that they have found that business in India is more fluid than in countries like China in terms of procedures and formalities. Although they found that this fluidity makes sourcing in India more appealing, the appeal was balanced by the challenges inherent to a developing economy. Most participants commented that India has problems with transport and infrastructure. However, participants also mentioned that the country is working to improve its infrastructure, and they believe that this will, in turn, improve logistics.

Functionality

Participants think that Indian suppliers have a high degree of technical capability in manufacturing certain types of apparel products, and that a number of the country's more well-known factories are continuously seeking to acquire the right equipment. They also indicated that Indian suppliers tend to have an interest in implementing technological innovations.

In contrast, other participants thought that Indian suppliers use less advanced technology compared to other countries, such as China, and explained that though India is known for advanced technology in general, suppliers in the apparel business are often still what they consider to be "home spun."

Quality obviously surfaced as an important component of a supplier's functionality for the participants. Regardless of the size or scale of a supplier's operations, participants expect to receive a quality product. Participants talked about quality as an expectation not only at the end of the production cycle, but throughout the entire production process. Some noted that their Indian suppliers are enthusiastic about making continual improvements in quality. Participants expected that their suppliers exhibit a high level of functionality, that is, the right equipment, technical capability, and procedures that result a high-quality product. Yet meeting their needs does not come without a price tag, in that participants emphasized the importance of considering functionality relative to costs and profit.

Price

According to the participants, a buyer's primary goal is to increase profits, and to do so by securing good prices from their suppliers. Participants pointed out that though there are typically dozens of suppliers around the world that can provide what they need, only a few can do so at the right price. Therefore, for the participants, the key is to find those few suppliers. Most respondents mentioned that they do business with Indian suppliers because they can get their product at lower cost there, primarily due to the country's availability of inexpensive labor. For the participants, India offers affordable and reasonable prices, even for those yarns that require treatment before usage.

However, as India's economy continues to grow, prices are becoming less competitive, creating a challenge for some participants. Such an increase in production costs has in some cases forced them to look for alternatives. Interestingly, though price is important to the participants, most talked about the importance of not sacrificing too much for it. Many participants qualified their statements about price by explaining that they prefer to select a supplier who offers moderate prices with good service, rather than one who offers low prices but no service.

Service

Service was critical to the participants, and many described seeking competent suppliers who offer good service. Most participants have traveled to India several times, and explained that Indian suppliers are not only capable of providing the required products but also better service than other countries. According to participants, elements of good service include fast response time, accessibility, and commitment. Participants expected quick responses from their suppliers, and most described experiences indicating that their Indian suppliers generally meet this expectation.

Participants indicated that, on the whole, the impression they get from their Indian suppliers is one of genuine interest in making sure they are satisfied. Participants commented that their Indian suppliers often treat them with respect and place particular emphasis on being available all the time. Yet, some participants pointed out that this dedication can sometimes lead to problems, namely the potential to over-commit. Commitment, as well as honesty, is required for both parties. As buyers, participants expect that their suppliers will do what they have committed to do, and at the same time, their suppliers expect them to commit to an order.

Partnership

Participants placed a great deal of importance on working with the right supplier. They described how, by focusing on key suppliers, they can go beyond a superficial buyer–supplier relationship to build an actual partnership. When asked to describe the key to building and maintaining long-term relationships with their suppliers, many participants used terms like "marriage" and "partnership." They explained that long-term success is the result of contributions made by both parties.

To establish a partnership, participants cited communication as the critical link between the two parties. According to the participants, regular communication can help to avoid any misunderstandings during the production process, decrease the chances of error, and ultimately increase output.

SOURCING FROM INDIA: BENEFITS AND CHALLENGES

All participants considered supplier selection as a crucial step when involved in sourcing apparel products. One selection criterion that was consistent among almost all of the participants was the supplier's expertise in the specific product category, especially their expertise in producing a variety of products from basic, to novel, to innovative. They saw this particular criterion as somewhat unique to their Indian suppliers, and one that is not easily found in other countries. Yet innovation was not the only benefit. As revealed in the interpretation, participants work with Indian suppliers because of category expertise, a high level of convenience, functional capabilities, effective pricing structures, and good service.

Although they emphasized the benefits of sourcing from India, participants also described some of the challenges they face. Participants were concerned that their suppliers continue to use old equipment and technology, despite the country's reputation for high technology. The participants were also concerned about their Indian suppliers' difficulty with saying "No," as accepting every job can lead to problems in the production process. Other concerns are in keeping with previous research on the industry in India, including logistical difficulties (Gupta 2006; Joshi and Singh 2010) and the impact of the ATC along with an appreciation of the country's currency (*Apparel Exports May Fall Short of Target* 2008; Karandikar 2005).

Relationship attributes: a focus on partnership

Results reveal that when working with their Indian suppliers, US buyers seek to build relationships in the form of *partnerships*. Considering the key relationship attributes described in the existing literature—

trust, knowledge, communication, commitment, follow up, and continuance—participants weighed each attribute's value differently based on their own experiences. Although participants pointed to all attributes as important for building, maintaining, and strengthening partnerships with their Indian suppliers, analysis of attribute importance revealed variations. Most participants considered effective communication, trust, and commitment as the most important, or necessary, to build partnerships with their Indian suppliers.

Partnership types

Further analysis of participant responses revealed variations in the type of partnerships that participants seek with their Indian suppliers. Four types of partnerships were therefore defined based on the interpretation: *Convenience Driven*; *Price Sensitive*; *Functionality Driven*; and *Service Driven*. The four types highlight the issues revealed by participants' experiences with their Indian suppliers. Each type also reflects the importance placed on different relationship attributes by the participants relative to working with Indian suppliers.

Over one-third of the participants (35 percent) are *Service Driven* when working with suppliers in India. The participants in this category placed a high value on service-oriented suppliers and tended to partner with certain suppliers based on their service offerings. Service-driven participants sought quick response, availability, and flexibility from their suppliers. This finding supports the literature on buyer–supplier relationships that has emerged alongside the advent of fast fashion retailing (Bruce and Daly 2006) and highlights the importance of communication to the service-driven partnership.

Participants who focused most of their effort on building partnerships with suppliers based on pricing structure fall within the *Price-Sensitive* type. Comprising the second largest group, at 26 percent of the sample, these participants are price-sensitive in that they preferred suppliers who can provide them quality products at the lowest price. This group reflects the emphasis on low-cost sourcing often cited as a core reason for working with suppliers abroad (Lowson 2001) and puts priority on developing a high level of trust that the supplier will also come through with the expected level of quality.

Just behind the price-sensitive partnership type were those participants who seek to build the *Functionality-Driven* type of partnership (22 percent). This group was focused primarily on the supplier's level of functionality, and whether it uses new technology, has the latest equipment, and meets quality requirements. For these participants, knowledge (Ganesan 1994) was the key relationship attribute that they emphasized when working with their Indian suppliers.

Participants most interested in the accessibility of the supplier illustrate the *Convenience-Driven* partnership type. The smallest group, at 17 percent of the sample, these participants tended to select Indian suppliers based on their accessibility and availability and emphasized the importance of commitment (Hartley *et al.* 1997) throughout the production process.

This study sheds light on the experiences of buyers currently sourcing from India. Results revealed that these buyers view their Indian suppliers as partners in the sourcing process and thus seek to build long-term, partnership-based relationships with them. Findings also indicate that these buyers highly value the unique combination of offerings provided by suppliers in India as compared to other low-cost sourcing countries such as China or Vietnam. Further research on the Indian supplier's experience would shed light on the benefits and challenges of global sourcing partnerships from the perspective of businesses within this country.

References

Anderson, M. G. and P. B. Katz. 1998. "Strategic Sourcing." *Mercer Management Consulting* 9(1): 1–13.

Apparel Exports May Fall Short of Target. 2008. Apparel Exports May Fall Short of Target [online]. http://economictimes.indiatimes.com/News/News_By_Industry/Cons_Products/Apparel_exports_may_fall_short_of_target/articleshow/2691219.cms (accessed January 17, 2009).

Apparel Sourcing from India and China. 2008. *Apparel Sourcing from India and China [online].* http://www.fibre2fashion.com/industry-article/pdffiles/articlepdf/apparel-sourcing-from-india-and-china.pdf (accessed January 24, 2009).

Bruce, M. and L. Daly. 2006. "Buyer Behavior for Fast Fashion." *Journal of Fashion Marketing and Management* 10(3): 329–44.

Cho, J., and J. Kang. 2001. "Benefits and Challenges of Global Sourcing: Perceptions of US Apparel Retail Firms." *International Marketing Review* 18(5): 542–61.

Curran, L. 2007. "Clothing's Big Bang: The Impact of the End of the ATC on Developing Country Clothing Suppliers." *Journal of Fashion Marketing and Management* 11(1): 122–34.

Curran, L. 2009. "The EU Clothing Market in 2008: Opening the Floodgates?" *Journal of Fashion Marketing and Management* 13(3): 305–10.

Doyle, S. A., C. M. Moore and L. Morgan. 2006. "Supplier Management in Fast Moving Fashion Retailing." *Journal of Fashion Marketing and Management* 10(3): 272–81.

Forker, L. B. and P. Stannack. 2000. "Cooperation vs. Competition: Do Buyers and Suppliers Really See Eye-to-Eye?" *European Journal of Purchasing and Supply Management* 6: 31–40.

Ganesan, S. 1994. "Determinants of Long-term Orientation in Buyer–Seller Relationships." *Journal of Marketing* 58(2): 1–19.

Gereffi, G. 2001. "Global Sourcing in the US Apparel Industry." *Journal of Textile and Apparel, Technology and Management* 2(1): 1–5.

Goel, S. 2007. *Indian Apparel Industry—Outsourcing Intelligence Report (2007–08)* [online]. http://www.marketresearch.com/search/ results.asp?sid=79921552-406579804-486042572&query=Indian+Apparel+Industry+-+Outsourcing&cmdSubmitLt=Go. (accessed March 4, 2008).

Gupta, R. 2006. *Indian Textile Industry: Prospects and Challenges* [online]. http://www.indianmba.com/Faculty_Column/FC236/fc236.html (accessed January 18, 2008).

Hartley, J. L., B. Zirger and R. R. Kamath. 1997. "Managing the Buyer–Supplier Interface for On-time Performance in Product Development." *Journal of Operations Management* 15(1): 57–70.

Joshi, R. N. and S. P. Singh. 2010. "Estimation of Total Factor Productivity in the Indian Garment Industry." *Journal of Fashion Marketing and Management* 14(1): 145–60.

Karandikar, S. K. 2005. *Indian Apparel Industry: Opportunities Unlimited* [online]. Maharashtra Economic Development Council. http://www.medcindia.org/cgi-bin/Mar05/Industry%20Monitor.HTM (accessed January 14, 2008).

Lowson, R. 2001. "Analysing the Effectiveness of European Retail Sourcing Strategies." *European Management Journal* 19(5): 543–51.

Ministry of Textiles. 2009. *Note on Indian Textile and Apparel Clothing Export* [online]. http://texmin.nic.in/ (accessed October 17, 2010).

Taplin, I. 1999. "Continuity and Change in the US Apparel Industry: A Statistical Profile." *Journal of Fashion Marketing and Management* 3(4): 360–68.

Teng, S. G. and H. Jaramillo. 2005. "A Model for Evaluation and Selection in the Global Textile and Apparel Supply Chain." *International Journal of Physical Distribution & Logistics Management* 35(7): 503–23.

Teng, S. G. and H. Jaramillo. 2006. "Integrating the US Textile and Apparel Supply Chain with Small Companies in South America." *Supply Chain Management: An International Journal* 11(1): 45–55.

Textile News—India. 2007. *India—Textile, Apparel Sourcing Set to Rise 12%: CII-Ernst and Young report* [online]. Yarns and Fiber Exchange. http://www.yarnsandfibers.com/news/index_fullstory.php3?id=13880&p_type=General (accessed January 17, 2009).

Thomas, A. and O. Jonathan. 2007. *Customer Relationship Management, from a Buyer's Perspective in a B2b Relationship* [online]. http://epubl.ltu.se/1402-1773/2007/208/ (accessed January 24, 2008).

Wuyts, S. 2009. "Extra-Role Behavior in Buyer–Supplier Relationships." *International Journal of Research in Marketing* 24(4): 301–11.

10

BUSINESS AND INDUSTRY

Colin Gale and Jasbir Kaur[1]

This chapter primarily focuses on two subjects – national industrial policies for the textile and clothing industry, and supply chain management. These topics have been chosen because they provide a broad industrial and commercial backdrop to fashion and textiles. They are applicable to each sector individually but equally are the context in which a wide range of interactions take place *between* fashion and textiles.

COMPANIES AND COUNTRIES

In recent years many large corporations, long associated with apparel and textiles, such as DuPont or Coats (previously Coats Viyella) have sought to entirely or partly withdraw from parts of the clothing and textiles industry, while in the process of restructuring their business. This can often result in smaller companies being formed through management buyout or acquisition by a third party. The industrial, corporate and company landscape is always changing and various reasons underlie this such as

- straightforward losses;
- predicted reductions in profits;
- increasing competition in one area of business activity;
- corporate refocusing in order to enter or develop more profitable business activity.

Problems such as these cause any company large or new, small or old to embark on reviewing their business activities or constructing their business plans.

The mindset of the twenty-first century professional is also dogged by a few recurrent thoughts – globalization, technology and branding. Collectively these have become the mantra of competition, spurred by the fear that one day the money and jobs will dry up. Of course, to the wholehearted optimist they are, more positively, keys to success. This modern psyche has a strong influence on business practice in fashion and textiles as it does in other sectors. Explicit themes of competition and survival have resulted in various action plans, initiatives and techniques. Over the past few decades logistics and management have increasingly fused with computing and communications. The result is at least two areas of business activity which are continuously and consciously addressed by politicians, journalists and business people alike:

- supply chain management;
- the formulation of industrial policy.

Also during the 1990s other manufacturing and retail concepts came to the fore as a consequence of a simultaneous increase in market competition and technology innovation. The resultant techniques and practices dealt with efficiency, economy, reducing overheads and meeting customer, or buyer, needs more closely.

- 'just in time' manufacture or supply;
- flexible manufacturing;
- customization.

The activities and practices mentioned above are manifested in different ways depending on how

---

[1] In Colin Gale and Jasbir Kaur (2004) Business and Industry. In Fashion and Textiles: An Overview. Oxford: Berg. 87-117.

companies evolve, how large a company is, product type, manufacturing process and so on. As broad themes of modern industry they can be considered to be 'in the grain' of many of the more specific or piecemeal examples given in this chapter.

INDUSTRIAL POLICIES AND GOVERNMENT STRATEGIES

A ten-year strategic plan commissioned by the Australian Textile, Clothing, Footwear and Leather (TCFL) Forum, raises some interesting points about the way the textile and clothing industry is perceived, not only in Australia, but more universally. For example their report points out how the disappearance and decline of large-scale traditional manufacturing, sector job losses and economic downturns generates the impression of an industry in severe decline. In turn this has a negative impact on attracting investment, new ideas and 'new people'. The report points out that new markets are emerging and that the pattern of industry has undergone a global change. What amounts to an optimistic thesis in the report is that the perceived 'decline' of the industry is, essentially, the globalization of the manufacturing supply chain. Consequently and in turn the Australian industry is in transition, taking on a new shape. The transition is hampered by the previously mentioned effects of negative perceptions, but also by a reactive rather than proactive industry. Equally the structural nature of the industry is such that it is difficult to implement forceful or purposeful change across the sector. The plans and visions of the Australian strategy – much the same as in all other countries prey to offshore manufacture – are to develop:

- niche markets;
- consumer-oriented industries;
- innovation;
- design;
- branding;
- internationalization;
- collaboration;
- national coordination.

Slightly reminiscent of the Australian call for 'new people' in the industry, in the UK designers are an emergent entrepreneurial group who want to enter the industry but for various reasons are often frustrated. While there has always been a pattern of designers founding companies, a more traditional route was to seek employment in an existing company. One factor now evident is that significant growth in design education coupled with industrial decline has led to large numbers of creative textile and fashion designers with few obvious local employment opportunities as designers. Vocational choices for this group can become quite stark and a proportion therefore elect the route of establishing design-led or designer-maker businesses. A number of problems were identified that hampered the growth of this sector:

- offshore producers not meeting standards and expectations;
- a reluctance of small to medium-sized manufacturers to:
  - work with designers.
  - see them as sources of future business.
  - market themselves to designers.

It was identified that, in general, designers want manufacturers nearby so they can have more control over what is produced. Also three problems needed resolving:

- connecting designers and small supplier;
- how to convince larger companies to supply the design sector;
- raising the profile of small manufacturers.

At a fundamental level a more general problem for many national industries is that how and where work is situated; its type and duration; and conventional sector employment are all changing. One example is the problem of recruitment. In the recommendations of a strategy document by the UK Textile and Clothing Strategy Group (TCSG, 2000), companies are exhorted (among many things) to:

- seek opportunities for student placements;

- establish relationships with schools and colleges to present a positive image of the industry;
- offer competitive employment packages.

Such activities and commitments cannot be lightly undertaken and similar expectations of industry are, no doubt, made elsewhere. However such actions are often a significant draw on resources. Thus many companies may not be able to commit to such policies. The difficulties of change, recruitment and growth that exist in the apparel/textiles sector might be usefully compared with the area of technical textiles. Most advanced industrial nations see this sector as highly successful and an area of future growth. In a report on the US market for technical textiles (Chang and Kilduff, 2002) various convincing factors are identified:

- the size and cutting-edge nature of local demand;
- the high quality of US textile engineers;
- the technical strengths of supporting educational and research institutions;
- the technical and commercial strengths of suppliers.

Such factors are most likely to lead to a highly collaborative technocracy with significant employment mobility across the sector. There is a good relationship with the educational sector and a continuously renewed and refreshed skilled workforce. The nature of the industry itself would already dictate the need for a high degree of logistical management including advanced process control, project management and efficient supply chain management. In a sense the technical textiles sector has many of the features and attributes that strategy documents suggest the apparel manufacturing sector should have. However even with these advantages there are no guarantees.

In a survey of the textile and clothing industry in the EU, Werner Stengg divided the industry into high-, medium- and low-quality segments. The high-quality segment (HQS), in the year 2000, accounted for over 50 per cent of EU exports. This segment was dominated by the trade in technical textiles. Most clothing products fell into the medium-quality segment (some 35 to 40 per cent of exports) and this included items such as tracksuits, brassieres, tights and slips, jerseys, cardigans, and shawls and ties. Fashion and design can however add value and, it seems, provide a further definition of quality beyond technical excellence.

It is interesting that industrial policy statements often see technical textiles as the salvation of textiles and clothing industries, but also see them as having little to do with the needs of fashion. Technical textiles are deemed to be mainly focused on performance characteristics suited to other industrial applications. Presumably there is a perception or assumption that fashion textiles:

- are primarily about aesthetic expression and comfort;
- have fairly rudimentary and straightforward function;
- are scientifically and technically 'simple';

and that

- the needs of fashion are already amply met by existing textile types and fabrics;
- any new needs will be met by technology transfer, trickle-down or spin-off.

Certainly much of the technical textiles sector looks for new and emergent markets and the fashion textiles sector, in this respect, may look resolved and oversubscribed while also offering proportionately much lower profit gains. This situation seems unlikely to change unless clothing becomes very hi-tech. In which case consumer demand may drive fashion-technical textiles more than the fashion industry itself. Such a change would be dependent on the ability of the fashion industry to implement technological product innovation as much as stylistic variation.

COLLABORATIVE COMMERCE

The ever-growing pressures of competition affect all aspects and types of business. From fibre production to fashion retail there is a need to seek economies, increase efficiency and improve communication. The beneficiaries of the increasingly competitive environment have been those that sell logical solutions, automated systems and communications technology. They promise to reduce costs, use resources better, improve the speed of doing business and so on. IT products used throughout the clothing and textiles industry include the likes of supply chain management systems, CAD/CAM systems, retail systems and e-commerce. The current success and stability of the IT industry has allowed it to develop increasingly complex and sophisticated systems.

Freeborders describes itself as a company that delivers software enabling its customers to 'streamline product development processes and collaborate more efficiently'. It promises reductions in product cycle times, and design and development costs, helping customers 'meet the ever-increasing demand to bring products to the market quickly'. The company's Product Lifecycle Management software, and Collaborative Product Management software, are used by over 350 retailers, brands and manufacturers around the world. The company has a prestigious list of customers – Liz Clairborne, Gap, Levi Strauss & Co., Nike, Saks, Burlington Industries, Dillards, J. Crew and many more. Customer interests include both manufacture and retailing and range across the various fashion and textile markets.

> At top companies per-unit product costs are extraordinarily low, inventory and distribution are managed in a far more efficient manner, and pricing and markdown strategies have dramatically improved net margins. (Pearson and Knudsen, 2003)

Pearson and Knudsen develop a thesis of future practice that builds on recent trends such as last-minute and flexible manufacturing. They suggest that currently used product data management (PDM) systems might be evolved into systems based on total product life cycle – from design, through manufacture to retail. PDM systems are themselves the consequence of a gradual evolution, therefore a further evolution is, in itself, unlikely to be contentious.

> With the rise of internet technologies, however, a new class of applications is emerging in product development – enabling greater management of a wider number of product-related activities. Known as Product Lifecycle Management or PLM, these applications better support collaboration both internally and externally with supply chain partners, something PDM systems typically did poorly. PLM is helping enable best-practice processes, while tying line and product creation back to the financial plan and the global supply chain. (Jerrard et al, 2002)

The overall ambitions of collaborative commerce (or c-commerce) are in a sense to move the consumer's deliberative act of buying, as near as possible, into one of commissioning; general retail and point of sale data triggering the supply chain in the process fulfilling all parties' dreams and changing 'they might buy' into 'they want to buy'. The logic of rapid response, c-commerce, flexible manufacturing and mass-customization as tools of competition and survival seem the inevitable end-game of information management and automation in the fashion and textile industries.

TECHNOCRACY VERSUS CONSUMERISM AND FASHION

Some significant questions are raised by the idea of handing over more and more manufacturing and design 'control' to consumers. The structural consequences of this for the textile and clothing industries are unforeseeable, and as a phase of industrial development it is a relatively recent ambition. There are no early signals of the longer-term effects. For example there might be industrial and employment benefits. Quick response, customized and commissioned goods might stop or even reverse the trend of offshore manufacture in some sectors. The path of business would be smoothed, stressful and expensive mistakes in supply, manufacture and retail, done away with and so on.

Another issue is that consumers have over the years showed a strong ability to reject the best laid plans of industry. In lifestyle and fashion sectors, many different factors can influence why something is fashionable or unfashionable at a particular time. Fashion 'statements' can also be a reaction to, or rejection of, conformity, tradition or the norm. That garments or styles become unfashionable is a commonsensical observation. Equally consumers are often resistant to being 'manipulated' by retailers and corporations. Also they tire of, or do not believe, brand identities and associations. Geraldine Bedell, commenting on Nike's loss of market position and a plunge in their share values, points out the significant influence of a youth-oriented fashion image.

> On both sides of the Atlantic, however, the story is the same: it's not easy for a global company whose trainers are on every high street and in every suburban mall, to remain fashionable. Young people like brands that are (a bit) rebellious, and Nike is perilously close to being the establishment (Bedell, 2003)

With respect to 'knowing your customers' (the second thorn in the side of a totally technocratic solution), the net effect of consumer behaviour is that retail data about consumers' purchases and preferred product characteristics can always, and quickly, become redundant. As for fashion culture, its play with iconic garments and fabrics is not neutral but one laden with value judgements or even political sentiment. The language of fashion is often linked to other social realities that can activate or disrupt retail activity. The consumer shopping for apparel or fashion may thus make decisions not based on formal garment properties. Indeed their decisions may be entirely unlinked to 'retail' descriptors of choice, taste or trend and be rooted in deeper sociocultural currents.

Unforeseeable, sometimes swift, consumer interest in a garment or look has implications for the stock on offer and the 'verity' or predictive potential of data held about consumers' choices. Fashionability is certainly a factor that can maintain and stimulate consumer interest in mainstream products and services. The irony is that equally it can do the opposite. The mechanisms and logistics of customization in many ways seem opposite to the idea of fashion and/or the survival of fashion brands.

THE STORE

In a sense many of the ambitions of coordinating the supply chain to retailing will depend on new retail technology and consumer reactions to it. A technology called radio frequency identification permits data to be stored in clothing tags. The system has been used in Prada's store in Manhattan's SoHo neighbourhood. Sales associates can find out such things as stock levels or the material composition of a garment using handheld computers. The so called 'smart tags' are typically in use in tracking goods in warehouses, so their introduction into the retail environment potentially moves closer to the concept of product life-cycle management. Various criticisms of the use of such technology can be raised, particularly if data about customers' shopping behaviour is held. To some extent these mirror existing general concerns about computer technology, privacy, and intrusive or aggressive selling techniques. The up-side is that sales staff can be more helpful and efficient. In the Prada store, customers can hang up their chosen goods in boxes and then see the clothes and accessories projected onto a plasma screen in the dressing room, by using a touch screen they can then mix and match their chosen items or find out more information about them. There is even talk of one day offering customers virtual wardrobes over the web. Integrating such technology into retail environments raises lots of interesting possibilities for shoppers, staff and company. But like many innovations to do with new technology, sometimes the vision is easier to achieve than the reality.

> 'Overall, it seems that the technology wasn't used to enhance the consumer experience, but help the sales people on the floor,' said Mitch Kates, a principal with Kurt Salmon Associates, a retail consulting firm. 'The technology is cool, but it can also be intimidating.' (CNN, 2002)

Prada's commitment to retail innovation is unquestioned (Koolhaas, 2001) but it seems that if the retail environment is to become a high-tech zone, some older and proven criteria need to be retained. The American National Textile Center has funded a project that looks into the role of emotion in the success of global textile product retailing. A 'feeling of excitement experienced during shopping was the important emotional response linked to store loyalty' (NTC, 2002). Some of the implications of the study are that the textile and clothing industry may ultimately need to adapt as much to changing global retail opportunities as it has to a global manufacturing market. This will undoubtedly provide further incentives for manufacturers to be proactive in establishing coordinated yet highly flexible relationships with retailers.

INFORMATION AND TECHNOLOGY

Identifying 'channels' and products and putting one with the other is, of course, the ancient premise of any market. In the global business environment, not only is such information key, it is in itself a new type of commodity. Sometimes information is sold, sometimes it is free. Information is variously broadcast, narrowcast and packaged in all kinds of ways in all kind of media. Information can swiftly move from being secret and valuable to being public and given away free.

For many large companies there is no simple vertical supply chain. In these circumstances a 'quiet pond' with a limited number of trusted business partners, sharing information resources, possibly doing business 'as and when', looks very attractive. These new types of consortia will use a variety of c-commerce and supply chain management software to coordinate their activities. The history of e-commerce during the time of this shift in business culture underscores the move to consortia. Prior attempts to offer supply chain management through e-commerce sites has moved to providing intranet/network based equivalents.

> Sources indicate that approximately 1,500 e-marketplaces were set up during the late 1990s and that about 90 percent have since gone out of business.
> (Global Sources, 2002)

While e-marketplaces have found it difficult to prosper, overall companies that sell IT reliant solutions to the clothing and textiles sector can benefit from a fractured and disparate industry as much as from a cohesive industry with fewer companies in it. The demand for better control of the supply chain, industrial collaboration, and the closing of the gap between retail and manufacturing have met with various reactions from traditional suppliers of manufacturing technology and software. The actions and announcements of companies that supply the clothing and textile industry, in many ways, directly reflect the concerns and preoccupations of the industry itself. Lectra Systèmes, the French supplier of CAD/CAM systems upgraded its software offerings and systems to include:

- prototyping;
- management of fashion collections and product development cycles;
- data exchange through the supply chain;
- cutting room management;
- customized apparel production;
- sell before producing;
- colour management and communication.

Lectra identifies seven strategic challenges facing its customers including reducing time to market; dealing with globalization; securely communicating across the supply chain; and mass customization. Interestingly Lectra states that it has considerably revamped its technology and services to provide 'new technological answers' for its customers. They identify mass customization as a key factor of the 'new economy', where the Internet and a total systems model are applied to the life of a manufactured item. In this situation:

- retailers are seen to minimize costs and improve customer relations;
- manufacturers reduce the risk of investment and inventory;
- designers offer more styles and combinations;
- information on customer preferences are vertically available in the entire textile chain.

It seems almost ironic that at a time when the complexity of the global economy gives rise to industrial confusion and business hazard, there is an almost universal consensus on 'the way forward' for mainstream clothing and textile industries. Everyone it seems – from retailers to policy-makers, from manufacturers to the suppliers of equipment and software – agree that remarkable control of an individual product will solve 'the problem'. Currently it seems there are few voices of scepticism countering this view. If the nature of 'the problem' were simply about locally saving losses in manufacture, investment, etc. the proposed solution might well work. However, for the majority of nations and companies, 'the problem' is also about gaining or securing advantage in the marketplace. And ultimately if everyone in the marketplace uses the same 'solutions', market advantage will be difficult to gain other than by conventional means, such as capital investment and good management.

From the point of view of aesthetics and style it is interesting to conjecture what 'the way forward might bring'. Customization and supply chain management are themes driven by business, managerial and technological culture. The product life-cycle management approach suggests that designers will be able to offer more variations of product, using what might be called a 'recombinant' approach to design by adapting and recycling product data. It may prove that certain formal properties are 'cheaper' to offer as factors leading to design variation than others, for example colour. This in a sense is a restrictive model of customization, but the opposite is also possible. Customization may prove to do for apparel what fully automated factory production did for other sectors, not only did it reduce factory workforces and labour costs, it permitted a technological evolution of manufacturing processes. In the automobile industry this seems to have introduced (or at least reintroduced) the possibility of quite fanciful design. To believe that technology produces 'greyness', mediocrity or the sub-standard proved to be a nineteenth-century fear. However that technology produced the same cultural menu everywhere was a twentieth-century observation. Whether customization and c-commerce prove to be the antithesis of fashion or spur it on, only time will tell.

References

Bedell, G. (2003), 'The changing face of the brand', *The Observer*, 19 January, at www.observer.co.uk/magazine/story/0,11913,841548,00.html.

Chang, W. and P. Kilduff. (2002), *The US Market for Technical Textiles*, Small Business and Technology Development Center at www.sbtdc.org/research/textiles.pdf.

CNN (2002), 'A glimpse of retail tech future at Prada', at www.cnn.com/2002/TECH/biztech/11/03/retail.tech.ap/index.html.

Global Sources (2002), 'Supply Chain Management: Collaborating for Online Solutions', at www.globalsource.com/MAGAZINE/FAS/0204/PECOMM4.HTM.

Jerrard, R., D. Hands and J. Ingram. (2002). *Design Management Case Studies*. London: Routledge.

Koolhaas, R. (2001), *Projects for Prada Part 1*, Milan: Fondazione Prada.

NTC (2002), 'The Role of Emotion in Success of Global Textile Product Retailing', Project No. I01-A31, National Textile Center, at www.ntcresearch.org/current/year11/yr11_proj.htm.

Pearson, S. and Knudsen, D. (2003), 'Critical Trends and Emerging Solutions', just-style.com. at www.freeborders.com/company/press/coverage/03_31_03.shtml

TCSG (2000), *A National Strategy for the UK Textile and Clothing Industry*, Textile and Clothing Strategy Group.

FURTHER READING

Imo, Beatrice Elung'ata, Olive Mugenda and Keren Mburugu, Challenges Facing Apparel Traders in Nairobi, Kenya and Strategies for Flourishing in a Liberalized Market, *Fashion Practice*, Volume 2, Issue, 1, Taylor & Francis.

Brookshire, Jung-Ha (2017), *Global Sourcing in the Textile and Apparel Industry*, New York: Bloomsbury.

Gale, Colin and Jasbir Kaur (2004), *Fashion & Textiles: An Overview*, Berg: Oxford.

Glock, R. and G. Kunz (2005), *Apparel Manufacturing: Sewn Product Analysis*, Upper Saddle River: Pearson/Prentice Hall.

Hugos, M. and C. Thomas (2006), *Supply Chain Management in the Retail Industry*, Hoboken: John Wiley & Sons.

Kunz, Gace I. and Myrna B. Garner, (2016), *Going Global: The Textile and Apparel Industry* Fairchild: New York.

Londrigan, M. and J. Jenkins. (2018). *Fashion Supply Chain Management*. New York: Fairchild Books.

Rosenau, J. and D. Wilson (2014), *Apparel Merchandising: The Line Starts Here*. New York and London: Bloomsbury Publishing.

Rossi, A., A. Luinstra and J. Pickles (2014), *Advances in Labour Studies: Towards Better Work: Understanding labour in apparel global value chains*, New York: ILO with Palgrave Macmillan.

Stephens, D. (2017), *Reengineering Retail: The Future of Selling in a Post-Digital World*, Vancouver: Figure 1 Publishing.

White, Nicola and Ian Griffith (2000), *The Fashion Business: Theory, Practice, Image*, Oxford: Berg.

Figure 12 Outside LaCoste. Photo Courtesy of Brent Luvaas.
Source: Brent Luvaas

PART III
Sustainability and Social Responsibility

Figure 13 DWI Handaanda. Photo Courtesy of Brent Luvaas.
Source: Brent Luvaas

INTRODUCTION

Tasha L. Lewis

CONTEXT

The terms sustainability and social responsibility, as the subject of the readings in this chapter, have become a significant discussion point for a range of stakeholders and critics focusing on the global fashion system over the past two decades. Given that the fashion industry is considered to be one of the worst industry offenders in terms of its negative impact on the environment (Fletcher, 2013), increased scrutiny has focused on the fashion industry's unethical, environmentally damaging and wasteful production and consumption habits as well as the detrimental, non-renewable impact on the planet. This debate has now expanded into the public domain beyond the scrutiny of academia and environmental agencies, reflecting a widespread industry concern about unethical and non-sustainable practices across the global supply chain (Markkula and Moisander, 2012).

Sustainability and fashion have a complex relationship involving a range of issues and a host of stakeholders throughout the production-consumption cycle who are responsible for the implementation of more ethical practices in the fashion industry. As a recent report explained:

> The sustainable garment of the future would be designed carefully and made from renewable material. It would be pesticide free and produced by workers in decent working conditions. It would washed at low temperatures and have fashion upgrades to extend its fashionable life. Finally it would be recycled, reused or composted.
> To make this vision a reality all the industry players need to act, including the consumer (Fashion for the Future, 2007).

Not only is the responsibility to implement sustainable fashion shared by a range of people, but the social, environmental and economic issues, and the means of implementing sustainable fashion are various and complicated involving systemic changes to established production and consumption practices and consumer behavior.

The main issues contributing to unsustainable fashion production and consumption involve textile production characterized by the overuse of water, chemicals and energy; labor conditions of workers from the farming of raw materials for textiles, to sweatshop or retail work exploitation; animal welfare in terms of leather and fur production and usage; large carbon footprints generated during the production and transportation of materials and finished garments to reach global markets; wasteful resource consumption and the increasing number of non-biodegradable garments discarded into landfills. There would seem to be a critical need to overhaul the product development and manufacturing process for textile and garments, in addition to mindless consumption habits and review the social, cultural, economic and ethical agendas that drive this industry. These sustainability challenges facing the fashion industry, and their possible solutions, are analyzed in the five readings in this section, and each will be outlined below in the context of the broader discussion on sustainable and ethical fashion and its CSR response.

Underpinning these complex issues of production and consumption for this three trillion dollar global fashion industry contributing 2 per cent to the world's GDP (Fashion United, 2018) is a significant "oxymoron" (Clark, 2008: 427). This oxymoron is considered to be the "paradox" between fashion's economic and socio-cultural standing, wherein 'cheap fashion means disposable fashion, and encourages more consumption creating a vicious cycle' (Black, 2008: 14) in the excess production, consumption and obsolescence of garments. High-speed, fast fashion production is fuelling insatiable consumption. These unethical production and consumption practices are generating growing volumes of garment waste as people buy more than they need and regularly dispose of unwanted clothes. Research shows, for example, that one in four women own more than ten pairs of jeans, but only wear four of them regularly (Bomgardener, 2016).

LABOR PRACTICES

Fashion is a major source of work and millions of people depend on the industry for their livelihoods across the supply chain, from textile making to retail sales and marketing. Globally, the fashion sector employs millions of people with every third worker across Asia now being employed upstream in the industry. Labor practices across the industry highlight a set of ethical issues including fair wages, working hours, worker treatment and rights, health and safety, gender equality and child employment. The exposure of labor violations across the global production and consumption circuit for the fashion industry has resulted in drastic changes for a number of high profile brands at all price points. Nike, for example, was at the forefront of criticism in terms of shortcomings in its labor practices surrounding product manufacture with calls for more responsible organizational practices overall from employees, union and opinion formers. Equally, celebrity turned anti-sweatshop activist, Kathie Lee Gifford worked with the U.S. government to enact laws that would protect children from sweatshops after being accused of using child labor from Honduras to make her clothing line sold exclusively at Walmart (Strom, 1996). The consumption of fashion products supports a global economy in the trillions of dollars, so there is little room for reform proposals to slow down consumption in order to avoid environmental harm. Hence, calls from NGO's and influencers to clean up supply chains and ensure worker safety and rights need to be compelling, more visible, and actionable.

In the past 20 years, this type of high profile shaming of unethical brands by activists and NGO's has put pressure on fashion and clothing brands such as Nike, GAP and H&M and luxury brands in the Kering Group resulting in a recalibration of their value chains and purchasing systems along more transparent and traceable sustainable lines. It has also led to the implementation and use of codes of conduct such as The Ethical Trading Initiative (ETI), protecting labor rights and conditions while setting standards for the remuneration and treatment of garment workers in the hope of creating advocates for ethical and environmentally friendly sourced and manufactured garments. Industry consortia, such as the Sustainable Apparel Coalition (SAC) and the Zero Discharge of Hazardous Chemicals (ZDHC) are also now attempting to provide specific guidelines that allow fashion firms to evaluate their sustainable standing and impact. However these voluntary requirements for sustainability are not explicitly defined and the comprehensive implementation of such codes of practice is difficult to enforce due to the sheer number of factories throughout the globe and the need to closely monitor all of them. So, labor violations currently remain a major problem for the apparel industry. As a result, the industry response in terms of the human cost is still woefully inadequate despite cross-sectoral pressure, as seen in the shocking 2013 Rana Plaza factory collapse in Bangladesh, killing 1,134 garment workers and injuring 2500 (Reinecke and Donaghey, 2015). This was the largest apparel manufacturing disaster in history (Taplin, 2014), representing a scale of crisis that the apparel industry had not witnessed since the 1911 Triangle Shirtwaist Factory fire in New York City (Miller, 2003).

Debates about the unethical working conditions of garment workers are based on an interpretational understanding of what constitutes issues such as a living wage, a legal working age; fair working hours and tolerable workplace conditions. The need to keep pace with changing fashion trends and deliver a timely, on-trend product at the right price point can lead to sourcing strategies that compromise labor standards as low-cost producers in mainly developing countries are pressured to meet deadlines, quality standards and comply with corporate codes of conduct. In this section, Liat Smestad also discusses how these challenges manifest in the industry (2009), "The Sweatshop, Child Labor, and Exploitation Issues in the Garment Industry". This article by Smestad provides a comprehensive and searching analysis of these aspects of the ethical fashion debate with a particular focus on the issue of child labor. Refusing to frame the exploitative issue of child labor in Third World garment factories as a simple social and cultural reality, Smestad broadens the scope of the analysis to locate this unethical form of exploitative sweatshop labor as an economic and situational phenomenon centered on the unavoidable question, "Why do young people work?".

Of course, the problems that plague apparel manufacturing are not new and the historical contexts are essential to grasping the opportunity for large-scale transformation. We can no longer be comfortable with moving apparel manufacturing and its accompanying problems around the globe in search of low cost and low barriers for regulation. Both Pietra Rivoli (2014) and Michael Lavergne (2015) have traced the historical development of apparel manufacturing in the western hemisphere—from the Industrial Revolution, which was driven by innovations in textile manufacturing, to modern-day offshoring and large-scale sourcing from developing nations. From these historical accounts, we understand how we have arrived at the current state of a fragmented supply chain reliant on a global division of labor that depends on a low-cost work force to meet consumer demand for an affordable fashion product. However, the present state of fashion is also contending with the value of re-shoring manufacturing and bringing production closer to a consumer market that is demanding faster delivery of products within a season. A more local product can mean a more sustainable product when transportation and other resources are taken into account. There is a strong case for making more things closer to where consumers live and shop, but there is also the question of scalability and infrastructure as building new factories and recruiting workers to staff then may prove challenging. Nevertheless, fashion brands are finding more sustainable ways of operating within the local as seen in Smedstad's illustrative case study of American Apparel (AA) one of America's largest manufacturing outfits. Despite the controversial antics of its CEO, Dove Charney and its provocative advertising campaigns, American Apparel is recognized for its enlightened labor practices operating through its domestic factory vertically integrated supply chain that as Smedtad explains are, "located in downtown Los Angeles and all aspects of the business—from design and concept to the actual physical labor of sewing a garment—are carried out under the roof of one 800,000 square foot." Providing job security on a living wage for the local population, in addition to avoiding garment overproduction the brand's revolutionary business model, has been lauded by commentators and adds to its brand ethos for its young urbanite consumer.

PRODUCTION, DESIGN AND CONSUMPTION CHALLENGES

Awareness of sustainability and ethical practices are now on the fashion consumer's agenda and are beginning to impact on consumption patterns. Yet, as fashion purchasing is based on visual, emotional connections and aspirational desires rather than solely on functionality and basic needs, significant changes in design and production practices are needed. Such changes can influence consumers and enable them to make more conscious purchasing choices. Fashion companies and brands can take various routes to enabling sustainable fashion output and are increasingly taking a "cradle to grave" approach from textile production and design to garment aftercare and disposal. Other fashion brands have successfully applied the "cradle to cradle" concept in recalibrating the design and production process by advocating that the fashion industry can reduce its environmental impact not by recycling more but by producing and disposing of less instead (McDonough and Braungart, 2010). Most recently, fashion companies from luxury to value brands such as Stella McCartney, H&M and Zara (Hendriksz, 2017) are all examining and implementing the circular fashion system in a move away from a "take-make-dispose" mentality to more circular operations recommend by the Ellen MacArthur Foundation's Circular Fibres Initiative (Ellen MacArthur Foundation, 2017).

Yet, whilst consumers across global research surveys profess to support more conscious fashion production and consumption, the reality still lags far behind. Some studies have found that consumers do not always believe that fashion brands can be sustainable as they 'green-wash' their ethical fashion narratives (Winge, 2009) in exaggerated marketing eco-claims (Beard, 2009). Other findings suggest that consumers are confused by the large array of technical terms and issues involved in the sustainable fashion debate and that fashion brands (Thomas, 2009) often mis-communicate this in their labeling and marketing campaigns (Peirson-Smith and Evans, 2017). So, fashion consumers clearly need more knowledge and tools to navigate the plethora of options available in the fashion marketplace in order to make more conscious decisions about purchases. Elizabeth Cline's *'Overdressed'* (2013) and Kate Black's *'Magnifeco'* (2015), are both consumer-directed guides intended to educate and empower the conscious shopper. However, this knowledge needs to be more clearly and comprehensively articulated and transparently applied in practice through labeling and blockchain technology tracking (Mori, 2018), for example, across the supply chain so that consumers are not just better informed, but are able to action sustainable behavior in their retail choices and after care of garments.

There are various approaches to effecting sustainable fashion through garment after-care, for example. Hence, the "upcycling", process as one option seeks to add value to discarded materials through redesign and remanufacturing. Underlying this business model is also a social motivation to bring a new form of apparel production to the island of Haiti. Like many developing countries, Haiti is a recipient of large quantities of used clothing exported from developed countries. Most of Haiti's used clothing inventory originates in the United States, and globally, the U.S. is the largest exporter of used clothing (UN Comtrade, 2014). I visited Haiti and experienced firsthand the bustling market in Port-au-Prince where mounds of imported secondhand clothing were visible as far as I could see – t-shirts, sweatshirts, jeans, table linens, men's blazers. After leaving the market, I visited a factory where used clothing was laundered and deconstructed in preparation for the upcycling process. I found myself with razor blade in hand helping to deconstruct a blazer and thinking how we could redesign clothing to make this more impactful. Our clothes are not really created for disassembly, but what if they were like automobiles, so that at the end of life they can be scrapped for parts and materials that add value for other product inputs. The deconstruction process was the most time-consuming part of the production process and required special worker training in order to maintain the integrity of the fabric. The upcycling process also yields a certain amount of leftover textile waste, which presented an additional challenge for maintaining the sustainable, zero-waste model of a fashion startup I visited in Haiti. The Haiti experience illustrates that exporting secondhand clothing, which is still how most clothing from developed countries is disposed of, is really not an entirely sustainable way to handle the overconsumption in our own market. How long can these countries manage what we discard in their own supply chains?

There are also more 'visible' routes for consumers to dispose of their used clothing and many of them are successful business models that manage to both incentivize consumers to return their unwanted clothing and to also purchase new items. One of the premier take-back programs is operated by womenswear brand, Eileen Fisher. The company began its 'Green Eileen' program in 2009 to support its sustainability goals and it was so successful that it now has select store locations across the United States dedicated to selling the brand's pre-loved items (Khalamayer, 2016). The company resells the take-back items after dry cleaning and repairs are completed. The customer is also rewarded with a $5 certificate for each garment returned which can be used towards the purchase of a new item. The company is also taking steps to scale up its recycling efforts for the clothing it take backs from customers but does not meet the quality standards for resale in its Green Eileen store locations. This closed-loop solution is a perfect example of 'extended producer responsibility' in which a product manufacturer broadens its supply chain to directly address issues of product end-of-life, so that the burden of disposal is not solely left up to the consumer.

Outdoor performance and casual clothing company, Patagonia, has also gone to great lengths to create and reclaim its apparel in a sustainable manner as part of its 'Worn Wear' program which also offers customers a reward incentive for the return of used items. In this section, Hepburn provides an intricate profile of Patagonia's path to a better apparel supply chain, interweaving personal accounts of interactions with the brand as well as key points in its history. Patagonia has long been hailed a leader in sustainable clothing across four decades of its existence. Yet, Sharon J. Hepburn in the article, "In Patagonia: A Complicated Greenness", considers this to be a contested situation as Patagonia paradoxically stimulates consumption of garments based on the dual, mythic narrative championing sustainability and nature as transformative through the production and consumption of clothing. Patagonia sells greenness according to Hepburn both in terms of the practical nature of its garments in the way that they are produced, managed and recycled, and at the same time appeals to its niche consumer's eco-aspirations through their aspirational promotional campaigns thereby stimulating sales—calling into question the efficacy of the brand's eco stance.

Consumer dissonance with eco fashion and fashion's sustainability paradox is demonstrated by Annamma Joy, John F. Sherry, Jr, Alladi Venkatesh, Jeff Wang and Ricky Chan in "Fast Fashion, Sustainability, and the Ethical Appeal of Luxury Brands". When interviewing consumers about their concerns regarding sustainability and social responsibility related to fashion, many claimed to support sustainable and socially responsible products, but those factors are often not the main motivation for their purchasing decisions. As Joy et al. explain, the consumers that they interviewed, "routinely availed themselves of trend-led fashionable clothing that was cheap: i.e. low cost to them, but high cost in environmental and societal terms. They also exhibited relatively little guilt about fast fashion's disposability, seeing little discrepancy between their attitudes toward sustainability and their fashion choices." This demonstrates that consumers are receiving the "message" about what makes a garment sustainable, but that purchasing behaviors were driven by price and the thrill of routinely changing their identity with an affordable fast fashion wardrobe. Eileen Fisher and Patagonia emerge as sustainability champions based on innovative design and development process aimed at assuring garment longevity through durability, quality and style. While these firms have done the difficult work of shaping their companies and products over time to align with a more conscious niche consumer, the majority of apparel brands have not yet reached this stage.

CSR AND ETHICAL FASHION RESPONSES

Sustainable practices are a part of an organization's corporate social responsibility portfolio, which has becoming a metric used by more investment firms to assess the overall risk of a company or sector. Producer and consumer aspirations are framed within the context of social responsibility in this section by Valerie Rangel in "Dress and disaster: Fashioning creative responses to disaster", the author moves away from analyzing social responsibility in fashion in the context of "labor rights, fair trade manufacturing and sourcing practices as well as marketing and environmental issues." Rangel instead examines the fashion organization and the designer's reaction to disasters and crises in their creative efforts and socially responsible behaviors rather than being relegated to a form of publicity based tokenism, as part of their CSR role. Engagement with, and the management of social issues, Rangel suggests, enables fashion organizations and designers to go beyond a surface commitment to a community in crisis by producing cause related fashion or providing one-off financial support to forging a deeper, lasting relationships with community stakeholders that will assure economic, cultural and social currency.

Ben Barry in "Selling Whose Dream? A taxonomy of aspiration in fashion imagery", explores the fashion and CSR dynamic by examining how fashion photography is used in the context of social responsibility. Assessments included portrayals of body ideals, inclusionary creative direction and styling, as well as evidence of sexism. Topics such as 'body ideal' and 'inclusion' and 'diversity' are often overlooked when social responsibility is linked to the fashion industry, but this article reveals why these socially-oriented issues have salience and deserve attention if change is to occur in the industry by making social responsibility a regular part of fashion business practice. The women interviewed in Barry's study related most to empowering, honest and socially responsible imagery and very much desired this from fashion brands. Interestingly, Designer and Project Runway winner, Christian Siriano, is one of a handful of designers extending notions of the ideal body in fashion terms. Siriano caters to a long list of celebrity clients, including former first lady Michelle Obama, but this has not narrowed his view on what is fashionably acceptable in terms of the perfect body shape. Siriano regularly uses plus-size models in his runway shows, creating a collection for mass retailer Lane Bryant, and in 2016 designing a red carpet gown for Saturday Night Live actress/comedian Leslie Jones when other designers refused to outfit the celebrity. Consumer demand for a more authentic and honest representation of models used in fashion advertising is a strong starting point for an industry that has traditionally dictated and 'pushed out' to the consumer what is considered the ideal and visually presented this through various media channels. Fashion gatekeepers that are sensitive to changing consumer sentiment will be able to fulfill realistic as opposed to idealistic consumer needs. In the future, fashion designers and brands ignoring calls for inclusion, body diversity and social awareness might have a narrower appeal and encounter diminishing significance among more conscious, demanding and empowered consumers.

While designers like Siriano exploit the creative power of fashion to foster inclusion, Rangel's article in this section also proposes that this creative power can be harnessed to address the needs of those in disaster situations. The idea that fashion can somehow positively impact disasters is impressive and a valuable addition to how we conceive of social responsibility as individual consumers and as companies. The use of clothing as a portable shelter during natural disasters can provide those in harm's way with an immediate protective environment that maximizes the functional benefits of clothing. Cause-related marketing that encourages purchase of products that give back to society is another form of social responsibility but can we really shop our way to a better world? This is only a possibility if products are designed and produced with higher standards and under better labor conditions and offered fair prices paid to all involved in the supply chain.

This cause-related model was the driving force behind the fashion up-cycling startup business that I researched in Haiti in 2013 and 2014 – a clothing company founded in the immediate aftermath of the 2010 earthquake in Port-au-Prince. The founders wanted to produce in Haiti by making use of local resources, including the skilled apparel work force, in order to export and sell upcycled garments that represented both sustainability and social responsibility in terms of equitable labor practices. When the founders were interviewed about their desire to enter the fashion industry with only their international development majors to guide them (Lewis and Pringle, 2015), their response resonated as an honest and attainable motivation to make the fashion industry better for all of those that admire it, aspire to work in it and depend on it for their livelihood. As they observed, fashion was "a means to express individuality and believed that the most beautiful and highest-quality clothing came from the creative genius of ethical partnerships that served people and planet" (Lewis, 2015: 116).

Environmental evidence points toward a resource-limited fashion industry, which requires urgent, immediate action on a global scale from a range of stakeholders in a range of approaches to making sustainable fashion into a reality, as a recent industry report observed:

> Sustainability will evolve from being a menu of marketing-focused CSR initiatives to an integral part of the planning system where circular economy principles are embedded throughout the value chain. More fashion brands will plan for recyclability from the fibre stage of the supply chain and many will harness sustainability through tech innovation in order to unlock efficiency, transparency, mission orientation and genuine ethical upgrades (BoF, 2018).

It is now clear that sustainable fashion and ethical approaches to fashion production and consumption are now firmly on the political, economic, social, organizational agendas and that a variety of approaches can be adopted at all levels of the industry to effect change in a less fragmented and more holistic way—harnessing new technology and innovation aligned with an mindful, committed consumer.

References

Beard, N. D. (2008), "The branding of ethical fashion and the consumer: a luxury niche or mass-market reality?" *Fashion Theory*, 12 (4), 447–467.

Black, K. (2015), *Magnifeco: Your Head-to-Toe Guide to Ethical Fashion and Non-Toxic Beauty*, Gabriola Island, British Columbia: New Society Publishers.

Black, S. (2012), *The Sustainable Fashion Handbook*. London: Thames and Hudson.

Bomgardner, M. (2016), "Can everything old be made new again? Brands and regulators confront the complexities and technological challenges of the circular economy", *Chemical and Engineering News (c&en)*, 94(26): 29. Retrieved 2017 from: https://cen.acs.org/articles/94/i26/everything-old-made-new-again.html

Clark, H. (2008), SLOW+ FASHION—an Oxymoron—or a Promise for the Future…?. *Fashion Theory*, 12 (4), 427–446.

Cline, E.L. (2013), *Over-dressed: The Shockingly High Cost of Cheap Fashion*, New York: Penguin Press.

Fashion for the future (2017), Retrieved 2018 from: https://www.forumforthefuture.org/sites/default/files/project/downloads/fashionsustain.pdf

Fletcher, K. (2013), *Sustainable Fashion and Technology: Design Journeys*, 2nd edition, London: Routledge.

Hendriksz, V. (2017), "Fashion Industry Leaders Vow to Move Towards Circular Economy", *Fashion United*, 12 May, Retrieved 2018 from: https://fashionunited.uk/news/fashion/the-fashion-industry-vows-to-move-towards-a-circular-system/2017051224498

Laverne, M. (2015), *Fixing Fashion: Rethinking the Way We Make, Market and Buy Our Clothes*, Gabriola Island, British Columbia: New Society Publishers.

Lewis, T.L. and A. Pringle. (2015), Local Buttons: Sustainable Fashion and Social Entrepreneurship in Haiti, *Nka Journal of Contemporary African Art*, 37, pp.116-125.

Ellen MacArthur Foundation (2017), "Make Fashion Circular Report" Retrieved 2017 from: https://www.ellenmacarthurfoundation.org/programmes/systemic-initiatives/make-fashion-circular/report

Khalamayer, A. (2016), Eileen Fisher has Designs on Keeping Clothes out of Landfills. *GreenBiz*, 21 November, Retrieved 2018 from: https://www.greenbiz.com/article/eileen-fisher-has-designs-keeping-clothing-out-landfills

Markkula, A., and J. Moisander. (2012). Discursive confusion over sustainable consumption: a discursive perspective on the perplexity of marketplace knowledge. *Journal of Consumer Policy*, 35(1), 105–125.

McDonough, W., and M. Braungart. (2010), *Cradle to cradle: Remaking the way we make things*. New York: North Point Press.

Miller, J. (2003), Why economists are wrong about sweatshops and the antisweatshop movement. *Challenge*, 46 (1), 93–122.

Mori, C. (2018) Is Blockchain the Answer to Supply Chain Transparency? *The Fashion Revolution*, Retrieved 2018 from: https://www.fashionrevolution.org/usa-blog/is-blockchain-the-answer-to-supply-chain-transparency/

Peirson-Smith, A. and S. Evans. (2017), "Green words and Eco Language: an examination of the consumer perception gap for fashion brands promoting sustainable practices" *Fashion Practice: The Journal of Design, Creative Process & the Fashion Industry*. 9 (3): 1–25.

Remy, N., E. Speelman and S. Swartz (2016) Style that's Sustainable: a new fast fashion formula. https://www.mckinsey.com/business-functions/sustainability-and-resource-productivity/our-insights/style-thats-sustainable-a-new-fast-fashion-formula.

Rivoli, P. (2005), *The Travels of a T-Shirt in the Global Economy: An Economist Examines the Markets, Power, and Politics of World Trade,* Hoboken, NJ: John Wiley & Sons, Inc.

Reinecke, J., and J. Donaghey. (2015), After Rana Plaza: Building coalitional power for labour rights between unions and (consumption-based) social movement organisations. *Organization*, 22 (5), 720–740.

Taplin, I. M. (2014), Who is to blame? A re-examination of fast fashion after the 2013 factory disaster in Bangladesh. *Critical Perspectives on International Business*, 10 (1/2), 72–83.

Thomas, S. (2008), From "green blur" to ecofashion: Fashioning an eco-lexicon. *Fashion Theory*, 12 (4), 525–539.

United Nations Commodity Trade Statistics Database (COMTRADE). (2014). *Worn clothing and other worn textile articles; rags 269*, Retrieved October 20, 2014 from: http://comtrade.un.org/db/

Winge, T. M. (2008), "'Green Is the New Black': Celebrity Chic and the 'Green' Commodity Fetish." *Fashion Theory* 12(4): 511–24.

11

SELLING WHOSE DREAM?
A taxonomy of aspiration in fashion imagery

Ben Barry[1]

In 1984, legendary fashion photographer Irving Penn remarked that he saw his role at *Vogue* as 'selling dreams not clothes' (Bailey and Harrison 1986: 13). Penn's comment represents the belief that consumers aspire to images in the media because they represent the ideals and goals that people desire (Hirschman and Thompson 1997). In the context of fashion, media images present an idealized form of beauty – thin, young and Caucasian – to which most women can aspire but never achieve (Kilbourne 2000). The goal of creating this unattainable image is to create desire and demand for fashion products. Karl Lagerfeld explained, 'Unreachable beauty is a reminder to make an effort. Maybe you cannot reach what you see, but you can make an effort. But if you see something, and you can reach what you see, then you do not have to make an effort anymore . . .' (Barry 2012: 110). By ensuring women cannot attain the image, the fashion industry intends for women to continually purchase products to fulfil their hope of achieving the ideal (Barry 2007).

The few researchers (e.g., Borland and Akram 2007; Phillips and McQuarrie 2009) who have discussed the concept of aspiration in fashion have relied on one operationalization – the model's thin body size. Disentangling the association between thin models and aspiration is critical given recent anecdotal evidence that suggests people are disillusioned with the thin aesthetic promoted in fashion. Consumers expressed outrage when the CEO of Abercrombie & Fitch said he only wanted 'attractive all-American' people wearing his clothes (Doucette 2013) and when Ralph Lauren airbrushed a model in an advertisement to make her waist appear smaller than her head (Klein 2009). A movement is also underway in the fashion industry to cast plus-size models; for example, *Vogue Italia* featured three plus-size models on its June 2011 cover (White 2011). This introduction of size diversity, alongside with some women's negative response to thin models (Borland and Akram 2007), suggests that a discrepancy may exist between what industry professionals believe comprises aspirational images and what women actually believe comprises such photographs.

THE ASPIRATIONAL ASSUMPTION

Fashion imagery is considered to be aspirational because it portrays models with physical attributes (e.g., thin, youthful faces) consumers desire to emulate (Borland and Akram 2007). Scholars assert that women aspire to these images and the models featured in them because western society places significant social value on women's appearance and, in particular, their ability to possess an extremely thin body (Wolf 1992; Wykes and Gunter 2005). The pressure to achieve a thin body is rooted in the inferences made between a woman's embodiment of thinness and her subsequent success in relationships, careers and life in general (Kilbourne 2000; Striegel-Moore and Bulik 2007).

Given the pressure for women to emulate the appearances of models, researchers have studied the influence of fashion models on women's attitudes and

---

[1] From Ben Barry (2014), Selling Whose Dream? A Taxonomy of Aspiration in Fashion Imagery, in Fashion, Style and Popular Culture, Intellect, Volume 1, Issue, 2, pp. 175–92.

behaviours using social comparison theory (Dittmar and Howard 2004; Halliwell and Dittmar 2004). Social comparison theory posits that in the absence of an objective standard, people evaluate their own attributes and abilities by comparing themselves to others (Festinger 1954). These comparison targets might be perceived as better or worse than the individual making the comparison. An upward comparison occurs when the target is viewed as better on comparison attributes. Upward comparisons are typically motivated by the desire to self-improve. Downward comparisons occur when the target is viewed as worse on the comparison attributes and these comparisons are often driven by the desire to maintain positive self-views (Wood 1989; Wood and Taylor 1991). Since fashion models are presented as standards of beauty and success, they are likely targets for upward social comparisons (Halliwell and Dittmar 2005).

Associating aspiration solely with thin models sidesteps the fact that some female consumers have positive reactions to models that reflect diverse sizes, ages and races. Researchers have found the women, with high levels of thin-ideal internalization, report positive feelings about their bodies as well as the advertisements after viewing average-sized versus thin fashion models (Diedrichs and Lee 2011; Dittmar and Howard 2004). Scholars have also found that consumers favourably evaluate models with appearances similar to their own. J. M. Kozar and M. L. Damhorst (2008) and Kozar (2010) concluded that middle-aged and senior women preferred the attractiveness of mature rather than younger models. Similarly, other scholars have found that when ethnicities match between viewers and models, viewers have positive responses to models and advertisements (Aaker et al. 2000; Lee et al. 2002). These findings challenge the narrow operationalization of thinness with aspiration by suggesting that some consumers positively view average-size, mature and non-Caucasian models.

THE ASPIRATIONAL TAXONOMY

While the literature review revealed that women's aspirations are not necessarily linked to thin models, scholars remain unsure about what makes an image aspirational because they have not studied the elements that evoke this concept. To organize how consumers perceive a particular construct in advertising imagery, researchers have developed taxonomies. Taxonomies are formal systems for classifying and categorizing complex phenomena according to a set of common conceptual dimensions (Patton 2002). By creating an organized scheme, taxonomies promote increased clarity in defining and comparing diverse, complex attributes (Sofaer 1999).

Analysis of focus groups transcripts revealed an interesting interplay between the criteria that comprised women's evaluations of aspiration in fashion photographs and the distinct image elements that triggered them. Two themes were identified that provided a structure for the analysis: (1) aspirational *criteria* and (2) aspirational *targets*. Aspirational criteria are defined as the cognitive rubric that women used to evaluate whether or not a fashion image reflected their aspirations. These criteria included women's perceptions that the image was honest, empowering and socially responsible. Aspirational targets were defined as the elements in an image that triggered women's aspirational criteria. These included the model's physical traits (i.e., size, age, height and race), the creative direction of the advertisement (i.e., hair, make-up, clothing, accessories and setting) and the model's visual cues (i.e., facial expression and pose).

ASPIRATIONAL CRITERIA: HONEST
Aspirational target: Physical traits

Participants aspired to fashion images when they perceived the models' physical features to authentically represent their appearance. The model – and her respective shape, age, race and height – triggered women's perceptions of honesty because she reflected the likelihood of participants replicating 'the look'. Women defined 'the look' as the outfit (i.e., the proportions of the garments) and the styling (i.e., accessories, hair and make-up) that were displayed by the model. Some women perceived photographs to be honest when they shared physical traits with the model because they could imagine how 'the look' complimented them.

Other women perceived images to be honest when consecutive photographs, such as in one editorial or magazine edition, displayed several models with a diversity of physical characteristics. They could imagine these looks on their bodies because they perceived different aspects of themselves in the various models. Conversely, women believed that images were dishonest when the models did not reflect their physical traits or only reflected the current ideal of beauty. They could not physically identify with the models and subsequently visualize the looks on them. Furthermore, the amount of digital manipulation that was performed on the model's face and body influenced women's perceptions of honesty.

Aspirational target: Creative direction

The creative direction triggered women's perceptions of honesty because the model's aesthetic influenced whether they deemed the photograph to be an authentic fashion image. Participants asserted that images in which the clothing was perceived as 'fashionable' and hair and make-up was perceived as 'glamorous' triggered their imagination. They asserted that they enjoyed viewing fashion images because the creative direction provided them with an opportunity to engage in fantasy and escapism. Conversely, women considered fashion images as dishonest when the clothing and styling conveyed a 'frumpy' or 'boring' aesthetic. These photographs failed to inspire fantasy and escapism.

Aspirational target: Visual cues

Participants explained that the model's visual cues triggered whether or not they believed that their internal qualities were accurately depicted. Women viewed models that were standing erect and making eye contact to communicate 'confidence' and 'strength'. In contrast, models that were lying down, leaning against a wall, and whose eyes were looking away from the viewer conveyed that they were 'passive' and 'weak'. Some women remarked that representing models as weak suggested that their purpose was to be controlled by men for sexual pleasure. While most participants asserted that this depiction was dishonest because it failed to represent women's strength, some mature women disagreed; they argued that sexuality is an integral aspect of mature women's character, and promoting mature models as sexually desirable was an honest representation.

ASPIRATIONAL CRITERIA: EMPOWERING

Aspirational target: Physical traits

Participants aspired to fashion images when they felt 'beautiful' and 'confident'. The model's physical characteristics elicited feelings of empowerment because they influenced whether women felt assured or insecure about their beauty. Women were empowered when the models reflected physical traits that opposed the beauty ideal because the lack of conformity to idealized beauty inspired them to embrace and celebrate their unique features. Conversely, women were disempowered when models reflected the beauty ideal or only reflected the beauty ideal in one editorial or magazine. Women perceived these models to illuminate how they failed to conform to the beauty standards valued in fashion.

Aspirational target: Creative direction

The creative direction activated women's feelings of empowerment because the model's aesthetic and the image's composition influenced whether they imagined themselves as 'sophisticated' and 'adventurous'. Women felt empowered when the model wore fashionable clothes and was featured in a luxurious context because they perceived these elements to convey 'elegance' and 'excitement'. Conversely, women felt disempowered when the model's clothing and setting were unfashionable and unglamorous; they explained that such an aesthetic suggested that the model's life was 'simple' and 'boring'.

Aspirational target: Visual cues

The visual cues of the models triggered women's feelings of empowerment. They felt empowered when models had facial expressions – evidenced by wrinkles, smiles and other facial movements – because it demonstrated that they were 'intelligent'. When digital manipulation erased a model's facial expression, women were not empowered because they questioned the model's intelligence; to them, these models appeared to be 'thoughtless' and 'superficial'. Being thoughtless, participants explained, was particularly disempowering because it reinforced the sexist stereotype that women's social value is based on their physical appearance.

ASPIRATIONAL CRITERIA: SOCIALLY RESPONSIBLE

Aspirational target: Physical traits

Women in this study aspired to fashion images based on the perceived societal benefits conveyed in the photographs. They evaluated the physical traits of models in order to understand the messages about beauty and body image that were communicated to consumers. Participants perceived idealized models to promote unhealthy ideals of beauty and subsequently trigger low self-esteem and body dissatisfaction. Women viewed models of diverse sizes, ages and races to challenge the singular notion of beauty promoted in fashion; according to them, diverse models conveyed the healthy message that all women were beautiful. Participants also explained that the amount of digital manipulation to a model's body and face promoted realistic or unrealistic beauty standards. They asserted that extreme airbrushing of models caused women to partake in dangerous dieting and cosmetic surgeries because it produced an unattainable ideal.

Aspirational target: Creative direction

The creative direction prompted participants' evaluations of whether fashion images were socially responsible because they perceived the styling and setting to legitimize women's inclusion in or exclusion from the fashion industry. Women perceived mature or curvy models that were styled in unfashionable clothing and depicted in unglamorous settings to be socially irresponsible. The images communicated that women who did not meet the beauty ideal were excluded from fashionable clothing and glamorous lives.

Participants explained that the model's visual cues evoked their readings of social responsibility because the pose and expression conveyed how women were valued or devalued in society. Models that were posed lying down and looking up at viewers were considered to communicate the message the women's societal role was for sexual pleasure. They explained that overtly sexualized visual cues fostered a culture of sexism and violence against women because they reduced women to the status of a sexual object.

INDUSTRY IMPLICATIONS

While many consumers are aware that carbon dioxide pollutes the air, this research suggests that many women are also aware that fashion imagery pollutes the mind and body. Social responsibility has been associated with the fashion industry through issues of counterfeiting (Hilton et al. 2004), labour practices (Bonacich 1998) and environmental sustainability (Hethorn and Ulasewicz 2008), but scholars have not linked social responsibility to fashion media. Study findings suggest that women connect social responsibility with fashion images because they view the thin ideal, digital manipulation and objectified representations in fashion photography as fuelling body dissatisfaction and sexist attitudes. These concerns about the health impact of imagery mirror the arguments of scholars who call for advertising images to be socially responsibility when promoting tobacco or alcohol (e.g., Daube 2012). Since women in my study hold the fashion industry responsible for the negative societal consequences associated with viewing their images, I propose that promotional and editorial imagery be incorporated into the corporate social responsibility (CSR) agenda of fashion brands.

When the CEO of Abercrombie & Fitch endorsed the thin ideal as the company's ideal customer, a range of protests evolved that were directed against Abercrombie & Fitch along with a petition to persuade the brand to design for plus sizes (LeTrent 2013; Temin 2013). These consumer protests and the resulting media coverage have been partially credited with the current decline of Abercrombie & Fitch's sales and stock shares (Yousuf 2013). A business case, not only a moral obligation, might therefore exist for fashion brands to produce images that reflect a range of body shapes beyond thin ideal. Society and industry do not appear to be rewarded by the current system of producing fashion images; a new philosophy and practice must be introduced in order to facilitate a sustainable future.

References

Aaker, J., A. Brumbaugh and S. A. Grier. (2000), 'Non-target market effects and viewer distinctiveness: The impact of target marketing on advertising attitudes', *Journal of Consumer Psychology*, 9: 3, pp. 127–40.

Bailey, D. and M. Harrison. (1986), *Shots of Style: Great Fashion Photographs Chosen by David Bailey*, London: V&A Publications.

Bakewell, C., V. Mitchell and M. Rothwell. (2006), 'UK generation Y male fashion consciousness', *Journal of Fashion Marketing and Management*, 10: 2, pp. 169–80.

Barry, B. (2007), *Fashioning Reality: A New Generation of Entrepreneurship*, Toronto: Key Porter Books.

Barry, B. (2012), 'New business model: Are fashion companies missing out on the bottom line when they only use one kind of model?', *Elle Canada*, June, pp. 108–14.

Bonacich, E. (1998), 'Latino immigrant workers in the Los Angeles apparel industry', *New Political Science*, 20: 4, pp. 459–73.

Borland, H., and S. Akram. (2007), 'Age is no barrier to wanting to look good: Women on body image, age and advertising', *Qualitative Market Research: An International Journal*, 10: 3, pp. 310–33.

Daube, M. (2012), 'Alcohol and tobacco', *Australian and New Zealand Journal of Public Health*, 36: 2, pp. 108–10.

Diedrichs, P. and C. Lee. (2011), 'Waif goodbye: Average-size female models promote positive body image and appeal to consumers', *Psychology and Health*, 26: 10, pp. 1273–91.

Dittmar, H. and S. Howard. (2004), 'Ideal–body internalization and social comparison tendency as moderators of thin media models' impact on women's body–focused anxiety', *Journal of Social and Clinical Psychology*, 23: 6, pp. 747–70.

Doucette, E. (2013), 'Is Abercrombie and Fitch the newest member of the mean girls?', http://www.forbes.com. Accessed 26 July 2013.

Elliott, R. and C. Elliott. (2005), 'Idealized images of the male body in advertising: A reader-response exploration', *Journal of Marketing Communications*, 11: 1, pp. 3–19.

Festinger, L. (1954), 'A theory of social comparison processes', *Human Relations*, 7: 2, pp. 117–40.

Halliwell, E. and H. Dittmar. (2004), 'Does size matter? The impact of model's body size on women's body-focused anxiety and advertising effectiveness', *Journal of Social and Clinical Psychology*, 23: 1, pp. 104–22.

Halliwell, E. and H. Dittmar. (2005), 'The role of self-improvement and self-evaluation motives in social comparisons with idealized female bodies in the media', *Body Image*, 2: 3, pp. 249–61.

Hethorn, J. and C. Ulasewicz. (2008), *Sustainable Fashion: Why Now? A Conversation Exploring Issues, Practices and Possibilities*, New York: Fairchild Books.

Hilton, B., J. Choi and S. Chen. (2004), 'The ethics of counterfeiting in the fashion industry: Quality, credence and profit issues', *Journal of Business Ethics*, 55: 4, pp. 345–54.

Hirschman, E. C. and C. J. Thompson. (1997), 'Why media matter: Toward a richer understanding of consumers' relationships with advertising and mass media', *Journal of Advertising*, 26: 1, pp. 43–60.

Kilbourne, J. (2000), *Can't Buy My Love: How Advertising Changes the Way We Think and Feel*, New York: Free Press.

Klein, K. (2009), 'Digital anorexia', http://www.opinion.latimes.com. Accessed 26 July 2013.

Kozar, J. M. (2010), 'Women's responses to fashion media images: A study of female consumers aged 30–59', *International Journal of Consumer Studies*, 34: 3, pp. 272–78.

Kozar, J. M. and M. L. Damhorst. (2008), 'Older women's responses to current fashion models', *Journal of Fashion Marketing and Management*, 12: 3, pp. 338–50.

Lee, C. K., N. Fernandez and B. A. Martin. (2002), 'Using self-referencing to explain the effectiveness of ethnic minority models in advertising', *International Journal of Advertising*, 21: 3, pp. 367–79.

LeTrent, S. (2013), 'Attractive & fat ad spoofs Abercrombie', http://www.cnn.com. Accessed 26 July 2013.

Patton, M. Q. (2002), *Qualitative Research and Evaluation Methods*, 3rd ed., Thousand Oaks, CA: Sage Publications.

Phillips, B. J. and E. F. McQuarrie. (2009), 'The aspiration assumption: Women's consumption of fashion advertising', *Advances in Consumer Research*, 36: 1, p. 154.

Phillips, B. J. (2011), 'Contesting the social impact of marketing: A re-characterization of women's fashion advertising', *Marketing Theory*, 11: 2, pp. 99–126.

Sofaer, S. (1999), 'Qualitative methods: What are they and why use them?', *Health Services Research*, 34: 5/2, pp. 1101–18.

Striegel-Moore, R. H. and C. M. Bulik. (2007), 'Risk factors for eating disorders', *American Psychologist*, 62: 3, pp. 181–98.

Temin, D. (2013), 'How a CEO can wreak a brand in one interview: Lessons from Abercrombie & Fitch vs. Dove', http://www.forbes.com. Accessed 26 July 2013.

White, B. (2011), 'Vogue Italia stay ahead of the curve: Three plus-sized models cover Vogue Italia's latest issue', http://www.fashion.telegraph.co.uk. Accessed 26 July 2013.

Wolf, N. (1992), *The Beauty Myth: How Images of Beauty Are Used Against Women*, New York: Anchor Books.

Wood, J. V. (1989), 'Theory and research concerning social comparisons of personal attributes', *Psychological Bulletin*, 106: 2, pp. 231–48.

Wood, J. V. and K. L. Taylor. (1991), 'Serving self-relevant goals through social comparison', in Jerry Suls and Thomas A. Wills (eds), *Social Comparison: Contemporary Theory and Research*, 23–49. Hillsdale, NJ: Lawrence Erlbaum.

Wykes, M. and B. Gunter. (2005), *The Media & Body Image*, London: Sage.

Yousuf, H. (2013), 'Teens ditch Abercrombie & Fitch, stock tanks 18%', http://www.buzz.money.cnn.com. Accessed 30 August 2013.

12

FAST FASHION, SUSTAINABILITY, AND THE ETHICAL APPEAL OF LUXURY BRANDS

Annamma Joy, John F. Sherry Jr, Alladi Venkatesh, Jeff Wang, and Ricky Chan[1]

SUSTAINABILITY: THE SOCIAL CONTRACT

Sustainability involves complex and changing environmental dynamics that affect human livelihoods and well-being, with intersecting ecological, economic, and sociopolitical dimensions, both globally and locally. Langenwater (2009: 11) lists some essential principles of a sustainable policy for companies: "Respect for people (at all levels of the organization), the community, and its supply chain; respect for the planet, recognizing that resources are finite; and generating profits that arise from adhering to these principles." Organizations are embedded in society, and reflect the value they offer society, which raises profound issues. As Beard (2008: 448) states, "The difficulty (in the fashion industry) is to see how all the suppliers of the individual components can be ethically secured and accounted for, together with the labour used to manufacture the garment, its transport from factory to retail outlet, and ultimately the garment's aftercare and disposal." With a global reach, the fashion industry supply chain is highly fragmented and inherently complex; as a result, fashion manufacturing is even less transparent than agribusiness (Mihm 2010; Partridge 2011).

WHY IS FAST FASHION UNSUSTAINABLE?

Fast fashion—low-cost clothing collections based on current, high-cost luxury fashion trends—is, by its very nature, a fast-response system that encourages disposability (Fletcher 2008). A formerly standard turnaround time from catwalk to consumer of six months is now compressed to a matter of mere weeks by such companies as H&M and Zara, with heightened profits to match (Tokatli 2008). Fast fashion companies thrive on fast cycles: rapid prototyping, small batches combined with large variety, more efficient transportation and delivery, and merchandise that is presented "floor ready" on hangers with price tags already attached (Skov 2002).

To keep customers coming back, high street retailers routinely source new trends in the field, and purchase on a weekly basis to introduce new items and replenish stock (Tokatli and Kizilgun 2009). The side effect of such continual and rapid turnover: a new form of seemingly contradictory mass exclusivity (Schrank 2004). Moreover, lower manufacturing and labor costs mean lower costs overall, which result in lower prices, which, in turn, equal higher volume. Even companies such as Zara, which once manufactured all their goods in Europe, resulting in better quality control, now outsource at least 13 percent of their manufacturing to China and Turkey. Shipping time from China to Europe may take three weeks, but it only takes five days from Turkey (Tokatli 2008). Admittedly, fast fashion companies do employ stables of in-house designers: more eye-catching designs lead to trendier, must-have fashions, which lure consumers into paying full price now rather than deferring gratification until the year-

---

[1] In Joy Sherry Venkatesh Wang and Chan (2012) Fast Fashion Sustainability and The Ethical Appeal of Luxury Brands Fashion Theory Volume 16 3 Taylor & Francis.

end sales arrive. When faced with tight delivery demands, fast fashion companies will even use higher-cost local labor and expedited shipping methods. In due time, future financial returns will far outweigh current costs (Cachon and Swinney 2011).

Avid consumers are now primed to browse fast fashion stores every three weeks or so in search of new styles (Barnes and Lea-Greenwood 2006). According to a former Topshop brand director, "Girls see something and want it immediately." The fast fashion industry—in common with the technology industry, which similarly produces a constant stream of ever-improved, ever more alluring, products—exists courtesy of such impulsive behavior, employing the planned obsolescence practices recently identified by Guiltinan (2009: 20): limited functional life design and options for repair, design aesthetics that eventually lead to reduced satisfaction, design for transient fashion, and design for functional enhancement that requires adding new product features. Fashion, more than any other industry in the world, embraces obsolescence as a primary goal; fast fashion simply raises the stakes (Abrahamson 2011).

Young consumers' desire for fast fashion is coupled with significant disposable income (or, alternatively, the availability of credit). Fast fashion exploits this segment, offering of-the-moment design and the immediate gratification of continually evolving temporary identities—a postmodern phenomenon (Bauman 2005). Fast fashion has been referred to as "McFashion," because of the speed with which gratification is provided. The framework is global, and the term "McFashion" is, to a degree, appropriate. According to Ritzer (2011: 1), "'McDonaldization' is a term that became fashionable in discussing changes in capitalist economies as they moved toward greater rationalization. Types of production matter: manufacturing reliant on artisanal craft is a distinct system, as are those of mass and more limited production." "Craft" denotes highly skilled labor, using simple tools to make unique items, one item at a time, and accessible to only a select clientele. Hermes' affluent customers, for example, might wait for several years to acquire a particular bag (Tungate 2009). With fast fashion, new styles swiftly supersede the old, defining and sustaining constantly emerging desires and notions of self. As Binkley (2008: 602) argues, the idea of "multiple selves in evolution" is central to fast fashion lovers. Fast fashion replaces exclusivity, glamour, originality, and luxury with "massclusivity" and planned spontaneity (Toktali 2008).

THE RISE OF ANTI-CONSUMERISM

Some consumers, however, are disenchanted with mindless consumption and its impact on society (Kozinets and Handleman 2004). Terms that are often used to represent this anti-market stance are: consumer resistance, rebellion, boycotting, countercultural movements, and non-consumption (Shaw and Riach 2011). Consumers are also aware that individual consumption fosters organizational production, creating an ongoing cycle of appetite, simultaneously voracious and insatiable. Bauman (2000) calls it "liquid consumption." Fluidity of identity and uncertainty are the trademarks of such a system, often leading to an anti-consumerism position (Binkley 2008). According to Binkley (2008: 601), "While anti-consumerism defines a broad set of ethical and political positions and choices, it also operates on the every-day level of mundane consumer choice, through critical discourses about the market itself, where small decisions serve to anchor subjectivities in constructed and heavily mediated narratives of lifestyle, self-hood, community, and identity." Anxiety and responsibility can weigh heavily on consumers. In the process of being catapulted to a postmodern lifestyle, "identity" as Bauman notes (2005: 116–28), in liquid modernity becomes "an endlessly cultivated and optimized polyvalency of mobility, a skilled adaptability to a permanent state of ambivalence and unsettledness." Such ambivalence allows individuals to continually reinvent themselves. Multiple evolving selves, as we argued earlier, are built on constantly evolving fashion styles created by fast fashion. But herein lies the paradox: the very possibility of reinvention can now serve to disenchant the consumer, as a means of revealing consumption's potential to harm others and the environment; such information can now realign consumers with ecologically sustainable fashion (Beard 2008; Elsie 2003).

METHODOLOGY: SEARCHING FOR SUBCONSCIOUS VALUES

In our study, we interviewed both male and female fast fashion consumers aged between twenty and thirty-five in Hong Kong and Canada on their own ideas of style and fashion, to highlight the issues involved in their approach to consumption. Hong Kong is a long-time manufacturing powerhouse in the fashion industry, home to at least one centenary company: Li & Fung, a self-described "network orchestrator" (Mihm 2010: 59) founded in 1906, and now the largest outsourcing firm in the world, linking to 83,000 suppliers worldwide (Fung *et al.*, 2008). Canada, by contrast, falls at the opposite end of the fashion industry continuum, playing no major role. Unsurprisingly, given its potent lure, fast fashion has taken root within Hong Kong's and Canada's respective youth cultures with equal vitality.

Our overarching finding is that consumers from both Hong Kong and Canada, while concerned about the environmental and social impact of their non-fashion purchasing decisions, did not apply such principles to their consumption of fashion. They talked in general terms of saving the environment, were committed to recycling, and expressed dedication to organic food. In the strict fashion context, ethical fashion refers to "the positive impact of a designer, a consumer choice, a method of production as experienced by workers, consumers, animals, society, and the environment" (Thomas 2008: 525). Yet, these very same consumers routinely availed themselves of trend-led fashionable clothing that was cheap: i.e. low cost to them, but high cost in environmental and societal terms. They also exhibited relatively little guilt about fast fashion's disposability, seeing little discrepancy between their attitudes toward sustainability and their fashion choices.

Our finding is unsurprising; other studies have similarly documented irrational consumer choices that are poorly connected to, or completely disconnected from, consumer values (Moisander and Personen 1991). The moral-norm activation theory of altruism proposed by Schwartz (1973) states that environmental quality is a collective good, and therefore will motivate consumers to embrace environmentalism in all aspects of life. The rapid rise of fast fashion implies otherwise. Schwartz' theory presumes that consumers will thoughtfully evaluate the life cycle of different products, and will then select whichever product has the least environmental load. However, in our study, participants had little overlap with the "ethical hard liners" (those living entirely in line with their commitment to sustainability, and thus purchasing only eco-fashion) discussed by Niinimaki (2010: 152) in her study of eco-fashion in Finland. Two themes predominate in our analysis: "speed and style at low cost" and "disposability and limited durability." These options enable consumers to constantly alter their identity.

THE ADVENT OF CHEAP CHIC

Often participants combined several themes in their descriptions. Speed was described as part of the fast fashion industry mode. Updated looks, greater variety, and limited editions, along with the speed of their availability, make this industry very attractive to many consumers—initially a younger crowd, but now attracting older segments as well. Some participants even talked of speed that resembled that of the fast food industry, although they recognize the problems associated with creating goods for mass cultural consumption (Stillman 2003).

TODAY'S TREASURES, TOMORROW'S TRASH

Disposability plays a key role, along with speed and style, in fast fashion. The reference to ten washes is derived from fast fashion companies themselves, who openly proffer the number as a benchmark, after which an item will no longer be expected to retain its original value, due to poor-quality materials and manufacturing. The companies pay no price for such revelations, nor do most customers experience regret in tossing out clothes based on this principle. Leticia, a Hong Kong office worker, did, however, have guilt pangs: "I fill up big garbage bags of things and then throw them away. It is a lot of wasted goods—some of which I may not even have worn more than once. I do feel guilty, but I have a small apartment and I cannot keep them." She rationalizes her actions on the basis of limited space, but shows no attempt to reducing her shopping sprees. Of the thirty participants in both locales, only six talked overtly about the societal downside of fast fashion.

UNDERSTANDING SUSTAINABILITY: IS ECO-FASHION A VIABLE OPTION?

Responses to what sustainability meant to individuals were robust, with details of how personal acts of consumption led to sustainability. Henry, a Canadian student, said, "Sustainability means to live a life where you are not taking any more from the earth than what you are giving back. You are trying to minimize the environmental footprint that you leave behind." It is important to him; he notes that he does not buy books anymore, but is involved in e-learning. He believes in not turning on the washing machine unless there is a full load, and even hang-dries his clothes. Yet, he experiences no guilt in buying clothes designed to have no long-term value. David, a young Canadian student, observed: "Sustainability is the level at which humans are able to live and co-exist indefinitely with the natural world without harming or causing damage to either side." For him, partnership with nature is a mechanism by which he is reminded to act in sustainable ways. He recycles bottles for money, conserves electricity, and uses water very carefully. Yet, he too shops for fast fashion items regularly. Alicia, who works in a grocery store in Canada, talked about how important it was to be vegetarian, given large-scale agribusiness' detrimental impact on the environment. But Alicia was oblivious of the links between environmental issues and her obsession with fast fashion.

When participants were asked if they would buy eco-fashion, the quick response was only if the clothes were stylish. Usually the choices available to them were only T-shirts. Even when other items were available, as in offerings by companies, such as American Apparel, that use organic cotton, participants saw the clothing as frumpy. As Linda, a student from Hong Kong, said, "I would never buy these clothes, because they are just as boring as [those from] Gap. It is so out of sync with what is happening now on the catwalks." When we probed further, Paula, a Canadian participant, said, "You need to get the designers weighing in on this issue and using organic cotton and the proper dyes and so on. If Marc Jacobs did it, we would all be buying these clothes." Change is possible, but it has to come from the fashion domain. Aesthetics is crucial to the appeal of eco-fashion.

LUXURY FASHION: DREAMS AND DESIRES

When we asked participants about luxury fashion, the three main themes that emerged were dreams, exclusivity, and beauty/art. Fast fashion allows dreams of luxury to come true. Style is achievable even if quality is compromised; if an article of clothing is not really "beautiful" and "elegant" as is the genuine item, consumers can nonetheless afford the fast fashion option. For our participants, the idea of owning exclusive, unique items from a luxury brand is both an aspirational dream and a desire; yet, even as aspirations motivate them to pursue their dreams, pragmatism prevails.

HERITAGE AND QUALITY

While the dream quality is essential to a luxury product, in some instances, a long history and heritage further intensify a brand's strength. Louis Vuitton, for instance, prides itself on having provided royalty with luggage. Quality is assured in all aspects of its business (or so is the claim), since Louis Vuitton Moet Hennessy has designed exclusive objects for the nobility. While Patek Philippe may not have served the nobility, it does have a rich tradition of creating exclusive and extraordinarily well-crafted dream products. Creating such products takes time, which in turn limits availability; highly trained artisans work with carefully chosen, exclusive materials that are not produced en masse.

The dreamlike quality of luxury products has its origin in elaborate craft ateliers where generations of artisans have created one-of-a-kind products. Heritage and quality appeal because they do not conjure up pollution, dwindling natural resources, and global warming—most of which are associated with the oil and transportation industries. There is little exploitation of labor, since most ateliers are attached to big fashion houses located in major fashion cities, such as Paris and Milan, although outsourcing to countries such as China and India is raising the specter of sweatshop operations.

BEAUTY AND ART

The final theme of beauty, elegance, and art is important as well. It is clear from the observations of the participants that they dream of exclusivity, beauty, art, design, and heritage—all of which are associated with luxury brands. Yet, this ideal seems distant. They love the glamour and style, but lament the expense. They see that the next best alternative is to buy fast fashion items. These items approximate the look, but at a fraction of the cost. Consumers compromise on quality, the factor central to undermining sustainability. If the items used featured high-quality material and stitching, they would not fall apart after ten washes. Yet fast fashion companies highlight a limited product life span as a special attribute. Consumers are trained to continuously purchase and consume fast fashion replacements. Durability in fast fashion apparel is the kiss of death.

CONCLUDING REMARKS AND IMPLICATIONS

In this article, we have explored the perceptions that consumers in both Hong Kong and Canada have of sustainability, fast fashion, and luxury fashion, and have shown that sustainable fashion is not a priority for them. The bulk of the data suggest that young people separate fashion from sustainability. They definitely support the idea of sustainability, but do not apply such ethics when it comes to sustainable fashion. Their moral imagination (Werhane 1998) seems quite impoverished in this category. This state of moral stasis may gradually change. As Carrigan and Attala (2001: 577) note, "Perhaps in time new generations of consumers will not only think more ethically, but also act more ethically."

References

Abrahamson, Eric. 2011. "The Iron Cage: Ugly, Cool and Unfashionable." *Organization Studies* 32: 615–29.

Barnes, L. and G. Lea-Greenwood: 2006. "Fast Fashioning the Supply Chain: Shaping the Research Agenda." *Journal of Fashion Marketing and Management* 10(3): 259–71.

Baumann, Z. 2005. *Liquid Life.* Cambridge: Polity Press.

Beard, N. 2008. "The Branding of Ethical Fashion and the Consumer: A Luxury Niche or a Mass Market Reality?" *Fashion Theory* 12(4): 447–68.

Binkley, S. 2008. "Liquid Consumption." *Cultural Studies* 22(5): 599–623.

Cachon, Gerard P. and Robert Swinney. 2011. "The Value of Fast Fashion: Quick Response, Enhanced Design, and Strategic Consumer Behaviour." *Management Science* April: 57(4): 778–95.

Carrigan, M. and A. Attala. 2001. "The Myth of the Ethical Consumer—Do Ethics Matter in Purchase Behaviour?" *Journal of Consumer Marketing* 18 (7): 560–77.

Elsie, M. 2003. "Managing Brands in the New Stakeholder Environment." *Journal of Business Ethics.* 44: 235–46.

Fletcher, K. 2008. *Sustainable Fashion & Textiles: Design Journeys.* Oxford: Earthscan.

Fung, V. K., W. K. Fung and Y. J. Wind. 2008. *Competing in a Flat World.* Upper Saddle River, NJ: Wharton.

Guiltinan, J. 2009. "Creative Destruction and Destructive Creations: Environmental Ethics and Planned Obsolescence." *Journal of Business Ethics* 89: 19–28.

Kozinets, R. and J. Handleman. 2004. "Adversaries of Consumption: Consumer Movements, Activism, and Ideologies." *Journal of Consumer Research* 31 (December): 691–704.

Langenwater, G. 2009. "Planet First." *Industrial Management* 51(4): 10–13.

Mihm, Barbara: 2010. "Fast Fashion in a Flat World: Global Sourcing Strategies." *International Business and Economics Research Journal* June 9(6): 55–63.

Moisander, Johanna and S. Personen. 2002. "Narratives of Sustainable Ways of Living: Constructing the Self and Others as a Green Consumer." *Management Decision* 40(4): 329–42.

Niinimaki, Kirsi. 2010. "Eco-Clothing, Consumer Identity and Ideology." *Sustainable Development* 18: 150–60.

Partridge, D. J. 2011. "Activist Capitalism and Supply Chain Citizenship: Producing Ethical Regimes and Ready-to-Wear Clothes." *Current Anthropology* 52(S3): S97–S111.

Ritzer, G. 2011. *The McDonaldization of Society*, 6th edn. Newbury Park, CA: Pine Forge Press.

Schrank, A. 2004. "Ready to Wear Development? Foreign Investment, Technology Transfer, and Learning by Watching in the Apparel Trade." *Social Forces* 83(1): 123–56.

Schwartz, S. 1973. "Normative Explanations of Helping Behaviour: A Critique, Proposal and Empirical Test." *Journal of Experimental Social Psychology* 9(4): 349–64.

Shaw, Deirdre and Kathleen Riach. 2011. "Embracing Ethical Fields: Constructing Consumption in the Margins." *European Journal of Marketing* 45(7/8): 1051–67.

Skov, L. 2002. "Hong Kong Fashion Designers as Cultural Intermediaries: Out of Global Garment Production." *Cultural Studies* 16(4): 553–69.

Stillman, T. 2003. "McDonald's in Question: The Limits of the Mass Market." *The American Behavioral Scientist* 47(2): 107–67.

Thomas, S. 2008 "From "Green Blur" to Eco Fashion: Fashioning an Eco-Lexicon." *Fashion Theory* 12(4): 525–40.

Tokatli, N. 2008. "Global Sourcing Insights from the Clothing Industry: The Case of Zara, a Fast Fashion Retailer." *Journal of Economic Geography* 8: 21–38.

Tokatli, N. and O. Kizilgun. 2009. "From Manufacturing Garments for Ready to Wear to Designing Collections: Evidence from Turkey." *Environment and Planning* 41: 146–62.

Tungate, M. 2009. *Luxury Worlds.* London: Kogan Page.

Werhane, P. 1998. "Moral Imagination and the Search for Ethical Decision-making in Management." *Business Ethics Quarterly* (Special Issue): 75–98.

Zaltman, G. 1997. "Rethinking Market Research: Putting People Back In." *Journal of Marketing Research* 34(4): 424–32.

13

IN PATAGONIA (CLOTHING):
A complicated greenness

Sharon J. Hepburn[1]

My task here is to chart the path of Patagonia to their present point, and to say that despite their protestations, they produce ecofashion, even "slow" fashion (after Clark 2008). They provide (relatively) sustainably produced clothing that does what fashion in general does: it lets a person express their style and taste in dress, and express aspects of how they situate themselves within discourses such as those of gender, class, taste, and various social issues. In this case what people wearing Patagonia clothing—the people moved by the popular catalog—are at least in part expressing are values regarding nature, to be sustained, but also as a place of transformation.

FOUR DECADES OF A COMPANY

Beginnings of the business: Mountain hardware and othermade clothing

From the late 1950s and through the 1960s, Yvon Chouinard made climbing hardware (not clothes) and along the way founded Chouinard Equipment. Chouinard presented the policy of the nascent company in their inaugural catalog in 1972, beginning the practices—the subject of this article—which carried through to the Patagonia company of today, weaving together images of items for sale with narratives and photos that create and evoke meaning beyond the purely utilitarian. In 1972, Chouinard told potential buyers that he aimed to create "the cleanest line" (1999: 9), in this case, the way to climb that left the least damage to the rock face. The company produced climbing hardware that left no trace, and which allowed the customer to be "a step closer to organic climbing for the natural man" (Chouinard 2005: 31).

Chouinard starts to make clothes, and the patagonia company is formed

Chouinard Equipment's first steps in selling clothing happened by chance and were a way to support the marginally profitable climbing hardware business. Chouinard relates the company history in *Let My People Go Surfing* (2005), in which he tells many stories (in a style that leads Moser-Wellman 2001: 127 to call him a "business artist") through which he builds an image of his values, and a shared mythology, that the company was based on. Chouinard Equipment started making their own climbing clothes and accessories in the early 1970s, which were to be "uncommon Clothes for uncommon People" (2001 Spring catalog: 3), beginning a note of self-declared specialness and exclusivity that persists today.

The business to support climbing was becoming a business in its own right, and Chouinard decided to separate it from the tool company for two reasons. First, he did not want "to dilute the image of Chouinard as a tool company by making clothing under that label" (2005: 38), an early indication of his ambivalence towards "fashion." And second, he did not want the clothing linked just to mountain climbing. Already, he recounts, "we had a vision of a greater future than that" (2005: 38). That vision became Patagonia, the clothing company. "Our intent" he says "was to make clothing

---

[1] From Sharron Hepburn, In Patagonia (Clothing): A Complicated Greenness, 2013, Fashion Theory, Volume 17, Issue 5, Taylor & Francis.

for those rugged, southern Andes/Cape Horn conditions" (2005: 38) of the place named Patagonia. The company label depicts the Mount Fitzroy skyline and blue ocean, representing the depths and heights of nature, and all the sports that took place within it. In 1975, the heroically envisioned Patagonia clothing company financially floundered, and the partnership collapsed, leaving Yvon and his wife Malinda as sole owners with the task of stabilizing the company.

They continued to sell clothes made by others, but started to develop a line of technical clothing to meet the conditions of high-altitude climbing, where weather changes can be fast and deadly. At the time, climbers wore cotton, wool, and down. Chouinard, however, was inspired by the clothing of North Atlantic fishermen, and designed his first synthetic pile sweater, which was more practical than natural fibers as it dried quickly and retained heat even when wet. Hardly objects of design beauty (described as "infinitely homely" in the 1998 Fall catalog, p.10), the first pile garments "were made from fabric intended for toilet seat covers" (by Malden Mills) and were available only in "an ugly tan and equally hideous powder blue" nonetheless, "Ugly as they were . . . the pile jacket soon became an outdoor staple" (2005: 50). The big moves forward in the technical line were in 1984, when a soft, non-piling fleece (Synchilla) was developed, and in 1985, when polyester (capilene) underwear with much better wicking abilities than the polypropylene (diaper liner) garments was developed (Chouinard 2005: 50–3). The technical line, the theoretical core of the business, for "core customers," has developed such that in 2011, there are different kinds of jackets, underwear, etc., for the degrees of breathability vs. waterproofness most suitable for who you were, what you are going to do, and where.

A transition to producing sportswear (though not, please, fashion) in the early 1980s

Although most catalog space through to the mid–late 1980s went to education about the benefits of layering, and technical products "for hardcore enthusiasts," people who "take their sport to the extreme" (2001 Spring catalog, Canadian insert: 1) the clothes that sold best were the least technical. The popular beach shorts and fleece-lined bomber jackets suited just fine for average people who wanted to do average things in attractive, well-made clothing. This clothing market sustained the company then (Chouinard 2005: 54), and continues to maintain the company profits well beyond the level that their "core customer," the extreme sport enthusiast, could do. And yet—in the words of its founder, some of its agents, and in the narratives of the catalog—Patagonia remains ambivalent about this.

Sportswear for uncommon–not fashionable–people

Patagonia is not interested in "fashion" but they explicitly insist their product be of high quality, and implicitly, increasingly, want it to look good, and not be "ordinary." And they do claim their ability "to make function and technical integrity look way cool" (2001 Holiday catalog: 16). In the early 1980s they moved away from the norm of the industry by making clothes in colors other than the rust, tan, or forest green that dominated the outdoor clothing industry. Says Chouinard, "we drenched the Patagonia line in vivid color . . . teal, French red, mango, seafoam, and iced mocha," moving the "still rugged" clothing from "bland-looking to blasphemous" (2005: 54). It was this bold coloring, not just the technical clothing line that set the company on the path to its present fortunes. Chouinard admits that the new profits were driven by "fashion consumers" as well as the outdoor community. He knew that growth was mostly from the "nontechnical" part of the line, and admits that he "worried that our image might become too soft and sports-wear oriented" (Chouinard 2005: 66). This worry was indirectly conveyed to catalog readers through the narratives, which came to be called "field reports," narratives not about the clothes for sale, but about what you did in them, and why, and the ethical issues of production. These field reports continue to be a primary vehicle through which the company consciously weaves and reweaves of the threads of their self-image and creed, which consumers are implicitly welcomed to participate in as they read.

Patagonia sportswear today: Elegance and sex-fleece

Patagonia sportswear today is presumably for those times you are not hanging in mid-air in immense nature, when you are not traveling in "extreme" destinations, or otherwise not in situations other—ordinary—people would want to escape from. The clothes are, presumably, for when you are working to sustain your "dirtbag" life, or for when you (like me, perhaps) simply need to be ready for the conditions you might face when, say, carrying your laptop down to a coffee shop (for which Patagonia now has numerous options, including a US$69 "barista tote," in three colors). And the sportswear is, the 2001 Spring catalog advises, for when you have "had enough haute couture."

ENVIRONMENTAL POLICIES AND PRACTICES

Patagonia is well known for its commitment to wilderness conservation and sustainable practices. The company reviews their policies at all levels—from offices, to cafeterias, to factories—to assess and minimize environmental impact. Employees can have two months away from work with pay each year to do an internship related to the environmental ideals of the company (Esposito 2009: 203; Haas and Hartman 1995; McSpirit 1998). There is no doubt that the company works far beyond what Simon and Alagoma refer to as the "truncated notions of environmental citizenship" (2013: 325) in government educational programs such as Leave No Trace: Patagonia considers not only the "traces" left in rock faces and campsites, but also the traces left in the environment by the production and consumption cycle. Doug Tompkins, a one-time partner of Chouinard (and founder of Esprit clothing, and North Face outdoor clothing), and wife used most of their profits to buy up wilderness in Patagonia (the place, not the company), which they are donating to the Chilean government and people to create nature sanctuaries (Robbins 2011). One percent of all Patagonia sales, or profits (whichever is higher) go to environmental projects.

Well in advance of most other companies, Patagonia calculated the environmental impact of producing the fabrics they used (Hartmann 2008; Hartman and Haas 1995). Synchilla, the fleece they have been making since 1985 came out on top, being made entirely from recycled bottles these days. They found cotton to be the most polluting, as were most "natural" source textiles, as is often the case (Scaturro 2008: 470). In response, Patagonia started to use only organic cotton, absorbing a large portion of the extra cost. These tales of corporate practice and commitment are told in the catalog, alongside "field reports." Sometimes they *are* the field report. And the consumer reading the catalog reads these on pages opposite superbly beautiful and evocative photographs of small man in immense nature, and turning the page she can find the Patagonia products for sale.

DILEMMAS OF DREAMS, DESIRE, AND DEMAND

Thomas (2008: 533) explains the notion of "greenwash": just as whitewash covers up things we would rather not see, greenwash is a marketing ploy, to be or to profess to be green, simply because it sells and some consumers want greenness, or want to be seen to be wanting it. Patagonia is known as a company that aims to use sustainable practices. Say Conley and Freidenwald-Fishman, in *Marketing That Matters*, Patagonia's openness about the pollution they cause "created a high level of trust among its employees and managers" (2006: 177) and presumably among customers too. In *Companies with a Conscience* (1994), Scott and Rothman include Patagonia as one of the twelve companies examined that "make a difference." Whether or not Patagonia's narratives are greenwash, it is hard to deny that greenness helps sell their product, and perhaps that, as Corbett argues more pointedly, the narratives actually help "work around any guilt related to consumerism" while encouraging people to pile up more of the "latest and greatest outdoor stuff" (2006: 111). And they can feel fashionable while they do that, as green can indeed be "the New Black" (Prothero *et al.* 2010; Winge 2008).

But it is—I argue now—a double greenness: it is not only the greenness of production processes to protect nature, but also greenness as a more ethereal, aesthetic quality with parallels in Western literary discourses, that links the wearer with images of the sublime *in* nature, and the sublime experience *of* nature. But the irony is that this very aesthetic, at the heart of how Patagonia displays their goods in the catalog, quite likely, very likely, inspires people to buy the product, whether for doing extreme sport, or going to the coffee shop. As Chouinard intended, who the catalog reader believes their fellow customer is, and what they represent, encourages a feeling of affinity—or desired affinity—that can inspire a purchase.

While the product is made in an environmentally conscientious way, it is still a product being bought, which had to be made, and it took resources to do so. And we must ask—as Patagonia asks us to—was that purchase necessary? And then the question comes, what else am I—and 1,000s of others—buying here? The answer should be clear by now, but Chouinard himself tells us the answer. The catalog yields more sales when there is a particular balance of text, photo, and product. If the text and dramatic images of nature and extreme sportsmen falls away, "ironically" the sales drop. Although the opposite of what Chouinard claims to want, this juxtaposition with the full knowledge of what proportions increase sales, facilitates creating "addiction" to the product, says Todor, giving Patagonia's strategy as an example of an effective technique to get customers "hooked" on your product (Todor 2007: 99). So it is safe to say that (some, many, or all) people are buying what is conveyed in the images/writing when they buy their Patagonia clothing.

I am not saying anything is, necessarily, intentional "greenwash" here. My point is that a conundrum is almost unavoidable in a capitalist, consumer society. The very effort to educate consumers, demonizing excess consumption, can, when tied to an ideal and an attractive product, encourage people to buy things they otherwise would not.

The early Chouinard products made no visual statement about ecology in general, and certainly a jacket made of fabric intended for a toilet seat cover—while it could say "use what's available, be frugal"—it also did not scream "minimalism" or "protect the earth," or "wear natural fabrics." In fact the fabric radiated fakeness, but if it were read as a statement, it would be read as some sort of empathy with the outdoor activities, of being in nature, or of looking like you were prepared to be there, whether or not you ever were. The early Patagonia company stayed close to the values of "use what's necessary," in clothes and other things, but do not waste your time or money on pointless things. But at that time they had no overtly expressed concern with ecological issues as such. Through the early 1990s until the present, as explained above, Patagonia increasingly wove this concern with the environment into their production practices and catalog narratives. Joining with the earlier indexing of the clothing with "being in nature," Patagonia effected what I am here calling a double greenness, that of "green" practices, combined with a particular vision of wilderness, these two linked by a re-creation (through images and narratives) of a sublime mythology with a few centuries of literary and artistic precedents.

This double greenness sells Patagonia clothing, but in doing so it becomes what I would call a *complicated* greenness. If people buy the clothes pictured in juxtaposition to the two discourses of greenness, then these are at least in some part selling them, and therein lie the seeds of the contradiction, and thus, complication.

In his 2012 book *The Responsible Company: What We've Learned from Patagonia's First 40 Years*, Chouinard (and Stanley) lay out an inspiring (to me) manifesto for responsible capitalism. In 2012 they posted an advertisement in *The New York Times* on Black Friday (the biggest shopping day of the year in the USA) saying "Don't Buy This Jacket," encouraging people to not buy what they don't need. In 2013 Patagonia's webpage explaining their Common Threads Initiative aimed at sustainable consumption, flatly states that "Everything we make—everything anyone makes—costs the planet more life than it gives back" (Patagonia.com 2013), a stronger version of Patagonia's earlier "everything we do pollutes" (Conley and Freidenwald-Fishman 2006: 177). And a Patagonia Vice President of world retail told me, acknowledging the dilemma, that his job requires him to fly all over the world, and Chouinard flies down to Patagonia (the place) to fly-fish a few times a year: don't buy the jacket but do fly the gas-consuming plane to go where you might sell it, or might have worn it. In his 2012 manifesto Chouinard states his faith that customers of all consumer goods will insist on environmental laws becoming more restrictive, and even that investors in all businesses will be demanding high levels of environmental accountability, and that to "compete, a company will have to be at least as responsible as its competitors" (Chouinard and Stanley 2012: 35).

CONCLUSION: IN PATAGONIA (THE PLACE, NOT THE CLOTHES)

Through four decades Patagonia has moved from serving the needs of "dirtbag" kindred spirits, to being dependent on serving the sportswear tastes of urbanites living the style of life the founders rejected. Yet the narratives and photos of the catalogs conjure images of the encounter with immense nature, reminding the reader on some level of the elation they can return to, if only in memory, and often the memory is revived—or even created—by the next Patagonia catalog that arrives in the mail. The tamed reader/consumer buys the dreams attached to the clothes.

Patagonia is selling greenness, but not just greenness in production practices. Green purchasing acts can spring from the pragmatic—to protect the environment in which me must live—to the aesthetic—the sublime aesthetic—to save nature as the environment in which we can find redemption and freedom: purchasing can arise from the desire to protect nature for its own sake, not just so that we can *be,* but so that we can *become,* in various ways. In this complicated intermeshing of dreams and desire, to be like the people we imagine the Patagonia customer to be, we may literally "buy into" a process that carries forward the very economic and ecological trajectory we (and Patagonia's responsible capitalists) would ideally curtail.

References

Chamberlain, Adam. 2003. "Winter Road Trip." *Patagonia Catalogue* Winter: 2.
Chouinard, Yvon. 1999. "Introduction." In N. Gallagher (ed.) *Patagonia: Notes from the Field*, pp. 8–11. San Francisco, CA: Chronicle Books.
Chouinard, Yvon. 2005. *Let My People Go Surfing: The Education of a Reluctant Businessman.* New York: Penguin Group.
Chouinard, Yvon and Vincent Stanley. 2012. *The Responsible Company: What We've Learned from Patagonia's First 40 years.* Ventura, CA: Patagonia Books.
Clark, Hazel. 2008. "SLOW + FASHION—an Oxymoron—or a Promise for the Future...?" *Fashion Theory* 12(4): 427–46.
Conley, Chip and Eric Freidenwald-Fishman. 2006. *Marketing That Matters: 10 Practices to Profit Your Business and Change the World.* San Francisco, CA: Berrett-Koehler Publishers.
Copp, Jonathan. 2005. "Field Report: Les Droites." *Patagonia Catalogue* Winter: 32.
Corbett, Julia B. 2006. *Communicating Nature: How We Create and Understand Environmental Messages.* Washington, DC: Island Press.
Esposito, Mark. 2009. *Put Your Corporate Social Responsibility Act Together.* Mustang, OK: Tate Publishing.
Haas, Erika J. and Harvey Hartman. 1995. "Patagonia Struggles to Reduce Its Impact on the Environment." *Total Quality Environmental Management* Autumn: 1–7.
Hartman, Harvey and Erika J. Haas. 1995. "Patagonia Struggles to Reduce Its Impact on the Environment." *Environmental Management* Autumn: 3–7.
Hartmann, Patrick. 2008. "Virtual Nature Experiences as Emotional Benefits in Green Product Consumption: The Moderating Role of Environmental Attitudes." *Environment and Behavior* 40(6): 818–842.
Long, John. 2010. "Out of Mud and Hail." *Patagonia Catalogue* Spring: 3.
McSpirit, Kelly. 1998. "Sustainable Consumption: Patagonia's Buy Less, But Buy Better." *Corporate Environmental Strategy* 5(2): 32–40.
Patagonia.com. 2013. "Common Threads Initiative." Patagonia.com. http://www.patagonia.com.au/environment/what-we-do/commonthreads-initiative/ (accessed May 3, 2013).
Prothero, Andrea, Pierre McDonagh and Susan Dobscha. 2010. "Is Green the New Black? Reflections on a Green Commodity Discourse." *Journal of Macromarketing* 30(2): 147–59.
Robbins, Jim. 2011. "When the Rich Go Wild." *Condé Nast Traveller* 46(9): 51–65.
Scaturro, Sarah. 2008. "Eco-tech Fashion: Rationalizing Technology in Sustainable Fashion." *Fashion Theory* 12(4): 469–88.

Scott, Mary, and Howard Rothman. 1994. *Companies with a Conscience: Intimate Portraits of Twelve Firms that Make a Difference.* New York: Carol Publishing Group.

Simon, Gregory L. and Peter S. Alagona. 2013. "Contradictions at the Confluence of Commerce, Consumption and Conservation; or, an REI Shopper Camps in the Forest, Does Anyone Notice?" *Geoforum* 45: 325–36.

Thomas, Sue. 2008. "From 'Green Blur' to Ecofashion: Fashioning an Eco-Lexicon." *Fashion Theory* 12(4): 525–40.

Todor, John I. 2007. *Addicted Customers: How to Get Them Hooked on your Company.* Martinez, CA: Silverado Press.

Winge, Theresa M. 2008. "'Green Is the New Black': Celebrity Chic and the 'Green' Commodity Fetish." *Fashion Theory* 12(4): 511–24.

14

THE SWEATSHOP, CHILD LABOR, AND EXPLOITATION ISSUES IN THE GARMENT INDUSTRY

Liat Smestad[1]

LABOR EXPLOITATION: THE CONNECTION BETWEEN THE CHILD AND THE SWEATSHOP

During the latter half of the twentieth century, the sweatshop has come to symbolize not only the greed of industry but also the impossible poverty in which many live all over the world. Allegations of misconduct at major retailers like Wal-Mart stunned many and brought the issue of child labor and exploitation to the forefront of discussions on the ethical responsibility of consumers in an increasingly global economy (HRM Guide 2005).

While labor abuses are not found only in the fashion industry, clothing manufacturing has become the focal point for much of the difficult discussion about ideas like *fair trade, union wages, globalization,* and *consumer responsibility*. Shocking allegations of labor exploitation at manufacturers such as Hanes, Puma, and Wal-Mart helped to raise awareness about the harsh economic realities faced by many across the globe (Harvard University n.d.). It is during the decade of the 1990s that the sweatshop becomes a singular representation for labor exploitation worldwide; furthermore, it becomes, for many, the primary association they have with the concept of child labor. And this association has, perhaps, impeded ethical progress by conflating two interrelated but unequivocal realities. The first reality is that of labor abuse where some companies are accused of routine physical abuse, employee endangerment, and wage manipulation—practices that have become definitive of the sweatshop. The second and perhaps harsher reality is that concepts of poverty are culturally dependent and are deeply connected to situations of human circumstance. The static nature of the sweatshop makes it less a cause of this poverty and more a symptom. The inability of sweatshops to account for the behaviors and conditions that perpetuate poverty and labor abuse reminds us that our collective ethical sensibility must be vigilant against our naive cultural biases. Ethel Brooks classifies the issue of child labor as alluring, an issue that can appeal to "a large and diverse number of people throughout the world." She goes on to claim:

> That children especially are conceived as innocent, pre-rational, and pre-economic, and therefore as extreme victims of global political economic flows, makes space for activism and protest by children and about children. Why has there been such a strong focus on child labor as particularly emblematic of the new sweatshop? (Brooks 2007: 1)

This article is an attempt to isolate critical issues in the child labor exploitation debate and attempts to answer Brooks' questioning of the sweatshop emblem. Essential to this investigation is the idea that child laborers do not represent a uniquely vulnerable class of workers and that the exploitation that child laborers endure indicates a variety of complex circumstances such as poor education, high poverty, a lack of social services, and cultural attitudes. This will reveal the sweatshop as an economic—not merely social—problem.

---

[1] Liat Smestad, (2009) The Sweatshop, Child Labor and Exploitation Issues in the Garment Industry, Fashion Practice, Taylor & Francis.

At the heart of the child labor dilemma is the issue of *exploitation*. The word exploitation refers to "the use or working of something, especially for a profit."[1]

It seems that child laborers are always at the forefront of reports on labor exploitation; children frequently represent the complacent employee. The child usually works for a successful Western retailer, leading many to conclude that companies employ children because they are easy to manipulate or abuse. But this stereotype belies the true issue: there are persons who are unable to say no to horrific working conditions, long hours, and low wages because opportunity is so scarce and economic necessity so strong. What becomes necessary is recognition of the breadth of social and economic experiences in the world. To risk understanding the complexity of child labor is to acknowledge the economic and social vulnerability of workers young and old. Social and economic vulnerability plays a crucial role in worker exploitation, but social and economic vulnerability are not natural causes themselves. Which is to say, *something* makes these workers socially or economically vulnerable to low-wage, dangerous jobs.

When critiquing child labor one must first determine whether the child and his/her family (or guardians) can afford for the child to *not* work. Any number of issues could influence this decision including the availability of public assistance programs, the composition or number of dependent parties residing with the family, the location of the family, the level of education individual members of the family have attained, etc. None of these are issues over which labor regulation, global economic trends, or industry standards have any control. It is reasonable to think that some families have a non-negotiable need that requires a child to work. In such situations, exploitation is subordinate to the overwhelming task of survival.

Grootaert and Patrinos point out that "In many societies a 10-year-old whose work makes a major contribution to the household's income is not considered a child" (1999: 2). In this regard, poverty rearranges the activities and priorities of childhood. The nature of *why* young people work is very different and is dependent, to an extent, on factors in their personal lives of which we may not be aware but which have significant impact on the decision to work.

To understand the reality of personal choice—the role personal choice plays in the global market place and our sense of global ethics—may mean accepting that our own ideas about children and labor will get turned upside down when we confront the difficult choices families must make around the world. As Moore says:

> Norms around access to assets and distribution of assets within families and between generations profoundly and directly affect children . . . clearly broader norms and practices that affect adults also affect children . . . In addition to affecting the ways in which resources are allocated and accessed, these norms are themselves resources, transmitted to greater or lesser degrees with ongoing implications for poverty transfers. (2003: 540)

II. THE SPECTER OF THE SWEATSHOP

While sweatshops exist physically, their primary function is metaphorical: they represent not only labor abuse but have also come to signify poor quality and workmanship, deplorable ethics, and insufferable human rights violations. However, sweatshops are a bit more complex than a mere physical place or cultural symbol; sweatshops are not malevolent spaces that appear out of nowhere. Instead, a sweatshop is a physical place, an industry phenomenon, a cultural indicator, an economic model, and the mascot for labor abuse worldwide. The fashion industry is notorious for its connection to sweatshops. In fact, the sweatshop seems to be specially designed for fashion because it combines the intensely intricate handiwork of fashion construction with the modern assembly line.

As with child labor, experts define terms in different ways. MIT economics professor Michael Piore claims, "These days, the term *sweatshop* is applied very loosely to almost any set of conditions considered inhumane or unfair" (Piore 1997: 133). In his study entitled "The Economics of the Sweatshop," Piore calls the sweatshop, "symptomatic of a particular economic logic, the manifestation of a specific organization of work . . . The sweatshop is characterized by very low fixed costs"

(Piore 1997: 135). Piore's definition is corroborated by Bud Konheim, CEO of Nicole Miller, Inc., a clothing design firm hailed by UNITE[2] as a model for how to run an ethically clean, no-sweat operation. Additionally, the line is produced entirely in New York with US union employees. In a Fall 1986 interview with Sally Singer (reproduced as "Rat-Catching: An Interview with Bud Konheim" in *No Sweat,* 1997), Konheim describes the sweatshop in much the same way Piore does—as a symptom of economic and industrial progress, claiming:

> I know what a sweatshop is in the U.S. A sweatshop goes into business when you ask your main contractor to make a thousand dresses by Friday. Although he is too busy, he takes the work and subcontracts it to a factory that has nothing to do. Why is this factory not busy? Because it is a sweatshop. It is not a sweatshop because it has low labor costs or abuses immigrant workers, but because it makes bad things. By the time the goods come back, the seams are wrong, the fit is not quite right—either that or I never get the garments because the operation has been closed down for unpaid taxes or violations of fire regulations. I lose out. (Singer 1997: 128)

Singer follows up Konheim's description of a US sweatshop by asking about conditions abroad; Konheim responds:

> I have been to factories all over the Pacific rim—Korea, Japan, Hong Kong, Szechwan, Singapore. I have seen workers in all kinds of situations but have never seen what I would call hazardous or abusive conditions. But the issue is complicated. Take child labor. Child labor is child labor: it is disgusting. I went to Morocco and saw seven year olds working in the kilim factories. In Morocco, that is not against the law, that is fine for them. I found it disturbing... However, nobody in Morocco is picketing in the streets about their daughters working in a rug factory. It is not slavery and the families have donated the girls to do this kind of work. Little boys working in leather dyeing are running around in tanning acid; it cannot be good for them, but this is what they do. So am I going to rewrite the social conduct of Morocco?" (Singer 1997: 128)

What these different *sweatshop* definitions do is provide one with a spectrum of possibility; there are many possible ways to define a sweatshop and in these definitions are also the possible causes that contribute to making a sweatshop, one being a cultural sensibility, which allows children to work. What these definitions lack is a clear sense that sweatshops are an issue exclusive to child labor abuse. Instead, the sweatshop is a conglomeration of separate but related practices, which are independent of country, and without regard to the age of the laborer it employs. Thus, eliminating a sweatshop only eliminates the jobs contained in that sweatshop. Unfortunately, this leaves needy workers with fewer choices for employment and allows the behaviors and practices that establish the sweatshop to root elsewhere.

To make a significant impact on the lives of child laborers one must accept that, in some instances, there is nothing that can prevent the child from working. Family debts and cultural or religious traditions lie well outside the sphere of public regulation. At times, rewriting the history of child laborers means rewriting the history and customs of a culture. In the USA, the definition of child and child labor has changed significantly since the Fair Labor Standards Act (FLSA). The FLSA instituted the national minimum wage and standards for overtime pay; it also strictly prevented children from working in oppressive labor environments. One effect of the FLSA was to define clearly *who* should be considered a worker. Furthermore, it defined child labor as oppressive, claiming:

> "Oppressive child labor" means a condition of employment under which (1) any employee under the age of sixteen years is employed by an employer (other than a parent or person standing in place of a parent employing his own child or a child in his custody under the age of sixteen years in an occupation other than manufacturing or mining or an occupation found by the Secretary of Labor to be particularly hazardous for the employment of children between the ages of sixteen and eighteen years or detrimental to their health or well being) in any occupation. (FLSA Sec. 3(e)(2)(III))

The text of the Act states that all employment under the age of sixteen is deemed oppressive and that, between the years of 16–18, only the Secretary of Labor has the power to deem employment oppressive. In this instance, the US government takes initiative and defines not only what constitutes labor (the FLSA also defines industry, goods, compensation, commerce, etc.) but also who can perform that labor. The FLSA, thus, embodies the American cultural attitude that children's work is dangerous for all involved.

But global life operates contrary to the standards of the FLSA and this helps to clarify the global role of reform. For, while it is not possible to have control over whether a family must rely on the labor of a child to survive, it is possible to have some measure of control over labor standards: wages, working conditions, and benefits. Many argue that child labor is part and parcel of a free market capitalistic consumer economy: manufacturers who need to turn out a quality product at a low price (in order to maximize profit and growth) often move industry work away from restrictive US labor forces (laws, unions, and wages) to countries where labor laws are less restrictive, making it possible for the company to cut costs by cutting worker wages and benefits; a process made easier by employing a young workforce. Ethically, there are some who will argue that labor is good for the child and the economy of that child's country. Some argue that steps to eradicate child labor cause more damage than good by eliminating a significant source of income. Furthermore, without a job many of these children would be forced into illegal "professions," like theft or prostitution, which guarantee no money, only danger. When critiquing child labor, one must contend not only with poverty, but the circular relationship poverty has to personal circumstance.

To this end, Rothstein draws out another complication: markets and industries. Rothstein claims that labor exploitation cannot be as cut and dried as one group taking advantage of another. In Rothstein's view, exploitation is less a definition and more a game of numbers, a very complicated game of numbers that directly contradicts many claims about child labor exploitation. To this end, Rothstein discusses what he calls "the disparity in sweatshop wages" (Rothstein 2005: 42), pointing out that in some places (Mexico, for example) labor wages are four times higher than in other places (Indonesia, for example) in terms of the garment industry.

Rothstein's arguments raise an interesting question: why would an Indonesian contractor like Nike, for example, contract also in Mexico where wages are at least four times higher? With this example, Rothstein shows us that our questioning of labor exploitation and wage structures is too simplistic for the reality of labor exploitation. Ideas that advocate that exploitative labor practices are the same everywhere and confined to a finite set of practices or attitudes do not account for the discrepancies Rothstein introduces. This is precisely the logic at work in the child labor–sweatshop conflation. One must consider exploitation as a total system to reconcile the complexities of labor abuse.

LABOR ABUSE: THE REAL ISSUE

A reasonable critique of child labor exploitation attempts to link personal choice to larger realities. Global finance and the complex nature of economies make it difficult to characterize child labor as wholly exploitative. Similarly, it cannot be true that the labor of children is exploited only because they are young and vulnerable; the situation has more texture than a simple power struggle. Everything from the gender and personal/social circumstance of the worker to global industry regulation affects just what constitutes labor exploitation and so affects how we deal with said exploitation when it occurs. Rothstein challenges people's ideas of the company as the master manipulator claiming:

> While labor standards vary from country to country, technology for assembling apparel does not—that is dictated from New York, for all countries. Apparel manufacturers consider many issues in deciding where to site facilities; labor costs are one, but relatively small differences in labor costs are not. (Rothstein 2005: 42)

So if it is not just children who are being exploited; if it is not just in one area of the world where labor is being exploited; if technology is regulated but wages are not, then how can taking jobs away from people who need them be the answer? Rothstein, like many others, is beginning to take the pressure off laborers and beginning to put it on industries. Rather than seeking to eradicate these jobs, perhaps a better strategy would be to make the jobs better. As Rothstein points out, there are many issues a manufacturer considers when relocating, cost of labor being one of them, but they are not the only costs. What Rothstein's arguments point out is that the worker may cost the company, but the worker is the least of the company's concerns. In this way, it would seem that relocating to another country merely to exploit a relatively small sector of the population seems not only egregious, but unprofitable.

The worker, for the company, is a fixed value, meaning that no matter where the company settles or how much production costs, the company will *always* have to pay a worker some salary to have a company at all. In this way, workers are more important to companies than arguments about exploitation acknowledge. Rothstein's examples are crucial to our argument because they refute popular ideas about exploitation and introduce new ideas about the nature of exploitation and how to combat it. Once one accepts the elasticity of the term *child laborer*, one must accept that exploitation cannot be solely about age. Rothstein then deconstructs ideas about unfair labor wages, claiming that what we understand as exploitation is really the interaction of business practices on a global scale. These examples show us that our ideas of free market economy are impossibly naive, pointing out that "Even if a modest increase in Indonesia's minimum wage tempted manufacturers to move their facilities to, say, Mexico, the temptation would be frustrated if Mexico simultaneously enforced a comparable increase in its minimum" (Rothstein 2005: 3).

What Rothstein's article on sweatshops brings to the discussion of child labor exploitation is a controlled examination of a difficult issue. Much of the literature on labor exploitation (especially child labor) veers toward emotional response. Rothstein does not lack an emotional response, but he wants to understand how cultural, financial, and historical circumstances also come to bear on our emotional response. This is because he understands that our emotional response to labor exploitation does very little if it constantly leads us astray. In fact, it is not that Rothstein either defends or condemns sweatshops or the use of child labor therein. Rather, he continues to turn the issue around and refine his sense of the nature of exploitation—how it manifests in a workforce. To call the issues of child labor and labor exploitation a prism is apt, for history often provides us with a conflicting sense of ethical responsibility. It is widely known that in America—and elsewhere—children were a viable part of the early industrial labor force. How then, in less than 200 years, did the ethical imperative change so drastically? Rothstein links this shift to FDR and the FLSA, "Until Franklin Roosevelt intimidated the Supreme Court, justices prohibited sweatshop regulation on constitutional grounds" (Rothstein 2005: 3). Again, we contend with a cultural perspective, not economic reality.

CONCLUSION

The general ethos of this article refrains from making casual recommendations on serious global matters. The goal is not to reveal the ills of an industry but openly to investigate viable scenarios, which exist within the fair labor debate. What is revealed is the tension between an idealistic sense of justice and a distorted sense of poverty as witnessed on a global scale. What becomes necessary is an approach to labor reform, which acknowledges the myriad ways in which global issues in economy, law, and politics affect individual choices. One must fight for the establishment of good working conditions.

References

HRM Guide. 2005. "Wal-Mart Fined for Child Labor Violations." *HRM Guide* February 15. http://www.hrmguide.com/relations/walmart-child-labor.htm, accessed June 27, 2009.

Moore, Karen. 2003. "Enduring Poverty and the Conditions of Childhood: Lifecourse and Intergenerational Poverty Transmissions." *World Development* 31(3): 533–54.

Piore, Michael. 1997. "The Economics of the Sweatshop." In Andrew Ross (ed.) *No Sweat: Fashion, Free Trade, and the Rights of Garments Workers*, pp. 135–43. London: Verso.

Rothstein, Richard. 2005. "Defending Sweatshops: Too Much Logic, Too Little Evidence" [electronic version]. *Dissent Magazine* Spring: 1–8.

Singer, Sally. 1997. "Rat-Catching: An Interview with Bud Konheim." In Andrew Ross (ed.) *No Sweat: Fashion, Free Trade, and the Rights of Garments Workers*, pp. 123–35. London: Verso.

Notes

1. *Webster's College Dictionary,* s.v. "exploitation."
2. UNITE is the acronym for the Union of Needletrades, Industrial and Textile Employees.

15

DRESS AND DISASTER:
Fashioning creative responses to disaster

Valerie Rangel[1]

In 2010, *Vogue* magazine (Italia) featured a fashion spread inspired by the BP Deepwater Horizon oil spill on the Gulf of Mexico that depicted models in high fashion clothing drenched in oil and dirt, spitting up seawater and in some cases lifeless and washed ashore. Titled *Water and Oil* these provocative images by photographer Steven Meisel drew immense criticism from many readers and bloggers. As one blogger noted 'Oil and Water don't mix. Nor does fashion and natural disasters' (Kelsey 2010). In using the medium of fashion to capture the devastation caused, to what extent did *Vogue*'s images engage with the issues at hand? Did the glamorization of the event speak to the reality of the tragedy? Was the creative outcome constructively aligned to meet personal and social needs? What does the fashion industry contribute to ameliorating the impacts of disaster and to what extent is the response socially responsible? The focus of this article is to examine the creative responses undertaken by the fashion industry in response to disaster and the extent to which their creative initiatives can contribute to enhancing the lives of individuals affected by disaster. Addressing these issues will enable us to understand how the fashion industry might contribute to the impacts of disaster in ways that are meaningful and socially responsible.

Empathizing and supporting disaster victims forms an important part of the fashion industry's corporate social responsibility (CSR) agenda. Yet, the industry's response to disaster has largely remained ignored in literature on fashion and dress. Researchers (Dickson et al. 2009; Fletcher and Grose 2012; Minney 2011; Paulins and Hillery 2009) addressing social responsibility in fashion have typically centred on labour rights, fair trade manufacturing and sourcing practices as well as marketing and environmental issues. While these researchers have contributed to our knowledge of social responsibility within the fashion industry, research addressing the specific area of disaster response has yet to be conducted. In a similar vein, much of the literature on disasters (Fischer 2008; Gillespie and Danso 2010; Rozario 2007; Stohr and Sinclair 2006) is often devoted to the reconstruction efforts of architects, urban planners and non-profit agencies and very little is mentioned about the efforts of fashion industry professionals and their contribution towards disaster response and recovery.

RESPONSE TO DISASTER

The increasing frequency of natural and manmade disasters in recent years, ranging from hurricane Sandy (2012) and the Japan earthquake (2011) to the Deepwater Horizon oil spill (2010) and hurricane Katrina (2005), have drawn attention to the widespread destruction of life and property and the need for critical social and economic intervention. Although responses to disaster typically include the involvement of engineers and architects, an increasing number of contemporary artists such as Mella Jaarsma, Hussein Chalayan and Lucy and Jorge Orta have attempted to use the medium of clothing to draw public attention,

---

[1] From Valerie Rangel (2014), Dress and Disaster: Fashioning Creative Responses to Disaster in Fashion, Style & Popular Culture, Volume 1, Issue 2, pp 161–173, Intellect.

promote social awareness and encourage creative solutions to the problems of disaster.

British cultural activist and artist Lucy Orta's work centres on the mobile and transformative properties of clothing, and ways in which they can be manipulated, transformed and reconstructed to have multiple meanings for users impacted by disaster. In her 1998 *Refuge Wear* series, Orta created weatherproof clothing equipped with food, water, medicines and other essential supplies that could convert to wearable mobile shelters with the intention of providing shelter and comfort to individual wearers. From the *Habitent* (1992-1993) designed to meet the survival needs of an individual to the more elaborate *Collective Survival Sac* (1996) that allowed individuals to connect to larger communities, Orta's designs reflect a serious attempt at exploring how clothing can serve as a vehicle for disaster intervention. Orta's work speaks not only to the physical but also the psychological well being of individuals affected by disaster. For example, in the *Identity + Refuge* workshop of 1995 Orta encouraged residents of a shelter to redesign second hand clothes in new and innovative ways. For Orta, the creative process of redesigning clothes was not only therapeutic in helping disaster victims overcome feelings of helplessness and dependency, but it also empowered them by imparting them with creative skills and the opportunity to earn an income (2010: 35).

The work of Turkish Cypriot fashion designer Hussein Chalayan reflects similar attempts at redefining the role of clothing to address problems of survival, shelter and homelessness. In his Fall/Winter 2000 collection titled *Afterwords,* Chalayan attempted to capture the realities of disaster victims who are compelled to flee with little or no belongings. Inspired by the Turkish invasion of 1974 and the subsequent migration of Cypriots to Britain, this collection, presented as a performance, began with models sitting on chairs around a central coffee table. As the performance progressed, the chairs transformed into suitcases while the grey coloured chair slipcovers were altered into dresses for the models and the circular wooden coffee table was converted into a multi layered conical skirt. Although Chalayan's collection was devoted more to the concept of disaster rather than to wearable solutions, it made a significant impact in drawing attention to the notion of clothing as architecture and initiated thinking around the themes of displacement and shelter.

The themes of alienation, displacement and loss of identity caused by disaster are also central to the work of Indonesian artist Mella Jaarsma. For example, in her *Shelter Me* series, Jaarsma explored the parallels between clothing and architecture by creating elaborate three dimensional movable shelters out of wood, flexible bark and zinc that protectively enclosed the wearer. Reminiscent of ancient Chinese shrines, Jaarsma's costume like installation symbolized the need for physical, emotional and psychological security and was designed to draw attention to the vulnerability and isolation of disaster victims.[1] Although Orta, Chalayan and Jaarsma's work offers ideological rather than pragmatic solutions to disaster, they are able to effectively raise critical awareness and stimulate social debate. Their ability to render meaning is largely determined by their position within the artistic sphere rather than the commercial sphere. Their work has and continues to be radically different from mainstream practices where there is greater concern to create products that ensure profitability.

One of the most common responses by the mainstream fashion industry to support disaster survivors has been through fashion fundraisers and the sales of cause-related fashion merchandise such as 'T' shirts, handbags, scarves and accessories.[2] However, as an increasing number of retailers use the sales of cause-related fashion merchandise to show allegiance to disaster relief efforts, there has been considerable criticism that these initiatives lack a deeper social commitment and are no more than a marketing ploy designed to capitalize on public sentiment. Intervention efforts by the industry have also frequently highlighted the existing tension between the need to provide social value and the need to increase product demand. For instance, in the wake of hurricane Sandy the clothing retailer American Apparel launched an advertising campaign that announced 'In case you're bored during the storm, 20 percent off everything for the next 36 hours' (Blank 2012). Such responses not only fail to empathize with the suffering and trauma of individuals impacted, but it also underscores the trivialization of disaster by retailers for their own self-promotion.

This criticism also extends to high fashion runway shows where it has become common for designers to capitalize on the spectacle of disaster to draw public attention to their work. For example, in his 2011 Fall/Winter haute couture collection, designer Giorgio Armani sought to pay tribute to the victims of the 2011 earthquake in Japan by featuring one of a kind couture creations inspired by traditional Japanese textiles and kimonos. Not only did the opulent fabrics and exquisitely designed garments in this collection evoke an aura of sophistication and luxury that seemed far removed from the realities of those impacted by the earthquake, but also, by placing the garments within the realm of the couture system, Armani's collection served as a reminder of the visible disconnect between the exclusive world of haute couture and the functional everyday clothing needs of disaster victims.

This proclivity to treat disasters as lucrative brand building opportunities is further amplified in fashion photography. For example, in the wake of the deadly Sichuan earthquake of 2008, the Chinese magazine *New Travel Weekly* featured skimpily dressed models posing in the rubble of collapsed buildings. Although the magazine was promptly closed down due to the insensitive nature of the photographs, these images are reminders of the capitalist methods by which fashion marketers' tap into catastrophic events to enhance production and consumption of their clothing. It could be argued that these photographs represent an attempt at injecting reality and credibility into fashion photography. However, the overtly sexual representations of the models in the photographs suggests a reading of fashion that is more concerned with the creation of desire than with addressing and exposing critical issues related to disaster.

Historian Kevin Rozario (2007) has argued that in today's society, disasters are presented as sensational spectacles where the focus is on the visual rather than moral significance of the event. Spectacle has always been an inherent part of the fashion experience. From spectacular runway settings and exclusive locales to pop star performances and high-tech extravaganzas, fashion has always been governed by excess, theatricality and fantasy. However, what we are currently witnessing in fashion is a new form of consumer culture where design is dominated by the visual spectacle with a marked irreverence towards social sensitivity and practicality.

CREATIVITY AND DISASTER

In order to assess the fashion industry's response to disaster, it is important to acknowledge the role and influence of creativity. Understanding the notion of creativity is vital as it has the potential to provide new ways for the fashion industry to address the complex problems associated with disaster in society and to stimulate positive change.

A good example of design that fits in within the framework of creativity and addresses the needs of individuals impacted by disaster is the *Emergency Bra* by Dr Elena Bodnar. Inspired by the Chernobyl nuclear disaster of 1986, the *Emergency Bra* is quite literally a bra that can be separated and converted into two face masks designed to filter out harmful pollutants released by biological explosions and natural disasters. The bra also has an inbuilt radiation sensor in the front opening that changes colour in the presence of elevated radiation levels. Despite the obvious humour and sexual overtones of this design, it exemplifies the way in which a simple and inexpensive item of everyday clothing can be creatively redesigned in ways to equip and protect the wearer from the impact of disaster. But more importantly, it is a striking example of how creativity in fashion can contribute towards stimulating desirable responses to disaster.

Another example of design that bridges the gap between aesthetics, innovation and functionality while addressing the needs of marginalized communities in society is the *Empowerment Plan*. Founded by designer Veronika Scott, this Detroit based non-profit organization provides homeless individuals with an inexpensive wind and water resistant *Element S(urvival) Coat* that transforms into a sleeping bag at night to keep homeless individuals warm and safe from the elements of nature. By reusing excess insulation materials from the housing and automobile industry, the *Element S(urvival) Coat* provides a cost effective and sustainable solution to addressing the issue of homelessness. As winner of the 2011 International Design Excellence Award, the *Element S(urvival) Coat* makes a significant contribution towards the physical well being of homeless individuals and in doing so, offers tremendous potential for use by victims of disaster.

CAUSE-RELATED CONSUMPTION

In a 2013 survey conducted by Cone Communications that examined global attitudes, perceptions and behaviours towards cause-related merchandise, 91 per cent of consumers indicated that their support for a brand was positively influenced by the brand's involvement with a social cause (2013: 18). These figures imply a strong correlation between consumers purchasing behaviour and the fashion industry's involvement through cause-related merchandising. This relationship reinforces the role of the consumer in disaster recovery efforts, implying that it is their consumption of cause-related merchandise that makes response efforts for disaster successful.

For many consumers, the attraction to cause-related merchandise lies not only in the 'use value' or 'aesthetic value' of the fashion merchandise but also to a large measure in the social image that people wish to project of themselves. Alison Lurie (1981), Fred Davis (1992) and Anne Hollander (1993) have suggested that fashion is very much like verbal communication that has the power to convey messages about the wearer's identities and self-image. Thus, the consumption of cause-related merchandise enables consumers to project a self-image of empathy, altruism and social responsibility.

At the same time, the high level of scepticism among the general public about the objectives of cause-related marketing, results in diluting its symbolic meaning and thereby decreases its value. Alison DaSila, the executive vice president for Cone Communications points out that although consumers today are eager to assist with a cause, they are '. . . more sophisticated about who and what deserves their hard earned dollars. They're no longer blindly buying the cause ribbon or environmental seal of the day. They want to understand their individual and collective impact before purchasing' (Cone Communications 2013: 37).

These developments are telling of the trend among manufacturers who today no longer claim 'charity' as the defining norm of cause-related merchandise, but instead make deliberate efforts to frame cause-related merchandise as a legitimate business activity. According to Evangeline M. Heiliger (2012), the aim in doing so is to make the capitalist mode of production seem good and ethical. Heiliger notes that by framing cause-merchandise as 'ethical consumption' the industry strategically sets up consumers of the merchandise as '. . . more thoughtful, mindful and moral than other types of consumers' (Heiliger 2012: 159). This deliberate positioning of cause-related merchandise not only portrays consumers as legitimate supporters of social change, but it also lends credibility to the retail efforts of manufacturers. To what extent then, are these initiatives committed to the fashion industry's corporate social agenda? How can they be better aligned to improve responses to disaster?

CORPORATE SOCIAL RESPONSIBILITY AND DISASTER

Understanding an organization's priorities as it relates to social causes is not easy and varies across the industry. What might appear at first glance as a genuine involvement in social causes could well be a *façade* that conceals other private motives of an organization. One such example is the Fashion Delivers Charitable Foundation, a non-profit fashion organization that collects excess clothing inventory and discontinued products from apparel manufactures and directs them to charitable organizations that in turn distributes them to individuals. Despite the seemingly well-intentioned efforts of the organization and its members, it can be argued that their altruistic actions stem from their need to dispose of overstock and overrun merchandise rather than a genuine sense of responsibility to help victims of disaster.

In a study on CSR, John L. Campbell (2007) noted that the extent of an organization's involvement and engagement with social issues was dependent on its level of financial performance, its involvement with philanthropic organizations and the influence of state regulators and the press. While these factors influence an organization's participation in CSR, there are no official standards to assess the level of engagement and commitment towards a cause. Consumer responses from an online survey on CSR reveal that although 93 per cent of Americans viewed companies having a social agenda favourably, only 16 per cent of the respondents were convinced about the positive impact of CSR on social issues (Cone Communications 2013: 36). These low levels of consumer confidence suggest that the effectiveness of CSR initiatives is largely dependent on the voluntary affirmative actions of member organizations.

Rozario (2007) has argued that despite the destruction caused by disasters, they should be considered as positive forces since they present an opportunity for individuals to rethink existing social, environmental and public policies. At a time when business involvement in communities and social causes is becoming increasingly important to consumers, now is the time to rethink how social responsibility towards disaster can be addressed by the fashion industry. Some strategies for social responsibility in fashion as it relates to disaster could include:

- *Community engagement*: The success of social responsibility in the fashion industry can only be made possible with the active involvement of relief organizations, members of society and disaster victims. Participation of the community enables designers to gather input, share ideas and implement strategies to increase the effectiveness of their design ideas.

- *Cross-disciplinary collaboration*: A multidisciplinary approach between fashion and other design disciplines could also serve as a unique opportunity for designers to collaboratively analyse, explore and address disaster-related issues.

- *Commitment to CSR*: There is need for the industry to move away from the stylized manipulation of disaster imagery and marketing campaigns that claim support of disaster. What are needed instead are systematic strategies that nurture authenticity, innovation and sustainability. The fashion industry needs to go beyond monetary assistance to provide physical and psychological support to disaster survivors. Stereotypical responses preclude designers from conducting a thorough investigation into how fashion can be used to develop a holistic and meaningful response to disaster. These responses will only come to fruition when designers question the motives underlying their current social initiatives and recognize that fulfilling the needs of disaster victims can deliver both economic and social currency.

References

Blank, Jessica (2012), 'Hurricane Sandy sales: Good business or bad taste?', http://abcnews.go.com/blogs/business/2012/10/hurricane-sandy-sales-good-business-or-bad-taste/. Accessed 16 January 2013.

Campbell, John L. (2007), 'Why would corporations behave in socially responsible ways?: An institutional theory of corporate social responsibility', *The Academy of Management Review*, 32:3, pp. 946–67.

Cone Communications /Echo Research (2013), *Global CSR Study* (pdf), Cone Communications Public Relations & Marketing: Boston, MA, pp. 1–68. http://www.conecomm.com/global-csr-study. Accessed 20 July 2013.

Davis, Fred (1992), *Fashion, Culture, and Identity*, Chicago: University of Chicago Press.

Dickson, Marsha A., Suzanne Loker and Molly Eckman (2009), *Social Responsibility in the Global Apparel Industry*. New York: Fairchild Books.

Fischer, Henry W. III (2008), *Response to Disaster: Fact Versus Fiction and its Perpetuation: The Sociology of Disaster*, 3rd ed., Maryland: University Press of America.

Fletcher, Kate and Lynda Grose (2012), *Fashion and Sustainability: Design for Change*, London: Laurence King Publishing Ltd.

Gillespie, David F. and Kofi Danso (eds) (2010), *Disaster Concepts and Issues: A Guide for Social Work Education and Practice*, Virginia: Council on Social Work Education.

Heiliger, Evangeline M. (2012), 'Ado(red), abho(red), dissapea(red): Fashioning race, poverty, and morality under product (Red)™', in Shira Tarrant and Marjorie Jolles (eds), *Fashion Talks: Undressing the Power of Style*. New York: State University of New York Press, pp. 149–64.

Hollander, Anne (1993), *Seeing Through Clothes*, Berkley: University of California Press.
Kelsey, Emily (2010), 'Italian Vogue's oil spill fashion shoot', http://kelseyemily.blogspot.com/2010/08/italian-vogues-oil-spill-fashion-shoot.html. Accessed 12 December 2012.
Lurie, Alison (1981), *The Language of Clothes*, New York: Henry Holt and Company.
Merriam-Webster (2013), 'Creativity', http://www.merriam-webster.com/dictionary/creativity. Accessed 1 September 2013.
Minney, Safia (2011), *Naked Fashion: The New Sustainable Fashion Revolution*, London: New Internationalist Publications Ltd.
Orta, Lucy (2010), 'Questioning identity', in Abbie Coppard, Gabi Scardi and Lucy Orta (eds), *Aware: Art Fashion Identity*, 33–39. Italy: Damiani.
Paulins, V. Ann and Julie L. Hillery. (2009), *Ethics in the Fashion Industry*, New York: Fairchild Books.
Rozario, Kevin (2007), *The Culture of Calamity: Disaster and the Making of Modern America*, 1st ed., Chicago: University of Chicago Press.
Stohr, Kate and Cameron Sinclair (eds) (2006), *Design Like You Give a Damn: Architectural Responses to Humanitarian Crisis*, London: Thames and Hudson.

Notes

1. In *This Land is Ours* (2007), Jaarsma created tent like structures with digital photographs of disaster printed on them as a reminder of the homes destroyed by the earthquake in Yogyakarta, Indonesia. The tents also served as a satirical comment on the role of NGO's and the way in which their desire to claim control of the devastated landscape dominated their efforts to address the trauma and loss of the community.
2. Other examples include projects such as Rosa Loves (that focuses on raising monetary support through the design of 'T' shirts), The Urban Forest Project (where prominent designers created products that addressed environmental issues) and the Awareness Bracelets (popularized by Lance Armstrong showing solidarity towards a cause).

FURTHER READING

Beard, Nathaniel Dafydd, "The Branding of Ethical Fashion and Consumer: A Luxury Niche Market Reality, *Fashion Theory*, Volume 12, Issue 4, Taylor & Francis.

Blackburn, R.S. (ed.) (2015), *Sustainable Apparel: Production, Processing and Recycling*, Cambridge, UK: Woodhead Publishing.

Brown, S. (2013), *Refashioned: Cutting-Edge Clothing from Upcycled Materials*, London: Laurence King Publishing Ltd.

Clark, Hazel, "Slow + Fashion –an Oxymoron – or a Promise for the Future…?, *Fashion Theory*, Volume 12, Issue 4, Taylor & Francis.

Clark-Esposito, Deanna (2018), *A Practical Guide to Fashion Law and Compliance*, New York: Bloomsbury.

Dickson, M.A., S. Loker and M. Eckman. (2009), *Social Responsibility in the Global Apparel Industry*, New York: Fairchild Books.

Hethorn, J. and C. Ulasewicz (eds.) (2015), *Sustainable Fashion What's Next?: A Conversation about Issues, Practices and Possibilities (2nd ed.)*, New York: Fairchild Books.

Kruger, H., D-K. Plannthin, E. H. Dahl and T. Hjort (eds.) (2012), *Guidelines II: A handbook on Sustainability in Fashion*, Denmark: Sustainable Solution Design Association.

Pinkhasov, M. and R.J. Nair. (2014), *Real Luxury: How Luxury Brands Can Create Value for the Long Term*, New York: Palgrave Macmillan.

Rissanen, T. and H. McQuillan (2016), *Zero-waste Fashion Design*, New York: Fairchild Books.

Winge, Theresa, "Green is the New Black: Celebrity Chic and the 'Green' Commodity of Fetish", *Fashion Theory*, Volume 12, No. 4, Taylor & Francis.

Figure 14 Justin O' Shea, Thom Browne. Photo Courtesy of Brent Luvaas.
Source: Brent Luvaas

Part IV

Brick and Mortar Retailing and Shopping

Figure 15 Luanna Perez-Garreaud. Photo Courtesy of Brent Luvaas.
Source: Brent Luvaas

INTRODUCTION

Catharine Weiss

Brick and Mortar Retailing and Shopping remain inspirational and transformative in their practices and methods. Contemporary retailers' link traditional and transformational identities to their brands through elements such as artisanship, celebrity and product affiliations, connections between the shopping experience and location, and operational practices aligned with social responsibility. With a mission to connect with the consumer, merchants continue to re-create a reason for the shopper to patron the store. Yet, the idea of tradition and transformation, something that perpetuates the shopping experience, is never lost for brands that understand its importance. Tradition and transformation become the essential elements that propel the merchant forward and enable retail survival.

For many retailers, tradition is the backbone of the store with stories from the past, reflected in design aesthetic, the store's physical space, manufacturing, and unique founding families. Tradition aligns itself with quality, value, and trust. As consumers change over time, the face of brick and mortar retailing also needs to change. Transformation provides the conduit for retailers to re-imagine themselves and it offers new ways of communicating and working with the consumer. The dynamics of a traditional yet transformed store gives a retail brand an updated identity. The idea that tradition creates brand loyalty can be traced back to companies such as Nordstrom's, Filenes, Strawbridge and Clothier, Marshall Fields, Bendel's and many of the iconic department stores in the industry. Although some merchants have not survived the melding of corporate offices into conglomerates, there are retailers that continue to provide transformational practices as they have evolved with their customer, offering new ways of doing business.

These themes, transformation, luxury, identity and customer exchange; will shape the following chapter. It will highlight retail practices either laced with tradition or uniquely produced for the contemporary customer. It will include five separate articles providing important insight. One article will reference research about the luxury company Hermes and its branded Birkin bag. Here, the author depicts stories of the bag and its acclaimed status through celebrities and the media. The chapter will also include research that renders new meaning to local retailing and aesthetics used by Uniqlo in its promotional campaigns. In order to create the local acceptance of a foreign brand the company used local and cultural nuances to promote the store. Additionally, the chapter will include research on obesity and the current perception of fashion students in academe. The author's research reveals the alarming negative perception of contemporary fashion students regarding this social problem. Lastly, the chapter will include research about the history of manufacturing and retailing in the Canadian marketplace. As Canadian merchants become more and more powerful within today's retail environment, (Hudson's Bay makes a bid for Macy's) the growth of their market sector, whether in manufacturing or retail, becomes a vital issue to study. (Reuters, 2017) Therefore, the articles in this chapter present compelling examples of research in brick and mortar retailing and shopping activities that are important in the field and for its future.

IDENTITY

Transformation, as a way of assigning meaning to the individual during his or her shopping experience, continues to play a pivotal role for luxury retailers such as Hermes. The tradition of Hermes' quality and craft continues to be sought after as the notion of "celebrity-ness" aligns itself with the brand through film and the backdrop of fashion narratives. The infamous Birkin bag, Hermes' signature piece, is reflected in the media as an obsession, a coveted acquisition, and status-assigning accessory. Anita Boyd describes this obsession in her article "Oh, Honey! It's not so much the Style, it's what Carrying it Means': Hermès Bags and the Transformative Process." (Boyd, 2014) The author takes us on a journey through various cinema and television scenes where characters somehow affix their own status through the acquisition of a Birkin, whether through their own personal means or as a gift. Using scenes from "Sex and the City" and other cinematic films, the depiction of women and their quest for a Birkin becomes humorous at best.

The factor that remains distinctive is that Hermes and the luxury brand market rely heavily on an identifiable meaning once the consumer acquires and wears their products. The Birkin has developed a fashion culture of its own, representative of wealth and high society. With a price point of $50,000 upwards, many urban women would forego a down payment on a condominium in the city to own and wear a Birkin with pride. Hermes, in its own portrayal of fine luxury and craft, offers this iconic bag in discrete yet alluring ways that increase the impression of the unattainable. Waiting lists to buy the bag, which is fully made by hand, creates a mystique that the company is known for and generates high demand among elite consumers. Interestingly, Hermes corporate has not intentionally endorsed this coveted status. The appeal of the Birkin bag is derived from a fashion legend and built on various cultural portrayals in movies and television, which has been used to establish its unique position in the luxury market as the ultimate possession.

LOCATION

Myles Ethan Lascity discusses the uniqueness of Uniqlo and its innovative connection with the local consumer. Uniqlo has attempted to build its own transformation through its in-store experiences and relational spaces. With each urban location comes a re-branded identity specifically assigned to the location of the store. Using contextual meaning in local geography and social nuances, it has enhanced the shopping experience to reflect the taste of the native community. This not only provides a connection for the consumer through experiential shopping, but also provides an entry point for a retailer that may have a difficult time capturing a new customer base in a new market. Lascity's research reflects the notion that consumers assign meaning to cities and geographic locations. With these meanings come a loyalty and trust. Retailers that use these local nuances in order to brand their own identity walk a fine line between what they represent as a company and how they are trying to attract the customer. However, according to the author, providing a shopping experience that includes local substance has been successful for this Japanese merchant. (Lascity, 2016) The company, in its initial store opening promotions, created excitement with unique contests and local celebrities. Drawing from local flavor and regional distinctions, it allowed the company to present itself in an identifiable way to the consumer and reduce its intimidation factor as a foreign brand. This tactic built trust within the local community and, more importantly, with its customer base.

Uniqlo has also created "fantastical" storefronts that include large glass windows and towering floors filled with merchandise. (Lascity, 2016) Competing against larger American department stores, the company has creatively and effectively transformed itself given its own urban placement. Many foreign retailers have not been so lucky in capturing the American market. Often, because of increased competition at Uniqlo's particular price point, the entry into this market was risky, but Uniqlo positioned itself as a European value brand, offering basics and some fashion forward pieces at substantially lower prices than their competition. They specifically opened in urban areas instead of suburban locations. The article is invaluable in its depiction of an alternative way of promoting retail for the value market.

LEADERSHIP

Mamp and Marcketti review both tradition and transformation in their article about Bonwit Teller. Their brief history of Hortense Odium, President and Chairwoman of Bonwit's from 1934 to 1944, serves as an interesting example of innovation and success. Bonwit's had a tradition of luxury and exclusive customer service, but it was not always the case and did not start that way at its inception. Founded in 1840 and managed by primarily male senior executives, the retailer did not reflect a customer centric appeal that it was known for during Odium's leadership. Odium's husband, owner of Bonwit's in 1934, asked his wife to take on several leadership roles. She literally had no experience for the job other than as an avid shopper herself. Coming from a certain level of sophistication bestowed upon her through her family and marriage, she transformed the store with new product categories and leadership styles that turned the business into a customer centric experience. Her innovative and transformative ideas played an important role in creating the timeless retail brand. Odium also carefully managed and, in many cases, protected her staff, which was unheard of at the time. She created new departments and product offerings that filled the needs of both local consumers and tourists, while also becoming one of the first female retail leaders of her time. Although history does reflect her reluctance in taking on the role, her leadership in retail was founded on common sense and female sensibilities. (Mamp & Marcketti, 2015)

GROWTH

Cynthia Cooper details the development of the fashion industry in Canada in her article called "The Garment Industry and Retailing in Canada." (Cooper, 2010) The author provides the reader with a series of benchmarks that followed the industry's growth from its beginning in the 1830s. To date, fashion manufacturing is one of the largest industries in Canada and is also one of the economic mainstays for provinces such as Quebec. Much of Canada's apparel manufacturing growth was connected to advancements in technology, as well the availability of immigrant workers and women prepared to take on lower paying roles. The industry became increasingly automated as the author states, "by 1905, 80 to 90 percent of Canadian men's clothing was factory made." The author goes on to review growing and shrinking markets during several decades that followed suit with the US apparel industry. Two significant occurrences changed the sector according to the author: 1) the 1930s depression, which exacerbated manufacturing closures and, 2) the post war boom, which led the industry towards new growth. The latter situation helped develop Canadian manufacturing and established the foundations for the retail industry today. Moreover, during the postwar period, many of the traditional factories replaced their logistics with more efficient means of production. The market also struggled later in the 20th century with competition from cheaper imports coming from the US and China. In response, governmental agencies were set up to combat the competition, bringing Canada into "a more competitive position during the 1970s as exports tripled in 1967." The author reviews how these changes in the marketplace continue to fuel contemporary growth as Canadian manufacturing becomes a more viable and less risky alternative to the current administration's push to bring manufacturing back to the US.

Cooper supports her argument by highlighting many of the great companies that excelled in areas of retail and manufacturing expertise in Canada, such as Peerless and Utex. Canadelle, which began in 1939, was the maker of the Wonderbra and Playtex brands, for example. None of these giants stood out more than T. Eaton, Co. During the 1950s, the retailer and manufacturer also became one of the biggest employers in the country. It existed for more than 130 years, and the store name became synonymous with old world merchants and was also a mail order company known just as "Eaton's." Sears ended up buying out some of the Eaton stores during the late 20th century.

In addition to Eaton's, another great name in the world of Canadian retail is Holt Renfrew. The retailer collaborated with Dior, who at the time was one of its vendors, to ensure that the designer's apparel was made locally for Canadian customers. Other prominent companies emerged in the Canadian market such as Hudson's Bay which as Canada's oldest merchant, with origins in the 1600s fur trade, was eventually renamed The Bay.

Today some of the outstanding Canadian retailers are names such as the national chain Reitman's. Both a merchant and manufacturer, the chain owns over 800 stores across the country. Much of its production actually occurs within Canada's borders. Another important chain is the store called Boutique San Francisco with over 140 shops. Several of the more recent retailers have either collaborated with US merchants or expanded their businesses into the states. To date, some of the most influential apparel brands are lululemon Athletica and Canada Goose. With the ever-increasing opportunities that NAFTA provides, this market segment continues to increase its diffusion into the American economy as well as across the globe. The industry has also allotted better funding towards infrastructure and improvements within its own borders.

IMAGE

Traditional roles through image and identity have plagued fashion and fashion retailers in the sense we continue to produce gender and physical stereotypes. The industry is rife with issues concerning marginalization and sexualization of women, more specifically the issue of size. Countries such as France have banned thin models representative in fashion images and on the runway. Retail media channels and some advertisers have followed suit out of necessity and public outcry. The impact of the fashion image and stereotypes subsequently created by those images are inherently the responsibility of the industry. Fashion also has an obligation to teach the leaders of tomorrow. As more and more companies take a stand against the issue of fat shaming and incorporate social responsibility into their business model, the last place one would expect this issue to occur would be on a college campus. In an article by Deborah Christel, the author researches the notion of fat shaming and preexisting perceptions of obesity. (Christel, 2014) Tradition, here, is located in idea that being fat is unattractive in western culture. Moreover, her research was conducted on fashion students and majors-the leaders of retails future. Her findings become critical in an overlooked area of industry transformation. As fashion works towards an unbiased playing field, realistic product offerings and identifiable imagery, Christel's research reflects on the need for a further change in cultural perception within the confines of academe. If we are in fact training our fashion leaders of tomorrow, then the author brings to light a critical step in reforming what we can do to make changes on a broader scale.

SUMMARY

Fashion retailers continue to find new ways to build on traditional views and societal nuances. Using their own history or the history of a geographic area, retailers re-brand and transform their images to accommodate the flavor of the local customer. The marriage of celebrity and the fashion brand will only increase as consumers continue to affix themselves in a world of social media and publicity. The alignment of product acquisition and the identity of a brand promoted by a famous bloggers, influencers, brand ambassadors, celebrities or sports heroes, continues to work well for brick and mortar retailers. Transformation also comes in the way we manage both company and staff as merchants innovate their management styles and practices to be customer and employee centric. Great managing executives, such as Hortense Odium, woman that offered leadership style and creativity way before her time, provide insights for contemporary leadership structures. We can align the same ideas regarding innovation and customer experience as we review the promotional strategies of Uniqlo, creating a very different shopping experience catering to the unquenchable taste of a fickle consumer. Other transformations are slow but necessary as the findings presented in the chapter focussing on obesity and ways of thinking at the college level are critical and could be transformative in the future. Finally, fashion retail and manufacturing sectors, such as those found in Canada, become increasingly important as potential growth areas for trade and expansion with retailers and manufacturing given that Canada offers an affordable and close alternative for the American industry. It has also earned its own acclaim with iconic retailers in the global arena such as Eaton's and The Bay and currently with one of the hottest 'athleisurewear' brands in the world, lululemon. The Canadian retail sector continues to grow and has now become a strong contender in the global economy demonstrating how.

References

Boyd, A., 2014. Oh, honey! It's not so much the style, it's what carrying it means': Hermès bags and the transformative process. *Intellect*, 1 (Fashion Style and Popular Culture), pp. 81–96.

Christel, D., 2014. It's your Fault you're Fat: Judgements of Responsibility and Social Conduct in the Fashion Industry. *Clothing Cultures by Intellect*, 1(3), pp. 303–320.

Cooper, C., 2010. The Garment Industry and Retailing in Canada. In: P. Tortora, ed. *Berg Encyclopedia of World Dress and Fashion*. London: Berg Encyclopedia of World Dress and Fashion: the United States and Canada, pp. 110–121.

Lascity, M. E. (2016). *Stores, Shoppers and Mediated Images: The Relational Space of Uniqlo*. Philadelphia: NA.

Mamp, M. & S. B. Marcketti. (2015). "Creating a Woman's Place: The bonwit Teller Presidency of Hotense Odium, 1934 to 1940." *Fashion, Style and Popular Culture*, 2(3): NA.

Reuters. (2017). "Canada's Hudson's Bay Makes Takeover Approach for Macy's: Sources". *Reuters*, February 3, p. 1.

16

THE GARMENT INDUSTRY AND RETAILING IN CANADA

Cynthia Cooper[1]

The apparel industry is the tenth-largest manufacturing sector in Canada. Apparel is manufactured in all provinces and territories. Quebec accounts for 55 percent of production, while significant concentrations of firms are found in Ontario, Manitoba, and British Columbia. Montreal is the third-largest apparel manufacturing center in North America, after Los Angeles and New York.

Canada's apparel industry produces a wide range of garments for consumer and specialized markets. Major areas of production include men's, women's, and children's fashion clothing, including knitwear, outerwear, denim, pants, shirts, and blouses; intimate apparel and sleepwear; tailored clothing; active sportswear; fur and leather goods; occupational clothing; technical outerwear; hosiery and knitted goods; and other fashion accessories.

While small firms predominate in the industry, Canada also has many large and highly sophisticated manufacturing companies. The majority of these companies are Canadian owned. Only about 2 percent of apparel firms are foreign owned, which are mainly subsidiaries of U.S. multinational corporations. Although computer-assisted technology has made inroads in several stages of apparel production, the apparel-manufacturing industry remains fragmented and labor intensive.

Statistics Canada reports that in 2005, the Canadian apparel industry comprised some 2,150 establishments, employed about seventy thousand workers, and shipped CAN$6 billion of apparel, of which some 40 percent was exported, mainly to the United States. For the same year, the Canadian apparel market was valued at CAN$10.4 billion. In 2007, retail markets are expanding rapidly for plus-size clothing as well as environmentally friendly organic clothing and the tween market for those approximately seven to fourteen years old.

EARLY DEVELOPMENT OF THE GARMENT INDUSTRY IN CANADA

Canada's garment industry developed in the nineteenth century. Company records are sparse or nonexistent, and little other evidence survives to document their activity. The industry developed primarily in the cities of Montreal and Toronto and its surrounding areas, including Hamilton, and to a lesser extent in Winnipeg, Edmonton, Vancouver, and Halifax. Montreal and Toronto were suited to become early centers for this industry because of proximity to markets and imported supplies, Montreal particularly because of an abundant rural and immigrant labor supply. In the 1901 census, these two cities together accounted for 55 percent of clothing produced in Canada. By 1928, the provinces of Quebec and Ontario accounted for about 95 percent of the country's garment production. While the industries in the smaller cities cannot compare in the value of their output, apparel manufacturing was still statistically a key sector of employment. The development of the industry in Canada, like elsewhere, is inextricably linked to technology and gender. The numerous Canadian sewing machine manufacturers made technology very accessible to enterprising manufacturers. Women filled the lesser-skilled positions of sewing machine operators, with

---

[1] From Cynthia Cooper, The Garment Industry and Retailing In Canada, Berg Fashion Library.

Canada's industry following gendered patterns of lower wages for women's work. Men almost always held the higher-paying skilled jobs of cutter, presser, and special machine operator. Even through the first half of the twentieth century, men received higher wages than women who performed the same jobs; owners, unions, and society at large agreed this was necessary so that men could support their families.

Immigration and ethnicity also structured and influenced developments in the industry in Montreal and Toronto. Between 1900 and 1920 the Canadian government's open immigration policy drew new labor into these cities. An influx of Jewish immigration gradually shaped not only the clothing workforce in these cities but also its residential communities; in both Montreal and Toronto, the location of the industry developed according to the residential areas of its growing Jewish workforce. The scant research that examines the development of the industry prior to 1871 focuses primarily on Montreal. In the 1830s, the city's population was expanding rapidly, creating a labor pool, a market, and an exchange economy. The first manifestations of larger-scale clothing production are seen with dry goods establishments, which began to manufacture garments on their premises for sale. An excellent example of this transition from retailer to manufacturer is that of the Moss Brothers, English Jews who arrived in Montreal in the 1830s. Their large establishment sold imported English ready-made clothing. By the 1840s they were manufacturing their own merchandise, using outside contractors. By 1856 they had established a five-story factory, the city's largest plant, employing 800 people. Markets for this early ready-to-wear were essentially rural, as urban dwellers continued to have easy access to custom clothing manufacturer. Other large establishments followed in the 1860s. A variety of modes of production existed simultaneously. Menswear was the most developed and specialized sector of the industry throughout the nineteenth century.

Shirt-making was one of the first sectors to be organized into industrial large-scale production. By 1905 it was estimated that 80 to 90 percent of Canadian men's clothing was factory made. The industry was slower to take on the manufacture of the full range of women's clothing. Hoop skirts, or crinolines, were being industrially produced in both Montreal and St. John in the 1860s in shops that were simultaneously manufacturers, wholesalers, and retailers. Whitewear (petticoats, corset covers, and drawers) was soon being factory produced. From 1900 to 1905 whitewear production doubled in Canada due to better and faster machinery. The corset industry also began relatively early. Toronto's Crompton Corset Co. was a key Canadian manufacturer; Dominion Corset Co., founded in Quebec City in 1886, became a leader throughout North America, Europe, and Australia until it closed in the 1970s.

The knitted goods sector included companies like Knit-to-Fit, founded in Montreal in 1902, which remained in business for seventy-five years. Its initial products were one-piece knitted undergarments for both men and women. Stanfield's in Nova Scotia, a company still running in the twenty-first century, began producing knitted undergarments in the 1890s.

Western Canadian companies dominated the workwear sector. The Winnipeg Shirt and Overall Company was founded in 1889. The Great Western Garment Company, whose factory ran in Edmonton from 1911 to 2004, claimed to be the largest garment manufacturer in the British Commonwealth throughout much of its existence.

TWENTIETH-CENTURY DEVELOPMENT OF THE GARMENT INDUSTRY

Until the end of World War I, the demand for factory-made clothing progressed steadily. Many small shops closed, as larger, vertically integrated businesses increased their production and gained a greater market share. Following the war, this trend was somewhat reversed; small entrepreneurs were able to compete successfully with larger factories. The industry progressed through the 1920s with both large factories and contract shops existing side by side. Business failure in the clothing industry was very common. Contract shops often stayed afloat for only a very short period of time. Through the 1920s, an average 12 percent of menswear businesses and 19 percent of women's wear shops closed each year.

The 1930s brought very difficult economic times with the Great Depression. As markets for clothing were constricted, factories and contract shops alike employed workers for fewer weeks of the year and applied a variety of other cost-cutting measures to wages. Workers fought back by joining unions and striking, making this decade a key period for labor unrest.

The postwar economic boom fueled a period of growth, modernization, and increased efficiency in the apparel industry. It marked the beginning of a new era in which some of the traditional craft skills and sweatshops were gradually replaced by assembly lines and larger manufacturing companies. Technical change occurred steadily but more slowly than in other sectors of industry until it began to progress more rapidly in the 1970s. Styling and design became an increasingly significant aspect of the manufacturing process. From 1952 to 1981, rates of profit were seen to increase.

Perhaps the most significant development in the Canadian apparel industry in the second half of the twentieth century is the substantial increase in world trade in apparel, mostly originating from low-wage, developing countries and destined for high-wage, developed countries. By 1948, import protection for the clothing industry became more structured as Canada negotiated with seven countries in the General Agreement on Tariffs and Trade (GATT).

Through the 1950s the industry's concern about imports expanded to include not only those from the United States and Britain but also from Japan and Eastern Europe, followed by Korea, Hong Kong, and Taiwan. Industry representatives increased pressure on the Canadian government to establish import quotas. Negotiations with the Asian nations culminated in quotas known as *voluntary export restraints*. Gradually from the 1950s through the end of the 1960s, Canadian manufacturers found the growth of cheap imports from Asia and the United States was directing them into a higher-style and quality-market niche, for both the large domestic and small export markets.

In the 1960s, in reaction to the import trends, provincial and federal governments multiplied their initiatives to promote Canada's industry and create an export market. In 1968 the federal Department of Industry, Trade, and Commerce sponsored presentations of Canadian fashion in New York, which were very successful in stimulating sales. It led to a federal review of the industry in 1970, following which it established its Fashion Canada agency, giving it a mandate to promote the quality of Canadian apparel both at home and abroad. A year later it established the Textile and Clothing Board as an advisory arm for the industry. In 1971, exports were reported to have more than tripled since 1967. The 1980s marked a decade of significant growth for the Canadian apparel industry, interrupted by the Canada–U.S. Free Trade Agreement (FTA), which Canada entered in 1989, and the recession of the early 1990s. The industry underwent significant restructuring. Between 1988 and 1993, some eight hundred Canadian firms closed. Then from 1993 to 1995, shipments and employment increased. So did imports; by 1995, when the Agreement on Textiles and Clothing (ATC) stipulated how MFA quotas were to be gradually phased out over a ten-year period, imports were back above 40 percent of the market share.

The drop in domestic market share from increasing imports, as well as the creation of a single North American marketplace, encouraged many Canadian manufacturers to develop an export orientation. The FTA and the North American Free Trade Agreement (NAFTA), entered in 1994, played a role in shaping a significant export market in the United States for Canada's apparel production. From the enacting of the FTA in 1989 to 1997, exports to the United States had quadrupled. In 2007, exports made up 40 percent of Canadian output. Canadian apparel companies have been adjusting to the new trade environment by shifting and focusing their production on selected North American niche markets, where geographical proximity gives them a competitive advantage.

CANADIAN GARMENT MANUFACTURERS

Menswear has remained the strongest sector in Canadian clothing manufacturing. Peerless Clothing in Montreal is North America's largest maker of men's suits and continues to do a substantial proportion of its manufacturing at its Montreal facility. Montreal-based Ballin, founded in 1946, is considered the leading manufacturer of better men's trousers in North America. Riviera Inc., a well-known high-quality trouser manufacturer, was established in 1917. In other sectors, Canadian manufacturers with significant longevity and a high national or international profile include the Utex Fashion Group, founded in 1943, a global manufacturer and marketer of men's and women's outerwear and menswear. Nygård International, a Winnipeg manufacturer founded in 1967, has grown to be the largest sportswear manufacturer in Canada and third largest in North America. Joseph Ribkoff International, a manufacturer of women's high-end clothing, celebrated its fiftieth anniversary in 2007. Ribkoff continues to manufacture apparel in Canada and exports extensively.

Gildan, founded in 1946, is a global marketer and manufacturer of knit apparel. Gildan remains Montreal based but in 2007 moved all its manufacturing outside of Canada. McGregor Hosiery was one of the early knit hosiery manufacturers and remains based in Toronto in the early twenty-first century.

Leading names in denim manufacture include Parasuco, a Montreal-based international jeans label originally established in 1975 as Santana. Western Glove Works Ltd. of Winnipeg has been in existence since 1921, selling Silver Jeans throughout North America, Europe, and Asia, as well as manufacturing other high-end private-label brands.

Canada has also had a history of excelling in the lingerie sector. Canadelle, founded in 1939, is a leading manufacturer of WonderBra and Playtex brands. Montreal-based Arianne Lingerie, founded in 1939, is a globally competitive lingerie brand. In swimwear, Christina America is one of North America's largest manufacturers.

Several Canadian garment manufacturers no longer in business have also had a significant presence in the industry in the latter half of the twentieth century in terms of their longevity, success, and renown. Auckie Sanft founded his company in 1935 and remained in business until 1997. Montroy Coat, known for outerwear, was founded in 1928 and closed in 1987.

Irving Samuel, founded by Samuel Workman in 1946, ran until 1995. Monarch Wear of Manitoba claimed to have been the national leader of Canadian manufacturing for half a century and in the 1970s was the largest jeans manufacturer in Canada; it closed in 1980. All these companies also collaborated with independent Canadian designers to manufacture their lines in the 1960s and 1970s.

THE T. EATON CO.

The T. Eaton Co. deserves a special mention in a history of Canadian garment manufacturing and retailing. This company was a key player in three different sectors. As a department store, it operated for 130 years, from 1869 to 1999. Eaton's, as the firm was popularly known, became a household name in Canada as a mail order company. As one of the early large manufacturers it led the way in vertical integration.

Eaton's introduced its first mail order catalog in 1884. Timothy Eaton was thus able to offer goods from his Toronto store to rural families throughout western Canada, now more accessible with railroad transportation. While a wide variety of merchandise was sold through the catalog, apparel was the dominant commodity and generated the largest sales volume.

Eaton's had been producing small amounts of clothing for the store in the 1870s, but following the first mail order catalog, it launched into manufacturing shirts, women's undergarments, and boys' clothing. By 1893, Timothy Eaton had established a four-story factory in Toronto for women's coats, capes, and skirts; three years later another factory was built for menswear. By 1904, with its new large factory and specialized machines, it was the leader in Toronto's clothing industry. Becoming the most successful of the emerging vertically integrated garment makers, Eaton's expanded its facilities twice more in that decade, making it the largest single center of garment production in the country at the time.

In the 1920s and 1930s, it was estimated that Eaton's had half the market share of all Canadian department stores. Eaton's was at the top in department store sales until 1951, when its competition began to increase. By 1950, with thirty thousand employees, Eaton's was

Canada's third-largest employer, after the railways and the federal government. Because of its size and spread across the country, it had an inevitable influence on retail wages in large cities and smaller communities.

By 1958, Eaton's gradually stopped manufacturing its own goods. It ceased its mail order operations in 1976 because of lack of profitability. It continued through these decades as a strong department store, however, and by 1994 the Eaton family still owned ninety stores in nine Canadian provinces but was beginning to experience serious financial and identity difficulties. Although the Eaton's company went out of business in 1999, its name lives on in shopping complexes in Montreal and Toronto, situated where the stores were formerly located.

MAIL ORDER AND GARMENT RETAIL IN CANADA

Mail order catalog sales were a very important means of garment retail in Canada from the end of the nineteenth century onward, particularly from the 1920s to the 1960s. The first Eaton's catalog, published in 1884, was a thirty-two-page booklet listing department store merchandise. In 1903, catalog sales became a separate operation with its own merchandise assortment. By 1905, Eaton's Winnipeg was issuing its own catalog for customers in the Canadian West, where mail order kept customers in remote communities supplied with essentials. Mail order retailers adapted their offerings and publications to their markets. Eaton's Winnipeg offered its western customers greater variety in outdoor garments, cold-weather clothing, and workwear for men, than Eaton's Toronto, which targeted a female readership. Its portrayals of women and clothing varied in order to appeal to a vast, heterogeneous clientele in the central and eastern parts of Canada, including both rural and urban dwellers.

The Hudson's Bay Company published a catalog from 1896 to 1913. Woodward's fared well in British Columbia from 1898 to 1953, and Army and Navy offered its discount line via mail order from 1919 to 1986. Montreal's Scroggies and Dupuis Frères also published their own mail order catalogs. Scroggies was offering catalogs in French by 1905, placing it twenty years ahead of its competitors in reaching a French-speaking market. Eaton's launched the French version of its mail order catalog in 1928.

In 1953, Simpson's forged a partnership with the U.S. company Sears and Roebuck, and Simpson's-Sears took over Simpson's mail order operation. Its market share increased dramatically after 1976, when Eaton's discontinued its catalog. Sears Canada took over from Simpson's-Sears in 1978. Sears remains the only major Canadian department store with a national presence that continues to produce a print catalog. It has service centers in Belleville, Ontario, and Regina, Saskatchewan. Sears' mail order operation also offers apparel and other general merchandise at its online store.

DEPARTMENT STORES AND GARMENT RETAIL IN CANADA

Department stores have long played a significant role in the history of garment retailing in Canada. In 1930 they accounted for 42 percent of the market share in women's clothing and 27 percent in menswear. In 1951 the market share of women's apparel had dropped to 33 percent, yet millinery and women's wear industry representatives claimed that the three largest department store groups, Eaton's, Simpson's, and Morgan's, determined seasonally whether or not a manufacturer remained in business. Even by 1977, industry advisors remarked that retail buying power was highly concentrated in department store chains. In the early twenty-first century department stores maintain a strong overall 26 percent of the apparel retail market.

In Canada's major cities, department store buildings were urban landmarks, defining apparel shopping districts. Eaton's Toronto, which opened at the corner of Queen and Yonge in 1883, competed with Simpson's on the opposite street corner as of 1896, creating a retail center for well over a century. Henry Morgan's, founded in 1845, established itself in a prominent new building in Montreal in 1891. When Simpson's opened in Montreal in 1905 in the former Murphy's department store, they both anchored a retail mile on busy St. Catherine Street, known as the city's prime fashion center.

The Eaton's company built up to a significant nationwide department store chain. It took hold of the Montreal market in 1925, when it acquired Goodwin's department store. When renovations were complete in 1931, the nine-story building was thought to be the finest in the chain. Eaton's extended its reach in the West in the same decade with stores in Regina in 1926, Saskatoon in 1928, and Calgary and Edmonton in 1929. In 1957, The Hudson's Bay Company (HBC), Canada's oldest retailer, established in 1670 by royal charter for the fur trade, diversified its activities in 1870 to encompass a network of retail stores. From 1881 to 1892, it opened large stores in Winnipeg, Calgary, Vancouver, and Edmonton, followed by Victoria and Saskatoon in the 1920s. The company reinforced its role in the department store retail arena in 1960, with the purchase of Morgan's stores, and began national expansion as The Bay, although they retained the Morgan's name until 1972.

In 1953, Simpson's continued to operate five existing department stores throughout Canada under that name; over the next few decades it would open many new stores under the name Simpson's-Sears. By 1973, the company began to name new stores Sears to avoid confusion with the distinct operation of the Simpson's company. In 1978, Simpson's stores were bought by HBC, and their names changed to The Bay by the late 1980s. Sears bought out the Eaton's department stores that closed in 1999.

Holt Renfrew, which began as a furrier in Quebec City and expanded its operations to include department stores in the major cities of Quebec, Ontario, and western Canada, offered superior custom-design services in its Montreal store. In the 1940s, its Salon Marie-Paule featured creations by Montreal designer Marie-Paule Nolin, who managed a couture workroom of some twenty employees in the store. This arrangement with a local designer has no other known parallel in the history of Canadian department stores and fashion design. From 1951 through the 1970s, Canadians could have Dior couture garments made locally, under a licensing agreement with Holt Renfrew. A workroom of fifteen couture seamstresses created these garments in the Montreal store.

Holt Renfrew still operates nine stores in central and western Canada in the early twenty-first century and occupies the niche of high-end fashion department store, grouping several designer boutiques under one roof. HBC operates five hundred stores across Canadaunder The Bay and Zellers banners, with significant apparel sales. HBC was the fifth-largest Canadian employer in 2003. Sears is Canada's largest and most well-known mass-market department store chain.

BOUTIQUES AND CHAIN STORES IN CANADA

In the 1950s, suburban malls developed rapidly, drawing customers away from downtown cores. Boutiques were on the rise as an alternative to the more traditional department stores and the more expensive specialty shops. Department stores reacted by expanding the number of "boutique" spaces within their walls. Window displays and visual merchandising in clothing stores became much more sophisticated.

Of the 1960s boutiques, outstanding examples were Unicorn and Poupée Rouge in Toronto. In Montreal one incarnation of the boutique Le Château followed this model, offering fashion-forward youthful styles. Numerous Canadian manufacturer-retailers developed through the 1970s, the presence of their boutiques in shopping malls giving them extensive market exposure. By the late 1970s, industry advisors were noting that retailers who were not directly involved in manufacturing were increasingly dictating the design aspect of the manufacturing process because of their market knowledge.

In the 1980s, the market became saturated for Canadian apparel retail. Many of Canada's top fashion retailers expanded into the United States, only to suffer significant losses. The 1980s U.S. expansion of Dylex, the largest clothing manufacturer-retailer in the country and one of its one hundred largest companies, proved disastrous and the company has since folded. Dylex enjoyed two decades of success in Canada and at its apogee owned or had interests in twenty-seven hundred stores.

The apparel market in Canada was particularly hard hit by the 1990–1991 recession. In the 1990s, there was an influx of U.S. retailers into the Canadian market, where they now dominate. A wave of consolidations took place, as newer vendors with discount lines moved in and large department store chains like Eaton's closed their doors.

In 2007 in Canada, apparel specialty chain stores dominated the market, with more than 33 percent of the market share. Many of these chains are in fact manufacturer-retailers.

MANUFACTURER-RETAILERS AND DOMINANT RETAIL CHAINS

Canadian apparel retailing has given rise to several successful chains of manufacturer-retailers. National chains include Reitman's, a family-operated manufacturer-retailer founded in 1926 in Montreal, which has over three hundred forty stores under the flagship banner and more than eight hundred stores in total. In 2002, Reitman's bought out another retailer, the Shirmax Organization, which had been in business since 1957. Le Château, founded in 1959, has found its niche in quick production turnaround time, facilitated by having about 40 percent of its production done in Canada. It continues to operate many Canadian and some U.S. stores.

Boutiques San Francisco, which began in 1978, had as many as 140 stores in Quebec and Ontario in the early 2000s. Jacob and Groupe Dynamite each have a thirty-year history, and each operates some two hundred stores in the United States and Canada. Tristan, with similar longevity, operates some seventy stores in Canada and the United States. Since 1984 Aritzia has promoted a unique boutique concept and has expanded into several locations in the United States as well as across Canada. Other large well-known retail chains include Laura, founded by Laura Wolstein as a single store in Montreal in 1930; its 136 stores across the country sell well-known brands as well as its private-label merchandise.

Some Canadian chains have ventured further afield. Parachute, which began in 1978 and ran until 1993, was the concept of design team Nicola Pelly and Harry Parnass. This manufacturer-retailer expanded into the United States in 1980 and at its height was found in five hundred points of sale around the world, including two hundred in Europe. Roots was established in Toronto in 1973 by Michael Budman and Don Green of the United States and now has more than one hundred and ten stores in Canada and the United States, with thirty Asian locations. Vancouver-based Lululemon Athletica opened its first store in 2000 and has since opened more than fifty locations across Canada, the United States, Australia, and Japan. La Senza, created in 1988 by Lawrence Lewin, operates five hundred stores in thirty countries.

THE CANADIAN APPAREL INDUSTRY IN TRANSITION

In the first decade of the twenty-first century, Canada's apparel industry is definitely in transition, primarily due to the rise in imports following the removal of tariffs and quotas on imported clothing in 2005, in a market where worldwide capacity is twice worldwide demand. Manufacturers continue to lose market share to offshore suppliers. The market share of domestic shipments has declined from 59 percent in 1995 to 33 percent in 2005. The market share of imports, in contrast, has gone up from 41 percent in 1995 to 67 percent in 2005, a 65 percent increase.

Between 1995 and 2005, the total apparel market, driven by rising imports, has risen 18 percent. Total shipments and domestic shipments have followed a pattern of decline since 1995. Statistics Canada records that between 2000 and 2005, Canadian apparel shipments have decreased 24 percent. To offset the continuing decline of the domestic share of total apparel shipments, domestic manufacturers continue to engage in sustained export market expansion. Although there have been slight declines in export volume each year from 2000 to 2005, the export share of total shipments in 2005 showed a 91 percent increase over that of 2000.

Statistics Canada reports that in 2005 the apparel industry allocated some CAN$100.3 million for new machinery, equipment, and buildings. The Canadian apparel industry's investments in machinery, equipment, and upgrading labor skills reflect the industry's drive to sustain its international competitiveness. Currently duty remission programs, managed by the federal Canadian Apparel and Textile Industries Program (CATIP), are designed to help the most vulnerable sectors of the apparel industry adjust to increased competition from low-wage countries and extend to outerwear, shirts, and blouses as well as to fabrics.

References

Baril, Gérald. (2004). Dicomode: Dictionnaire de la mode au Québec de 1900 à nos jours. Montreal: Fides.

Gannagé, Charlene. (1986). *Double Day, Double Bind: Women Garment Workers.* Toronto: Women's Press.

Hiebert, Daniel. (July 1990). "Discontinuity and the Emergence of Flexible Production: Garment Production in Toronto, 1901–1931." *Economic Geography* 66, no. 3: 229–253.

Industry Canada. (1997). Consumer Products Industries Branch. *Apparel. Part I, Overview and Prospects.* Ottawa: Industry Canada.

Johnson, Laura C., and Robert E. Johnson. (1982). *The Seam Allowance: Industrial Home Sewing in Canada.* Toronto: Women's Educational Press.

Kinnear, Mary. (1987). *First Days, Fighting Days: Women in Manitoba History.* Regina: University of Regina.

Kuz, Tony J. (1974). *Winnipeg 1874–1974: Progress and Prospects.* Winnipeg: Manitoba Department of Industry and Commerce.

Larocque, Peter J. (2004). "'The Work Being Chiefly Performed by Women': Female Workers in the Garment Industry in Saint John, New Brunswick in 1871." In Alexandra Palmer (ed.), *Fashion: A Canadian Perspective,* 139–165. Toronto: University of Toronto Press.

Lewis, Robert. (2000). *Manufacturing Montreal: The Making of an Industrial Landscape, 1850 to 1930.* Baltimore: Johns Hopkins University Press.

MacKay, M. Elaine. (2004). "Three Thousand Stitches: The Development of the Clothing Industry in Nineteenth-Century Halifax." In Alexandra Palmer (ed.), *Fashion: A Canadian Perspective,* 166–81. Toronto: University of Toronto Press.

Mahon, Rianne. (1984). *The Politics of Industrial Restructuring: Canadian Textiles.* Toronto: University of Toronto Press.

Palmer, Alexandra. (2004). "The Association of Canadian Couturiers." In Alexandra Palmer (ed.), *Fashion: A Canadian Perspective,* 90–109. Toronto: University of Toronto Press.

Beth Tzedec Reuben and Helene Dennis Museum. (2003). *A Common Thread: A History of Toronto's Garment Industry.* Toronto: Beth Tzedec Reuben and Helene Dennis Museum.

Routh, Caroline. (1993). *In Style: 100 Years of Canadian Women's Fashion.* Toronto: Stoddart.

Steedman, Mercedes. (1997). Angels of the Workplace: Women and the Construction of Gender Relations in the Canadian Clothing Industry, 1890–1940. Toronto, New York, and Oxford: Oxford University Press.

Textile and Clothing Board. (1977). *Clothing Inquiry: A Report to the Minister of Industry, Trade, and Commerce.* Ottawa: Textile and Clothing Board.

Tulchinsky, Gerald. (1990). "Hidden among the Smokestacks: Toronto's Clothing Industry, 1871–1901." In David Keane and Colin Read (eds.), *Old Ontario,* 257–284. Toronto and Oxford: Dundurn Press.

17

CREATING A *WOMAN'S PLACE*:
The Bonwit Teller Presidency of Hortense Odlum, 1934 to 1940

Michael Mamp and Sara Marcketti[1]

INTRODUCTION

From the nineteenth century onward, a myriad of new retail stores developed within the United States (Hendrickson 1979). These establishments provided shoppers, particularly women, assortments of fashion products that helped shape the American culture of consumption. Ready to wear flooded the marketplace and prompted the democratization of fashion (Kidwell and Christman 1974). Authors have explored the role that women played as consumers and entry-level saleswomen in stores in both America and abroad. However, less is documented regarding female management and leadership contributions in retail. Stories of legendary men such as Marshall Field, Harry Selfridge, John Wanamaker and James Cash Penney abound. Conversely, aside from scholarship regarding Dorothy Shaver and her career at Lord & Taylor, documentation of female contributions in retail is limited. Shaver is credited as the first female President of a major American retail company and the 'first lady of the merchandising world' (see Amerian 2011; Webber-Hanchett 2003). However, Hortense Odlum, who served as first President and then Chairwoman of Bonwit Teller from 1934 to 1944, preceded Shaver by ten years (Anon. 1970). Furthermore, although Bonwit Teller operated for close to 100 years, 1895 to 1990, the history of the store remains somewhat obscure.

The New York-based Bonwit Teller was founded by Paul Bonwit as a women's specialty store in 1895 (Crawford 1941). In the early part of the twentieth century, Bonwit's was known as a retailer that provided luxury goods to a discerning clientele (Keist and Marcketti 2013). Mr. Bonwit was a merchant who demanded the finest of fashions for his customers and his passion for style and quality established his namesake business as a premier choice for New York's elite (Crawford 1941). A promotional catalogue produced by the store in 1928 stated: 'It was his [Paul Bonwit's] ambition to create the first great store devoted exclusively to the finest apparel and accessories for women and misses' (Anon. 1928). Bonwit executed his store with the focus of a specialty boutique yet on the scale of a department store. The store occupied several different locations until 1930 when the permanent flagship was established at 56th Street and 5th Avenue, an address in the New York retailing world that became synonymous with luxury fashion.

However, once at the new location, the exclusivity that Bonwit's was known for vanished in a cavernous space previously occupied by A.T. Stewart and Co. department store, a larger and more diversified business. Moving exhausted financial reserves, and Mr. Bonwit was unable to sufficiently update the store interior or fill it with enough products. At the same time, sales had softened as a result of the Great Depression. Bonwit defaulted on his loans and Atlas Corporation, operated by Floyd Odlum, acquired the company in 1931 (Anon. 1940a). Odlum, a lawyer and

---

[1] From Michael Mamp and Sara Marcketti (2015), Creating a Woman's Place: The Bonwit Teller Presidency of Hortense Odlum, 1934–1940. Fashion, Style & Popular Culture, Volume 2, Issue 3, pp. 301–19, Intellect.

venture capitalist by trade, was unsure of what to do with a women's store; however, he noted that the company in the years leading up to 1930 generated nearly 500,000 dollars in annual profits (Anon. 1934a). This' previous financial success intrigued Odlum, and so he decided to ask his wife, Hortense, for advice as to what was wrong with the store.

What started as a casual enquiry from husband to wife in 1932 led to an exciting new career for Hortense Odlum. At first, she served as consultant from 1933 to 1934, then as President of the firm from 1934 to 1940 and finally as Chairwoman of the board from 1940 to 1944 (Farshall 2012). Without previous work experience, and little education, Odlum, at the age of 40, re-established Bonwit Teller as an icon of the American retail industry (Mamp 2014). Her clear focus on customer service and stylish quality merchandise offered at diverse price points was in tune with consumer demands of the 1930s.

HUMBLE BEGINNINGS

Hortense Odium was born in 1892, the third of six children to Hector and Ella McQuarrie, in the small town of St. George, Utah, where her father was an elder in the Mormon Church and a farmer. Her proclivity for shop keeping was evidenced at an early age, as she would make cornhusk dolls that she then sold to neighbourhood children in a makeshift store she had set up in her backyard in exchange for pins, matches or eggs (*Memories* 1935).

In 1915, Hortense met a lawyer from Colorado named Floyd Odium. They were married that same year and the first of two children (Stanley and Bruce) was born in 1916. Their first year of marriage was one of scrimping and saving to support their new family on Floyd's salary of 50 dollars per month. Hortense said of this period, 'my budget ignored such needs as clothes and amusements. We were clothed in so far as the demands of decency required... it didn't matter that we couldn't afford even a daily paper' (Odium 1939: 32).

Floyd Odium's company gave him a raise to 75 dollars per month and then asked him to relocate to their New York office. Floyd ascended the corporate ladder to the position of Vice President and then started his own company in 1923 with 40,000 dollars that, by 1930, had grown into a value of over 120,000,000 (Anon. 1941). His company, Atlas Corporation, sold holdings before the stock market crash of 1929 and was then able to use that liquidity to acquire several new companies for a fraction of their value before the crash. In just fourteen years, Floyd Odium became one of the ten wealthiest men in America (Anon. 1941).

In December 1932, Floyd told Hortense that Bonwit's was 'on the rocks' and asked her opinion regarding what was wrong with the store; she replied, 'I can't tell you anything about what's wrong with Bonwit Teller because I've never been in it' (Odium 1939: 7). When her husband's persisted as to why, she replied, 'I suppose I never heard anything about it that made me think I'd find what I wanted there' (Odium 1939: 7).

One of the first suggestions that Odium made for Bonwit Teller was to relocate the millinery department to the first floor of the store. Paul Bonwit, who continued to serve as President of the firm until October 1934, and his executive team were against it. However, Odium was undeterred and maintained that 'women know what women want in a store' (Anon. 1934b: 14). Odium's instinct was correct; the new department opened and millinery sales tripled (Anon. 1934a).

In the summer of 1933 Odium went on her annual pilgrimage to her native Utah for a few weeks (*Memories* 1935). When she returned to New York she found that an entire floor of the store had been blocked off to save money on utilities, displays were dull and the morale that she had 'worked her heels off to improve' had returned to its previous state (Odium 1939: 48). It occurred to the Odiums that if Hortense's improvements to the store were going to have any real lasting impact, she needed to have more authority in the business. They developed a plan to gradually retire Paul Bonwit permanently from the business and to install Hortense as President. Hortense officially became President in October of 1934 and Bonwit publically retired for health reasons.

COOLER AND BIGGER

Odium quickly repainted and cleaned up the store but also went about cooling the store with air conditioning. In the 1930s air conditioning was not yet widely available. The first air-conditioned car was not manufactured until 1939, and only the wealthy had the pleasure of affording private residence air conditioning. Most businesses did not employ the technology until the mid- to late 1940s (Green 2012). The Great Depression initially stalled the widespread adoption of air conditioning and World War II further delayed progress of the invention first developed in 1902 to cool an overheating printing press (Scanlon 2004). However, in May of 1938 more than 1300 employees gathered to celebrate as Odlum 'cut a silver cord putting the motors into operation' (Anon. 1938a: 35). The store capitalized on this event and announced the innovation in an advertisement on the fifth page of *The New York Times*, which featured a quote from Odlum, 'we have air conditioned every inch from entrance to eaves. And that means a cool comfortable healthful summer for employees as well as pleasant shopping for all our customer friends' (Anon. 1938b: 5). A cool environment in May 1938 ensured good business for the summer, particularly as retail stores often experienced decreased sales in the hot months of July and August (Biddle 2011).

As business increased under Odlum's tenure, more departments were added to the store and additional space was required. In mid-1938, construction began at the store that would add two additional floors at a cost of 85,000 dollars. This added 12,000 square feet of space that according to Odlum would be used 'to handle increasing business and to permit reallocation of a number of selling departments as well as to provide additional space for service departments' (Anon. 1938c: 39).

These additional departments and services allowed Odlum to gain market share and attract customers to the store. In the throes of the Great Depression, and within three years of becoming President, business dramatically increased and the sales staff grew from about 600 to over 1400 people (Anon. 1937a). Between 1935 and 1937 total sales volume at the store increased 62 per cent and profits grew an astounding 305 per cent (Anon. 1938d). These financial achievements allowed Bonwit's to payback a 300,000-dollar bank loan in 1937 (Anon. 1938d). Additionally,

The New York Times reported in 1939 'one of the largest realty deals consummated recently in the 5th Avenue district' when Bonwit Teller acquired sole ownership of the building they occupied and purchased the space outright from the landlord (Anon. 1939a: 51).

DIVERSIFIED PRICING, ASSORTMENT AND SERVICES

Salon De Couture

Odlum focused, starting in 1934, on the development of a new department at the store that provided access to the finest fashions of Paris and custom designs called the Salon de Couture. The newly designed space occupied the entire fourth floor of the building and was decorated by a celebrated female interior designer of the time, Agnes Rowe Fairman, whose work for Bonwit Teller 'achieved an atmosphere of that described as a Parisian couturier's salon' (Anon. 1934c: 12). Odlum recognized, being a discerning woman of means herself, that Bonwit's was not offering exclusive enough products for New York's social elite. Competitors such as Saks Fifth Avenue's Salon Moderne, headed by Sophie Gimbel since 1931, were very successful, and Bonwit's was not effectively competing in this arena (Anon. 1969).

Fira Benenson, who went by the professional name of Countess Illinska, was hired as head designer for Bonwit's Salon de Couture and served in this capacity from 1934 until 1948 (Anon. 1977). Benenson created made-to-order clothes, and showed small customizable collections each season of her own designs to Bonwit customers. The Salon de Couture also fulfilled requests for orders with Paris fashion houses such as Schiaparelli, Mainbocher, Lanvin and Chanel with the assistance of Gladys Tilden, Bonwit's liaison in Paris.

Rendezvous and Debutante

Odlum was not just interested in meeting the needs of her wealthiest customers. Personally, she understood the needs of a woman on a budget. When she and Floyd first moved to New York they were invited to a Thanksgiving dinner at the home of a wealthy colleague.

Floyd had no dark shoes so he painted a light pair with shoe polish. This was met with complaints of the smell of fumes during dinner. Hortense wore an ill-fitting dress that did not suit her because it was the only thing she could find on her limited budget (Odlum 1939). According to Odlum:

> Because I had been one of them, I knew that there were countless women with modest budgets who knew and wanted to wear good clothes, good in the sense of design and fabric as well as practicality. Their numbers had been increased by the first years of the depression. There was an enormous market waiting for any merchant who would take the time and trouble to find out what its needs and preferences and financial limits were. (1939: 95–96)

Odlum observed that the moderate dresses offered at Bonwit's were covered in decoration in order to compensate for the fact that they were poorly made or designed. She stated:

> There isn't a dress in that department that a well-dressed woman would want to wear. I've never seen so many Christmas tree ornaments on clothes. Our moderate priced merchandise must be the best we could find in the markets. (Odlum 1939: 72, 115)

It was Odlum's assertion that women would respond to dresses that were of better fabrication with clean line and minimal ornamentation that would allow the wearer to be stylish yet practical, offering length of and versatility in wear. She worked and pleaded with her buyers and manufacturers (most of whom were men) to deliver this kind of merchandise. Despite their protests she insisted and finally a product arrived in spring 1934 and was presented in newly branded departments called Rendezvous and Debutante.

College Girls Department

Another new department established in 1934 was dedicated to women in college (Anon. 1934d). Starting in the 1920s a broader access to higher education resulted in more than one million Americans attending college by 1930 (Farrell-Beck and Parsons 2007). By this time, more women than ever before achieved a high school diploma and subsequently female enrolment at co-educational and female-only colleges across the country increased (Blackwelder 1997). Under Odlum's direction, Bonwit's began to market specific apparel products to these women. Advertisements for the new shop featured an adoption of masculine fabrications and casual silhouettes and modest price points (Anon. 1935). The College Girls Department proved to be a long-term success. Twelve years later, in 1946, a fashion show on the eighth floor of the store featured products developed by Bonwit's buyers and designers who had visited colleges such as Wellesley, Mount Holyoke, Smith, Bennington and Vassar as inspiration for the collection (Pope 1946).

Beauty salon

Aside from improved assortment, a more attractive store, more engaged salespeople and a customer-centric attitude, Odlum also recognized the need for the addition of services. In October of 1934, one of the first additions made soon after Odlum's appointment to President was that of a beauty salon (Anon. 1934e). Other stores such as Saks Fifth Avenue already had salons; however, Odlum recognized that this service was distinctly lacking in a store that sold products only for women (Kopytek 2011).

721 Club

Odlum realized that there was an opportunity to increase sales during the holiday shopping season. Women, who were most often busy shopping for others during the holidays, were also the recipients of gifts. In order to appeal to men shopping for women, the 721 Club originated in 1934 (Anon. 1937b). The club, advertised as the 'gift headquarters for men' was located on the fourth floor of the store and hosted an annual cocktail reception to launch the beginning of the season, referred to as a 'stag' party (Anon. 1938e: 34).

The club was very well received. What started during Odlum's first holiday season as President in 1934 with 100 members grew to over 500 members by 1937 (Anon. 1937b). In order to shop at the 721 Club you had to be a credit account holder or the husband of an account holder. Each season, Bonwit's would also hold a preview for women to get a glimpse of the new gift assortment. Women shoppers were able to leave behind a wish list that itemized their current sizes to make shopping for the men in their lives even easier (Anon. 1951). The club was staffed with attractive women in green dresses and maintained an air of exclusivity via a private entrance, red lacquered doors and a sign above the entrance that read '721 Club, For Men Only' (Anon. 1951). The club became one of Odlum's longest-lasting initiatives and continued annually until 1971, when pressure from the Human Right's Commission of New York persuaded several New York department and specialty stores to do away with male-only shopping services or clubs (Anon. 1971).

Bonwit's was the pioneer of the specialized Christmas shop for men. In 1952, Saks Fifth Avenue opened the male-only Stag Club, borrowing its name from the Bonwit's annual opening party (Anon. 1952). In 1954, cosmetics firm Elizabeth Arden also opened a male-only private shop called 1 East Fifty-fourth Street, which was named after the store's address, copying Bonwit's 721 Club naming strategy (Anon. 1954a). Other retailers offered male-only shopping services in the form of specialized salespeople such as Lord & Taylor's Red Rose Shoppers and Bergdorf Goodman's Christmas Angels, but without a private club-like atmosphere with coffee and pastries in the morning and cocktails in the afternoon (Anon. 1959). Upon the closing of the 721 Club in 1971 a long-term patron lamented that it was 'the only place you can get a decent drink on Fifth Avenue' (Anon. 1971).

CONSUMER AND EMPLOYEE COMMITTEES

Odlum's hiring decisions, merchandising strategies and personal transition from housewife and mother to business leader and champion of women in business evidenced a feminist approach. *The New York Times* reported that she was 'assembling a staff of executives, almost entirely feminine' (Anon. 1939b: d4). To develop a holistic feminine point of view in her business, Odlum turned to the most important female voice, that of the customer. She did this first through the creation of an open-door policy that made her personally accessible to any customer who wanted to lodge a complaint (Anon. 1938g). By 1935 Odlum created the Consumer Advisory Committee. In the beginning Odlum brought with her the uncomplicated point of view of a customer. She realized that to retain this perspective she would have to connect with customers on a regular basis.

The Consumer Advisory Committee provided Odlum and her team with valuable insight. The committee met on a monthly basis as Odlum would host a lunch in her office with a variety of both charge and cash customers, who, according to Neimark, received a gift for their participation. The consumer-focused committee was such a success from both a store operations and publicity standpoint that the concept was expanded in 1937 to store employees. Starting in 1937 Odlum met with salespeople who were elected by their co-workers for monthly lunches on a six-month rotation; the following autumn a separate non-selling advisory committee was also formed with employees from non-sales functions. It is clear that Odlum appreciated her employees both in word and in action. In December of 1938 bonuses totalling 25,000 dollars were paid to employees based on their length of service and department managers were given a two-week paid vacation (Anon. 1938g).

GOALS ACHIEVED

By January of 1940, Bonwit's achieved annual sales of over 10,000,000, a 190 per cent increase in volume since the beginning of Odlum's Presidency in 1934 (Anon. 1940b: 47). On the anniversary of her sixth year as President the store achieved this financial milestone, which was a record for the company not seen since the early days of the 1920s (Anon. 1940c). Having achieved what she set out to do, Odlum stepped down as President at the end of 1940. William Holmes, whom she hired as the store's General Manager and Vice President, was promoted to fill the open position and stated, 'there will be no change whatsoever in our policy and we will carry on all the principles Mrs. Odlum has laid down for us' (Anon. 1940d: 45).

Odlum became Chairwoman of the board and served in this capacity until 1944, when she permanently retired. According to Ira Neimark, 'the general public perception of Bonwit Teller during the late 1930s was the best high fashion retailer on Fifth Avenue. It was no doubt due to Hortense Odlum's vision'.

In many ways the story of Hortense Odlum's merchandising strategies at Bonwit Teller is not unique. During the Great Depression, other retailers of the period were looking for ways to diversify pricing and attract customers with different services and promotions. However, hers is the story of a woman, who, with no previous training or work experience, applied a feminine perspective to her business and achieved a positive outcome. She fully embraced her role as President of the store and simply approached the job from a customer's point of view. She also appreciated the feminine opinions of her employees and customers. Her vast life and economic experiences up until her career at Bonwit Teller informed her understanding of what women of various walks of life needed and wanted from a store of their own.

Women were not just shoppers and saleswomen but some, like Odlum, were able to crash through the proverbial glass ceiling. For Hortense Odlum, a keen fashion sense, an understanding of what her customers wanted and a proclivity for hard work saved Bonwit Teller during the Great Depression. Her story, and many others of forgotten female leaders, is worth remembering.

References

Amerian, Stephanie Marie (2011), 'Fashioning a female executive: Dorothy Shaver and the business of American style, 1893–1959', Ph.D. dissertation, Los Angeles: University of California.
Anon. (1928), 'Park Avenue fashions Bonwit Teller, 1928', Store Promotional Catalogue, Special Collections Department, Iowa State University Library, Ames.
Anon (1934a), 'Lady from atlas', *Time*, 22 October, p. 61.
Anon (1934b), 'Mrs. Odlum heads Bonwit Teller', *New York Times*, 9 October, p. 14.
Anon (1934c), 'Bonwit Teller adds department', *New York Times*, 1 April, p. 12.
Anon (1934d), 'Mrs. Odlum: Bonwit Teller's chief began work 2 years ago', *Newsweek*, 20 October, p. 34.
Anon (1934e), 'Beauty salon to open, Bonwit Teller department will receive customers Monday', *New York Times*, 14 October, p. 30.
Anon (1935), 'Bonwit Teller "College Special"', *Harper's Bazaar* (advertisement), August 1935, p. 121.
Anon (1937a), 'Mrs. Odlum cites sharp sales gains, volume has tripled in three years she has been president of Bonwit Teller', *New York Times*, 30 September, p. 32.
Anon (1937b), 'Store's club has party, men shoppers see fashion show for Christmas season', *New York Times*, 3 December, p. 39.
Anon (1938a), 'Air conditioning celebrated', *New York Times*, 24 May, p. 35.
Anon (1938b), 'Bonwit Teller: The mercury goes down but spirits go up', *New York Times* (advertisement), 29 May, p. 5.
Anon (1938c), 'Store to add two floors, Bonwit Teller will begin $85,000 addition in May', *New York Times*, 19 April, p. 39.
Anon (1938d), '$223, 672 cleared by Bonwit Teller', *New York Times*, 23 March, p. 36.
Anon (1938e), 'Party for men shoppers, Bonwit Teller arranges event to help Christmas buyers', *New York Times*, 2 December, p. 34.
Anon (1938f), 'We rest our future on the human side of storekeeping', *New York Times* (advertisement), 9 October, p. 5.
Anon (1938g), 'Store pays $25,000 bonus, each employee shares on basis of length of service', *New York Times*, 20 December, p. 47.
Anon (1939a), 'Building acquired by Bonwit Teller', *New York Times*, 13 December, p. 51.
Anon (1939b), 'Mrs. Odlum's career prospers amid a shattering of tradition', *New York Times*, 5 March, p. d4.
Anon (1940a), 'Odlum makes a deal', *Time*, 35: 14, p. 61.
Anon (1940b), 'Record sales set by Bonwit Teller, total for year ended Jan. 31 put at $10,006,325 by Hortense M. Odlum', *New York Times*, 20 March, p. 47.
Anon (1940c), 'Mrs. Odlum marks sixth year in post, Bonwit Teller head reports volume at record level', *New York Times*, 2 October, p. 40.
Anon (1940d), 'Holmes elected by Bonwit Teller, becomes president of store, succeeding Mrs. Odlum, who is made board chairman', *New York Times*, 17 October, p. 45.
Anon (1941), 'Atlas into hearst', *Time*, 10 March, p. 86.
Anon (1951), 'Women get past a men only sign, preview granted to shoppers at exclusively male shop in Fifth Avenue store', *New York Times*, 27 November, p. 35.
Anon (1952), 'Saks to open gift service', *New York Times*, 1 December, p. 35.
Anon (1954a), 'Two new gift shops bar women buyers', *New York Times*, 1 December, p. 37.

Anon (1969), 'Sophie is retiring, and so is her custom salon at Saks', *New York Times*, 26 May, p. 50.

Anon (1970), 'Hortense Odlum of Bonwit Teller head of store here from 1934–1944 is dead', *New York Times*, 13 January, p. 24.

Anon (1971), 'Christmas shopping services for men only turn coed', *New York Times*, 7 December, p. 58.

Anon (1977), 'Fira Benenson, fashion designer', *New York Times*, 24 October, p. 32.

Biddle, J. (2011), 'Making consumers comfortable: The early decades of air conditioning in the United States', *The Journal of Economic History*, 71: 4, pp. 1078–94.

Blackwelder, J. (1997), *Now Hiring: The Feminization of Work in the United States, 1900–1995*, College Station: Texas A&M University Press.

Crawford, M. (1941), *The Ways of Fashion*, New York: G.P. Putnam's Sons.

Farrell-Beck, J. and J. Parsons. (2007), *Twentieth Century Dress in the U.S.*. New York: Fairchild.

Farshall, A. (2012), 'Utahan brings touch of personal service to Manhattan store, triples business', *Salt Lake Tribune*, 15 April, p. 84.

Green, A. (2012), 'A brief history of air conditioning', http://www.popularme-chanics.com/home/improvement/electrical-plumbing/a-brief-history-of-air-conditioning-10720229. Accessed 18 February 2015.

Hendrickson, R. (1979), *The Grand Emporiums the Illustrated History of America's Great Department Stores*, New York: Stein and Day.

Keist, C. and S. Marcketti. (2013), 'The new costumes of odd sizes: Plus-sized women's fashions, 1920–1929', *Clothing and Textiles Research Journal*, 31: 4, pp. 259–74.

Kidwell, C. and M. Christman. (1974), *Suiting Everyone: The Democratization of Clothing in America*, Washington: The Smithsonian Institution Press.

Kopytek, B. (2011), 'The department store museum', http://departmentsto-remuseum.blogspot.com/2010/11/saks-fifth-avenue-new-york-city-new.html. Accessed 18 February 2015.

Mamp, M. (2014), 'Female presidents of Bonwit Teller, Hortense Odlum (1934–44) and Mildred Custin (1965–70)', Ph.D. thesis, Ames: Iowa State University.

Marcketti, S. (2010), 'The sewing room projects of the works progress administration', *Textile History*, 41: 1, pp. 28–49.

Memories (1935), *Packet of materials presented to Hortense Odlum to mark the opening of the McQuarrie Memorial Museum*, St. George, Utah.

Odlum, H. (1939), *A Woman's Place the Autobiography of Hortense Odlum*, New York: Scribner & Sons.

Pope, V. (1946), 'Togs born of reconnaissance on college campuses show a trend to plaids at Bonwit Teller's', *New York Times*, 2 August, p. 16.

Scanlon, L. (2004), 'The birth of cool, the history of modern air conditioning', *Technology Review*, 107: 2, p. 84.

Webber-Hanchett, Tiffany (2003), 'Dorothy Shaver: Promoter of "The American Look"', *Dress*, 30: 1, pp. 80–90.

18

STORES, SHOPPERS, AND MEDIATED IMAGES:
The relational space of Uniqlo

Myles Ethan Lascity

INTRODUCTION

As Uniqlo, the Japanese clothier known for its basics, has moved into and through the U.S. marketplace, the brand has been following a "flagship market entry" strategy. The brand first opened a Global Flagship store in 2011 on the corner of New York's famed Fifth Avenue and 53rd Street. The three-story store is massive, covering 89,000 square feet of floor space; for comparison, an American football field is 57,600 square feet. There are two smaller flagship stores in Manhattan — the Herald Square location is 64,000 square feet and the SoHo store is 36,000 square feet. Uniqlo has since built larger stores in other metro areas, including Philadelphia (29,000 square feet) and Chicago (60,000 square feet).

Beyond the size, the store experience is fantastical from the start. Stores rise above the street level in a cascade of glass and color. From Fifth Avenue, shoppers can gaze upon Uniqlo fashions that rise and fall as store visitors take the elevators. On Chestnut Street, the Philadelphia flagship lights up with rainbow colors behind a historic stone façade. These flagships need to be eye-catching to help Uniqlo stand apart from the competition of other retailers. However, by bringing the larger-than-life stores to Fifth Avenue, Herald Square, and Chestnut Street, Uniqlo helps to define shopping districts and urban images.

Researchers have long known that geography helps color shopping experiences (Kotler, 1973) — both within specific cities (Gilbert, 2006:16–26; Hollander, 1970:19–20) and within specific districts (Fernie et al., 1998). As Uniqlo grows across the United States, it is integrating into the familiar shopping districts across the United States. From its initial U.S. enclave in Manhattan, Uniqlo has moved onto San Francisco, Chicago, Boston, Philadelphia, Los Angeles, Denver, Seattle, and Washington, D.C. This growth has come with numerous flagship stores — in Herald Square, Union Square, Michigan Avenue, Newbury Street, and Chestnut Street — with smaller locations pushing into the suburbs.

In this chapter, I argue that there is a two-way process at work, where stores like Uniqlo both reflect and help create the shopping districts. In doing so, I pull together brand, fashion, and urban studies literature. Urban studies have noted this two-way process (see Ryu and Swinney, 2012; Teller et al., 2010; Warnaby and Bennsion, 2006); however these studies emphasize place branding over retail branding. Instead, I'll be relying on the idea of "relational space" and how digital technology has connected cities across the globe (McQuire, 2008:20–1). Through Uniqlo's use of relational space the brand is able to create a global network that helps to connect and frame the places it chooses to locate. Relying on consumer interviews and an analysis of Uniqlo's social media campaigns, it is possible to see how consumers use brands to connect global cities while at the same time experiencing some form of variation.

UNIQLO AND RELATIONAL SPACE

In 2014, Uniqlo announced the openings of five stores in Los Angeles (Uniqlo, 2014a), six stores in Boston (Uniqlo, 2014b), and three in Philadelphia (Uniqlo, 2014c) within days of each other. The brand's website showed that the locations in the three cities are being greeted similarly, with announcements of "From Tokyo to [insert city here]"; contests where social network users could use "local vocab" (such as hoagie, jawn, or Yuengling in Philadelphia) for a chance to win a $100 gift card to Uniqlo; and videos with local celebrities. Uniqlo's promotions of these cities helped not only to advertise the brand, but also to frame the city. Researchers have long noted that people attach meanings to cities and other geographic locations (Lynch, 1960; Kavaratzis, 2004), and here Uniqlo's promotion can be seen as part of this development. As Lynch points out the "mental image" of the city is created by the physical space (Lynch, 1960: 9–12), but also through a host of other means, including residents, media portrayals, and activities. McQuire points out that digital technology has helped restructure the city and its "relational space" (2008:20–1). Instead of a city only being experienced in person or through a single medium, such as postcards or film, digital technology can constantly reframe them and transmit their images across the globe. McQuire suggests that relation space can be reworked at different "velocities" (2008:23); in the case at hand, Uniqlo's brick-and-mortar stores take time to build, but their social media advertisements take only seconds to distribute.

During Uniqlo's expansion into Philadelphia, Boston, and Los Angeles, the brand offered frames of each city and the local consumers. This framing was conducted by a variety of means, including a social media campaign, videos with local celebrities, and sponsored BuzzFeed content. These promotional devices allowed Uniqlo to leverage both local celebrities and average shoppers to promote the brand and imbue its new locations with a sense of familiarity. Here both the company could shape the city through its presence and advertising, but by drawing shoppers into a social media campaign these shoppers became enmeshed in the retail and city brand.

Uniqlo's social media outreach became more prominent during its 2015–2016 expansions and its #WhereUniqlo social media campaign. The campaign aimed to promote specific locations in the United States by asking social media users "show us where you wear your Uniqlo," by tagging Instagram photos with #WhereUniqlo. This promotion included a website that divided photos by city; these cities either already had Uniqlo locations, such as New York, Philadelphia, and Boston, or a store that was opening soon, such as Chicago, Seattle, and Toronto.

Behind the scenes, Uniqlo connected with various social media influencers offering them things such as free clothing and gift cards to take and post Instagram photos with the hashtag. As described to one recipient,

> As part of the #whereUniqlo social campaign, which aims to showcase Uniqlo fans and influencers at cool events, Uniqlo is looking to send a handful of influencers to the Philadelphia Museum of Art to enjoy the current Japanese art and culture exhibit "Ink and Gold: Art of the Kano" and the associated Wednesday Ink and Gold Tattoo Parlor nights.
>
> We'd love for you to visit the museum sometime between now and when the exhibit's run ends on May 10. As an influencer, we'd give you **2 free museum admission tickets** and a **$50 Uniqlo gift card** for participating. All that we ask is that you share at least 2 Instagram posts from the museum using the hashtag #whereUNIQLO. (emphasis in original)

This influencer was also invited for a "personal shopping experience" at the location of their choosing. The same rules applied; in return for a personal tour of the store and a "small gift" (a.k.a. a canvas tote bag), the influencer was asked to take two photos of the store and post them to Instagram with the #whereUNIQLO hashtag. Clearly the idea was to help imbue Uniqlo with a uniquely local flair — in this case through activities that could only be found in Philadelphia.

Likewise, the geographic sections of the #WhereUniqlo site offered specificities to each city Uniqlo would be expanding to in the next two years. Headlines included, "Seattle, We couldn't be happier," "See you soon, Denver," "Hello, DC!," and "Oh, Canada," while introductory promotions were dotted with local references. For Seattle, the site reads, "We've been enjoying getting to know your city — from boating on the Sound to experiencing all of the sights and tastes of Pike Place … ." In comparison, Uniqlo noted that it would be opening outside of Washington, D.C., "just in time for the next Cherry Blossom Festival." Instagram photos were also used to promote the local-ness of the brand. The best example was from Seattle where a couple was photographed in front of the Space Needle. The Denver page featured a view of the Rocky Mountains. Other photos included a picture of a well-dressed man passing through a turnstile in the New York subway, as well as photographs and references of Los Angeles and San Francisco.

Freberg et al. (2011) have suggested that social media influencers have a type of capital that companies can use in their public relations efforts. This capital is dependent upon social media users' perceptions of the influencer's relevance and expertise. This, in turn, helps create more personality-driven connections to the brand. Here, Uniqlo used local influencers in an attempt to ingrain itself into local fashion scenes. In the same way that Uniqlo attempted to leverage a hashtag campaign, celebrity videos and BuzzFeed articles to connect the store to Boston, Los Angeles, and Philadelphia, were where the #WhereUniqlo campaign attempted to reinforce previous connections and built new connections to Seattle, Denver, Toronto, and Washington.

SHOPPERS BUILDING BRAND IMAGE

By utilizing a social media campaign and hashtag, Uniqlo is helping to set up several of the velocities of relational space that McQuire noted. First, the physical presence in each city helps to offer some connections between the various metro areas through each hosting prominent Uniqlo locations. Second, Uniqlo's own advertising helps to transfer and change the city's image. Finally, Uniqlo encourages social media users to post photos relating to specific cities, thereby creating a more rapid way for users to reframe a city's image. This process works to draw shoppers into the brand and helps give Uniqlo a local, human face.

Similarly, residents of cities have been noted to have an influence on city branding (Aitken and Campelo, 2011; Mittilä and Lepistö, 2013; Swinney et al., 2012). Aitken and Campelo suggest that co-creation between the residents and the marketers is fundamental to place branding and the resulting image is "dynamic, authentic, and, most importantly, collective" (2011: 927). Individuals are constantly presenting themselves within the geographic space and their image is fundamental in how outsiders understand the location. New York wouldn't be the same place without New Yorkers and when New Yorkers shop at Uniqlo they help to some of their New York-*ness* and cultural affinity to the brand.

As individuals influence both place brands and retail brands, they also create a link between the two. Those who live in a particular area are obviously more likely to frequent stores nearby, unless — perhaps — the store is set up as a particular tourist destination (Zukin, 2005: 204). Otherwise, we can see consumers as a physical link between geographic and retail brands. Fashion studies have already acknowledged the role geography plays in dress and consumption (Bernstein and Kaiser, 2013; Gilbert, 2006; Kaiser, 2013) and seeing consumers as a link between the two would suggest brands are subject to similar influences.

During interviews with Uniqlo shoppers, several explained Uniqlo's brand image by linking geography and a customer base. Illeana, a twenty-one-year-old design and merchandising major, suggested that the "typical Philadelphia customer" would appreciate Uniqlo's basics. Generally speaking, when individuals talked of the "typical Philadelphia customer" it was a full-figured, black consumer with limited financial means. Due to the stereotype of the Philadelphia shopper — the idea that Philadelphia is a "fat" city (McQuade, 2012) — some consumers noted that Uniqlo's slimmer fitting clothing might be problematic.

Teddy, twenty, a Vietnamese international student in Philadelphia, liked Uniqlo for its tighter fit, which he attributed to it being a Japanese brand. However, Teddy pointed out that Uniqlo might work in Philadelphia, but wouldn't work in more rural parts of the United States. Teddy believed people in Philadelphia have a style closer to that of people in Hanoi — where he's also shopped Uniqlo — compared to people in rural areas of the United States who wear looser, more comfortable clothing than he believed the store provides.

Meanwhile, Sadie, a biomedical engineering student, further emphasized the link between location, style, and brand. She felt the typical Uniqlo shopper would be "very urban and easy going," comparing the user image to that of Los Angeles residents. The typical customer, according to Sadie, wasn't very East Coast and not "prim and proper." Sadie's description is particularly useful, since she noted the stereotypical differences between locations.

Illeana, Sadie, and Teddy all made assumptions about consumers based on their geographic locations. Illeana judged the "typical Philadelphia shopper," while Teddy and Sadie both assumed consumers in different locations have different styles. For Sadie, she drew a contrast between Los Angeles and East Coast consumers. Teddy did the same between cosmopolitan and rural consumers. However, Uniqlo is currently located within both Los Angeles and East Coast cities and is pushing into less urbanized areas.

The link between city and local consumer is highlighted in the case of Celeste, a native New Yorker studying architecture in Philadelphia. Celeste originally shopped Uniqlo on vacation in Kyoto and waited to visit the Manhattan outlet. "A lot of the clothes seemed fine," Celeste said, "but it wasn't a novelty store." The fact that the store was nearby made it more common and less exciting. However, she still preferred to be seen in Uniqlo than other clothing stores. Celeste noted that some stores — namely Aeropostale in Times Square — attracted a lot of tourists. And while she didn't frequent the Uniqlo stores in New York City, she felt it was a hipper place to shop and one in which she felt comfortable taking visitors. "[Uniqlo is] a place that you want to be seen," Celeste said. "I'd sooner my friends know I'm shopping at Uniqlo than [Aeropostale]." By distinguishing Uniqlo as a "place that you want to be seen" and following through with that belief, Celeste helped to create a sense of "New York-ness" for the brand; this is the physical embodiment of what Uniqlo attempted to do via its #WhereUniqlo campaign.

Still, the fact that Uniqlo is commonplace in New York, but growing into other urban markets, makes it more likely that potential consumers will associate the brand with New York City's global fashion scene than with more mundane aspects. In fact, both Celeste's experience with the brand in Kyoto and Teddy's experience with the brand in Hanoi speak to such a linkage. Teddy especially linked Uniqlo to cosmopolitanism and suggested that Hanoi had more in common with it than rural parts of the United States. Whether Teddy is correct in his assumption is beside the point. Rather, the link of geography to the brand is significant to Teddy's understanding of the brand. The fact that Uniqlo is located in both Hanoi *and* Philadelphia says something about the shoppers in both cities. And, the fact that Uniqlo is not in rural Ohio means something to Teddy as well.

BRANDS AND THE CITY

The fact that Teddy, Celeste, and Illeana made assumptions about Uniqlo and its shoppers from the store locations is not an entirely new concept, since fashion has had a long relationship to urbanity. Fashion and branding studies have been especially interested in urbanity since the economic capital tends to be concentrated in cities and thus allows a "luxury" such as fashion (Wilson, 2006). Others have noted that both retailers and the fashion industry are tied to a city's geography and the networks within a city are important to development of these industries (Fernie, Moore and Lawrie, 1998; Williams and Currid-Halkett, 2011). Uniqlo has located stores in prominent cosmopolitan areas, many of which have had a historical involvement with fashion (Gilbert, 2006: 10–16), and further, the brand opened in rather specific areas within those cities.

Part of Uniqlo's draw as a fashionable retailer is because of the locations of its stores. This works on global, national, and local levels. On the international level, Uniqlo's prominence in Japan and other counties makes it a more desirable brand and product. While Tokyo is a relative newcomer to the club (Kawamura, 2006), its fashion scene ranks with the likes of Paris, Milan, and New York. Uniqlo's slogan of "From Tokyo to [insert city here]" manages to connect the latest host city to Tokyo's fashion environment. The process helps build the relational space so that Uniqlo becomes its own network that both connects and reshapes the locations around its stores.

In the United States, the growth of Uniqlo from New York and San Francisco to the other urban areas also helps to give the brand national fashion bona fides. New York City is still the United States's predominant fashion hub (Williams and Currid-Halkett, 2011) and brands often work to tie themselves to the city. As such, Uniqlo's New York City flagship stores help develop its brand image and promote stores in Philadelphia, Boston, and other cities. The same connections can be made for the Philadelphia flagship stores to its suburban mall-based locations.

At the same time, the face that these locations can host Uniqlo location alters the perception of the city. Tokyo and New York's fashion scenes might help to create Uniqlo's brand meaning, but the fact that the chain opened flagships in Philadelphia and Boston after New York helps to make the host cities more fashionable. There is an implicit declaration that *this city* (whether it be Philadelphia, Boston, or Chicago) is cosmopolitan enough for a Uniqlo location. It creates a distinction between cities that have a Uniqlo: New York, San Francisco Los Angeles, Philadelphia, Boston; Chicago, Denver, Seattle, Washington, Toronto; and those that are not (yet): Miami, Houston, Atlanta, Pittsburgh. This connection works on the local level as well. Beyond the Philadelphia flagship, stores were located in five area malls; this raised the profile of those shopping centers, while excluding places that Uniqlo passed over.

The expansion of chains and brand names has often been criticized as a homogenizing force that swamps and replaces local cultures. Ritzer's (2004) discussion of "McDonaldization" is perhaps the most well known. This process, according to Ritzer, works to make modern life — among other things — calculable and predictable (2004: 13–14). As chains have circled the globe, corporations have found ways to imbue themselves with local qualities — whether this is through product variety or advertising campaigns. Ritzer suggests that ingrained in this process are tensions between cultural "something"-ness and cultural "nothing"-ness, and between ongoing globalization and local adaptations (2004: 165–81). This process of standardization and differentiation can be seen in Uniqlo's efforts.

Still, it would be a mistake to suggest that Uniqlo is homogenizing clothing and the shopping experience around the world. This is partially due to Uniqlo's advertising practices. Uniqlo's branding is what Ritzer would call "glocalized" in that the company is exporting a similar style, but with unique traits (2004: 169–81). In general, globalization has not had the homogenizing effects once feared. Instead an active audience has made sense of more globalized processes and responded in diverse fashions — whether that has been to accept, reject, or moderate the messages (Norris and Inglehart, 2009: 15–21). As some scholars have noted, brands and products are experienced through unique lenses that can make consumers see McDonald's feel familiar or exotic (Caputo, 1998) or Coca-Cola as both a local and global drink (Miller, 1998).

As Uniqlo creates a glocalized brand image, individuals will develop different understandings of the brand. This becomes more pronounced with larger differences. For example, media reports said that the Philadelphia flagship had "the largest kids sections in the entire Uniqlo chain at 2,300 square feet" (Kauffman, 2014). Spatially, the entire second floor of the Philadelphia store is dedicated to children's clothing. The Philadelphia flagship also offered space that promoted the SPRZ NY line — initially, the store was the only shop outside of the Fifth Avenue flagship to have such an assortment.

Practically speaking, a shopper who becomes familiar with Uniqlo from the Philadelphia flagship store would come to expect to find both a plethora of children's clothing and the SPRZ NY lineup. And simply moving to the suburban stores could make this challenging, since Uniqlo doesn't offer the same product mix at all of its locations. These differences would be further exacerbated by size and distance, as shoppers of the New York flagships would come to expect more variety in offerings than the smaller locations provide. Similar situations exist during the brand's Instagram campaign or reliance on local influencers. Each provides opportunity for consumers to see the brand in a different manner.

CODA

Brands are, at all times, in a dialogic relationship with their geographic locations where they both influence and are influenced by their surroundings. Further, consumers do not act in a vacuum where they are only exposed to a particular set of brand messages, but rather they are forced to make sense of the brand based on their experiences with it. These variations help to create uniqueness in situations that might otherwise appear similar; for Celeste it was seeing Uniqlo as a place to take friends and Teddy seeing the brand as intended for other urbanites. Neither assumption was based on only global or local elements. And despite the fact that global and local elements are often seen at odds with one another, it is important to note they cannot be pulled apart from each other. Global forces, in this case Uniqlo brand managers and its parent company, have the ability to frame geographic areas through advertisements and locating within these environments. At the same time, local forces, such as shoppers and consumer perceptions of their respective cities, provide nuances that cannot be found in a different setting.

References

Aitken, Robert and Adriana Campelo. (2011). "The Four Rs of Place Branding." *Journal of Marketing Management*, 27(9): 913–33.

Bernstein, Sara Tatyana and Susan B. Kaiser. (2013). "Fashion Out of Place: Experiencing Fashion in a Small American Town." *Critical Studies in Fashion and Beauty*, 4(1): 43–70.

Caputo, John S. (1998). "The Rhetoric of McDonaldization: A Social Semiotic Perspective." In M. Alfino, J. S. Caputo and R. Wynyard (eds.), *McDonaldization Revisited: Critical Essays on Consumer Culture*, 39–52. Westport, CT: Praeger.

Fernie, John, Christopher M. Moore and Alexander Lawrie. (1998). "A Tale of Two Cities: An Examination of Fashion Designer Retailing within London and New York." *The Journal of Product and Brand Management*, 7(5): 366–78. doi: 10.1108/10610429810237637

Freberg, Karen, Kristin Grahma, Karen McGaughey and Laura A. Freberg. (2011). "Who Are the Social Media Influencers? A Study of Public Perceptions of Personality." *Public Relations Review*, 37:90–2. doi: 10.1016/j.pubrev.2010.11.001

Gilbert, David. (2006). "From Paris to Shanghai: The Changing Geographies of Fashion's World Cities." In C. Breward and D. Gilbert (eds.), *Fashion's World Cities*, 3–32. New York, NY: Berg.

Hollander, Stanley C. (1970). *Multinational Retailing*. East Lansing, MI: Michigan State University.

Kaiser, Susan B. (2013). "Place, Time and Identity: New Directions in Critical Fashion Studies." *Critical Studies in Fashion and Beauty*, 4(1):3–16.

Kauffman, Leah. (2014). "Exclusive: UNIQLO to Open Three Stores in Philadelphia This Area Year." *Philly.com*, May 7. http://www.philly.com/philly/blogs/style/Exclusive-UNIQLO-will-open-three-stores-in-Philadelphia-area-this-year-.html. Accessed November 3, 2015.

Kavaratzis, Michalis. (2004). "From City Marketing to City Branding: Toward a Theoretical Framework for Developing City Brands." *Place Branding*, 1(1): 58–73.

Kawamura, Yuniya. (2006). "Placing Tokyo on the Fashion Map: From Catwalk to Streetstyle." In C. Breward and D. Gilbert (eds.), *Fashion's World Cities*, 55–68. New York, NY: Berg.

Kolter, Philip. (1973). "Atmospherics as a Marketing Tool." *Journal of Retailing*, 49(4): 48–64.

Lynch, Kevin. (1960). *The Image of the City*. Cambridge, MA: The MIT Press.

McQuade, Dan. (2012). "Philly: Fat, Unhealthy and Drunk." *Philadelphia Magazine*, April 4. http://www.phillymag.com/news/2012/04/04/philly-fat-unhealthy-drunk. Accessed December 3, 2015.

McQuire, Scott. (2008). *The Media City: Media, Architecture and Urban Space*. Los Angeles, CA: Sage.

Miller, Daniel. (1998). "Coca-Cola: A Black Sweet Drink from Trinidad." In D. Miller (ed.), *Material Cultures: Why Some Things Matter*, 169–87. Chicago, IL: University of Chicago Press.

Mittilä, Tuula and Tanja Lepistö. (2013). "The Role of Artists in Place Branding: A Case Study." *Place Branding and Public Diplomacy*, 9(3): 143–53.

Norris, Pippa and Ronald Inglehart. (2009). *Cosmopolitan Communications Cultural Diversity in a Globalized World*. New York, NY: Cambridge University Press.

Ritzer, George. (2004). *The McDonaldization of Society: Revised New Century Edition*. Thousand Oaks, CA: Pine Forge Press.

Ryu, Jay Sang and Jane Swinney. (2012). "Aligning Business Owners for a Successful Downtown Brand." *Journal of Place Management and Development*, 5(2): 102–18. doi: 10.1108/17538331211249983

Swinney, Jane, Chunmin Lang and Rodney Runyan. (2012). "An Exploration of Rural Community Branding Efforts from the Perspective of Community Residents." *International Journal of Rural Management*, 8(1): 35–47.

Teller, Christoph, Jonathan R. Elms, Jennifer A. Thomson and Andrew R. Paddison. (2010). "Place Marketing and Urban Retail Agglomerations: An Examination of Shopper's Place Attractiveness Perceptions." *Place Branding and Diplomacy*, 6(2): 124–33.

Uniqlo. (2014a). "Uniqlo to Open Five New U.S. Stores in Los Angeles: Opening Dates Announced." April

20. http://www.uniqlo.com./us/company/news/2014/20140430-01.html. Accessed November 3, 2015.

Uniqlo. (2014b). "Uniqlo to Open Six New U.S. Stores in the Boston Area: Opening Dates Announced; Pop-Up Shop to Open This Summer in Faneuil Hall." May 7. http://www.uniqlo.com/us/company/news/2014/20140507-01.html. Accessed November 3, 2015.

Uniqlo. (2014c). "Uniqlo to Open Three New U.S. Stores in Philadelphia This Year: Opening Dates Announced." May 7. http://www.uniqlo.com/us/company/news/2014/20140507-02.html. Accessed November 3, 2015.

Warnaby, Gary and David Bennison. (2006). "Reciprocal Urban Place Marketing and Co-branding? Retail Applications." *Place Branding*, 2(4): 297–310.

Williams, Sarah and Elizabeth Currid-Halkett. (2011). "The Emergence of Los Angeles as a Fashion Hub: A Comparative Spatial Analysis of the New York and Los Angeles Fashion Industries." *Urban Studies*, 48(14): 3034–66. doi: 10.1177/0042098010392080.

Wilson, Elizabeth. (2006). "Urbane Fashion." In C. Breward and D. Gilbert (eds.), *Fashion's World Cities*, 33–9. New York, NY: Berg.

Zukin, Sharon. (2005). *Point of Purchase: How Shopping Changed American Culture*. New York, NY: Routledge.

19

'OH, HONEY! IT'S NOT SO MUCH THE STYLE, IT'S WHAT CARRYING IT MEANS':
Hermès bags and the transformative process

Annita Boyd[1]

INTRODUCTION

The prestigious Hermès company began its life as a saddlery in Paris in the mid-nineteenth century, providing goods for noblemen and royalty. After the introduction of the automobile the business extended its production of hand-made leather goods to include luxury luggage, and later, fine couture. It is particularly known for its silk scarves and women's handbags, but retains its link to its equestrian past via its logo of the horse-drawn carriage. Two of their bags have become synonymous with the name Hermès. Grace Kelly (Princess Grace of Monaco) carried the famous Hermès bag known as the 'small tall bag with straps' (Steele and Borrelli 1999: 115). After being photographed for the cover of *Time* magazine using the bag to cover her pregnancy bump, it was renamed the Kelly bag in 1956 (Johnson 2002). The bag therefore, despite its royal connection, is associated with a kind of sexual deception in its representation. The Kelly emerged in 1935 and the Birkin in 1984, after Hermès president, Jean Louis Dumas, offered to make singer, Jane Birkin, a bag that would accommodate her belongings more comfortably (even though she had to pay for it!). She has since abandoned the Birkin, claiming it was too clumsy for her. It has now become one of the most covetable handbags in the world.

In *Intolerable Cruelty* (Cohen, 2003) Marilyn Rexroth (Catherine Zeta-Jones), serial divorcee, carries a red ostrich Hermès Birkin in her opening scenes, whilst dressed in stylish red dresses signifying her character's fire and sexuality, and adorned in a gold multi-strand necklace. Upon learning that the private detective she hired has footage of her husband's cheating, she declares, 'I'm delighted you found this material'. Then as she picks up the Birkin and holds it close to her chest, she says, 'This is going to be my passport to wealth, independence and freedom'. She is referring to the evidence of his infidelity but it is no coincidence that the line coincides with the clutching of her bag. The Birkin also accompanies her to Miles Massey's (George Clooney) law office where she attends a meeting with him and her husband to discuss divorce proceedings. The bag is associated with wealth, ambition and above all, sexual deception. She carries a pink Hermès Constance bag later when she meets her friend 'after she fails to get alimony from her ex-husband' (rochasgirl, 13 August 2006).

SEX AND THE CITY

'It's not a bag. It's a Birkin!'

Hermès sales assistant, *Sex and the City*

Samantha: Look at that one! Isn't it adorable?
Carrie: Which one?
Samantha: The red one in the middle. I love it.
Carrie: The Birkin bag? Really? That's not even your style.

---

[1] From Annita Boyd, (2014) 'Oh Honey! It's Not So Much the Style, It's What Carrying It Means': Hermes Bags and the Transformative Process in Fashion, Style & Popular Culture, Intellect, pp. 81–96.

Samantha: Oh, honey! It's not so much the style, it's what carrying it means.
Carrie: It means you're up for 4,000 bucks!
Samantha: Exactly! When I'm tooling around town with that bag, I'll know I've made it!
Carrie: OK, let's go. The visiting hours are over. (*She pulls Samantha away from the shop window*)
Samantha: Bye Bye Birkin!
(Frankel, 2001, Season 4, Episode 11)

In the voice-over of the episode 'Coulda Woulda Shoulda' (Frankel, 2001) of Sex and the City (Star, HBO, 1998), Carrie Bradshaw (Sarah Jessica Parker) describes the characters as being at a crossroads, and their destination: 'a place called who we hope to be'. This speaks of aspiration and Hermès embodies it in myriad forms. After being told she must sign on for a five-year waiting list for a Birkin, Samantha (Kim Catrall) tries to jump the queue by claiming it is for Lucy Liu whom she is representing, and promising that it will be carried by her to a premiere and photographed at length. Days later she is confronted with the horror of seeing on the street, 'a fucking nobody in a tracksuit carrying the one we want! Is Hermès short for "we take our good old fucking time?"'. Samantha reads this as not only an insulting injustice but also a denial of her entry into a certain class. Earlier she tells Liu, 'When I'm representing you, it's class all the way!' Unfortunately Samantha not only abuses her position but also the publicist at Hermès in an effort to get what she wants. Samantha's inability to acquire a Birkin signals failure for her. Her statement, 'When I'm tooling around town with that bag, I'll know I've made it', says much more about her own perception of achievement than others'. Sam's lack of 'classy' behaviour and loss of composure is incompatible with the cachet Hermès is meant to carry. And Samantha never gets to carry the Birkin. Even when she visits the Hermès store, the bag is snatched away from her by the sales assistant before she can hold it (if she does not own it, she cannot touch it). Her lack of entitlement to the Birkin is reinforced throughout the text. Her object of desire is continually 'out of reach'. And despite her paying for the bag eventually, her deceptive measures ensure that she does not get to keep it, as it bypasses her and goes straight to Lucy Liu.

THE HERMES BRAND

The potential Hermès customer must demonstrate an observable degree of consumer sophistication to be deemed a suitable candidate for the purchase of a Kelly or a Birkin. To this end, Hermès has established the waiting list. Customers may even be told that the list is closed. The inability to simply walk in off the street and buy one of these bags means that they cannot be purchased upon an impulsive whim. Considerable time and expense is channeled into manufacturing each unique bag, which is handmade by a single master craftsman/woman and bears his/her mark. Susanne LeBlanc (2012) identifies this as a commitment by Hermès to slow fashion, selecting sustainable materials and business models that oppose mass-market production.

Hermès president, Jean-Louis Dumas, insists that the brand 'preserves a certain distance while at the same time being determined to remain contemporary. The notion of permanence gives us an aristocratic distinction which has, we must admit, an intimidating side' (Dumas, quoted in Tungate 2005: 151). Indeed, Hermès manufactures, and relies upon, a certain cultivation of taste in order to maintain its exclusivity. In the article, 'Pricey Purchases and Classy Customers: Why sophisticated consumers do not need the protection of trademark laws', Goodwin (2004: 255) argues that, 'in unique situations where the goods at issue are very expensive and rare, the traditional test of consumer sophistication should trump the other factors in the likelihood of confusion analysis'. The premise of this argument is that Hermès customers are so highly skilled at recognizing authentic bags and their channels of distribution and sale, that it is unlikely that they would confuse mass-produced counterfeit items for real. In such cases, the chance of being misled by a fake trademark with a less than perfect product, and inexpensive price in the context of the market, is not probable. Nevertheless, Hermès is quick to prosecute not only against any counterfeited trademark, but also when there is a perceived infringement of its image, even when the seller markets his bags as satirical rubber (rather than leather) knock-offs, as in the case against Steven

Stolman in the United States (Bellafante 2003). There is even a special guide purchasable on eBay written by an ex-Hermès employee (Cynthia Lane Schames), which educates the naive consumer about the finer points of authenticity in legitimate Birkin buying – her employment history in New York and Paris being evidence of her unique authority. It is this specialist knowledge, skill and class possessed by bona fide Hermès clients that prohibit such mistakes.

> There are two types of purchasers of knockoff Birkin and Kelly bags – those waiting for the real thing and those who know they will never own the real thing. Either way, these purchasers are aware of the Hermès name, its reputation for quality, and its prestige. This sophistication cuts against Hermès's claim of infringement because both types of consumers are much less likely to be confused than other purchasers. (Goodwin 2004: 266)

MEDIUM

The episode of *Medium* entitled 'Twice Upon a Time' (Schwary, 2006) has Allison Dubois (Patricia Arquette) imagining a different existence for herself. She dreams what life would be like if she had married her teenage sweetheart – and a different life it is indeed. Allison becomes the high-profile lawyer she might have been, had she not given up law school to work for the District Attorney's Office as a consultant psychic on difficult and unsolved cases. In her alternate life, she lives in an expensive apartment with her husband from whom she appears distant; has no children, and clothes herself in high fashion couture. Despite her wealth and career, she is not fulfilled.

The episode features a scene wherein Allison is dressed in a Chanel suit, complete with a four-strand pearl necklace, and carries a Hermès black Birkin. The Birkin here is used instead of the briefcase one would perhaps expect in such a functional context. The Birkin in particular becomes a marker of transformation for Allison (who in her other reality could never afford such a luxury). It takes near centre-frame as she visits District Attorney Manuel Devalos. Allison places the highly-polished bag upon the desk between herself and Manuel, indicating her higher-class position. For the most part of the scene, he stands on the left whilst she is seated on the right. This appears to indicate a bid for power.

In her 'normal' life Allison Dubois, usually carries a slouch tan shoulder bag, often worn across her body. This speaks practically and affordability. She wears smart and unpretentious suits to work with a small pendant around her neck. Despite her husband, Joe, being a systems design mathematician in the aerospace industry (read 'rocket scientist') and presumably earning a more than decent wage, the Dubois family lives a modest existence. The moral outcome in this episode hangs on the 'money (and Birkins) don't buy happiness' trope.

LE DIVORCE

> 'I know my son – faithful only to Hermès'
> Amélie Cosset, *Le Divorce*

Le Divorce (Ivory, 2003) opens with animated icons of French beauty and culture, closing with an image of a red Hermès Kelly bag flying across the screen. The Kelly bag in this film betrays a sexual secret. It is given to American, Isabel Walker (Kate Hudson) as a gift by Edgar Cosset (Thierry Lhermitte) for being his mistress. A married and wealthy French politician, he is her sister's husband's uncle.

Isabel's first scenes depict her wearing a brown, leather fringed shoulder bag, worn across the body, in much the same manner as Alex and Allison do. It is in keeping with her casual Bohemian look and long flowing wavy hair. But the acquisition of the Kelly bag signals an outward transformation in other areas too: we witness a rapid increase in her level of sophistication, knowledge of French wines, conservative chic tailored suits, and her free flowing hair is replaced by a straight stylish bob. This transformation is noticed and remarked upon by Edgar at least twice. Isabel's change is also noted by others: 'You look like someone who reads Marie Claire'. She replies, 'Have you any idea what this cost!'. Of course this is not just a reference to its monetary value, but also a metaphor for the social cost to her reputation for being Edgar's mistress. Upon another meeting with Edgar the bag it positioned between them. When he leaves the room, Isabel places her padded bra inserts inside the bag. The Kelly, as a containment metaphor for sexual deception, is reinforced. Isabel masquerades as an image of a woman suitable to Edgar's tastes. The more she adopts the mask, the more she is recognized for who she 'really is'. It seems Isabel remains dis/tastefully conspicuous whilst carrying such an outrageously expensive purse (estimated value, $45,000). It betrays her 'true' identity at every turn. A young man with whom she has already had a flirtation remarks, 'That's not yours. You stole it from some rich old lady!'. The text is at pains to point out Isabel's unsuitability to wear the Kelly, and simply that she would never be able to afford it. The text invites us to prefer the 'real' Isabel, postponing the inevitable moment where she too will cast it away, as foreshadowed in the opening-credit sequence and confirmed in the closing scenes.

Author, Olivia Pace (Glenn Close), is Isabel's employer. Upon seeing her new bag, she knowingly remarks, 'Oh a Kelly! You must have an admirer, and he must be rich and French'. She is well aware of Edgar's history of 'gift-giving', having received a Kelly from him herself as a younger woman. She later expounds upon Edgar's attraction to Isabel, proclaiming him as 'a bit worldly, a bit knowing, famous, older – I suppose that's sexy, especially to a young person. It's like fornicating with God!'. Isabel vicariously enjoys the power Edgar wields but there are limits to this power.

At her book signing, Olivia inscribes Edgar's copy: 'To the Kelly man' and draws a little sketch of a Kelly bag. He enquires: 'Do you still have yours?' to which she replies, 'No, I lost it a long time ago', signifying that she has no need of it any longer. She cast it off, no longer wanting it as an outward sign of sexual dependence upon an unfaithful and deceitful man. For her, she has outgrown the need to play games of furtive love and expensive gifts as 'pay off' for keeping the secret.

Edgar uses the Kelly as a means of courting favour and controlling his mistresses. The downside of this is that he needs to police the locations in which the bag can be seen, if he is to preserve his secret. His constant monitoring begins to annoy Isabel who just wants to enjoy the bag.

> Edgar: It's not a bag for a bookshop.
> Isabel: It's convenient and beautiful.

At a classical concert he reiterates:

> Edgar: I've told you, a purse of this kind is not suitable for every occasion! A simple black evening bag would be more appropriate.
> Isabel: What is suitable? The French talk about religion, morality, sex. Why not money?
> (Ivory, 2003)

Thus, the question of suitability is debated throughout, not just through dialogue but also with disapproving and knowing glances: 'Such are the wages of sin!' (with a look to the bag). Isabel's own admission that she would oblige Edgar with sexual favours, even without expensive gifts, strongly indicates that she is not a fitting recipient of the bag.

Whilst at dinner, in an effort to divert her attention away from the cost of the bag, Isabel's sister, Roxy, declares to her mother, Margeeve (Stockard Channing), 'She got it on sale'. The notion that a Kelly can be purchased 'on sale' is a humorous misnomer. Their often bespoke and handmade qualities preclude any such instance. Should Margeeve entertain any truth to this statement, she too would demonstrate her unsophistication as a potential Hermès customer, and hence, unsuitability. The bag in this situation reveals as much about character, as it seeks to conceal.

Shin'ya Nagaswa (2008: 34) reveals how the significance of the customer experience with such luxury brands as Hermès, 'reflects the characteristics of the upper-class societies of the nations where the brands were founded' and that the 'concept of aristocratic value is reflected in the products'. Later, Margeeve takes the Kelly to lunch with Edgar's family, where she learns the truth about its history.

The French–American opposition continues throughout, as scenes depicting the ways French women wear scarves as a symbol of their culture function alongside others, where the French, civilized manners are posed against more crude, unseemly 'American' enactments (for example, the preference for sugar cubes over grains). Edgar's parting gift to Isabel is a Chanel scarf and he eventually confesses, 'I'm much too old for you', as Isabel's mother similarly declares: 'My favourite thing in Paris is this purse you gave me. It was too middle-aged and too lady-like for you'. Thus, the Kelly functions as a synechdoche of unsuitability. But her mother does not retain the bag either, reaffirming that neither she nor Isabel are suitable contenders for its ownership.

GILMORE GIRLS

'A beautiful leather, grown-up thing.'

Rory Gilmore, *Gilmore Girls*

Another text that features a Hermès bag as a gift is an episode of *Gilmore Girls* (Sherman-Palladino, The WB, 2000–2006). In 'Welcome to the Dollhouse' (Douglas, 2005) Rory Gilmore (Alexis Bledel) receives a pink ostrich-leather Birkin from her rich boyfriend, Logan (Matt Czuchry). Rory's wealthy and class-conscious grandmother, Emily (Kelly Bishop), is envious that her humble granddaughter who is ignorant of the bag's status value has received such a gift, whilst such a coveted object has escaped her own clutch. When Rory innocently discloses the news of this present, Emily cannot conceal her surprise and repeatedly exclaims, 'Well, well, well – a Birkin bag! A Birkin bag. A Birkin bag for Rory!', thereby signalling her perception that this a much too extravagant purchase and inappropriate gift to bestow upon her granddaughter. Rory is blissfully unaware of its potential impact, and after Emily proclaims, 'That's a very nice purse', she asks, 'Oh, maybe I shouldn't use it?', upon which, Emily replies, 'No. A Birkin bag is meant to be used, and seen!'

Emily is clearly in tune with the transformative powers of Hermès bags, as Samantha in *Sex and the City* is. The question is, though, why Emily, as a wealthy older woman who has the means to purchase a Birkin, does not own one. In later scenes she continues to express her extreme desire for 'the most sophisticated bag in the world' and her outrage at Rory's ownership of one. She reminds her husband that, despite her hints, he has still failed to buy her a Birkin. Emily may believe the bag should be a gift from a suitor, and perhaps a too indulgent an item to purchase for oneself. Aware of its capacity as an instrument of social power, she interprets Logan's gift to be an outward sign that his and Rory's relationship is about to undergo a social transformation – marriage.

The couple's relationship status, however, is not about to transform and the gesture is misread by Emily. Logan's real motive for gifting the bag is ambiguous but his intention is definitely to impress. As he enters the room the oversized orange carry bag is conspicuous and the clearly visible Hermès trademark provides the viewer with a moment of anticipation for the reveal. It is surprising though that Rory, as an aficionado of popular culture, is not familiar with the Hermès brand. She says, 'You know, I think my computer cord would fit in this perfectly,' but Logan advises, 'Ah, this is not a computer cord kinda purse'. Just as Edgar in *Le Divorce* directs Isabel on appropriate use for a Hermès bag, so too does Logan for his girlfriend. The Birkin's significance goes unnoticed by Rory who appreciates the bag as simply, 'a beautiful leather, grown-up thing'. How telling this observation is, as several times throughout the episode attention is drawn to how young she is, most importantly by Emily, who, whilst snooping in Rory's bedroom, finds the Birkin. She jealously holds the bag close (as Marilyn Rexroth does in *Intolerable Cruelty*) and says, 'A twenty-one-year-old girl has a Birkin and a grown woman doesn't!', thereby reinforcing her opinion that Rory is an unfitting recipient. Like Isabel, Rory is deemed by others not to be mature enough to carry the bag. But Rory happily keeps it, remaining ignorant of its magic. Her charming *naïveté* and eschewing of social-climbing ironically function as a justification for her suitability as an owner. Indeed, she is an 'authentic' character. Emily remains without – her irritating personality and excessive desire for a Birkin, preclude her ownership.

Steele and Borrelli (1999: 107) argue according to a branding expert that cult bags acquire their status via three criteria: '(1) legitimacy within the fashion industry, (2) great advertising, and (3) celebrity support'. Hermès has all three, especially the first. Hermès lines are decidedly distinct in style from other cult handbags. The Kelly and the Birkin have a rigidity and a strength of line not found in the popular slouch bags that even though expensive, do not approach a price anywhere near a Hermès (a crocodile Birkin with pavé-set diamonds will set you back around $200,000, but you might pick up a more modest number for around $10,000 if you are lucky). There is certainly something different about them. They hark back to an earlier era.

Hermès is more than fashion. Fashion is transient, changeable, disposable and recyclable. Hermès has always prided itself on its unique classic design, its longevity, quality and exclusivity. It is about retrained luxury, understatement and durability. The May 2007 edition of *Harper's Bazaar* states that current perceptions of luxury are changing, describing the new luxury as, 'going back to the old idea of the super-exclusive, the rare; things that simply cannot be mass-produced. The one defining aspect they share is that they are unique, one of a kind, hand-built' (Huckbody 2007a: 37). The Luxury Institute included Hermès among the top social status brands for 2006 (Huckbody 2007a: 36). This notion of understatement 'whispers' throughout this issue of *Harper's Bazaar*. In a photographic feature entitled 'Quiet Luxury, Shhhh: Winter's best takes on classic pieces' (Smith 2007: 191) we are re-introduced to the Hermès Kelly bag in light green (price on application, of course). We may also be green with envy of its perfect complement of the model's pale neutral-toned House of Cashmere jumper and Emporio Armani pants, complete with Fendi, Cartier and Tiffany & Co. jewelry.

'Jean Louis Dumas insists that "Hermès is not a fashion house"' (Dumas, cited in Tungate 2005: 151). Its price tags alone keep it well out of range of most mortals. 'Pierre-Alexis Dumas, fifth-generation Hermès and successor to his father as artistic director, says silk scarves "capture the spirit of the time without giving in to fashion"' (Dumas, cited in Huckbody 2007b: 76) – a similar sentiment to that of Jean Louis. It is because Hermès seems so out of reach to us all, it is the royalty of leather goods and couture, as evidenced by Queen Elizabeth often seen wearing their scarves about her head, and also her player, Helen Mirren, in the film, *The Queen* (Frears, 2006), adorns herself with the equine-inspired silk squares. Tungate notes that Gaultier's first prêt-à-porter collection for Hermès featured 'delightfully perverse harnesses and riding boots' (2005: 150).

Hermès and film have also become synonymous with French culture with a glass tower boutique in Tokyo that 'offers not only the full range of Hermès goods, but also regular screenings of French films' (Tungate 2005: 150). One of the members of the *Purse Blog* declares in reference to *Le Divorce*, 'The bag was the best thing about that movie . . . and then it got flung off the Eiffel Tower!!' (QuirkyCool, 24 March 2006) thus identifying the bag as essential to the film. A strange equation seems to be emerging here: Hermès = French = class = wealth = culture = film = sexuality/sexual deception.

It is well known that Sigmund Freud identified the purse as a metaphor for a woman's sexual parts, but film seems to have run with this on an unprecedented scale, as this observation from the *Purse Blog* reveals:

> In the movie 'Dream Lover' with James Spader and Mädchen Amick, I think Mädchen Amick is carrying an Hermès . . . not completely sure. (The purse that James Spader empties during that part of the movie to confirm that she's still wearing her diaphragm.) It looks like an Hermès. Does anyone remember? (Buttery, 24 March 2006)

Diaphragms and padded bra inserts – intimately personal feminine objects, concealed in expensive leather containers. The link with bags, sexuality and desire is strengthened by the reply to the above post by a woman who is almost breathless at the mention of Spader and Hermès in the same sentence!

CONCLUSION

Hermès is, at the very least, provocative and ambiguous. Its high-end products and the cultural and social effects it relays will not go unnoticed by the savvy consumer, whether they are purchasers of bags, or consumers of images. However, it remains that in both many fictional representations and narrative forms, and real life situations, certain characters and individuals will be deemed unsuitable as bearers of Hermès merchandise. The aura that is carefully crafted and purposefully manufactured works to maintain its exclusivity. The entwining of notions of class with conservative cultural values and restrained sexuality complicates this formula of suitability. In addition, knowledge about how to discern a fake from a real Hermès bag is tied in with notions of an authentic personality. There is a distinct code in operation at the level of character and reader, and a certain pleasure in the spectacle of something that surpasses its role as simply an item of wardrobe.

References

Bellafante, G. (2003), 'Hermès goes after the purse snatchers', *Sydney Morning Herald*, 15 August, http://www.smh.com.au/articles/2003/08/14/1060588523598.html. Accessed 14 August 2013.

Cohen, Joel (2003), *Intolerable Cruelty*, USA: Universal Pictures.

Douglas, J. (2005), 'Welcome to the Dollhouse', *Gilmore Girls*, Season 6, Episode 6, USA: Warner Bros. Entertainment.

Frankel, David (2001), 'Coulda Woulda Shoulda', *Sex and the City*, Season 4, Episode 11, USA: HBO.

Goodwin, M. E. (2004), 'Pricey Purchases and Classy Customers: Why sophisticated customers do not need the protection of trademark laws', *Journal of Intellectual Property Law*, Fall, 12, pp. 255–82.

Huckbody, J. (2007a), 'Planet Luxury: Are You On It?', Australian *Harper's Bazaar*, May, pp. 36–42.

Huckbody, J (2007b), 'Outside the Square', Australian Harper's Bazaar, May, pp. 76–78.

Ivory, James (2003), *Le Divorce*, USA: Twentieth Century Fox Corporation.

Johnson, A. (2002), *Handbags: The Power of the Purse*, New York: Workman Publishing.

LeBlanc, S. (2012), 'Sustainable Fashion Design: Oxymoron No More?', *BSR*, October, http://www.bsr.org/en/our-insights/report-view/sustainable-fashion-design-oxymoron-no-more. Accessed 8 May 2013.

Nagaswa, S. (2008), 'Creating Customer Experience in Luxury Brands – Comparison of Hermès, Louis Vuitton and Coach', *Waseda Business & Economic Studies*, No. 44, pp. 25–39, http://dspace.wul.waseda.ac.jp/dspace/bitstream/2065/33710/1/WasedaBusiness%26EconomicStudies_4 4_Nagasawal.pdf. Accessed 14 August 2013.

Schwary, Ronald, L. (2006), 'Twice Upon a Time', *Medium*, Season 2, Episode 22, USA: Warner Bros. Entertainment.

Smith (2007), 'Quiet Luxury, Shhhh: Winter's best takes on classic pieces', Australian *Harper's Bazaar*, May, p. 191.

Steele, V. and Borrelli, L. (1999), *'Status' Handbags: A Lexicon of Style*, New York: Rizzoli, pp. 104–28.

Tonello, M. (2008), *Bringing Home the Birkin*, New York: Harper Collins.

Tungate, M. (2005), *Fashion Brands: Branding Style from Armani to Zara*, London: Kogan.

FURTHER READING

Belisle, D., 2011. Retail nation: Department stores and the making of modern Canada. UBC Press.

Clifford, M., 2003. Working with Fashion: The Role of Art, Taste, and Consumerism in Women's Professional Culture, 1920-1940. American Studies, 44(1/2), pp.59-84.

Edwards, Bronwen, *Department Store*, Berg Fashion Library

Entwistle, Joanne (2009) Understanding High Fashion: Retailing and Buying. In *Aesthetic Economy in Fashion Markets and Value in Clothing and Modeling*, 83-106, Oxford: Berg.

Hancock II, Joseph H. "Chelsea on 5th Avenue: Hypermasculinity and Gay Clone in the Retail Brand Practices of Abercrombie & Fitch, *Fashion Practice*, Volume 1, No. 1. Taylor & Francis, 2009.

Halepte, Jaya, (2011), *Retailing in Emerging Markets*, New York: Fairchild.

Lavrence, C. and K. Lozanski. 2014. "This Is Not Your Practice Life": Lululemon and the Neoliberal Governance of Self. Canadian Review of Sociology/Revue Canadienne de Sociologie, 51: 76–94. doi:10.1111/cars.12034

Okonkwo, U., 2010. Luxury brands & celebrities: An enduring branding romance.

Santink, J.L., 1990. Timothy Eaton and the rise of his department store. Univ of Toronto Pr.

Shaw, David and Dimitri Koumbis (2017), *Fashion Buying, From Trend Forecasting to Shop Floor*, London: Bloomsbury.

Wang, S. S., K. D. Brownell and T. A. Wadden, 2004. The influence of the stigma of obesity on overweight individuals. International journal of obesity, 28(10), pp.1333–1337.

Figure 16 Mia Moretti Photo Courtesy of Brent Luvaas.
Source: Brent Luvaas

PART V
Media and Omni-Channel Retailing

Figure 17 Photo Courtesy of Brent Luvaas.
Source: Brent Luvaas

INTRODUCTION

NIOKA WYATT

The combination of fashion production and consumption, coupled with the integration of new technological advancement throughout the supply chain from proprietary software systems speeding up textile production to augmented reality enhancing fashion retail experiences, has the potential to propel the future growth and development of innovative fashion companies and offers new commercial opportunities (Genova and Moriwaki, 2016). As with all modern industries, the growth of the fashion sector across a century or more into a viable trillion dollar international industry, has evolved on the back of ongoing technological development enabling the mass production of consumer goods (Tortora, 2015). Implementing relevant technology for the right purpose can assure a competitive advantage. This is based on the refinement of logistical processes implementing a more efficient production and delivery system and enhancing the consumer experience by personalizing products and elevating shopping experiences, both online and offline, in the interests of taking the consumer value proposition of fashion brands at all price points to another level.

Technology has serviced the needs of fashion companies throughout the value chain across the past century or so, fueling consumption and the intrinsic need for consumers to acquire products at faster and cheaper rates. Automation in factories replaced textiles and garments produced in domestic settings; the sewing machine changed clothing production from the 19th century onwards, while the invention of metal zippers impacted on how clothing was constructed in the early 20th century, and the late 20th early 21st century has seen the invention of a range of high-tech fabrics that can adapt to the demands of modern lifestyles. Each wave of disruptive technological change usually involves operational and economic challenges. This enables industries to remain competitive in the existing system with lower cost, more efficient ways of doing business. Yet, these changes are often resisted and not embraced by all industry sectors. It would also appear that the larger brands and traditional areas of the fashion industry have been slow to embrace this change with new operators popping up to lead the way, particularly in the retail arena. Undoubtedly, one of the major forces shaping the business of fashion across the next decade and beyond will be technological advancement. Fashion businesses in future will need to rely on the multi-channel approach of implementing technology to support their business strategies. These digital transformations will impact on traditional retail and consumer behavior to streamlining processes and modernizing operations across the fashion industry, but as yet they are still a work in progress. As a *Business of Fashion (BoF)* editorial observed,

> The fashion industry fetishises technology as if it were a seasonal trend, not an ongoing revolution. Technology is changing everything, from product development to manufacturing to logistics to human resources to sales. Still, most fashion companies relegate technology to a subset of their marketing and sales departments, treating it as a side-project rather than integrating technology into core business thinking. (BoF, 2015)

Due to the rapid development of the digital landscape, geo-location based software, and wearable technology, the future of fashion technology will serve as a catalyst to encourage imagination, ingenuity, and innovation; all crucial elements in pushing forward technological and social progress (Walker, 2006). However, the realization that technological change offers new opportunities, or significant threats if this is ignored, appearing to percolate through and across every level of the fashion industry and throughout its value chain system. Technology-driven initiatives in the fashion industry are all about connecting with, and understanding consumer needs and can be distilled into five main themes in terms of the digitization of: fashion design and production; product innovation; data management and decision making; directive distribution; marketing and e-commerce purchasing solutions. These will be now be briefly examined in turn as a framework for the readings in this section that deal with many of these technologically-oriented issues facing the fashion industry and the myriad of brands that it contains and reflects on they will conduct the business of profitable survival in the future. This chapter will evaluate the radical shift facing the fashion eco-system supported by industry examples and grounded case studies.

DIRECTIVE DISTRIBUTION AND SUPPLY VIA PRODUCT LIFECYCLE MANAGEMENT (PLM)

Starting at the back end of the fashion chain – technology has the potential to monitor, analyze and enhance supply chain efficiency. To this end, the fashion industry in the late 1990s introduced enabling software systems such as Product Lifecycle Management (PLM) and Enterprise Resource Planning (ERP) to speed up production, and these systems still use in operational terms across the contemporary fashion system. Essentially, PLM is a database designed to track the progression of products throughout the supply chain system. The PLM database can store designs for easy manipulation, create technical packets, compare prices from global manufacturers, assess the costs of products, and manage the overall brand architecture of the line. Yunique PLM, for example, is a system offered through Gerber technology enabling the fashion eco-system to communicate and streamline the decision-making process. Sourcing teams can monitor bids and progress throughout the logistical process of production, track fabric and color approvals throughout the line, identify carryover products, and generate new styles. Traditional Product Data Management (PDM) systems manage products that are developed in Excel or handle communication through email. Innovative PLM systems are creating seamless approaches to managing processes faster and more accurately. Fruit of the Loom (FOL), a vertically integrated underwear manufacturer and subsidiary of Berkshire Hathaway Corporation, owned by Warren Buffett, was able to connect their WebPDM software to Gerber's Accumark® pattern design, grading, and marker making software. During implementation of PLM systems, companies often experience downtime in production and the overall operation of the supply chain process. Hence, employees are normally trained in stages in order to maintain a high percentage of productivity, while incorporating processes to handle any lapses due to downtime that the company may encounter.

Also, the Vanity Fair Corporation (VFC) infuses PLM systems in their product development process. The company utilizes 3-D fits to manage the technical process, while documenting decisions derived during these fit sessions. Fashion companies can integrate live models, mannequins, or innovative avatars representing the targeted size of the consumer. The avatars are the exact dimensions of a live model in both petite and full figured sizes. The importance of utilizing an avatar model in the fit process is highly important to ensure that products are delivered to consumers in the appropriate dimensions, materials, styles, and color-ways. During the fit process, companies can make three or more adjustments to prototypes. When VFC implemented the 3-D system, their technical fit process declined 40%. In most cases, the company receives an initial prototype and a final top of a production sample, constituting a representative style of what the end consumer will receive. The virtual fit model visualizes the avatars dancing, running, or catwalking down the runway, while incorporating and extending 3-D images for e-commerce platforms and advertisements. As one main role of a live fit model is to provide feedback regarding the overall aesthetic, touch, and feel of the material then one of the disadvantages of 3-D fits is the lack of evaluation about the feel of the fabric on a live model. Gerber and other companies are researching ways to simulate materials on the skin of avatars. Nevertheless, companies are able to select the movement of the avatar in various elements such as rain or windy atmospheres. From an efficiency perspective, Tukatech's 2017 version of TUKA3D also allows companies to reduce the number of samples and shipping time from China, India, and other global production centers.

As with most new technological applications, these heritage enterprise systems need to be constantly updated to ensure efficient ways of operating and that they keep up with innovative practices by integrating existing technology with new updates both inside and outside of the organization. Technological updates are essential if a fashion company is to survive and prosper and it is critical for specific activities, such as product launches, to ensure that goods and information move correctly through the relevant departments and areas. This is particularly important given the number of people involved and the complex decision-making executed at speed as the fashion collection makes its début

Information is pushed, pulled and shared at each juncture and technology needs to efficiently display this data in order to help designers, press and buyers make better decisions, whether at a runway show in Paris, a tradeshow in Berlin or a press day in London as the process of launching products encompasses more than just promotions and marketing. It begins at the very point of a product's inception and continues throughout the development, production, buying and merchandising processes, into PR and marketing and onto retail (Mullon 2015). Also, updates in the form of proprietary software system such as Product Launch Planning (PLP) that harvest data in real time, have been adopted by brands such as ASOS, Burberry and Levis to enhance supply chain efficiency and enable speedy decision making so that the company can respond immediately by delivering products as and when needed.

Product innovation and design

The fashion industry's operations and product range is also being impacted by the expansion of the Internet of Things (IoT) as the next wave of Fashion 4.0 referring to those wearable objects that are connected to the internet by a range of digital devices (Greengard, 2015). According to Business Insider (BI), the IoT comprises connected objects that enable the collection and exchange of data through embedded sensors, such as brassieres or watches that track your heartbeat, or the latest version of Amazon Eco connected to cloud based voice service Alexa to play music or access useful information that sold over 5.2 million units globally.

As an example, Google Glass was an early IoT with a fashion dimension, however its initial execution failed due to fears of radiation waves close to the skin and its unappealing design. Consumers also expressed privacy concerns because of the image and information tracking functions. Although a number of fashion companies selected Google Glass to test record their fashion shows with influencers, the connections often failed due to software updates interrupting the event. More successful IoT wearable examples are demonstrated in the crossover between fashion and sport over heath with Nike + shoes that tracked performance through I-phone technology. Also, the sports watch such as the FitBit – also parenting with Tory Burch - is also gaining traction on the pure luxury timepiece as a symbol of a healthy lifestyle among executives. In addition to physical objects, IoT applications are also being developed in the form of high performance textile technology enabling smart bags or t-shirts, such as Loomia's soft flexible circuit that can be integrated into fabric for heating, sensing or tracking.

Currently, Google Glass is revamping their core product features although its prototype launch was short lived. Also, the retail fashion market is now experimenting with virtual reality (VR) augmented reality (AR) in providing heightened customer experiences in store and at events. AR is the real-time use of information in the form of text, graphics, audio and other virtual enhancements integrated with real-world objects, differentiated from the more fixed hardware dependent Virtual Reality headsets and haptic accessories. While L'Oreal successfully launched its augmented reality based app, Modiface, simulating real-time skincare and makeup assessments, Coach, in partnership with Simon Malls and Facebook, enabled customers in New York to watch its real-time runway fashion shows using VR headsets in store (Lockwood, 2017).

Consumers today are compellingly drawn to "newness" with individual's social status often attributed to purchasing the latest technology in the form of an I-Phone, Apple Watch, or Fitbit, where fashion is expressed in terms of the aesthetic ad symbolic value of digital devices. Across the 20th century, technological devices, such as cameras and watches, were designed and marketed in terms of functionality rather than on their aesthetic elements. This trend has seemingly been reversed with aesthetic concerns playing a greater role among the fashion conscious. In a related study, Pan et al. (2015) interviewed participants from the United States, China, and Korea to identify and evaluate the digital devices that participants purchased in terms of influencing product choices, including newness versus patina, conspicuous consumption versus functionality, and imitation versus personal style. Their findings suggested that newness versus patina related to the consumption of objects that are relegated to being short-lived fads such as Google Glass. In the same study (Pan, 2015) one of the interviewees explained how his wife purchased a Louis Vuitton (LV) I-Pad case that was almost the same cost as the I-Phone. This luxurious case was a social symbol among her co-workers in meetings and at other business functions. During a recent conversation a friend also shared her distress at losing her LV I pad case that had been a personal gift for completing graduate school. As an executive at Uber's Philadelphia headquarters, she explained, "the case to carry my I-Pad allowed me to express my status in a professional manner." Although it was a regular leather case adorned with the printed Louis Vuitton signature logo, the product was an ideal purchase for this most desirable gadget of the year. Consumers experience emotional and develop personal attachments when purchasing luxury products including the crossover between technology and fashion, such as an I-Phone with a lack of concern for functionality or practicality. In some cases, consumers may own digital device for a number of years, however the intention to purchase a new product tend to change if they have an upward shift in lifestyle or income. Hence, imitation as a definer of personal style through acquired possessions allows consumers to have a sense of belonging to a specific group or socio-economic class. Many consumers also falter in the Apple 'family' trap by purchasing a bundle of branded products, including the I-Phone, Apple watch, MacBook, and I-Pad and often dress-up and personalize this technological ownership.

BIG DATA MANAGEMENT AND DECISION-MAKING

Data analytics are now driving decision-making in the fashion industry for detailed updates about current trends and customer needs. Access to, and analysis of the right data has always been essential to running a business and enabling relevant supply to meet demand using spreadsheets and sales data. In a past analogue age, collecting information was time consuming and slow and industry research relied on small samples. Now, in the digital age, driven by huge computer power with seemingly limitless storage and data management software, vast amounts of data can be accessed, analyzed and applied to help businesses operate based on new insights that add value to their offering and enable them to interact efficiently with consumers. This means that fashion companies can make more accurate forecasts based on predictive models about new trends and emerging consumer needs and wants. Historically, trend analysis relied on a team of experts making predictions from small datasets, which was labor intensive and expensive. With the arrival of big data acquisition and analysis vital and reliable information about consumer preferences will be generated on which can be based winning decisions for fashion companies and brands such as what color combinations will work next season; what will sell in certain geographical locations over others and what sort of retail experiences consumers desire. Companies can use data mining and cognitive computing to predict trends based on consumer mindsets. Big data usage will also enable designers to know how to fully satisfy consumer demands before they trend or change from fast fashion to providing near instantaneous access to catwalk offering as H&M did in Paris Fashion Week (H&M, 2017). Data analytics also assist in evaluating and planning fashion retail design and management of stores using location analytics and consumer online offline shopping preferences and some online niche fashion retailers to heighten the online retail experience are also using algorithms. San Francisco based Stitch Fix operates a personalized shopping service where it provides customers with a box of clothing options after submitting their style profile based on size, color preferences, lifestyle and budget, The consumer then provides feedback on the selections once they have selected or returned the garments, which are kept on online for future purchasing decisions. So, no longer is data just the enabler of business – it has a significant value in itself as it holds the key to successful future business operations in the fashion industry. For many fashion companies this is still a work in progress and many fashion companies, notably in the luxury sector are still playing catch-up but should be mindful of the need to fully activate their data analytic capacity.

MARKETING AND E-COMMERCE PURCHASING SOLUTIONS

Technology has revolutionized the ways in which we shop and connect on a global scale. The growth of synchronized technology has facilitated the development of omni-channel platforms and increased the usage of mobile shopping as more fashion consumers – three out of four - are browsing and ultimately shopping online. The convenience and reliability of large online retail platforms, such as Zalando and Amazon, for example are increasingly becoming the first port of call for fashion consumers, spurring these online retail giants to offer their own private labels and in the case of Amazon to collaborate on a line of 'athleisurewear' as a measure of active fashion consumer presence on these sites.

Social shopping via intelligent systems

The swift arrival and successful presence of online fashion platforms have disrupted the way that consumers are buying fashion and accessories across all sectors as they offer luxury retailers wider customer access. Collaboration with online platforms for fashion companies provides opportunity for grater personalized customer engagement to enhance sales, but also extend their omni-channel offerings and heighten value added customer experiences with Tmall for example, partnering with New York Fashion Week 2017 offering live-streaming of catwalk shows of its high-end brand collaborators. In this sense, for mass, niche or luxury brands the questions is not *whether* to provide this retail extension for the customer but *when* to do so, despite the fact that some premium brands are still concerned about rescinding control over their offering.

FASHION RETAIL MOBILITY IN DEVELOPED AND DEVELOPING MARKETS

Mobility holds the key to future fashion retail, while smartphones represent a significant amount of fashion sales on a global scale. Fashion consumers are opting for this more immediate, convenient way of locating and buying fashion items as mobile phones increasingly become extended wallets making speedy payments via apps or in store. Both Tommy Hilfiger and Chanel have partnered with and Farfetch offering an integrated mobile futuristic shopping experience enabling customers, notably targeting millenials, to view, engage with and purchase items via their apps, while also to link and share their purchase through their social media accounts. Increasingly, Asian countries are leading the way in mobile take up and application for fashion retail. In South Korea and Japan mobile accounts for over half of shopping transactions, while in China this figure is over 80 percent, assisted by the exponential growth of payment apps WeChat and Alipay.

Emerging countries such as India also now represent a very large market share because of their potential consumer markets and increasing Gross Domestic Product (GDP). Lakshmy's (2014) investigation in the Indian market on the trends, consumer buying behavior, design, screen size, and social influences of smart phones found it to be the second largest industry for digital subscribers accounting for 12% of the world's subscribers. Low cost mobile phones constitute 91% of overall mobile phone sales, leading to growth opportunities in view of a growing middle class with disposable income. Equally, Nigeria relies on a shared telephone network in order to conduct business on a global scale. Many consumers do not own mobile phones, however a fee is paid to the owner to conduct business when stores are running low on various merchandise. Neuwirth noted that, "System D is referred to an informal economy which references the black market. Neuwirth coined the term System D as the DIY economy that focuses on the underground market which contradicts his beliefs because business owners are operating their mode of entrepreneurship in an open economy that is not Westernized. "It's totally open and right there for you to find." Proctor and Gamble's largest business sector is large frequency stores operating in System D markets and earns 20% of revenue from the growing economy. Similarly to various cellular operators in the United States, cell phone carriers sells airtime to consumers and not monthly plans. A majority of the cell phones are shipped from Guangzhou or Shenzhen, China where a large percentage of electronics and small parts are produced. One of the disadvantages for consumers in System D markets is the production of counterfeit merchandise. Due of the low wages earned in System D areas, consumers cannot afford to purchase branded cell phones. Recognizable brands such as Apple and Samsung are not affordable in System D economies. As a result, consumers purchase Nextel products. Across time, the System D economies will evolve similarly to the technology in developed markets. As the Internet, social media, and the development of broadband continue to flourish and become more globally accessible, emerging markets will embark on retail fashion opportunities in this growing arena.

While Americans and Europeans have also embraced the evolution of smart phones to satisfy their retail habits the take-up rate has been relatively slower with 15% of mobile phone owners using their devices to purchase goods but this trend is moving in the right direction with a predicted increase of 23% usage for the next 5 years. The Pew Research Center (2017) reported that 12% of Americans claimed to be dependent on their smartphones with 50% also owning a tablet. Hence, companies are partnering with Silicon Valley experts to manage the various interfaces and tracking the customer experience when purchasing from a variety of devices. In 2017, over 50% of QVC (home shopping channel) customers purchased products on their mobile devices. The buying pattern for consumers at QVC in North America, as a grounded example, initially begins with a desktop search. Following this, a consumer may continue their search process on their I-pad finally making a decision to purchase the chosen product on their digital device.

THE GROWTH OF FASHION APPS

Mobile applications are also enabling closer producer-consumer retail relationships. As a situated example, RetailMeNot, Inc. is an application (app) designed for consumers to gain information about sales, coupons, and other promotions. Cotter Cunningham, the innovator of Whaleshark recognized the future of digital coupons and founded the company. RetailMeNot, Inc. went public in 2013 and has global presence in Canada, United Kingdom, Spain, Germany, Italy and the Netherlands operating under various subsidiaries. Each month, the app shares over 800,000 offers from retailers and 70,000 brands are in the global digital network. The app incorporates a Global Positioning System (GPS) or network location sources when connected to a network such as WIFI. When the GPS is enabled, push notifications are distributed to a consumer's digital device as long as permission is granted from the user. RetailMeNot also offers rebates when a consumer walks into a certain number of stores. In 2016, the company received over 675 million visits, 19 million mobile visits, mobile site traffic increased 47%, and 45 million people subscribed through email. Information gathered from the website found that RetailMeNot attributed $4.8 billion in retail sales to consumer transactions from paid digital offers in its marketplace in 2015 and more than $600 million of which were linked to its in-store solution.

WECHAT IN CHINA

Social platforms are stimulating retail fashion sales globally and have overcome distribution barriers in developing and emerging by offering convenient, safe, direct ways to shop online. The overwhelming success of WeChat is one example, enabling Chinese consumers to network, shop, engage in banking, and interface with millions of brands without leaving the site. WeChat China , whose parent company is Tencent Holdings, Ltd., focuses on developing and enhancing user's retail experiences based on a seamless shopping experience where consumers can make purchases without leaving the site, as with Instagram. According to a China Channel report, only one percent of WeChat's users are over the age of 55, with over 800 million active users (Brennan, 2017). While Instagram's social architecture focuses on videos and following influencers, WeChat's platform allows users to access secured banking, group chats, and a streamlined shopping experience for groceries and garments. One of WeChat's strategy for growth focuses on targeting an overseas Chinese consumer living in global markets such as Europe. The company's goal is to capture a percentage of the international arena by marketing the social and marketing component of the application in areas that are frequently visited by Chinese tourists, as an alterative offering to traditional banking options. As a grounded example of a WeChat success story, Tao Lian "Mr. Bags" is a Chinese handbag blogger who partnered with French luxury brand Givenchy to sell an exclusive limited edition of 80 pink handbags. Since 2011, Mr. Bags captured an entourage of 1.2 million followers on WeChat using a three part promotional strategy. Firstly, Mr. Bags published an article covering the handbag promotion. Secondly, the blogger focused on the product's main selling features and those of the French luxury brand collaborator. Thirdly, selling the limited edition bags for 14,900 RMB ($2,170) as a marketing strategy stimulated swift sales selling out in twelve minutes and generating 1.192 million RMB (US$173,652). In addition, the increasingly luxury conscious Chinese customer gained bragging rights for purchasing an exclusive product around Valentine's Day as a form of conspicuous consumption. Furthermore, due to the special holiday launch more male followers purchased these products for their wife, mistress, or girlfriend. As a way of stimulating consumer desire, Mr. Bags also reminded potential consumers of celebrities who owned Givenchy bags by frequently posting up their images. Also, the scarcity tactic was used as the company ensured that the cost of their bags would exceed the daily limits imposed on WeChat, while each customer was limited to 15 minutes online contact time per sale, which further stimulated product desire.

However, issues associated with managing synchronized web interfaces poses challenges for retailers in view of the complexity in a growing proliferation of payment providers, operating standards and the management of a wide range of enabling technologies - cloud base to physical devices. Also, data security will be the main concerns for users and providers. Blockchain technology offers a solution to this with a more secure approach to conducting the business of fashion consisting of a decentralized network that securely and directly exchanges information, documents and data enabling more transparency for fashion companies. It also prevents fraud across a fast, low risk, low cost payment sevice whilst nurturing consumer trust. In application, both the Payaoni and Provenance brands have found this useful in terms of demonstrating their sustainably sourced fashion stories (Provenance, 2018). Also, redefining the consumer as producer is one of the important manifestations of this trend enabling the brand to offer a more two-way, inclusive and personalized offering.

FASHION AND ARTIFICIAL INTELLIGENCE (AI)

The business of fashion is also set to benefit significantly from the manifest application of Artificial Intelligence (AI) - whereby computer systems replace tasks traditionally completed by humans across the supply chain enhancing speed, and quality of operations in from forecasting and merchandising to product delivery. Despite detractors questioning its relevance to the creative process, AI offers the ability to enhance design and product development closely aligned with consumer preferences as typified by fashion design start-up Stitch Fix, using AI to generate creative moodboards. In terms of customer-relations management, AI is also being used by Burberry's chatbots offering an immediate response for consumer enquiries. Offline, AI can also enhance the store experience for consumer via digital changing room mirrors and sizing technology in store.

The readings in this chapter highlight the range of companies implementing innovative technological applications ranging from online consumer co-creation and social media engagement via apps and blogs; to streetstyle photographs in emerging fashion markets using traditional photographic and smartphone technology. Building up and maintaining customer loyalty and a fan following using social media is the focus in the reading "Yoga, Facebook, and Fandom: Examining Brand Devotion by lululemon Customers using Social Media" authored by Caroline Czajkowski and Tasha L. Lewis. The authors demonstrate in an empirical investigation of yogawear company lululemon, that active online brand engagement is a beneficial usage of enabling technology that strengthens the brand's image and identity. Yet, it is not without its risks in terms of controlling and containing criticism about a new collection that fails to live up to expectations, for example. However, as this reading demonstrates, careful control of social media engagement with its customer/fan base is critical to the competitive survival of a fashion brand.

Juanjuan Wu in, "Co-design Communities Online examines a closer level of consumer involvement in the fashion design and production process: Turning Public Creativity into Wearable and Sellable Fashions". Focusing on two fashion brands Zazzle and Threadless that base their business on co-designing communities Wu demonstrates how emerging co-design hubs are rapidly becoming a viable options for mass customizing brands not only as a successful business model, but also as a way of stimulating and injecting innovation and creativity into their brand offering, while providing an outlet for sharing ideas and strengthening relationships among young likeminded online communities of interest.

Continuing on the theme of fashion co-creation and product design, Kendra Lapolla in "Modcloth: a case study in co-creative branding strategies" examines how an American online vintage and vintage inspired retailer actively engages and involves its young female millennial consumer using the brand's website hosting a range of collaborative conversations. This consumer centric and dialogue-driven approach to brand management based on dialogue, access, transparency and risk assessment uses targeted and relatable technology to facilitate innovation and creative expression as a new personalized, inclusive and nuanced approach to fashion branding.

In a different cultural and spatial context, Brent Luvaas challenges the western centric mythic worldview of streetstyle blogs in his anthropological examination, "Shooting street style in Indonesia: a photo essay". In a quest to locate and visually articulate style on the streets of Jakarta and Bandung, Luuvas comes to questions the real value and purpose of this western obsession, reflecting that it may be founded on an empty sign system without meaning that tells us very little about what is in fashion or in style. Alternatively, Luuvas emerges from the experience of streetstyle photographer in this non-western location reflecting on the rich personal style that he witnessed of colorful fabrics of the female hijabers, and the more politicized culturally appropriated male dress often based on customized black t-shirts. This enabled him to reflect on the diverse cultural influences that Indonesia represents and which operate in the absence of technologies that their geographic peers are so reliant upon to access and define fashion.

TECHNOLOGICAL CHALLENGES AND OPPORTUNITIES FOR THE FUTURE FASHION INDUSTRY

New technology offers many opportunities for the fashion industry across the supply chain from product lifecycle management (PLM), 3-D printing and fitting devices, digital printing, virtual reality, augmented reality, e-commerce systems and marketing initiatives through crowdsourcing, retail technology, applications (apps), and social media platforms. The growth of technological advancements also leads to data security risks for consumers. Target, Home Depot, and Chick-Fil-A, Sony and the United States Postal Service have all been victims of data breaches. Nevertheless, fashion companies will have to invest in tighter security measures to ensure that shared information enabling a heightened fashion retail experience is also safe and protected to ensure trust and reliability in customer-brand relationships.

Ultimately, technological applications in the fashion system will ensure greater collaboration across the supply chain among different players. Inevitably, anxieties emerge about job replacement and reskilling, for example, which are encountered each time any industry incorporates new technological approaches to doing business. These are real issues and the industry will have to plan ahead for the inevitable restructuring and retraining that will be need to adjust to these new realities, but which may also result in releasing more time for fashion professionals to pursue new creative and innovative design opportunities and pathways.

References

Brennan, M. (2017). "The 2017 WeChat User Behavior Report", *China Channel*, Tencent Penguin Intelligence, Retrieved 2018 from: https://chinachannel.co/1017-wechat-report-users/

Business of Fashion (2015). "Is fashion missing the technology revolution?: Editorial" *Business of Fashion (BoF)* 5 April. Retrieved 2017 from: https://www.businessoffashion.com/community/voices/discussions/is-fashion-missing-the-technology-revolution

Elison, J. (2018). "Chanel and Farfetch team up to shape the fashion retail experience", Retrieved 2018: https://www.ft.com/content/b7dafa04-1330-11e8-8cb6-b9ccc4c4dbbb

Genova, A. and K. Moriwaki. (2016). *Fashion and Technology: A Guide to Materials and Applications*. London: Bloomsbury Academic.

Gerber Technology (n.d.). "Elevating Supplier to Collaborative Partners." Retrieved 2017 from: http://www.gerbertechnology.com/fashion-apparel/interior/product-lifecycle-management/cutter-buck/.

Greengard, S. (2015). *The Internet of Things*, Cambridge Massachusetts: MIT Press.

H&M (2017), "Unveiled: The First Looks from the H&M Studios". *H&M Website*. Retrieved 2017 from https://www.hm.com/om/magazine/culture/h-m-inside/2017/01/unveiled_-the-first-looks-from-hm-studio-ss-17

Lakshmy, S. (2014), "Empirical study on cluster analysis of the smartphone segment". *International Journal on Customer Relations*, 2(2), 32–36. Retrieved 2017 from https://ezproxy.philau.edu/login?url=http://search.proquest.com/docview/1845261593?accountid=28402

Lockwood, L. (2017), "Coach, IMG and Simon Malls Partner of Virtual Reality Experience", *WWD*, 14 February, https://wwd.com/fashion-news/fashion-scoops/coach-img-and-simon-malls-partner-on-virtual-reality-experience-10802073/

Meola, A. (2016), "What is the Internet of Things (IoT)?" Retrieved 2016 from http://www.businessinsider.com/what-is-the-internet-of-things-definition-2016-8

Mullon, E. (2015), "Technology can transform the backbone of fashion", *Business of Fashion (BoF)* 5 April, Retrieved 2017 from: https://www.businessoffashion.com/community/voices/discussions/is-fashion-missing-the-technology-revolution/op-ed-embracing-digital-is-a-matter-of-survival

Pan, Y., D. Roedl, E. Blevis, and J. Thomas (2015), "Fashion thinking: Fashion practices and sustainable interaction design". *International Journal of Design*, 9 (1). Retrieved from https://ezproxy.philau.edu/login?url=http://search.proquest.com/docview/1682231529?accountid=28402

Pew Research Center (2017), "Pew Research Center: Mobile Fact Sheet". Retrieved 2017 from http://www.pewinternet.org/fact-sheet/mobile/

Provenance, (2018), "Increasing transparency in fashion with blockchain". *Provenance website*, Retrieved 2018 from: https://www.provenance.org/case-studies/martine-jarlgaard

Smith, A. (2017). "Record Shares of Americans now own smartphones, have home broadband". Pew Research Center. Retrieved 2017 from http://www.pewresearch.org/fact-tank/2017/01/12/evolution-of-technology/

RetailMeNot (2015), "Annual Report" RetailMeNot Inc. Retrieved from https://materials.proxyvote.com/Approved/76132B/20160229/AR_275102/#/12/

Tortora, P.G. (2015), *Dress, Fashion and Technology: from prehistory to the present*, London: Bloomsbury Academic.

Walker, S. (2006), *Sustainable by design: Explorations in Theory and Practice*. Sterling, VA: Earthscan.

SHOOTING STREET STYLE IN INDONESIA:
A photo essay

Brent Luvaas[1]

INTRODUCTION

In March 2012, I started a street-style blog, *Urban Fieldnotes* (http://www.urbanfieldnotes.com), as both a research instrument for studying the practice of street-style blogging and an open-source forum for documenting my preliminary thoughts on the subject. Then, after shooting and posting style pics in my home base of Philadelphia for some ten months, in January 2013 I had the opportunity to expand the scope of the project considerably, when I was invited to a workshop in Jakarta, the bustling capital city of Indonesia on the densely populated island of Java. Indonesia is a profoundly diverse place, with no shortage of sartorial styles to call its own. The Southeast Asian nation is an archipelago of some 17,000 islands and is home to more than 200 distinct ethnic groups, with their own languages, customs, textile and clothing traditions. It is also home to the world's largest Muslim population, with some 88% of its more than 230 million citizens subscribing to the faith. But this is only part of Indonesia's style story. Indonesia has one of the world's fastest growing fashion industries. Garment production and textiles, now the second-largest sector of Indonesia's economy (Chongbo, 2007), is helping drive an impressive economic growth rate of some 6% per year over the last decade. Accompanying this growth has been a massive expansion of Indonesia's middle class, from around 4% of the population in 1998 to estimates as high as 40% today. Indonesia now has dozens of high-end couture designers, a thriving cottage industry of hundreds of local independent clothing labels (Luvaas 2012), and an upwardly mobile population hungry for new designs and products. Needless to say, I was eager to see what I could find shooting street style there.

I should probably also mention that Indonesia is a place where I lived for more than two years, first as an exchange student in 1996 and later as a researcher for my book *DIY Style* (Luvaas, 2012) in 2006. I knew its fashion scene pretty well before heading there to shoot street style, and I had just published an article (Luvaas 2013) on personal-style bloggers in Indonesia, a group hundreds strong and growing, with some national semi-celebrities like Diana Rikasari and Evita Nuh in their midst. But try as I might, I could not find any active street-style blogs in Indonesia. There had been one, *Jakarta Street Looks,* a few years back, but it had already quietly fizzled out. The only other remaining one I could find, *Jakarta Street Journal,* was devoted largely to industry events and contained only a few, sparsely updated posts on style outside of those events. I wanted to know why. Why does one of the world's fastest growing fashion industries, with its own expansive community of personal-style bloggers produce so few *street-style* bloggers? What is it about Indonesia that makes it less prone to that particular – and enormously popular – type of representation?

PLACING THE 'STREET' IN 'STREET STYLE'

Does fashion trickle down from the elite (Veblen 1994; Bourdieu 1984) or bubble up from 'the streets'

---

[1] From Brent Luvaas (2013), Shooting Street Style in Indonesia: A Photo Essay, Clothing Cultures, Volume 1, Number 1, pp. 59–61, Intellect.

(Polhemus 1994; Aspelund 2009)? And do the styles on the sidewalk really inspire the fashions on the catwalk, as decades of literature in fashion studies have now claimed? If so, then Indonesia's fashion industry is in bad shape. Its streets are a congested mess of motorbikes and rickshaws. Its sidewalks are packed with food vendors and pirated CDs. Fashion, as we understand it in the western world – that practice of stylized experimentation characteristic of the upwardly mobile and the creatively inclined (Polhemus 1978), simply does not happen on the streets of Indonesia. There is no room for it. The very notion that fashion starts on 'the streets', a premise, incidentally on which street-style blogs depend, presumes a romanticized model of street life passed down in the European tradition from Baudelaire, an intoxicating blend of dandies and scoundrels that defy the bourgeois conventions of the settled and the genteel.

This is not what Indonesian streets look or feel like. The streets in Indonesia are not pedestrian zones where smartly dressed *flâneurs* go to promenade (Benjamin 2002). Parades of edgy, avant garde style do not happen there – indeed, it is an open question as to whether they happen anywhere at all. As Sophie Woodward (2009) has argued, street style is largely a 'myth', fabricated and promoted by fashion magazines, and yet it is a western myth, modelled on a very specific type of European pedestrian zone. To the extent that parades of style happen in Indonesia, they happen in malls. And that is where I had to go to shoot street style there. Malls, with their canned lighting and brand-name chain stores, malls that recreate the mythology of 'the streets' indoors.

CURATING COOL

The street-style bloggers I have interviewed for my larger project often imagine themselves as documenting trends on city streets the way curators of some turn-of-the-century museum of mankind salvaged the traditions of disappearing tribes. But there is a significant difference: archivists attempt to get representative samples. Street-style photographers document exceptions. They are interested in 'style', that 'superadded, rare, desired quality' (Johnson-Woods and Karaminas 2013: 13), that applies to probably no more than one in a hundred people. And how do street-style photographers recognize style? The answer I have invariably received from every street-style photographer I have interviewed is this: they just do. Photographers sense a quality in a person – a particular stance, a mode of presentation, a way of moving through the world – that is distinctly bold and stylized, and they react to it, the more instantaneously the better. When you think about it too much, the theory goes, you tend to get it wrong.

So what problems, then, does shooting in a foreign context pose to a street-style photographer? How does one recognize style in a place where the bodily hexis (Bourdieu 1980) of cultural elaboration is so utterly different? Does 'cool' cross borders? Does it even make sense to talk about 'cool' in a place so far from urban America, that racially charged milieu in which the stylized indifference of 'cool' became a fixture of the modern personality (Leland 2004)? I do not know. I can tell you, however, that in Bandung and Jakarta, my style radar – cultivated over months of shooting in Philadelphia – was malfunctioning. I hesitated. I questioned myself. I felt ill-equipped to pick out the stylish among the many.

HIJABER STYLE

What Indonesian street style lacked in 'cool', at least as I had understood it back home, it made up for in colour and conviction. Colour is everywhere on the streets – and in the malls – of urban Indonesia: colour, that is, and prints, some employing local patterns, some sampling from an international repertoire of tie dye, paisley and plaid. Urban Indonesian women, it would seem, have turned to colour and print in a big way, taking risks with both of a sort I have seldom seen in the United States – batik with hounds tooth, ikat with stripes. Colours ranged from bright pink and orange to rich blues and golds. And the women taking the biggest risks bar none were the 'hijabers', those modest Muslim women making their declarations of faith into expressions of personal style.

Hijabers have become much more visible in Indonesia in recent years. During the authoritarian Suharto regime, which ruled Indonesia from 1965 to 1998, Islam was continually minimized in political life, some might say 'suppressed' (Hefner 2000; Rudnyckyj 2009). Suharto's New Order government considered hardline (*santri*) Islam a threat to national sovereignty and sought to promote the 'tolerant', mystically oriented traditionalist (*abangan*) brand of Javanese Islam (see Geertz 1960; Beatty 1999) in its stead. But when student revolt brought down the regime in 1998, a new era of openness and freedom of expression, commonly known as *Reformasi*, took hold, and in keeping with an increasingly familiar brand of irony, it also brought more fundamentalist strands of Islam into the open. Far more women began to cover their heads, a practice often frowned upon by the older generation of the Javanese majority (see Brenner 1996), and seen as almost a rebellious act throughout much of the 1980s and 1990s, a declaration of faith against common social expectations. During my first time in Indonesia, back in 1996, I would estimate that about one in twenty women I came across in Java covered their heads. In 2013, it must have been closer to one in three. But this does not mean women were dressed more conservatively or 'traditionally'. On the contrary, as anthropologist Carla Jones (2010) has documented, the rise of piety has produced numerous innovations in Islamic fashion. Designers like Dian Pelangi and Irna Mutiara design exclusively for observing Muslim women, producing brightly coloured, intricately draped garments that have garnered international attention. Workshops are held in upscale Jakarta suburbs, providing make-up and self-presentation tips to the Muslim and upwardly mobile (Jones 2010). And every bookstore I stepped into this past January had a section devoted to 'hijab style', full of books of tips and tricks for tying and draping, often stacked high on the bestseller tables. There is even a network of personal-style bloggers in Indonesia, known as the Hijabers Community, devoted exclusively to hijab style. And designer Dian Pelangi, a member of that community, recently put out her own book of street-style photographs, titled, appropriately *Hijab Street Style*.

I found the visibility of hijabers in public space rather inspiring. These women are bold and striking. But it brought forth a number of questions for me. Has, for instance, the increasing presence of Islam in public life enabled expressions of fashion for women once frowned upon as immodest or imprudent? Has the professed modesty of the hijab made forms of expression acceptable that once were taboo? And do women experience this development, this stylization of Islam, as a new liberation or constraint? Why, after all, has Islam's fashion explosion been so specific to women? Why has there not been a comparable phenomenon for men?

IMPORTING SUBCULTURE

Where men's fashion has been most conspicuously articulated in Indonesia is in a decidedly more secular realm, that of 'alternative' urban styles labelled locally as 'indie' or 'underground'. As Wallach (2008b), Sen and Hill (2000) and Baulch (2007), among others, have documented, these are imported subcultural styles that came to Indonesia first through a variety of unofficial circuits: from cassette tapes dubbed off of passing European tourists, from mail order catalogues sent for from abroad, through to well-worn magazines passed hand to hand among friends. Punk and metal were already present in Indonesia by the early 1980s, but they became further elaborated on in the 1990s as both an alternative to the commercial schlock pumped out by a state-controlled media industry (Baulch 2007; Luvaas 2013), and as a cry of protest against the authoritarian Suharto regime (Wallach 2008a; Lee 2011). Underground scenesters were deeply involved with the protests that eventually brought down the regime in 1998, and once it had fallen, such styles only proliferated more rapidly. In a newly open media environment, with an Internet infrastructure firmly in place by the end of the 1990s, nearly every variety of imported subcultural expression was able to move freely and easily throughout the urban centres of the archipelago. Today, Indonesia is a hotbed of punk, post-punk, new wave, no wave, noise and every variety of metal imaginable. There is hardly a music or fashion scene anywhere not represented somewhere in the archipelago. And yet, underground looks remain a male-dominated mode of expression, with somewhat conservative, even ascetic tendencies (Wallach 2008b). In Indonesian subculture, the simple black T-shirt reigns supreme.

CONCLUSION: THE TROUBLE WITH REPRESENTING PLACE THROUGH STREET-STYLE PHOTOS

So what can I say about style in Indonesia after shooting there for three weeks this past January? What can I claim to have learned about place, space and meaning from documenting a people through their stylized exceptions? Well, perhaps there is not all that much I can say that has not already been said thousands of times already: that Indonesia is vast and varied; that its quiltwork of cultures is impossible to accurately characterize without a great deal of hedging; that it is highly syncretic and appropriative, drawing from multiple other places and cultures, whether by inspiration or imposition. There is no 'Indonesian' style, just as there has never been an Indonesian culture or character. There is no singularity of vision. And yet there are tendencies and moods that I hope emerge from these photos, patterns just on the verge of crystallization. Hijabers, for instance, with their colourful play on high fashion excess and modest piety, have risen to public prominence in the last decade. But so have punks, indie kids and metalheads. There has long been something fundamentally democratic at work in Indonesian fashion, a sheer irrepressible diversity of influences, none ever able to fully dominate another. But the democratization of Indonesian style tells us little about Indonesia's place in the larger fashion world, a place still tenuous and marginal at best. Indonesia has been largely left out of representation in the street-style blogosphere, just as it has in the fashion world more generally. Street style, as currently conceptualized, remains foreign to Indonesia for reasons articulated here, and Indonesia, consequently, remains off the street-style map. I hope these pictures succeed in evoking something of the dynamism and variety of style in Indonesia today.

I hope they succeed in making visible something of what still remains without representation.

References

Aspelund, Karl (2009), *Fashioning Society: A Hundred Years of Haute Couture by Six Designers*, New York: Fairchild Publications.

Baulch, Emma (2007), *Making Scenes: Reggae, Punk, and Death Metal in 1990s Bali*, Durham, NC and London: Duke University Press.

Beatty, Andrew (1999), *Varieties of Javanese Religion: An Anthropological Account*, Cambridge: Cambridge University Press.

Benjamin, Walter (2002), *The Arcades Project*, Cambridge, MA: Belknap Press of Harvard University Press.

Bourdieu, Pierrre (1980), *The Logic of Practice*, Stanford, CA: Stanford University Press.

Bourdieu, Pierrre. (1984), *Distinction: A Social Critique of the Judgment of Taste*. Cambridge, MA: Harvard University Press.

Brenner, Suzanne (1996), 'Reconstructing Self and Society: Javanese Muslim Women and 'The Veil'.' *American Ethnologist*, 23(4): 673–97.

Chongbo, Wu. (2007), 'Studies on the Indonesian Textile and Garment Industry', *Labour and Management in Development Journal*, 7(5): 1–14.

Geertz, Clifford. (1960), *The Religion of Java*. Chicago, IL and London: University of Chicago Press.

Gilbert, David. (2006), 'From Paris to Shanghai: The Changing Geography of Fashion's World Cities', in C. Breward and D. Gilbert (eds.), *Fashion's World Cities*, Oxford: Berg, pp. 3–32.

Hefner, Robert W. (2000), *Civil Islam: Muslims and Democratization in Indonesia*, Princeton and Oxford: Princeton University Press.

Johnson-Woods, Toni and Vicki Karaminas (2013), *Shanghai Street Style*, Bristol and Chicago: Intellect.

Jones, Carla (2010), 'Materializing Piety: Gendered Anxieties about Faithful Consumption in Contemporary Urban Indonesia', *American Ethnologist*, 37: 4, pp. 617–37.

Lee, Doreen (2011), 'Styling the Revolution', *Journal of Urban History*, 37: 6, pp. 933–51.

Leland, John (2004), *Hip: The History*, New York: Harper Perennial.

Luvaas, Brent (2012), *DIY Style: Fashion, Music, and Global Digital Cultures*, London and New York: Berg.

Luvaas, Brent (2013), 'Indonesian Fashion Blogs: On the Promotional Subject of Personal Style', *Fashion Theory*, 17: 1, pp. 55–76.

Polhemus, Ted (1978), *Fashion and Anti-Fashion*, London: Thames and Hudson.

Polhemus, Ted (1994), *Streetstyle: From Sidewalk to Catwalk*, London: Thames and Hudson.

Rudnyckyj, Daromir (2009), 'Spiritual Economies: Islam and Neoliberalism in Contemporary Indonesia', *Cultural Anthropology*, 24: 1, pp. 104–41.

Sen, Krishna, and David T. Hill. (2000), *Media, Culture and Politics in Indonesia*. Oxford: Oxford University Press.

Veblen, Thorstein. (1994), *The Theory of the Leisure Class*, London: Dover Publications.

Wallach, Jeremy (2008a), 'Living the Punk Lifestyle in Jakarta', *Ethnomusicology*, 52: 1, pp. 98–116.

Wallach, Jeremy (2008b), *Modern Noise, Fluid Genres: Popular Music in Indonesia, 1997–2001*, Madison: University of Wisconsin Press.

Woodward, Sophie (2009), 'The Myth of Street Style', *Fashion Theory*, 13: 1, pp. 83–102.

21

CO-DESIGN COMMUNITIES ONLINE:
Turning public creativity into wearable and sellable fashions

Juanjuan Wu[1]

MASS CUSTOMIZATION

Mass customization, as an innovative business strategy, provides a feasible solution to meet customers' needs more precisely while maintaining economies of scale through combining the best elements of mass production and customization (deRoulet 1993). Mass customizers only produce what has already been ordered. Thus, they achieve what traditional mass producers cannot: lower or no inventory, higher margins, quicker cash flow, and no markdowns (Anderson 1998). Duray et al. (2000) stressed that the essence of mass customization lies in two key dimensions: 1) the mass customizer must find a means for including each customer's specifications in the product design; 2) mass customizers must utilize modular design to achieve manufacturing efficiencies that approximate those of standard mass production.

According to Gilmore and Pine (1997), consumers can be involved in customizing the representation of a product (cosmetic customization), changing the nature of a product (transparent customization), manipulating a product to suit their own needs without additional interaction with the producer (adaptive customization), and changing both the nature and representation of a product (collaborative customization). Based on four entry points of customer involvement (i.e. design, fabrication, assembly, and use) and modularity (customized vs standardized), Duray et al. (2000) identified and named four dimensions of mass customization: "fabricators," "involvers," "modularizers," and "assemblers."

A consumer-driven model developed by Anderson-Connell et al. (2002) suggested four paths for apparel mass customization: "clothes clones" refer to copying a customer's favorite clothing item and partially modifying the attributes upon the customer's request; "totally custom" involves the customers in designing the garment, fabric, colors and offering customized fit; "co-design" integrates a professional associate's contribution with the individual customer's design; and "design options with standard sizes" provides a menu of design components for the individual customer's selection to create a customized garment.

CO-DESIGN

Co-design is the process of involving consumers in co-creating a product, which combines individual consumer's specifications with a company's pre-designed modules. The co-design process allows individual customers to customize a product to meet their needs more precisely while allowing near mass-production efficiencies in production. Co-design is a core component in the offerings of mass customizers. In the co-design process, "customers are integrated into value creation by defining, configuring, matching, or modifying their individual solution from a list of options and pre-defined components" (Piller et al. 2005). Fiore et al. (2001) defined apparel co-design as "the process

---

[1] From Juanjuan Wu, (2010) Co-Design Communities Online: Turning Public Creativity into Wearable.

that a customer follows to choose an individualized combination of product style, fabric, color, and size from a finite group of options." This research defines three phases in apparel mass customization:

Phase I: Apparel Mass Customization: One-to-one interactions between the mass customizer and the consumer co-designer in a retail store.

In Phase I, the mass customizer interacts with individual consumer co-designers one-to-one in a retail store environment. Besides a customized fit and a variety of design options, the assistance of a sales associate is a common feature of Phase I mass customization. The sales associate can assist with analyzing body scanning data, selecting appropriate size, or taking measurements. The sales associate also works with the customer to provide suggestions for not only what the customer wants but whether the design they desire is feasible to produce (Rabon 1996). After consulting with the professional associate, the consumer co-designer selects from and assembles pre-designed components, such as cut, fabric, color, and size. The consumer co-designer may also be able to add one-of-a-kind features. The mass customization programs of Levi Strauss, Second Skin Swimwear, and Brooks Brother provided examples of Phase I interactions between the consumer co-designer and the mass customizer.

Levi Strauss launched its first mass customization program, "Personal Pair," in 1994 (Carr *et al.* 2002). Trained sales clerks in a Levi Strauss store would take customer measurements for a customized fit. Customers could then individualize their jeans from a selection of five color choices in both tapered and boot-cut legs. Levi's retailing stores are supplied with 500 pairs of prototypes (Abend 1996). However, Levi's mass customization program was closed in 2003 after evolving into "Original Spin."

Second Skin Swimwear and Brooks Brothers also implemented mass customization in their retail stores. Rabon (1996) described the co-design process in a retail store of Second Skin Swimwear. It started with a customer trying on sample suits in a Second Skin Swimwear retail store. When a customer identified a style and fit, she was scanned by a digital camera from the front and side while wearing the garment. Customers could request any changes or add-ons to the sample suits, such as straps, ruffles, control panels, etc. The cut of the patterns could be adjusted as well. Once the design was decided upon, it could be constructed from more than 100 fabrics. Second Skin Swimwear has about twenty tops styles and twenty bottoms styles, as well as a selection of twenty one-piece suit styles with sizes ranging from three to six (Rabon 1996). Brooks Brothers' customers can create and visualize twenty-five suit silhouettes in anywhere from 300 to 500 different fabrics (Rabon 2000).

Phase II: Apparel Mass Customization: the mass customizer simultaneously interacts with a great number of consumer co-designers online.

Compared to the co-design process in Phase I, where mass customization takes place in a retail store that relies on face-to-face interactions between the customer and the mass customizer, in Phase II dot-com mass customizers offer more convenience, possibilities, and a greater capacity to interact with their customers. Through the use of digital design toolkits, the mass customizer is empowered to simultaneously interact with millions of consumer co-designers.

A digital or online design toolkit provides an online interface that has various functions to aid the co-design process. In Phase II co-design interactions, the online design toolkit replaces the professional associate of Phase I to present design options and to facilitate the selection of options and design decisions of the consumer co-designer. For example, a typical online design toolkit in Phase II mass customization has functions that enable consumer co-designers to easily select from possible design options (size, color, fabrics, style) with a simple click. More advanced design toolkits (see Phase III) offer co-designers functions to manipulate design elements (color, line, shape, orientation, font) or upload images. Design results can often be instantaneously visualized on screen as the co-designer proceeds along the co-design process.

Online mass customizers have mushroomed over the past decade. Various fashion products are now co-designed online, such as shirts (e.g. Shirtcreations, MyTailor, Brooks Brothers), jeans or pants (e.g. Land's

End, indiDenim), suits (e.g., MyTailor, MyCustomTailor), T-shirts (e.g. cafepress.com, customlnk, Zazzle, Threadless), wedding dresses (e.g. CustomCoutureBridal), and shoes (e.g. NIKEiD, MIAdidas, Reebok). Many of these online mass customizers can be categorized as Phase II mass customization, including Land's End, indiDenim, Shirtcreations, MyTailor, Brooks Brothers, MyCustomTailor, and CustomCoutureBridal. Nike experienced success with their customized sneakers. According to Swartz (2002), customized sneakers accounted for 20% of online sales on the NikeiD website.

The consumer co-designer selects a basic style or category to start the co-design process. They then configure the design details by selecting from limited options in fabrics, colors, pant rise, pockets, leg cut, collar styles, cuffs, back details, etc. The options for design details vary across product categories. For example, IC3-D provided selections of fits, fabrics, leg, ankle, waist, pockets, fly, nickel, and even gets as detailed as thread. For example, Shirtcreations.com allows their customers to create their unique monogram on the pocket by inputting their initials or other letters. The monogram can take on different font styles and colors. And Nike, which introduced customized sneakers in 1999 (Ives and Piccoli 2003), offers personal ID designs in various colors. The online environment also opens up new channels for communication and interaction between the mass customizer and the consumer co-designer, such as Land's End's online chat and indiDenim's blog.

However, as many online mass customizers redesigned their mass customization websites (e.g. NikeiD), many others mass customization programs have been discontinued, such as IC3-D and Americanfit.com. Because mass customization is generally connected to additional premium price and extra time and effort involved in the co-design process, concerns relating to whether there was enough market demand for customization have been raised by researchers (Ives and Piccoli 2003). Customers could also get confused by too many choices (Ives and Piccoli 2003; Piller et al. 2004, 2005; Pine et al. 1995) and by uncertainties regarding the behavior of a co-design provider (Piller et al. 2005). Still other researchers questioned the integrity of consumer co-designed products (Ives and Piccoli 2003; Relph-Knight 2008), which might account for returns caused by post-purchase dissatisfaction.

Phase III: Apparel Mass Customization: the mass customizer simultaneously interacts with a great number of consumer co-designers and co-designers interact with each other within the online community.

In Phase III, online interactions happen not only between the mass customizer and co-designers, but also among co-designers. Interactions and communications among consumer co-designers mark a critical departure from both Phase I and II co-design practices, which rely on a linear relationship between the customer and the mass customizer. These many interactions in various forms (e.g. commenting, evaluating, criticizing, promoting, buying, selling) among different parties create a sense of community in which customers can take on multiple roles as co-designers, buyers, sellers, and marketers. These communities also function as social networks where strangers meet, make friends, and find a sense of belonging.

This research refers to those communities participating in the co-design process as "co-design communities." Co-design communities of new startups have been thriving online in recent years. Threadless and Designbyhumans are two T-shirt co-design websites that have built co-design communities of similar nature: not only do the communities participate in the co-design process by offering criticisms, they also vote on submitted co-designs to help select winners of co-design contests.

In an interview with Frank Piller (2008), responding to the question "What are recent trends you see with regard to mass customization?" Scott Killian, co-founder of Yerzies, DemandMade, and FanBuz, stated: "If the first wave of innovation we saw online was about letting users create or configure a customized item, then the second wave is clearly about the intersection of social networking and mass customization. Although Etsy.com isn't a mass customizer, they have proven that users are not content to merely sell the items they've created; they want affirmation and interaction with other users."

Recognizing this new trend, many influential mass customizers also started to launch community-building programs. For example, NikeiD introduced community features in 2009 into their customization program, such as enabling customers to rate and post review comments on a design. Reebok offers a built-in e-mail function so that consumer co-designers could share their designs with others. Many online mass customizers offer forums, newsletters, blogs, chat rooms, and customer reviews and comments to encourage interactions among their consumer co-designers. Many of them also utilize other widely-used social-networking websites such as Twitter, Facebook, and YouTube to build their co-designer communities.

This observational research of two online co-design providers, Zazzle and Threadless, investigates co-design community features and interactions between the company and co-designers, as well as among co-designers.

ZAZZLE

Zazzle, a mass customization website, is characterized by its vibrant online co-design community. Zazzle was co-founded by two brothers, Jeff and Bobby Beaver, along with their father Robert, in 1999 (e-mail interview with Jeff Beaver, co-founder and CPO, June 2009). The Zazzle website was publically launched in 2005. The idea for Zazzle came from their own unmet needs when the two brothers attempted to make a T-shirt to advertise a fraternity party. They realized how difficult it was to get high-quality custom T-shirts in small quantities (Piller 2009). Of course, after Zazzle took off, it set no limit for a minimum order. Zazzle grew 65% from 2008 to 2009 with more than 500,000 registered users generating approximately 150,000 new products each day (e-mail interview with Jeff Beaver, June 2009).

In the T-shirt category, Zazzle provides various styles for co-design: for men or women, kids or pets, fitted or loose, long sleeves or short, plain or with stripes, scoop or ringer neck, in typically four to six colors. Using Zazzle's interactive design toolkit, customers can type in any text or add their own images to a designated area on either the front or back of a T-shirt they choose. The placement, size, and the orientation of the image and text are adjustable. Co-designers can experiment with hundreds of fonts and colors to complete a unique design or they can simply upload their own image or mix it with existing graphics for a unique design. Beaver (e-mail interview with Jeff Beaver, June 2009) contended:

> The ability for a seller to allow a consumer to customize their product before they make a purchase is an extremely powerful component of the Zazzle value proposition for almost all sellers. When your customer has a level of involvement with the design and creation of that final product, and when that product as a result becomes unique and personal, the interaction and connection between that customer and your brand becomes so much more powerful, deeper, and more valuable.

Zazzle's co-designers can upload their own images to customize a T-shirt. To make it even easier for amateur co-designers, CafePress, another notable T-shirt mass customizer founded in 1999, provides dozens of graphic templates. Co-designers can alter one or more components of a graphic to change its color or to change a portion of its color. On Zazzle, any T-shirts designed and sold by other consumer co-designers are available for customization and redesign. In this sense, the choice of graphic templates is unlimited. Consumer designers become smarter by building upon each other's creativity, and instantaneous visualization of the design result reduces uncertainties in the design process. Instantaneous visualization is a critical feature of advanced design toolkits that are often used by Phase III mass customizers. In an e-mail interview, Jeff Beaver pointed out, "The network effects of a vibrant and engaged community is a foundational premise in the Zazzle business model. The ability for designers (sellers) and buyers to communicate and collaborate around the products they buy and sell is one of the key drivers of engagement and conversions on the website." Under this model, the success of a business does not only rely on savvy businessmen but also on smart customers. As Bobby Beaver, co-founder of Zazzle, put it in an interview by *Fox Business News* in April

2009: "We're just the framework, which enables it all to happen." With a technologically advanced framework, smart customers become even smarter with support from a whole community with its creativity unleashed (Beaver 2009).

Zazzle's community starts from its homepage with a top-ten list of products, bestsellers, featured stores, hot searches, and upcoming holidays. On Zazzle's community page, customers can rate and comment on products to exert their influence over what is hot in the community.

Featured co-designers on the community homepage get a link to their individual store page where they promote and sell their designs. All Zazzle co-designers can become sellers by customizing a store page for their own use, which functions as a normal online store. Both individual co-designers and well-known brands, such as Disney and Star Wars, have set up stores on Zazzle. And co-designers do not just design for money. According to Beaver (e-mail interview with Jeff Beaver, August 2009), the Star Wars fan art section of the Star Wars store is a collection of designs that are produced by fans featuring Star Wars materials. In these cases, the co-designers have chosen to forego any rights to their designs in exchange only for the glory of seeing their products offered for sale. Any designs in any stores can be sold the way they are or they can be customized by other co-designers. The owners of these stores can also build their own sub-communities by creating their own "fan clubs" and "commenting walls."

More dynamic community interactions can be found on "Zazzle Pulse," and the site's forums and blogs. Zazzle Pulse broadcasts what is happening in the community moment by moment. Automatically refreshed features include just-shipped products; running commentary by designers, sellers, and buyers; recently changed stores; most viewed new products; most recently published products; busiest contributors; and pictures of Zazzle users with their products.

Zazzle makes money when their customers buy and makes even more when their customers sell. Zazzle also has a low return rate of less than 1%. However, returned products are mostly destroyed because they are custom and unique and are difficult to resell or reuse (e-mail interview with Jeff Beaver, August 2009).

THREADLESS

If the community is only one part of Zazzle, it is what Threadless, another very successful T-shirt co-design website, is built upon. Threadless was co-founded by Jake Nickell and Jacob deHart after the two met on an online design forum called Dreamless in 2000. "We thought it would be interesting to have an ongoing competition through which the winning designers could win prizes and the winning designs would be our product," recalled Jake (Bryant 2004). The business model for Threadless revolves around design competition and building a community. The community fully participates in co-designing, evaluating, selecting, criticizing, promoting, and buying co-designed T-shirts. Any registered users can submit a design using the preconfigured template provided by Threadless. The template includes a basic T-shirt in twenty-five colors, which can be changed into any other color or customized with patterns or graphics. One unique feature of designing at Threadless is that there is no designated area for graphics. Graphics can be applied anywhere on the T-shirt template in order to maximize creativity. A total of eight unique colors can be used with numerous combinations of halftones for multiple shades.

As a pre-submission tool, consumer co-designers can use Threadless's "Critique" feature to take advantage of the design expertise of its community to have their work critiqued before submission.

Along with their submission, co-designers name their design and tell their story. Thus, each design is linked with a known co-designer who actively listens, communicates with others, manages the design, and creates meaningful experiences for those who participate in the co-design process. After the submission, the Threadless community will score and comment on the design over a period of seven days. The limited timeframe creates a sense of urgency, which is similar to eBay's bidding timeframe. Based on the ratings and feedback from the community, the Threadless staff finally decides which top designs get printed on T-shirts and sold on its website and in retail stores. In each seven-day season Threadless rolls out a new line of approximately thirteen T-shirts; this poses a real challenge for its shops to keep up.

The printed designs that pass the screening of both the Threadless community and staff will receive US$2,000 in cash and have their name printed on the label of the T-shirt they designed—reminiscent of *haute couture*—along with other prizes. Community votes also choose one best T-shirt design each month, with an award of US$2,500 and the potential for a US$20,000 design-of-the-year award. Threadless also has a system that awards its members with points for referred sales. Co-designers can have their own blog to introduce themselves, showcase their photos, and communicate with peers using the comment or voicemail functions. Moreover, co-designers are constantly interviewed and featured on the website to promote their images, as well as to strengthen community ties. Another attractive community feature is the Tee-V, which serves as a TV station for Threadless that "showcases the random awesomeness that is always taking place in Threadless land" (Threadless 2009). In recent programs, Threadless staff have starred in a short comedy film production, with the ending left to be finished by its customers. Similar to their T-shirt competition, Threadless produces the most creative screenplay idea to finish the film and gives a cash prize to the winner. It sends out a message to Threadless's users in a high-tech way: sometimes, making a sale can be secondary, sharing creativity, no matter the form, is what is behind the business model.

However, the business model of Threadless is technically a variation of mass customization because the designs submitted by consumer co-designers cannot be directly bought but need to be pre-approved by the community and company staff for final production. Piller (2006) refers to the system of Threadless as "custom mass production." It may reduce the risk of producing random designs by random consumers, which can potentially lead to low post-purchase satisfaction and a high return rate.

The community relationships Zazzle and Threadless foster are multidimensional. Not only is the relationship between the business and its customers important, but also the relationship between customers is crucial. How customers are connected to each other determines the way they design, sell, and buy. This observational research of Zazzle and Threadless led to the development of a third model that depicts and predicts the interactions among consumer co-designers and between the co-designers and the mass customizer in online co-design communities

In Phase III, the interactions between the mass customizer and consumer co-designers remain similar to those in the Phase II, but interactions among co-designers characterize Phase III apparel mass customization. Co-designers interact with each other in various ways, such as through design competitions, evaluations, comments, suggestions, criticism, promotions, buying or selling. Meanwhile, they entertain, engage in networking, and find a sense of belonging in the co-design community.

As pointed out by Beaver (e-mail interview with Jeff Beaver, June 2009), "The concepts of crowd-sourcing and user-generated commerce are very much in their infancy." But they are spreading quickly into various fields like a virus powered by digital technology. The new generation dot-coms have begun to realize that consumers can no longer be treated as faceless market segments. Recognizing that consumers have individual needs for experience sharing, fun seeking, and relationship building means big business not only for T-shirt mass customizers, but also for most other mass customizers and retailers of shoes, health insurance, automobiles, food, housing, music, and other categories of apparel.

References

Abend, J. 1996. "Custom-Made for the Masses: Is It Time Yet?" *Bobbin* October: 52.

Anderson-Connell, L. J., P. V. Ulrich and E. L. Brannon. 2002. "A Consumer-driven Model for Mass Customization in the Apparel Market." *Journal of Fashion Marketing and Management* 6(3): 240–58.

Anderson, L. J. 1998. "Mass Customization: A Business Strategy." Paper presented at the Apparel Research Seminar of the American Apparel Manufacturers Association Task Group, September 1999, Atlanta, GA.

Beaver, Bobby. 2009. "Online Tea Party Merchandise Sales Soar." *Fox Business Interview* April 15. http://video.foxbusiness.com/4394234/?category_id=1292d14d0e3afdcf0b31500afefb92724c08f046 (accessed December 18, 2009).

Bryant, S. 2004. Interview on Crowndozen, October 21. http://crowndozen.com/main/archives/001396.shtml (accessed June 13, 2009).

Carr, L. P., W. C. Lawler and J. K. Shank. 2002. "Reconfiguring the Value Chain: Levi's Personal Pair." *Journal of Cost Management* November/December: 9–17.

deRoulet, D. G. 1993. "Mass-Customization: It's Not an Oxymoron." *Transportation & Distribution* 34(2): 40.

Duray R., P. T. Ward, G. W. Milligan and L. W. Berry. 2000. "Approaches to Mass Customization: Configurations and Empirical Validation." *Journal of Operation Management* 18: 605–25.

Fiore, A. M., S. Lee, G. Kunz and J. R. Campbell. 2001. "Relationship between Optimum Stimulation Level and Willingness to Use Mass Customization Options." *Journal of Fashion Marketing and Management* 5(2): 99–107.

Gilmore, J. H. and B. J. Pine, II. 1997. "The Four Faces of Mass Customization." *Harvard Business Review* 75(1): 91–102.

Huffmann, C., and B. E. Kahn. 1998. "Variety for Sale: Mass Customization or Mass Confusion?" *Journal of Retailing* 74(4): 491–513.

Ives, B. and G. Piccoli. 2003. "Custom Made Apparel and Individualized Service at Land's End." *The Communications of the Association for Information System* 11: 79–93.

Piller, F. 2005. "Re-Post: Analysis: Why Levi Strauss Finally Closed It's 'Original Spin' MC Operations." *Mass Customization & Open Innovation News* December 22. http://mass-customization.blogs.com/mass_customization_open_i/2005/12/repost_analysis.html (accessed June 15, 2009).

Piller, F. 2006. "Threadless.com—When Mass Customization Meets User Innovation Meets Online Communities." *Mass Customization & Open Innovation News* June 1. http://mass-customization.blogs.com/mass_customization_open_i/2006/06/threadlesscom_w.html (accessed August 8, 2009).

Piller, F. 2008. "Demandmade Launches YERZIES.Com, Extending Apparel Customization Beyond Screen Printing By Providing Users Access To Advanced Manufacturing Methods." *Mass Customization & Open Innovation News* December 2. http://mass-customization.blogs.com/mass_customization_open_i/clothing/index.html (accessed November 7, 2009).

Piller, F. 2009. "Niching the Niche: Observations from My Visit at Zazzle's Silicon Valley HQs." *Mass Customization & Open Innovation News* April 20. http://mass-customization.blogs.com/mass_customization_open_i/2009/04/niching-the-niche-observations-from-my-vistit-at-zazzles-silicon-valley-hqs.html#comments (accessed June 10, 2009).

Piller, F., P. Schebert, M. Koch and K. Moslem. 2005. "Overcoming Mass Confusion: Collaborative Customer Co-design in Online Communities." *Journal of Computer-Mediated Communication* 10(4). http://jcmc.indiana.edu/vol10/issue4/piller.html, (accessed August 2, 2009).

Piller, F., K. Moeslein and C. M. Stotko. 2004. "Does Mass Customization Pay? An Economic Approach to Evaluate Customer Integration." *Production Planning & Control* 15(4): 435–44.

Pine, B. J., D. Peppers and M. Rogers. 1995. "Do You Want to Keep Your Customers Forever?" *Harvard Business Review* March/April: 103–14.

Rabon, L. C. 1996. "Custom Fit Comes of Age." *Bobbin* August: 42–8.

Rabon, L. C. 2000. "Mixing the Elements of Mass Customization." *Bobbin* January: 38–41.

Relph-Knight, L. 2008. "'Co-design' Can Work Well, But Let's Not Push It Too Far." *Design Week* April 17: 6.

Swartz, J. 2002. "Thanks to Net, Consumers Customizing More." *USA Today* October 29.

Threadless. 2009. http://www.threadless.com/tv (accessed June 16, 2009).

Ulrich, P., L. J. Anderson-Connell and W. Wu. 2003. "Consumer Co-design of Apparel for Mass Customization." *Journal of Fashion Marketing and Management* 7(4): 398–412.

Zazzle. 2009. http://www.zazzle.com/mk/welcome/first/thecompany (accessed June 5, 2009).

22

MODCLOTH:
A case study in co-creative branding strategies

Kendra Lapolla[1]

CO-CREATION AND BRANDING

Researchers acknowledge a demand for new information regarding co-creation and branding. Specifically, brand researchers recognize social, inclusive and interactive qualities of co-creation as a new paradigm for branding (Hatch and Schultz 2009; Lusch and Vargo 2006; Payne et al. 2009). For example, R. F. Lusch and V. L. Vargo (2006) express a need for shifting to a Service-Dominant logic based on the value of active relationships built in co-creation. Prahalad and Ramaswamy (2004: 2) also reinforce the need for a shift from the 'traditional system of company-centric value creation' used in the past 100 years to a 'premise centered on co-creation of value'. Attempts should be made to push thinking 'away from the traditional consumer-brand dyad to the consumer-brand-consumer triad' (Muniz and O'Guinn 2001). The concept of 'enterprise branding' proposed by M. Hatch and M. Schultz (2009) explains this new brand paradigm as co-creation between all stakeholders 'engaged by its purpose and in its activity'.

Co-creation employs engaged participation and communication skills between brand and consumer. S. Abbott (2007) explains co-creation as a way to bring 'consumers into a closer relationship with the brand by inviting them to take part in the creative process'. I. Nam et al. (2008) agree that a co-creative experience includes an active consumer who is able to contribute to the 'design, delivery, and creation of the customer experience'. This is also supported by E. B.-N. Sanders and C. T. William (2001) that state participation in the 'fuzzy front-end of the development process' is necessary for human-centred co-creation. While the literature contains varying degrees of co-creation, the common thread is that co-creation requires active participation and interaction from all members involved.

Communities provide an opportunity for members to actively participate in co-creation through a series of collaborative conversations. Past brand community studies focus on the interaction and dialogue of all members involved in the community (Hatch and Schultz 2010; Muniz and O'Guinn 2001). Specifically in some branding studies, the term co-creation is used to describe 'customer-supplier dialogue and interaction' (Payne et al. 2009: 381). The co-creation of value framework created by Payne et al. (2008) stresses the need for these encounters between customer and supplier that will contribute to a 'long-term view of customer relationships' through individualized communication. A. M. Muniz and T. O'Guinn (2001) further support this by explaining brands are socially constructed through actively involved consumers.

This article attempts to build additional research using the co-creation building blocks by Prahalad and Ramaswamy (2004) for brand co-creation. This article addresses research questions, such as, how do consumers actively participate in co-creative branding? What are potential access points for encouraging brands to become more co-creative?

---

[1] From Kendra LaPolla, ModCloth: A Case Study in Co-Creative Branding Strategies, in Global Fashion Brands, Intellect, pp. 85–102.

THE CREATIVE CUSTOMER

A change in the mindset of customers is causing online retailers to be more creative and collaborative in the communication of the brand. The shifting position of these new customers is 'from isolated to connected, unaware to informed, from passive to active' (Prahalad and Ramaswamy 2004: 2). Through years of generative research, Sanders (2006) has found a deeper user engagement may come from the idea that everyday people don't want to be just 'consumers'. What they really desire, is to become 'creators'.

The desire to be a more creative consumer manifests itself in a demand for a variety of new fashion online retail experiences. These new retail experiences give consumers an active voice in the brand and provide a social platform to interact. J. Wu (2010) identified Zazzle and Threadless as specific examples that support consumer co-creation through the interactive features used by their online communities. Design contests also promote dialogue within the online community. In a study of online design competitions, J. Füller et al. (2011) examined a jewelry competition titled 'Swarovski Enlightened™' and found that co-creation experiences can positively impact quality and quantity of design submissions, as well as the likelihood of participating in a future co-creative competition. J. Quillin and K. Peck (2012) support this by saying, 'Information-hungry customers want to feel like they are a part of a brand's intimate circle and want to take part in how a brand takes shape and the products it markets'.

Nam et al. (2008) empirically tested customer satisfaction of co-creative marketing approaches and found both satisfaction and trust can be achieved from co-creation and as a result relationship strength and loyalty would be affected positively. Giving consumers the ability to create individual designs and vote on favourite ideas is a way to support brand co-creation.

CO-CREATION BUILDING BLOCKS

According to Prahalad and Ramaswamy (2004), there are four main building blocks for value creation in a co-creation process. These four building blocks are Dialogue, Access, Risk Assessment and Transparency.

In this framework, the building blocks provide new 'points of interaction between the consumer and the company – where the co-creation experience occurs, where individuals exercise choice, and where value is co-created' (Prahalad and Ramaswamy 2004: 33).

DIALOGUE

Prahalad and Ramaswamy (2004: 23) identify dialogue as 'interactivity, deep engagement, and a propensity to act-on both sides'. Dialogue requires a conversation between both the customer and the company. It should focus on common interests and issues. This in turn builds a loyal community that is maintained by additional dialogue and conversation. Prahalad and Ramaswamy (2004: 23) further describe dialogue by saying, 'It entails empathic understanding built around experiencing what consumers experience, and recognizing the emotional, social, and cultural context of experiences. It implies shared learning and communication between two equal problem solvers'. For a strong dialogue, both the customer and company should be equally heard.

Online retailers initiate dialogue with their customers through social media, blogs and online customer service options. Free People has a Free People Me Style Gallery which allows an online community to submit photos of themselves wearing Free People stylized outfits. Not only does this initiate communication between the brand and customers, it creates conversation between the online community members to share ideas, comment, and like others' outfits. Free People's BLDG 25 blog is another way the brand creates a dialogue with its customers by encouraging customers to comment and discuss posted articles. Another example, Zappos is an online retailer with a successful online customer service feature that uses customer initiated dialogue. The live help feature allows customers to ask questions or give comments about products.

ACCESS

Access is the second building block of co-creation. Access in this case refers extensively to the access customers have for involvement with the brand. In a traditional value chain, a company would focus on creating a product the customer could own through a purchasing process. This was the main access for gaining ownership with the brand and products. Prahalad and Ramaswamy (2004: 25) say, 'Increasingly, the goal of consumers is access to desirable experiences- not necessarily ownership of the product. One need not own something to access an experience. We must uncouple the notion of access from ownership'. For successful co-creation, companies should understand that customers want more than access to ownership. They want access to experiences with the company as well. In this way, access should be understood from a broader perspective.

Mass customization is a form of access that online retailers are providing to consumers. Laudi Vidni, is an online retailer that allows consumers to create custom leather handbags by selecting shape, leather and details. Laudi Vidni, which is 'individual' spelled backwards, focuses on the consumer's personal wants. These made-to-order bags are hand-crafted in Chicago, Illinois by skilled crafts-people and individually customized by the consumer.

RISK ASSESSMENT

Risk refers to how it could harm the customer or company. Traditionally, internal managers were thought to better handle a company's risk more than its customer. This is why marketers often focus on only communicating the benefits to customers. When customers are active co-creators they may assume more responsibility for risk and subsequently, demand more information about the products and services offered (Prahalad and Ramaswamy 2004: 27). Customers as active co-creators may assume more responsibility for the success of the company. In turn, strategies that seem risky may have less perceived risk if the customers are closely involved in a co-creation process.

Crowd-sourcing is an example of how online retailers are using consumer input to lessen the risk of offering new products. CutOnYourBias.com engages consumers in a virtual collaboration with select fashion designers. Consumers create designs from set selections of fabric and styles on a crowd-sourced social commerce platform. The winning designs are then manufactured in an upcoming collection.

TRANSPARENCY

Information about all aspects of the company must be transparent to the customers. Prahalad and Ramaswamy (2004: 30) further state, 'Firms can no longer assume opaqueness of prices, costs, and profit margins. And as information about products, technologies, and business systems becomes more accessible, creating new levels of transparency becomes increasingly desirable'. Companies used to benefit from 'information asymmetry between the consumer and firm', but that mentality is quickly disappearing (Prahalad and Ramaswamy 2004: 30).

Online retailers create transparency of the brand through unbiased online product reviews. Product reviews often allow customers to comment on the fit, price and even quality of the garment. Other customers can use the reviews as a way to evaluate purchasing decisions.

MODCLOTH CASE STUDY: COMPANY PROFILE

In the short history of ModCloth, the company has quickly grown with a consistent co-creative focus. ModCloth is an online retailer equipped with a trendy, user-centred website that sells hip clothing to millennial women (Hesseldahl et al. 2010). In 2006, Susan and Eric Koger started ModCloth to manage Susan's vintage clothing collection (Barnard et al. 2012). They worked from a family member's living room selling clothing online and using a cell phone number for customer service (Hesseldahl et al. 2010). J. Barnard et al. (2012) say, 'The site blossomed naturally to include both independent and major designers, and is flourishing in sales and in social spaces'. ModCloth now has three offices in Pittsburgh, San Francisco and Los Angeles with 350 full-time employees (Gannes 2012). Inc. Magazine identified ModCloth as 'America's Fastest-Growing Retailer' for 2010, and founders

Susan and Eric were named in 'Forbes 30 under 30' list (Brennan 2012).

There is a strong online social presence with over 692,000 Facebook fans, 97,000 Twitter followers, and over 1,300,000 Pinterest followers (Barnard et al. 2012). Currently, ModCloth has nearly two million visitors to their website each month (Hesseldahl et al. 2010). ModCloth is on the forefront of digital shopping by focusing on opportunities for consumers to shop on their smart-phones. They are able to deliver convenience, choice and value for money in a quick click, faster than mortar franchises like Gap and Limited Brands (Barnard et al. 2012). Beyond shopping, this growing access to the Internet has provided ModCloth with the ability to develop new platforms for co-creation activities with its customers.

ModCloth's co-creative platform is different from some other online retailers who are targeting young, millennial women because the brand is rooted in consistent dialogue and social engagement between the consumers and company. For example, online retailers like Gilt, ideeli and Blue Fly provide flash sales and discounts on designer merchandise. This is a trickle down approach to telling the consumer what they want to buy with giving them little input to effect product innovation or advertising. In the case of ModCloth, the consumers are able to initiate design inspiration for new products, marketing, social media and more. These social experiences work especially well with these young, millennial women because they prefer collective and communal shopping experiences (Dias 2003; Dennis et al. 2010).

MODCLOTH CASE STUDY: A NEW CO-CREATIVE FRAMEWORK FOR BRANDING

For this research, a case study was created by using observational research of ModCloth. The main objective of the data generation was to show examples that illustrate how consumers participate in co-creation and to look for accessible opportunities to enter into co-creation. Data was collected from the company website, online community comments, and additional secondary sources. Analysis of the data supported a new co-creative framework that emphasizes dialogue as the foundation of co-creative branding strategies. Examples from ModCloth show dialogue is the connection to access, risk assessment and transparency.

DIALOGUE: A FUNDAMENTAL ENTRY POINT

ModCloth encourages open dialogue with their customers through contests. The 'Name It & Win It' Contest engages customers in naming the styles of garments soon to be for sale online. The winner of the best name for the garment receives that garment in their size (ModCloth 2012b).

ModCloth also initiates open dialogue with customers through social media and an online style gallery. With ModCloth's new style gallery, customers are able to communicate new outfit ideas by posting styled outfits on the website. This online style gallery combines user content, commerce and community in one place (Gannes 2012). Other customers can view the outfit ideas and be directly linked to the garment item and price if they would like to purchase it (ModCloth 2012a). L. Gannes (2012) says, 'The "Style Gallery" ties into ModCloth's efforts to make customers feel the site is their online home'. This gives the customer responsibility for visual merchandising and demonstrates their strong voice within the company dialogue. Some visitors access the page more than ten times a day (Gannes 2012). ModCloth is also using social media websites, like Pinterest, to further create a dialogue. C. Horton (2012) says, 'ModCloth joined Pinterest in the fall of 2011, but it's already one of ModCloth's top unpaid referral sites in terms of traffic and revenue'. There are approximately 7000 pins that have been tagged on Pinterest, and '99 per cent of them are from advocates of the ModCloth brand' (Horton 2012).

DIALOGUE + ACCESS

Access to the brand is created from a preliminary dialogue between the brand and consumers. ModCloth offers access to their brand by inviting the customers into the creative process with their 'Make the Cut'

Contest. This private label collection is a collaboration between the company and the customers, offering access to a new design experience. The brand initiated communication by inviting aspiring designers to submit their sketches and ideas for garments. Co-founder, Susan Koger, then selected 25 finalists from the 1900 submissions and continued the dialogue by asking customers to vote for their favourites on the ModCloth Facebook page (Joyner 2012). The 25 finalists were narrowed down to seven designs based on more than 10,000 votes, 1000 comments, and two of the founder's favourites (Joyner 2012). These seven designs went through 'extensive development, from selecting fabrics to construction samples and creating dress patterns' (Paranjpe 2012).

This proved to be a successful opportunity for customers to have access to a creative experience and maintain influential communication with the brand. Selection of the final designs came from a connected dialogue between the brand and customers. There were initially 200 garments produced of each of the seven designs by a third-party manufacturer in California (Joyner 2012). About 40 per cent of the available inventory was sold on the first day (Plichta 2012). The garments were available for purchase on the ModCloth website each with a custom 'Make the Cut' tag that included the designers name (Paranjpe 2012). In an interview with Joyner, co-founder Eric Koger says,

> The way most of the industry works is, they produce a design on a large scale, then they send it out to stores and hope customers buy it. Ours is a more lean and agile approach. We involve the customer and get feedback earlier in the process (2012).

DIALOGUE + RISK ASSESSMENT

ModCloth uses dialogue to evaluate the risks of new products and ideas for the brand. There is an inherent risk in predicting what to buy for future seasons as the fashion industry is in a constant state of fluctuation. Further, for those in the retail business it can be difficult because of 'minimum purchase requirements, travel limitations, and sometimes buying stock based on technical sketches, it's difficult to determine what, how many, which color to buy six months in advance of the season' (Barnard et al. 2012). In 2010, ModCloth launched 'Be the Buyer' to collect customer interest and feedback on potential styles before placing an order as a way to lessen the risk (Barnard et al. 2012).

ModCloth's 'Be the Buyer' programme can better predict the potential best sellers by inviting the customers to give feedback and help assess the risk of each style (Figure 3). Through this programme, customers are given fourteen days to vote on potential designs that ModCloth might consider selling (Bennett 2012). By using a 'Pick It' button customers can vote for the designs they like, and those with the highest amount of votes are produced and sold (Bennett 2012). ModCloth produces in smaller quantities that creates less waste because only the most popular styles are produced in limited, predetermined quantities (Barnard et al. 2012). One month after the launch of the 'Be the Buyer' programme, there was a 25 per cent increase in traffic to the ModCloth website (Bennett 2012). Barnard et al. (2012) suggest, 'Customers are more apt to purchase something they provided input for, and ModCloth makes the extra effort to alert them if an item they voted for has gone into production'.

DIALOGUE + TRANSPARENCY

Transparency becomes visible through dialogue between the brand and consumers. ModCloth illustrates transparency within their company through the online reviews of their products. ModCloth has an interactive review space that upholds transparency about the company and its products. ModCloth also has a team of 'Social Butterflies' that respond to positive and negative reviews posted on their Twitter account (Bennett 2012). The openness with ModCloth's product reviews builds a sense of trust and transparency about products customers may potentially purchase.

A FRAMEWORK TO ENTER IN CO-CREATION BRANDING

As shown in observation of ModCloth, dialogue should be the core of a co-creative brand. This new co-creative branding framework emphasizes dialogue as a connection to access, risk assessment and transparency. Placing dialogue at the foundation of the framework provides focus for introduction into brand co-creation.

Any entry point into co-creative brand experiences should use dialogue as the gateway. For example, brands wanting to venture into assessing risk through crowdsourcing should first start with smaller contests to test consumer response, build trust and further initiate a dialogue with the online community. The start to building these relationships is by encouraging an open dialogue between members of the online community. In another example, brands could strengthen the relationship by following up in additional conversations with online product reviews. This way the dialogue continues and others are encouraged to join the conversation.

This case study of ModCloth serves as an example of co-creative implementation in branding and additionally supports the modified co-creation building blocks originally introduced by Prahalad and Ramaswamy (2004). The co-creation building blocks (dialogue, access, transparency and risk assessment) by Prahalad and Ramaswamy (2004) provide a background to study co-creation in branding. The case study of ModCloth illustrates examples of consumers actively participating in co-creation and suggests that dialogue provides an entry to co-creative experiences. Exposure to access, risk assessment and transparency are initiated using dialogue as a bridge. ModCloth is unique in this way because all co-creation starts with a dialogue between every stakeholder involved.

References

Abbott, Susan (2007), 'Customer experience crossroads: Co-creation and fashion brands', 5 April, http://www.customercrossroads.com/customercrossroads/2007/04/cocreation_and_.html. Accessed 20 March 2010.

Barnard, Jonathan, Jennifer Ladds and Jinah Kim. (2012), 'How to Do Social Shopping Right: A Case Study – Moxie Pulse', November 9. http://www.zenithoptimedia.com/zenith/how-to-do-social-shopping-right-a-case-study-moxie-pulse/. Accessed December 3, 2012.

Bennett, Hubert. (2012), 'Social Commerce Case Study: ModCloth', November 7. http://insparq.com/social-commerce-case-study-modcloth-2/. Accessed December 4, 2012.

Brennan, Bridget. (2012), 'The Retailer Winning the Battle for Millennial Women', November 16. http://www.forbes.com/sites/bridgetbrennan/2012/11/16/the-retailer-winning-the-battle-for-millennial-women/. Accessed December 4, 2012.

Dennis, Charles, Alesia Morgan, Len Tiu Wright and Chanaka Jayawardhena. (2010), 'The Influences of Social e-shopping in Enhancing Young Women's Online Shopping Behaviour', *Journal of Customer Behaviour*, 9(2): 151–74.

Dias, Laura Portolese (2003), 'Generational buying motivations for fashion', *Journal of Fashion Marketing and Management*, 7: 1, pp. 78–86.

Füller, Johann, Katja Hutter and Rita Faullant (2011), 'Why co-creation experience matters? Creative experience and its impact on the quantity and quality of creative contributions', *R&D Management*, 41: 3, pp. 259–73.

Gannes, Liz (2012), 'ModCloth Launches an In-House Pinterest', 19 November, http://allthingsd.com/20121119/modcloth-launches-an-in-house-pinterest/. Accessed 4 December 2012.

Hatch, Mary Jo and Majken Schultz (2009), 'Of bricks and brands. From corporate to enterprise branding', *Organization Dynamics*, 38: 2, pp. 117–30.

Hatch, Mary Jo and Majken Schultz (2010), 'Toward a theory of brand co-creation with implications for brand governance', *Journal of Brand Management*, 17: 8, pp. 590–604.

Hesseldahl, Arik, Olga Kharif, Douglas MacMillan and Rachael King (2010), 'Best Young Tech Entrepreneurs 2010', 4 April, businessweek.com/ss/10/04/0419_best_young_tech_entrepreneurs/index.htm. Accessed 3 December 2012.

Horton, Chris (2012), 'Case Study: 4 Brands that Use Pinterest the Right Way', 25 April, marketing-technology-for-growth/bid/136311/Case-Study-4-Brands-that-Use-Pinterest-the-Right-Way. Accessed 30 November 2012.

Joyner, April (2012), 'ModCloth: Getting customers to design their own clothes', 3 May, http://www.inc.com/magazine/201205/modcloth-demo-cratizing-fashion-company-watch.html. Accessed 30 November 2012.

Lusch, Robert F., and Stephen L. Vargo (2006), 'Service-dominant logic: Reactions, reflections and refinements', *Marketing Theory*, 6: 3, pp. 281–88.

ModCloth (2012a), 'Just the Fox, Ma'am Sweater', www.modcloth.com/shop/pullovers-sweaters/just-the-fox-ma-am-sweater. Accessed 18 December 2012.

ModCloth (2012b), 'The winners of name it & win it: Good tidings & titles', http://blog.modcloth.com/2012/

12/07/the-winners-of-name-it-win-it-good-tidings-titles/. Accessed 15 December 2012.

Muniz Jr., Albert M., and O'Guinn, Thomas C. (2001), 'Brand Community', *Journal of Consumer Research*, 27(4): 412–32.

Paranjpe, Anjelika. (2012), 'Be the Designer: ModCloth's Brand New User-Generated Clothing Collection', May 29, Brit.co www.brit.co/be-the-designer-modcloth-s-brand-new-user-generated-clothing-collection/. Accessed December 3, 2012.

Payne, Adrian, Kaj Storbacka, Pennie Frow and Simon Knox (2009), 'Co-creating brands: Diagnosing and designing the relationship experience', *Journal of Business Research*, Advances in Brand Management, 62: 3, pp. 379–89.

Plichta, Aire. (2012), 'Modcloth continues mission to democratize fashion; launches second crowdsourced clothing collection', 20 August, http://www.prweb.com/releases/2012/8/prweb9812715.htm.

Prahalad, C. K. and Venkat Ramaswamy. (2004), *The Future of Competition: Co-creating Unique Value with Customers.* Boston, MA: Harvard Business School Publishing.

Quillin, Jessica and Krista Peck. (2012), 'Digital emotiveness: The new key to participatory marketing', 4 April, http://fashionscollective.com/FashionAndLuxury/04/digital-emotiveness-the-new-key-to-participatory-marketing/. Accessed 9 December 2012.

Sanders, Elizabeth B.-N. (2006), 'Scaffolds for building everyday creativity', in Jorge Frascara (ed.), *Design for Effective Communications: Creating Contexts for Clarity and Meaning*, 65–77. New York, NY: Allworth Press.

Sanders, Elizabeth B.-N. and Colin T. William (2001), 'Harnessing people's creativity: Ideation and expression through visual communication', in J. Langford and D. McDonagh-Philp (eds), *Focus Groups: Supporting Effective Product Development*, 137–48. New York, NY: Taylor and Francis.

Wu, Juanjuan (2010), 'Co-design communities online: Turning public creativity into wearable and sellable fashions', *Fashion Practice*, 2: 1, pp. 85–104.

23

A STUDY OF HOW SMALL AND MEDIUM-SIZED ENTERPRISE TAILORS UTILIZE E-COMMERCE, SOCIAL MEDIA, AND NEW 3D TECHNOLOGICAL PRACTICES

Frances Ross[1]

This survey updates a study conducted six years ago on Savile Row and London bespoke tailors to explore their adaptation to new technology in anthropometrics (measurements), manufacturing, and e-commerce. The original survey conducted interviews with sixteen bespoke tailors and observation of their physical and virtual environment and were published in *The Journal of Textile Institute* (September 2007).

The current research used observation and content analysis of the original tailors, plus new Google search links of companies describing their creative process as Bespoke and Semi-bespoke. The following factors were assessed:

1. Terminology to describe new forms of tailoring.
2. Use of social media/blog to purchase/advertise.
3. Use of new technology for measurements/patterns/manufacture.
4. Good web-atmospherics communicating contemporary and traditional tailoring values.

Although this second study focuses on bespoke tailors (mainly in London) and their current practices, the findings have much broader international implications for small and medium-sized enterprise (SME) fashion companies. SME stands for small and medium-sized enterprises as defined in European Law. This study provides an insight into how SMEs can offer a personalized service through their websites for current and new customers, which could lead to increased market share.

It is evident from fashion reports in the national and trade press (*Drapers Record* 2003; *ShortList* January 27, 2011) that there is a new generation of male consumers aged 25–39 with a large disposable income who have a discerning fashion style and a good knowledge of textiles and production techniques. They demand not just luxury apparel but also innovation in all aspects of men's tailoring production and consumption.

The bespoke industry is divided in two. One group includes famous names, such as Henry Poole, who have helped create and sustain the heritage and traditions that surround Savile Row. The second group includes fashion icons, such as Oswald Boateng, who have innovative up-to-the-minute retail environments both on and offline, while still offering luxury apparel. Oswald belongs to the group of tailors from the 1980–90s who were known as the "New Tailors" as they were pushing the boundaries of traditional tailoring while keeping Savile Row bespoke values (Jerrard *et al.* 2003).

Today a web presence alone is not sufficient for any SME company to operate or promote themselves. Luxury fashion brands still find it challenging to communicate store atmosphere and excellent service via online communication (Okonkwo 2005). But an SME who operates single and multiple-channel strategies can provide a range of valuable benefits for customers while

---

[1] From Frances Ross, (2012) A Study on How Small and Medium-Sized Enterprise Tailors Utilize e-Commerce, Social Media, and New 3-D Technological Practices, Fashion Practice, Volume 4, Issue 2, Taylor & Francis.

still maintaining heritage, luxury status, and service. This can be achieved by innovative use of new technologies and digital tools such as 3D body-scanning, style advice, co-design, and interactive screening, which enables an online company to equal or surpass that of the physical retail environment (Okonkwo 2009; Ross 2010). This is a key strategy for SME fashion companies and in particular the bespoke tailoring market, as additional channels can provide additional income.

However, for garments that need to provide an exceptionally good fit, design, and service, such as men's suits, the anthropometric data generated by sizing systems such as body-scanners bridges the gap between "custom-made" and "mass-produced" (Apeagyeri and Otieno 2006). Ross uses the market descriptor "demi-bespoke or semi-bespoke" to cover this category based on previous studies (2007: 281).

The discussion commences with a synopsis of the original study and key findings compared with literature on bespoke innovations in design, measurement sizing, and manufacturing. This is followed by observations, analysis, and evaluation of the thirty-eight tailors surveyed and their current practices and utilization of 3D technology, terminology, and online innovations.

HISTORIOGRAPHY OF BESPOKE, MADE-TO-MEASURE, AND READY-MADE

When the study was originally conducted with sixteen tailors their market position and descriptors were listed as on Table 2.

At that time there were mainly two definitions to describe the suit-making process. The first was Bespoke: "A bespoke suit is cut from a pattern made specifically for a particular client (i.e. the material is spoken for), whereas a made-to-measure suit is cut from a standard pattern and amended to suit the contours of the individual" (Ross 2007: 283, quoted from the Foreword of Walker 1998). The second definition was Made-to-Measure, which was made popular in the early 1900s by Montague Burton, who developed an emporium of high street tailoring services for the mass market. Timothy Everest's website, whose own tailoring practices incorporates ready-to-

Table 2 Original 2006–7 bespoke tailors survey

Tailors	Market Descriptor
Alan Canon-Jones	Traditional Savile Row style
Chris Kerr and Eddie Kerr	Traditional Savile Row style
Charlie Allen	The New Tailors
John Pearse	The New Tailors
Timothy Everest	The New Tailors
Gordon Millings	Traditional Savile Row style
Antonio Pipitone of Zegna	Italian Bespoke/Demi-bespoke Tailors
Bradley Bond of Beale & Inman	Italian Bespoke/Demi-bespoke Tailors
Thomas Mahon Englishcut	Traditional Savile Row style
Andrew Ramroop of Maurice Sedwell	Traditional Savile Row style
David Lewis of Holland & Sherry	Traditional Savile Row style fabrics
Susannah Hall & Lisa Braton	Designer/Demi-Bespoke Tailors
Angus Cundey of Henry Poole	Traditional Savile Row style
Jonathan Quearney	Traditional Savile Row style
Manager Oswald Boateng	The New Tailors
Mark Powell	The New Tailors

wear collections for Marks & Spencer, bespoke, and made-to-measure, describes the latter:

> "Made-to-Measure" is used to describe a highly individualised garment that is hand-made to your specification. The process involves an initial personal consultation with one of our tailors in order to discuss your needs and the desired style and trims of the garment you wish to commission. Unlike bespoke, where the cutter will draft your pattern from scratch, made-to-measure garments are adapted from existing (pattern) blocks. (timothyeverest.co.uk/made-to-measure, accessed January 20, 2011)

The terms "demi-" and "semi-bespoke" combine traditional ready-to-wear with technical elements of craftsmanship in finish; this mixture of bespoke and made-to-measure industrial manufacture were just emerging at the time of the first study. Whereas the current study establishes the descriptor "semi-bespoke" to the tailoring process categories.

SHIFTING CONSUMER AND INDUSTRY PERCEPTIONS

The study identified the shift in consumer attitudes and behavior towards the top end of tailoring. The target market had become more democratized and less niche. This larger younger male market were not so entrenched in the ritualized tradition of bespoke one-to-one tailoring services and hand manufacture methods; they were more readily accepting of suits made in the new "demi-bespoke" or "semi-bespoke" method as described on the tailor's website (www.jasperlittman.co.uk, accessed February 10, 2011), and Ross (2007) interviews. This change in attitude was also initially documented by the *Drapers Record* (2003) and more recently by *ShortList* (January 27, 2011). This "semi-bespoke" notion had a parallel in luxury womenswear, described as "demi-couture" a similar development of the "demi-bespoke" concept in the women's couture industry.

Cornellani, the Italian menswear company, has a machine, which provides bespoke services. The measurements are taken for the pattern in London but in the near future it will be possible to scan the person's body shape and feed this into a computer, with the customer's fabric selection. The computer will draw up a template of the customers shape and dimensions, allowing a visualization of how the fabric flows on the customer.

LITERATURE DISCUSSION

Very little has been written specifically on menswear or bespoke tailoring except a design management case study on one of the "New Tailors," Charlie Allen. This uses a rigorous design audit to assess how a suitable SME branding strategy can expand a business portfolio of bespoke, made-to-measure, ready-made, and wholesale distribution (Jerrard *et al.* 2003). This was conducted in the early 1990s and was revisited in the current survey.

At a slightly later period (2003) Professor Powell wrote how traditional high-end menswear was lagging behind the new technology utilized by the seamless Italian knitwear companies in manufacture and the retail environment. Her main point was that although Savile Row "bespoke" was still considered the ultimate in customized craftsmanship products ". . .the lifestyle and preferences of the future may demand a different style of customization . . .Consumers of all ages are looking for streamlined silhouettes with a youthful appearance created by garments that fit and flatter the body." Today this is supplied by 3D tailoring utilizing body-scanning, pattern-cutting, and semi-bespoke manufacture (Ross and Jenkyn-Jones 2009; Ross 2010). Brooks Brothers combines the traditional with the new by turning round customized suits in two weeks from scanning to finish. This illustrated the potential of "semi-bespoke" for Savile Row and other tailors wishing to expand their share of the market (Powell 2003).

Another recent article entitled "breaking the tailoring rules" listed London tailors from the Savile Row tradition who were utilizing new techniques. The most interesting example being Cad & the Dandy: "There is a thoroughly modern approach, measurements are taken on the Mac or they can be submitted via its website, which also offers the chance to design and fine-tweak the details of your suit online" (*Short-List* January 27, 2011).

ANTHROPOMETRICS

In considering new technology and fit with 3D scanning and pattern-making, Apeagyeri and Otieno (2006) discuss how 3D can improve fit for the average-size body but advises that an asymmetrical body shape customer should go for a traditional made-to-measure or bespoke fitting, as tailors pride themselves on being able to visually correct any body fault in their suit design and construction.

Anthropometrics (the study of measuring the human body) has been considered by tailors and scientists for decades, but instead of using traditional methods of measurement, a good fit can now be achieved digitally. The big question for Savile Row and education is how to do this accurately? The conclusion of the study responds to this question with "Use of the 3D data will clearly enhance made-to measure learning and teaching with 3D-2D pattern cutting and 2D grading being taught on 3D scanned toiles or scanned bodies" (Taylor and Unver 2011: 12).

ONLINE RETAIL ENVIRONMENTS

In terms of new online environments such as Web 2.0 and 3.0 tools that enable the consumer to receive style advice and participate in the co-creation of their suit design, Ross (2010) studies the possibilities through the "pink market" for civil-partnership suiting and other gay styling that could provide a growth niche market for online mass-market tailors. Although there is a buzz about social media platforms and how they change fashion business and consumers behavior, apart from Ross (2010) discussing the importance of social media in the menswear market and a recent online thesis by Han Nguyen (2011) on the subject of Facebook, You Tube, and Twitter as social platforms for high street fashion, there is currently little published that studies this culturally new technological phenomena.

From the perspective of experiential web-atmospherics there is a body of knowledge that includes Kurniawan (2000), Schenkman and Jonsson (2000), and Mahlke (2008). However, recently Manganari *et al.* reviewed the subject in "A Store Atmosphere in Web Retailing" (2009). A conceptual model of consumer responses to the online store environment was tested, which paralleled with the physical store environment in terms of sensory perception, accuracy of product information, and virtual social presence. This enforces an earlier study of virtual communities that states virtual behavior can be classified into four types of human needs: interest, relationship, fantasy, and transaction (Kim and Jin 2006), all of which can be fulfilled by e-tailoring.

NEW TERMINOLOGY

Consideration of new terminology to describe new forms of tailoring showed that none of the original sixteen tailors used text or images that reinforced this factor. They preferred texts that illustrated the traditions and quality of "bespoke," "made-to-measure," and "ready-to-wear." This is despite knowledge acquired from the original interviews that disclosed new terminology practices and descriptions (Ross 2007).

The literature review identified two Italian companies that utilized 3D technology but did not currently communicate this to the consumer (Ross 2007). This indicates that new technology is not what sells upscale suits but the more traditional notions of craftsmanship, tailors' measurements, and personal service. However, as shown in Figure 1, column 1, the twenty-two newly surveyed tailors showed more acceptance of new terminology with 30 percent having direct reference to the term "semi-bespoke." The term "demi-bespoke" seems to be completely replaced by "semi-bespoke" in all sites viewed.

DATA ANALYSIS: 3D TECHNOLOGY

None of the original sixteen surveyed had subsequently embraced or at least communicated the use of digital technology to the public. However, 26 percent of the new e-tailor sites visited presented these technological practices. Quotation examples taken from the websites are shown in Table 3. www.sousterandhicks.com highlight "3d computer cutting, digital pattern

Table 3 Examples of 3D technology from websites

Descriptors	Website
"Classic and contemporary styles are available, enabling us to create an individual garment just for you. Your size and figuration details are carefully taken and then transferred to the *computer cutting system where your pattern is drafted onto paper digital patterns, your garment is then hand cut, and beautifully tailored by machine*" (Souster and Hicks, January 30, 2011)	www.sousterandhicks.com

drafting" but still emphasized the garment being 'hand cut' and used the semantics "beautifully tailored by machine" which is an attempt to hide the mass market machine-made component of the manufacturing process. Also whether the measurements "are carefully taken" by hand or 3D body scanning is not made clear.

The first example in Table 3 is the most interesting comprehensive 3D technology website as it communicates heritage, craft, and contemporary bespoke technology. David Mason is the current Director of Nutters of Savile Row, which was originally established in 1969 by Tommy Nutter, London's tailoring rebel, who dressed many celebrities of the 1970s. Tommy died of AIDS in 1992 but David Mason revived the brand by digitalizing the original pattern blocks along with employing two of the original pattern-cutters of the Tommy Nutter period (shop.goodwood.com/products/nutters-of-savile-row-for-goodwood, May 5, 2011).

This website embraces all the new formats of 3D technology "body scanning" measurement, "design," "pattern cutting," "garment manufacture," and "virtual try on" discussed in the literature (Powell 2003; Ross 2010; Taylor and Unver 2011; *ShortList* January 27, 2011) and clearly illustrates that the tradition of Savile Row can be updated to include new technological practices while still offering craftsmanship, quality, and a luxury service.

DATA ANALYSIS: WEB ATMOSPHERICS

A good description of classical and aesthetic website design as discussed by Kurniawan (2000), Schenkman and Jonsson (2000), and Mahlke (2008) came from the Nutters of Saville Row for Goodwood website. This had been designed with a menu on the left hand side of the site with crisp, capital san-serif typography reversed white out of black. High-resolution photographic images in a lifestyle composed shot plus three different colorway waistcoats to select from. When the apparel was clicked on a larger magnified photograph of the garment in six primary colorways appeared. Textual information for those customers wanting to read more was on the right-hand side with 1.5 line-spacing to make the text easily readable. The checkout was accessible and the speed of moving from one section to another was rapid and satisfactory. The generic Nutters of Savile Row site also was also a good example of "classic" web-aesthetics, well set out with good-quality photographs but this time utilizing mono images and text for the archive gallery that included famous faces including the Beatles, Mick Jagger, and Andy Warhol. The general aesthetic feel was of nostalgia and heritage but with a contemporary twist.

DATA ANALYSIS: SOCIAL MEDIA/BLOGS

A significant development since the first survey was conducted in 2006 was the general uptake of social media/blogs to purchase or advertise menswear. Many managed successfully to balance the traditional bespoke quality and luxury service with new experiential online sites that would appeal to the younger and less traditional consumer. The research demonstrates that 58 percent of the total thirty-eight sites were using a combination of Blogs, You Tube, Facebook, and Twitter. Interestingly, this represents a fairly even split of 61 percent of the other websites observed and

53 percent of the original sixteen tailors surveyed. This underwrites Powell's study of digital tailors and her predictions for the future (2003). In 2006 only two of the sixteen tailors were using blogs and social media was not readily available to the general public. Now ten websites had active blogs, eight used Twitter feeds, eight had Facebook sites, and Henry Bailey's site used a full combination of social media that included Delicious, a social bookmarking service, Twitter, Facebook, and You Tube.

INDUSTRY PERSPECTIVE

Professor Ramroop has trained and practiced as a bespoke tailor in Savile Row since a young man and has many very wealthy customers, some of whom fly in their own planes for a suit fitting. However, he tells me that there are numerous opportunities in information technology (IT) that can bring about new and improved tailoring practices. For example he now uses Skype fittings for a jacket which is quite different from practices in 2006. "The client can put his jacket on for a Skype viewing and I would make comments about the fit." The suit is sent on after the initial measurements and pattern-cutting for a fitting with the customer. The advantage of Skype is the visual opportunity of communicating with the customer virtually but still giving a Savile Row quality service. They are operating with client fittings in over fifty-eight countries so far! The use of Skype in this way can be considered similar or have parallels with the 3D technological "Virtual fitting-room" but in a more directly personal way. He says that he "wants the customer to maintain that level of service and not get the impression he is buying online." Professor Ramroop explains, "Customers who purchase high class bespoke tailoring expect this level of service" (interview, March 28, 2011). He started to utilize Skype as an additional IT service about a year ago, first in Japan then with customers in Washington, DC, and then Texas. He said "Any customer spending in excess of £5,000 (US$7,929.59 on April 6, 2012) would expect that personal service even if they were time scarce" (interview, March 28, 2011).

Ramroop has "current plans to develop a middle range Maurice Sedwell (his company brand name in Savile Row) made-to-measure suit, which he refers to as 'semi-bespoke' on the website." He said that he "considered his clients who pay a price of £5,000+ (US$7,929.59+) for his suits are getting them 100% handmade" (interview, March 28, 2011). Specifically, this means only a small amount up to 10 percent is machine work, the rest is still hand sewn.

Professor Ramroop admits his website is not yet updated in terms of current web-atmospherics but this is planned for the near future. Questioned about his objectives for the new site he states that the new website is to be informative rather than an e-commerce, e-tailoring site. The purpose is to drive the customers to come to the store or make an inquiry via e-mail and he added "we have a different email address so we can track and monitor who they are; and where they are from; and if they are a serious bespoke customer; all from their enquiries" (interview, March 28, 2011). In terms of "aesthetics" the web-atmosphere has continuity with the store and the corporate color green and the gentleman's club wood panel feel is communicated.

There was a discussion on the term "co-design" where a customer can choose online from certain specific pre-set configurations of colors, cuts, patterns, and threads as the provenance of high-end bespoke tailoring. The customer can co-design within those parameters anything they like. However, Ramroop's view is "that this sounds similar to what any customer and good bespoke tailor creates as a co-designed bespoken outfit for their clientele" (interview, March 28, 2011).

CONCLUDING DISCUSSION

Returning to the questions set for the study: the use of social media/blogs to purchase and advertise. Social media platforms were identified as a substantive method of promoting and ordering suits. This is definitely the biggest innovation and change in practice in the five years since the original bespoke survey was conducted, with Facebook, You Tube, and Twitter as clear favorites. Blogs are now much more commonplace and considered an important part of an SME brand image and communication platform.

Use of new technology for measurements/patterns and manufacture highlights another generation of tailors willing to use 3D technology and CAD for pattern-cutting and some parts of manufacturing, but mainly in the younger middle-market ranges. Body-scanning is becoming slightly more popular but mainly with the knowledgeable younger male consumer identified by *ShortList* (January 27, 2011) and observed in this study. However, it is forecast that as future tailors and menswear designers graduate with embedded 3D skills many more tailors will operate offline and online retail environments using 3D-2D pattern-cutting, 2D grading, and 3Dscanned toiles or body measurements as Taylor and Unver (2011), Ross (2010), and Powell (2003) suggest.

The question of web-atmospherics communicating contemporary and traditional values shows that some tailors are utilizing "classical" aesthetics and creating web-atmospherics that give positive experiential values to the browser wishing to obtain more information, or purchase suits direct. There is much evidence that communicating the heritage and quality of bespoke tailoring is still more important to the consumer, than new 3D technological practices except in tailoring sites specifically aimed at the less traditional male consumer. However, there is room for improved web design practice from many sites visited and experimentation with "style advice" and "co-design" configuration options would add more value to consumers visiting a SME tailor online.

References

Apeagyeri, P. R. and R. Otieno. 2006. "Usability of Pattern Customising Technology in the Achievement and Testing of Fit for Mass Customisation." *Journal of Fashion Marketing and Management* 11(3): 349–65.

Drapers Record. 2003. *Suit* Issue. *Drapers Record* May 17: 37–8.

Hackley, Chris. 2003. *Doing Research Projects on Marketing Management and Consumer Research.* London: Routledge.

Jerrard, R, D. Hands and J. Ingram. 2003. *Design Management Case Studies.* London: Routledge.

Kim, H.-S. and B. Jin. 2006. "Exploratory Study of Virtual Communities of Apparel Retailers." *Journal of Fashion Marketing & Management* 10 (1): 41–55.

Kurniawan, S. H. 2000. "Modelling Online Retailer Customer Preference and Stickiness: A Mediated Structural Equation Model." 4th Pacific Asia Conference, April 18–20, Kyoto, Japan.

Mahlke, Sascha. 2008. "Visual Aesthetics and the User Experience." SchlossDagstuhl Seminar Proceedings, October 24, Berlin, Germany.

Manganari, E. E., G. J. Slomkos and A. P. Vrechopoulos. 2009. "A Store Atmosphere in Web Retailing." *European Journal of Marketing* 53(9–10): 1140–53.

Nguyen, Han. 2011. "Facebook Marketing in the Fashion Industry." *Arcada.* publications.theseus.fi (accessed June 13, 2012).

Okonkwo, U. 2005. "Can Luxury the Fashion Brand Store Atmosphere be Transferred to the Internet? www.brandchannel.com/images/papers/269_lux_goods_online.pdf. [give date accessed]

Okonkwo, U. 2009. "Sustaining the Luxury Brand on the Internet." *Journal of Brand Management* 16(3–5): 302–10.

Payne, G. and J. Payne. 2004. *Key Concepts in Social Research.* London: Sage.

Powell, N. 2003. "Italian Style." *Journal of Textile and Apparel, Technology and Management* 3(1): 1–9.

Ross, F. 2007. "Refashioning London's Bespoke and Demi-bespoke Tailors: New Textiles, Technology and Design in Contemporary Menswear." *The Journal of the Textile Institute* 98(3): 281–8.

Ross, F. 2010. "Leveraging Niche Fashion Markets through Mass-customisation, Co-design, Style Advice, and New Technology: A Study of Gay Aesthetics and Website Design. *Fashion Practice* 2(2): 175–98.

Ross, F. and S. Jenkyn-Jones. 2009. "Same-Sex Suits; Co-design, Style Advice and the Identification of the Gay Aesthetic Experience." Conference proceedings from MCPC Helsinki, Finland, October 4–8.

Schenkman, B. O. N. and Fredrik U. Jonsson. 2000. "Aesthetics and Preferences of Web Pages." *Behaviour & Information Technology* 9(5): 367–77.

Taylor, Andrew and Ertu Unver. 2011. "An Experimental Study to Test a 3D Laser Scanner for Body Measurement and 3D Virtual Garment Design in Fashion Education." University of Huddersfield Repository http://eprints.hud.ac.uk (accessed January 31, 2011).

Walker, R. 1998. *The Savile Row Story and Illustrated History.* London: Prion Multimedia Books.

24

YOGA, FACEBOOK, AND FANDOM:
Examining brand devotion by lululemon customers using social media

Caroline Czajkowski and Tasha L. Lewis

INTRODUCTION

Brand logos and images are the most visible aspects of the retail world. Having a brand that stands out among the rest is one of the keys to success. Many customers have brands they prefer, and in some cases this preference can turn into a fierce devotion. Those loyal consumers are repeat buyers, are vocal about their love for the brand, and will defend the brand and their devotion to it. Enabled by social media platforms, these brand enthusiasts sometimes form online communities where they discuss the brand and its products, ask questions, and offer advice and answers. This study explores the phenomenon of this brand devotion through the case study of lululemon athletica, and examines the company's conscious use of social media to encourage and maintain a brand-devoted community.

Lululemon opened its first store in 1998 in Vancouver, Canada; in little under a decade, the company's popularity had exploded. In 2006, the company operated 46 stores with annual revenue of about US $100 million (Morse et al., 2006), but by 2016 lululemon operated over 250 stores in Canada, the United States, Australia, and New Zealand, with annual revenue reaching US $266 million. Lululemon began as a niche women's yoga apparel manufacturer and retailer but has since expanded its product line to cover the active lifestyle of its brand devotees. In the process, lululemon has also appealed to sportswear and casual wear markets, with a growing number of customers willing to spend increasing amounts of money on its products (Urstadt, 2009).

The case study of lululemon presented here will explore how social media is used by and for brand-devoted customers to foster a compelling and resilient zeal for the market leader in yoga apparel. The digital experience of its customers is a priority for lululemon and reinforces the in-store community-building that the brand has embraced. A glance at the company's Facebook page is an indicator of its strong social media presence. In 2016, lululemon's Facebook page had over 1.5 million "likes." By comparison, competing Canadian fitness apparel brand Lolë had just over 83,000 "likes," and U.S.-based Gap Inc.'s Athleta brand trails lululemon with just over 313,000 "likes."

FASHION BRANDING, RELATIONSHIPS AND EMOTION

Lululemon's brand success was driven without the aid of traditional means of advertising; instead the company focused on brand-building through local yoga studios and a strong core of innovative customers to serve as attractors to the brand (Tushman, 2010). Lululemon stores are seen as a prioritized consumer touch point for the brand and store employees are granted a good deal of autonomy to customize the store experience for their local customers. This customer-centric approach to its brick-and-mortar strategy also extends to the digital space and customers have responded with a deep attachment to the brand through both the physical and virtual channels.

When consumers are intimately tied to their preferred brands this type of attachment can be termed as "brand love," which is "the degree of passionate emotional attachment a satisfied consumer has for a particular trade name" (Carroll and Ahuvia, 2006: 81). Marc Gobé (2009) looks at how consumers attach emotion to products, and how emotional aspects can be used to set a company's products apart from others to attract customers and retain customers' loyalty. Consumers can make emotional attachments to brands, sometimes forming a type of relationship with them. In return, companies understand the need to form relationships with their customers. Many companies have some form of customer relationship management (CRM) in place to keep their customers happy. CRM encompasses how companies create, maintain, and strengthen relationships with their customers (Vence, 2007), and may be a contributing factor to why customers are so devoted to certain brands.

While companies do what they can to manage and shape customer relationships, customers can also form relationships with each other. These types of relationships can start with a small group of people and grow into a larger community that can be labeled a "brand community" (McAlexander et al., 2002; Petrescu and Korgaonkar, 2011). Muniz Jr. and O'Guinn (2001) describe a brand community as "a specialized, non-geographically bound community, based on a structured set of social relationships among admirers of a brand. It is specialized because at its center is a branded good or service" (2001: 412).

SOCIAL MEDIA AND BRAND COMMUNITIES

Brand communities are abundant on the Internet, especially via social media. Social media encompasses how people connect with each other on the Internet, using platforms like Facebook, Twitter, and YouTube. Petrescu and Korgaonkar (2011) state that social media is focused on the social aspects of behavior, such as "communication, information sharing, keeping in touch with friends, and finding new friends" (2011: 212). The popularity of fashion brands in the social media space may be explained by "the increasingly important role that such sites play in influencing consumers' online purchasing decisions" (Kimberley, 2010: 1). Social media is increasingly being used as a way for customers to leave feedback and suggestions on their favorite products ("Social Media Is Fashion's Newest Muse" 2010). These types of posts have opened the door for interactive communication between companies and their customers, and many companies have begun to listen. Smith et al. (2012) found that lululemon engaged in an active social dialogue with its customers on Facebook and that the content the brand posted was not one-sided but tended to foster conversations expressing opinions and questions. Lululemon's content is managed by a dedicated web team as part of its Guest Education Centre (GEC) which monitors the company's Facebook page, responding to customers and sharing information about new products. Due to evidence of this growing and carefully managed dialogue on the lululemon Facebook page, this case study explored the following questions in relation to both the customer and company strategies for using social media:

- *How do customers create loyal followings around a certain brand using social media?*
- *What role, if any, does the company play in encouraging extremely loyal customer behavior via social media?*

FACEBOOK DATA

The comments posted on lululemon's Facebook "wall" on Thursdays over a three-month long period in fall 2011 were analyzed. Facebook was chosen due to the ability to track conversations, as well as its popularity as the preferred social media channel used by lululemon and its customers at the time. Lululemon posted new products on its own website each Thursday and posted images or links on their Facebook page, directing customers to the new products. Many users commented on Facebook on the same day about the new items that appeared on lululemon's website. Due to the noticeable number of comments spurred by new product arrivals, the sample comments used for analysis were taken from comments posted on Thursdays. The three-month period was from September to November 2011, which included the end of the back-to-school sales period and included the very beginning of the holiday sales period. It was expected that this busy sales season would yield an increased amount of consumer and company traffic on lululemon's Facebook page.

For this study, only the main posts on lululemon's "wall" were examined, leaving out customer comments, or cascades, that were generated in response to those posts. The comments were excluded from the data count because the cascades varied in topic and oftentimes became unrelated to the original post. On lululemon's Facebook page, the setting for the comments was changed to show posts from everyone (the default setting on lululemon's Facebook page is to show only comments posted by lululemon). Once all the comments from the given date were fully visible, the pages were saved as a PDF file to be used for analysis.

CONTENT ANALYSIS

A content analysis was performed on the data from the posts, which were analyzed to determine if any recurring themes linked them (Bouma, 2002). The posts were first categorized into "comments" or "questions" and then according to the topics they addressed, such as products, customer service, or general expression of opinion of the brand. The types of posts and topics lululemon responded to on the Facebook page were also noted. Two researchers coded the data independently and compared the results, focusing on emerging categories for the first round of analysis. After initial coding categories were determined independently, and the categorization terms were discussed, aligned, and reconciled into themes that allowed for classification of the data.

FINDINGS

The total number of customer posts during the study period was 454, averaging 35 customer posts per day (see Figure 18). The total number of lululemon responses to customer posts was 206. This shows that a little under half, 45 percent, of all customer posts received responses from lululemon. Customers posted more comments than questions on lululemon's Facebook page. Both comments and questions were sorted based on whether the tone was found to be positive (e.g., "I love this" or "I really like this"), neutral (non-emotional statements), or negative (e.g., "I'm disappointed" or an overall negative statement). Overall, the majority of both comments and questions

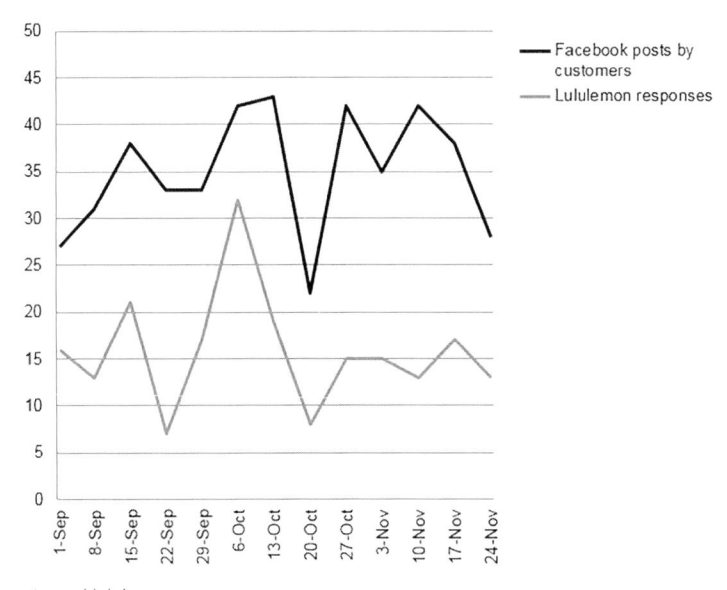

Figure 18 Customer posts and lululemon responses.
Source: Tasha Lewis

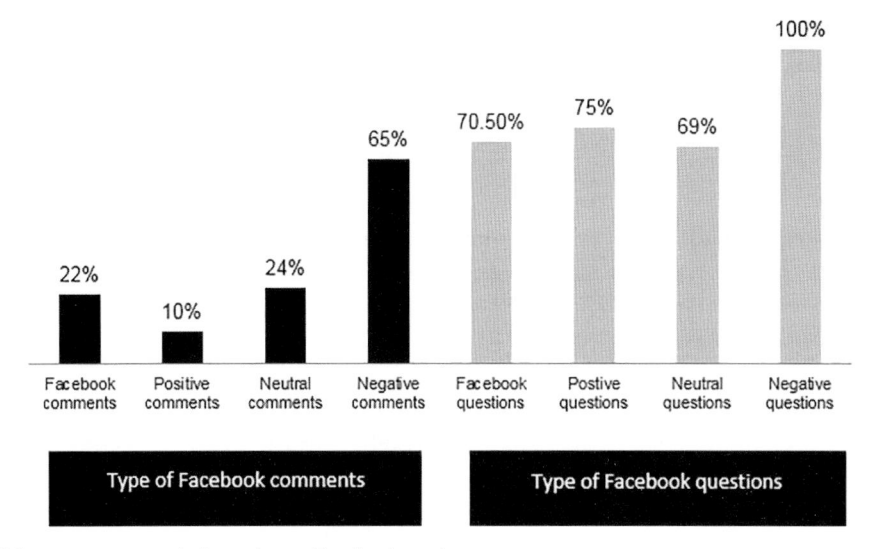

Figure 19 Lululemon response rate to customer Facebook posts.
Source: Tasha Lewis

were neutral in tone. Lululemon's average response rate was 45 percent and the results showed that lululemon responded to 100 percent of the negatively toned questions posted by users (see Figure 19).

Lululemon responded most often to customer questions and inquiries about a specific product. In addition to responding to customer comments and questions, lululemon also posted thirty-six of their own comments on Facebook during the study period. Customers responded to lululemon's posts a total of 854 times during the study period (see Figure 20), and responded most often to lululemon's most frequent post type, posts about new products available on the company's website.

FANDOM: CUSTOMER LOYALTY EXPRESSED VIA SOCIAL MEDIA

The first research question of this study sought to explore how customers create a loyal following around a certain brand using social media. The data from Facebook can provide insight into the answer for this question. A total of 454 customer comments were posted on lululemon's Facebook page with 206 responses from lululemon, and lululemon's 35 posts generated 854 responses from customers. These numbers show a large amount of traffic on the page created by customers. Example excerpts from the data show that customers appreciate lululemon's customer service and take to social media to voice their satisfaction.

> *Facebook user*: "Chinook Centre customer service is amazing WOW!!! I went tonight and bought a few things. I wish I knew the names of the associates but honestly all of them were so helpful. Thank you, thank you, thank you!! BEST customer service EVER!!!"

As was seen in this study, Facebook was frequently used as a customer's first point of contact when they had questions or comments. To evaluate whether customers create a loyal following around the brand using social media, the data also showed that customers assemble around the brand due to a perceived or actual quality or functionality of the product. Comments within the data include the following:

> *Facebook user*: "My most comfortable, best fitting, greatest quality & best looking gear EVER!!!! ... and I do try everything folks! :)xo"

Comments also showed that customers do feel they can express their opinions in terms of suggestions for products, such as color. Some customers would respond directly to lululemon employees asking them

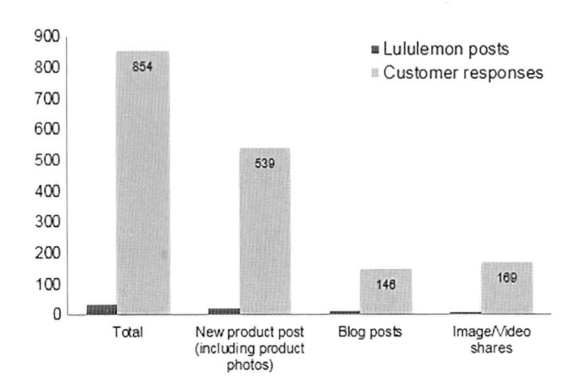

Figure 20 Customer responses to lululemon posts.
Source: Tasha Lewis

what they liked about a certain product, and others would do so without being prompted by lululemon, choosing to share their ideas on the Facebook page:

> *Facebook user*: "Here's an idea: Instead of squeezing out yet another shade of berry pink, aqua, or royal blue this year, let's go GREEN! Can you make some clothes in green? How come you never make green? It's autumn, let's see some nice earthy leafy greens. Please? I would be most grateful."

Customer contributions in general on Facebook suggest that some customers feel personally involved in the brand. It was even noted in the data that some users are quick to serve as peer-educators by answering fellow customers' questions before, or even instead of, lululemon employees.

LULULEMON'S ROLE IN ENCOURAGING CUSTOMER LOYALTY

The second research question of this study aimed to determine what role, if any, the company plays in encouraging extremely loyal customer behavior via social media. The study examined the company's level of involvement in maintaining an online community, and the results show that lululemon has a high level of involvement in maintaining that community. During the study period, the company posted to its Facebook page an average of almost three times per day, which generated an average of almost seventy responses per day from customers. Lululemon's total number of responses during the study period was 206, which is an average of 16 responses a day.

As mentioned, lululemon's Facebook page seemed to serve as a first line of communication for customer service support. The company's GEC team responds to customer's questions and comments using their own experience with the brand to help customers.

> *Facebook user*: "GEC, do the arms/sleeves on the don't worry be happy pullover fit tight and does the pullover fit TTS in the body? Thanks :)"
>
> *Lululemon athletica*: "Hey [Facebook user], I haven't had a chance to try on the pullover yet but I chatted with an educator this morning who said that she found it true to size and didn't find the arms to be tight. Hope this helps! ~[Lululemon employee]"

These types of responses show that lululemon closely monitors its Facebook page, informing customers of new products and responding to their questions and comments in a very personalized tone, thus maintaining a high level of involvement in this online community. Additionally, when issues with a product arise, these are treated as escalated issues and employees responding on Facebook urge the customer to contact lululemon's GEC by phone to resolve any problems. For example, look at the following:

> *Facebook user*: "I ordered the long sleeve cabin II in black swan and it arrived today with the security tag on it! Why would this happen? Why would you put security tags on merchandise? Isn't that the stores responsibility when merchandise arrives? Also, why is this the only cabin tee that reverses to the same color? What is the point?"
>
> *lululemon athletica*: "Hi [Facebook user] Thanks for reaching out to us. Sorry to hear you received your Cabin Long Sleeve with the security tag on. We would love to fix that for you. Please call us at the GEC at 1-877- 263-9300 option#2 and an educator will be able to sort that out for you. As far as the black swan colour being the same colour on both sides that was a choice our designers made when they decided what would look best

for this style. I would love to pass your feedback along to our designers. What colour would you like to see paired with the black swan?"

The option of calling the GEC was often suggested for problems customers encountered with orders or products. Even though lululemon does not explicitly advertise its customer service policies on Facebook, customers are educated on policies by reading other customers' posts and lululemon's responses on Facebook. In this way, lululemon can assert its role as an "educator" not just a retailer, which is a pillar of its customer service style (Morse et al., 2006).

The research also found attempts to involve customers in the brand's image. One such attempt is the company's posting of images of new items or links to its website. Lululemon's 35 Facebook posts generated 854 responses from customers, some of which were opinions about items that were posted. This parallels the company's view of its stores as an R&D center to gather customer feedback (Morse et al., 2006). Social media further enables this feedback process, for example:

> *lululemon athletica*: "This Just In » Cuddle Up Jacket, Scuba Hoodie*Print and Dog Running Pant! http://bit.ly/ThisJustIn_Oct20"
> *Facebook user 1*: "MUST HAVE!"
> *Facebook user 2*: "Oh that cuddle up jacket looks SOOOO cozy. Too bad about the price. :("
> *Facebook user 3*: "Nice—I want one!"
> *Facebook user 4*: "drool!"
> *Facebook user 5*: "The dog pants are my favourite pants of the year! So excited! I wore last year's in the rain last night and my legs were so warm and dry. But I will be picking up this year's version for sure!"

Not all responses to items are positive; however, both negative and positive responses are helpful in terms of future product releases (such as knowing whether to bring back a product or to give it a different name next time). Most of the feedback the company seeks is for its products, which make up a large part of its brand image. While the data showed evidence of attempts to involve customers, they do not reveal whether the company takes these suggestions into consideration or implements them.

THE FUTURE OF LULULEMON'S FACEBOOK FANDOM

Lululemon's careful management of its Facebook dialogue was tested during troubled times in 2013 when it was confronted with a major quality issue involving the sheerness of its Luon™ fabric, followed by controversial remarks by founder Chip Wilson. Dissatisfaction with the fabric was widely shared on social media and on lululemon's own product review pages before the company issued a product recall, with one customer even posting a photo on Facebook to show the sheerness of the fabric as it was held up to the light of a window (Larcker et al., 2014). The recall cost the company $17.5 million and its CEO Christine Day, who resigned in June 2013 (Binns, 2013). In the midst of the recall and ongoing quality complaints from lululemon's customers, company founder and chairman, Chip Wilson, during a television interview on Bloomberg, blamed product failures on some women's body types. Social media blasted Wilson and he apologized in a YouTube video that was posted on the company's Facebook page on November 8. Over 100 comments were posted in response to the video with both supporters and critics of Wilson's apology, as well as continued commentary on the noticeable decline in product quality. Lululemon replied to comments only eleven times in an effort to diffuse negative remarks (see Figure 21). A month later, Wilson resigned from his role as chairman at lululemon.

This study found evidence that lululemon recognizes the important role that social media can play in terms of customer loyalty and is actively using social media to embolden it. The company maintains a high level of involvement on Facebook and does attempt to engage customers for product feedback. Although it remains unknown to what extent lululemon takes customer suggestions into account, the turbulence of 2013 demonstrated that social media not only may be more than a tool for engaging customers around the brand but also serves as an empowering platform for customers to demand brand accountability.

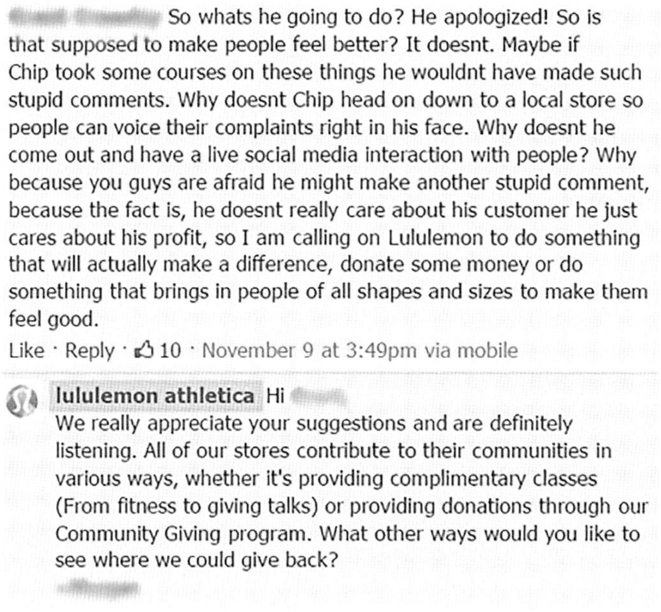

> So whats he going to do? He apologized! So is that supposed to make people feel better? It doesnt. Maybe if Chip took some courses on these things he wouldnt have made such stupid comments. Why doesnt Chip head on down to a local store so people can voice their complaints right in his face. Why doesnt he come out and have a live social media interaction with people? Why because you guys are afraid he might make another stupid comment, because the fact is, he doesnt really care about his customer he just cares about his profit, so I am calling on Lululemon to do something that will actually make a difference, donate some money or do something that brings in people of all shapes and sizes to make them feel good.
> Like · Reply · 👍 10 · November 9 at 3:49pm via mobile
>
> **lululemon athletica** Hi ▓▓▓
> We really appreciate your suggestions and are definitely listening. All of our stores contribute to their communities in various ways, whether it's providing complimentary classes (From fitness to giving talks) or providing donations through our Community Giving program. What other ways would you like to see where we could give back?

Figure 21 Facebook post in response to Chip Wilson's apology.
Source: Tasha Lewis

References

Alreck, Pamela L., and Robert B. Settle. (1999). "Strategies for Building Consumer Brand Preference." *The Journal of Product and Brand Management*, 8(2): 130–44.

Binns, Jessica. (2013). "Splitting from lululemon, CEO Reveals Details of Sheer-Pants Debacle." *Apparel*, June 11. http://apparel.edgl.com/news/Splitting-From-lululemon,-CEO-Reveals-Details-of-Sheer-pants-Debacle86839. Accessed July 9, 2015.

Bouma, Gary D. (2002). *The Research Process*. 4th ed. Australia: Oxford University Press.

Bourne, Leah. (2010). "Social Media Is Fashion's Newest Muse." *Forbes*, September http://www.forbes.com/2010/09/07/fashion-social-networking-customer-feedback-forbes-woman-style-designers.html. Accessed October 10, 2011.

Carroll, Barbara A. and Aaron C. Ahuvia. (2006). "Some Antecedents and Outcomes of Brand Love." *Marketing Letters* 17(2): 79.

Gobé, Marc. (2009). *Emotional Branding: The New Paradigm for Connecting Brands to People*. New York, NY: Allworth Press.

Keller, Kevin L. (2010). "Brand Equity Management in a Multichannel, Multimedia Retail Environment." *Journal of Interactive Marketing*, 24(2): 58–70.

Kimberley, Sara. (2010). "Fashion Retailers at Top of Social-Media Charts." *Marketing*, June, https://www.questia.com/magazine/1G1-228397975/fashion-retailers-at-top-of-social-media-charts. Accessed January 9, 2012.

Larcker, David F., Sarah M. Larcker and Brian Tayan. (2014). "Lululemon: A Sheer Debacle in Risk Management." *Stanford Graduate School of Business*, https://www.gsb.stanford.edu/sites/default/files/41_Lululemon.pdf. Accessed August 20, 2015.

Morse, Eric, Ken Mark and Patrick Walsh. (2006). "Lululemon Athletica: Primed for Growth." *Ivey Publishing*, Case Number 906M92.

McAlexander, James H., John W. Schouten and Harold Koening. (2002). "Building Brand Community', *Journal of Marketing*, 66(1): 38–54.

Muniz Jr., Albert M., and Thomas C. O'Guinn. (2001). "Brand Community." *Journal of Consumer Research*, 27(4): 412–32.

Petrescu, Maria, and Pradeep Korgaonkar. (2011). "Viral Advertising: Definitional Review and Synthesis." *Journal of Internet Commerce*, 10(3): 208–26.

Smith, A. N., Eileen Fischer and Chen Yongjian. (2012). "How Does Brand-Related User-Generated Content Differ across Youtube, Facebook, and Twitter?" *Journal of Interactive Marketing*, 26(2): 102–13.

Strauss, Marina. (2010). "Tweet to lululemon: Smaller Sizes Please." *The Globe and Mail*, June. http://www.theglobeandmail.com/globe-investor/tweet-to-lululemon-smaller-sizes-please/article1314995/. Accessed October 23, 2011.

Strauss, Marina. (2013). "Lululemon to Answer for 'Rubbing Thighs' Remark." *The Globe and Mail*, December. http://www.theglobeandmail.com/report-on-business/Lululemon-to-answer-for-rubbing-thighs-remark/article15818427. Accessed December 15, 2013.

Taylor, Timothy. (2011). "CEO of the Year: Christine Day of lululemon athletica." *The Globe and Mail*, November. http://www.theglobeandmail.com/report-on-business/rob-magazine/ceo-of-the-year-christine-day-of-Lululemon/article2247700/print/. Accessed December 2, 2011.

Tushman, Michael and David Kiron. (2010). "Leadership, Culture, and Transition at lululemon." *Harvard Business School*, Case Number 5-410-123.

Urstadt, Bryant (2009). "Lust for lulu." New York, August. http://nymag.com/shopping/features/58082/. Accessed October 25, 2010.

Vence, Deborah L. (2007). "CRM: You Know What It Stands for, But You May Not Know What It Means." *Marketing News*, 41(15): 12.

Walker, Rob (2008). *Buying In: The Secret Dialogue between What We Buy and Who We Are*. New York, NY: Random House.

FURTHER READING

Burns, Leslie Davis, Kathy Mullet, and Nancy O. Bryant (2016), *The Business of Fashion*, New York: Bloomsbury.

Business of Fashion (2018), "The State of Fashion 2018 Report", *Business of Fashion (BoF) and McKinsey & Co.*, Retrieved 2017 from: https://cdn.businessoffashion.com/reports/The_State_of_Fashion_2018_v2.pdf

Diamond, Jay, Ellen Diamond, and Sheri Diamond Litt (2015), *Fashion Retailing: A Multi-Channel Approach*, New York: Bloomsbury.

Mayer-Schonberger, V. and Cukier, K. (2013), *Big Data: A Revolution That Will Transform How We Live, Work and Think*, Boston: Houghton Mifflin.

Psarras, Evie (2014), "We All Want To Be Stars!: The Desire for Fame and the Draw to The Real Housewives, *Clothing Cultures*, Volume 2, Number 1, pp. 51–72, Intellect.

Poloian, Lynda (2014), *Retailing Principles: Global Multichannel and Managerial Viewpoints*, New York: Bloomsbury.

Quin, Bradley (2002), *Techno Fashion*, Oxford: Berg.

Seymour, S. (2012), *Fashionable Technology: The Intersections of Design, Fashion Science and Technology*, Copenhagen: Verlag.

Figure 22 Tattoos, Photo Courtesy of Brent Luvaas.
Source: Brent Luvaas

PART VI
Fashion Merchandising and Strategy

Figure 23 Denny Balmaceda, Photo Courtesy of Brent Luvaas.
Source: Brent Luvaas

INTRODUCTION

Joseph H. Hancock, II

The dawn of the 21st century saw a shift from retail stores to online shopping and then to the eventual rise of social media and various omni-channel outlets such as social media platforms, kiosks, and the rejuvenation of home shopping channels such as the Home Shopping Network (HSN) and Quality, Value, Customer Service (QVC). Now with more products than ever before available to shoppers an ironic scenario is taking place. Across the globe, brick-and-mortar retail stores and shopping malls are crying out that it is a retail apocalypse. Customer traffic has slowed down in various locations throughout the world and it appears that this is the end of retail as we know it with stores closing and some retail giants going into bankruptcy. But is this the decline of brick-and-mortar retailing? Or are we witnessing a new evolution of retail that makes us think we are just seeing the decline in retail brick-and-mortar?

With omni-channel retailing only representing about 10% of total retail it is clear that shoppers are still going to stores. And of that 10% only about 5% is clothing (citation here)! This includes such retailing as mobile-only commerce (m-commerce), Internet-only (e-commerce), infomercials, direct response television advertising, television shopping channels, catalogue sales, in-home demonstrations, vending machines, and multi-level marketing. Even more ironic you have had a complete shift in the research generated by consumer behavior scholars to focusing on this area that is not even truly representing a large part of the retail market. University departments and programs across the globe are switching the names of their retailing programs to things like the University of North Texas that calls their merchandising program "Digital Retailing." However if they examined industry trends it would be clear that they are only truly marketing themselves to a small portion of the retailing world that is the hottest trend. But like the news media that is telling everyone we are in a "retail wreck" (Cappetta and Ruhle, 2017) and that everyone going digital they are falling victim to the latest and greatest trends in industry instead of examining the larger picture…retailing just needs, to use fashion terminology - a facelift (Ibid).

EXPERIENTIAL RETAILING OR RETAILTAINMENT

When Youn-Kyung Kim, Pauline Sullivan and Judith Cardona Forney (2007) came out with their book *Experiential Retailing: Concepts and Strategies That Sell* they were ahead of their time. The book outlines how retail stores relate to consumer through a variety of methods that includes the symbols that relate to, rituals of consuming, how retail entertains, themes retailers use to relate to consumers, lifestyle retailing, strategies and most importantly branding. The overall theme of the text is how retail embodies parts of consumers' cultures in order to relate to them and get them into brick-and-mortar stores. The authors in the text emphasize the need for retailers to create an experiential retailing experience for customers to want to come back and shop. Today this notion has changed to what most are calling retailtainment or more closely defined as a retailer's ability to entertain customers either through store experience or in actual product to get them into stores to purchase and repurchase from them again.

Atmospherics (Kim, Sullivan & Forney, 2007: 163) play a key role in this process engaging a consumer's senses such as smell, taste, sight, hearing and touch. For example a retailer's ability to just engage the senses creates excitement in consumers to actually want to come into the store. And while a person may think Abercrombie & Fitch is passé, the company did a great job with creating this sort of excitement in the late 1990s and the early to mid-2000s with their nude magalogues and shirtless greeters at the entrances to their stores that drew customers in by the millions (Hancock 2009). Only when this strategy tired and was criticized by the media did it fail across the globe, but it allowed the brand to expand globally and become one of the world's top retailers during this time period.

But retailers still continue to create an aura of experience for customers that defeat the online experience. And while Ralph Lauren, the king of lifestyle merchandising is closing some of their brick-and-mortar locations across the world; the brand still generates excitement in their flagship stores that remain strong during this time of crisis. Through their niche brand divisions such as Ralph Lauren's Double RRL, the company continues to create unique experiences for their customers that cannot be paralleled by the website. Their flagship store located in Manhattan's Soho area is homage to the brand and cannot be replicated. As David Moskowitz, General Store Manager explains, in this space Ralph likes to tell stories reminiscent of an era gone by in history. That is why we also sell vintage pieces like Rolex watches, authentic military jackets, and Made in the USA collector Levis jeans that cannot be found anywhere else and customers come into to see them and while they are here purchase something new as well (personal communication, 4, August, 2017). And while these items may be found online or in social media for purchasing this experience of actually going to the store to touch and feel cannot be duplicated online or through media, it can only be found in stores. But the United States is not the only popular place for Ralph Lauren Double RRL, the brand has found large success among Japanese consumers as well, perhaps a store will someday be opened there too!

GLOBAL EXPANSIONS

The idea of opening a new store in a foreign market entices many retailers. As Rita Andrade explains in her article "Mappin Stores: Adding An English Touch To The São Paulo Fashion Scene," (Root, 2005: 176–187) the growth of stores across globe not only spreads goods and services to customers it also introduces a new culture into that region. She explains:

> The opening of an English department store in São Paulo was the consequence of urban modernization. From the nineteenth century until the first decade of the twentieth century, the major capitals of Latin America were Rio de Janeiro and Buenos Aires. In 1913, Mappin Stores allowed the members of an aspiring middle class and the bourgeoisie of São Paulo to experience "Englishness" – in a way that only the upper classes had previously – through the consumption of luxury goods (Andrade 2005: 176).

A similar experiencing of mass fashion cultures can be seen in the rise of what is sometimes referred to as *cheap chic* through brands such as H&M, ZARA, and Uniqlo. These three retailing giants have spread the culture of their countries and their fashion ideology across the globe representing the countries of Sweden (H&M), Spain (Zara) and Japan (Uniqlo). The success of each of these retail giants in the regions in which they exists really relies on the consumers in each area to accept that particular retailer's clothing styles and fashion appeal.

Uniqlo expected major growth in the United States when it first appeared in New York's Soho district less than a decade ago. However the retailer has since closed stores in areas such as Philadelphia, where it has seen a major decline in sales because of what this author calls *over storing* the region with locations. The retailer is known for its basic clothing styles that are somewhat replicated in other brands that are popular in the United States such as The Gap, Banana Republic, Club Monaco and J.Crew. Additionally the retailer's lack luster stores that offer a white space with oak floors only mimic that of The Gap in the 1980s (where this author worked for over a decade of his life) and somewhat today. That said, even the designer collaborations that Uniqlo did with such stars as Pharrell Williams, while doing very well in such cities as New York, did not draw the crowds it expected in areas such as King of Prussia, Pennsylvania, that houses the second largest mall in the United States. That said, Uniqlo closed this location in July 2017 and left the mall leaving only its Montgomeryville and Philadelphia Center City locations open.

DESIGNER COLLABORATIONS AND ATHLEISURE

Generating excitement in retailing goods and services through celebrity endorsement is not new. For those of us who can remember the late 1970s and early 1980s, retail stores like Kmart with their Jacqueline Smith Collection, Sears with their Cheryl Tiegs and Evon Goolagong fashions defined a new change in the retail climate. When Target introduced its first in a series of designer collaborations with the likes of Mossimo in his Red and Black labels and Isaac Mizrahi for its women's clothing, shoppers went crazy acting as if this was a new concept. Target quickly reacted introducing designer brand extensions all over the store in departments such as infants with Philippe Stark and Nate Berkus for home.

But the trend continues to grow for brands such as Target as Edwina Luck, Gjoko Muratovski and Lauren Hedley discuss in their article titled "Co-branding Strategies for Luxury Fashion Brands: Missoni for Target (2014: 41-56). The authors discuss how Missoni is a luxury Italian knitwear brand and it partnered with Target in September 2011 releasing a large, one off, mass-market collection that ranged from apparel to home wares. The collaboration received extensive media coverage and was consequently extremely sought after. The online sales site crashed within hours of opening while shelves were cleared in stores minutes after trading began. Within hours more than 40,000 items from the collection were posted for sale online at greatly inflated prices. The authors reveal that sales of the Missoni collection increased following the collaboration and the value of the publicity generated at estimated US$100 million.

The lack of available stock, despite the enormous hype created, reinforced Missoni's luxury image. Missoni was able to gain massive awareness of the brand despite not employing any of its own communication channels in the promotion of the collaboration. However the co-branded collaboration was distinctively Missoni, potentially inciting comparison and confusion with the signature line. Their study demonstrates how co-branding strategies can offer a viable opportunity for luxury brands to increase their market share, while they maintain their market position.

Additionally, Anne Peirson-Smith in her article, "Comme on Down and Choos Your Shoes: A Study of Consumer Responses to the Use of Guest Fashion Designers by H&M as a Co-Branded Fashion Marketing Strategy (2014: 57-82), focuses on the social construction intended to concretize the abstract symbolic nature of fashion in the global marketplace. As the fashion system is increasingly image driven, designers are personified, individualized and aestheticized, also branded and co-branded by the cultural intermediaries whose job it is to align and position them within a consumer niche of shared values and lifestyles. These symbiotic relationships borrow interest from each other as trickle-down and bottom-up brands cohabit in the interests of establishing brand visibility and credibility amongst aspirational consumers. Her study examines consumers using focus groups and interviews suggesting that the intentions of co-branding strategies is to motivate consumers to trade upwards by implementing celebrity designer crossover collections has been largely successful in engaging fashion brand fans, there is evidence of increasing consumer agency, cynicism and saturation with regard to this strategy in view of changing economic conditions and evolving consumer needs. Most importantly for both the Target and the H&M studies is to see that while both these retailers have online presence, most consumer flocked to stores to purchase the goods from them demonstrating the strength of retail's brick-and-mortar stores and how they continue to be the main place where consumers go to make their purchases.

So why are stores closing and what is really going on in the market of fashion? The answer lies in the article by Jennifer Craik, "Fashioning Sports Clothing as Lifestyle Couture" and her discussion of the rise of athletic apparel in the market place. Her article investigates how sports clothing has shifted from specialist apparel to enhance sporting performance to become a mainstay of stylistic trends in fashion and the basis of contemporary everyday dress. Sports clothing is not only the dominant form of clothing and footwear manufacture and marketing but also an increasingly important segment of designer fashion. So-called sports couture has taken the functionality out of sports clothing and transformed it into hyper chic.

Her essay exemplifies the current state of the retailing industry where brands such as Lululemon Athletica dominate the market with their athleisure clothing lines. In fall of 2016, athletic apparel carried the global apparel industry. The jogger became a dominant category for retailers across the spectrum and demonstrated that both men and women wanted comforted in the clothing they wear. The realization is not so much that one type of retail format for selling clothes – the brick-and-mortar store – is dead. The fact remains that the global arena of fashion are failing to give consumers new goods that are unique and that they do not already own. Bianca Wouch-Wilker a Sales Manager for Mundi-Wesport a leading manufacturer of women's and men's accessories revealed that the only categories doing well in fashion today or athleisure and cosmetics…the surviving retail stores are those discount off-price retailers like TJMaxx, Marshalls, and Home Goods because they are offering the same goods that other brick-and-mortar retailers are offering but at cheaper prices, as she states, "I mean wouldn't you buy things cheaper if you could?" She goes on to state that our global market place over saturated with stores not because stores are dead but because they are all offering basically the same thing. Most retailers don't have anything unique and are not offering unique experiences so wouldn't you just go to the off-price store to buy it. Unless a store offers exclusive products and services then really there is no reason to go, just buy it online and save yourself the trip (personal communication, 4, August, 2017). Until stores start to offer a unique experience or until fashion finds its way back into the lives of consumers we are in a retail rut and this industry definitely needs – a facelift!

References

Cappeta, Michael and Stephanie Ruhle (2017), "Retail Wreck? Over 1,000 Stores Close in a Single Week," *NBC News*. http://www.nbcnews.com/business/consumer/retail-wreck-over-1-000-stores-close-single-week-n767556, (accessed 9, August 2017).

Craik, Jennifer, "Fashioning Sports Clothing as Lifestyle Couture", *Berg Fashion Library*, http://dx.doi.org/10.2752/9781847881212/UNIFEXP0013, (accessed, 9, August 2017).

Farfan, Barbara (2017), "2016 US Retail Industry Overview: Statistics, Types of Retailing, Largest Chains", *The Balance*. https://www.thebalance.com/us-retail-industry-overview-2892699, (accessed 9, August 2017).

Hancock, Joseph (2009), "Chelsea on 5th Avenue: Hypermasculinity and Gay Clone Culture in the Retail Brand Practices of Abercrombie & Fitch," *Fashion Practice*, Vol. 1, Issue 1, pp. 63–86.

Kim, Youn-Kyung, Pauline Sullivan, and Judith Forney (2007), *Experiential Retailing: Concepts and Strategies That Sell*, New York: Fairchild Books.

Luck, Edwina, Gjoko Muratovski, and Lauren Hedley (2014), "Co-Branding Strategies for Luxury Fashion Brands: Missoni for Target", in Joseph H. Hancock, II, Gjoko Muratovski, Veronica Manlow, & Anne Peirson-Smith (eds), *Global Fashion Brands: Style, Luxury & History: Style, Luxury & History*, pp. 41–56, Intellect, United Kingdom.

Peirson-Smith, Anne (2014), "Comme on Down and Choos Your Shoes: A Study of Consumer Responses to the Use of Guest Fashion Designers by H&M as a Co-Branded Fashion Marketing Strategy", in Joseph H. Hancock, II, Gjoko Muratovski, Veronica Manlow, & Anne Peirson-Smith (eds), *Global Fashion Brands: Style, Luxury & History: Style, Luxury & History*, United Kingdom, pp. 57–82. Intellect.

25

MAPPIN STORES:
Adding an English touch to the São Paulo fashion scene

Rita Andrade[1]

ENGLISH INFLUENCES IN THE TROPICS

The decision to choose São Paulo for the site of a new English department store stemmed from the fact that commercial relations had existed between Brazil and England since the eighteenth century, during the colonial period and following independence from Portugal. European influences had been prevalent since 1763, when Brazil's capital was transferred to Rio de Janeiro in order to accommodate expanding commercial activities. This shift began the development of the southeast and, a few decades later, its inhabitants had assimilated to the new modes of European-style consumption. Rua do Ouvidor (Ouvidor Street) in Rio de Janeiro reflected the eagerness of Brazilians and wealthy immigrants who desired to further their socioeconomic status. In spite of this ideology, which deemed European culture superior to native ways, the Rio de Janeiro of the nineteenth century was a far cry from the cities that served the population as a cultural and architectural model (Mauad 1997: 207).

The opening of Brazilian ports to "friendly nations" in 1808 would initiate a unique link between Brazil and Europe, especially the United Kingdom. In 1815, Dom João IV declared Brazil a kingdom and established a series of administrative measures that gave the former Portuguese colony the status of a nation (Basbaun 1968: 103). Rio de Janeiro's aristocracy, eager to imitate the Portuguese in habits and titles, began to create a metropolis with commercial establishments, including fragrance stores, jewelry bazaars, and fashion showrooms. With the defeat of Napoleon in Portugal, Dom João IV returned to Portugal and left in his place Prince Dom Pedro, who declared Brazilian independence from Portugal in 1822, thus becoming the first Emperor of Brazil (Basbaun 1968: 104–6). With this relatively peaceful emancipation from Portugal, Brazil began to trade with the United Kingdom (Boris 2001: 78).

During the colonial period, a prohibition of the production of manufactured goods had slowed this commercial exchange. Exports of raw materials, like coffee and cotton, facilitated the import of manufactured goods, such as fabrics (Dowbor 1994: 33–56). At this time, injunctions from 1785 had ordered the closing of all existing factories in the colony, a move that hindered Brazil's ability to produce fine textile articles that would compete with other markets (Basbaun 1968: 102). Only the manufacture of thick cotton fabrics to dress slaves was permitted, thereby forcing inhabitants to import fine fabrics from Portugal. Despite emancipation and a shift in power, the challenges were great. England delayed the nation-building process.

While many owned tobacco, cotton and coffee fields at the end of the nineteenth century, some entrepreneurs established industries that made fabrics, ceramics, hats, and shoes. Gold mining was a resource for a few of the Brazilian provinces. In 1874, a textile factory using domestic raw materials was founded in Rio Grande do Sul. The following year, more than

---

[1] From Rita Andrade (2005) Mappin Stores: Adding An English Touch to San Paulo Fashion Scene. In Regina Root (ed) The Latin American Fashion Reader. Oxford: Berg.

twenty-five silk, felt, and straw factories had opened (Basbaun 1968: 108).

Large landowners who supported slavery, as well as obstacles imposed by Portugal, delayed Brazil's industrialization. Following independence, the elite of São Paulo and Rio de Janeiro contributed to this delay by continuing the dependency on manufactured goods. England supplied Brazil with prime materials, which natives assembled. The submission to the interests of England on behalf of the leading Brazilian classes evolved into a kind of subaltern culture that found its expression in the imitation of the habits, dress and patterns of consumption of the European upper classes.

SÃO PAULO: ITS ORIGINS AND ITS MODERNIZATION

By the first half of the twentieth century, *paulistas* (people born in the city of São Paulo) and *paulistanos* (those born in the State of São Paulo) already exhibited the influences of modernity and industrialization. Casa Mappin would play a pivotal role in the dissemination of the customs and styles proper to this experience. As Mappin's seventieth anniversary book reads, "Mappin, besides being a place to shop, was a habit in the Paulistano's lives. One did not go there only to buy clothing or to obtain the last novelty in home ware. Above all, the store was a place to meet and to be entertained" (Alvim and Peirão 1985: 113). As a backdrop, the modern city favored the advent of equally modern goods.

Into the first decade of the twentieth century, Rio de Janeiro was Brazil's capital and commercial center. Novelties from Europe arrived at the city's port and Ouvidor Street became a popular marketplace for these items. According to Cohen (2001: 31), French influences prevailed as evidenced by a large group of French traders who "specialized in fine textiles, millinery, perfumes, fashion and costumes objects, jewels, books and many other items." This may explain the hesitation on the part of the English to direct business there, but as Cohen illustrates, it might have more to do with the fact that British investments have often been associated with the industry trades rather than retail. But that did not stop British entrepreneurs from inaugurating their Mappin & Webb store at 100/101 Ouvidor Street in 1911 (Cohen 2001: 99; Alvim et al. 1985: 22). Built like its London flagship model, one of which the company had already installed in Buenos Aires, the store would later become known as Casa Mappin.

FASHION AND THE MODERN CITY

One can still recognize the British influences on São Paulo's cityscape. Urbanization campaigns in the nineteenth and early twentieth centuries incorporated English-style buildings, as evidenced by the façades of banks and trade houses. In 1899, Canadian Light, the first power company in the city, allowed a series of developments that included the illumination of public spaces, the establishment of a trolley car system, and electricity for industrial use. At the onset of the twentieth century, São Paulo had also been transformed by the wealth amassed by coffee plantations and invested in the city. The affluent coffee barons moved their families from the countryside to mansions in the city, their new urban lifestyle bringing them in close proximity with fine European goods and services. In 1910, the Estação da Luz (Station of Light) was imported in its entirety from England, still serving residents today. Modern methods of transportation and the importation of red bricks for stations and other buildings gave the city its English appearance. Social customs soon followed: five o'clock tea, theater concerts and daily promenades were part of the lives of elegant *paulistanos*, although their habits were not influenced by those of London alone. As the city sought all things English, immigrants from Portugal to Turkey and from all social backgrounds helped reshape city life.

By the 1920s, both immigrants and the new coffee aristocracy enjoyed a sort of European lifestyle. The city boasted teahouses, car rides and the City Hall Theatre (Teatro Municipal). So what better place than São Paulo, with its population that viewed "Englishness" as a synonym of elegance, to launch an English department store? There was misery, but also a promise of sophistication. Paulistas were thirsty for the styles of Europe and they had the buildings and means of transportation with which to make a department store feasible in their city.

That a department store appeared in São Paulo almost eighty years after its appearance in Europe might suggest that this city possessed a subaltern culture. According to Homi Bhabba, relationships between the North and the South can be viewed in light of their established specifications (Bhabba 1994). The Mappin Store did not just launch a branch in São Paulo; instead, it carefully synchronized its appearance with the modernity – and social hybridity – experienced in the Brazilian city. Was, then, the launch of this department store a confirmation of the elite's readiness to consume or had a new consumer-based culture with particular fashion tastes already been established?

São Paulo, it is worth highlighting, was a city preoccupied with its own industrialization, as some of its inhabitants had abandoned the coffee and other agricultural production that still persisted in much of South America. Its industrial growth was so rapid that São Paulo became known as a "Brazilian Manchester." Mappin Stores was at the heart of the city, or the Triângulo, at which point the XV de Novembro, São Bento and Direita Streets met. Sevcenko writes: "From 4 p.m. on, many paraded by the circuit of fine stores in the Triângulo, its apex the five o'clock tea salon at the Mappin Store prior to the six o'clock rush hour. The city's center smelled of perfume and skirt ruffles communicated feminine waves, a hustle and bustle, circumscribing the Triângulo in a desirable space" (Sevcenko 2000 [1992]. 51). One located English influences in the education, culture, tastes and habits of wealthy *paulistanos*. Most of all, this influence was evident at the level of material culture, in those very luxury items coveted by São Paulo's high society.

THE DEPARTMENT STORE AND MODERN LIFE

A product of the late nineteenth century, the department store catered to clients who desired to experience and consume luxury in a seemingly private but yet so public atmosphere. The concept had first emerged in France and England of the 1830s and 1840s. In Paris, as well as in the north of England, a change in architecture and urban planning all contributed to the birth of a business that gathered various articles under one roof. In this initial phase, production was usually determined by demand. In England in the 1830s, the majority of goods were still produced in sweatshops or small workshops.

Two department stores that appeared in the north of Britain claimed to be the first: Bainbridge's of Newcastle upon Tyne and Kendal; and Milne & Faulkner of Manchester (Lancaster 2000: 7). In France, the *magasin des nouveautés* preceded the opening of Paris's Bon Marché, anticipating its sales, customer service, and luxurious spaces. As Aristide Boucicaut, the founder of Bon Marché would declare, this store had been "specially constructed and entirely intended for a great trade in *nouveautés*" (Miller 1981: 20). All stores marked a shift in the shopping patterns and behaviors of their clients. Lancaster describes what might have happened on any given day: a lady visits the store to buy fabric to make a dress but she also needs thread, bows, ribbons. As she looks for the right ones, she comes across other novelties that might match her first purchase, like a pair of gloves or socks (Lancaster 2000: 10–11). With all her needs and desires in one place, the client hardly ever left with just one item. The Mappin Store of São Paulo would market similar novelties, although it would soon find the need to shift its marketing strategies.

MAPPIN STORES: THE HEIGHT OF SOPHISTICATION

Mappin Stores first opened its doors in São Paulo on 29 November 1913. The main newspapers, like *O Estado de São Paulo,* assigned whole pages to the big event. It was not only the opening of another English shop; it was Brazil's first department store. The origins of the business dated back to eighteenth-century Sheffield, England where since 1774 the store Mappin & Webb had sold silver, ceramics and other fine goods (Alvim et al. 1985: 21). When contemplating the market overseas, São Paulo did not immediately come to mind. Late nineteenth-century Buenos Aires had the reputation of being the Paris of South America and it was home to the largest English community outside Great Britain. Mappin and Webb was thus established in Buenos Aires and Rio de Janeiro before the setting up of São

Paulós branch in 1912. The nature of the business in São Paulo was, however, very different from that of the shops in Europe, Buenos Aires and Rio de Janeiro, as it did not just specialize in silver and crystal but instead branched out to become a true department store.

In a short period of time, Mappin was a place where one could find fine clothes, fabrics, trimmings, accessories, furniture, and household appliances. It was the very experience of elegance, the perfect meeting point for afternoon tea or a ladies fashion show. Salespeople (usually women) attended to the needs and requests of loyal customers and served coffee. A client could sit down as goods were brought to her. Attendants picked out the latest arrivals. Because items purchases were noted in notebooks with information about family accounts, one's socioeconomic status was noted at the time of payment. Thus, the Mappin shopping experience adapted the desire for that certain "Englishness" to particular class-based hierarchies that predominated in Brazilian culture.

Soon after the launch of Mappin & Webb in the three South American cities, São Paulo was the one chosen to house Mappin Stores, an English anonymous society formed by Mappin & Webb and Debenhams. The Brazilian undertaking, called Mappin & Webb (Brazil) Ltd., consisted of three English partners: Walter John Mappin, Herbert Joseph Mappin, and Henry Portlock. In 1913 those three partners joined Sir John Kitching, manager for the English shop Debenhams, to found Mappin Stores in São Paulo (Alvim et al. 1985: 21–4). Mappin Stores and Mappin & Webb were housed in the same building at XV de Novembro Street, in the very heart of the city and they stayed there until 1919, when Mappin Stores moved out to the Praça do Patriarca (where it existed until 1936). The launch of this new branch attracted the following note from the English newspaper *Times of Brazil*, published on 1 August 1919: When the prefect [Mayor] arrived, shortly before 9.30 p.m., the ground floor and the upper galleries were thronged with visitors. Dr. Washington Luiz was met at the Rua Direita entrance by Mr Kitching, managing director of the Stores, . . . The prefect [Mayor], in a brief address congratulated Mr. Kitching on the enterprise which had given São Paulo such a magnificent establishment and wished that it might meet with the success that it undoubtedly deserved.

As this description suggests, the Mappin Stores inaugurated a much welcome establishment that far surpassed others in its elite clientele. Similar store concepts, such as the Casa Alemã (German House) launched by Daniel Heydenreich and located on 25 de Março Street since 1883, targeted a less economically privileged consumer (Alvim et al. 1985: 35).

During the first two decades of the twentieth century, the coffee baron families settled in new mansions on what had been farmland previously (Rolnik 2001: 26–7). Today's Paulista Avenue, on which one finds São Paulo's business center, gave way to rows of European-style mansions with more "Latinized" features. The new residential areas were called Campos Elíseos (the French Champs Elysées) and Garden Cities. By building them in clusters, São Paulo's streets took on the feel of European sophistication; however, this push marginalized the working class to the city outskirts.

The interests of skilled immigrants, businessman and wealthy *paulistanos* were at the core of Mappin Stores' early years. Following the 1929 depression and the sale of Mappin shares to an English tradesman in 1936 there was an attempted name change. The Casa Anglo-Brasileira (Anglo-Brazilian House) concept, however, proved impractical as the Mappin name was fixed in the *paulistano* imaginary. The 1940s witnessed the popularization of the department store, a reflection of the boom in the region's industrial and commercial infrastructure. The increasing influence of the United States brought new businesses and an emphasis on mass consumption. By the 1950s, Mappin Stores saw an end to its elevated status as the company implemented a more aggressive marketing-style approach that paralleled that of businesses in the United States.

MAPPING FASHION

When consulting the Mappin Historical Archive, the wide array of advertisements that the store placed in São Paulo's main newspapers stands out. With these images and descriptions, Mappin proposed its own brand of modernity – one that made its way to the consumer (and hence, the city at large) at every instant. Furthermore, it is a fashionable identity targeting a cosmopolitan society with the elegance of European social circles. It also appears to be quite French, using French words to name colors, styles, garments and emphasizing the praised Parisian fashions of *Vogue* magazine – even though there is no evidence to suggest that these garments actually came from France. While there is ample evidence to document that these fashionable goods were imported from England, Mappin preserved its use of English terms only to denote types of fabrics. In the imaginary of the time, this approach preserved the fashionable crowd's sense of elitism grounded in that center of fashion, Paris; while maintaining a certain Englishness. The profusion of fashion magazines in São Paulo counted on these associations, especially as more and more members of the middle and upper classes traveled to Europe to purchase these fashions on their own account.

Richard Sennett explains that the term "sophistication" was first used in nineteenth-century France and Britain as a compliment amongst the bourgeoisie, denoting "the one who could [be] recognize[d] as 'well educated', or as one who has 'good manners', in spite of any language, national customs or age barriers" (Sennett 1988: 175–6). Sophistication was indeed one of Mappin Store's most marketable qualities, as this testimony by Olga Rubião, a middle-class woman born in the 1920s, indicates. She remembers the kinds of clothes sold at Mappin, saying: "I preferred Mappin's ready-made clothes that had been imported from England, such as cashmere pullovers and overcoats. But the dresses were so unfashionable. British women had no taste and some of their garments seemed a bit too conventional."

Her statement reflects a distancing effect that Mappin's marketing department would promote rather than downplay A lecture room included a bookshop that sold mainly foreign English titles. Mappin placed its advertisements in the English-language newspapers of São Paulo, such as the *Anglo Brazilian Chronicle*. In October 1937, Casa Mappin announced the arrival of new book titles available at the department store; of the 35, all titles were in English.[10] Another popular section of the store was its Tea Salon, where the elite – politicians, plantation owners, bankers and writers like Mario de Andrade – enjoyed meeting. The Tea Room, or Salão de Chá as it was also known since its inauguration in 1919, was also the site of the more popular fashion shows in Brazil.

Mappin's Tea Room, which took up the store's first floor of the XV de Novembro Street section, was later moved (along with the rest of the store) to Praça Ramos de Azevedo in 1959. Its popularity, however, had seen its peak in previous decades and it was transformed into a new banquet-style Sala Verde (Green Room) with an "American spirit" and visited by secretaries of state and military officers.

In a short period of time, Mappin had transformed its fine goods reputation into a place for "being seen" by other elegant members of society during a fashion show or afternoon cup of tea. Mappin's storefront displayed those items that were transforming the lives of elite Brazilian households. The department store simultaneously marketed the exclusivity of the upper classes, when announcing in 1915, for example, the option to tailor for its clients Carnival costumes. Other fashions, such as an advertisement for women's blouses indicates that same year, implied that wealthy *paulistanos* also possessed the best of France and England. The May 1915 advertisement categorizes these washable – read as "modern" – garments with Parisian chic and British design: "New model in washable white silk, modern collar"; "Modern blouse in washable white silk"; "Chic blouse in silk taffeta, modern style"; and "Shirt Blouse in sheer wool and silk, English cutting, various colors" . . . The Mappin of the 1920s would leave an indelible mark on the cityscape and an impression on the customs of São Paulo's inhabitants. The pursuit of an English chic style would persist in the Brazilian cultural imaginary for decades, even after the Mappin brothers sold their company shares to Alfred Sim following the 1929 stock market crash (Alvim et al. 1985: 94–7).

In the end, Mappin conquered both its Brazilian and European clientele with the distribution of catalogs and by furthering its advertisement campaigns. Each time a new product arrived in Brazil, Mappin Stores was at the forefront, publishing notes that invited its customers for a private showing. Gradually, some Brazilian craftsmen and newly arrived immigrants were hired to produce specialty items. Mappin also added well-known tailors to its staff so as to expand its repertoire of services. To best appeal to the Brazilian client, these nationally produced goods and garments still possessed British style and design. The department store continued to import fashions from France and England, especially fabrics that could be tailored into individualized designs.

From the moment that Mappin integrated its sale of imported fabrics with a growing local clothing industry, it became more like an American department store. Mappin's catalogs expanded its city-based clientele to the countryside and thus initiated a special delivery system to provide its products to customers who could not enter its store as frequently. Each catalog contained instructions on made-to-fit measurements and suggestions regarding sizes for newly introduced ready-to-wear clothing. By 1939, Mappin had relocated to a new building at Praça Ramos de Azevedo, opposite the City Hall Theatre, where it still stands as a landmark in the downtown area (Alvim et al. 1985: 104).

Grounded in São Paulo's Anglo-Brazilian identity, Mappin department stores would continue to disseminate fashionable forecasts and news of newly arrived goods. Well educated in British modes, the Brazilian elite relished in Mappin's presentation of their status and relationships with other classes. Although the founding partners had long left Brazil, a new group of shareholders appropriately named the Casa Anglo-Brasileira Society expanded on and promoted what many perceived as that certain "Englishness" in Brazilian society. With its rising middle-class clientele and a locally based staff, the store deepened its presence in the cityscape, only to be concluded by the announcement of Mappin department store's bankruptcy on 29 July 1999. Today, the name Mappin continues to represent a small part of Brazil's national heritage, a symbol that remains uniquely *paulista*.

References

Alvim Z. and S. Peirão (1985), *Mappin setenta anos*, São Paulo: Editora Ex Libris.
Basbaun L. (1968), *História sincera da república – das origens à 1889*, São Paulo: Alfa-Omega.
Bhabba H. (1994), *The Location of Culture*, London: Routledge.
Cohen A. A. (2001), *Ouvidor, a rua do Rio*, Rio de Janeiro: AA Cohen.
Giroletti D. (1995), "'The Growth of the Brazilian Textile Industry and Transfer of Technology'", *Textile History*, 26(2): 215–31.
Lancaster W. (2000), *The Department Store: A Social History*, Leicester: Leicester University Press.
Mauad A. M. (1997), 'Imagem e auto-imagem do segundo reinado', in L. F. Alencastro (ed.), *História da vida privada no Brasil. Império: a corte e a modernidade nacional*, vol. 2, São Paulo: Companhia das Letras.
Miller M. B. (1981), *The Bon Marché: Bourgeois Culture and the Department Store 1869–1920*, London: Allen & Unwin.
Rolnik R. (2001), *São Paulo*, Coleção Folha Explica, São Paulo: Publifolha.
Sennett R. (1988), *O declínio do homem público – as tiranias da intimidade*, São Paulo: Companhia das Letras.
Sevcenko N. (2000), *Orfeu extático na metrópole. São Paulo sociedade e cultura nos frementes anos 20*, São Paulo: Companhia das Letras.

26

FASHIONING SPORTS CLOTHING AS LIFESTYLE COUTURE

Jennifer Craik[1]

Sportswear exists because American women were the first to live the modern, fast-paced life. (designer Michael Kors, quoted by Seeling 2000: 578)

SPORTS CLOTHING AS FASHION

This chapter explores how sports clothing has shifted from specialist apparel to enhance sporting performance to become a mainstay of stylistic trends in fashion and the basis of contemporary everyday dress. Sports clothing is not only the dominant form of clothing and footwear manufacture and marketing but also an increasingly important segment of designer fashion. So-called sports couture has taken the functionality out of sports clothing and transformed it into hyper chic.

In the post-war period, sports clothing developed both more refined and specialist genres and influenced increasingly the commercialization and democratization of fashion into everyday streetwear and high street fashion. Sportswear has become a huge international business with brands becoming synonymous with sporting apparel both in and out of sporting arenas. Brands such as Reebok, Nike, adidas, Puma, Ripcurl, Billabong, Hot Tuna, Quiksilver, Speedo, Jantzen and Canterbury have become the currency of youth-oriented "hip" style (O'Mahony and Braddock 2002; Quinn 2002; Chalmers 2003; Weinstein 2003). In addition to sports clothes, sportswear has proliferated into an unimaginable array of associated paraphernalia, such as heart monitors, sports watches, computerized devices, sports radios and CD-players, sports bags, sports drinks, sports cosmetics and body products, sports cars, sports bikes, sports underwear and socks, sports shoes, sports parkas, sports exercise equipment, training devices and facilities.

The marketing and selling of this paraphernalia and sporting merchandise in general has become extremely sophisticated: e-selling, club merchandise, high street chain merchandising, specialist stores (e.g. Niketown in Chicago) and sports superstores and malls. Sports clothing has become an integral part of subcultures and youth identification with sporting heroes vying with movie and pop stars as role models and whose dress sense has influenced youth clothing since the 1950s. Increasingly, everyday fashion and prosaic dress has its origins in sportswear since sporting apparel offers clothes that are cheap, practical, casual, multipurpose and stylish (Kidwell and Christmas 1975; cf. Joseph 1986: 177–80; de Teliga 1995; Danielsen 1999). This trend has been explained in terms of the apparent blurring of class and status, the rise of leisure time and decline of formality in everyday life.

Functional imperatives have dominated over form and design or aesthetic sensibilities increasingly shaped by the elements and details of sports clothing. In Chapter 6, we discussed the important contribution made by Coco Chanel to transforming sports fabrics and clothing into high fashion and thereby reshaping ideas about comfort and style. In the United States,

---

[1] From Jennifer Craik (2005) Fashioning Sports Clothing as Lifestyle Couture: Sport Clothing as Fashion. In Uniforms Exposed: From Conformity to Transgression. Oxford: Berg. Pp 161–174.

Claire McCardell played a similar role in the post-war period. She experimented with jerseys, knitted fabrics and nylon that she manufactured into clothes with a practical cut and more relaxed styling, thereby influencing the consumer culture of clothing and influencing the designers who followed (O'Mahony and Braddock 2002: 14). By the 1960s, sports clothing had become an integral component of designer fashion. This occurred first in North America, but quickly spread to Europe, then globally.

From the 1950s, sports clothing dominated the cinema, popular music and consumer culture. American popular culture became a major influence elsewhere reflecting an obsession with leisure, informality and less conservative social mores. Wetsuits, for example, were developed in California as part of the culture of surfing with the development of neoprene fabrics to cope with cold water and long immersion (Hall, Carne and Sheppard 2002). Innovations in swimwear soon followed.

To meet demand, many clothing companies specialised in "sportswear" and leisurewear. Some also became heavily involved in the development of new artificial fibres that were cheaper than wool and cotton as well as having other advantages; they were lightweight, resisted water and dirt, and streamlined the body. Companies like Du Pont, Courtaulds and ICI developed new synthetic fibres, based on nylon, rayon or polyester, such as dacron, orlon, tricel, bri-nylon, terylene, courtelle and a lycra forerunner – fibre K – that were quickly popularized. Synthetic fibres and fabrics were marketed as "miracle" materials with "easycare", "wash and wear" properties.

Because of their "resistance to outdoor exposure", light weight, durability, and wash and wear character, they were perfect also for sports clothing, and made appearances in swimwear, skiwear, anoraks and many sports uniforms (gymnastics, baseball, basketball and so on), though other sports resisted their allure, e.g. athletics, boxing, hockey, football. Skiwear, however, adopted these new fabrics with alacrity and, as skiwear was emulated in fashion, streetwear followed suit. Quilted nylon anoraks and polyester ski pants were popularized both for practical reasons (e.g. warmth) and for fashion (as après-ski wear) (Handley 1999: 63).

The image of Emma Peel in the British television series, *The Avengers,* dressed in a body-hugging futuristic flying suit had a major impact on redefining the ideal female form and popularizing body-hugging fashions and fabrics (O'Mahony and Braddock 2002: 16). These fabrics also influenced developments in camping and outdoor equipment (such as sleeping bags) again popularizing outdoor, sporting lifestyles.

Increasingly, acrylics (e.g. terylene, orlon, dacron and crimplene) were adopted in sport and on the street with their benefits of being drip-dry, permanently pleated, non-fading and durable. These wonder fabrics were weatherproof, breathable and durable as well as being adaptable for hot or cold environments in which sport occurred (O'Mahony and Braddock 2002: 41–4). Their uptake in sport quickly led to fashion knock-offs such as 1960s one-piece stretch jumpsuits, pantyhose, sleepwear, underwear revolutions, skivvies and stretch slacks. Indeed, (Handley 1999: 75) regards the 1960s and early 1970s as "the heyday for synthetic fashions". A big breakthrough in securing public acceptance of synthetics was the growing use of synthetics by Parisian – and later American - designers. And, as American fashion was dominated by casual wear, synthetics quickly became the staple of everyday clothing.

Perhaps it was the impact of 1960s pop culture and "Swinging London" fashion that catapulted experimentation with these new fabrics and new approaches to design and wearability into global prominence. According to (Handley 1999: 89–112), the period saw the growth of a specific teenage culture with distinctive consumer habits, new designs that were skimpy, bold and body revealing and new looks that were ultra-fashionable, lurid, synthetic and neon. Above all, they were sporty. A revolution in streetwear and sportswear was occurring. By the 1970s, sportswear-influenced fashion had been elevated to the status of haute couture and renamed sports couture, a label attributed to the American designer, Roy Halston, who reworked sportswear as fashion for the mainstream market. He favoured understated elegance using jersey and body-hugging fabrics for tube dresses, jumpsuits, pantsuits and cashmere twinsets (Danielsen 1999;

Seeling 2000: 417). Halston "gave sportswear a sophistication which had seemed impossible beforehand" (Seeling 2000: 588).

As marketing companies mastered the art of making sports clothes "cool" for the youth-oriented market, sports labels have increasingly produced "diffusion lines" alongside sports performance gear aimed specifically at the mainstream market. According to O'Mahony and Braddock (2002):

The latest designer sports labels are aimed at the 18–34 age group, with the result that anyone wearing them can seem young, healthy and active by association. Sports-inspired fashion advertisements suggest links with a clean-living active life: sport is fashionable, and sporty references give collections a contemporary edge. (O'Mahony and Braddock 2002: 132)

At the moment when it seemed that synthetics had swept away all before them, a convergence of factors in the 1970s burst the bubble. Synthetics became synonymous with bad taste, tackiness and superficiality: "disco dacron" became a term of abuse, despite the popularity of commercial bands like ABBA and John Travolta's groundbreaking performance in John Badham's *Saturday Night Fever (1977)*. Manufacturers were desperate to revive the fortunes of synthetics with all kinds of marketing and promotional campaigns. Although the public turned away from synthetics, companies continued to experiment with new fabrics, especially by developing blends that disguised the essential ingredients of the fabrics and could incorporate some natural fibres. In particular, new approaches were developed to produce better fabrics for sports clothing, especially action sports clothing for elite athletes. Low cost, high quality leisurewear was now available in turn producing a "more practical mix-and-match aesthetic" (Danielsen 1999). Thus ironically, at the time when the masses turned away from synthetics, major advances were occurring in the sporting arenas that were to revolutionize approaches to fabrics in the future.

(Handley 1999: 129–42; cf. Quinn 2002: 141–61) attributes the breakthrough to the impact of Japanese designers such as Rei Kawakubo, Issey Miyake, Yoshiki Hishinuma and Junya Watanabe on western fashion in the 1980s. They used radically different ideas of line, cut and combination with technological savvy and technical sophistication in producing sculptural body outfits using the latest developments in fibre manufacture. Instead of sewing machines, clothes were made by industrial technique polyester, shrunken nylon, microfibre taffetas and monofilament gauzes undergo unspecified chemical and heat treatments to emerge as textured cocoons for the body. Waves or wrinkles are technologically fixed into the fabrics or, conversely, creaseless, glassy acetates produce wrinkle-free clothing. (Handley 1999: 134)

So there was a convergence of factors: clothing designed for enhancing sporting performance was taken up by high-street fashion; revolutions in fabrics to improve comfort, durability and environmental conditions were challenging traditional natural fibres and fabrics; and subcultures associated with certain sports (e.g. surfing, skiing, ski-boarding, bushwalking, riding, cycling) had become the defining parameters of youth culture.

THE LYCRA REVOLUTION

By these techniques, fabrics were more responsive to the body -acting like the pores of skin, almost a second skin – and therefore perfectly suited to designing performance-enhancing sports clothing, such as the skiwear of the winners of the 1988 Winter Olympics. Epitomizing this fabric revolution – as far as public opinion was concerned – was lycra, which is perhaps the wonder fabric of postmodernity (O'Mahony and Braddock 2002: 143; Quinn 2002: 192–4). Developed in 1958, it was not popularized in fashion until the 1980s. However, as a synthetic elastic, it had an immediate uptake in foundation garments (corsets and bras) because of its profound "stretch and recovery" qualities and because it could be blended with anything.

In 1964 the lycra body stocking was invented; swimwear manufacturers immediately adapted this for swimwear because it was body hugging, lightweight, colourful and moisture repellent. Other sports and leisure manufacturers soon followed, e.g. skiwear. This trend really took off in the mid-1970s coinciding with the new body-conscious culture of self-improvement, body sculpting and healthy living. Lycra could be found in exercise wear, sportswear, lingerie and fashion. Films like teen-oriented *Grease* (1978) and *Fame* (1980) reflected the convergence and triggered the manufacture of sportswear as leisurewear on an unprecedented scale. By the 1980s, lycra leggings, bodysuits, tops and tights were everywhere from the catwalk, the starting blocks and the gyms to shopping centres, offices and backyards (Joseph 1986; Schreier 1989). It was not too long before specialist clothes for sport could be worn in a multiplicity of venues: gym wear, dance wear, aerobics wear, swimwear and even evening wear all drew on the same synthetic body-hugging elements (see Schulze 1990; Li 1999; Skoggard 1998; O'Mahony and Braddock 2002: 143; Sawyer 2002; Taffel 2003; Zamiatin 2003a).

The popularity of underwear as outerwear, a trend from the 1980s and still fashionable, further enhanced this convergence. Lycra became a key attribute of postmodern popular culture because of its flexibility, suitability for a relaxed, pleasure-seeking lifestyle and connotations of sexuality and eroticism. Inevitably it infiltrated popular music and celebrity culture – a mainstay of stage clothes for example (e.g. Madonna, Kylie Minogue, Cher). If a celebrity wore a designer label garment, increased sales were sure to follow. The success of Tommy Hilfiger, Stussy and Massimo in the 1990s has been largely attributed to celebrity promotion (Danielsen 1999). The fusion between sportswear and streetwear was deepened with the fad for the styles of American basketballers and rappers. Streetwear became black, baggy and bold – and accompanied by the ubiquitous baseball cap and "athletic" shoes or sports shoes (Chalmers 2002; Weinstein 2003; Zamiatin 2003c). The widespread acceptance of the highly charged allure of urban black culture produced globalized fashions for teens, especially young males based on the sportswear and streetwear of sporting heroes (cf. Maynard 2004: 34–6). In turn, selected sports stars were used as the face of sport labels' promotions, such as Michael Jordan for Nike. Nike was the first company to exploit the sportswear as fashion promotional tactic, leading the industry for more than a decade "in both technological innovation and style" (Quinn 2002: 186). Simultaneously, Nike produced advanced sports gear for professional sports people and parallel lines aimed at amateur sport and leisure, "urban streets and city parks":

Nike's signature Lycra and fleece silhouettes leapt into mainstream casual wear, creating a look that went beyond sporty associations to identify the wearer as an active, trendy, health-conscious individual. Nike's body-hugging designs were produced in vibrant colours or basic black – creating shapes and tones that mirrored those worn on the nightclub scene. (Quinn 2002: 187)

Before long, Nike gear was the cool gear for clubbers and ravers. As other companies began to compete for the youth market for sportswear, Nike invested in designing a "swift suit" that could give the body aerodynamic properties and thereby enhance performance (O'Mahony and Braddock 2002: 127; Quinn 2002: 187–8). Other companies soon followed. Clothes that emanated from sport-music contexts were turned into fashion for everyday everywhere (Li 1998; Skoggard 1998). This has spawned a proliferation of brand names and companies specializing in sports goods and popularized on the street by brand-name trainers visibly promoting sports brand names.

These trends persisted through the 1990s with the ubiquitous lycra and sportswear never far from headline fads and celebrities. The designer label Prada, for example, was credited with turning nylon into the cashmere of the 1990s (Handley 1999: 163). Miuccia Prada has experimented with new lightweight fabrics that breathe and float to produce a "synthesis of design and function" leading to "new styles and types of clothing" (Danielsen 1999). While Prada is associated with couture, her Prada Sport line is aimed at the well-heeled mass consumer who can also display her comfortable yet sexy outfits for leisure or for active pursuits (Quinn 2002: 192–4). Inspiration from sports clothing has become the defining theme of fashion hybrid clothing – between sports clothes and pure fashion -is where action clothing, prêt-a-porter and the rarefied world of haute couture meet. Fashion also influences sports clothes in its turn, and sports collections are becoming more glamorous. Track runners can now wear aerodynamic one-piece garments in low-resistance synthetics; beaded stretch tulle may be used for sports tops, and sequinned hotpants for running. Practical and decorative, they are suited to action and fashion alike. (O'Mahony and Braddock 2002: 140–1)

BODY TECHNOLOGIES

The development of full bodysuits for competitive swimming raised the stakes still higher. Released to coincide with the 2000 Olympics, the new bodysuits created controversy because of their acute figure-hugging qualities and rumours that they were performance-enhancing apparatuses rather than simply swimming costumes. The suits – based on the swimming capacities of a shark and the unusual characteristics of sharkskin – were designed to streamline the body's silhouette, cut down drag and resistance through the water, compress the muscles into performance and control bodily deviations from maximum performance (O'Mahony and Braddock 2002: 119–24). Despite the initial controversy, the suits quickly transformed the sport of swimming.

The revised fastskin FSII, designed for the 2004 Athens Olympic Games, "mimics sharkskin and employs the same 'computational fluid dynamics' used in the design of Formula One racing cars and America's Cup yachts" (Jeffrey 2004b: 3). Not only does the new Speedo suit follow the flowlines around the body", but also the suits are now "gender and stroke specific" (Jeffrey 2004b: 3). So confident of the suits, Speedo launched an international advertising campaign featuring leading swimmers (including Grant Hackett, Michael Klim, Jenny Thompson, Lenny Krayzelburg and Inge de Bruin) as "human fish" with "shark gills" simulated on their necks (Cowley 2004: 69).

Once again, the bodysuit technology has been adapted for other sports (e.g. athletics, netball) and other garments (e.g. lingerie, gym wear). So-called gym wear combines the latest in action sports clothing design with high street fashion and recognizable brand names and motifs. Leggings and legwarmers are one example of an undergarment that has become high fashion and everyday wear (O'Mahony and Braddock 2002: 143; Thompson 2003). Epitomized by beach volleyball uniforms, almost all this sports clothing contains synthetic fibres (Schulze 1990; Sawyer 2002; Taffel 2003). Microfibre technology has transformed the properties of many sporting items, from bodysuits to shoes to footballs.

The latest chapter of the sports clothing saga is the promise of wearable technologies, that is, through smart-fibre technology for the manufacture of smart clothes (Handley 1999: 140–2; Marzano 2000; Harkin 2002; O'Mahony and Braddock 2002: 48–52; Quinn 2002: 191–2; Fynes-Clinton 2003). Products such as Fabrican, an aerosol spray-on fabric, are already being used in fashion, for example, by the New York-based label DDCLAB to produce super-tough hip urban wear. Other fabrics have been Teflon-coated, Kevlar-treated or Tyvek-infused to produce practical, lightweight and extremely durable clothes that have been endorsed by American film and music celebrities.

These new age fabrics can offer thermal control, built-in air conditioners, performance-enhancing attributes and control mechanisms, and body adjustment or maintenance – hydrating, vitamin, perfume or steroid release, for example. In the lead-up to the 2004 Athens Olympic Games, the Australian Olympic team had an exclusive deal with Nike to provide uniforms that included a "pre-cool vest" constructed to incorporate eighteen ice packs that allow "athletes to perform for 19 percent longer before their body temperature reaches the critical point where it compromises their efficiency" (Jeffrey 2004a: 3). While Nike believed its vest was state-of-the-art, the Australian Institute of Sport advocated the adoption of its "new high tech cooling jacket that uses a phase-changing polymer rather than ice to reduce the athlete's core body temperature", a jacket it claimed was "vastly superior to our old ice vest . . . We believe that technology is outdated". Although the ice vest was favoured at the 2004 Athens Olympics, one could confidently predict that high-tech vests will make their appearance in international competition very quickly. Other components of the Olympic team uniform include other heat-countering features such as "ventilation panels, lightweight materials and breathable fabrics". Applications of new technologies into competitive sports uniforms illustrate the rapid uptake of innovation and refinement of traditional approaches to sportswear.

Still at the experimental stage are sports uniforms and sports clothing that incorporate inbuilt communication systems in clothing. Although the circuitry currently creates a problem for laundering, ultimately such garments will be manufactured with machine-washable circuitry. Already Phillips has manufactured underpants and bodysuits for athletes and clubbers with body-monitoring sensors, flashing lights and pagers (Marzano 2000: 55, 91; O'Mahony and Braddock 2002: 80–4). The possibilities for applications in sports clothing as well as streetwear are clearly mind boggling.

Even the staid tracksuit has undergone a revolution. It was one of the earliest applications of new synthetic fibres to sportswear, producing fleecy jersey that kept sports people warm, comfortable and dry, first manufactured in the 1960s. From the late 1970s, tracksuits incorporated then switched to synthetic fabrics that were lighter, water resistant, warmer and more stylish. During the 1980s, the tracksuit was popularized for leisurewear (indeed, it has been regarded as Australia's national costume) and in the 1990s, the tracksuit gained popularity for travellers and among elderly people, e.g. preferred clothing in nursing homes. Although this could well have been the death knell for the tracksuit – unstylish (baggy, faded and misshapen) beyond belief – it has been revived in celebrity circles as the fashion look of hip hop artists, rappers, pop stars, sports celebrities and film stars. The tracksuit in the new millennium is ultra cool streetwear. The tracksuit worn by the soccer star, David Beckham, at the Manchester Commonwealth Games opening ceremony in 2002 confirmed its high fashion status: here was a specially designed shiny white tracksuit with cubic zirconium detail highlighting, among other things, the brand name, adidas -surely synonymous with cutting-edge sports clothing and sporting excellence (Sawyer 2002).

FROM STYLISH SPORTS CLOTHING TO SPORTY STYLE

Over time, but especially during the twentieth century, clothes have become looser, are more informal and more suited to leisure and recreational activities "all-purpose clothing [has] transcended role demarcation" (Joseph 1986: 178). Sports clothing has been the obvious beneficiary of this trend. As well as using sports uniforms for other activities, designers are increasingly designing and producing sports-influenced casual clothing (e.g. T-shirts, leggings, sports shoes, lycra swimwear and exercise wear, sports jackets, facsimile sports jerseys, football strips and baseball caps). These garments and their details focus on the utilitarian and the egalitarian with the "emphasis as much on the structural quality and everyday practicality as on the visual surface of the garment" (Danielsen 1999).

Designer cargo pants, military-style trousers, jumpsuits, hooded jackets, fleecy vests and zippered tops proliferate in recent collections. These borrow heavily from winter wear and mountaineering apparel, with brand names like Himalayan and Patagonian. Sports clothing has become the mainstay of many designers and the last resort in hard times. There is an increasing incidence of specialised wear for leisure activities for those who may not actually be sports people – for fishing, horse riding, golf, tennis, martial arts, yoga, and so on. The quasi-uniform has been derived from the appropriate sports uniform and outfits then commercialized into specialist activity wear and popularized as leisure and recreation fashion.

One of the notable success stories of sports clothing being mainstreamed is that of sports shoes (O'Mahony and Braddock 2002: 105, 169–74; Quinn 2002: 197–9). While soft shoes or slippers for sport were systematized in the invention of plimsolls (or tennis shoes), it was relatively recently that manufacturers reworked the design of sports shoes to maximize flexibility, support and sport-specific requirements by rethinking support and cushioning. What they did not count on was the translation of the sports shoe into youth culture to become the generic shoe of young people. They have become the tip of new trends, necessitating constantly updated models and features – with fashion and style as much in mind as practicality for sport.

Manufacturers of sports shoes produce and retailers stock only limited numbers of high-end street designs to make purchases more exclusive: "We only get a limited number usually in the low hundreds, of each style, which can sell out in a couple of weeks. Then we move onto the next one. It keeps up the excitement over the shoes" (Zamiatin 2003c: 37). At Niketown, a sportswear mega-complex, some buyers acquire special edition shoes as an investment – never to be worn. Indeed, collecting sports shoes and sneakers has become a popular hobby with enthusiasts owning up to 500 pairs and specialist websites and magazines serving the collectors (Lunn 2003: 9).

According to (Alderson 2002: 29), an estimated 430 million pairs of sports shoes are sold annually accounting for a quarter of the footwear market. Yet only a fifth of these are worn for sport; the rest are "lifestyle" purchases. In the United States, the "athletic footwear" industry has been valued in excess of $16 billion a year (Lunn 2003). Perhaps not surprisingly, couture designers have joined the fray producing "status sneakers" for the "fashionista" and bowling shoes (a cross between a "nanna" shoe and a trainer) for the chic urban worker. Sportswear manufacturers must not only produce garments that enhance performance and are durable but also be equally concerned with producing goods that are received as looking stylish: cool vies with function in the sports clothing war and, all too often, cool has won out.

Not always though. Some sports have resisted new approaches to uniform and sports clothes' design – for example, tennis, baseball and football. So while some sports embrace new developments, others lag behind. Thus we find that cycling, skiing, scuba diving, swimming, luge and so on have adopted one-piece outfits as standard wear while other sports resist. One case in 2004 concerned the decision of the Cameroon soccer team to wear a one-piece microfibre bodysuit in the African Cup of Nations in Tunisia. As a result, they were docked vital championship points on the grounds that football's governing body, FIFA, had rules insisting on a two-piece outfit (BBC Sport) 2004. The Cameroon team's defence was that they had merely joined the two pieces together. Despite this setback, it can be predicted that the sport of soccer will, in time, permit one-piece bodysuits in new climatically suitable and ergonomically appropriate fabrics.

According to Quinn (2002), we are seeing a new dialogue between sports technicians and fashion designers forever disrupting the historical narrative of fashion, making it less apparent where the boundaries between fashion and sport now lie. From sportswear, fashion has learnt to protect and equip the body, while from fashion, sportswear has learned to decorate the body and tailor clothing to follow its shape . . . The combined sense of utility, functionality, performance and transformability inherent in sportswear is moving fashion forward. (Quinn 2002: 199)

But is this as radical as some commentators suggest? (Quinn 2002: 200) concludes that the sports-techno revolution in fashion is overdue – a belated recognition of the centrality of characteristics of "functionality, performance and transformability" in clothing. In a sense, this is a revival of fundamental principles of clothing design developed among early societies such as the waterproof, weatherproof clothes of the Inuit (parkas and sealskin boots) and Scandinavians (two-thumbed mittens knitted from human hair to repel water and provide a wet and dry thumb for fishermen) (O'Mahony and Braddock 2002: 92, 4, 111–12). The wheel of fashion may have turned full circle with the sports obsession redrafting our ideas about clothing, dress and bodily performance in general.

References

Alderson Maggie. 2002. "Status Sneakers." *The Sydney Morning Herald* (18–20 April): 29.
Braddock Sarah and Marie O'Mahony. 2002. *Edge: The Influence of Sportswear*, Catalogue. Copenhagen: Oksnehallen.
Chalmers Emma. 2003. "Sneak Up on Style." *The Courier-Mail* (25 February): 14.
Cowley Michael. 2004. "Revealed at Last: How Hackett Dominates the 1500m." *The Sydney Morning Herald* (6–7 March): 69.
Danielsen Shane. 1999. "Sporty but Nice." *The Australian* (1 February): 15.
De Teliga Jane. 1995. "Rough Cuts." *The Sydney Morning Herald* (2 May): 33–4.
Fynes-Clinton Jane. 2003. "Tune in, Turn on to Smarter Fashion." *The Courier-Mail* (5 February): 16.
Hall Carne, Marjorie and Sylvia Sheppard. 2002. *California Fashion*. New York: Harry N. Abrams.
Handley Susannah. 1999. *Nylon. The Manmade Fashion Revolution*. London: Bloomsbury.
Harkin Fiona. 2002. "Smarty Pants." *The Weekend Australian Magazine* (9–10 November): 42–3.

Jeffrey Nicole. 2004b. "Sharkskin Suits Our Olympic Hopefuls." *The Australian* (10 March): 3.

Joseph Nathan. 1986. *Uniforms and Nonuniforms. Communication Through Clothing*. New York: Greenwood.

Kidwell Claudia and Margaret Christmas. 1975. *Suiting Everyone: The Democratization of Clothing in America*. Washington, DC: Smithsonian Institution Press.

Li, Xiaoping. 1998. "*Fashioning the Body in Post-Mao China*." In Anne Brydon and Sandra Niessen (eds), *Consuming Fashion. Adorning the Transnational Body*, pp. 70–89. Oxford and New York: Berg.

Lunn, Jacqueline. 2003. "Anyone for Tennis?" *The Sydney Morning Herald* (2–3 August): Metropolitan 9.

Marzano, Stefano (ed.). 2000. *New Nomads*. Rotterdam: 010 Publishers.

Maynard, Margaret. 2004. *Dress and Globalisation*. Manchester: Manchester University Press.

Quinn, Bradley. 2002. *Techno Fashion*. Oxford and New York: Berg.

Sawyer, Miranda 2002. "Suiting Themselves." (7 December): 72–3.

Schreier, Barbara. 1989. "*Sporting Wear*." In Claudia Kidwell and Valerie Steele (eds), *Men and Women: Dressing the Part*, pp. 92–123. Washington, DC: Smithsonian Institution Press.

Schulze, Laurie. 1990 "*On the Muscle*." In Jane Gaines and Charlotte Herzog (eds), *Fabrications. Costume and the Female Body*, pp. 59–78. London and New York: Routledge.

Seeling, Charlotte. 2000. *Fashion. The Century of the Designer 1900–1999*. Cologne: Konemann.

Skoggard, Ian. 1998. "*Transnational Commodity Flows and the Global Phenomenon of the Brand*." In Anne Brydon and Sandra Niessen (eds), *Consuming Fashion. Adorning the Transnational Body*, pp. 57–70. Oxford and New York: Berg.

Taffel, Jacqui. 2003. "*Loosen Up*." *The Sydney Morning Herald* (22–23 February) Metropolitan: 9.

Weinstein, Richard. 2003. ""Reboot"." *Sport Monthly* (March): 84–93.

CO-BRANDING STRATEGIES FOR LUXURY FASHION BRANDS: Missoni for Target

Edwina Luck, Gjoko Muratovski, and Lauren Hedley[1]

The main object of this study is the co-branding alliance between Missoni and Target in 2011. As a means of rationalizing the results of this retrospective analysis, we have reviewed the luxury fashion branding literature in relation to marketing and brand management theory. In the process, we have focused on four aspects: (1) the implications of customer perception of co-branding collaborations between luxury fashion brands and high street retailers, (2) luxury fashion branding, (3) co-branding strategies and (4) the market implications of such strategies. In this study we have highlighted some of the key factors that determine the implications for customer perception of luxury fashion co-branding strategies and we have presented a list of recommendations for planning such strategies.

THE ETHOS OF LUXURY FASHION BRANDING

Recent research into luxury fashion branding has attempted to identify specific elements that in combination have been the foundation for success for the market's leading brands with regard to perceptions of leading brands and equity (Zhan and He 2012), teen attitudes (DeAraujo Gil et al. 2012), and value perceptions (Shukla and Purani 2012). While researchers appear to agree on certain individual factors such as distribution exclusivity and targeted communication strategies, other elements such as appropriate price and brand positioning strategies appear to be in contention. Moreover, disagreement emerges over the level of importance placed on individual elements in comparison to the cohesive collaboration of all contributing factors.

The literature clearly identifies the necessity for a strong focus on developing a clear and distinct brand identity focusing and agreeing on intangibility brand elements such as history, culture, spirit, corporate identification and reputation of a brand (Atwal and Williams 2009; Beverland 2004; Dubois and Paternault 1995; Fionda and Moore 2009; Kapferer and Bastien 2009; Keller 2009; Nueno and Quelch 1998; Wetlaufer 2004). Along these lines, A. M. Fionda and C. M. Moore (2009) argue that brand identity is reflective of brand values such as 'fashionability' and heritage, which then determine a brand's unique approach to distribution, awareness and positioning. This is consistent with the factors identified by Okowono (2007) that work to develop both functional and emotional appeal for consumers through heritage of craftsmanship and a global reputation.

The importance of developing a unique and compelling brand image is championed by J.-V. Kapferer and Bastien (2009). They argue that traditional approaches to positioning, in which brands develop a unique selling proposition relative to other competitors in the market, goes against what is at the heart of luxury. Rather than carving out a niche based on a recognized business opportunity, a brand's image must be 'born of

---

[1]From Edwina Luck Gjoko Muratovski and Lauren Hedley (2014) Co-branding Strategies for Luxury Fashion Brands: Missoni for Target Global Fashion Brands Intellect pp. 41–56.

itself' and founded on its individual creative eccentricities (2009: 316). This, however, is in direct contrast to the observations of C. M. Moore and G. Birtwistle (2004), suggesting that luxury fashion brands must compete with rivals particularly by developing a high fashion collection necessary to facilitate editorial content. Furthermore, they also recognized the importance of a flagship store located amongst other luxury fashion brands and participation in major fashion shows hosted in New York, Milan, London or Paris as both present crucial opportunities for the brand to interact with the media and a perception that is a reflection of perceptions that holds strong consumer associations of uniqueness (Keller 1993).

While the brand identity forms the brand's existence (Louis and Lombart 2010), creating a personality for a brand allows for meaning to be encompassed (Kapferer and Bastien 2009. This allows for other emotive elements such as loyalty (Southgate 1994), trust and relationships to be established. On the basis of this, it can be argued that successful luxury fashion branding likely lies somewhere in between branding elements and personality aspects. However, the boundaries of high-end fashion and luxury are being blurred as brands are extending their exclusivity by creating limited edition collections. This allows short-term value-conscious customers access to a high-end brand.

In comparison, the studies that we have outlined in Table 4 are based on theoretical models that are seen as critical to a luxury brand's success factor.

In order for luxury brands to maintain their status, they must ensure that they are offering outstanding products at a premium price, alongside targeted marketing communications (Fionda and Moore 2009; Okonkwo 2007). Furthermore, studies show that luxury fashion consumers seek unique and exceptional products that are reflective of the brand's individual aesthetic and heritage (Dion and Arnould 2011). In addition to this, Fionda and Moore (2009) have identified product quality, craftsmanship and attention to details as key features that, alongside innovation and creativity, reflect the status of a luxury fashion brand and differentiate it from less prestigious counterparts.

Nevertheless, the thirst for luxury is built on the desire for exclusivity with a luxury fashion brand's communications strategy integral in creating and maintaining this desire beyond the target market. This strategy aims to engage consumers who do have the means to seek out the brand above all others (Kapferer and Bastien 2009). However, I. Phau and G. Prendergast (2000) argue that exclusivity must be maintained, through both premium pricing strategies and limited distribution, so as to prevent erosion of the brand's

Table 4 Success factors of luxury fashion brands

Fionda and Moore (2009)	Kapferer and Bastien (2009)	Moore and Birtwistle (2004)	Okonkwo (2007)
• Clear brand identity • Luxury communications strategy • Brand signature • Prestige price • Exclusivity • Luxury heritage • Environment and consumption experience • Luxury culture	• Brand identity over positioning • Be superlative, never comparative • No flaws, no charm • Resist client demands • No equality with clients • Make it difficult for clients to buy • Role of advertising not to sell • Advertise to those not targeted • Raise prices continuously to increase demand	• Clearly defined brand positioning • Coordinated distribution ensuring maximum market coverage • Brand extension facilitated by strong brand identity • Flexible management to allow foreign market opportunities • Media relations management to build and maintain brand reputation	• A distinct brand identity • Innovative, creative, unique and appealing products • Consistent delivery of premium quality • Exclusivity in goods production • Tightly controlled distribution • A heritage of craftsmanship • A global reputation • Emotional appeal • Premium pricing • High visibility

prestigious identity. In addition to this, M. Chevalier and G. Mazzalovo add that a luxury brand is founded from the process of maintaining 'well-controlled scarcity' while the brand itself remains highly desirable and recognisable (2008: 14).

According to K. L. Keller (2009), abiding by such a model can limit a luxury fashion brand's growth potential, particularly in the trade-off between exclusivity and accessibility in an effort to maximize market coverage. Furthermore, Keller (2009) asserts that it is necessary to differentiate across market segments and price points in order to achieve growth in sales and brand equity. In essence, this entails following the branding guidelines presented by the studies discussed above in that each sub-brand develops a unique brand identity and strategy. In addition to this, Y. Truong et al. (2009) argue that luxury status must be maintained relative to each market so that consumers at every level perceive the brand as aspirational because it remains somewhat inaccessible. However, a successful 'masstige' strategy of this kind could prevent brand dilution if middle-class consumers are only allowed to access the brand infrequently (Truong et al. 2009).

CO-BRANDING STRATEGIES

Co-branding is a strategy in which two existing brands are paired together to create a single product offering. S. J. Dickinson and T. Heath (2008) qualified that co-branding can apply to the cooperation of two brands extending to advertising, product distribution or product development activities. Researchers in the field generally agree that the recent increase in popularity of co-branding strategies is founded on the notion that leveraging an existing brand to achieve growth is more efficient that creating a new brand (Dickinson and Heath 2008; Chang 2008). Specifically, J. H. Washburn et al. (2000) highlighted co-branding strategies as a means of gaining additional market exposure, sharing costs with a partner, and defending against competitors. Moreover, each brand engaging in a co-branding strategy seeks to capitalize on its partner's reputation and core competencies in order to create a competitive advantage (Dickinson and Heath 2008; Chang 2008, 2010).

In Table 5 we can see a more comprehensive set of objectives for brands engaging in this strategy. This includes organizational objectives of gaining financial and operational benefits, expansion of the brand's customer base, and strengthening of the brand's competitive position (Chang 2008; Dickinson and Heath 2008).

Studies into co-branding have largely focused on the success factors for brands engaging in this strategy, with partner selection and suitability widely identified as critical in ensuring successful branding alliances. For example, research conducted by Ahn et al. (2010) investigated the dimensions that determine the suitability of brand pairings, identifying the importance of complementarity, substitutability and transferability of brands engaging in the alliance. The study emphasized the importance of partnering with a brand that maintains the same usage situation, user identity and perceived brand equity. W.-L. Chang (2010) additionally highlighted the importance of evaluating and selecting partners based on business criteria such as financial and operational feasibility considerations and complementary business cultures. Furthermore, L. Leuthresser et al. (2003) asserted that successful

Table 5 Identified aims of co-branding strategies

Chang (2008)	Dickinson and heath (2008)
• Expand customer base • Achieve financial benefits • Respond to expressed and latent needs of customers • Strengthen competitive position • Introduce new products with a strong image • Create new customer perceived value • Gain operational benefits	• Achieve market place exposure • Share expenses • Gain access to new markets • Enhance reputation

co-branding alliances are based on the idea that both brands contribute value by pairing their potential customer bases with the new product. In line with this, their study championed the importance of clearly defining the co-brand's customer base, comprehensive evaluation of the benefits to the customer, and clear division of responsibilities for delivering these benefits to the end customer.

Leuthresser et al. (2003) identified achieving market response, in terms of sales profits and market reach, as potential advantages of this strategy. However, the study also argued that potential disadvantages include giving a competitive advantage to the alliance partner, creating potential competition, trusting the alliance partner with important product characteristics, and limiting potential market reach in comparison to a line or brand extension strategy. On another note, in their study on the issue, A. d'Astous et al. (2007) highlighted the benefits of sharing costs associated with launching the co-branded product. For example, the new product has the advantage of being offered to existing customers of both partner brands and can further benefit from the increased brand recognizability over other products. Nevertheless, this study also identifies the risk of potential customer confusion between the individual partner brands, affecting the partner brand image in the long term. The implications for customer perception of this strategy in conjunction with luxury fashion branding is evaluated in the following section.

CASE STUDY: MISSONI FOR TARGET

The collaboration between Missoni and Target was announced on the 21st of July 2011 via an otherwise non-descript fashion blog titled All the way up here. The blog was authored by a blogger named Marina' with posts dating back to early April 2011. The blog went on to exclusively release the date when the collaboration was to hit stores and included a preview of the collection. The blog became a platform for promotion of the collaboration leading up to, and immediately following its release date. Eventually, the brand ambassador 'Marina' was introduced to the public as a seven-metre tall doll dressed in Missoni clothing (Hutzler 2011).

This seemingly anonymous blog allowed for the utilization of the re-blog function of Tumblr blogging and the real-time nature of Twitter to generate enormous buzz around the collaboration amongst the fashion media and the new customers (Connor 2011). Such was the hype created, that long queues of customers were formed outside Target stores prior to their opening on the day of the launch – 13 September 2011. The collection was released online two hours prior to in store but the website subsequently crashed due to the overwhelming demand before stores had even opened. The scene was similar in store with shelves cleared within twenty minutes of opening in some locations (Bickers 2011).

The collection included 400 distinctively Missoni pieces. This was the largest of Target's co-branding collaborations, encompassing men's, women's and children's apparel, home items luggage, and even bicycles. Prices ranged from US$2.99 to US$599.99 for a patio set. Apparel pieces averaged under US$40, significantly less than the Missoni signature collection with most pieces retailing for in excess of US$1000 (Abraham 2011).

The unanticipated demand for the collection meant that the promotion lasted for days rather than for more than a month as was originally intended, despite additional stock made available in some stores (Stych 2011). This gross underestimation was despite exceptionally high demand already experienced in the pop-up store established in New York one week prior to the collection's national release. The temporary store, also 'Marina's' location, was expected to remain open for three days but instead sold out of stock after six hours and was forced to close (D'innocenzio 2011).

Ongoing implications of the co-branding strategy: The backlash

Angela Missoni identified building awareness as a key objective of the co-branding collaboration, which appears to be achieved with estimates that the strategy generated publicity to the value of AU$100 million. That strategy also appears to have succeeded in the immediate term with sales for following collection of the Missoni signature line increasing by 10 per cent on the previous season (Moore 2011).

However, many customers of the co-branded collection were left disgruntled by the overall consumer experience, generating significant backlash on social media channels (Brooks 2011). Many online customers had their orders cancelled by Target due to unavailability of stock despite already being charged for the items. Adding to customer frustration, within hours of selling out, Missoni for Target pieces began to be posted for resale online. By the 15th of September up to 44,000 items were listed as for sale on eBay, with many sellers demanding extraordinarily inflated prices. Bicycles that retailed for US$399.99 were sold within days for US$2500, a more than 600 per cent mark up, and remain available on the site for up to US$1000 (Bickers 2011).

The implications of this backlash were immediately debated and while some theorized that Missoni loyalists may now reject the brand as it is now in reach of a mass audience with concern that their original signature pieces may be confused with the co-branded collaboration (Bickers 2011). Conversely, others insist that the relative inaccessibility achieved a 'digital velvet rope' effect that was able to preserve the Missoni exclusivity, even at the mass market level (Dishman 2011).

EVALUATION AND ANALYSIS

This co-branding strategy afforded Missoni to expand its customer base into new markets with significant financial gains, in line with generic objectives of co-branding strategies (Chang 2008; Dickinson and Heath 2008). The venture, however, did not respond to the needs of the brand's existing customers. Missoni did not deliver a unique product to this new market with an individually strong brand image; instead it offered a mass market adaptation of its existing product line.

Missoni's signature line is perhaps one of the most recognizable labels within the luxury fashion industry. Hence, for any co-branded collaboration to be identified as Missoni it was imperative that the offering remain faithful to the uniquely vibrant zigzag knitwear pattern synonymous with the Missoni aesthetic. This therefore complicates the creation of differentiation and separation between the signature and co-branded offerings necessary to ensure that inexpensive co-branded pieces are not perceived as equal alternative to the luxury priced signature line (d'Astous et al. 2007).

The luxury fashion branding literature clearly identifies the importance of developing and maintaining a distinct brand identity (Fionda and Moore 2009; Okonkwo 2007). The positioning of the Missoni for Target collection was in stark contrast with the luxury position traditional to the Missoni brand. The collaboration maintained the brand aesthetic of the Missoni main line, though the quality was undoubtedly compromised. Similarly, the pricing strategy of the co-branded collaboration did not align with its standard prestige strategy and distribution to the mass market contradicted the main line's exclusive distribution.

However, the execution of the strategy brings into question potential disparity between the superficial positioning of the co-branded collaboration and the intended perception outcome. In reality, the Missoni for Target collection was exclusive relative the proportion of customers aspiring to buy (Keller 2009). The promotion of the collaboration was extremely successful in gaining mass awareness despite the limited merchandise available. In this sense, Missoni for Target adopted a luxury communications strategy by appealing to customers that were outside of the target market. Moreover, the exorbitant prices demanded for pieces of the collection that were later posted online further served to position the offering as out of reach for many customers (Kapferer and Bastien 2009). By creating massive hype prior to the collections release, Missoni for Target ensured that offering was inaccessible in a similar manner to standard luxury fashion brands (Wu and Hsing 2006); this in return created the emotional allure, which is usually reserved for its signature line. The mass communications strategies to ensure extensive brand awareness was further aided by the enormous media coverage following the collections dramatic sell out.

Perhaps most ingeniously, Missoni did not use any of its own communication channels to gain awareness for the collaboration. Instead information was disseminated through the *All the way up here* blog and Twitter feed in combination with high profile events held to generate further publicity. The media coverage of this collaboration was unprecedented and likely meant that the total publicity achieved through the venture was an enormous return on investment. For Missoni this also meant that distance was maintained between the high street collaboration and its signature line communications.

The immediate repercussions for customer perception appear to be positive, as demonstrated by increased sales in for Missoni's signature line. The Missoni for Target collaboration was, in reality, all about Missoni, with Target acting as a trusted distribution channel for the collection. While the line was priced at a Target level, all of the merchandise and communications spoke of Missoni. Hence, Target's reputation as a reliable high street retailer brought credibility to the collaboration, with the Missoni parent brand remaining unaffected by its lower budget image (Washburn et al. 2000). The consequential backlash regarding the online sales bungle and lack of merchandise was ultimately aimed primarily at Target as it was recognized as responsible for this aspect of the collaboration, further shielding Missoni from any negativity.

For existing Missoni customers this collaboration served to reinforce the brand's desirability, while for new customers who are now aware of the brand, it continues to remains out of reach. The potential concern for existing customers may be that their signature Missoni pieces may now be compared or confused with the low priced co-branded collection (d'Astous et al. 2007). This is the pitfall of co-branding. While the co-branded offering must be truly reflective of the signature brand, association that is too close may offend existing customers who bought the signature collection on the basis of its prestigious reputation, and much higher price.

Perceptual theory gives reason to the extreme success in achieving sales of the co-branded collaboration. As observed by Berger et al. (2007), likelihood of purchase of a new product variety is expressly linked to perceived category expertise.

Missoni has demonstrated its proficiency in luxury fashion over its lifetime, and hence consumers perceive that its co-branded lower-end offering can be trusted to also be of high quality.

It is imperative that such co-branding ventures be implemented by luxury fashion brands on an extremely rare basis. If entering the mass market is seen as a long term, ongoing opportunity, the brand puts its luxury position in significant jeopardy. Co-branding in a luxury fashion context must be considered only as a momentary opportunity to gain significant awareness and build the brand's reputation.

RECOMMENDATIONS AND CONCLUSIONS

This study examined the consumer experience as a valuable tool for evaluating co-branding strategies, while raising questions about the implications related to brand credibility. Based on the preceding evaluation of the Missoni for Target collaboration, several recommendations have been developed for luxury fashion brands seeking to implement a successful co-branding venture in the future:

Co-branding strategy is a single opportunity

Maintaining a luxury fashion brand's prestige positioning is determined by a cohesive brand image. Venturing into the mass market too frequently, or as an ongoing brand extension has the potential to erode a brand's luxury status and alienate its primary target market (Truong et al. 2009; Rajagopal 2008).

Communicate beyond target market

The primary objective of implementing a co-branding strategy must be to gain mass market awareness of the luxury fashion brand (Dickinson and Heath 2008). As such, it is necessary for communications to reach beyond the co-branded collaboration's target market in order to gain maximum ongoing awareness of the signature line and consequently increase its desirability (Kapferer and Bastien 2009).

Maintain inaccessibility

A co-branded collaboration must be positioned as a prestige brand relative to the mass market (Keller

2009). Luxury positioning is founded on creating desire among those who are not able to obtain the brand (Chevalier and Mazzalovo 2008). Rationing of the co-branded collection not only increases desire for the collaboration but also the signature collection as its inaccessibility is further highlighted.

Differentiate from signature line

It is imperative that luxury fashion brands create separation between their signature and co-branded collections to minimize confusion between the two and demonstrate value to existing customers (d'Astous et al. 2007). Nevertheless, the co-branded collection must be recognized that it comes from a luxury fashion brand, but it should not replace the luxury line (Dion and Arnould 2011).

Choose the right partner

Luxury fashion brands should seek to align with a high street retailer that is experienced in delivering similar co-branding collaborations and trusted by the new target market. Ensuring credibility with a high street partner is significant, though luxury fashion brands must maintain prominence in the collaboration with the high street retailer acting as a trusted distribution channel (Ahn et al. 2010).

This case investigation found that engaging in a co-branding strategy could positively impact customer perception of a luxury fashion brand. Missoni's success is contingent on the brand adhering to the recommendations presented, which articulates to creating exclusivity despite trading in the mass market. Therefore this strategy has been found to be viable for luxury fashion brands for the future, based on the condition that it is only implemented fleetingly. For the fashion industry, this strategy presents as feasible in creating mass awareness while maintain luxury positioning: something that has not been examined in great detail in this fierce industry.

References

Abraham, Tamara (2011), 'Sneak preview of Missoni's designer style at Target prices (so will you be bagging the babygro or the bicycle?)', *Daily Mail*, August 11, http://www.dailymail.co.uk/femail/article-2024687/Sneak-preview-Missonis-designer-style-Target-prices-bagging-babygro-bicycle.html. Accessed 8 December 2013.

Ahn, SooKyung, Huenjung Kim, and Judith Forney. (2010), 'Fashion collaboration or collision? Examining the match-up effect in co-marketing alliances', *Journal of Fashion Marketing and Management*, 14: 1, pp. 6–20.

Amatulli, Cesare and Gianluigi Guido. (2009), 'Determinants of purchasing intention for fashion luxury goods in the Italian market: A laddering approach', *Journal of Fashion Marketing and Management*, 15: 1, pp. 123–136.

Atsmon, Yuval, Demetra Pinsent and Lisa Sun. (2010), *Five trends that will shape the global luxury market*, McKinsey & Company, http://csi.mckinsey.com/Knowledge_by_topic/Consumer_and_shopper_insights/globalluxury.aspx. Accessed 7 December 2011.

Atwal, Satnam and Alistair Williams. (2009), 'Luxury brand marketing – the experience is everything!', *Journal of Brand Management*, 16: 1, pp. 338–46.

Benigson, Moira. (2010), 'The key to successful collaboration', *Retail Week*, 17 September, http://www.retail-week.com/comment/the-key-to-successful-collaboration/5017134.article. Accessed 12 December 2013.

Berger, Jonah, Michaela Draganska and Itamar Simonson. (2007), 'The Influence of Product Variety on Brand Perception and Choice', *Journal of Marketing Science*, 26(4): 460–472.

Beverland, Michael B. (2004), 'Uncovering "Theories-in-use": the case of luxury wines', *Journal of Management Studies*, 42: 5, pp. 1003–29.

Bickers, James, (2011), 'Missoni for Target line sells out, raises questions', *Retail Customer Experience*, 15 September, http://www.retailcustomerex-perience.com/article/184615/Missoni-for-Target-line-sells-out-raises-questions. Accessed 12 December 2013.

Bold, Ben (2002), 'Is Gucci for the masses damaging the brand?', *Marketing Magazine*, 10 October, p. 15.

Brooks, Tory (2011), 'Missoni for Target – Challenges of Online Retailing', *The Online Economy*, 4 November, http://www.onlineeconomy.org/missoni-for-target-challenges-of-online-retailing. Accessed 12 December 2013.

Chang, Wei-Lun (2008), 'A Typology of Co-branding Strategy: Position and Classification', *Journal of American Academy of Business*, 12: 2, pp. 220–226.

Chang, Wei-Lun (2010), 'A Taxonomy Model for a Strategic Co-Branding Position', *The Journal of American Academy of Business*, 16: 1, pp. 165–170.

Chevalier, Michel, and Gerald Mazzalovo (2008), *Luxury Brand Management*, Singapore: John Wiley & Sons.

Connor, Emily (2011), 'Marina – Doll, Blogger, Celebrity – Target's Unique Approach to Missoni Fashion Line Launch', *Business2Community*, 14 September, http://www.business2community.com/trends-news/marina---doll-blogger-celebrity---target's-unique-approach-to-missoni-fashion-line-launch-058944. Accessed 12 December 2013.

Danziger, Pam (2008), 'Luxury Consumption Index (LCI) in Free Fall', *Marketwire*, 31 October, http://www.marketwire.com/press-release/luxury-consumption-index-lci-in-free-fall-915650.htm. Accessed 7 December 2011.

d'Astous, Alain, François Colbert and Marilyne Fournier (2007), 'An experimental investigation of the use of brand extension and co-branding strategies in the arts', *Journal of Services Marketing*, 21: 4, pp. 231–240.

Dickinson, Sonja and Tara Heath. (2008), 'Cooperative Brand Alliances: How to Generate Positive Evaluations', *Australasian Marketing Journal*, 16: 2, pp. 22–38.

D'innocenzio, Anne (2011), 'Shoppers furious as Target's Missoni problems continue', *Today (Style)*, 22 September, http://www.today.com/id/44624643/. Accessed 12 December 2013.

Dion, Delphine and Eric Arnould. (2011), 'Retail Luxury Strategy: Assembling Charisma through Art and Magic', *Journal of Retailing*, 87: 4, pp. 502–520.

Dishman, Lydia (2011), 'The Genius of Target's Missoni Madness', *Forbes*, 14 September, http://www.forbes.com/fdc/welcome_mjx.shtml. Accessed 12 December 2013.

Dubois, Bernard and Claire Paternault (1995), 'Understanding the world of international luxury brands: the dream formula', *Journal of Advertising Research*, 35: 4, pp. 69–77.

Dwyer, Michael (2011), 'Anti-crisis in the bling economy', *The Australian Financial Review*, 15 November, p. 61.

Fionda, Antoinette. M. and Christopher. M. Moore (2009), 'The anatomy of the luxury fashion brand', *Journal of Brand Management*, 16: 5, pp. 347–363.

Geylani, Tansev, J. Jeffrey Inman and Frankel Ter Hofstede. (2008), 'Image Reinforcement or Impairment: The Effects of Co-branding on Attribute Uncertainty', *Journal of Marketing Science*, 27(4), pp. 730–744.

Hosea, Maeve (2008), 'Couture collaborations: Hitting the street', *Brand Strategy*, 8 April, pp. 50–51.

Hutzler, Kayla (2011), 'Missoni avoids brand dilution with secret Target partnership', *Luxury Daily*, 19 August, http://www.luxurydaily.com/missoni-maintains-luxury-status-by-keeping-quiet-about-target-line/. Accessed 12 December 2013.

Kapferer, Jean-Noel and Vincent Bastien. (2009), 'The specificity of luxury management: Turning marketing upside down', *Journal of Brand Management*, 16: 5, pp. 311–322.

Keller, Keith L. (1993), 'Conceptualizing, measuring, and managing customer-based brand equity', *Journal of Marketing*, 57: 1, pp. 1–22.

Keller, Keith L (2009), 'Managing the growth tradeoff: Challenges and opportunities in luxury branding', *Journal of Brand Management*, 16: 3, pp. 290–301.

Kemp, Simon (2008), 'Perceiving luxury and necessity', *Journal of Economic Psychology*, 19: 5, pp. 591–606.

KPMG International (2011), 'Resurgence in demand for luxury goods', *Issues Monitor*, 9: 1, pp. 9–16.

Lee, H. (2011), 'Designer's rack up their high street credentials', *Sassybella*, http://www.sassybella.com/designers-rack-high-street-credentials/. Accessed 7 December 2011.

Leuthresser, Lance, Chiranjeev Kohli and Rajneesh Suri. (2003), '2 + 2 = 5? A framework for using co-branding to leverage a brand', *Journal of Brand Management*, 11: 1, pp. 35–47.

Liu, Shuk-ching and Tsan-ming Choi (2009), 'Consumer attitudes towards brand extensions of designer-labels and mass-market labels in Hong Kong', *Journal of Fashion Marketing and Management*, 13: 4, pp. 527–540.

LxKnitwear (2012), 'Missoni History', *Lx Knitwear*, 14 February, http://www.lxknitwear.com/articles/44-article/66-missoni-history.html. Accessed 8 December 2013.

Marketing Week (2011), 'Fashion designers reaching out to the high street cultivating new consumers or losing their edge?', *Marketing Week*, http://www.marketingweek.co.uk/sectors/retail/fashion-designers-reaching-out-to-the-high-street-cultivating-new-consumers-or-losing-theiredge?/3024742.article. Accessed 12 December 2013.

Martin, Richard (2012), 'Missoni', *Fashion Encyclopedia*, 14 February, http://www.fashionencyclopedia.com/Ma-Mu/Missoni.html. Accessed 12 December 2013.

Miller, Karen W. and Michael K. Mills. (2012), 'Fashion Marketing and Consumption of Luxury Brands', *Journal of Business Research*, 65: 10, pp. 1471–1479.

Missoni (2012), 'History', *Missoni*, http://missoni.com/ing.html. Accessed 2 February 2012.

Moore, Booth (2011), 'Sitting down with three generations of Missoni', *Los Angeles Times*, 30 October, http://articles.latimes.com/2011/oct/30/image/la-ig-missoni-20111030. Accessed 12 December 2013.

Moore, Christopher M. and Grete Birtwistle. (2004), 'The Burberry business model: Creating an international fashion luxury brand', *International Journal of Retail & Distribution Management*, 32: 8, pp. 412–422.

Mower, Sarah (2011), 'Preen reigns supreme at Debenhams', *The Telegraph*, 13 April, http://fashion.telegraph.co.uk/news-features/TMG8446339/Preen-reigns-supreme-at-Debenhams.html. Accessed 12 December 2013.

Nueno, Jose, L. and John, A. Quelch (1998), 'The mass marketing of luxury', *Business Horizons*, 41: 6, pp. 61–68.

Okonkwo, Uche (2007), *Luxury Fashion Branding: Trends, Tactics, Techniques*, Hampshire: Palgrave Macmillian.

Phau, Ian and Gerard Prendergast. (2000), 'Consuming luxury brands: The relevance of the "Rarity Principle"', *Journal of Brand Management*, 8: 2, pp. 122–138.

Rajagopal (2008), 'Measuring brand performance through metrics application', *Measuring Business Excellence*, 12: 1, pp. 29–38.

Schiffman, Leon, David Bednall, Aaron O'Cass, Aangela Paladino and Leslie Kanuk. (2005), *Consumer Behaviour*, Frenchs Forest: Pearson Education Australia.

Shukla, Paurav. and Keyoor Purani (2012), 'Comparing the importance of luxury value perceptions in cross-national contexts', *Journal of Business Research*, 65: 10, pp. 1417–1424.

Stych, Ed (2011), 'Target says some stores will restock Missoni collection', *Business Journal*, 14 September, http://www.bizjournals.com/twincities/news/2011/09/14/missoni-target-more-stock-coming.html. Accessed 12 December 2013.

Surchi, Micaela (2011), 'The temporary store: a new marketing tool for fashion brands', *Journal of Fashion Marketing and Management*, 15: 2, pp. 257–270.

Swerdloff, Alexis (2011), '60 Seconds With: Rosita Missoni', *The Wall Street Journal*, 12 February, http://online.wsj.com/news/articles/SB10001424052748704422204576130313988378624. Accessed 12 December 2013.

Truong, Yann, Rod McColl and Phillip J. Kitchen (2009), 'New luxury brand positioning and the emergence of Masstige brands', *Journal of Brand Management*, 16: 5, pp. 375–382.

Van Praet, Nicholas (2011), 'Luxury brands start feeling the pinch', *Financial Post*, 29 November, http://business.financialpost.com/2011/11/29/luxury-brands-start-feeling-the-pinch/. Accessed 12 December 2013.

Washburn, Judith H., Brian D. Till and Randi Priluck. (2000), 'Co-branding: Brand equity and trial effects', *Journal of Consumer Marketing*, 17: 7, pp. 591–604.

Wetlaufer, Suzy (2004), 'The perfect paradox of star brands: an interview with Bernard Arnault of LVMH', *Harvard Business Review*, October, pp. 79–117.

Wu, Couchen and San-san Hsing. (2006), 'Less is More: How Scarcity Influences Consumers' Value Perceptions and Purchase Intents through Mediating Variables', *Journal of American Academy of Business*, 9: 2, pp. 125–132.

Wu, Shwu-Ing and Chen-Lien Lo. (2009), 'The influence of core-brand attitude and consumer perception on purchase intention towards extended product', *Asia Pacific Journal of Marketing and Logistics*, 21: 1, pp. 174–194.

Zhan, Lingjing. and Yanqun He. (2012), 'Understanding luxury consumption in China: Consumer perceptions of best-known brands', *Journal of Business Research*, 65: 10, pp. 1452–1460.

28

COMME ON DOWN AND CHOOS YOUR SHOES:
A study of consumer responses to the use of guest fashion designers by H&M as a co-branded fashion marketing strategy

Anne Peirson-Smith[1]

INTRODUCTION: H&M STREETSCENE

Picture the scene – actually it is not too difficult and does not take too much imaginative effort – as it has rapidly become a regular media story – much editorialized and photographed, blogged and tweeted about and now an established part of the fashion consumer Zeitgeist. It is Saturday in a major global city – take your pick – New York, London, Paris, Shanghai, Seoul, Hong Kong. Imagine – there you in are in your city of choice and you're walking down the street at 7:30 a.m. Here you see a long queue of shoppers snaking round the block of a mall at street level in the central shopping area. Curious as to what's behind this collective show of dedication to some strange cause – and ever the street anthropologist (or is it frustrated investigative journalist?) – you make your way to the front of the queue – to the source of this magnetic draw. After passing a long line of a hundred or more anticipatory females of varying demographic profiles, you find yourself at the gleaming plate glass, red and white plastic portals of that current temple of high street consumerism – H&M.

Most of the worshippers appear good humoured despite the cool, overcast morning with a hint of rain in the air, and you can feel the sense of anticipation in the air like that of children eagerly awaiting the arrival of Santa Claus or the Easter Bunny. Reaching the front of the queue, but not joining it, you ask one of the pole-positioned twenty-something girls in skinny jeans, Hello Kitty t-shirt, BAPE customized denim jacket and Ugg boots (and wait – is that a sleeping bag that you can see peeping out from her Coach leather backpack) how long has she been waiting to get to the front of the queue? 'Oh I've been here all night', she smiles casually pushing her Ray-Ban aviators back up onto her well-groomed hair. 'It's so worth it you know, because I'm about to purchase my big dream fashion item – a pair of Jimmy Choos!' Her voice rises to a state of frenetic, breathy ecstasy as she adds, 'Look there they are in the window!' You crane your neck to see above the heads of the couple of girls immediately behind her who scowl at you grimly as if you are attempting to pull off some kind of subtle queue-jumping stunt. You gasp and raise your eyebrows in response to what you can see.

There in the window is a sight to make even the most hard-bitten urban Cinderella's heart melt. Before you is a high pyramid of purple Jimmy Choo monikered shoe boxes displaying five styles of shoe (two stiletto-style sandals, two stiletto high boots and a low kitten heeled shoe) surrounded by sleek mannequins intently pawing each others' shoes, whilst also adorned with the said objects of desire. 'Which ones will you buy then?' you ask. 'Oh those leopard skin and black patent super high stilettos – they'll be mine – and my friends will be

---

[1] From Anne Peirson-Smith (2014) Comme on Down and Choos Your Shoes: A Study of Consumer Responses to the Use of Guest Fashion Designers by H&M as a Co-Branded Marketing Strategy, Global Fashion Brands, Intellect, pp. 57–82.

so like, "Wah! You look amazing" when I wear them out tonight'! She responds with an almost religious fervour and reverence for the object of her desire, mixed with more than a hint of lustful glee.

The contemporary retail trend to use guest celebrity fashion designers notably by high street fashion brands as a central promotional marketing strategy is the focus of this article. Specifically, this article examines the efficacy of the current fashion retail trend to use guest celebrity fashion designers by high street fashion brand, mass market retailer, Hennes & Mauritz (H&M) from 2004 onwards as a co-branding promotional strategy resulting in global urban scenes of customers queuing for hours in all weather conditions pre-opening, followed by locust-like scenes of frenzied shoppers emptying racks and shelves of designer branded items in seconds with resulting media buzz. The analysis will be based on a qualitative, ethnographic investigation into H&M's designer crossover collections launched in its major global flagship stores such as Hong Kong based on feedback from a series of focus groups and on the spot interviews at the launch of selected H&M co-branded designer collections.

FASHION BRANDING

A brand is based on the association that people make with a company in addition to its tangible material aspects so that it exists in the minds and hearts of the consumer (Olins 2000; Ind 2001). The rationale of branding 'is to establish a differentiated identity for the line of clothing being marketed in a highly competitive, crowded marketplace niche so that Zara's knitwear, for example, sets itself apart from H&M's or Mango's version' (Peirson-Smith 2013:180). Brand management focuses on brand identity (logo, name) created by the designer encapsulating the brand mission or rationale and the brand image – the resulting perception in the mind of the consumer. Hence, brand managers aim to establish a relationship with consumers and control their perception of the brand identity through multi-modal communicative forms and channels from print to social media. This brand identity is managed in three ways: through the brand's ethos or what it represents at its core, the values that it ascribes to and the brand personality 'that enable the brand to be instantly recognisable and much desired' (Devereux and Peirson-Smith 2009: 66). Brand managers attempt to control the overall character of the brand, making it unique from others, bringing it alive, giving it a raison d'etre with a consistently identifiable look and feel (Peirson-Smith and Hancock 2013).

In response to this brand product positioning, the brand image is the overall consumer perception of the brand (ethos, values and personality) driven by the brand personality and its relative positioning in the market (Aaker 1997). Branding is the result of interplay between these different elements in the push from the producer and the pull of the consumer affecting the values and symbolic meanings attached to the brand and its acceptance or rejection by the consumer as active agent (Arvidsson 2005). Effectively, branding 'takes a lifeless garment and transforms it into something with a desirable and irresistible power to persuade the customer to acquire it' (Peirson-Smith 2013: 181).

So, brand managers create a universe in which to situate the brand, project its identity intertextually and invite the consumer to exercise creative agency by engaging within the co-creation of meaning for the brand (Bridson and Evans 2004; Lury 1999). In the specific case of fashion branding, the designer's creative output and the strategy of using a 'celebrity' designer crossover will set in motion the material and intangible 'platforms for action that enable the production of particular immaterial use-values: an experience, a shared emotion, a sense of community' (Arvidsson 2005: 248). Arguably, the brand in itself is not important. Rather, it is what it can do for the consumer, or more precisely it is what the consumer does with it that is important.

Frame and narrative theory

Frame theory is also useful here in attempting to understand the production process and consumption response that underlies this celebrity guest designer strategy adopted by H&M. Frames are the fundamental cognitive structures signposting the representations of reality, which Goffman saw as a basis for understanding how we 'locate, perceive, identify and label a seemingly infinite number of concrete occurrences defined in its terms' (Goffman 1974: 21) in the process of making sense of the vast array of mediated information processed on a daily basis. Goffman considered that frames are unconsciously assimilated into communication exchange as he saw framing as an innate social and communicative process. Yet, this only accords with one part of the picture – and places emphasis on the creator of the discourse and the sender of the message. These are the cultural mediators – actively and professionally responsible for selecting and positioning the visual and verbal message. As Gitlin notes, 'frames are principles of selection, emphasis and presentation composed of little tacit theories about what exists, what happens, what matters' (1980: 6). The emphasis on the selection of frames by the promotional intermediaries accords with their professional brief as Entman observes,

> To frame is to select some aspects of perceived reality and make them more salient in communicating text, in such a way as to promote a particular problem, definition, causal interpretation, moral evaluation and/or treatment recommendation. (1993: 54)

In this way, the promotional intermediaries responsible for the marketing campaigns and how it is communicated to the consumer and consciously communicate using frames or schemata to reflect their position (and convey their belief system) using cognitive devices such as keywords, issues, stereotyped images, which thematically reinforce their position in competing stakeholder markets.

Clearly, the views articulated through the framing of designers will on the one hand represent the worldview of those representing the case, and also the choice of frame is based on professional considerations of what will capture media attention and connect cognitively and affectively with consumers – especially pushing their emotional buttons and linking them to the brand more closely.

For the H&M co-branding campaigns, we can identify some common frames that have assisted in effecting meaning behind this persuasive retailing endeavour in the process of signalling their difference from the high street competition – both the brands being promoted and the consumer once they have bought into this cultural system emotionally and functionally.

Framing the celebrity brand narrative

Storytelling as a sense-making device (Weick 1995) is a human trait and a communicative tool that is used rhetorically to persuade others and to influence events (Fisher 1984) premised on audience identification and involvement. Hence, stories are often used to make sense of organizational life and to communicate that sensibility created through a range of communication channels and modes. In many ways, brand identity building is all about storytelling (Hancock 2009). In an age of celebrity culture (Marshall 1997), consumers aspire towards and buy into celebrity brands to be part of their dream story or to make that story part of their own lives as they want to cast themselves in leading roles or live like they imagine their favourite celebrities do.

RESEARCH METHODOLOGY

As an active agent the consumer will interpret the brand's signifiers or image in their own way. In anticipation of this, brand managers ensure that all brand communication and messages are consistent and coherent. Hence, as Fisher (1987) suggested, all narratives form the basis of our sense-making and fail or succeed on the basis of their ability to be internally structurally consistent and credible for their audience. This suggests that the crossover designer brand relationships with H&M must attain some sort of credibility and credence with the consumer in order to make sense and to align with the brand's identity and impact on the brand's image all based on consumer perceptions as 'the effects of co-branding on the consumer should be paramount in decisions concerning this strategy' (Okonkwo 2007: 171).

The next section will test this notion out by presenting qualitative research findings from the consumer's perspective by matching up eight promotional frames or narratives identified as being embedded in the H&M crossover campaigns 2004–2012 with the consumer response elicited in the focus groups (Morgan 1988, Kawamura 2011). The intention was to determine the prospects' responses to the H&M designer collaborations, and to identify the range of motivations underpinning the consumer's cognitive, affective and behavioural engagement. To elicit this data, twenty student respondents (5 males and 15 females) across five focus groups representing an age range from 18–23 and featuring a range of representative ethnicities (from Hong Kong, Mainland China, the Philippines, India, Sweden, Poland, United Kingdom, North America, Australia, Canada, France, Germany and New Zealand) were interviewed. In addition, on the spot open-ended interviews with customers (Weiss 1984) were conducted both outside and inside H&M stores during the M for Madonna, H&M loves Kylie (July 2007), Comme des Garçons (November 2008), Jimmy Choo (November 2009), Versace (November 2010), Matthew Williamson (S/S 2008), David Beckham (2012), Sonia Rykiel (December 2008), Marni (November 2011), and H&MxMMM (November 2012) collection launches in Hong Kong. Responses were coded and analysed according to the themes covered below (Harding 2010). These include: limited edition; affordable luxury; glamour; quality, uniqueness, fashion heritage, design principle and reciprocity.

1. Limited edition

H&M's foray into guest-designed lines from Lagerfeld's A/W 2004 to Maison Martin Margiela (MMM) A/W 2012 collection have not only been limited in stock numbers as 'one-off' phenomena and also only released in selected global stores. This constructed scarcity principle articulated through the frame of 'get it now whilst stocks still last' – a frame originally borrowed from low price point retailing – appears to add to the special value of the branded items on offer arousing the intensity of the desire to purchase (Cialdini 2001). It intends to add excitement to the purchasing experience at point of sale, with most of the H&M guest designer lines being emptied from racks and shelves within a few hours and usually resold on eBay within the day.

The interviewees did generally concur that the idea that the items from each collection would be highly desirable, certainly adding to H&M's brand cachet and to their desirability as one of the focus group respondents observed:

> People always like limited editions because they are unique, and if you get that, it means that . . . for example if there are 10 items, and you get one of them, then it means that just 9 of the others can have that, and you will feel like you are so privileged and I can tell you that makes me feel really good and superior to everyone else. (Janice, Hong Kong, student, 20)

Another respondent also supported this idea regarding the worth of the superior affect afforded by accessing and purchasing the celebrity crossover item and speculated that this motivated H&M customers to withstand the rigours of standing in line for hours on end outside of the H&M store:

> I think that people are prepared to sacrifice their time and comfort to queue overnight and sleep outside in the street to get a chance to buy the H&M Versace jeans or the H&M Matthew Williamson suit and tie because it really matters to them to be seen as unique and special and to stand out from the crowd because they have been able to get something that no-one else has. Exclusivity really works and matters in this place. (James, Hong Kong, student, 21)

Outside the store for the Versace-H&M launch, one respondent said, 'In this life when everything is the same it's great to be able to find something different and exclusive. I'm planning to buy the big Versace cushions as they will dress up my home in a unique way' (Eunice, Thailand, 20).

The exclusive nature of the designer collections also yields a significant exchange value beyond the symbolic value. As a measure of this, another respondent queuing for the Comme des Garçons collection explained that this collection had real commercial value in the marketplace,

> Quite a few people will buy as many outfits as they can from this collection as it's a famous Japanese designer and Hong Kong people admire Japanese designers. So, many of us will put these items straight onto the internet for sale as it's the start of the day and I will most likely make a profit today . . . maybe three

times the price that I will pay and that will be a good money. (Den, Hong Kong, 22)

Another respondent from the Philippines explained as she emerged from the store with ten large white bags with items worth over HK$5000 that she had travelled specially to Hong Kong to select pieces from the Marni collection for her customers of her boutique in Manila as 'their desire for these items is so high and they are more than willing to pay the price which covers the cost of my travel expenses too. They will be so happy'.

2. Affordable luxury

The notion of affordable luxury and fantasy is encapsulated in the framing of most of the H&M crossover collections including the Roberto Cavalli guest designer relationship in 2007, for example, who promised as the first invited Italian designer to 'add a dash of festivity and dreams' to H&M customers' life.

The focus group respondents largely believed this to be a major driver in the success of the celebrity collections, as noted by Stephen (Australia, 19):

> Yes the pricing really works, especially when H&M cross-over with famous brands like Comme des Garçons because people usually have to spend like thousands on items for Comme des Garçons, so now they only need to spend HK$200–300, so they will think they will have to have this because it is a rare opportunity to get a high luxury fashion item.

This sentiment was mirrored by the interviewees lining up for many of the collections as Dot (Hong Kong, 26) said 'We would never be able to afford the real thing in the Versace shop so we can have a luxury outfit at non-luxury prices'. Equally, as Candice (Singapore, 24) noted:

> In our age group (i.e. 20s to 30s), we normally cannot afford high-end fashion brands such as Roberto Cavalli, Jimmy Choo, or Sonia Rykiel. Therefore, we may not take the initiative to search for the information about these brands. However, when they have crossover fashion lines with H&M, the price of the products become affordable for us, so the distant between the brands and us has shortened.

There also appeared to be an expectation that the exchange value of the designer goods would not exceed a certain threshold and should be good value as if the H&M brand principle was also a critical part of the commercial exchange relationship:

> I noticed that people still tend to buy the designer clothes at a cheaper price, even in the cross-overs with the famous brands because I saw the $2000 Comme des Garçons cross-over with the H&M trench coat, and no one bought it, because it was slightly more expensive because the customers have the perception of, although you are Comme des Garçons but with H&M, but H&M doesn't deserve this amount of money. (Win, China, 23)

3. Glamour and lifestyle aspirations

> 'Celebrity culture, the art, movie and music world . . . As a designer you must have your eyes, ears, everything open'. (Margareta van den Bosch in Fisher 2009)

Glamour was feted as the hallmark of both the Versace and Jimmy Choo inaugural shoe and accessory range offering consumers the borrowed interest and brand identity associations from A-List designers.

In a similar manner, Madonna's womenswear (S/S 2006) and Kylie's beachwear (Summer 2007) invested their respective pop celebrity crossover collections with a rock chick and pop princess quality that adds other cultural systems – the music and pop culture industry – to this aspirational frame.

Queuing overnight for the Versace collection, Dina from India explained that she had a long list of items from friends and family that she was intending to buy for them in time for the Christmas season as 'some of the pieces are so sexy and so Versace and we love that'.

4. Quality lines

One of the core brand values of quality that H&M places great emphasis on in all of their external communications and promotional collaterals is a key promotional frame encapsulated in the guest designer relationships with Stella McCartney and Matthew Williamson, for example. McCartney's aesthetic of cool, feminine, wearable designs most typically aligns with the target H&M customers who are also offered sharp tailoring in the process for A/W 2005 – from the frame of her own signature line or her former Chloé wardrobe. Similarly, Matthew Williamson's men's and womenswear line offered in all featured stores for two seasons in 2009 was framed as an opportunity for the designer to benefit from H&M's penchant for matching quality and craftsmanship in the signature line to educate the consumer about fashion and style (Dehn 2012). Yet, many are keen to note, including Lagerfeld and Jimmy Choo themselves, that this was a specially invited line with a different finish, and was not a diffusion line for their brand whose signature shoes are made in Italy.

The focus group respondents questioned the quality of the fabric and production of the garments and one shared a disappointing experience when the hem of a Marni skirt came unravelled after one wear whilst another said that the buttons on the Matthew Williamson jacket had fallen off after a few weeks. As Janice (Canada, 20) observed:

> In fact, like last time I went to H&M for that Sonia Rykiel collection, I don't know why, but the bangles are not well produced – such cheap plastic and disappointing as it looked like they came from a cheap market stall.

There was a sense with the interviewees at the store that they had convinced themselves of the superior quality of the goods that they were lusting after and buying into. 'Look at that bag' Tammy (from Beijing, China) noted pointing at the black Versace tote, 'It's such good leather – you could not get any better in the actual shop'.

5. Uniqueness

A more esoteric and conceptual frame was crafted for the Comme des Garçons winter 2009 avant garde and intellectual collaboration, 'founded on artistic inspiration and her philosophy of pursuing the ultimate form of creation based on a sense that H&M is surprising and educating consumers – even taking them outside of their comfort frame and broadening its target base', which was also the case with the 2012 MMM collection.

In the same vein, the Viktor & Rolf 2006 collection was aimed at a more discerning fashion crowd or at bringing a new one up to speed, as Tim Blanks at Style.com noted,

> Viktor and Rolf suggest a number of opportunities for customers as well as designers at H&M. This is a clever collaboration. The challenge: V&R are cherished within the international fashion crowd but still a bit unknown outside it. This will put an end to that. Whilst V&R, whose roots are based in couture, but love to play with opposites, embraced the opportunity to 'communicate our vision to such a large audience of H&M devotees'. (Blanks 2006)

The unique liaison between high street and haute couture was seen by many respondents as an interest generator and one that creates significant desire. Yet, other respondents in the focus group viewed it as a cynical marketing ploy that duped the consumer into thinking that they had acquired the real designer item. 'The consumers are fooled into thinking that the designer and atelier have had a big input into the collection but in reality it's not true and it's like buying fake goods really' (Jac, France, 20).

On a pragmatic note, some of the focus group respondents were also keen to point out that whilst the MMM collection was interesting, it was essentially unwearable for most young people given the sizing as Matt (Hong Kong, 21) noted:

> I really admire Maison Margiela and its really fascinating to see a reworking of the collection across the decades like a museum but I tried the men's coats and jackets on and I looked like a crazy person or a clown as even the XS size drowned me.

Significantly, much of this collection including the iconic duvet coat remained on the racks to become remainders or were relocated back to other global stores.

6. Fashion heritage

In a sense, the entire guest designer relationship is premised on the notion of providing customers with a rare gift or opportunity to buy into the story of the couture fashion brand of the moment as was the case with the recent Spring 2010 collection with Sonia Rykiel knits that evoked the 1960s modernist Parisian left bank look and origins of her original boutique. Equally, the most recent A/W 2012 MMM collection featuring replicated selected pieces such as the sock jumper from 1998 and other past collections from the 1980s onwards offered the chance to acquire a piece of fashion history.

There was a sense amongst the focus group respondents that the range of crossover collections representing a variety of styles and taste determined their level of cultural capital amongst the consumers who had to be in the know about many of the less well-known designers such as Sonia Rykiel or MMM. 'I think why it works is because the customers show their knowledge of fashion. You must be in the know about style, and knowing that you're in the know so you're part of a club'. The idea of a fashion club was also highlighted by the responses from the on-site interviews and observations as quite a number of customers from a range of countries across the collections said that they had checked on the H&M app, website and also with local fashion blogs to determine the content and to plan their personal or commercial purchases beforehand.

7. Design principle

H&M's CEO is on record as saying that H&M is committed to good design: garment design was allegedly one of the reasons that Lagerfeld entered into the strategic crossover alliance (Tungate 2006). Whilst most respondents and interviewees admitted that the design of the products would not be the same as the actual designer brand, they all believed that the collections represented good design and felt and looked well designed.

However, the focus group respondents were more cynical and savvy about the design process: 'H&M shoppers just don't know that perhaps things they get in H&M with those famous designers, they just don't know that maybe these collections are not designed by that designer but it's designed by their team or associate' (Karly, Hong Kong, 21).

8. Reciprocity – Gift giving

Some focus group respondents noted that H&M's celebrity collections could be interpreted as a gift for their customers, given that they were the first high street brand to launch and continue this strategy. As such, there seemed to be a recognition that this impacted on the brand image in a favourable way. As one respondent noted, 'Now that I think of it – Zara don't do it, Mango don't, Cotton On and Forever 21 so they are giving their consumers something special I guess' (Carmen, China, 20).

DISCUSSION

Throughout all of these promotional frames or brand stories runs the notion that H&M attempts to position itself as the key fashion driver with its finger on the pulse of style and fashion trends of the now as it is in control of the selection and invitation process for each of the guest designers who to a person gush gratefully in the news releases and media interviews arranged around the launch of their one-off collections as to how enthusiastic and grateful they are to be occasioned this creative opportunity and chance to widen their market as the ultimate credibility booster.

In response from the consumer perspective, it would appear that these eight frames and brand narratives are largely recognized and bought into both symbolically and tangibly by H&M consumers. In addition, they go a significant way to explaining the cognitive, affective and behavioural responses that do appear to turn regular consumers of H&M merchandise into avid fans of the designer crossover collections. They appear to be successful in aligning with the aspirations of the consumer in terms of providing access to limited-edition, well-designed, affordable luxury items that appear to make sense of their lives given the current prevalence of celebrity culture. Beyond that, these collections also appear to increase H&M's brand equity on the back of the existing high-end designers' credibility, thereby strengthening H&M's brand equity and loyalty. Respondents appeared to associate value for money and good design with the H&M brand, which is also aligned with H&M's mission as a consequence of the content of both the designer and the regular collections, suggesting that the former transfers associational or symbolic value to the latter enhancing brand loyalty in the process.

Many of the focus group consumers and customers at the site of the designer collections appeared to be affectively connected to the celebrity designer crossover collections in terms of how it made them feel more positive about themselves with regard to others. In many ways, being able to purchase from the designer collections empowered them and made them feel more 'superior' and 'in the know about fashion unlike people who just throw on clothes' (Ang, Philippines, female shopper, 36). Yet, there was no evidence that H&M's regular customers would become the designer's customers other than in an aspirational way, although one shopper did say that having 'bagged my Versace gold party dress I'm now off to cosmetics store, Sasa, to buy my Versace perfume to complete the outfit' (Tara, United Kingdom, 38), suggesting that the designer buying relationship could be extended to related affordable designer diffusion lines. On the other hand, it was interesting to encounter consumers wearing designer outfits or bags who were in line to supplement their authentic designer wardrobes with the crossover items as one well-informed respondent in the store explained,

> I'm here to buy a few Marni H&M items and I love the look of the pea coat and the graphic fabric of the skirts as they add an interesting twist to the collection and it was worth the wait in line to get my hands on these items. I think that we've all got over the head to toe designer look that was so prevalent here in the 1980s and 1990s. Actually, that looks so over the top and dated now and it was all so insecure. But you do see it in some Asian cities still and in Mainland Chinese first and second tier cities but their time will come too and that look will evolve as mine has. (Cath, Canada, 33)

However, the 'lustomers' also appear to have their own frames or agendas when participating in the performance of queueing and frenzied shopping at the crossover launches. As we have seen, some of the participants' motivations in this spectacle are more cognitively and less affectively oriented, purely purchasing their quota of designer goods in each size to either sell in their own local or regional boutiques, sell on eBay or the Internet and to take them home as gifts in a variety of geographic and cultural locations. In this way, the designer collections fully represent the global commodification of fashion items with a high exchange value.

References

Aaker, Jennifer (1997), 'Dimensions of brand personality', *Journal of Marketing Research*, 34: August, pp. 347–56.

Arvidsson, Adam (2005), 'Brands: A Critical Perspective', *Journal of Consumer Culture*, 5: 2, pp. 235–57.

Blanks, Tim (2006), 'Viktor and Rolf for H&M', *The Fashion Spot.com*. http://forums.thefashionspot.com/f60/viktor-rolf-h-m-44141-16.html. Accessed 3 March 2011.

Bridson, Kerrie, and Jody Evans (2004), 'The secret to a fashion advantage is brand orientation', *International Journal of Retail and Distribution Management*, 32: 8, pp. 403–11.

Ciadini, Robert B. (2001), *Influence: Science and Practice*, 4th ed., Boston: Allyn & Bacon.

Devereux, Mary and Anne Peirson-Smith. (2009), *Public Relations in Asia Pacific: Communicating Effectively across Cultures*. London and Singapore: John Wiley & Sons Ltd.

Entman, Robert M. (1993), 'Framing: Towards a Clarification of a Fractured Paradigm' *Journal of Communication* 43(4), pp. 51–58.

Fisher, Walter R. (1984), Narration as Human Communication Paradigm: The Case of Public Moral Argument, *Communication Monographs*, 51, pp. 1–22.

Fisher, Walter R (1987), *Human Communication as Narration: Toward a Philosophy of Reason, Value, and Action*, Columbia: University of South Carolina Press.

Gitlin, Todd (1980), *The Whole World Is Watching: Mass Media in the Making and Unmaking of the New Left*, Berkeley, CA: University of California Press.

Goffman, Erving (1974), *Frame Analysis: An Essay on the Organization of Experience*, London: Harper and Row.

Hancock, Joseph (2009), *Brand Story*, New York: Fairchild Books.

H&M (2008), *Annual Report Part 1: H&M in Words and Pictures*, Stockholm: H&M.

H&M (2012), *Annual Report*, Stockholm: H&M.

Harding, Jamie (2010), *Qualitative Data Analysis from Start to Finish*, London: Sage.

Ind, Nicolas (2001), *Living the Brand*, London: Kogan Page.

Kawamura, Yuniya (2011), *Doing Research in Fashion and Dress: An Introduction to Qualitative Research*, London: Bloomsbury.

Lury, Celia (2004), *Brands: the logos of a global economy*, New York: Routledge.

Marshall, P. David (1997), *Celebrity and Power*, Minneapolis: University of Minnesota Press.

Morgan, David L. (1988), *Focus Groups as Qualitative Research Methods*, Volume 16, Thousand Oaks, CA: Sage Publications.

Okonkwo, Uche (2007), *Luxury Fashion Branding: Trends, Tactics and Techniques*, London: Palgrave Macmillan.

Olins, Wally (2003), *On Brand*, London: Thames & Hudson.

Peirson-Smith, Anne (2013), 'Wishing on a star – promoting and personifying designer collections and fashion brands', *Journal of Fashion Practice: The Journal of Design, Creative Process and the Fashion Industry. Special Issue: Fashion Branding*, 5: 2, November, pp. 171–202.

Peirson-Smith, Anne and Hancock IIJoseph H. Hancock II. (2013), 'Editorial', *Journal of Fashion Practice: The Journal of Design, Creative Process and the Fashion Industry. Special Issue: Fashion Branding*, 5(2), November, pp. 165–170.

Weick, Karl (1995), *Sensemaking in Organizations*, Thousand Oaks, CA: Sage.

Weiss, Robert (1984), *Learning from Strangers: The Art and Method of Qualitative Interview Studies*, New York: The Free Press.

FURTHER READING

Bailey, Sarah and Jonathan Baker (2014) *Visual Merchandising For Fashion*, New York: Fairchild.

Everett, Judith C., Kristen K. Swanson, and José Blanco (2018), *Guide to Producing a Fashion Show*, New York: Bloomsbury.

Granger, Michele M., Tina M. Sterling, and Ann Cantrell (2019), *Fashion Entrepreneurship*, New York: Bloomsbury.

Hancock II, J. H. (2016), *Brand / Story: Cases and Explorations in Fashion Branding*, 2nd Edition, New York: Fairchild Publications.

Kim, Youn-Kyung, Pauline Sullivan, and Judith Cardona Forney (2007), *Experiential Retailing: Concepts and Strategies That Sell*, New York: Fairchild Books.

Lantz, Jenny (2016), *The Trendmakers, Behind the Scenes of the Global Fashion Industry*, London: Bloomsbury.

Rath, Patricia Mink, Richard Petrizzi, and Penny Gill (2012), *Fashion Marketing: A Global Perspective*, New York: Fairhild Books.

Rosenau, Jeremy A. and David L. Wilson (2014), *Apparel Merchandising: The Line Starts Here*, New York: Bloomsbury.

Stark, Gill (2018), *The Fashion Show, History, Theory and Practice*, London: Berg.

Stephens, Doug (2013), *The Retail Revival: Reimagining Business of the New Age Consumerism*, John Wiley.

Figure 24 Photo Courtesy of Brent Luvaas.
Source: Brent Luvaas

PART VII
Fashion Branding

Figure 25 Eli Soul, Photo Courtesy of Brent Luvaas.
Source: Brent Luvaas

INTRODUCTION

Veronica Manlow

The process of branding is premised on the need to differentiate a product, person or organization from its rivals in a competitive marketplace in the mind of the consumer by highlighting its distinctive, unique features using strategically selected communication in the form of words and images to stimulate current and future sales. Across history farmers branded their livestock for recognition, while artisans and artists highlighted the quality of their artwork with a signature, symbol or stamp, for example (Clifton and Simmons, 2004).

    A brand can be defined as, "an entity with a distinctive idea expressed in a set of functional and experiential features with a promise of a value reward relevant to its end users, and an economic return to its producers (through the building of equity). A successful brand has a strong identity (mentally and physically), is innovative, consistent, competitively positioned, and holds a matching positive image in the consumer's mind" (Hameide, 2011:5-6). The branding process is the totality of what is communicated by a brand about its uniqueness in both tangible and intangible, rational and emotional ways - in terms of its image and how that messaging is understood by consumers in terms if its recognized identity (Hancock et al., 2014; xii). Fashion branding is based on "the context that surrounds the garment, as well as the image that designers retailers, manufacturers and promotional consultants create to encourage consumers to buy new items. Fashion branding can make fashion seem fun, exciting, innovative and unique' (Hancock, 2016: 6). Originally, couture fashion houses such as Worth evolved into brands as a means of protecting their copyright through franchising and licensing to department stores. The broadening of consumer access through 'named" branding followed across the 20th century with designers, such as Coco Chanel for example, using their name to market a range of related lifestyle good including fragrances, and the emergence of more affordable ready-to-wear deigns. Brand differential is signaled through tangible aspects that create brand identity – the brand name, trademark and logo, the product, packaging and presentation and visual merchandising in the physical or online store. In addition, the more abstract aspects of the brand's uniqueness are conveyed through promotional and advertising efforts, in addition to the brand producer's public reputation (Devereux and Peirson-Smith, 2009).

    Fashion brands differentiate themselves from each other in a highly competitive marketplace in communicating the unique benefits of their products and thereby adding monetary and social value or imagined value to work on the emotional connections that contribute to brand equity – the actual worth of the brand and the brand image - the perception of the brand by consumers and other stakeholders. In late capitalism, fashion branding is firmly associated with the intangible aspects of the brand, the experience that it offers and the lifestyle that it represents, rather than the actuality of the named product itself (Tungate, 2008).

    Increasingly, the brand story is conveyed through a range of communication channels and communicators – advertisers, public relations professionals and digitally based influencers. Brand narratives aim to connect with consumers by conveying shared values (Fog et al., 2005) whereby "a brand reaches full consumption potential when it makes an emotional connection with consumers, when the consumers and employers of the brand are able to understand the company's values and messages. Storytelling speaks to the emotions of the target market, which in return becomes loyal to the company." (Hancock, 2016: 8)

    Some of the brand's communication, how it is managed and how it is conveyed to the consumer is firmly under the brand's control, but as the scope of fashion has expanded globally, and as technology has rapidly advanced and become accessible to all--and ubiquitous in the form of social media, in one way brands have a less of a share in controlling their identity or have to manage their brands more consistently and conscientiously in order to assure that the brand image in the mind of the consumer is positively received. Print, broadcast and other channels of communication such as outdoor advertising—the advertisements that we see on public transportation for example—have not disappeared, they continue to be important for establishing and maintaining fashion brand identity, equity and image, but many brands are increasingly shifting their emphasis toward the use of digital media and key influencers such as bloggers and vloggers to communicate their message. Yet, in addition to momentous changes in, and the impact of communication technology and digital communication channels, fashion brands at the macro-level are navigating and often struggling to survive in a changing socio-economic world order requiring more critical brand management. These contextual issues will be examined next, before progressing to examine the more micro-issues surrounding fashion branding in the contemporary fashion system.

THE CONTEXT OF A NEW UNSTABLE WORLD ORDER

We live in a world of 'fake news' and in which the systems that traditionally provided stability: religion, the family, political parties, have been challenged, dismantled and/or reinvented (Hunt and Gentzkow, 2017). Globally, the pace of social change is rapid, and individual freedoms that were not imagined by the majority in the near past seem to be more easily accepted. Yet, there is another reality held by those who do not control public discourse or influence popular or elite cultures. On the one hand, we are subject to the threat of visible and dangerous reactionary forces making the world a more uncertain place. Terrorist groups, most notably Isis and Al Qaeda, are rising up and attracting new adherents who conduct random attacks on innocent civilians causing insecurity and fear on the streets of our cities. On the other hand, there are ordinary folk in places such as North America, famously described by Barack Obama in 2008 as "bitter" people who "cling to guns and religion or antipathy to people who aren't like them" (Davis, 2008). Intolerance and even hatred seem to be proliferating throughout the world from a wellspring of fear and anger via populist movements that spreads rapidly through social media and represents a threat to democracy. Presently, we face what might be called a global crisis in which there is a deep disorientation: uncertainty about the environment, the economy, and the instability of political systems. Humanitarian crises continue in the aftermath of war with ongoing conflicts in Syria, Iraq, Afghanistan, Yemen, South Sudan, Chad, just to name a few areas where fragmented political parties and rival factions continue to cause conflict. Throughout Europe we see a turn against globalization and the established order in politics and the media, and a backlash against immigrants. Brexit was an attempt to restore a national British identity, culture and worldview not challenged or diluted by "others", particularly immigrants, but also the controlling political elite. Worldviews are now increasingly polarized, so while far right French presidential candidate, Marine le Pen, espoused anti-Muslim rhetoric, linking xenophobia with the preservation of French civilization ("French First"), center right candidate François Fillon lamented the loss of colonialism, or at least reacted against criticisms of it, in stating that France "should not be blamed for just wanting to share and spread its culture to the people of Africa" (Gaillard 2016). Before Emmanuel Macron was elected as French President in May 2017 there was fear that we may even see the unraveling of the European Union, and post-Brexit this is still a possibility posing a threat to the operation of organizations doing business across and within Europe, including many high profile fashion brands. Meanwhile, across the pond, "Make America Great Again" and the U.S. presidential election of Donald Trump also became a reality, surprising many, including the American fashion industry (Zerbo, 2016). The industry's response was appropriately played out on the catwalk:

> here in the fashion world – populated by minorities, women, gays, immigrants, East Coast elites and all-around rebels – a lot of people are not fine. They are not OK. They are dismayed, angry, frightened. They do not like what they see happening in Washington. And they are processing it the way they know how: through fashion (Givhan, 2017).

Hence, fashion's leading media influencers, such as *Vogue* had openly supported and advised rival Hillary Clinton, while designer brands such as Marc Jacobs and his political tees or had Willy Chavarria's F/W 2018 show BELIEVERS was branded with a strongly politicized flavor:

> Graphics included a Ralph Lauren-inspired Polo Sport flip, with the USA flag turned upside down — a common symbol of a nation in distress. Hard-wearing garments and accessories like gloves and water bottles made references to sanctuary cities and relief counseling—something appropriate for the everyday crises of a post-Trump America (DeLeon, 2017).

Fashion mirrors social and political developments (Lemire, 2010) and it is touched by developments in these sectors as it operates against and within this socio-political context being a trillion dollar global industry employing millions across its supply chain. As contemporary women's wear buyer Bijou Abiola from Lord & Taylor put it, people are ready to fight back in fashion (Pulse, 2018). She spoke of several designers showing military inspired clothing during Fashion Week 2017 in New York, noting how politics impacts fashion trends with feminist messages from the Women's March making their way onto the runway, for example.

Fashion has now detached itself from an aristocratic past, although celebrities such as the Beckhams or the Kardashians are the new styled neo-royalty (Church Gibson, 2012). Centuries ago, luxury goods were rare and exclusive, but massluxe and massclusive brands now represent accessibility and offer more democratic forms within the domain of fashion.

Fashion embodies change (Crane, 2000). It is a principally a business and its democratic logic is a hyper-capitalist logic in a Post-Fordist world, although we see much smaller scale and increasingly influential manifestations, which may be ecological, sustainable and equitable. Goods of Conscience, for example, is a non-profit brand dedicated to keeping Mayan textile traditions alive through fair work conditions and wages. Here, weavers in Guatemala produce "social fabric" which is used to create garments designed by Father Andrew O'Connor in a workshop on the Lower East Side of New York.

Fashion is not only a social and cultural mirror; it is also a global force infiltrating and sometimes driving change in various domains. Politics, the media, entertainment, art, education, architecture, technology, just to name a few important sectors of society, once might have claimed a certain distance from fashion, but few would deny that representatives of these sectors can often be found worshipping at the altar of fashion (McRobbie, 1999).

What does fashion branding mean in the age of information availability, and in the age digital technology at a moment in history characterized by incremental uncertainty? Fashion can be viewed as a deregulated system where immediacy has become primary. More than ever, it requires a great deal of advanced strategic planning behind the scenes, in a variety of functions: design, production, logistics, finance, merchandising, marketing and engineering, for example, to create an experience of immediate access, gratification, engagement and personal transformation for the consumer. "Fast fashion" and the value brands that propagate it is "slow violence" for the factory worker in Bangladesh as the Rana Plaza disaster proved (Siegle, 2011), and indeed it is a contributor to the processes that lead to the environmental consequences that disproportionately affect the poor such as displacement of indigenous people through deforestation in Brazil or pollution of water sources through toxic drift, as described by Rob Nixon (2013).

In the past, there was an orderly and predictable fashion system, which required some degree of patience on the part of the consumer who had to wait for the next season to access verdicts from the fashion press, for clothing to arrive, for styles to trickle down from the couture houses, especially if she was not a member of the social elite (Craik, 1994). The fashion cycle has increasingly accelerated to meet the demands of an insatiable consumer. Fast fashion, street style, bloggers and other influencers compete with the fashion establishment: both luxury and street brands with a long heritage, and the editors, buyers, fashion photographers and forecasters who operate within the confines of the fashion system, bypassing the rules and creating a new fashion landscape characterized by immediacy and all that it implies: variability, change, excess, diversification, flexibility, and new forms of spectacle.

It is no longer editors and buyers who determine trends and who secure the success of some brands over others through the selections and endorsements they make in the media and in store. Bloggers, influencers and celebrities have undermined their once unquestioned authority and as New York fashion buyer, Bijou Abiola observed, celebrity Kim Kardashian and model and designer Gigi Hadid have such an important impact on fashion and its followers amongst a youth demographic that wearing an item of apparel or accessory on Instagram can immediately create a trend and a huge consumer demand that cannot be met by a department store such as Lord & Taylor, which habitually buys its offerings a full year in advance. Fashion forecasters typically and traditionally predict trends a year or sometimes several years in advance, but digital influencers now operate in the immediate present of the fashion system (Wiedmann et al., 2010; Duffy and Hund, 2015).

How then has branding adapted to these new fashion realities and rapidly changing landscape in which the fashion brand operates? Branding emanates from fashion brand in several ways: the form and aesthetics of the products it creates, a designer or creative director who is the visible face of the brand, if applicable (otherwise the named reputation of the brand takes precedent as in the case of Target or J. Crew), the stores in which the brand is sold, the people who sell the brand, as well as those who are less visible and work behind the scenes at retail level. In addition to the retail store environment, there is often a website and many people working collaboratively to create a presence, identity, experience, aesthetic and functionality online. In the corporate office of a fashion brand, if it is a large enough firm, there will be many divisions involved in branding, most notably marketing/PR and merchandising. The materials and experiences they produce: advertising, packaging, fashion shows and presentations, fashion films, and collaborations, for example, all have an important impact on fashion branding (Cope and Maloney, 2016).

For most of contemporary fashion history, fashion editors and buyers carried great weight in consecrating brands by lending their expertise and prestige in deciding to endorse and to buy the products of one or another brand (Borelli, 1997). These original, all-powerful fashion influencers developed relationships with certain brands serving an ancillary role in a company's branding efforts. They also held the power to make a brand irrelevant by personally ignoring or dismissing it in print or at point of sale. Today, it is not only editors and buyers who make decisions about a brand, and whose communications send a clear message to consumers. There are new influencers: celebrities, models and bloggers, vloggers and prominent people with a variety of social networks who can become ambassadors or detractors such as such as bloggers Susie Lau of *Style Bubble* or Aimee Song of *Song of Style* and pure influencers Caroline Vreeland or Olivia Palerma. "Ordinary" individuals who have a following can become influencers too, thus not only forming their own opinions about brands, but by spreading a brand's message or creating counter narratives. Indeed, important influencers such as Alexa Chung may create their own brands or collaborate with existing ones, challenging established brands, bypassing retail stores, and doing business directly with their followers.

Many brands adapt content to social media and others create content specifically for individual social media platforms, for example, Burberry creates video content particularly for Instagram. Some brands maintain tight control of social media--this is almost always the case with luxury brands. Hermes has an interactive portal, for example, where customers can send photos and stories from which the brand selects content that it uses. Other brands allow user generated content on their social media platforms and Instagram platforms, such as Calvin Klein' celebrity led love-in with #MyCalvins or Marc Jacob's #CastMeMarc for aspiring models.

Partnering with digital influencers with vast numbers of followers can create instantaneous sales in the millions for brands when fans see them wear, use or endorse products. Brands have invited influencers, not just famous actresses like Gwenyneth Paltrow who is a brand ambassador for Chanel, or Uma Thurman for Louis Vuitton, but bloggers, models, celebrities from reality TV shows, and photographers to work for and partner with them in a variety of collaborations. Dolce & Gabbana has been drawing its runway models from the influencer crowd: bloggers, celebrities, singers, and YouTubers. H&M invited Swedish blogger Elin Klin to design a collection, and

Kate Spade invited blogger Garance Dore to design clothing and accessories. Chiara Ferragni, who Fashionista.com gives first position for her Blond Salad blog, designed a collection for Steve Madden shoes before creating her own line of shoes, which are sold in 300 retail stores. On the back of this success story, she is planning on opening her own store in Milan. Also, Ferragni has been on the cover of 25 international magazines and is a brand ambassador for Pantene. Equally, Club Monaco hired street style photographer Tommy Ton to design handbags, accessories and photograph them in the street for the brand.

Yet, luxury brands such as Hermes have generally approached social media with caution given that their brand ethos is based on exclusivity, quality and heritage, consequently often still engaging in one way communication: never directly responding or interacting with followers and only benefiting passively from their retweets, follows and shares. By way of contrast, Burberry was an early digital adapter using live streaming runway shows and allowing instant purchases (Phan, Thomas and Heine, 2011). In recognition of reportage suggesting that 40% of all luxury purchases are now being made online (Dauriz et al., 2016) the brand spend over 60% of their marketing budget on social media strategies. *The Art of the Trench* web campaign, launched in 2009 for example, featuring photos of customers wearing the iconic Burberry trench coat became one of the brand's most important facets in its social media presence, established its leadership in the digital domain, setting a powerful precedent for other fashion brands to follow suit.

Tommy Hilfiger from the time he began his career has had a strong "democratic" orientation to fashion, and close ties with popular culture. He prides himself on being focused on what Lauren Sherman (2016) terms "fashion immediacy." His chief marketing and brand officer, Avery Baker describes a quest for "closing that gap between the visibility of a fashion show and the moment of purchase" and indeed he accomplished this on a large scale. Items shown on the runway during #TommyNow in September 2016 were available immediately at Tommy Hilfiger stores and at 40 other locations in a total of 70 countries. Hilfiger created a unique space called Tommy Pier for his show featuring Gigi Hadid's collection. This two day event at the South Street Seaport recreated a street fair environment complete with carnival rides, pop-up shops, and free food and entertainment for 2,000 guests, half of them industry people and the remainder customers and brand followers who responded within an hour to his online invite. Alongside this physical brand retail experience he created a virtual experience by live streaming a "shoppable" video in Times Square, on his Tommy.com website, on Facebook, and on 175 partner websites. The brand also provided links to the video on Instagram, Snapchat and Pinterest. Also, Hilfiger has re-booted the brand's image by collaborating on two capsule collections with Gigi Hadid, drawing on the range and reach of her social networks, as well as the brand's existing followers and fans.

Fashion has the capacity to become a system where immediacy is its primary mode, and many brands are making this commitment, if not fully at least across a variety of technological innovations from 3-D printing of fashion accessories to Artificial Intelligence (AI) employed to manage big data for faster forecasting, planning and merchandising. The role of branding is to tell these fashion forward stories and highlight achievements by ramping up their social media presence. Branding provides the underlying code and the manifestation of a brand's system of values; its worldview.

Branding itself, no matter the communication or technological tools used to tell the fashion brand story, continues to have a social, cultural and psychological impact enabling the fashion to evolve and operate profitably, by generating income and creating jobs. However, some things do not change: the symbolic importance of branding in people's lives through consumption and visible display will inevitably continue to be used to reinforce status and identity (Bridson and Evans, 2004).

A dramaturgical approach (Goffman, 1959) can also usefully help us understand branding as a performance in which agents interpret and interact with and manage branded content in environments such as stores, on websites and in experiences outside the shopping context so that brands perform well in the marketplace based on creating a memorable customer experience. As Gad observes,

> The implementation of a brand strategy consists of two parts. One is the conversation content and the other is dramaturgy or the dramatic composition of the implementation…that includes scripted surprise (Gad, 2016: 99)

Customers are also playing their art in this performance and in assuming more empowered roles, taking a more active role in deciding what to buy, what messages to accept, reject or redefine, and where they will find these messages: from the brand itself or via blogs, vlogs, on reality TV shows, for example. By communicating their own opinions using social media they become influencers in small or large social networks. Branding in this new context can be seen as a heterotropic or interdependent site of knowledge. Robert J. Topinka (2010) who builds on Foucault's work on order and knowledge production sees heterotropic space as sites combining contradictory elements, whereby "epistemes collide and overlap creating an intensification of knowledge" in this way destabilizing "the ground on which knowledge is built." This is the new fashion eco-system located within a conflicted consumerist global society in which brands find themselves, and must find their way by closer negotiation with influencers and consumers.

The selected readings in the following section illustrate pertinent issues facing fashion branding past, present and future by largely dealing with the fashion branding process vis-à-vis the stories and mythologies built by the founders of several fashion brands and ways in which the positive associations with their names bolsters the brand image, identity ethos and persona. Tasha Lewis and Natalie Gray focus on Russell Simmons the founder of Phat Farm contextualizing the brand to examine the landscape in which hip hop fashion was born. They trace the evolution of hip hop fashion from clothes styles created through the artful combination of a variety of clothing brands by artists and fans of the new genre of music in the neighborhoods of the Bronx and Brooklyn in the 1970s and 1980s. Eventually brands such as Tommy Hilfiger, Polo and Timberland became brands of choice and as thus became associated with hip-hop although this was not their consumer base. In the 1990s brands, which specifically identified as hip hop brands such as Rocawear, Phat Farm and Sean Jean emerged as hip-hop artists who founded them became famous. Within this seminal decade, hip-hop fashion and style became mainstream and the brands responded in a variety of ways, some catering to a more mature hip hop consumer whose tastes had changed and others less concerned about "authenticity." In the selection by Veronica Manlow, readers will have a chance to discover the straightforward branding strategies behind three larger established mass-marketed American brands: Ralph Lauren, Tommy Hilfiger and American Apparel, all of whom pride themselves on being true representations of American culture and ideals, and whose identities however different and sometimes contradictory, as in the case of American Apparel, are unambiguously and unapologetically American. One finds a more nuanced reality in reading Anne Peirson-Smith's article about the evolution of two smaller Chinese brands, one a Hong Kong based designer brand founded by two siblings in 2006 which describes itself as an international fashion label, Daydream Nation, and the other, Rose Studio, a couture brand founded by Guo Pei in Beijing in 1997 which now has an atelier in Paris. These Chinese brands reflect a more complex transformative cultural journey as they navigate local and global identities and utilize brand storytelling ultimately to become "global commodities" as recognition of success and survival. In the reading on Elizabeth Hurley written by Lee Barron we move into the domain of influencer turned fashion brand. Barron traces Hurley's career from model to actress to designer allowing the reader to see the process by which she turned the cultural capital she had amassed coupled with an image and identity she carefully cultivated into Elizabeth Hurley Beach. Through the brand and celebrity engagement with her customers through traditional and social media channels she provides a window into her life and an invitation to live the 'Elizabeth Hurley Beach lifestyle' by acquiring a range of glamorous clothing and accessories that are all skillfully marketed and branded. Raf Simons is a trained Belgian designer who has risen to the top in his field designing both menswear under his own name, and latterly with his distinctive womenswear collections for Jil Sanders, and graduating briefly to the post of creative director at Christian Dior. Nick Rees-Roberts explores his evolution taking the time to trace the influences and inspirations that contributed to his genius. Rees-Roberts brings fabrics and designs to life for us as he draws the connections between aesthetic decisions and the cultural context in the world of art, pop culture, music and architecture that Simons inhabited. We see how Simons respected the foundations of the venerable House of Dior but introduced "neo-modern" codes, sometimes playful and sometimes subversive, in the form of reconfigured silhouettes, color and technology, infusing the brand with surprising new references from sources not explored before in the brand's history.

From these more conventional to heterotopic sites of resistance between producer and consumer we witness brand making and creation of fashion, be it mass marketed, couture or somewhere in between, as a process that is meaningful both to the designers and to consumers, from a distance or up close, depending on the ways in which the brand communication and brand narrative is approached. Fashion branding involves the attempt to creation of order and knowledge through the selling of dreams and the fulfillment of aspirational consumer desires. In the following pages, we gain access to a variety of approaches in a constantly renewing fashion system, which is always ready to incorporate new brands at the expense of the old in the vast arsenal of its collective memory subject and is now having to engage in the process of more interactive brand storytelling with consumers and influencers.

References

Borrelli, L. (1997), Dressing Up and Talking about It: Fashion Writing in *Vogue* from 1968 to 1993, *Fashion Theory*, 1: 3, 247-259.

Bridson, K. and J. Evans. 2004, The secret to a fashion advantage is brand orientation, International journal of retail & distribution management, 32, 8: 403–411.

Church Gibson, P. (2012), *Fashion and Celebrity Culture*. London: Berg.

Clifton, R. and J. Simmons. (2004), *Brands and Branding*. The Economist Volume 45, London: Wiley.

Crane, D. (2000), *Fashion and Its Social Agendas: Class, Gender and Identity n Clothing*, Chicago: University of Chicago Press.

Craik, J. (1994), *The Face of Fashion*, London: Routledge.

Cope, J. and D. Maloney (2016). *Fashion Promotion in Practice*, London: Bloomsbury Books.

Dauriz, L., N Remy and N. Sandri. (2016). *Luxury Branding in the Digital Age*, McKinsey, Retrieved 2017 from: https://www.mckinsey.com/industries/retail/our-insights/luxury-shopping-in-the-digital-age

Davies, C. (2008), Obama 'Sorry' for God and Guns Jibe. *The Guardian*, April 12. Retrieved from: https://www.theguardian.com/world/2008/apr/13/barackobama.uselections2008

Davis, F. (1994) *Fashion Culture and Identity*, Chicago: University of Chicago Press.

Devereux, M. M. and A. Peirson-Smith (2009), *Public Relations in Asia Pacific: Communicating Across Cultures*. London and New York: Wiley.

DeLeon, J. (2017), Willy Chavarria's FW18 collection ramps up the anti-Trump attitude. *HighSnobiety*, Retrieved 2018 https://www.highsnobiety.com/p/willy-chavarria-fall-winter-2018/

Duffy, B. E., and E. Hund. (2015), "Having it All" on social media: Entrepreneurial femininity and self-branding among fashion bloggers. *Social Media+ Society*, 1(2).

Fog, K, C. Budtz and B. Yakaboylu (2005), *Storytelling: branding in practice*. Berlin: Springer-Verlag.

Gad, T. (2016), *Customer Experience Branding: driving engagement through surprise and innovation*, London: Kogan Page.

Gaillard, B. (2016), France : Pour François Fillon, la Colonisation S'apparente à un "Partage de la Culture." Jeune Afrique, August 31. Retrieved from:http://www.jeuneafrique.com/353496/societe/france-francois-fillon-colonisation-sapparente-a-partage-de-culture/

Givhan, R. (2017) "How Donald Trump Had Affected the American Fashion Industry." *The Independent*, February 10. https://www.independent.co.uk/life-style/fashion/donald-trump-affect-american-new-york-fashion-week-us-presidential-election-win-a7565576.html Accessed 2017.

Goffman, E. (1956). *The Presentation of Self in Everyday Life*. New York, NY: Random House.

Hancock, J. H. (2016). *Brand / Story: Cases and Explorations in Fashion Branding*, 2nd ed. New York, NY: Fairchild Publications.

Hancock, J. H., G. Muratovski, V. Manlow and A. Peirson-Smith (2016), *Global Fashion Brands*. Bristol: Intellect Books.

Hameide, K. K. (2011), *Fashion Branding Unraveled*, New York: Fairchild Books.
Hunt, A. and M. Gentzkow. (2017), "Social Media and Fake News in the 2016 Election." *Journal of Economic Perspectives*, 31 (2): 211–36.
Indvik, Lauren. 2016. The 20 Most Influential Personal Style Bloggers: 2016 Edition. *Fashionista.com*. March 14. Retrieved from: http://fashionista.com/2016/03/style-bloggers-2016
Lemire, B. (2010), *The Force of Fashion in Politics*, Farnham, Surrey: Ashagate.
McRobbie, A. (1999), *In the Culture Society: Art, Fashion and Popular Music*, London: Psychology Press.
Nixon, Rob. 2013 *Slow Violence and the Environmentalism of the Poor*. Cambridge, MA: Harvard University Press.
Phan, M., R. Thomas and K. Heine. (2011), Social Media and Luxury Brand Management: The Case of Burberry, *Journal of Global Fashion Marketing*, 2:4, 213–222
Pulse (2018), Top New York fashion buyer to speak at GTBank Fashion Weekend, *Pulse*, 26 October, Retrieved 2018 from: https://www.pulse.ng/lifestyle/fashion/bijou-abiola-top-new-york-fashion-buyer-to-speak-at-gtbank-fashion-weekend-id5660910.html
Sherman, L. (2016), How Tommy Hilfiger is Rewiring for Fashion Immediacy. *The Business of Fashion*. Retrieved from: https://www.businessoffashion.com/articles/intelligence/tommy-hilfiger-gigi-hadid-fashion-immediacy-direct-to-consumer
Siegle, L. (2011), *To Die For: Is Fashion Wearing Out the World?* London: Fourth Estate.
Topinka, R. K. (2010), Foucault, Borges, Heterotopia: Producing Knowledge in Other Spaces. *Foucault Studies*, 9, , pp. 54–70.
Tungate, M. (2008), *Fashion Brands: Branding from Armani to Zara*, 2nd edition, London: Kogan Page.
Wiedmann, K. P., N. Hennigs and S. Langner. (2010), Spreading the Word of Fashion: *Identifying Social Influencers in Fashion Marketing*, *Journal of Global Fashion Marketing*, 1: 3, 142–153.
Zerbo, J. (2016) How this election jolted fashion into action, *Dazed,* 8 November, 11 June Retrieved from http://www.dazeddigital.com/fashion/article/33635/1/how-2016-election-jolted-the-fashion-industry-into-action-vogue-politics. 2018**.**

29

THE MATURATION OF HIP-HOP'S MENSWEAR BRANDS:
Outfitting the urban consumer

Tasha Lewis and Natalie Gray[1]

INTRODUCTION

The hip-hop music genre began amidst the street gang culture of the Bronx. By the 1970s, gangs had divided up their turfs and this was the battleground backdrop where hip-hop took root and flourished. The sound eventually spread downtown, across to Brooklyn and in subsequent decades, across the globe. The first popular commercial rap "song," *Rappers Delight* by the Sugar Hill Gang, was released 1979 (Light 1999). While the music has gained popularity over the last thirty years, and made megastars out of some of its artists, hip-hop fashion has steadily paralleled their success and extended the impact of the music. Relying on their musical success, many artists developed their own clothing lines. The unique fashion taste and aesthetic expanded beyond its urban roots and by the mid-1990s, hip-hop brands were part of the retail assortment in specialty and department stores across the USA. As these definitive street styles filled the closets of middle-class youth, hip-hop fashion leaders continued to challenge societal dress codes by adopting a more sophisticated, tailored look that contrasted its urban roots but signified the entrepreneurial success of some of hip-hop's iconic celebrities.

In the 1990s, the arrival of some of hip-hop's music executives and artists, like Russell Simmons, Sean "Diddy" Combs and Jay-Z, to great levels of wealth and entrepreneurship allowed for the creation of apparel brands that fed the demand for the hip-hop fashion aesthetic that had long been creatively mixed with designer labels and urban fashion trends by its wearers. Consumption of luxury brands like Gucci, Fendi, Louis Vuitton, and Prada were not new to hip-hop, but the idea of creating brands specifically for hip-hop consumers was, and it has paid off for pioneer brands like Rocawear (Jay-Z), Phat Farm (Russell Simmons), and Sean John (Sean "Diddy" Combs). A little over a decade later, these brands, plus graffiti artist Mark Ecko's Ecko Unlimited brand, were described as having potential for further growth in international markets and capable of changing the landscape of American fashion design (Lockwood and Greenberg 2004).

What is *hip-hop* fashion? There is no one consistent look, but rather a popularization of styles based on a subculture group's aesthetic preferences. The extent of this style diversity is clearly outlined by Lewis (2003) and lists the trends found among hip-hop's "b-boys" and "b-girls" in the 1980s into 1990s. This extensive list includes such items as "leather jackets with fake Gucci and other designer insignia," . . . "tracksuits," . . . and "oversized T-shirts" (Lewis 2003: 169). Echoing Gwendolyn O'Neal's (1997) research are the words of rapper Jay-Z in a *Black Book* (Kitwana 2004: 114) interview. He defends hip-hop's adaptation of upper-class, bourgeoisie tastes and states that "instead of emulating an elite lifestyle, they're trying to live it on their own terms" (2004: 114). Spiegler (1996) notes that "hip-hop music, language, and fashion also change because looking good and sporting the latest styles are both very important to core members of the culture" (1996: 34). *Black Book* magazine continues:

---

[1] From Tasha Lewis and Natalie Gray, (2013), The Maturation of Hip Hop's Menswear Brands: Outfitting the Urban Consumer, Fashion Practice, Volume 5, Issue 2, Taylor & Francis.

In the last decade, hip-hop has become a capitalist's dream. Given its wide visibility and knack for trend setting, its stars are at the forefront of promoting a wide range of high-end products, making it nearly impossible to distinguish the point where hip-hop ends and conspicuous consumption begins. (2004: 14)

Hip-hop is a powerful mix of influences, especially for clothing—allowing for the interaction of two theories of fashion diffusion: both trickle-down and trickle-up. The trickle-down, or upper-class, theory of fashion leadership proposes that new styles are adopted or started by groups in higher social classes and these styles are later adopted by those in the lower social classes (Simmel 1904). This theory explains the early emergence of hip-hop fashion in the 1980s and 1990s when consumers adopted aspirational labels, not typically marketed to them.

Preppy looks trickled down to African-American youth in the first national wave of hip-hop influence. "This group of black yuppy wannabes or 'buppies' were drawn to Hilfiger because of its all-American, WASP-y, country club feeling—it was exclusive and aspirational" (Kitwana 2004: 114). The immense popularity of the brand among members of the hip-hop subculture provided Hilfiger with substantial capital and widespread brand awareness. This success eventually allowed the brand to pursue global expansion (Lockwood 2010: 30).

Some other designer labels also took note of the trendsetting influence of hip-hop culture and embraced elements for their own collections; thus marking the beginning of hip-hop's "trickle-up" influence on fashion. In 1991, Isaac Mizrahi incorporated hip-hop accessories like wide-brimmed hats and African-inspired medallions into his runway show. Anne Klein even introduced a clothing line especially based on rap music and launched the line at Bloomingdale's with live performances of rap music. (Solomon and Rabolt 2009: 85).

Hip-hop has also adopted and then transformed traditional or "old world" luxury symbols and made them modern-day, "cool" commodities. Rapper LL Cool J (Todd Smith) wore a Kangol hat back in the 1980s, when few Americans knew anything about the European hat maker—but its association with hip-hop would invigorate the brand.

Hip-hop's influence continued to grow into the 1990s and subcultural leadership also explained the trends of the mid-1990s that were reinterpreted from hip-hop culture for mass retailers, or what can be called the "commercialization" of a style.

HIP-HOP CONSUMERS

The transformation of the hip-hop "look" to a mass fashion trend, while removing many of the original connotations, pushed hip-hop fashion and its pioneer labels like Rocawear and Phat Farm to iconic brand status. According to Torelli *et al.* (2010), iconic brands are heavily laden with symbols for consumers "who frequently rely on them to communicate to others who they are or aspire to be" (2010: 115). These early menswear brands were based on the lifestyle and preferences of the youth cohort that witnessed hip-hop's global expansion from the Bronx. Styles offered by the brands reflected the current trends in hip-hop at the time—including baggy jeans, oversized T-shirts, sport jerseys, and tracksuits. The brands also possessed aspirational connotations by their association with hip-hop celebrities who had reached levels of unprecedented success.

In 1996, consumer data hinted at the growing influence of hip-hop on American youth. One survey found that over 50 percent of youth aged 12–20 and 38 percent of those aged 21–24 were strong followers of rap music; and another survey showed teen fashion preferences for hip-hop-inspired styles like baggy clothes, hooded sweatshirts, and pro sports apparel (Spiegler 1996: 31). However, a few years into the millennium, when hip-hop's menswear market was estimated to be worth US$10 billion (Clark 2003: 2), a noticeable shift in style preferences was emerging as hip-hop consumers, particularly males, began looking for more tailored clothing (Bailey 2005: 38). Hip-hop brands were slow in responding to this shift, a miss confessed by hip-hop music mogul and founder of Phat Farm clothing, Russell Simmons, who noted that the change in dress among hip-hop's most elite artists, like Jay-Z, from baggy shirts and jeans to suits and

French cuff shirts, should have prompted hip-hop brands into swift action. A few labels did make an effort to translate hip-hop's shifting upscale aesthetic into male fashion, including Simmons himself who introduced the Phat Farm Collection of men's suits. Rapper Jay-Z added a premium sportswear line called Wash House into his Rocawear label, Sean "Diddy" Combs even opened a flagship store on 5th Avenue stocked with men's suits and accessories, and graffiti artist Mark Ecko began his Cut & Sew premium collection (Bailey 2005: 38). The youth of the 1990s, who grew up listening to rap music and wearing the styles seen in hip-hop videos, were in their early twenties and mid-thirties in 2005, and likely looking for clothing that was more sophisticated or professional.

This psychographic is not exclusively African-American; rather it contains multiple demographic profiles, including Hispanic, Asian, Native, and even White Americans, who as youth consumed hip-hop music and culture (McBride 2007; Stoute 2011). Consumers in their teens to early fifties are likely purchasers of hip-hop fashion, with a core group in their late twenties through early forties (Simmons Market Research Bureau, unpublished data). The hip-hop clothing market is predominantly made up of menswear brands, and categories of male consumers in the core age group include: *elite men* who are global travelers (median age = 42) and *male students and grads* who are just entering the workforce (median age = 26) (Miller 2012). The diversity of the hip-hop psychographic also has economic implications. With a steady increase of college graduates likely seeking professional white-collar jobs, hip-hop may still be the soundtrack of their life, but their job roles may not always allow them to wear the casual street styles of hip-hop fashion on a regular basis.

APPEALING TO TODAY'S URBAN CONSUMER: RUSSELL SIMMONS' URBAN GRADUATE

Noting the lack of fashion choices for the maturing hip-hop demographic, hip-hop's most notable innovator of men's fashion, Russell Simmons, decided to put his signature aesthetic back on the market. Russell Simmons says, ". . . these hip-hop aficionados, who aspired to own a Bentley and wear as many diamonds as they could, also wore clothes from the Tommy Hilfiger and Ralph Lauren collections" (Greenberg 2003b: 4). In 1992 Simmons started Phat Farm, a mix of traditional American and hip-hop style for men, with the tagline "Classic American Flava." This unique mix is the reason Simmons said the upside-down American flag was the logo for the label (Greenberg 2003b: 4). In describing the brand mythologies associated with both Polo Ralph Lauren and Tommy Hilfiger, Manlow (2011) notes that each brands' designers "deconstruct America and reassembles it according to his parameters" (2011: 92). This is also clearly the case for Simmons—although he references the elite, upper-class American lifestyle, he is also adept at differentiating his brand using the hip-hop culture that is part of his American experience. His Phat Farm advertisements prominently featured African-American males outfitted in Oxford shirts, blazers, denim or khakis, and accessorized with sneakers and a baseball cap against the backdrop of a yacht or golf course.

In 2004 Simmons sold Phat Fashions to Kellwood, the retail conglomerate of such conservative labels as Sag Harbor and Briggs, for US$140 million. This purchase seemed to be following the trend of hip-hop labels being acquired by larger, more conservative brands—in 2003 hip-hop brand Enyce was acquired by Liz Claiborne as part of the company's efforts to gain a portion of the US$10 billion men's urban market (Clark 2003: 2). After the sale of his Phat Fashions labels, Simmons stated that he had learned much from the all-American conservative brands, but that "those brands have gone ice cold" and that "Phat Farm is posing a tangible challenge to the dominant brands of the Nineties" (Wilson 2004: 152). Simmons was correct in his understanding of the mass appeal of his labels, and perhaps unknowingly wise in his decision to sell them off. Mass acceptance in the fashion cycle is followed by a phase-out stage (Dickerson 2003). Having capitalized on the rise and peak of hip-hop fashion, Simmons was reportedly moving into jewelry and automobiles as new ventures (Wilson 2004: 152). However in 2010, Simmons returned to menswear and his retail partner, Macy's, announced that his latest menswear line,

Argyleculture, would have floor space next to Tommy Hilfiger and Ralph Lauren. Argyleculture, according to Simmons, is a line for the male consumer who has matured in his tastes and is looking for an edgier style. He describes his line as having:

> Heathery argyle sweaters with a little silk to make them pop, cool corduroys with a different cut, off-colored denims, blue blazers with gold buttons and collars with a burgundy underside, simple argyle sweaters with a fresh point of view, and Oxford shirts with soft liberating fabrics. (Moin 2010: 2)

In a recent interview regarding Argyleculture, when asked to define his urban graduate customer, Simmons expertly outlined the history of hip-hop clothing and the impact of its influence on the urban-minded consumer:

> At one moment 80% of the hip hop audience was non-African-American. Those people were very entrenched in this cultural phenomenon that was heavily based in African-American culture and a great percentage of this 80%—about 50% to 70%—grew up and really identified so much that they think of their childhood as a Jay-Z record or a RUN-DMC record. They think of those things as inspiration for their youth and they take a lot of that with them. and more than that, there is a culture that 50% or more identify with—the entire culture, not just the record, that contributed to the soundtrack of their youth . . . That whole idea of urban culture finding a space in the mainstream and becoming the mainstream is a reality. So this post-racial America that is an aspiration for many, it's real for a few, but it's an aspiration—it's good because you have a huge piece of America that is underserved. There's a large underserved community of people who are not being spoken to by lily-white American brands, and they can be lily-white themselves but certainly they don't want to be that boring. Somebody grew up and didn't want to buy Ralph Lauren. Somebody grew up and thought Tommy Hilfiger was [for] the previous generation or worse, it was just bland. Those are good brands by the way, but there is something that speaks their language . . . All of the cool kids in the last 20 years that grew up on urban culture buy into a lot of American mainstream products and they need something that speaks a little bit more of their language. And that's what this mission is. The urban graduate is there but under-served.
> (Russell Simmons, personal communication)

Simmons is making a very strong reference to the cultural branding around his new label, which is following the life cycle of his male consumer. He also demonstrates an awareness of the multicultural appeal of his brand based on the mass cultural adoption of hip-hop culture throughout the USA.

BRAND EQUITY AND DECLINE OF BRANDS

Kaplan (2008: 1) noted that the hip-hop clothing market was being plagued by declining sales, which was evidenced by the bankruptcy and even closings of specialty stores like Against All Odds and Up Against the Wall (Bailey 2005), which catered to hip-hop consumers. These changes were likely signals of the continual shifting in hip-hop styles toward a broader consumer base and influence.

Like Simmons' Argyleculture, Sean John by Sean "Diddy" Combs was also allotted significant floor space in Macy's, as of 2010, when the retailer entered into an agreement with Combs to be the sole distributor his sportswear line (Lipke 2010). The brand is being presented as a contemporary menswear line in a section of the store called "Impulse," strategically placed between the young men's and designer collections. Combs commented that the placement represents "the way the line has evolved from the sweat suits we were known for. Now we go from the block to the boardroom" (Lipke 2010). Russell Simmons has witnessed the arrival of all of the brands that followed his lead in later years and he commented on why some have failed and others have remained and thrived—mainly due to brand equity:

> The old regime that forced its way in the doors had to build a brand bigger than the artist that had credibility of its own. You can't just put an artist's name on a clothing company. The early brands, myself, FUBU, Mecca, Enyce—I was not a brand because I was Russell Simmons as much as I had become credible after years

of losses. Brand equity doesn't just transfer from one brand to another. You are a singer don't just give me clothes it takes time. It was about a consistency and vision. It gets a little kick-start but that is as much a curse as it is a kick start. You have to be a competitor . . . I have to look at Ralph and say can I compete with him, I have to look at Lacoste, I have to look at Tommy, I have to look at Calvin, I have to look at all the men's designers and say am I men's designer? Not Russell Simmons the singer, Russell Simmons the yogi, Russell Simmons the philanthropist, it's Russell Simmons the designer. It takes time and consistency. To our audience we say who we are but then we have to prove it. (Russell Simmons, personal communication)

By benchmarking his success against other iconic American menswear brands, Simmons manages to maintain a strategic place in the menswear market and his placement in Macy's between two of those brands, Ralph Lauren and Tommy Hilfiger, serves as a visual reminder of the cultural niche he has established. Simmons was also owner of one of hip-hop's most successful women's brands, Baby Phat, and when asked if he would be adding women's clothing to his Argyleculture brand, his response was that he did believe there was a component and that he "had a vision for it"; however, the menswear line was his current priority due to the variety of the assortment. Clear evidence that he had been researching the climate of the women's hip-hop market was his comment on the recent debut of the womenswear collection Dw by Kanye West,

Kanye [West] . . . I think he'll deliver something. You could hardly call him a hip hop designer but Kanye is a designer. He's for real. No one knows that. The rest of the world needs to know it but he's needs to prove it. His name got us to look at it and they gave him terrible reviews . . . but they are paying attention. And he is going to deliver. I believe in him. (Russell Simmons, personal communication)

FUTURE OF URBAN BRANDS

Peter Shapiro's *Rough Guide to Hip-Hop* (2005) defines the roots of hip-hop as a "celebration of the art of survival, as an art form that sprang from the hopes and desires of kids who were damned" (2005: 182). In just over thirty years, hip-hop has evolved from its roots as an underground music genre into an unprecedented global phenomenon that shatters cultural, geographic, and socioeconomic barriers.

Along with the dispersion of the hip-hop culture amongst diverse groups of Americans, the rapidly changing nature of fashion in our postmodern society makes it difficult to determine the next fashion phase for hip-hop. Hip-hop has been infused with traditional American labels, sportswear, and *haute couture*; so where will the next wave of designers turn for inspiration? Many of hip-hop's artists opted to create their own labels, but a resilient few, like those created by Russell Simmons, Jay-Z, and Sean Combs, have proven to be iconic brands with staying power.

The demand for a taste of the "American Dream" on one's own terms, as communicated through hip-hop, has reached global scale (Chang 2007: 58). The association of hip-hop music with American culture and its global popularity, especially among youth—also bodes well for brands that embody hip-hop culture, making increased global consumption a possibility. In Shanghai among 15–25 year olds, 37.1 percent identify rap and hip-hop as their musical preference (Smith 2007). These statistics are similar to those found among American teens in the mid-1990s (Spiegler 1996: 30) and can suggest the next wave of hip-hop clothing consumers.

Over the last decade many students and working-class Chinese have been writing rap as a form of self-expression . . . Before that, kids listened to hip-hop in English but maybe less than 1 percent could actually begin to understand . . . Wang Li, a 24-year-old from Dongbei, became interested in hip-hop when he heard American rap group Public Enemy in the mid-'90s. He said rapping helped him deal with bitterness that comes with realizing he is one of the millions left out of China's economic boom. (Wang 2009)

For new brands, such as Simmons' Argyleculture, that recognize and target a mature hip-hop enthusiast, a receptive global environment makes it easier to penetrate markets where hip-hop culture has already been cultivated. While hip-hop's lifestyle and message has grown in popularity amongst international youth culture, this global group of young consumers will also mature and likely seek brands that still resonate with the culture.

References

Bailey, Lee. 2005. "It's Time for Urban Renewal—Insiders Say the Once—Hot Hip-Hop Apparel Business is in Flux. One Thing is Clear: The Old Rules Don't Apply." *DNR* February 14.

Chang, Justin. 2007. "It's a Hip Hop World." *Foreign Policy* November/December: 58–65.

Clark, Evan. 2003. "Claiborne Said Eyeing Enyce." *Women's Wear Daily* November 11.

Dickerson, K. G. 2003. *Inside the Fashion Business.* Upper Saddle River, NJ: Pearson Education.

Kitwana, Bakari. 2004. "Hip Hop & High Society." *Black Book* Spring: 112–17.

Lewis, VanDyk. 2003. "Dilemmas in African Diaspora Fashion." *Fashion Theory* 7(2): 163–90.

Light, Alan. 1999. *The VIBE History of Hip Hop.* New York: Random House.

Lipke, David. 2010. "Diddy's Big Deal." *Women's Wear Daily* May 6: 1. http://search.proquest.com/docview/275991770?accountid=10267 (accessed February 21, 2012).

Lockwood, Lisa. 2010. "The Stroll and Chou Years." *Women's Wear Daily* September 10. http://search.proquest.com/docview/851541549? accountid=10267 (accessed March 3, 2012).

Lockwood, Lisa and Julee Greenberg. 2004. "The Mega Branding of Hip-Hop." *Women's Wear Daily* February 11. http://search.proquest.com/docview/231159670?accountid=10267. (accessed December 10, 2005).

McBride, James. 2007. "Hip-Hop Planet." *National Geographic* 211(4). http://search.proquest.com/docview/200960448?accountid=10267 (accessed March 15, 2012).

Miller, Richard K. 2012. "Male Consumers." *Consumer Behavior.* http://search.ebscohost.com/login.aspx?direct=true&db=bth&AN=27788326&site=ehost-live (accessed March 20, 2012).

Moin, David. 2010. "Macy's Relaunches Simmons Argyleculture." *Women's Wear Daily* September 29. http://search.proquest.com/docview/757008945?accountid=10267 (accessed March 2, 2012).

O'Neal, Gwendolyn. 1997. "African-American Aesthetics of Dress." In Ann Marie Fiore and Patricia Ann Kimle (eds) *Understanding Aesthetics for the Merchandising and Design Professional*, pp. 108–9. New York: Fairchild Publications.

Shapiro, Peter. 2005. *The Rough Guide to Hip-Hop.* London: Rough Guides.

Simmel, George. 1904. "Fashion." *International Quarterly* 10 (October): 130–55.

Smith, Clyde. 2007. "China Youth Culture Study of 15 to 25 Year Olds." *ProHipHop: Hip Hop Marketing & Business News* September 28. http://www.prohiphop.com/2007/09/china-youth-cul.html (accessed March 29, 2012).

Solomon, Michael R. and Nancy J. Rabolt, 2009. *Consumer Behavior in Fashion.* Upper Saddle River, NJ: Pearson-Prentice Hall.

Spiegler, Marc. 1996. "Marketing Street Culture: Bringing Hip-Hop Style to the Mainstream." *American Demographics* November: 29–34.

Stoute, Steve. 2011. The Tanning of America: How Hip-Hop Created a Culture That Rewrote the Rules of the New Economy. New York: Gotham Books.

Torelli, Carlos J., Hean Tat Keh and Chi-Yue Chiu. 2010. "Cultural Symbolism of Brands." In Barbara Loken, Rohini Ahluwalia and Michael J. Houston (eds) *Brands and Brand Management*, pp. 113–29. New York: Routledge.

Wang, Jimmy. 2009. "Now Hip-Hop, Too, Is Made in China." *The New York Times* January 23. http://www.nytimes.com/2009/01/24/arts/music/24hiphop.html?pagewanted=all (accessed March 29, 2012).

Wilson, Eric. 2004. "Phat Fashion." *W* March: 152.

THE HABITUS OF ELIZABETH HURLEY:
Celebrity, fashion, and identity branding

Lee Barron

In 2005, as in 1994, Elizabeth Hurley was the focus of widespread media coverage and the two temporal moments, separated by little more than a decade were based exclusively upon the act of wearing clothes. In 1994 it was for a modified couture black dress; in 2005 it was for modeling a bikini drawn from her soon-to-be-launched swimwear and beachwear collection. In assessing Elizabeth Hurley's continuing cultural significance, Bowyer argues that "the media's obsession with Elizabeth Hurley is such that scarcely a day goes by without her appearing in a magazine or newspaper" . . . a "flashbulb courtesan who enslaves the paparazzi like no British women since Princess Diana" (2003: 15, 254). However, the focus of much of this media reporting persistently has little or nothing to do with the professional activities of Elizabeth Hurley. Rather, it focuses almost exclusively upon her lifestyle as a "professional celebrity" (*BBC News,* 2002). Indeed, news reports concerning her fashion range went hand-in-hand with even more media coverage dedicated to her 40th birthday on June 10 2005.

This article has everything to do with her professional activities. It is focused on the manner in which her multifaceted career is now centrally located within the world of fashion; not merely as a model advertising the wares of other producers, but now as a designer creating and advertising her own "look." I argue, revisiting applications made by Bourdieu to fashion, principally by Craik, that she represents a potent contemporary purveyor of a specific "habitus" via her own clothing range and accessories: Elizabeth Hurley Beach, launched in 2005, in which she is simultaneously present in both the "front" and "back" regions of the enterprise. In this sense, Elizabeth Hurley represents the fusion of fashion *and* embodiment, a figure inextricably linked to sophisticated couture, but now also as a designer, establishing and marketing her own "tasteful look." Although perhaps stretching the conceptual framework somewhat, I wish to explore the ways in which the elusive concept of habitus can be applied to fashion at the level of agency, literally in this case, in relation to a single "fashionable" individual. Because, whatever its successes and longevity (it is sold in exclusive clothing stores across the world), with the establishment of Elizabeth Hurley Beach, Elizabeth Hurley has created a marketable and identifiable "brand" that is built entirely on her image and persona. Therefore, Elizabeth Hurley Beach not only represents a range of glamorous clothing and accessories to wear but, through marketing techniques and media coverage, it also represents a set of instructions on how to wear her garments, and essentially how to replicate, albeit fleetingly and imaginatively, the essence of *being* Elizabeth Hurley.

ELIZABETH HURLEY: ACTRESS BECOMES MODEL

There are few media celebrities whose key moments of cultural impact can be identified with such precision as that of Elizabeth Hurley's. This moment was the 1994 premiere of Mike Newell's film *Four Weddings and a Funeral* where she wore a Versace dress fastened together with safety pins, an image that made newspaper front pages the following day, and an event all the more striking because she had no connection with the film whatsoever. As Smith comments, "It was perhaps the only time in movie history that a frock has been a career turning point" (A. Smith 2001: 88). Although she was an actress of some experience before this event, most notably within the Dennis Potter scripted television drama *Christabel* (1988), it is from this episode that her celebrity status would grow, so much so that this single event would ensure that Elizabeth Hurley would become indelibly part of popular culture and inspire "trillions of words" (Derrick and Muir 2003: 320). It was also the moment that forever forged the link between Hurley and the world of fashion.

Following the *Four Weddings and a Funeral* premiere, she would rapidly become a globally recognized figure and represent a key exemplar of Daniel Boorstin's classic definition of the "celebrity" as "a person who is well-known for their well-knownness . . . by differentiating their own personality from those of competitors in the public arena" (quoted in Turner 2004: 5). Although, Elizabeth Hurley has downplayed the significance of the Versace dress:

> I had no idea people would make such a fuss over it. Why should I? I've been wearing sexy dresses all my life. I was in Cannes at the time it all blew up and my press agent told me about it, so I had some idea of what was starting up, but . . . it's all so silly (Shone 1994: 34).

In Boorstin's frame of reference, the Versace dress was the engine for Hurley's cultural differentiation. However, she was also assisted by further supporting "players" in this process. As Evans (2005) points out, celebrity is not merely based upon the possession of "charisma," (or based on charisma at all) but rather, celebrity is a resource created by a host of "interlocking media" such as: the press, films, or television programs. As Rojek elaborates, celebrities are cultural "fabrications:"

> Their impact on the public may appear to be intimate and spontaneous. In fact, celebrities are carefully mediated through what might be termed chains of attraction. No celebrity now acquires public recognition without the assistance of cultural intermediaries who operate to stage-manage celebrity presence in the eyes of the public. "Cultural intermediaries" is the collective term for agents, publicists, marketing personnel, promoters, photographers . . . (2001: 10).

In Elizabeth Hurley's case, these cultural intermediaries were initially the paparazzi and Versace, agents that opened the way for subsequent cultural opportunities. As Anthony states of her role as Agent Kensington in *Austin Powers,* arguably her most successful film role: "she landed that part because her image was already marketable (and spoofable), courtesy of her role as the paparazzi's favored muse. She was a star of the photo opportunity long before she was given the opportunity to be a film star" (1999: 145). However, since the late 1990s, and certainly in 2005, Elizabeth Hurley has firmly taken over this management role for herself, and for very sound financial reasons. As Turner contends:

> Celebrity also makes money for the individual concerned . . . The celebrity can develop their public persona as a commercial asset and their career choices, in principle, should be devoted to that objective. As the asset appreciates—as the celebrity's fame spreads—so does its earning capacity (2004: 34–5).

And Elizabeth Hurley's career has perfectly embraced the post-Fordist work ethic of "perpetual innovation" (Kline *et al.* 2003). Since the mid-1990s she has engaged in a determined process of synergy located usually at a corporate level (Murray 2005; Tunstall and Palmer 1991). As Buckley and Gundle assert:

> *That* dress did wonders for her own profile, but it also enhanced the image of Versace: because of Elizabeth Hurley's appearance at the world premiere of *Four Weddings and a Funeral*. Front-page colour pictures in newspapers such as the 'Sun', the 'Mirror and the 'Evening Standard', as well as the broadsheets, turned Versace into a household name that functioned as a byword for show-stopping, sexy clothes (2000: 341).

Elizabeth Hurley's appearance at the film premiere resulted in synergism that manifested itself on a number of distinct levels. Firstly, it boosted Elizabeth Hurley's film career and led to a modeling career (at the age of twenty-eight); secondly, it raised Versace's profile, boosting "his reputation as the emperor of glam frocks" (Martin 1997: 97); and thirdly, it advertised *Four Weddings and a Funeral*. In the wake of this synergistic aura, Hurley (with Hugh Grant) established her own film production company, Simian Films, producing two films: the medical thriller *Extreme Measures* (dir. Michael Apted, 1996) and the Mafia-themed comedy *Mickey Blue Eyes* (dir. Kelly Makin, 1999). Because Hollywood glamour and celebrity are essential components "on which entertainment branding ultimately depends" (Murray 2005: 416), the move into film production was tied directly to the growing fame and reputation of Hugh Grant, which proved to be powerful lever for raising money for film deals.

GOODBYE VERSACE, HELLO ELIZABETH HURLEY BEACH: MODEL BECOMES DESIGNER

In 2005, Elizabeth Hurley, having produced two films, disbanded Simian films and moved: "From Hurley the model/actress/film producer to Hurley the entrepreneur with a product to sell. Elizabeth Hurley Beach, her own collection of bikinis, tops and summer dresses . . . now available at exclusive department stores in New York, London, Sydney and Moscow" (Grieg 2005: 142–5). The fact that she designs, produces, and models the garments, in a fundamental sense, means that Elizabeth Hurley Beach *is* Elizabeth Hurley.

Clothing has long been read as an integral aspect of symbolic communication, as Cunningham and Voso Lab argue: "clothing plays an important role in our lives . . . [because] . . . it is often through its meaning that we substantiate our sense of self and our place in society" (1991: 1). According to Craik (1994), fashion performs the functions of a "mask" disguising the "true" nature of the body or person. Hence, "fashion and dress articulate the body in culture: fashion produces discourses on the body and how to adorn it, dress is the translation of fashion into everyday practice" (Entwistle 2000: 237). Codes of dress represent "technical devices" that can express the relationship between a specific body and its lived "milieu," the space occupied by bodies and constituted by bodily actions, namely, Bourdieu's (1984) concept of habitus. Habitus refers to specialized techniques and embedded knowledge that enable people to navigate the different levels of life such as:

> The unconscious dispositions, the classification schemes, taken-for-granted preferences which are evident in the individual's sense of the appropriateness and validity of [their] taste for cultural goods and practices. . .as well as being "inscribed on the body" through body techniques and modes of self-presentation (Craik 1994: 4).

Such techniques and modes of self-presentation constitute a habitus or more simply, a "lifestyle" (P. Smith 2001), a way of being in the world. Although the concept of habitus is linked fundamentally with class, a "variant of class practice" (Lury 1996: 86), "habitus can, and indeed arguably must, be related to gendered practice, because it is a constructive conceptual tool for understanding how dress styles are gendered and how gender is actively reproduced through dress" (Entwistle 2001: 37). In relation to habitus, bodies are "made up," they are constructed through the acquisition of body techniques; it "manifests itself in our most practical activities, such as the way we eat, walk, talk" (Ritzer and Goodman, 2003). Regarding the source of such instructions, Craik states that social actors map out codes of conduct through fashion behavior and the fashion "role models" and instruction guides produced within popular culture. As Jenks points out, a sense of habitus may be rendered as "style" (1993: 14). Thus, the social actor's habitus of clothing creates a "face" that positively creates an identity and facilitates self-formation and self-presentation: "fashions symbolize sex, age, social position, and any given complex of acts, gestures, movements, and intentions" (Anspach 1967: 239). However, a fashion system that embodies the denotation of acceptable codes and conventions also sets limits to clothing behavior, it prescribes acceptable and prohibits "unacceptable" modes of clothing the body. Therefore, codes of dress are never static; the habitus constantly revises the "rules of the fashion game" (Craik 1994).

In 1994, Elizabeth Hurley arguably revised the rules of the "fashion game." The premiere of *Four Weddings and a Funeral* not only paved the way for film roles but also established Elizabeth Hurley as a major fashion figure, whose recognition factor (via a *Tatler* magazine cover) led to her joining and spearheading worldwide fashion campaigns for Estee Lauder; thereby consolidating her own global level of recognition in the process via mediated images of herself as model on the covers and pages of magazines devoted to film, fashion, and gossip/lifestyles. As Gilligan contends, models and film stars exist "not as a single iconic image, but as a multiplicity of images, a ceaseless flow of self transformation and masquerade" (2000: 246). Regarding Elizabeth Hurley, perhaps nowhere is this embrace of masquerade more observable than within the Serge Normant *et al.* fashion photography collection *Femme Fatale* (2001), which also includes models and actresses such as Cindy Crawford, Milla Jovovich, Isabella Rossellini, and Gisele Bundchen. Within *Femme Fatale,* Elizabeth Hurley is cast in the fashions and hairstyles of various periods in twentieth-century history that capture the multifarious looks and styles of Mata Hari, Josephine Baker, and a pastiche of the archetypal Bond girl.

However, Elizabeth Hurley is not a "postmodern" performer. Although her image is globally mediated, and, in the example discussed below, she has playfully toyed with her image, unlike Madonna or Kylie Minogue, she is not a "postmodern chameleon" nor is she a progressive image "bricoleur" (Gauntlett 2004; Tetzlaff 1993). Arguably Hurley's defining moment as a *bona fide* celebrity owes, in Wollen's terms, more to modernism than to postmodernism with its "decorative excess and stylistic extravagance" (Connor 1997: 213–14). Regarding *that* Versace dress, costing £2,580, and held together at the sides by twenty-four outsized gold safety pins, it represented a definitive "modernist" instance "of dressing oneself with attention to effect" (Barnard 1996: 9). Regarding identity, Kellner argues that within traditional societies, identity was perceived to be "fixed, solid, and stable" (1992: 141). However, within the "age of modernity" identity becomes more "mobile, multiple, personal, self-reflexive, and subject to change and innovation...Yet the forms of identity in modernity are also relatively substantial and fixed" (Kellner 1992: 143). This conception of identity is particularly applicable to Elizabeth Hurley's image,

because whatever guises she temporarily adopts, they are ultimately reducible to a connotative "master status," that of Elizabeth Hurley, "the quintessential English rose," "utterly English," "slightly naughty head girl," "the eternal sixth-former" (Anthony 1999: 145; Brinton 2003: 16; Gannon 2006: 36). And if, as Rojek asserts: "postmodernism associates modernity with the heaviness of being" (in Rogers 1999: 146), then this encapsulates the "essence" of Elizabeth Hurley, she endures as a cultural and fashion "icon" who remains always effectively *Elizabeth Hurley,* a factor which is fundamental to Elizabeth Hurley Beach.

Yet, Hurley herself had to engage in a process of image construction post-*Four Weddings*. It was widely noted that she lost weight and altered other aspects of her image, such as resculpting her eyebrows, a feature that would subsequently become something of a Hurley fashion trademark. Such celebrity-body media scrutiny and transformation would subsequently become an endemic aspect of the ascension to celebrity, from Jennifer Aniston, Jade Goody, and Nicole Richie to identify but a few examples. However, once it had been modified, Hurley's "fashion-system" would become highly symbolic, and specific. Her clothing acts as a particular sign system, as a set of cultural and bodily signifiers, as an act of "symbolic communication" and the transmission of an aesthetic role (Barnard 1996; Barthes 1990; Lurie 1981; Wilson 2003); all befitting a women who has been dubbed "quite literally the face that launched a thousand facelifts" (Grieg 2005: 142); a system synonymous with designer-clothed sophistication. As a universally recognized "celebrity," and as a model for Estee Lauder, Elizabeth Hurley represents an idealized feminine image. As Craik argues, fashion has emerged as one of the principal ways of providing "techniques of femininity" throughout the twentieth century because modeling came "to epitomize dominant characteristics of Western femininity: the importance of appearance; fetishisation of the body; the discipline and labour associated with 'beauty' and body maintenance" (1994: 70). Elizabeth Hurley herself perfectly illustrates this, when for example she revealed in an article within the fashion magazine *Elle,* which Bourdieu dubbed "an index of investment in the aesthetics of dress" (1984:

378), the range of measures, both cosmetic and physical, that must be undertaken in order to construct and maintain her image: "There can't be a girl in the world who doesn't long for a flatter stomach so immediately start eating less . . . [and] even though it's loathsome, take every opportunity to throw yourself on the floor to do some sit-ups" (Hurley 2000: 63). And her status as a mediated image following the Versace dress event in 1994 was such that:

> From that day to today, nearly eight years later, I've been photographed non-stop and paparazzied almost to death, my weight is constantly discussed nationally and my body dissected by complete strangers in the media almost on a daily basis (Hurley 2002: 95).

Hence, her position as an "idealized" (by some) woman can be articulated by the view that she "symbolically" connotes certain values, and conforms to a specific bodily habitus, those ways of being that are inscribed on the body through body techniques and modes of self-presentation. As Donatella Versace has stated of Hurley:

> One of the most important aspects is the way a person wears and carries a dress. It is a question of attitude and spirit, which Liz embodies as she wears clothes in such as glamorous and fascinating way. Not only does she have the body to wear Versace, but one can tell that she has the personality and just the right amount of attitude (*Arena* 2001 116).

If habitus is symbolically mediated and learned through experience, then Hurley ably demonstrates the process of such transmission as a possessor of a desirable, "fashionable" body, albeit a body that she acknowledges takes extreme discipline to both achieve and maintain. Body maintenance is a social component that she always emphasizes, that looking good means disciplined commitment:

> Ninety-eight per cent of the women who come up to me say, "What do you eat? How did you lose weight after your baby? Do you have any diet secrets?" And I think that they're quite relieved when I say that the only way to lose weight is to go on a strict diet. I have to be a little hungry all of the time, because if I ate what I liked, I'd be two dress sizes bigger (in Syson 2005: 85).

But if Elizabeth Hurley herself is subject to a socially prescribed set of beauty/style norms, she is now channeling her own fashion habitus through Elizabeth Hurley Beach, and on two fronts: as a model for the swimwear, and as a designer. As Craik (1994) argues, a salient feature of Western consumer fashion has been the rise of fashion designers as authoritative sources of advice about clothes and, by extension, related techniques of femininity. Fashion designers represent an expert group that possesses the ability to pronounce what is in vogue, and what most definitely is not. Craik argues that the reason for their continued success and influence stems from their role in defining body–habitus relations through the cut of clothes—they impose their will and extol a version of a fashionable lifestyle. Successful designers (usually men) have consequently become arbiters of taste within society. Elizabeth Hurley, then, adds to the growing presence of female fashion designers. And forging a specific gender image, a definitive habitus, is at the heart of her promotion of Elizabeth Hurley Beach, which is built centrally upon the cultural signifiers of her own body image and lifestyle. As she states with regard to the motivation for her clothing: "almost all of it is for me" (Shuckburgh 2005: 26).

Explaining the inspiration behind her swimwear range, she reveals: "I've always been obsessed with summer clothes and glamorous vacations. . .So to me, this collection epitomises jet-set glamour. It's quite aspirational" (Syson 2005: 80). And her lifestyle is undeniably one to which many might aspire. As Grieg asserts: "The pretty daughter of an Irish-Catholic army major from Hampshire has moved up to an extraordinary superstar life of first-class tickets, private jets, VIP treatment, front-row catwalk seats and invitations to go on safari with Sir Elton John" (2005: 142). Consequently, Elizabeth Hurley Beach offers the possibility of achieving a taste of such a "jet-set" life, if only imaginatively through the choice of purchasing her swimwear.

With regard to the public achieving of "iconic glamour," there are perhaps certain parallels with earlier fashion icons such as Princess Diana, whose "look" was marketed to the public within *The Princess of Wales Fashion Handbook*. As Craik (1994) points out, *The Princess of Wales Fashion Handbook* was about how the Princess of Wales acquired a sense of "style" and built up a wardrobe, makeup, and a set of looks. The book also took her "look" and used it as a role model for ordinary women, but with modifications to suit "flawed" unfashionable body types. Elizabeth Hurley Beach is similarly pitched to the "imperfect" as much as the "perfect," because there are "ways of wearing all the pieces to suit older and younger people" (Shuckburgh 2005: 26). As Hurley states:

> If you're among the vast majority of women who dread wearing bikinis, there are a few things you can certainly do to make it less traumatizing. The first thing is obvious: invest in a really good bikini that is as flattering as is physically possible. Almost everyone has a different size top and bottom, me included, so seek out brands (like mine!) for which you can buy the top and bottom separately. It makes a massive difference (2005b: 25).

Such apparent candor underscores the centrality of her personality within the clothing range. As she has stated: "this is not a licensed line, I've done it all myself. . . .I dealt with the designing, the production and distribution" (Fearon 2005: 14). Elizabeth Hurley Beach represents the marketing of her distinctive brand identity, an integral aspect for market success because branding "is essential as a recognised sign of value in a business world where customers have multiple choices, and where investors need a symbol of acknowledged capacity for value creation" (Castells 2001: 76) and is an essential component to delineate corporate personalities (Olins 2003). As Baudrillard illustrates:

> The concept of "brand," which is advertising's prime concept, sums up the prospects for a "language" of consumption rather well. All products . . . are now offered under brand names. Every product "worthy of the name" has a brand . . . The brand's primary function is to designate a product; its secondary function is to mobilise emotional connotations (2005: 209).

Branding, a corporate enterprise with at least a 100-year history, has become ever more central to business advertising whereby 'organizations develop brands as a way to attract and keep customers by promoting value, image, prestige, or lifestyle (Rooney 1995: 48). Certainly the ethos transmitted by the marketing and imagery associated with the swimwear emphasizes one prevailing principle: Elizabeth Hurley Beach is Elizabeth Hurley. It is her sculpted body that demonstrates the clothing, and a body much commented on for its "age-defying" aspects and the beachwear reflects this. Commenting in the glossy fashion magazine *Grazia* on "How I *Really* Got My Bikini Body" she states:

> In an ideal world we'd all eat healthily and exercise every day; sadly, we pretty much all fail on this count, so last-minute preparations have to be relied upon. I've found that if I stop drinking all alcohol and eat very little dinner (ie [sic], a slice of toast and marmite and an apple) for a week before going away my stomach definitely becomes much flatter (2005b: 24).

Within such articles, Elizabeth Hurley provides a range of "instructions" on how to enhance bodily perceptions: "I'm not a great water drinker but when you're eating less, drinking more water helps you feel less hungry. If you can bear it, warm water on an empty stomach makes you feel fabulous" (Hurley 2005b: 26). Elizabeth Hurley advances a regime of "body maintenance," whereby: "like cars and other consumer goods, bodies require servicing, regular care and attention to preserve maximum efficiency" (Featherstone 1991: 182). Subsequently, Elizabeth Hurley Beach promotes not simply a "look" but a "lifestyle" a clearly defined habitus, a means for others to engage in a process of "practical mimesis" (McNay 1999: 101). The emphasis on sexuality and a "beachwear body" is conspicuously apparent in her attitudes to swimwear choice: "I haven't worn a one-piece for years, although they can be flattering on some women. I like tiny string bikinis in hot colours" (Hurley 2004: 90).

The aura surrounding Elizabeth Hurley Beach is one of maintaining a fashionable 'front' in a process of distinctive dramaturgical comportment (Goffman 1971). Hence, the purposively "chic" range is deliberately "wearable" and focused on "fit and practicality," and includes string bikinis garnished with semi-precious stones such as turquoise, tiger's eye, and amethyst and Klimt-print kaftans. And buttressing the swimwear, is a range of accessories to the actual swimwear which represent essential aids to the creation of a fashionable front-region images because: "The vocabulary of dress includes not only items of clothing, but also hair styles, accessories, jewellery, make-up and body decoration" (Lurie 1981: 4). Elizabeth Hurley Beach therefore provides a complete fashion ensemble perfect for "exotic" beach locales.

Within supporting interviews and rhetoric, Elizabeth Hurley provides not only bodily advice but also clear instructions concerning how to wear her clothing, and how to correctly display the body to maximum fashion effect. For instance, she recommends techniques such as adjustable halternecks, the importance of color regarding swimwear, a self-action tanner and "never, ever point out your faults to anyone" (Hurley 2005b: 29). Thus, to achieve the requisite, ideal "beach look," discipline and the right attitude is compulsory:

> The feminine body is the site of severe conflict and prodigious labor. Body management constitutes a bewildering array of techniques aimed at realizing the *intelligible* and *useful* body that can cope with the practical circumstances of one's habitus. For women, in particular, this involves reconciling techniques of being female with techniques of femininity appropriate to a particular cultural milieu (Craik 1994: 69).

As both fashion image and clothing creator Elizabeth Hurley acts as an arbiter of "good taste," of "distinction" communicating "the ability to be discriminating" and to make distinctions between the "good" and the "bad" (P. Smith 2001: 137). Clothes consequently become tools of self-management whereby an appropriate "dress code" must be learned if mistakes and unsuitable sartorial choices are to be avoided. And the rules of Elizabeth Hurley Beach have been extensively mediated because:

> Fashion is news, and the news media cover it, both in editorial treatments and in paid advertising messages. This statement applies not only to newspapers and magazines, but also to broadcast media. Thus a vital means of communication between the industry and the consumer, and between related parts of the industry, is activated in the daily newspapers, in news magazines, in women's and men's magazines, in specialized fashion publications, in those segments of the trade press that affect the fashion business, in radio, and in television. The impact is enormous (Jarnow *et al.* 1981: 348).

And the establishment of Elizabeth Hurley Beach *did* become news. It made the front page of numerous tabloids, which extensively featured the photo shoots done to advertise and promote the range. Furthermore, and not surprisingly, Elizabeth Hurley Beach articles and photographs featured in leading fashion magazines such as *Vogue, Tatler,* and *Marie Claire,* and a range of American and European periodicals including: *Vegas, Russian Vogue, Angeleno,* and *Vanidades,* and health and lifestyle magazines such as *Shape*. The launch of Elizabeth Hurley Beach also involved numerous fashion events in which the swimwear and accessories were personally introduced by Hurley herself, flanked by models displaying her wares in Saks in New York, Harrods in London, and at David Jones in Sydney and Melbourne. Consequently, if, as Craik contends, the challenge for any aspiring fashion designer "is to gain the support of key fashion leaders, in particular fashion editors and department stores buyers" (1994: 60) then Elizabeth Hurley has achieved this with considerable aplomb, not only gaining the attention of buyers of exclusive department stores, but also the owners of these exclusive department stores; such as Mohammed Al Fayed, who was present at the Harrods launch. In the true spirit of entrepreneurial endeavor, Elizabeth Hurley herself has taken an active role in marketing her clothing and accessories because Elizabeth Hurley Beach has been plugged into the globally linked "network society" and the apparent flexibility of e-commerce (Castells 2001) with the creation of the Elizabeth Hurley Beach website, from which the clothing can be bought directly.

The website represents a crucial aspect of the Elizabeth Hurley brand. The "aspirational" quality she ascribes to her garments is immediately visually perceptible on entering the website. The home page shows a bikini-clad Hurley kneeling on a beach, acting as the forefront to a glamorous, tropical beach marked by an azure sky and sea; whilst a right-hand-side column shows a succession of images of Hurley, fading slowly in and out, and displaying a montage of the different garments and accessories available. Browsers can access to the fashion spreads that appeared in various fashion magazines and the swimwear section shows displays of the various bikinis available, but is also supported by fashion advice, often presented in a humorous, but instructional manner, accentuating the importance of perfect fit.

Accessing the website is to journey through the fashion world as created by Hurley. It is an exercise in habitus, in constructing a fashionable image, in purchasing swimwear, but also creating an ensemble of supporting items, from kaftans and trousers, skirts and sarongs, to beach bags and hats. All displayed in perfect detail, with the bonus of a "virtual" Elizabeth Hurley, in the form of her commentary, to aid in making the "right choices" to achieve the "right look." As she states: "While developing my first beachwear collection I have done a great deal of research and put much thought into how to look better on holiday" (Hurley 2005a: 25). Thus, Elizabeth Hurley Beach communicates explicitly the essence of a fashion-based habitus, stressing the "things to do or not to do," and ensuring the "'correctness' of practices and their constancy over time" (Bourdieu 1994: 96–8).

ADIEU CELEBRITY, HELLO THE "BIKINI BILLIONAIRESS?"

This article has explored what I believe to be the relevance of habitus as applied to the workings of fashion. In effect, Elizabeth Hurley represents a fusion of theory and fashion, with her image and career as the linchpin. She is a prime exemplar of the ways in which the boundaries between the worlds of celebrity and fashion are increasingly permeable. Her progression into the role of fashion designer serves as a potent example of a cultural icon in the process of using her recognizable brand name and glamorous image to diversify her career, a process she has been engaged in for some years, but which is now firmly located within the fashion industry because she has an established brand:

> Hurley's almost parodic image of glamour, which has kept her in the public eye for the past 15 years, will obviously be the appeal of her clothing. She is, to say the least, canny about the power of celebrity, despite her insistence that "I'm trying to build a brand, so I don't want people to associate me with every item of clothing." Nevertheless, she named the label after herself and posed for all the publicity shots (Freeman 2005: 15).

The progression into the production aspects of the fashion industry and the forging of a brand intimately connected to her celebrity and status as "identifiable persona" (King 2003) is perhaps an inevitable and *necessary* progression. She is still a perennial presence within the world's top fashion periodicals, for that is the medium in which she is most celebrated. Her relationship with Estee Lauder has been symbolically enshrined with the creation of a lipstick named after her. Furthermore, she served as the co-host of *Fashion Rocks,* a gala event held in benefit for the Prince's Trust, bringing together luminaries from the world of popular music and fashion design, in which she wore dresses by a range of designers including: John Galliano, Armani, Matthew Williamson, Dolce & Gabbana, Donna Karen, Prada, Stella McCartney, Alexander McQueen, Gucci, and of course, Versace. This connection with the world of fashion was further established by Elizabeth Hurley's foray into the world of "reality television," in *Project Catwalk,* on which she acted as the host and which featured aspiring fashion designers competing for the opportunity to display their creations during London Fashion Week, judged by fashion designers and writers such as Giles Deacon, Robert Cary-Williams, Julien Macdonald, and Lorraine Candy.

Elizabeth Hurley's newly acquired role as fashion designer reflects something of a contemporary trend. Within the "world of celebrity" a major synergistic development in recent years is the increasing frequency of figures from the fields of acting and popular music extending the reach of their careers into fashion. At one level, this involves modeling and product endorsements, such as Nicole Kidman advertising Chanel, Liv Tyler's association with Givenchy, Scarlett Johanssen acting as the face of Calvin Klein's Eternity Moment fragrance, and David Beckham's endorsement of Police Eyewear (Cashmore 2002), a process long-established within Hollywood (Stacey 1994). However, what seems to be an emerging trend is the number of media figures who are increasingly diversifying into the productive aspects of the fashion industry. For instance, Jennifer Lopez, in addition to an acting and music career, has expanded into the fashion industry with her JLo clothing/underwear/swimwear range. Similarly, numerous other pop performers have released clothing ranges, such as Gwen Stefani's L.A.M.B. (Love, Angel, Music, Baby) fashion range; P Diddy's "Sean John" menswear/womenswear fashion label; Jay-Z's Rocawear label; Beyonce Knowles's House of Dereon, Kylie Minogue's Love Kylie lingerie range, and Milla Jovovich's Jovovich-Hawk fashion line.

In relation to habitus, the motivation for such diversification is clear: to purchase such items may, symbolically at least, enables the consumer to share in the glamour of such celebrities, to mimic them to some degree, and imitation is a long-established aspect of the fashion world. As Jarnow *et al.* point out: "the great fashion designer, the late Coco Chanel, said . . . very clearly: 'If there is no copying, how are you going to have fashion?'" (1981: 29). And even more pertinent to the era of celebrity fashion are the words of Georg Simmel for whom "fashion is the imitation of a given example" (1957: 543). If then, "habitus arguably provides the principles by which people make choices and choose the strategies that they will employ in the social world" (Ritzer and Goodman 2003: 521), then perhaps as the twenty-first century progresses, it will increasingly be celebrities such as Elizabeth Hurley, moving into the production aspects of the industry, who may well prove to be the primary agents to influence the fashion choices people make.

But why should celebrities engage in such productive synergy? Why should Elizabeth Hurley establish Elizabeth Hurley Beach? The answer is unquestionably linked to the issue of her chief asset, her body. Whilst the beach range emphasizes glamour, leisure, and "jet-set glitz," the Elizabeth Hurley Beach promotional images present Elizabeth Hurley near naked in "string bikinis" displaying her still taut, glamorous, and "fashionable body" in a manner that inevitably results in widespread media attention and publicity. Thus, beachwear is the ideal fashion product to market because such a strategy brings maximum promotion for her clothing range and for herself. But, the motivation is also concerned with cultural and productive longevity.

John Gray argues that the world of celebrity is "inherently transitory" (2004: 209); that celebrities constantly come and go within media discourse. As a result, the ethic and ethos of flexible accumulation and "perpetual innovation" is a double-edged sword. For many commentators, the Western world shifted fundamentally away from a stable "Fordist" production system to a system of "flexible accumulation" typified by "the fleeting qualities of a postmodernist aesthetic that celebrates difference, ephemerality, spectacle, fashion, and the commodification of cultural forms" (Harvey 1989: 156). In the face of a society arguably caught in a "dromological" state of flux and flurry of ever-changing fashions this manifests itself in the constant search for "the next big thing." With regards to a modeling career in fashion, the future of that career *will* be curtailed by the requirements and standards of a youth driven industry (Craik 1994).

Moreover, if Elizabeth Hurley is indeed a "flashbulb courtesan," she is not alone. With regard to contemporary "fashionable faces," the paparazzi have found numerous new "muses" in recent years, indeed, in recent months and weeks. Established media figures must now share the stage with the next generation, from actresses such as Sienna Miller and Keira Knightley, "instant celebrities" in the form of Paris Hilton (complete with fashion and perfume range), the pantheon of "stars" perennially created by the "democratising" medium of Reality Television (Andrejevic 2002), to the media-dubbed 2006 England World Cup football team "WAGS" (Wives and Girlfriends), all of whom are also being increasingly drawn into the orbit of the fashion industry.

However, turning forty has not yet signaled the end of Elizabeth Hurley's appearances upon the covers of fashion and celebrity magazines, nor has it ended her modeling career, as it appeared to for Isabella Rossellini, who was dropped by Lancôme when she reached a similar age (Bailey 1998). Simian Films is seemingly no more and her (often critically derided) involvement with acting is becoming less visible; however, she has a continuing modeling career, having signed on for her thirteenth year with Estee Lauder (Preston 2006), thus

Elizabeth Hurley Beach may well prove to be, as Grieg suggests, the establishment of "Hurley Incorporated" (2005: 145). Thus, she can still have the best of both worlds for a time yet and continues to be Elizabeth Hurley Beach's visual, as well as creative, center. And in maintaining this dual role she illustrates the potency of a fashion habitus, as she is effectively both transmitter, and subject. As she states with regard to her modeling duties for Elizabeth Hurley Beach: "I'd love Kate Moss to model my bikinis but I couldn't afford her, so I just have to do some more exercise and do it myself" (Gannon 2006: 37).

References

Andrejevic, M. 2002. "The Kinder, Gentler Gaze of Big Brother Reality TV in the Era of Digital Capitalism." *New Media and Society* 4(2): 251–70.

Anthony, Andrew. 1999. "The Player." *Vogue*: 142–9.

Arena. 2001. "Goddess: Heartbreaker." *Arena* May: 109–16.

Anspach, Karlyne. 1967. *The Why of Fashion.* Ames, Iowa: Iowa State University Press.

Bailey, David. 1998. *Models Close-Up.* London: Channel 4 Books.

Barnard, Malcolm. 1996. *Fashion as Communication.* London and New York: Routledge.

Barthes, Roland. 1990. *The Fashion System.* Berkeley, CA: University of California Press.

Baudrillard, Jean. 2005. *The System of Objects.* London and New York: Verso.

Barnard, Malcolm. 1996. *Fashion as Communication.* London and New York: Routledge.

BBC News. 2002. "Liz Hurley: Life in the Spotlight." *BBC News* April 4 2002.

Bourdieu, Pierre. 1984. *Distinction: A Social Critique of the Judgement of Taste.* London: Routledge & Kegan Paul.

Bourdieu, Pierre. 1994. "Structures, Habitus and Practices." In *The Polity Reader in Social Theory*, pp. 95–111. Cambridge: Polity Press.

Bowyer, Alison. 2003. *Liz Hurley: Uncovered.* London: Andre Deutsch.

Brinton, Jessica. 2003. "In Full Bloom." *The Sunday Times: Style* June: 14–21.

Buckley, Reka and Stephen C.V. Gundle. 2000. "Flash Trash: Gianni Versace and the Theory and Practice of Glamour." Stella Bruzzi and Pamela Church Gibson (eds) *Fashion Cultures: Theories, Explorations and Analysis*, pp. 331–49. London and New York: Routledge.

Cashmore, Ellis. 2002. *Beckham.* Cambridge: Polity.

Castells, Manuel. 2001. *The Internet Galaxy: Reflections on the Internet, Business, and Society.* Oxford: Oxford University Press.

Craik, Jennifer. 1994. *The Face of Fashion.* London and New York: Routledge.

Connor, Steven. 1997. *Postmodernist Culture: An Introduction to Theories of the Contemporary*, 2nd edn. Cambridge: Blackwell.

Cunningham, Patricia. A. and Susan Voso Lab. 1991. *Dress and Popular Culture.* Bowling Green, Ohio: Bowling Green University Popular Press.

Derrick, Robin and Robin Muir. (eds) 2003. *People in Vogue: A Century of Portraits.* London: Little, Brown.

Entwistle, Joanne. 2000. *The Fashioned Body: Fashion, Dress and Modern Social Theory.* Cambridge: Polity Press.

Entwistle, Joanne. 2001. "The Dressed Body." In Joanne Entwistle and Elizabeth Wilson (eds) *Body Dressing*, pp. 33–59. Oxford and New York: Berg.

Evans, Jessica. 2005. "Celebrity: What's the Media Got to Do with It?" In Jessica Evans and David Hesmondhalgh (eds) *Understanding Media: Inside Celebrity*, pp. 1–11. Maidenhead: Open University Press.

Featherstone, Mike. 1991. "The Body in Consumer Culture." In Mike Featherstone, Mike Hepworth and Bryan S. Turner (eds) *The Body: Social Process and Cultural Theory*, pp. 170–96. London: Sage.

Fearon, Francesca. 2005. "Elizabeth Hurley Tells Us About Her New Swimwear Collection." *Hello* April, No. 864: 12–14.

Freeman, Hadley. 2005. "Jolly Hurley Sticks." *The Guardian Student* April 21: 14–15.

Gannon, Louise. 2006. "Elizabeth Hurley: 'I Loved Being Thin But Curves Are Good.'" *Grazia* January 16: 34–7.

Gauntlett, David. 2004. "Madonna's Daughters: Girl Power and the Empowered Girl-pop Breakthrough." In Santiago Fouz-Hernandez and Freya Jarman-Ivens (eds) Madonna's *Drowned World's: New Approaches to her Cultural Transformations, 1983–2003*, pp. 161–76. Aldershot: Ashgate.

Gilligan, Sarah. 2000. "Gwyneth Paltrow." Stella Bruzzi and Pamela Church Gibson (eds) *Fashion Cultures: Theories, Explorations and Analysis*, pp. 245–251. London and New York: Routledge.

Goffman, Erving. 1971. *The Presentation of Self in Everyday Life.* Middlesex: Penguin Books.

Gray, John. 2004. *Heresies: Against Progress and Other Illusions.* London: Granta Books.

Grieg, Geordie. 2005. "Million Dollar Babe." Tatler May: 140–9.

Harvey, David. 1989. *The Condition of Postmodernity.* Cambridge: Blackwell.

Hurley, Elizabeth. 2000. "The Devil in Miss Hurley." *Esquire* December: 160–6.

Hurley, Elizabeth. 2002. "One Sexy Mother-To-Be." *Elle* March (UK Edition): 92–8.
Hurley, Elizabeth. 2004. "Mother Nature." *Harpers & Queen* July.
Hurley, Elizabeth. 2005a. "Elizabeth's Beach Party." *You* magazine, The Mail on Sunday April 10: 20–5.
Hurley, Elizabeth. 2005b. "How I Really Got My Bikini Body." *Grazia* July 4: 24–9.
Jarnow, Jeanette. A., Beatrice Judelle and Miriam Guerreiro. 1981. *Inside the Fashion Business*, 3rd edn. New York: John Wiley & Sons.
Jenks, Chris (ed.). 1993. *Cultural Reproduction*. London and New York: Routledge.
Kellner, Douglas. 1992. "Popular Culture and the Construction of Postmodern Identities." In Scott Lash and Jonathan Friedman (eds) *Modernity and Identity*, pp. 141–78. Oxford: Blackwell.
King, Geoff. 2003. "Stardom in the Willenium." In, Thomas Austin and Martin Barker (eds) *Contemporary Hollywood Stardom*, pp. 62–73, London: Arnold.
Kline, Stephen, Nick Dyer-Witheford and Greig De Peuter. 2003. *Digital Play: The Interaction of Technology, Culture, and Marketing*. London: McGill-Queen's University Press.
Lurie, Alison. 1981. *The Language of Clothes*. London: Heinemann.
Lury, Celia. 1996. *Consumer Culture*. Cambridge: Polity Press.
Martin, Richard. 1997. "A Note: Gianni Versace's Anti-Bourgeois Little Black Dress." *Fashion Theory* 2(1): 95–100.
McNay, Lois. 1999. "Gender, Habitus and the Field: Pierre Bourdieu and the Limits of Reflexivity." *Theory, Culture & Society* 16(1): 95–117.
Murray, Simone. 2005. "Brand Loyalties: Rethinking Content within Global Corporate Media. *Media, Culture & Society* 27(3): 415–35.
Normant, Serge, Bridget Foley and Michael Thompson. 2001. *Femme Fatale: The Timeless Style of Beautiful Women*. London: Thames and Hudson.
Olins, Wally. 2003. *On Brand*. New York: Thames & Hudson.

Preston, Jane. 2006. "The World's Most Glamorous Farmer?" *Red* July: 60–4.
Rogers, Mary F. 1999. *Barbie Culture*. London: Sage.
Rojek, Chris. 2001. *Celebrity*. London: Reaktion Books.
Rooney, Joseph Arthur. 1995. "Branding: A Trend for Today and Tomorrow." *Journal of Product & Brand Management* 4(4): 48–55.
Ritzer, George and Douglas. J. Goodman. 2003. *Sociological Theory*, 6th edn. Boston, MA: McGraw-Hill.
Shone, Tom. 1994. "Flirtysomething." *The Sunday Times Magazine* July 31: 30–7.
Shuckburgh, Hannah. 2005. "Elizabeth Hurley: Flying High." *Easy Living* December: 22–8.
Simmel, Georg. 1957. "Fashion." *The American Journal of Sociology* LXII(6): 541–58.
Smith, Adam. 2001. "The Devil in Miss Hurley." *Empire* December: 84–91.
Smith, Philip. 2001. *Cultural Theory: An Introduction*. Oxford: Blackwell.
Smith, Melanie. 2004. "Celebs and THEIR clothes." www.nzgirl.co.nz/articles/3357
Stacey, Jackie. 1994. *Star Gazing: Hollywood Cinema and Female Spectatorship*. London and New York: Routledge.
Syson, Damon. 2005. "I Have Never Been So Happy." *Marie Claire* Elizabeth Hurley Interview. *Marie Claire* August: 80–8.
Tetzlaff, David. 1993. "Metatextual Girl: Patriarchy, Postmodernism, Power, Money, Madonna." In Cathy Schwichtenburg (ed.) *The Madonna Connection: Representational Politics, Subcultural Identities, and Cultural Theory*. New York: Westview.
Tunstall, Jeremy and Michael Palmer. 1991. *Media Moguls*. London and New York: Routledge.
Turner, Graeme. 2004. *Understanding Celebrity*. London: Sage.
Vale, V. and Mike Ryan (eds). 2004. *J.G. Ballard: Quotes*. San Francisco, CA: RE/Search Publications.
Wilson, Elizabeth. 2003. *Adorned In Dreams: Fashion and Modernity*. London: I. B. Tauris & Co.

CREATING AN AMERICAN MYTHOLOGY:
A comparison of branding strategies in three fashion firms

Veronica Manlow[1]

Myth is linked to fashion by von Samsonow (2009: 20) as the substance of fashion. "Myth supplies a highly constant baseline, an unchanging dimension, while fashion plays variations on top of it." Von Samsonow explores this synthesis of myth embodied in fashion in the interpersonal realm, as a means by which women fabricate and perform a feminine identity. Mythology is also infused in fashion in commercial processes enacted by firms involved in creating and marketing branded fashion products.

MARKETING CULTURE AND NATIONAL IDENTITY IN FASHION

National identity in fashion coexists with a new global culture. Branding in American fashion reflects this local and global reality. Since the mid-nineteenth century, for about a century, there was essentially one fashion and one center of fashion: Paris styles, which were created by couturiers, were copied. Marketing focused on the styles themselves and on their quality and newness. Poiret and Chanel, for instance, were influenced by a modernist aesthetic and not a specifically national identity (Lipovetsky 1994).

Gradually other fashion centers emerged and a distinct national identity became a defining feature that set one apart from Paris (see for example Breward 2004; Edensor 2002; White 2000). Paulicelli (2004) shows how Italian fashion emerged and how under various regimes it embodied a unique type of national identity infused with a particular ideology. While there had long been an American style in fashion, prestigious fashions originated in Paris and American fashion had its own local history. This changed considerably with the creation of an American style for an international market, particularly starting in the 1980s.

Hancock (2009) contends that brands communicate on multiple levels to provide people with stories to relate to their products. This study focuses on the images conveyed through marketing and communications by three American firms. Each firm draws upon a national identity that they reinterpret in reference to the brand's own identity. Though different each has created a brand with a distinctive American cultural identity. The construction of mythologies embedded in American culture in these firms is illustrated through reference to ethnography and interviews, visits to stores, and analysis of the firms' products. Research in the Tommy Hilfiger (hereinafter TH) firm was conducted over several years ending in 2006. Research at the American Apparel firm (hereinafter AA) was conducted over several months in 2007 and 2008. The author interviewed designers who work or worked at Polo Ralph Lauren (hereinafter PRL) but has not extensively studied the firm.

---

[1] From Veronica Manlow, (2011), Creating an American Mythology: A Comparison of Branding Strategies in Three Fashion Firms, Fashion Practice, Volume 3, Issue 1, Taylor & Francis.

MYTHOLOGY AND ITS CONNECTION TO BRANDING

Barthes (1972[1957]: 109) speaks of myth as part of a semiological system of communication, whereby an object is defined. It's a construct that attains significance through culture, and not due to the "nature" of things (1972[1957]: 110). While myths are historical and situated reality, they are taken to be normal, obvious, and true. Holt (2004) sees brand myths as a powerful force reflecting cultural content.

Mythologies are the conduit by which advertising and marketing reaches its target audience. A firm's basic message will be infused with meaning situated in a cultural context. The brand—particularly in fashion where image is a core part of what is being sold—must be linked to something outside of itself. The mythology of a brand, and the mythologies it creates in its products and the communications about its products, is a second-order semiological system, containing already formed signifiers.

CREATING AMERICAN MYTHOLOGIES

For some American firms the brand's image is linked to icons of American culture. Each reads the American cultural landscape differently: abstracting, re-appropriating, and inventing elements that resonate with the brand's own vision and objectives. Table 6 provides an overview of the master narratives that comprise each brand's mythology. Table 7 outlines the characteristics along social, cultural, and branding dimensions.

CASE STUDIES

Polo Ralph Lauren

Vision and culture of the brand

The PRL empire is closer to the world of fantasy—of cinema—than to the garment industry or indeed to the real world of America's elite. The mythology is built on Lauren's vision of an old-money lifestyle, which he polishes up and re-presents to the consumer. Designers work within a narrative framework set by Lauren to create a line of products within each brand that bespeak the broader PRL aesthetic, and the dynamic or theme of a particular season. Lauren offers to all the promise—the facade—of a particular American lifestyle: the WASP, the Ivy League, the country club, the socialite, the polo player, the successful businessman, the cowboy. This dream of upward mobility sold to a mass market, and on a smaller scale to the luxury market, relies upon visionary marketing and advertising. Lauren chooses

Table 6 Comparison of master narratives of three American brands

Brand	Master Narrative: Defining Concepts
Polo Ralph Lauren	WASP/preppy style. Timeless, elite American heritage. Wealth, luxury, privilege. Establishment. Nostalgia, classics
Tommy Hilfiger	Fresh American classics. Youthfulness, fun. The new American dream: multicultural, apolitical, happy, optimistic
American Apparel	Basic. Utilitarian. Raw sexuality. Anti-establishment. Progressive. Libertarian. Young. American

Table 7 Comparison of characteristics of three American brands

References	References	References	References	References	References	References	References
PRL	Traditional	Elite	Nostalgic	Exclusivity	Conservative	Lifestyle	All
TH	Contemporary	Mass	Popular	Diversity	Apolitical	Popular culture	Young/middle age
AA	Utilitarian	Industrial	Progressive	Hedonistic	Liberal/radical	Anti-marketing	Young hipster

not to dilute this image by linking the brand to popular culture; rather, he seeks "timeless" or at least long-standing symbols of privilege. The PRL aesthetic goes against the grain of fashion in another important way: its essential identity is ageless and styles can be worn by older and younger people.

What does PRL say that it stands for?

On the website the company presents its marketing strategy as its vision and mission. "Ralph Lauren has always stood for providing quality products, creating worlds and inviting people to take part in our dream. We were the innovators of lifestyle advertisements that tell a story and the first to create stores that encourage customers to participate in that lifestyle."

Leadership style and culture in the firm

The culture at the firm is described by many employees as harsh and competitive, with Lauren as an autocratic leader. The culture and the tone of the workplace is determined by Lauren. The office environment is carefully choreographed to reflect his, and only his, aesthetic. Individual expression within one's own physical space, or in one's own appearance, is not allowed. A former menswear designer at TH who worked for PRL says, contrasting Lauren with Hilfiger, that he is "elitist" and "snobby." (Manlow 2007: 203). Yet Lauren is a charismatic leader strongly identified with and admired by employees. Employees uniformly describe him as a brilliant man, worthy of admiration.

Marketing

Lauren creates an idealized America that status-conscious people who identify with American taste find appealing. Lauren has amplified a lifestyle marketing approach that rather than treat each product, product line or brand as a separate entity, creates a meaningful universe that comes into being through an all-encompassing philosophy of classicism and tradition (Martin 2007).

We see an editing and recasting of authenticity, a mythology "stolen and restored" (Barthes 1972[1957]: 125), or a hypermodern nostalgia. "My things, I've always thought, were in a lot of ways more English than the English," says Lauren (Gross 2003: 237). Lauren mixes improbable elements: English gentry, WASP, international polo player, cowboy, an aristocratic restraint with the freedom of the West, Old World with modern, tweed and denim, to form a new hyperreal aesthetic.

Tommy Hilfiger

Vision and culture of the brand

Like Lauren, Hilfiger deconstructs America and reassembles it according to his parameters. The TH brand has a core commitment to Americanism. The brand, though it resembles the PRL style, trades an American elitist heritage for one linked to popular culture, a dream of the past for one of the future. The Ivy League is prominent as is the New England WASP aesthetic, though the gates of entry are opened much wider—we see "multicultural" models in fun and happy advertisements. American popular culture is embraced.

Hilfiger also upholds conformity. There was a foray into the world of hip-hop during the middle to late 1990s. Nevertheless, the brand remains reverential to the New England WASP, which is in part why it appealed to urban youth, for whom such a life was always out of reach.

Hilfiger, who sees Norman Rockwell as a hero, believes that America is an uncomplicated place. Hilfiger says: "I love aircraft carriers, sailors lined up, and American flags billowing in the wind" (1997: 220).

In its outward image, values that are prominent in the firm, individual freedom and a communal ethos, are translated into an image of a tolerant, apolitical America. Hippies and peace symbols exist easily alongside icons of a consumer culture that they would have confronted in a distant past. Freedom is a fragrance that everyone can wear. In the employee "brand bible," Americans are described as free, inclusive, and determined.

What does th say that it stands for?

In the red, white, and blue "brand bible": "Defining Fresh American Style," the first line is: "It began as the great American dream." In the section entitled "Core Values" we see this statement:

> We believe in:
> The values embodied
> In the American dream—optimism,
> Determination and success
> Having fun and enjoying life
> Helping others succeed
> Treating people with respect
> Being a genuine company

Leadership style and culture in the firm

Like Lauren, Hilfiger is a charismatic leader capable of instilling high levels of devotion in employees. Collegiality and freedom of individual expression are the two most prevalent themes in the firm. At TH egalitarian practices, aimed at diminishing status differences, are built into the work process. Hilfiger is described as being "an average guy," a "buddy."

Employees are not required to wear TH clothing. Workspaces are decorated according to one's personal preference. When there is discord and competition, between design divisions and marketing or merchandising for example, it is downplayed and perhaps not acknowledged openly as this is not "acceptable" behavior for people who are "Tommyized" (a term some employees use).

Marketing

Marketing, as in the other firms, spans advertising via print and broad-cast media, social media, and outdoor venues, sponsorships of music events, and other promotions connected to celebrities and popular culture. Both Lauren and Hilfiger grew up in middle-class families, Lauren in the Bronx and Hilfiger in Elmira, New York. While neither Hilfiger or Lauren had an Ivy League education (Hilfiger says that he barely graduated high school and Lauren completed two years at Baruch College of the City University of New York) the Ivy League was to figure prominently in the branding of each firm. Lauren dreamed of becoming rich and being accepted in WASP circles. Hilfiger (1997: 9) instead speaks of his admiration for the way the Ivy League man *looked* in his chinos and Oxford cloth shirts.

American apparel

Vision and culture of the brand

Barthes (1972[1957]) spoke of the bourgeois norm as the essential enemy because it creates a falsely obvious reality. We have seen it in operation in the mythologies of TH and PRL. AA aggressively detaches the bourgeois norm from its foundation, upsetting what others may take to be a comfortable status quo. What it puts in the place of culturally accepted mainstream views about proper conduct and self-presentation is an amalgam of confrontational attitudes. AA, based in Los Angeles, projects a complex countercultural image, at once being progressive—committed to fair wages, good working conditions, and immigrant rights, and its vertically integrated made-in-America values—and politically incorrect. Freedom of expression, rebellion, and individuality take on a tone that may be bold, loud, uncontrolled, offensive, subversive, indifferent, detached, ironic. Traditional decorum and rules of polite discourse are routinely violated

AA refuses to subscribe to mainstream myths of a happy and wholesome America, but it nevertheless succumbs to American mythology in its own way. Charney, the firm's founder, is the superhero, the paragon of fairness, freedom of expression, and freedom of the market. He keeps jobs in America. He produces superior made-in-America garments, he protects democracy by paying fair wages, he brings freedom and dignity to the oppressed, he supports American values of hard work and individualism, allowing people to higher earn wages according to their level of production. Myths on the left are rare, and are limited to a few political notions (Barthes 1972[1957]). Although Charney's political position is not coherent, even to his own employees, he can perhaps only go so far in marketing based on his labor, employment, and production ideology. Enter raw, hedonistic sexuality as a force that Charney effectively uses to invigorate the brand.

What does AA say that it stands for?

American Apparel claims in its advertising and within the culture of the firm to be defined by the following practices:

Made in America
Immigrant rights
Labor advocacy
Environmental responsibility
Individual freedom/independence DIY
Sexual liberation/hedonism
Rejection of blatant consumerism (logos, trends, slick marketing)

Employees have described the brand as progressive, subversive, anarchic, anti-establishment, counter-cultural, provocative, politically incorrect, young, liberal, loose, non-corporate, vintage.

> We design for ourselves. Our clothing reflects true ideas. We stand for something. Vice, My Space, Hipsters, West Coast Punk, all subcultures. People gravitate from all directions. Even hip hop.

AA proclaims its rejection of establishment ideals but how can it at once be progressive, libertarian, anarchic, and hedonistic? This incoherence works well for AA. It is part of an appeal that it uses strategically to set itself apart from other brands.

Leadership style and culture in the firm

The culture of AA is animated by sex. Charney, its founder, has openly advocated sex in the workplace, has lived with more than one female employee at a time, and more recently with male employees as they are "easier," and has had several charges of sexual harassment brought against him, and then withdrawn. Applying a mainstream logic, one would tend to see the positions held by Charney as "abusive" or as constitutive of sexual harassment. Charney sees it quite differently and during the research the author found that employees did not see him as abusive. One might say, to be very polite, that Charney does not restrain himself. The author's first meeting with him began with a stream of expletives condemning academics. What might appear to an outsider as abusive was often described by employees as posturing, as high drama, as comedy, and not as insulting. The work environment can be described as so relaxed and unstructured that people often did not know who was in their department, what department they were in, what other people in that department did, and what had been done in the past. There was no rational system of record keeping in most departments, and there were no formal schedules or job descriptions. The factory, however, is run according to strict bureaucratic principles. Its location within the firm allowed for a laissez-faire culture amongst the non-factory employees—that is until Charney enters what one employee described as a combat mode. Employees are very devoted to Charney, to the company, and what it stands for. In this way, Charney qualifies as a charismatic leader, though not a typical one. Not many CEOs appear in their own advertisements—with full frontal nudity.

Charney has set up a factory paying garment workers the highest wages in the world, with a base salary of US$12 that can go up to about US$20 per hour depending on productivity. He offers on-site family medical care, subsidized meals and transportation, free bikes, fitness and yoga classes, and massages at one's workstation. In the on-premises factory Charney plays a non-sexualized paternalistic role. He is the hero, the great benefactor who never fails to proclaim demonstratively how much he has done for the workers, sometimes at the top of his voice, trembling, with arms outstretched.

When Charney ran through the factory in his underwear, to a cheering mass, he was seen by employees as a lovable prankster. This was a way of breaking down hierarchical boundaries while still asserting authority (insofar as Charney is the only person able to act in such a manner).

Marketing

AA's marketing is a reflection of its identity as a firm, and that of its products. Marketing like the clothing and the attitude at AA is basic. AA espouses an anti-marketing, anti-branding position, specifically hiring people with non-marketing backgrounds and calling the department "web design." Terry Richardson's documentary style photography, which rejects the use of professional models and photographers, is much admired by Charney. At AA there is a deliberate use of low-grade files to downgrade the quality of photos. Photos are done in-house by Charney or other employees, sometimes with an old Polaroid camera. Models are often ordinary-looking employees or friends of employees. When hired they may, like Lauren Phoenix, have accomplishments such as a porn film entitled *Anal Delinquents*. An employee in marketing states: "He hates the commercial fashion establishment viscerally. That is the reason we are here." Charney gravitates toward the irreverent, that which exists outside the boundaries of popular taste, be it in fashion, art, politics or pornography. According to an employee in marketing:

> There is absolutely no testing/research. No cool hunting. We make what we want to wear. We do what turns us on.

DISCUSSION

Each firm has a particular vision and culture that shapes the brand's communications. One can begin by looking at the overall vision of the brand. There are some similarities in the way the creative process unfolds, even though TH and PRL are far more bureaucratic in structure than AA. Each of these firms is headed by a designer who sets the tone of the culture of the work environment and personifies the image of the brand. Designers and others work within a narrative framework set by the founding designer that is connected to the overall mythology of that brand. The charisma of the leader becomes "routinized" in the brand.

The firms selectively extract ideas and ideals, and ways of being and expressing oneself within the context of American life. The Statue of Liberty, cowboys, Elvis Presley, the shores of Nantucket are examples of significations that brands can work with and which are edited to become something new and different. The significations the firms produce are dislocated or emancipated from any connection to the real, referential object (Baudrillard 2000[1976]).

PLR, TH, and AA are examples of firms that build an identity around the idea of being American. Each firm represents America through the products they create, sell, and market, and each contributes to a global vision of the American lifestyle. The mythology a firm adopts will influence the design of its products and will define its message. In a post-productivist consumer society dominated by simulations Charney does something quite interesting. He calls attention to something that remains hidden from view in the mythologies of other fashion firms: the fact that fashion is a material product that is produced through the labor of workers who do not share in the proceeds of the American "dreamworld" of the WASP and who are barred from access to this world, both real and imagined.

All three firms inhabit a new moment in the marketing of identity. Each has found success through marketing a coherent American identity, reflective of the past but cast in ways that are relevant to consumers today. Each brand, through its selective use of icons, ideals, and themes, creates an American brand culture that it launches through images and associations it claims as its own. Within these mythologies, built into clothing, stores, and messages of multiple types, we find the enactment of an American identity that can be purchased and worn.

CONCLUSION

The brands are very different and no one best represents America. In the myth-making activities of these three firms we see fragments of a hyperreal America melded with brand histories, consumerist ideologies, and new marketing strategies.

Mythologies not only provide a coherent structure to firms—even if that means, as in the case of AA, to not be coherent—they contribute to a system of logic present within the increasingly important and influential world of fashion, which has become a force that gives meaning and direction to the larger culture. The narratives of American life and values created by these three firms are taken to be genuine expressions of an appealing American lifestyle.

References

Baudrillard, Jean. 2000[1976]. *Symbolic Exchange and Death*. Trans. Iain Hamilton Grant. London and Thousand Oaks, CA: SAGE Publications.

Barthes, Roland. 1972[1957]. *Mythologies*. Trans. Annette Lavers. New York: Hill and Wang.

Breward, Christopher. 2004. *Fashioning London: Clothing and the Modern Metropolis*. Oxford: Berg.

Edensor, Tim. 2002. *National Identity, Popular Culture and Everyday Life.* New York: Berg.

Gross, Michael. 2003. *Genuine Authentic: The Real Life of Ralph Lauren.* New York: Harper Collins Publishers.

Hancock, Joseph. 2009. *Brand/Story: Ralph, Johnny, Billy, and Other Adventures in Fashion Branding.* New York: Fairchild Books.

Holt, Douglas. 2004. "How Brands Become Icons: The Principles of Cultural Branding." Boston, MA: Harvard Business School Press.

Lipovetsky, Gilles. 1994. *The Empire of Fashion: Dressing Modern Democracy.* Princeton, NJ: Princeton University Press.

Manlow, Veronica. 2007. *Designing Clothes: Culture and Organization of the Fashion Industry.* New Brunswick, NJ and London: Transaction Publishers.

Martin, Michael. 2007. "Heroes: Ralph Lauren." *V Magazine* September 7.

Paulicelli, Eugenia. 2004. *Fashion under Fascism: Beyond the Black Shirt.* Oxford and New York: Berg.

Von Samsonow, Elisabeth. 2009. "Myth and Fashion." In Gerda Buxbaum (ed.) Fashion in Context, pp. 20–5. New York: Springer Wien.

White, Nicola. 2000. *Reconstructing Italian Fashion: America and the Development of the Italian Fashion Industry.* New York: Berg.

32
RAF SIMONS AND INTERDISCIPLINARY FASHION FROM POST-PUNK TO NEO-MODERN

Nick Rees-Roberts

The sonic blast from Belgian dance band Technotronic's 1989 hit *Pump Up the Jam* signaled the start of the Raf Simons Spring/Summer 2014 show, part of the Paris men's fashion week in June 2013. The setting was unusual. Rather than present the collection in Paris, Simons chose the recently inaugurated Larry Gagosian art gallery at Le Bourget in the northern outskirts of the city. The gallery space, a vast 1950s industrial structure transformed by architect Jean Nouvel, is positioned opposite Europe's largest business airport, a revealing indication of the project's commercial stakes. Simons' decision to set a fashion show in a postindustrial gallery space shows the extent to which contemporary luxury and high-fashion houses strategically intersect with the global art and design markets through what Hal Foster has termed "the art-architecture complex"—the creative and commercial intersection of contemporary art and architecture configured as "a primary site of image-making and space-shaping in our cultural economy" (Foster 2011: vii).

Setting aside the conceptual experiments in formal tailoring present in previous collections, Simons reclaimed his pop culture heritage by returning full circle to the youthful freedom and graphic intensity of his first collections in the mid- to late 1990s. The 2014 collection playfully included black jersey "onesies" gesturing to the innocence of baby-grows and elongated print tops with advertising slogans in bold colors, combining a pop modernity (through the use of saturated colors and synthetic materials) with a sense of futuristic potential (through the reconfigured silhouettes and the unisex hints of gender subversion). The calculated juxtaposition of influences from pop culture with other inspirations from fine art, architecture, interior and industrial design has become Simons' authorial signature, evidenced by the menswear collections for his own label since 1995 and his output as creative director at Jil Sander (2005–12) and since then at Christian Dior, widely held to be the most prestigious creative position in the fashion industry. In the case of the Spring/Summer 2014 menswear collection, the conversation between fashion and the connective industries of art, architecture, communications, and design was not simply a rhetorical gesture. The choice of location provided a material representation of Simons' conceptual framework by taking advantage of the concurrent exhibition of works by mid-century modernist sculptor Alexander Calder and industrial designer Jean Prouvé, both celebrated in their time for their expressive, forward-looking manipulations of form, shape, and technology. The sequential procession of models was staged around Prouvé's large-scale structures with guests seated in and around the transparent "Total Filling Station" (1969) and the iconic "Demountable House" (1944). This imaginative use of the performance space was further enhanced by a number of Calder's whimsical kinetic sculptures, metal and wire mobiles that toy with notions of gravity and motion—"the idea of detached bodies floating in space" illustrative, in the artist's vision, of "the ideal source of form" (Calder 1951: 8–9).

Simons is one of the most celebrated contemporary fashion designers, part of a generation that emerged through the late 1990s and early 2000s, including Alber Elbaz, Nicolas Ghesquière, Lucas Ossendrijver, Phoebe Philo, and Hedi Slimane, all now in tenure in the leading Parisian design houses. They are collectively associated with an architectural vision—a shared focus on form, shape, and technology, which, I argue here, requires the critical attention of contemporary fashion scholars. As we shall see, Simons' designs both for his nominal label and for Christian Dior characteristically involve a collision between the elevated and the immediate, the classical and the futuristic, the conceptual and the wearable. In what follows, I shall attempt to chart Simons' trajectory from an interdisciplinary perspective, seeking to tease out his creative influences from across the spectrum of pop music and culture, contemporary visual art, and modernist architecture and interior design. Beyond that contextual framework and beyond the fundamentally collaborative nature of fashion design, I shall also examine Simons' own distinctive interrogation of the material object, paying formal attention to shape, tactility, and technology. Drawing on the study of a number of key designs archived by the MoMu Fashion Museum in Antwerp, I juxtapose the revision of couture history at Christian Dior with the groundbreaking ideal of masculinity that first shaped the streamlined silhouette dominating menswear of the 2000s.

SUBCULTURE

Simons trained as a furniture and industrial designer, securing an internship in 1990 at the Antwerp office of fashion designer Walter Van Beirendonck, where he worked on the interior design for the label's showroom. It was there that he met artist Peter de Potter and stylist Olivier Rizzo, both subsequent collaborators and contributors to the designer's aesthetic language. Van Beirendonck was part of the original wave of Belgian designers (the "Antwerp Six") emerging in the 1980s, collectively positioned as a conceptual avant-garde (Teunissen 2011). The creation of Belgian fashion *ex nihilo* was supported by Antwerp's drive to establish itself as a cultural hub (Martínez 2007), thereby fashioning a national brand that stuck to a second generation of designers in the 1990s and to the parallel emergence of Martin Margiela, whose deconstructionist challenge to fashion history caught the decade's *finde-siècle* zeitgeist of decadence and decay (Evans 2003: 35–7).

While working for Van Beirendonck, Simons was exposed to Paris fashion, the main platform for the international promotion of Belgian design, attending shows by Jean Paul Gaultier and Martin Margiela in 1989. More than the former's elaborate sense of spectacle, it was the latter's third collection (the "white collection" shown with black children in a Parisian playground) with its trashy conceptualism, graphic purity, and emotional resonance that captured Simons' imagination. His preference for monochrome was further influenced by the non-referential fashions of Austrian designer Helmut Lang, whose icy aloofness and contrived simplicity impacted heavily on the dominant trend for minimalist design through much of the 1990s, perhaps best epitomized by Jil Sander's iconic white shirt. Superseding the perceived brashness of late 1980s European fashion (the excessive styles made famous by Claude Montana, Thierry Mugler, or Gianni Versace), "it was Lang's cool, urban silhouettes, marrying basic shapes with edgy color combinations and advanced technological fabrics, which were both the crucial look for fashion insiders, and the key influence on other designers, eager to find a new vision of the modern" (Arnold 2001: 20).

Lang has described the challenge of his own designs, presented at experimental *séances de travail* rather than at conventional catwalk shows, along with the conceptual Belgian and Japanese fashions shown in Paris since the 1980s, as a "silent counter-movement" to the dominance of Saint Laurent, Mugler, and Gaultier, helping to configure the more modern, streamlined silhouette that took root later in the 1990s (von Olfers 2010: 54). Simons' early run of menswear collections, though influenced in shape and tone by Lang's reduced silhouettes and cool distance, reflected a more sinister frame of reference, bringing the austerity and precision of the mod suit into dialogue with a new range of codes and meanings. By 2005, Simons was perceived as one of the most influential designers of menswear (Horyn 2005), known for emblematic pieces such as the narrow-shouldered, skinny black suit, foreshadowing Hedi Slimane's aesthetic appropriation and commercial exploitation of a similarly razor-tight silhouette for the Dior Homme label (Rees-Roberts 2013). Other core Simons pieces include white sleeveless shirt tops, wide-leg trousers, oversize layering, and low-key street-wear with counter-cultural symbolism. Simons' early designs contrasted the rough-and-ready style (frayed sleeves on shirt tops) with the material delicacy of the fabric—a translucent cotton/linen mix with formal, starched collars. Simons' proposition for menswear is, in essence, antinomic: fashioned around material formality and symbolic severity (ciphered through the imagery of a disaffected youth culture) combined with an underlying fragility (alluded to through the use of delicate fabrics on vulnerable bodies).

The graphic simplicity of Simons' menswear was apparent from the start: the videos made to promote his first collections between 1995 and 1997 (shown at art galleries and design studios in Paris) were statements of intent, symptomatic of the emerging label's core aesthetic sensibility, cultural values, and formal shape. The detection of a more "feminine" feel to Simons' later menswear collections subverts the darker imagery that his label has consistently traded in: a fashionable silhouette of an alienated, youthful masculinity, now commonplace on the men's catwalk (Furniss 2011). Simons' first collection for Fall/Winter 1995–6 took its inspiration from English school uniforms with a characteristically tight silhouette in dark colors. The promotional video for the Spring/Summer 1996 collection continued the tight silhouette inspired by David Bowie in the late 1970s, showing three boys and a girl (fellow-designer and former girlfriend Veronique Branquinho) hanging out, playing records, and trying on clothes. It combines nods to both commercial music video (set to a soundtrack of songs by Britpop band Pulp including *My Legendary Girlfriend* and *Underwear*) and artistic home video (through the coyly voyeuristic presence of the camera and the sub-erotic display of bodies). Branquinho's effortless cool is counterbalanced by the hip boys, who show off Simons' collection of oversized knitwear, bomber jackets, and skinny ties worn under leather coats—a tribute to the styles of British pop culture after punk, incorporating hints of gender indeterminacy and an undertow of sexual transgression. "Pop music," as Jon Savage observes, "still requires the willing feminization of young men" (Savage 1995: xxiv).

The amateur video for Fall/Winter 1996–7 (*We Only Come out at Night*) filmed a group of friends watching horror movies, playing ghost games before getting dressed to go out. The display of Simons' black formal suits was couched in a broader set of musical references taking in 1980s pop classics from Visage, The Human League, and Kate Bush, whose own gothic sensibility complemented Branquinho's romantic androgyny. The last of the promotional videos shot for Simons' early menswear was the most ambitious: *How to Talk to Your Teen* (Spring/Summer 1997) continued the New Romantic pop frame of reference (with music by Depeche Mode, Japan, and Underworld) but crystallized the label's sensibility by shifting the generational focus specifically to teenagers, foregrounding the social tension between conformity and freedom, thereby underscoring the formal impact of uniformity and repetition on fashion. The interest in movement is conveyed through shots that are captured in slow motion of the teenagers dressed in school uniform, escaping to a secluded meeting place in a futuristic concrete tower. The scenario switches to sci-fi as they are transported to a sparse white interior, the setting for a display of the designs. A kaleidoscope effect culminates in the presentation of the monochromatic collection with the alienated models assembled in a sectarian circle. The inclusion of biker helmets signals the tonal shift from the world of sexually indeterminate English pop to European electronic minimalism, foreshadowing Simons' later show-length homage, *Radioactivity* (Fall/Winter 1998–9), to influential German synth band Kraftwerk, the pop prototype of a minimalist modernity—both forward-looking and stripped back.

While the designer's remapping of the visual coordinates of male youth has on occasion been interpreted as a transparent vehicle for social commentary (particularly the vision of global terrorism and social insecurity in the Fall/Winter 2001–2 and Spring/Summer 2002 collections), his menswear designs in fact juxtapose a more diffuse set of ideas, emotions, and states of being, blending the everyday quality and commercial potential of the clothing—the shrewd combination of pure lines and street styling—with less immediately legible references and inspirations drawn from across the spectrum of pop culture, visual media, and the applied arts.

Along with the publication in 2005 of a retrospective book of the designer's menswear, *Raf Simons Redux* (Frisa 2005), which sought to enshrine him as one of fashion's principal innovators, Terry Jones, founder of *i-D* magazine, provided a synthesis of the designer's creative impact on the industry, describing his references ranging from architecture to pop music as intended "to form garments that have celebrated the alienation and absorption of adolescence." Employing a regular group of models cast from the streets of Antwerp, Simons' early collections played with the shapes and volumes of menswear with a precision that took him "beyond the confines of the form" (Jones 2013: 74).

Surpassing both the limited templates of menswear and avoiding a glib citation of post-punk styles, Simons' early designs envisioned an alienating masculinity rather than reflecting back a mirror image of the here-and-now. Rather than nostalgically reproducing the surface allure of youth subcultures, the designer has consistently underscored an indefinable element through the transposition of the language of punk. Simons' adoption of the term "interzone" references proto-punk writer William Burroughs' seminal work, the disjointed and hallucinatory nonlinear narrative *Naked Lunch* (1959), as well as post-punk band Joy Division's later appropriation of the term for a song on their debut album *Unknown Pleasures* (1979). "Interzone" is intended to capture fashion's inherent porosity (the in-between space connecting art, design, and commodity culture) and the importance of interdisciplinary activity to Simons' creative practice. The term also alludes more precisely to a futuristic, marginal, and otherworldly ideal of masculinity, the screen prototype for which was David Bowie's gaunt alien figure in *The Man Who Fell to Earth* (Roeg (dir.), 1976). This menacing edge was apparent in Simons' contribution (*2001 minus 3*) to the Biennale di Firenze in 1998, co-curated by Terry Jones and Dante Ferretti. Simons presented a disturbing live installation in which three teenage boys were confined within a clinical, white reconstruction of the designer's own Antwerp apartment for the three-week duration of the event.

Simons' menswear is concerned as much with control and precision as it is with uniformity and repetition, a link to mod dressing and styling that Alexander Fury has noted in the designer's preference for buttoned-up shirts. An inherent atmospheric quality of a Raf Simons show is a "tension barely concealed beneath a tightly buttoned collar" (Fury 2013: 70–1). The "Confusion" collection (Fall/Winter 2000–1) blurred the boundary between uniform and formal menswear by including pleated, high-waist woolen trousers with wide bottoms and turn-ups, a veiled reference to Bowie's own mid-1970s take on earlier twentieth-century menswear through the persona of the Thin White Duke. Dressing men in uniform has also allowed the designer to exploit the historical fault line in both high fashion and subcultural style between social conformity and individual rebellion, a recurrent feature of Simons' work: "Repetition has become this obsession for me now . . . By sending out male models all wearing headscarves, I think I'm enhancing the sense of repetition but not necessarily decreasing any sense of individuality you might get from the guys I've cast" (Heath 2002: 370). The procession of half-naked (but nonetheless asexual) boys in the "Black Palms" collection (Spring/Summer 1999) illustrated the particular relevance to fashion of a conceptual understanding of difference within repetition—Gilles Deleuze's postulate of "indifferent difference" through the repetition of a unique series of objects as opposed to the generality of cycles (Deleuze 1994[1968]: 15). The show's visual impact was derived from its serial rotation of tall, white male bodies, all shrouded in loose black tailoring combined with elements of subcultural street-wear.

The "Teenage Riot" collection (Fall/Winter 1999–2000) built on this monochromatic formalism combined with counter-cultural iconography, employing the same set of models carrying placards with the inscription of signifiers of insubordination, such as incubation, disorder, and confusion, offset by the buttoned-up white dress shirts and formal black trousers. Voluminous capes were used dramatically to emphasize the models' pale white skin and jet-black hair. This deathly procession of disaffected youths included some striking elements of formal experimentation such as chunky black knitwear under sleeveless coats, and black leather tunics in the shape of bomber jackets. The collection's only minor color variation was a series of gray suits and red jumpers, continuing the same minimalist coding from the previous season's sci-fiencoded "Radioactivity" collection, based around Kraftwerk's heritage with its emblematic red shirts. Franky Claeys was responsible for the graphic design for all of Simons' collections in the later 1990s including the emblematic "Black Palms" collection in 1998, with its black and red imagery used to frame the collection of heavy-metal-style prints and tight silhouettes. Despite the overall graphic simplicity of such collections, "Radioactivity" also included intricate garments in clashing materials such as a black jumper covered in a spider's web pattern in wool on one side and leather on the other. Another fragile sweater, with a regular knitted collar, cuffs, and waist, had deconstructed sleeves with suede, cotton, and woolen chain-mail motifs, the garment designed to hang loosely on the body.

THE MAN-MACHINE

The Raf Simons menswear of the early 2000s transcended the stylistic reimagining of a post-punk youth to incorporate a didactic commentary on global terror and social dystopia with collections entitled "Riot Riot Riot" (Fall/Winter 2001–2) and a video (*Safe*) shot to accompany the Spring/Summer 2002 collection, capturing a bleached-out, dystopian environment with political slogans designed by Peter de Potter inscribed on the surface of the garments. The pallor of the garments was contrasted by vibrant splashes of red and the theatrical use of flare guns. The bright, sleeveless hoodies with ripped armholes harbored textual fragments with apocalyptic messages translating the imagery of male angst serially reproduced elsewhere on the garments.

A visual template for this collection was Todd Haynes' film *Safe* (1996), which deals with the cultural desire to give narrative shape to unexplained illness, toying with a provocative AIDS analogy. *Safe* follows the trajectory of an alienated suburban housewife, Carol White, played by Julianne Moore, who develops Environmental Illness, a form of chemical sensitivity that transports her from suburban normalcy in Los Angeles to a New Age institute in the desert of New Mexico, where she retreats to a post-apocalyptic igloo, conceived as a metaphor for the narrative's movement towards paranoia and isolation (Potter 2004: 145). Moore's flatly minimalist performance underscores the film's tonal blankness. Glyn Davis has explained its interplay of whiteness, illness, and heterosexuality, through which Carol's etiolated body slowly fades away, the preponderance of static distance shots that linger on her frail frame emphasizing this loss of identity (Davis 2000). The film's bleached aesthetic works to merge subjectivity and anonymity, the bipartite structure translating the shift from "questions of space" to "questions of

Simons' own video *Safe* transposed the tonal blankness of Haynes' film to a series of monochromatic images of interchangeable models wearing loosely cut, black and white casual clothing, including a number of *keffiyeh* headscarves, which led the collection to be read politically, as conveying a cross-cultural message. The dissolution of identity captured through the final scenes of Haynes' film was reframed by Simons' complementary vision of an anonymous, masked youth culture, marketed as the insubordinate fear generation, filmed in a bleached urban desert. Simons' abstract social commentary, reducing contemporary politics of the environment to an affectless and toneless look, communicated a vision of male youth framed by the stark contrasts of "blinding white and annihilating black" (Marchetti 2003: 55).

The use of theatrical staging to reinforce the visual impact of the collections was later apparent in the nature-related "Virginia Creeper" collection (Fall/Winter 2002–3), drawing on generic imagery from horror films. The artificial layering and padding of many of the garments interspersed different types of fabrics and technologies to construct an eerie image of the brutal industrialization of nature. The discursive press releases accompanying "Virginia Creeper" and "Consumed: A Reflection on Consumerism" (Spring/Summer 2003) reveal a designer attempting to articulate a revised aesthetic language beyond the familiar archetypes of post-punk pop culture, one concerned with the material affect and future sustainability of consumer fashion. A subsequent collection in 2008 was devoted entirely to the material world, showcasing the juxtaposition of natural and artificial fabrics such as neoprene in clashing colors.

Simons' forward motion is not solely concerned with shape-shifting; it also launches a critical inquiry into the haptic qualities of clothing. Touches of material futurism such as fluorescent neoprene gloves made an appearance in the Fall/Winter 2009–10 collection. Allusions to futurist modernism (with shades of the early-twentieth-century celebration of speed, industry, machinery, and youth) have also been made through the settings of many of the shows. The visionary "History of the World" collection (Spring/Summer 2005) wore its musical credentials on its sleeve (with a soundtrack including New Order). But, with its futuristic combination of white leather tunics, its setting at the spherical dome, La Géode, situated in the science and industry park at La Villette in Paris, and a press release name-dropping pioneering computer-scientist Alan Turing and futurist physicist Nikola Tesla, the collection drew attention to Simons' own self-conscious positioning within a temporal dialectic—the calculated fusion of past, present, and future. While Simons' fashionable re-imaging of the doom generation tapped into fears of globalization, unrest, and terrorism at the start of the twenty-first century, his early menswear designs were equally prospective, revealing the transformative potential of fashion imagery and pop culture.

Simons' time-travel through the preceding decades of European pop imagery combines references to the cold minimalism of British music culture after punk, particularly the anguished introspection of Joy Division, with the mood of Bowie's Berlin period, which was marked by the singer's turn in the mid-1970s to a neo-European modernism under the influence of Kraftwerk's detached image and controlled sound—a synth-pop conjuring up a vision of European pop as "modern, forward-looking, and pristinely post-rock" (Reynolds 2006: xxii). In his retrospective account of the estate of Peter Saville, the art director and graphic designer responsible for the iconic record sleeves for the Joy Division and New Order albums, Michael Bracewell posits "elegiac modernity" as the key locus, the set of all points through which the graphic designer expressed both "the passing of modernism and the replacement of modernist ideals with postmodern rearrangements of context and quotation" (Bracewell 2012: 209). Saville's combination of the modernist geometries of form with the postmodern consumption of imagery paralleled an overarching preoccupation with an "elegiac pop minimalism"—the combination of an "exquisite, highly poetic imagery with a kind of brutalist formalism" (Bracewell 2012: 218), a sensibility close to Simons' own. Given full access to the graphic designer's personal archive, the "Closer" collection (Fall/Winter 2003–4) included a tribute to Saville's work, transposing the language of fine art to the world of commodity communications. The reproduction of Henri Fantin-Latour's painting *A Basket of Roses* (1890) on the cover of New Order's 1983 release, *Power, Corruption and Lies*, was rerouted through Simons' own collection, re-inscribed on the front of T-shirts and on the back of leather coats. The collection was accompanied by the show's invitation in the shape of a record sleeve. The ephemera of catalogs and invitations are designed to complement the label's visual identity, dominated by monochrome black and white with disjunctive splashes of red, close-up photographic portraits of the models and the use of portentous post-punk language ("All shadows and deliverance" was the strapline for "The History of My World" collection).

INTERMISSION

Peter Saville's graphic designs sit on the cusp between "the passing of modernism" and "a postmodern environment of constant, simultaneous reclamations of the detailing and successive moods of pop-cultural history" (Bracewell 2012: 148). Postmodernism can be situated as part of the perverse legacy of Andy Warhol, whose prophetic vision of an "art-celebrity-fashion nexus" is now the status quo (Church Gibson 2011: 5). The Warholian cliché of surface representation and serial repetition is one that Simons has simultaneously challenged and perpetuated through a visual interpretation of the artist's legacy for his womenswear collections at Christian Dior. His use of Warhol's drawings from the 1950s as a leitmotif running through the Fall/Winter 2013–14 ready-to-wear collection resurrects the artist's more refined early art-works, such as spidery shoe drawings embossed on handbags or portraits of women embroidered on bustier dresses, part of a commercial partnership between Christian Dior and the Andy Warhol Foundation for the Visual Arts. This type of co-branding operation puts the fashion house into renewed dialogue with artistic creation—Christian Dior was himself an accomplished art collector and gallery owner—while allowing Simons to develop his personal interest in mid-century design and his activities as a private collector of contemporary art. His collection includes pieces by LA-based mix-media artist, Sterling Ruby, who is known for his scratch-paintings and installations (Rawsthorn 2012). As well as employing Ruby to design the interior of his Tokyo Aoyama menswear boutique in 2008, Simons used images from Ruby's splashed paint prints on the satin fabrics used to make a number of gowns for his couture debut at Dior in 2012.

A further collaboration with Ruby for the Fall/Winter 2014–15 Raf Simons menswear collection took the designer's engagement with contemporary art to a new level. Since Marc Jacobs' celebrated co-merchandising operation with Takashi Murakami for Louis Vuitton in 2002, art-fashion collaborations have become a routine part of fashion branding, co-opting artistic signatures for commercial appeal. Simons and Ruby, however, collaborated on the entire collection, blending color with craft by splashing bright paint onto oversized formal menswear. Danish fabric manufacturer Kvadrat, with whom Simons collaborated on a parallel textile collection, provided the durable material for the patched coats (Judah 2014).

Such collaborations investigate the potential interaction between the visual arts and fashion, while at the same time delineating the formal distinctions between both. Simons' practice goes beyond a straightforward art-fashion collaboration (in which fashion is elevated through artistic influence or in which art is commodified through product development) towards a properly interdisciplinary project testing the definitional parameters of both categories—interdisciplinary practice understood as not only conjoining forms of knowledge or techniques, but also undertaking "interrogatory work about what is left outside the boundaries of given disciplines [. . .] both the site of a productive joining and the marker of the boundary between" (Downing 2012: 216, 218).

The fashion brands housed in the main European conglomerates (LVMH, Kering, Prada Group, Richemont) are engaged in a cultural-economic exchange with the global art market, investing heavily to extend their influence across the interlocking forms of visual culture, digital media, communications, design, and architecture, to create a new intersectional definition of luxury, updating the historical dialogue between art and fashion (Geczy and Karaminas 2012). The management of this *neo-luxury* includes lucrative co-branding partnerships such as Dior's sponsorship—under Simons' helm—of the annual Guggenheim International Gala hosted by the museum in New York in 2013. Such cooperation would suggest that Simons' appointment as creative director at Dior was partly intended to facilitate the brand's expansion into the global art market while consolidating the designer's creative exchange with the visual arts. While the decorative aesthetic and theatrical sensibility of John Galliano, Simons' high-profile predecessor, had revitalized Christian Dior's heritage in costume design, the strategic appointment of a more circumspect couturier following the demise of the star-designer enabled the house to reinforce its artistic lineage and to project its intellectual aspirations. Simons' previous engagements with the art and culture industries had included curating a trans-medial exhibition of imagery of teenagers, *The Fourth Sex: Adolescent Extremes,* in Florence in 2002, and the *Transmission: The Avant-Garde Diaries* event in Berlin in 2011, which was promoted as a "digital lifestyle hub and event series" and sponsored by Mercedes-Benz to showcase emerging talent from across the visual arts. (Simons chose an exhibition of photography by Peter de Potter called *Image-Machine.*) The event sealed the corporate exchange between the fashion and automobile industries focusing on shared interests in engineering, innovation, and technology.

Robert Radford locates the creative dialogue between art and fashion in "the poetics of associated ideas" (Radford 1998: 155), a formulation shared by Valerie Steele who has described fashion as a "cannibalistic business" (Steele 2012: 25), channeling adjacent forms of visual media (from high art to pop culture) to feed its constant creative need for contextual stimuli. Prior to his total collaboration with Sterling Ruby on the Fall/Winter 2014–15 menswear collection, Simons' artistic engagement had involved embedding motifs from the work of earlier twentieth-century artists in his own designs for Jil Sander these included a chromatic tribute to Yves Klein's blue (Spring/Summer 2008) and a tonal tribute to ceramicist Pol Chambost (Fall/Winter 2009–10). Simons reproduced Leonard Tsughura Foujita's ink techniques showing women's faces on tunics in the Spring/Summer 2010 collection and transferred Pablo Picasso's ceramic designs onto sweaters in the Spring/Summer 2012 collection. These stylistic flourishes draw attention to the designer's own fashionable translation of the formal preoccupations with color, shape, and volume that inform the aesthetics of modernist design. In an interview for a piece on nostalgia in *Vogue* in March 2012, Simons described the allure of mid-century modernism and its influential transposition to his own Antwerp home, which contains furniture by George Nakashima and Isamu Noguchi and ceramics by Valentine Schlegel (Holgate 2012; Rawsthorn 2012). This contrived staging of the designer's own habitat aimed to complement his artistic reputation, but also, more strategically, to consolidate his neo-modern revision of mid-century fashions and fabrics at Jil Sander and to promote an ongoing reconfiguration of the couture heritage for the twenty-first-century consumer at Christian Dior. Simons' self-fashioning as an artist-by-proxy follows in art and fashion's shadow dance through the twentieth century, including Dior's own mid-century neoclassicism, which pushed him "towards clarity of outline and shape, emphasized by black, and carrying echoes of an ordered, formal world, where discretion rather than spontaneity was stressed" (Wollen 2004: 173). Notwithstanding the overall importance of the brand or the collaborative work of a design studio in the fabrication of ready-to-wear, Simons' dialogue with the visual arts strategically complements the authorship of his collections, a position rooted in the *haute couture* tradition with its emphasis on the articulation of an individual signature and creative worldview (Manzoni and Jourgeaud 2012: 5).

Unlike Jean Baudrillard's earlier use of the prefix "neo" to indicate an "anachronistic resurrection" of the past (Baudrillard 1998[1970]: 99), as symptomatic of cultural recycling, Simons' re-evaluation of the modernist design heritage transcends mere stylistic quotation and is more attuned to the resurfacing of pure form characterized by the "neo-modern" in contemporary theories of the built and designed environment. Tracing the historical convergence of fashion and architecture, Bradley Quinn describes how early-twentieth-century architects drew specifically on the formal functionality of menswear to argue against the perceived feminine ostentation and decoration of the previous century. Relying on core elements from engineering, mathematics and geometry, such as proportion, volume, and mass, both fashion designers and architects "produce environments defined through spatial awareness by working with and against the human form" (Quinn 2004: 6).

Jacques Rancière has argued that the continued relevance of the Bauhaus tradition of architecture and design, of the functionalist "paradigm of the flat surface," lies in its redefinition of "the place of artistic activities in the set of practices that configure the shared material world" (Rancière 2007[2003]: 103, 91). However, fashion's return to the forms of modernist architecture—"associated with smooth, pure and more often than not, white surfaces" (Brennan *et al.* 2001: 5)—is also part of a wider contemporary commodification of modernist design through the communications strategies of luxury branding and the minimalist aesthetics of corporate retail space, situated more broadly within an era of total design (Foster 2002: 14). The pure lines of Simons' later menswear collections, for example, interpreted as a type of constructed architecture (Menkes 2006), illustrate the designer's willingness to align himself with the stylistic heritage of the so-called "architectural" fashion designers Christian Dior and

Cristóbal Balenciaga. The recurrent articulation of spatial metaphors also shows Simons to be operating transversally, reshaping his aesthetic sensibility to suit his commercial circumstances, imagining a design strategy that would cut across the fine and applied arts, through what Rancière terms the *regime* of art, "a network of relationships which informs the way an object, act, process or practice is understood as art" (Davis 2010: 134). The philosopher's radical reimagining of aesthetic practice, as "a redistribution of the relations between the forms of sensory experience" (Rancière 2009: 24), bypasses the standard historicist separation of modern from postmodern, instead repositioning the artwork as an object of sensorial experience (Davis 2010: 136).

The interior design of Simons' retail outlets—both those for Jil Sander and the standalone boutiques for the Raf Simons label in Japan—suggests an affective manipulation of both commercial space and designed object, a sensory experience that enables the designer to transpose the material objects of fashion to another symbolic realm, one that seeks to convey the immaterial values of brand identity as they are processed through artistic and architectural paradigms. Ruby interpreted the Raf Simons boutique in Tokyo as a visceral canvas by installing huge photographic prints of abstract splashes of blue paint on the walls and on the furniture, so as to embed the clothing literally in the art. In contrast, Roger Hiorns' geometric structure for the label's boutique in Osaka carved out a sparsely hyperrealist space by dividing the boutique diagonally with a 9-meter mirror, surrounded by glass curtain walls displaying clothes that appeared to float in midair. Angular geometry and reflective surfaces were also the lynchpin of Simons' own spatial design for the Jil Sander boutique in SoHo, New York, in 2008 (Merkel 2010), conceived as an art gallery presenting the collection sequentially in a static recreation of a catwalk show. At the rear end, vertical rotating slats shrouded a white marble staircase, designed by artist Germaine Kruip, a creative touch echoed by the freestanding, mirrored dressing rooms. This vision of design was at once innovative and functional, translating into visual terms the tonal sobriety and austere sensibility of the label.

MINIMUM–MAXIMUM

Suzy Menkes' report of the Jil Sander Spring/Summer 2012 collection, presented in Milan in September 2011, highlighted the designer's "meticulous modernism" in translating the label's minimalist heritage (beginning and ending with his take on Jil Sander's iconic white shirt) to the Italian *alta moda* spirit of couture (Menkes 2011). Rather than simply consolidating Sander's reputation as a minimalist designer, Simons overturned the expectation by imagining a maximalist vision of the label that continued to emphasize her purist sensibility through experiments with color and form. Harriet Walker has traced the history of minimalism in fashion from the sartorial reduction associated with early-twentieth-century modernism (architect Mies van der Rohe's maxim "less is more" transposed to Chanel's fashionable functionalism), through the aesthetics of refusal associated with the artistic minimalism of the 1960s, to the purism of the late-twentieth-century minimalist fashion designs characterized by Calvin Klein and Donna Karan, both influenced by the American tradition of casual sportswear. Sander, who had founded her own label in 1978, became known principally for her androgynous silhouettes and the conjunction of functional sobriety with luxurious techno-fabrics such as neoprene, added for "architectural fluidity" (Walker 2011: 92).

In Simons' final collections for the Jil Sander label in 2011–12, a feminine ideal resurfaced referencing Christian Dior's neoclassical New Look, preempting the designer's subsequent tenure at the couture house and aesthetically remolding modern eveningwear by banishing the ubiquitous little black dress that had been a popular mainstay of the previous decade. The use of color blocking to offset the precise, functional tailoring of both the Jil Sander menswear and womenswear introduced a playful dimension to the label's recognizable austerity. The women's Spring/Summer 2011 collection flirted with classical Hollywood glamour by ironically accompanying the display of billowing neon polyester gowns with snatches of Bernard Herrmann's musical score for *Psycho* (Hitchcock (dir.), 1960). The collection included a floor-length evening dress in vibrant orange made from a polyester outer shell and a smooth silk lining, the synthetic fiber used to capture the garish color and the luxurious fabric to sheath the body. This subtle disjuncture between the haptic appeal and the visual quality of the garment was also to be found in the winter collections, such as Fall/Winter 2009–10, which combined fluid curves and mixed fabrics to modernize mid-century frock-coats and dresses, using panels of robust fabric, ergonomically encasing the body in a classically feminine shape. Simons' individual contribution to the label's heritage was notable for such daring splashes of color, "his embracing of bright neons, even romantic pastels, rendered in everything from neoprene to chiffon and gauze" (Walker 2011: 152). The abstraction of minimalism was undercut by the bold injections of vibrant color.

Simons' luxurious combination of classic tailoring and neon coloring for Jil Sander was also manifest in the label's designs for Tilda Swinton for her role as Emma in Luca Guadagnino's film *I Am Love* (*Io Sono l'Amore,* 2009). Simons' team collaborated with the film's costume designer, Antonella Cannarozzi, who was Oscar-nominated for her work in fashioning the supremely elegant wardrobe of a family of rich Milanese industrialists, including most notably the Fendi furs worn by Marisa Berenson. Alongside this spectacular inclusion of luxury, the Jil Sander pieces are memorable for their formal subtlety and chromatic expressivity. Swinton's character Emma, a Russian émigré and the adulterous wife of a rich textile industrialist, is delineated by Simons' austere tailoring, which on a purely narrative level indicates her social status, but which on a symbolic level distances her from the surrounding opulence through the maximal color coding. The film makes an obvious opposition between Berenson's "Italian" style—heavy on furs, jewels, and leather goods, despite wearing the French label Hermès—and Swinton's pared-down model of functional professionalism (although she too is adorned with an Hermès "Birkin" handbag). Emma's subjective transformation from an empty clotheshorse to a passionate woman is over-scored by Simons' designs, which act out, rather than merely accompany, the character's narrative arc. Karen de Perthuis has captured the formative role of fashion in *I Am Love,*
describing how Emma's transformation from style icon to woman in love is conveyed through the precise cuts, luxurious fabrics, and tonal range of Simons' designs, "the shifting palette of block colour signalling a clear emotional barometer" (de Perthuis 2012: 278). This is translated by the opposition between the formal tailored dresses variously used to denote Emma's social function (in dark colors) or to signify her emotional awakening (in bright red), and the more shapely gown (in tangerine orange) used to signal her sexual appeal, preempting a cathartic escape from the stifling carapace of high-bourgeois fashion at the end of the film. De Perthuis notes that Simons' costumes act as a uniform for Swinton's character, thereby linking the designer's purist fashions for Jil Sander to his menswear designs with their parallel focus on serial functionalism. The graphic simplicity of Emma's wardrobe is a perfect fit for the actor's much publicized fashion sense and the director's architectural sensibility, channeled through the location shooting at the 1930s rationalist Villa Necchi Campiglio and the retro graphic design of the film's credits, which include a series of black and white photographic shots of hibernal Milan prefacing the narrative.

THE HANGING GARDEN

Simons built his reputation on an abstract intellectualism centering on the communication of thematic concepts and masculine ideals, a visual language expanded through his precise tailoring and maximalist color blocking for Jil Sander. A more poetic vision came to the fore in his revision of the classic couture heritage of Christian Dior. Simons' final collection at Jil Sander in February 2012 set the tone for a more expressive vision of modernity in both the couture and the ready-to-wear collections for the house of Dior, which included a fresh interpretation of the cinched hourglass silhouettes and the classic bar suit jacket, reimagined by Simons as a sensual cross between a dress and a jacket (ready-to-wear Spring/Summer 2013). Following historically focused exhibitions on Dior's artistic and cinematic inspirations, the Christian Dior museum, located at the designer's family home, Villa les Rhumbs in Granville, organized a celebration of the artistic influence of impressionism on the designer's craft in 2013, tracing the house's use of floral imagery. The exhibition, suitably set in the superb belle époque villa, reunited two of Christian Dior's individual passions—architecture and flowers.

The late 1940s New Look was fashioned around the retrogressive link between femininity and nature, the precise shaping of the body in counterpoint to the expressive use of floral motifs drawn from the artistic models of the late nineteenth century—the impressionism of Claude Monet and the pointillism of Georges Seurat (Müller 2013: 9). Simons' first *haute couture* collections (Fall/Winter 2012–13 and Spring/Summer 2013) took inspiration from Dior's own preference for wildflowers: one bright red layered bustier evening dress embroidered with poppies evoked Monet's eponymous canvas from 1873 and another white organza dress with pointillist embroidery was redolent of the 1949 *Miss Dior* gown. Dior had himself always been resistant to the anti-ornamental strain of modernism, a productive tension running through Simons' revision of the house's couture heritage (Chenoune 2013: 14). The staging of his early catwalk shows for Dior complemented the conventional feminine template by blending the standard floral imagery with the architectural purity of the designs. The walls for the first couture show were lined with flowers, encasing the clothing within a poetic decor. In the Spring/Summer 2013 *haute couture* collection the neo-formalist experiments with shape and volume were conveyed through the imaginative manipulation of the performance space. Erected in the *Jardin des Tuileries* in January 2013, the structure was lined with external mirrors reflecting the image of the winter garden, a visual effect echoed inside through the bleak setting of bare trees used to delineate the winding catwalk, the sparseness of which was acoustically enhanced by the ambient minimalism of the contemporary indie-pop trio The xx.

Included in the Dior Impressions exhibition were examples of Simons' tribute to the house's pastel heritage, such as a layered polyester-tulle gown, finely embroidered with Oilier sequins and Swarovski beads in a floral motif (*haute couture,* Spring/Summer 2013), developing the designer's blending of the decorative, the luxurious and the synthetic. The exhibition opened with Simons' double-face bustier dress (*haute couture,* Fall/Winter 2012–13), made from white organza and embroidered with floral motifs—a *trompe l'oeil* effect of plastic violets embroidered on the front and a classical image of roses printed on the back. Dior's New Look was formally austere despite the flourishes of nostalgic femininity (Wollen 2004: 173). Nevertheless, the house continues to favor the promotion of its expressive sensibility. Christian Dior's *haute couture* collections between 1947 and 1957 simultaneously balanced two ideals of an elite femininity—that of the sophisticate and the ingénue (Palmer 2009: 36). There was a central paradox underlying his reactionary turn to the courtesans and coquettes of the belle époque as models for his sculpted silhouette of the mid-century *Parisienne*: despite the decorative ornamentation, his commercial success stemmed from an artistic sobriety (Pujalet-Plaà 2010: 222). Simons sought to exploit this historical tension between an archaic (Western) ideal of femininity and the contemporary international consumer of couture in the Fall/Winter 2013–14 collection, which was fashioned around the positioning of the brand in the global and digital age, preempting the emergence of a "new digital aesthetic" promoted by trend forecaster WGSN in their 2014 bulletin. The multicolored collection including 3D embroideries was divided into four continental zones to acknowledge the altered landscape of contemporary couture, particularly in light of the concurrent economic rise and consumer might of Brazil and China. The formal staging was radically juxtaposed by casual shots of the pre-show collection imagined by hip photographers such as Terry Richardson, whose own louche signature style provocatively rubbed up against the precious refinement of *haute couture.*

The Spring/Summer 2014 ready-to-wear collection was set in a faux-tropical garden, providing a lush surround for the designer's less reverential take on Dior's visual heritage. The collection, framed by an angular scaffold draped with neon wisteria and artificial flowers, was remarkable for its pop jewelry, its graphic use of language on floral prints and its double-face pleated bar jackets, a gender switch carried over from the designer's concurrent menswear. A final flourish consolidated the opposition between the ultra-modern suits and the ultra-feminine gowns: the models' curtain call was used to present an entirely new collection conceived as a summative snapshot of Simons' revision of the Dior heritage through the rotation of metallic silk ball gowns and monochrome pant suits. This collection marked the transition from a respectful homage to Dior's iconic silhouettes to a more complex actualization of the house's heritage in creative dialogue with Simons' own parallel vision of contemporary menswear.

MOVEMENT

In light of the Raf Simons Spring/Summer 2014 collection, it is possible to conclude this critical inquiry into the designer's trajectory by remarking that the overall focus of his menswear has shifted from the fashionable rerouting of subcultural icons, looks, and sensibilities to a more sustained exploration of form through graphic experiments with cut, proportion, and volume. This neo-formalist focus on the material product, including the futuristic use of artificial fabrics for synthetic panels and geometric inserts stitched onto traditional materials, has been accompanied by the questioning of masculine archetypes (the back and forth movement between alienated boys and suited men) and the inclusion of certain unisex elements into the designer's repertoire. This is indicative of a broader stylistic shift in men's fashion towards a preoccupation with shape and tactility influenced by womenswear—a trend marketed to male consumers as a technical (and therefore gender-appropriate) interest in engineering and fabrication. It is also illustrative of the broader "neo-geo" trend in twenty-first-century high fashion through the "influx of bright, geometric patterning" (Dimant 2010: 206). The incongruous presence of industrial fabrics such as neoprene, the synthetic rubber used to make practical consumables such as laptop cases and drysuits, seen on a series of detachable neon sleeves worn over formal suits in the Fall/Winter 2009–10 collection, follows Bradley Quinn's account of the contemporary manipulation of "techno" fabrics in fashion. He argues that such "crossover materials mark a specific moment in fashion, in which garments are beginning to be characterized by hybrid forms, and are in themselves emerging as complex, multifaceted hybrids" (Quinn 2012: 94). Simons' hybrid designs subvert the basic rules and conservative assumptions of menswear—the natural reliance on staples such as the structured suit jacket—by using a high percentage of synthetic fibers such as plastic (Spring/Summer 2008) and latex (Spring/Summer 2011), or polyamide and elastane, which provide the necessary elasticity required for the designer's shape-shifting. Simons' mixed ensembles best illustrate this material experimentation: Fall/Winter 2009–10 contained a tailored gray waistcoat with a fine blue stripe on the front and a neon blue verso in neoprene. Fall/Winter 2011–12 included a blue tailored dress shirt with wide-legged plastic trousers and a rubber bolero jacket. This vision of contemporary menswear is, in essence, bifacial—positioned on the cusp between the formal and the recalcitrant, the natural and the synthetic.

Simons' later menswear attempts to blend technology with formality through the static security of tailoring. The designer's use of geometric inserts and futuristic materials positions his designs alongside Lucas Ossendrijver's collections for Lanvin with their parallel emphasis on form and engineering. Simons' later menswear also subtly subverts the ideal of an alienated male youth that his label has been so instrumental in disseminating. The move beyond the limited templates and gendered constraints of men's fashion was pioneered by Simons' mentor Walter Van Beirendonck, who experimented with queer erotic apparatus and cross-gender fluidity, using corsets, high heels, and dresses in his various menswear collections (Steele 2013). In the more avant-garde forms of designers like Rad Hourani or JW Anderson, a unisex aesthetic seeking to transcend gender categories is emerging as a key signature in both luxury ready-to-wear and advanced contemporary fashion. Gender ambiguity (channeled through the expression of male femininity) was noted as a key trend at the Spring/Summer 2015 Paris menswear shows, across a broad spectrum of labels and houses, from the use of delicate male models (Dries Van Noten) or female models (Saint Laurent) to entirely genderless collections such as JW Anderson's revival of the heritage brand Loewe for LVMH (Flaccavento 2014). Simons' own transgender dynamic is noticeable in the cross-fertilization between the menswear for his nominal label and the womenswear for Dior: Fall/Winter 2012–13 included outsized floral shirts and Spring/Summer 2013 featured double-face men's suit jackets with a formal blue cotton front and a floral pleated effect on the back. Such designs incorporate elements from women's couture into a more amorphous vision of men's fashion, in touch as much with the material shaping of clothing as with the projected image of masculinity. Alongside this conceptual vision of menswear Simons has gained commercial visibility via co-branding deals with popular sportswear labels Fred Perry, Eastpak, Adidas, and Asics, each of which transposed the Raf Simons brand identity and design aesthetic to casual staples such as polo shirts, sneakers, and backpacks.

Raf Simons' high-profile nomination as creative director at Christian Dior in 2012 enabled the house to distance itself from (what was retroactively perceived as) an era of excess. Following John Galliano's dismissal from the house in 2011, the arch-theatrical vision of the star-designer was strategically positioned as passé in the context of the global economic crisis. His decorative aesthetic was seen as out of touch with the more sober modernity of a younger generation of more conceptual designers, who had come to prominence through the 2000s, known collectively for an architectural (rather than a thematic) vision of fashion: Phoebe Philo for Céline; Nicolas Ghesquière for Balenciaga; Alber Elbaz and Lucas Ossendrijver for Lanvin; Riccardo Tisci for Givenchy; and Hedi Slimane for Dior Homme and Yves Saint Laurent. Following the previous generation of star-designers (Tom Ford, John Galliano, and Marc Jacobs—Karl Lagerfeld both precedes and transcends such a chronology), this new generation has continued reviving the heritage of the traditional Parisian couture houses by transposing their discrete codes, identities, and values to the exigencies of the early-twenty-first-century global industry. Dior's nomination of Simons is characteristic of a wider trend in luxury fashion that emphasizes the self-effacement of the designer in favor of the brand and the product, striking a precarious balance between the designer's individual artistic signature and the cultural iconicity of the fashion house as it is channeled through corporate branding. This strategic articulation of design innovation and brand heritage has, in effect, been at the forefront of the financial consolidation of European luxury and high fashion since the mid-1990s. In her analysis of the cultural poetics of late-twentieth-century post-fashion, Barbara Vinken pointed to the destruction of the "Western Paris-based fashion system" (Vinken 2005: 64) based on the waning of the elitist, aristocratic model of *haute couture*. Its revival in modified form in the early twenty-first century, built on the successful branding of the European heritage of luxury goods, provides the commercial backdrop for the rise of a designer like Simons, able to continue developing his own creative signature through an independent menswear label, whilst in parallel reinterpreting the visual codes of an emblematic French design house and global brand.

Since the launch of his label in 1995, Raf Simons has caught the zeitgeist of contemporary fashion, supplying menswear with a versatile range of styles, shapes, and symbols that articulate ideas about masculinity, influenced by European pop culture and electronic music, fine art, modernist architecture, and graphic design. "It happened," Monsieur Dior noted simply in his autobiography in 1957, "that my own inclinations coincided with the spirit and sensibility of the times" (Dior 1957: 45). Likewise, Simons' nomination at one of the most prestigious of the Parisian fashion houses was a perfect fit, positioning him as heir to the artistic and architectural strand of the couturier's legacy, and making him instrumental in the brand's global projection of its creative heritage.

References

Arnold, Rebecca. 2001. *Fashion, Desire and Anxiety: Image and Morality in the 20th Century.* London: I. B. Tauris.
Baudrillard, Jean. 1998[1970]. *The Consumer Society: Myths and Structures.* London: Sage.
Bracewell, Michael. 2012. *The Space Between: Selected Writings on Art.* London: Ridinghouse.
Brennan, Ann Marie, Nahum Goodenow and Brendan D. Moran. 2001. "Resurfacing Modernism: An Editorial Overview." *Perspecta* 32: 5–6.

Breward, Christopher and Caroline Evans (eds). 2005. *Fashion and Modernity.* London: Berg.

Calder, Alexander. 1951. "What Abstract Art Means to Me." *Museum of Modern Art Bulletin* 18(3): 8–9.

Chenoune, Farid. 2013. "Meeting in Paradise: Dresses, Flowers, and Women." In Florence Müller (ed.) *Dior Impressions: The Inspiration and Influence of Impressionism at the House of Dior*, pp. 14–21. New York: Rizzoli.

Church Gibson, Pamela. 2011. *Fashion and Celebrity Culture.* London: Berg.

Davis, Glyn. 2000. "Health and Safety in the Home: Todd Haynes's Clinical White World." In David Alderson and Linda Anderson (eds) *Territories of Desire in Queer Culture: Reconfiguring the Contemporary Boundaries*, pp. 183–201. Manchester: Manchester University Press.

Davis, Oliver. 2010. *Jacques Rancière.* Cambridge: Polity Press.

Deleuze, Gilles. 1994[1968]. *Difference and Repetition.* Trans. P. Patton. New York: Columbia University Press.

de Perthuis Karen. 2012. "I Am Style: Tilda Swinton as Emma in Luca Guadagnino's *I Am Love.*" *Film, Fashion and Consumption* 1(3): 269–288.

Dimant, Elyssa. 2010. *Fashion and Minimalism: Reduction in the Postmodern Era.* New York: Harper Collins.

Dior, Christian. 1957. *Christian Dior and I.* Trans. A. Fraser. New York: E. P. Dutton.

Doane, Mary Ann. 2004. "Pathos and Pathology: The Cinema of Todd Haynes." *Camera Obscura* 57, 19(3): 1–20.

Downing, Lisa. 2012. "Interdisciplinarity, Cultural Studies, Queer: Historical Contexts and Contemporary Contentions in France." *Paragraph* 35(2): 215–32.

Evans, Caroline. 2003. *Fashion at the Edge: Spectacle, Modernity and Deathliness.* New Haven, CT: Yale University Press.

Flaccavento, Angelo. 2014. "In Paris, Ambiguity is in the Air." *The Business of Fashion.* http://www.businessoffashion.com/2014/06/paris-ambiguity-air.html (accessed July 14, 2014).

Foster, Hal. 2002. *Design and Crime (and Other Diatribes).* London: Verso.

Foster, Hal. 2011. *The Art-Architecture Complex.* London: Verso.

Frisa, Maria Luisa (ed.). 2005. *Raf Simons Redux.* Edizioni Charta: Milan.

Furniss, Jo-Ann. 2011. "Raf's Army." *Dazed and Confused* January: 78–89.

Fury, Alexander. 2013. "Fashionable Ways." In Fantastic Man (ed.) *Buttoned-Up: A Survey of a Curious Fashion Phenomenon.* London: Penguin.

Gay, Peter. 2008. *Modernism: The Lure of Heresy. From Baudelaire and Beckett and Beyond.* New York: W. W. Norton & Company.

Geczy, Adam and Vicki Karaminas (eds). 2012. *Fashion and Art.* London: Berg.

Heath, Ashley. 2002. "The New Raf Riff." *Arena Homme Plus* no. 16 (Autumn/Winter): 292–7, 370.

Holgate, Mark. 2012. "Out of the West." *Vogue* March: 318, 324.

Horyn, Cathy. 2005. "Raf." *The New York Times, T: The New York Times Style Magazine* September 18: 190–5.

Jones, Terry (ed.). 2013. *Raf Simons.* Cologne: Taschen.

Judah, Hettie. 2014. "Inside Raf Simons' Kvadrat Collaboration." *The Business of Fashion.* http://www.businessoffashion.com/2014/02/bof-exclusive-inside-raf-simons-kvadrat-collaboration.html (accessed February 16, 2014).

Manzoni, Isabelle and Bénédicte Jourgeaud. 2012. "Dior ouvre un nouvelle page." *Journal du Textile* no. 2124 (April 17): 2–5.

Marchetti, Luca. 2003. "White on White, Translucent Black Capes.. ." *View on Colour: The Colour Forecasting Book* no. 24 (June): 54–7.

Martínez, Javier Gimeno. 2007. "Selling *Avant-garde*: How Antwerp Became a Fashion Capital (1990–2002)." *Urban Studies* 44(12): 2449–64.

Menkes, Suzy. 2006. "Affirming the Male in a Long, Dark Winter." *International Herald Tribune*, January 30: 18.

Menkes, Suzy. 2011. "Playing with Mid-Century Modernism." *International Herald Tribune* September 26: 9–10.

Merkel, Jayne. 2010. "Interior Eye." *Architectural Design* 80(1): 114–19.

Meyer, James. 2001. *Minimalism: Art and Polemics in the Sixties.* New Haven, CT: Yale University Press.

Müller, Florence (ed.). 2013. *Dior Impressions: The Inspiration and Influence of Impressionism at the House of Dior.* New York: Rizzoli.

Palmer, Alexandra. 2009. *Dior: A New Look, A New Enterprise (1947–57).* London: V&A Publishing.

Potter, Susan. 2004. "Dangerous Spaces: *Safe.*" *Camera Obscura* 57, 19(3): 125–55.

Pujalet-Plaà, Eric. 2010. "Dior, Christian." In V. Steele (ed.) *The Berg Companion to Fashion*, pp. 219–23. London: Berg.

Quinn, Bradley. 2004. *The Fashion of Architecture.* London: Berg.

Quinn, Bradley. 2012. *Fashion Futures.* London: Merrell.

Radford, Robert. 1998. "Dangerous Liaisons: Art, Fashion and Individualism." *Fashion Theory* 2(2): 151–63.

Rancière, Jacques. 2007[2003]. *The Future of the Image.* Trans. G. Elliott. London: Verso.

Rancière, Jacques. 2009. *The Aesthetic Unconscious.* Trans. D. Keates and J. Swenson. London: Polity.

Rawsthorn, Alice. 2012. "What Makes Raf Run?" *W Magazine*(March). http://www.wmagazine.com/fashi

on/2012/03/raf-simons-designer-obsessions (accessed July 14, 2014).

Rees-Roberts, Nick. 2013. "Boys Keep Swinging: The Fashion Iconography of Hedi Slimane." *Fashion Theory* 17(1): 7–26.

Reynolds, Simon. 2006. *Rip It Up and Start Again: Postpunk 1978–1984*. London: Faber & Faber.

Savage, Jon. 1995. "The Simple Things You See Are All Complicated." In H. Kureishi and J. Savage (eds) *The Faber Book of Pop*, pp. xxi–xxxiii. London: Faber & Faber.

Steele, Valerie. 2012. "Fashion." In A. Geczy and V. Karaminas (eds) *Fashion and Art*, pp. 13–27. London: Berg.

Steele, Valerie. 2013. "Fashion Prescribes the Ritual." In W. Van Beirendonck (ed.) *Dream the World Awake*, pp. 135–43. Tielt: Lannoo Publishers.

Teunissen, José. 2011. "Deconstructing Belgian and Dutch Fashion Dreams: From Global Trends to Local Crafts." *Fashion Theory* 15(2): 157–76.

Vinken, Barbara. 2005. *Fashion Zeitgeist: Trends and Cycles in the Fashion System*. Trans. M. Hewson. London: Berg.

von Olfers, Sophie. 2010. "We are not concerned with approval: Helmut Lang in conversation with Sophie von Olfers." In S. von Olfers and S. Gaensheimer (eds) *Not in Fashion: Photography and Fashion in the 90s*, pp. 51–6. Bielefeld: Kerber Verlag.

Walker, Harriet. 2011. *Less is More: Minimalism in Fashion*. London: Merrell.

Wollen, Peter. 2004. *Paris Manhattan: Writings on Art*. London: Verso.

WISHING ON A STAR:
Promoting and personifying designer collections and fashion brands

Anne Peirson-Smith

This article highlights the micro, bottom-up branding endeavors that two independent fashion designers are engaged in for visibility and survival amidst this shifting production–consumption axis, namely Hong Kong-based independent label Daydream Nation by Kay and Jing Wong and Rose Studio by established Chinese *haute couture* designer Guo Pei in Beijing. At the same time, at a macro-level it highlights the shift from the dominance of a uni-centric notion of fashion to a multicultural, transnational clothing regime whereby "contemporary fashion systems may be recast as an array of competing and inter-meshing systems cutting across western and non-western cultures" (Craik 1994: 6). In doing this, the article supports the need for a reevaluation of the original notions of the fashion system. This is increasingly becoming a pluralistic, multi-way flow of production and trading vectors, rather than a traditional system of fixed production flows radiating outwards from a Western-centric point (Davis 1992; Niessen 2003; Skov 2010) as it was originally represented. In other words, a new geo-economic world order is emerging as traditional sources of fashion production such as China become a center of fashion consumption for luxury brands for new middle-class customers, thereby realigning the dynamics and geographies of trading relationships and how brands are communicated. Here the designer often relies on local state and media support to secure a foothold in the market. This conscious promotion of fashion designer as national commodity and as part of the narrative fabric of a nation begs some fundamental questions that this article addresses by analyzing the literature and examining two grounded cases. The lines of research inquiry include: does the fashion designer make the fashion center or does the fashion center make the fashion designer? And what role does a world-class Chinese fashion designer and couturier have on both the domestic and international stages? Also, why is going global such a prevalent aspiration, and how is it being managed by Chinese designers in terms of their personal and corporate branding?

To answer these questions, first, the article will examine the prevailing literature and examine the celebrity-oriented fashion system and its adherence to the promotion of a new fashion story as a central brand management strategy, followed by a discussion of fashion design development in Hong Kong and China as the frame of operation. Finally, the article will be rounded off with descriptive findings that test out these themes from grounded case examples of two design teams based on qualitative data resulting from ethnographic, semi-structured interviews with designers in their respective Beijing and Hong Kong studios from 2010–12.

THE FASHION STAR SYSTEM

The existence and contribution of design professionals in the creative or culture industries as producers is seen as being significant both by academics and practitioners in controlling the global and local flows of materials, visual and textual information in an unending circuit of cultural production (Hesmondhalgh and Pratt 2005). As can be seen in the evolution of various creative industries such as art and architecture, the global fashion industry has been built on the backs of individual "star" designer names to head up high-end fashion houses such as Gucci, Louis Vuitton, and Chanel, for example, where "personal image has helped to transform brands" (Tungate 2008: 57), or has become inseparable from the essence of the brand in some cases.

In his study of creativity and the art world, Becker (1982) demonstrated that artistic creativity is not so much an act of individual genius as it is the product of the cooperative effort of a number of people. Essentially, creative production is a collaborative, group-based process that is socially constructed, and regulated by a contextualized, complex social system. This consists of the "field" populated by those cultural intermediaries and powerbrokers located in the circuit of cultural production and consumption (Braham 1997; Du Gay and Pryke 2002). These experts define, judge, support, and disseminate creativity and creative works as cultural capital (Bourdieu 1993), in addition to, and in connection with, the "domain" embodying all of the shared conventions, codes, discourses, and creative products systemically defining the creative field itself (Csikszentmihalyi 1996).

As many fashion scholars have also observed (Crane 2000; Entwistle 2002; Kawamura 2005), the global fashion system as part of the creative industries functions on the collaborative interaction between various teams of knowledge workers involved in the production and supply chain. Essentially, these "boundary spanners" manage the "filters" and "flows" of the fashion system through print, broadcast, and social media channels. Their existence was made necessary because the fashion industry from the twentieth century onwards, in step with the growth of the newspaper and media industries needing pages and airtime to fill, has increasingly been directed by the workings of the influential, publicity-driven system. This works by trading on the discourse of novelty, located in this article in the promotion of endless seasonal fashion cycles, catwalk events, young designer competitions, and cover stories featuring the creators behind "image clothing" represented in "image words" (Barthes 1967: 3).

The patronage of, and support by, this publicity machine and its symbolic, cultural capital find a parallel with the economic capital that historically had to be secured for the production of creative work. Artists relied on the patronage of the wealthy sponsor to fund their talents across time (Wilson 2002). Whilst select designer brands may attract the economic capital of crossover sponsorship from other brands in co-branding relationships, fashion designers seek publicity and media recognition as sociocultural capital in order to mark out their difference to ensure and assure their survival in a highly competitive global market. In the aestheticized economy (Featherstone 2007), consumption practices are increasingly driven by an insatiable desire for the new in the ceaseless search for expressive lifestyles. For a demand-driven industry such as fashion there is a constant need to communicate the innovative designer collection based on reworked signifiers in the hope that it aligns with aspirational consumer values or Veblen's "honorific values" (Veblen 2007: 197).

In the creative sector, fashion in many ways often leads the way in dramatizing the mundane and highlighting the ordinariness of everyday life by celebrating its own existence through spectacle and by visually communicating its extraordinary nature. It provides spectacular narratives in its continuous cycle of collections and in the stories embedded in the publicity emerging from the management of the fashion brand. These two levels of fashion narrative perhaps exist and thrive in the absence of community myth-making (Debord 1994) at the heart of which is the creation and promotion of the star fashion designer and their anticipated genius collection inviting the consumer to become a cast member in their fashion story.

In a system of commodity aesthetics, the production and consumption of images are as important as the production and consumption of the products themselves, if not more so, as a way of differentiating companies and their products. This is as true across China and Asia as anywhere in the globalized and socially networked arenas that fashion designers and fashion brands currently operate in, whatever their scale of operation. It also suggests that the consumer as agent is engaged throughout this communication process by the creative boundary spanners or brand managers in terms of the novelty and fit of a designer collection. The emphasis in this brand relationship is focused on how the designer is positioned cognitively and affectively with the consumer. Economies of scale may come into play here as we might assume that large-scale enterprises have more cultural intermediaries at their disposal to both image and imagine the consumer, whilst smaller-scale enterprises are more constrained in this endeavor. Many fashion designers are still often unable to allocate resources to professional promotional activities. This is particularly true for those trying to establish themselves as newcomers to the market, or those who operate in a different cultural frame underexposed to this knowledge (Storey 1996). This gap tends to be filled in Hong Kong, China, and the Asian region by governmental agencies or state intervention such as the Hong Kong Trade Development Council (HKTDC) or the China Fashion Designers Association (CFDA). In this way, the celebration of the individual creative or "star" producer is used to signify national pride and achievement in fostering trade relations between and beyond the geographic entities in which these designers promote their brands. In the process of transglobal trade, national, cultural, and creative identities are often compromised and diluted in this exchange process. Often these designers are undervalued by local consumers in rapidly expanding markets in the face of seemingly insatiable demand for European luxury or mid-range brands as markers of wealth or gift-giving.

CREATIVE CENTERS AND FASHION DESIGNERS

Having made the transformation from the center of global fashion production to that of producer-consumer both Beijing and Hong Kong, whilst not necessarily world fashion cities (Gilbert 2006) are arguably world fashion centers in the new economic world order characterized by the transglobal flows of people and commodities across multiple "scapes" (Appadurai 1986) and "liquid times" (Bauman 2007) emerging as a viable niche by marking out and controlling its own creative boundaries and narratives. Although international fashion houses and global media organizations control a large stake in the ownership of cultural production this ignores the multifaceted dynamics of a culture industry that also operates at a micro level such as independent, design teams like Daydream Nation that are the subject of this article. This is especially pertinent in China as independent designers are battling it out with luxury brands on the catwalks of global fashion week events and in first-tier cities such as Beijing and Shanghai (Tian 2012).

CHINA AND HONG KONG'S FASHION SYSTEM

Therefore, the creative outcomes of star designers in any locality and geographic space are subject to the collective interplay of creative output by the designer, facilitated on their journey to the consumer by the professional and political filters exercised by the cultural boundary spanners or mediators. Bourdieu (1984) originally suggested that cultural intermediaries select and comment on the season's best with remarkable homogeneity due to shared universes. Fashion stories are created and recreated by the designers and those cultural mediators responsible for promoting the designer and their collections when exporting fashion brands overseas in the commercial arena of fashion trade fairs (Skov 2010) and in global reportage on fashion media events.

Through this transnational trading activity the cultural producers and political intermediaries are continuing an ongoing tradition of East–West mercantilism in the entrepôt trade between China and the world. It also represents part of a continuing tradition of seeking and assuring export markets for creative products and knowledge capital. Both China and Hong Kong in the past thirty years have desired to be recognized as espousing an innovative, creative fashion design industry capable of competing on the world stage. Their governments and individual designers strongly desire to activate this change from "workshop of the world to cradle of creative innovation" (Wu 2009: 127).

Hong Kong is perhaps only marginally ahead of China in attempting to realize this aspiration. The former British Territory's development as a fashion and design center from the 1960s onwards reflects the evolution of the textile and garment industry from manufacturing-based production center to a service-oriented economy through the invention and implementation of design technology and the promotion of homegrown Hong Kong fashion brands by the government and trade department. This trend also spawned the launch of Hong Kong Fashion Week and the setting up of fashion programs at education level from the 1980s onwards.

CHINA'S FASHION SYSTEM

Post-reform China from 1978 onwards echoed a similar aspirational trajectory in terms of fashion development, moving from a situation where garments were usually produced at home or by a tailor to the development of a parallel ready-to-wear domestic market alongside its export-oriented apparel industry. State-run factories, recognizing the potential for an emerging domestic market of fashion consumers, allied to the states' desire to foster an innovation-oriented country across various sectors including design, saw the implementation of fashion exhibitions and national competitions for "model" designers in addition to sending the winners overseas to disseminate their award-winning work via trade shows (Finnane 2008).

So, Hong Kong and China developed their first generation of fashion designers from the 1980s onwards in a similar state/government-run model based on a desire to export their own label framed as "Made BY China or Hong Kong" rather than those manufactured on the basis of cheap labor being "Made IN Hong Kong or China" (Keane 2007). Yet, many of these more mature designers have still largely operated as invisible operatives for fashion brands produced in each location whilst others bemoan the lack of individual recognition of their design talent such as Peter Lau or William Tang in Hong Kong (Skov 1997).

FASHION SYSTEMS AND FASHION CITIES: HONG KONG AND CHINA

Despite the integration of the apparel industry at the global level, designers from China and Hong Kong often go unrecognized or are underrepresented in some markets (Zhang 2011). Nonetheless, they measure their success in these terms—most hoping to exhibit at global fashion weeks and work in Paris, Milan, New York, or London. This aspiration appears to be based on a perception amongst designers operating in these locations that visibility and recognition on the global fashion stage hosted by the world fashion cities is critical to their success.

From the 1990s aspirational fashion designers in Hong Kong and China who gained access to the world fashion stage (through government-funded trade fairs or fashion shows) tended to design collections that used authentic Chinese signifiers and symbols as a mark of patriotism or as a way of visibly expressing difference from Western designers, often just replicating a Western-centric view of chinoiserie. The imagined geographies of these Hong Kong and Chinese designs focus on the monetary value—where high-end couture is usually showcased, and the new orientalism is on show also as a way perhaps of dissociating themselves with mass garment production. Yet, a new wave of designers often having been educated, employed, or well-traveled outside of Hong Kong and China are now reworking notions of Chinese design creatively and boldly integrating fashion, art, and performance and directing their own destinies.

The two design brands featured in this article represent the complexities and contradictions faced by national independent designers attempting to make a success of their business in this geographic location. Their design aesthetic represents two distinct approaches to fashion design and creativity as each target a different market demographic. Also, each has chosen a different route to gain market visibility. Whilst they both employ brand managers, Daydream Nation attend fashion trade fairs in Paris and showcase their work at London Fashion Week, whilst Guo Pei for Rose Studio shows her collections at government-sponsored fashion shows in China, Hong Kong, and the region, whilst also taking on high-profile commissions and private clients.

TELLING BRAND NEW FASHION TALES

The purpose of fashion branding is to establish a differentiated identity for the line of clothing being marketed in a highly competitive, crowded marketplace niche, so that Zara's knitwear, for example, sets itself apart from H&M's or Mango's version. Brand management starts from the idea of brand identity (logo, name) created by the designer encapsulating the brand mission or rationale. This brand identity is managed in three ways: through the brand's ethos or what it represents at its core, the values that it ascribes to, and the brand personality "that enable the brand to be instantly recognisable and much desired" (Devereux and Peirson-Smith 2009: 66).

In response to this brand product positioning, the brand image is the overall consumer perception of the brand (ethos, values, and personality) driven by the brand personality and its relative positioning in the market (Aaker 1997). Branding is the result of interplay between these different elements in the push from the producer and the pull of the consumer, all affecting the values and symbolic meaning attached to the brand.

Brand managers employ the media-scape not to convey a unidirectional message about the brand, but rather to create a universe in which to situate the brand, define its ethos inter-textually, and invite the consumer to exercise creative agency by engaging within the co-creation of meaning for the brand (Bridson and Evans 2004; Lury 2004). Fashion designers as brand producers, and brand managers as cultural boundary spanners are all in the business of intuitively and empirically predicting and embedding use value in the promotion and creation of the brand.

Given the global circulation of fashion brands, the geographic location of the brand and its cultural backstory are increasingly used to differentiate the brand (Schroeder and Salzer-Morling 2006). This also gives rise to the "cultural brand" (Holt 2002: 14), which tries to "embody a sum total of a group's cultural identity, including the surrounding myth, a string that ties consumers to their cultural roots, and associations (real and imaginary) of all the good and wonderful things that have been left behind as well as those that are possible in the future." In the fashion industry, brands as symbols of cultural identity (McCracken 1988) are contested sites amongst consumers depending on their nation of origin. In China and Hong Kong, fashion brands representing a Western cachet engender desirability especially in the luxury brand market, whilst locally designed fashion brands are often devalued in the domestic market highlighting the complexities of the producer–consumer relationship in the fashion system.

Daydream nation and Rose Studio: their brand stories

In examining Daydream Nation and Rose Studio the following qualitative analysis is based on personal, in-depth, ethnographic interviews using the same open-ended questions (Fontana and Frey 1994) with the two design teams during a three-hour interview session with each in Beijing and Hong Kong, in addition to attending and observing their fashion shows and promotional events from 2010–12. The interview questions centered on three main themes—brand ethos, brand identity, and communicating the brand materials. Hence, the three respondents comprising the two design teams were asked: What is your brand history and mission? What is your brand personality? What is your brand story and how is that communicated to your target customer? The qualitative results were manually sorted and analyzed according to these three main themes informing the discussion below.

The line of inquiry focused on the brand identity of each as the starting point of the designer-driven brand management process. Here the star designer, their story, and the narrative driving each individual collection are critical to the branding management effort. The brand management process assumes that consumers are more inclined to develop a positive relationship with the brand if they associate with its identity, ethos, and personality (Bickle 2009; Elliott and Wattanasuram 1998).

FASHION FABLES

In Hong Kong there is an upcoming brand called Daydream Nation, originally based in a small street-level store, and recently relocated to two outlets in the Hong Kong Arts Centre, Wanchai, and K11 art-oriented shopping mall, Tsim Tsa Tsui. Located on an industrial estate on the outskirts of Beijing, there is Rose Studio, atelier of *haute couture* designer Guo Pei, showcasing her couture collection. This is their story and it encapsulates a new adventure for a youthful Hong Kong label aspiring to conquer global markets and an emerging Chinese couturier catering for the local upwardly mobile Chinese middle-class elite.

Every successful brand has a story behind it (Hancock 2009) and memorable fashion brands tell good tales and construct engaging fables to gain visibility and establish memorable and lasting relationships with their consumer market. Yet, few brands create a myth from scratch and many fashion brands buy into existing stories. So, originality as in any creative domain will stand out and get noticed. This is a story of a Hong Kong brand that has recently emerged and the tale of a first-generation Chinese fashion designer, Guo Pei, who worked her way up through the garment production system to set up her own label over the past decade of China's exponential economic growth.

Fashion arts house Daydream Nation was launched in Hong Kong in 2006 by Hong Kong-born sibling designer team and Central St Martins graduates Kay and Jing Wong, both in their early twenties. Kay studied Print Textiles at Central St Martins where she worked with designer Jessica Ogden, followed by an MA in Constructed Textiles at the Royal College of Art, whilst Jing studied Theater Design at Central St Martins. On graduation they both returned to their Hong Kong birthplace to set up their new label

Guo Pei, the designer behind Rose Studio, was born in 1967 at the start of the Cultural Revolution. Growing up in the capital she enrolled in the mid-1980s in fashion studies at Beijing Second Light Industry School where her teachers had no real exposure to Western fashion trends. After graduating in 1986 she worked as a designer for a children's clothing company. As she explained, "My job was provided by the government at that time and I was paid just US$10 a day and then went to work at Tinma, a private factory manufacturing the new fashionable clothes for women" in a more colorful post-Mao era. Having earned her fashion industry stripes as an in-house designer, she followed her star and established Rose Studio in 1997, selling couture and evening wear for celebrities, the Beijing elite, businesswomen, executives and celebrities from CCTV (China's state-run television station), and the wives and daughters of Communist party leaders (Rose Studio 2010: 005).

In the past, product and manufacturing technology were the critical success factors for fashion companies. This has shifted latterly to the more intangible elements located in the domain of branding and retail management. Here the fashion brand has rapidly become the fulcrum of marketing strategies. Significantly, both design houses in this case employ marketing managers to manage their brand communication, highlighting the realization that their identity has to be carefully controlled and positioned through strategic communication. Great skills may not be enough in a crowded marketplace, so the brand narrative helps deliver and differentiate realistic and culturally relevant messages to entertain, inspire, and emotionally engage consumers in the context of brand relationship building experiences.

Taking a producer focus the next section will examine the brand management strategy and its three component parts—brand ethos, brand identity, and brand communication as they contribute to the overall brand narrative to provide alignment and sustained engagement with the consumer.

Brand ethos/brand mission

The brand ethos refers to the essential core or soul of the brand and what values it actually represents. This is often articulated through a proposition statement. Fashion brands such as Daydream Nation and Rose Studio start with a very individual vision, and then profess to follow that vision through in everything they do. This is often based on a very personal ethos, philosophy, and style underpinning the entire expression of the brand.

For Daydream Nation this is embodied in their brand statement on their website:

> We believe that daydreams are the lost children in society. Daydream Nation is a place where people see boats in buckets and hear sea waves in radio glitches.

> It is a way of life, vow to dream and dare to act upon it. Come dream with us. (Daydream Nation 2010)

Similarly, Guo Pei also aspires to creating a dream factory where her clients can realize and live out their fantasies through beautifully crafted unique garments.

As she noted in interview:

> The crafted couture that I create for my catwalk shows and my clients is not just a garment or a product. It's the realization of a dream. Every designer has a dream. . . .Then she shares that dream at the show and when her clients wear her clothes they enact the dream in their own lives and fulfill their dreams in the process.

Certainly, the theme of beauty is a key message that Guo Pei consistently repeats across many media interviews and in her promotional materials as a core ethos that appears to be at the heart of her work and inspiration, as opposed to being imposed upon her by her publicist.

For Daydream Nation the meta-story or brand ethos/spirit is further articulated in the words of one half of the sibling design team, Jing Wong, in terms of a rebellion against the conformity of a conservative Asian value system:

> Being born in the rigid Hong Kong educational system that stifles creativity we found it our mission to cultivate a culture of imagination. So, really our designs are a platform for daydreamers to dream out loud.

Each season the fashion storytelling brand created by the sibling design duo, dubbed by the local media as the Hans Christian Andersens of the fashion world (Chau 2009), use ready-to-wear garments and accessories to unveil quirky, fey narratives inspired by literary sources, poems, the environment, art, and music.

Guo Pei also uses fashion weeks in Beijing, Hong Kong, Taipei, and London as a vehicle to theatrically show off her grand designs in her shows that typically last thirty-five minutes, often invoking Chinese fairy tales or blending historic Elizabethan themes with Ming dynasty costumes. These are spectacular couture productions reminiscent of Thierry Mugler's theatrical creations. As Cathy Horyn for *The New York Times* wrote:

> for her third collection—held at the national stadium in the Beijing Olympic village before an audience of 2,600 people—Guo Pei flew the legendary model Carmen Dell'Orefice in from New York. Dell'Orefice was 78 when she agreed to wear a bejeweled sheath and an embroidered, fur-trimmed cape fit for a Ming empress, and heavy enough to require an escort by two men "and two boys in back pushing the train. (Horyn 2010)

The theme of beauty lay at the center of this show based on the Arabian Tales of 1001 nights, which Guo Pei was inspired by as a child. The atypical, radical use of a mature American model as the main agent of the show who the designer had seen in a magazine was intended to "challenge the audience and media to have a new kind of understanding about what is beauty" (Guo Pei interview, Beijing, 2010). This was not a branding strategy imposed on the designer, but rather an idea hatched by the designer herself and one that resides at the core of her aesthetic ethos.

Stylistic brand identity

The role of independently owned fashion boutiques as intermediary creative institutions are significant at point of sale "in building up the designer's status and visibility in the marketplace" (Rantisi 2011: 262) and in promoting and personifying the brand locally. Both Daydream Nation's whimsical, boho collections and cozy, artistic retail spaces with a hipster vibe are positioned as places dedicated to enhancing their own and their customers' creativity. Characterizing their style as "surreal and poetic," the aesthetics of their collections are driven by the narratives that they embody.

Likewise, Guo Pei's stylistic identity is theatrical, artistic, and made to be showcased on the catwalk in contrast to the predominant ready-to-wear market. Typically, it blends historic and transcultural references with ancient Chinese signifiers often in the embroidered finish of her garments, all of which she meticulously researches whilst traveling. Similarly, for Guo Pei the core essence of Rose Studio is classical *haute couture* with a theatrical East–West twist in design and finish "breathing life into art and art into life," as the atelier's promotional.

Managing brand identity: The brand communications process

The brand personality of both fashion houses is closely tied to and represents the designers at the creative core of the brand and is centrally featured in promotional materials and resulting media coverage. Since inception they have generated significant global media impact in feature articles. They also regularly feature in fashion blogs (Bubble, 2010).

Guo Pei regularly invites local and international journalists to her fashion shows to consciously manage her profile in addition to a web presence, whilst Lady Gaga's purchase of her shoes and outfits has generated significant independent global media coverage.

As Jing observed, whilst their customer base in Hong Kong is still small, Daydream Nation is a story that the local media here are proud to tell of Hong Kong kids made good in London who brought the kudos all back home. Hong Kong designers characteristically are not recognized or valued unless they train overseas and acquire external validation.

Both design teams are able to exercise a creative freedom and realize their grand sartorial ambitions because of their access to low-cost skilled labor in stark contrast to the reduction in expensive handwork in Western fashion houses. Guo Pei manages 140 skilled dressmakers in Rose Studio painstakingly hand-painting and embroidering *haute couture* gowns, with another 300 workers situated in a factory outside of the city. This enables her to create spectacular, media-worthy collections, rapidly becoming a thing of fable in European fashion houses, comprising such items as a bell-shaped dress made of gold panels encrusted with gold filigree thread that took 50,000 hours to embroider and which was showcased by invitation at Paris Fashion Week in 2010.

Beneficiaries of affordable craftspeople, Daydream Nation also employ a small group of local women, former local textile workers from the 1960s, to hand-finish their garments and make accessories in their Kowloon workshop. In this way, they claim they are also adding to and sustaining local, disappearing craft skills.

DREAMS COME TRUE: GLOBAL RECOGNITION

In terms of fulfilling ambitions to be globally recognized, both brands are increasingly networked with a range of cultural intermediaries—buyers, stores, and fashion media alike enabling their design collections to be actively communicated locally, regionally, and globally. Daydream Nation have collaborated with a range of other fashion brands providing items and accessories from their collections. They even caught the eye of a buyer for Chanel who selected monochrome accessories from their Fall/Winter 2009 collection that influenced Karl Lagerfeld's work that season. Also, they currently sell to nineteen countries.

Whilst they are positioned as star designers within their own domain and by the glocal media coverage they receive, the need to validate this by networking with celebrities is also a key part of the brand strategy. Both design houses engage in local celebrity styling, which generates publicity and validates their work by association, as does international celebrity recognition of their work. Guo Pei attained a much desired global dimension when Lady Gaga's stylist Nicola Formichetti, asked to borrow some clothes including a forty-pound crystal dress and vertiginous metallic platform shoes.

In addition, this highlights that brand management and publicity are critical precursors to establishing a brand profile. Guo Pei for example regularly invites forty-plus local and international journalists to her fashion shows to consciously manage her profile. Whilst this is a critical network for any fashion brand, potentially opening many doors, the media response and the wider global reach throughout the fashion network and its boundary spanners or intermediaries are largely uncontrolled and often serendipitous.

FUTURE FASHION FABLES

Both fashion brands have generated global media attention and fashion awards with orders coming in from overseas retail outlets and brands, in addition to a healthy local client base. Yet, they still aspire to extend their reach across global fashion and lifestyle networks seeking validation beyond their home base. For the future, Daydream Nation, true to their brand ethos, plan to organically develop an artistic hub in this designated creative city—facilitating cabarets, artwork, and a cafe culture—as a sort of bohemian hangout for likeminded people—creating a new nation or consumption community that takes root globally and "gives everyone permission to daydream," as Jing puts it. In contrast, Guo Pei extends her aesthetic desires "to become the top luxury brand in China, as famous as Karl Lagerfeld . . . and Rose Studio to be as big as Chanel. I really wish to push the China market forward and gain respect for the fine beauty and art of Chinese culture represented by my heart's work." Daydream Nation, on the other hand, seem content just to have been commissioned by Chanel to produce a line of hair accessories. These varied aspirations may reflect generational and educational differences at different stages of their careers as established versus emerging designers.

CONCLUSION

The tale of these two design houses is that of creative ambition mixed with pragmatic realism, beset with contradictions and challenges for the future of their brands based on their respective geographic locations. These fashion designers, at different stages of their careers, are making the most of the more liberalized economic climate by being able to develop their brands independently in Hong Kong and China for the seemingly insatiable fashion consumer.

Here, they have a role to play in promoting their brands in both domestic and international markets and place a value on that by hiring brand managers to execute this process through a variety of communication channels. Both teams are developing evolving niche markets for differing demographics in their own locality using non-conventional, extraordinary brand strategies in blending fashion with other art forms and novel, story-based branding practices that are also embedded in the fabric and design of their collections aligned with the branding effort. Global recognition also has its downsides and its creative price as their valued work has often been copied and stolen. Ironically, whilst global fashion brands are queuing up to service China's middle-class consumers' insatiable desire for conspicuous luxury (Sun 2011), Hong Kong and Chinese fashion designers aspire to having a foothold in other fashion capitals as evidence of a flying geese trend. The final question remains as to why this might be—is perhaps it a form of postcolonial insecurity and is this phenomena being undermined by a realigned global economy? To be successful in China and Hong Kong a brand needs a history. In the West, it is the attraction of the new and the exotic. Many Chinese designers in the past few decades have tried to gain visibility by emphasizing Chineseness in their designs to the point of caricature. But, a fusion of creative inspiration sources perhaps enables a collection to gain a wider appeal based on developing the brand's intangible attributes beyond tangible features and strong design principles. Both fashion brands analyzed here by reinterpreting this theme through creative individuality and engaging storytelling through brand management may yet realize their dreams to straddle both domestic and international arenas joining the newly aligned transglobal flow of fashion brands. One market may benefit the other by appealing to global consumers given the stellar potential of the other geo-economic frame in which they are fatefully located.

In terms of reevaluating the fashion system and fashion practice itself, it is the flow of ideas rather than things that has increasing currency for the fashion consumer and their relationship with the culture brand. So, the challenge for independent design teams will be to remain adaptive enough to survive in fashion's global firmament and in telling a creative brand story not only by top-down showcasing and promoting collections both locally and globally as this may not be the sole way to sustain market visibility and remain memorable. It will also, but not exclusively, be about democratizing the brand and giving the consumer the illusion of emotional connect and control of content through closer involvement using a hybrid communication strategy of traditional and digital marketing campaigns reflecting the makeup of the fashion industry itself. For many aspiring fashion designers in this geographic location these are still such things that dreams are made of, but it is a brave new world that they and their brand managers appear to be re-appropriating into the content and creativity of their brand narratives.

References

Aaker, Jennifer L. 1997. "Dimensions of Brand Personality." *Journal of Marketing Research* 34(3): 347–56.

Appadurai, Arjun. 1986. "Introduction: Commodities and the Politics of Value." In Arjun Appadurai (ed.) *The Social Life of Things*, pp. 3–63. Cambridge: Cambridge University Press.

Barthes, Roland. 1967. *The Fashion System*. Trans. Matthew Ward and Richard Howard. Berkeley, CA: University of California Press.

Bauman, Zygmunt. 2007. *Liquid Times: Living in an Age of Uncertainty*. London: Polity Press.

Becker, Harold. 1982. *Art Worlds*. Berkeley, CA: University of California Press.

Bickle, Mariane C. 2009. *Fashion Marketing: Theory, Principles and Practice*. New York: Fairchild Books.

Bourdieu, Pierre. 1984. *Distinction: A Social Critique of the Judgment of Taste*. Cambridge, MA: Harvard University Press.

Bourdieu, Pierre. 1993. *The Field of Cultural Production*. Cambridge: Polity Press.

Braham, Peter. 1997. "Fashion: Unpacking a Cultural Production." In Paul du Gay (ed.) *Production of Culture/Cultures of Production*, pp. 119–165. London: Sage.

Brïdson, Kerrie and Jody Evans. 2004. "The Secret to a Fashion Advantage Is Brand Orientation." *International Journal of Retail & Distribution Management* 32(8): 403–11.

Bubble, Suzie. 2010. "Daydreamer." *Style Bubble*—Suzie Bubble's blog, December 16. http://www.stylebubble.co.uk/style_bubble/2010/12/daydreamer.html (accessed February 3, 2011).

Chau, Winnie. 2009. "The Artful Designer." *Hong Kong Magazine* May 21. http://hk.asia-city.com/shopping/article/artful-designer (accessed June 15, 2010).

Craik, Jennifer. 1994. *The Face of Fashion*. London: Routledge.

Crane, Diana. 2000. *Fashion and Its Social Agendas: Class, Gender, and Identity in Clothing*, Chicago, IL: University of Chicago Press.

Csikszentmihalyi, Mikhail. 1996. *Creativity: Flow and the Psychology of Discovery and Invention*. New York: Harper Collins.

Davis, Fred. 1992. *Fashion, Culture and Identity*, Chicago, IL: University of Chicago Press.

Daydream Nation. 2011. Daydream Nation website. http://www.daydream-nation.com/ (accessed September 7, 2011).

Debord, Guy. 1994. *Society of the Spectacle*. Trans. D. Nicholson-Smith. New York: Zone Books.

Devereux, Mary and Anne Peirson-Smith. 2009. *Public Relations in AsiaPacific: Communicating Effectively Across Cultures*. London and Singapore: John Wiley & Sons.

Pryke. 2002. *Cultural Economy, Cultural Analysis and Commercial Life*. London: Sage.

Elliott, Richard and Kritsadarat Wattanasuran. 1998. "Brands as Symbolic Resources for the Construction of Identity." *International Journal of Advertising* 17(2): 131–44.

Entwistle, Joanne. 2002. "The Aesthetic Economy: The Production of Value in Fashion Modeling." *Journal of Consumer Culture* 2(3): 317–39.

Featherstone, Mike. 2007. *Consumer Culture and Postmodernism*. London: Sage.

Finnane, Antonia. 2008. *Changing Clothes in China*. New York: Columbia University Press.

Fontana, Andrea and James Frey. 1994. "The Art of Science." In N. and Y. L. Denzin (eds) *The Handbook of Qualitative Research*, pp. 361–76. Thousand Oaks, CA: Sage Publications.

Gilbert, David. 2006. "From Paris to Shanghai: The Changing Geographies of Fashion's World Cities." In Christopher Breward and David Gilbert (eds) *Fashion's World Cities*, pp. 3–32. Oxford: Berg.

Hancock, Joseph. 2009. *Brand Story*. New York: Fairchild Books.

Hesmondhalgh, David and Andy C. Pratt. 2005. "Cultural Industries and Cultural Policy." *International Journal of Cultural Policy* 11(1): 1–14.

Holt, Douglas. 2002. "Why Do Brands Cause Trouble? A Dialectical Theory of Consumer Culture and Branding." *The Journal of Consumer Research* 29(1): 70–90.

Horyn, Cathy. 2010. "Year of the Couturière." *The New York Times* Women's Fashion, December 5.

Kawamura, Yuniya. 2005. *Fashion-ology: An Introduction to Fashion Studies*. Oxford: Berg.

Keane, Michael. 2007. *Created in China: the Great New Leap Forward*. London: Routledge.

Lury, Celia. 2004. *Brands: The Logos of a Global Economy*. New York: Routledge.

McCracken, Grant. 1988. *Culture and Consumption*. Bloomingdale, IN: Indiana University Press.

Niessen, Sandra. 2003. *Re-Orienting Fashion: The Globalization of Asian Dress*. Oxford: Berg.

Rantisi, Nancy. M. 2011. "The Prospects and Perils of Creating a Viable Fashion Identity." *Fashion Theory* 15(2): 259–66.

Rose Studio. 2010. *Rose Studio: China Haute Couture.* Beijing: Rose Studio Publications.

Schroeder, Jonathan E. and Miriam Salzer-Morling. 2006. "Introduction: The Cultural Codes of Branding." In J.E. Schroeder and M. Salzer-Morling (eds) *Brand Culture*, pp. 1–12. London: Routledge.

Skov, Lise. 1997. "Hong Kong Fashion Designers as Cultural Intermediaries: Out of Global Garment Production." *Cultural Studies* 16(4): 553–69.

Skov, Lise. 2010. "Dreams of Small Nations in a Polycentric Fashion World." *Fashion Theory* 15(2): 137–56.

Storey, Helen. 1996. *Fighting Fashion.* London: Faber & Faber.

Sun, Celine. 2011. "China, Where Luxury Brands Are." *The South China Morning Post* Business Post, March 5: 3

Tian, Gan. 2012. "Independent Designers Strut onto International Catwalks." *China Daily* (online edition). http://usa.chinadaily.com.cn/china/2012-10/26/content_15847995.htm (accessed January 11, 2012).

Tungate, Mark. 2008. *Fashion Brands: Branding Style from Armani to Zara.* London: Kogan Page.

Veblen, Thorstein. 2007. *The Theory of the Leisure Class.* Teddington: Echo Library.

Wilson, Elizabeth. 2002. *Bohemians: The Glamorous Outcasts.* London: I. B. Taurus

Wu, Juanjuan. 2009. *Chinese Fashion: From Mao to Now.* Oxford: Berg.

Zhang, Jing. 2011. "All Eyes on China but Capital's Fashion Week Slips under the Radar." *South China Morning Post* Lifestyle Post Section: 3.

FURTHER READING

D-arienzo, W. (2016), *Brand Management Strategies: Luxury and Mass Marketing*. New York: Bloomsbury Publishing.

Hancock, J. H., G. Muratovski, V. Manlow and A. Peirson-Smith. (2016), *Global Fashion Brands*. Bristol: Intellect Books.

Hancock II, J. H. (2016), *Brand / Story: Cases and Explorations in Fashion Branding*, 2nd Edition, New York: Fairchild Publications.

Holt, D. (2004) *How Brands Become Icons: The Principles of Cultural Branding*, Boston: Harvard Business School Press.

Kompella, Kartikeya (2015), *The Brand Challenge: Adapting Branding to Sectorial Imperatives*, London: Kogan Page.

Rath, Patricia Mink, Richard Petrizzi, and Penny Gill (2012), *Fashion Marketing: A Global Perspective*, New York: Fairhild Books.

Moor, Liz (2007), *The Rise of Brands*, Oxford: Berg.

Okonkwo, U. (207) *Luxury Fashion Branding: trends, tactics, techniques*, London: Palgrave Macmillan.

Figure 26 Photo Courtesy of Brent Luvaas.
Source: Brent Luvaas

PART VIII

Fashion Communication

Figure 27 Photo Courtesy of Brent Luvaas.
Source: Brent Luvaas

INTRODUCTION

Anne Peirson-Smith

Fashion as the system responsible for "the collective imitation of regular novelty" (Barthes, 2006: 63) has been credited with serving various functions and purposes in protecting the human body from the environment, reflecting and signaling social class, mores, civilization and values, or in fulfilling an aesthetic role for its wearer. Yet, the communicative function of fashion has increasingly been recognized as having a significant purpose in fashion's story. As Roland Barthes observed in *The Fashion System*,

> we must add another function, which seems to me to be more important: the function of meaning. Man has dressed himself in order to carry out a signifying activity. The wearing of an item of clothing is fundamentally an act of meaning that goes beyond modesty, ornamentation and Fashion and the protection. It is an act of signification and therefore a profoundly social act right at the very heart of the dialectic of society (Barthes, 2006: 90-91).

As a social and cultural signifying practice, fashion affords the wearer the option to dress and fashion their corporeal body into a recognized style tribe, or to adopt a prevailing trend. But, at the same time, fashion signals individuality by adopting and interpreting a particular fashionable look. Beyond functional concerns, wearers buy fashion in terms of what it represents symbolically. The fashion system invests garments with symbolic meaning enabling the consumer to signal social and cultural capital attached to the notion of the new, while at the same time generating economic capital for the producer. Here, the notion of 'embodiment' is critical to this understanding of fashion. As humans we have bodies that we clothe – giving life to fashionable garments and clothing and acquiring form and purpose through the adorned body (Entwistle, 2015) and its active construction and the normalization of being dressed (Craik, 1994) in a particular way with an aesthetic, sensory and affective purpose and dimension. Embodiment enables endless options for action through a range of affordances. In this way, clothing can be seen as an extension of the embodied self, whereby the garment or accessory empowers the wearer or defines them and their assumed identity. Clothed bodies are also discursive constructs utilizing signifying surfaces (Jobling, 1999; Rocamora, 2009) whereby the fashion media and the cultural intermediaries who work in those institutions reinforce the legitimacy and regulation of the clothed body through their multi-mediated and subjective utterances.

Historically, across space and place, clothing and their component textiles have been used to delineate status and class based on a pre-ordained, divinely constituted and codified social order represented in the color coded garb of medieval European or Chinese nobility, for example, to the modern adoption of the formal male business suit in the late nineteenth century (Breward, 1995; Hollander, 1993; Lipovetsky, 2002). This mantle is now assumed in the use of celebrity endorsement by high end fashion brands creating aspirations for luxury labels that are often unaffordable for the majority of consumers. As Barthes explains,

> Every social condition had its garment and there was no embarrassment in making an outfit into a veritable sign, since the gap between the classes was itself considered to be natural. So, on the one hand, clothing was subject to an entirely conventional code, but on the other, this code referred to a natural order, or even better to a divine order. To change clothes was to change both one's being and one's social class, since they were part and parcel of the same thing (Barthes 2006: 60).

While this observation underlines the notion that fashion is not a recently invented modern phenomenon allied to class, civilization and consumerism, and its evolution is not located purely in a western frame (Craik 1994: 3), it also highlights the contextualized, yet ever changing nature and meaning of fashion across time and place.

In its signifying function, fashion has been metaphorically likened to a linguistic system in its own right (Lurie, 1981) with its own vocabulary, grammar and syntax that can be used to deliberately signal meaning on behalf of the wearer accordingly decoded by the onlooker. Fashion is constantly communicating meaning on behalf of the wearer or viewer and is an instant language as Barnard observes, "Clothes are selected for purchase, and for wearing, according to the meaning we believe them to have, or the messages we believe them to send" (Barnard 2007: 170). However, the simplistic transmission model of communication appears to be inadequate in explaining how fashion actually communicates. The notion of fashion as a pure language falls short of an adequate explanation for its raison d'etre in the absence of a fixed and structured system with vestimentary, linguistic meaning. A fashion outfit or item is a text that is open to subjective interpretation and subject to cultural construction (Peirson-Smith and Hancock, 2018). Fashion does not have an arbitrary, fixed meaning. Hence, as Barnard notes, "There is no meaning until the interaction between cultural values and items of fashion has taken place […] fashion is not a vehicle for conveying messages." (Barnard, 2007: 176). In this sense, fashion can be meaningful and communicative, but also operates as a signifying system and is not a simple transmitter of universally understood, pre-existing messages. Symbolic communication is based on the exchange of recognized or understood meaning in the process of socialisation between an actor expressing the message and the receiver who decodes the existing meaning of the garment, outfit or item. So, individuals and individuals within groups communicate messages as a way of making sense of their lives and their role and identity within that social system by constructing meaning and conveying this through material means, among other things, such as the ways in which they present themselves through the clothes that they wear and the way that they style their hair, for example. In this way, people tap into the prevailing beliefs, values and ideological systems of a given culture and society in which they reside or in which they find themselves situated by wearing clothes that adopt meaning within that specific cultural context. As Barnard notes, "Fashion statements, then, are one of the ways in which cultural structures and individual agency relate and in which they are both constructed and reproduced" (Barnard, 2007: 180).

On the one hand, fashion operates subjectively as an expression of individual agency and power. It can be used to communicate self concept aligned with the idealized self, involving aspirations of who a person wishes to become versus their social self in terms of how a person imagines they are perceived, versus the real self or who a person actually is. According to this schema, the aim of fashion consumption is to attain self-congruity, whereby the fashion item or outfit closely aligns with self-image.

On the other hand, fashion is also understood in accordance with the contemporary beliefs and values of a given group. Social groups are important in defining status in social contexts based on their reference points and in social connections to their related affiliations. Groups enable people to comparatively evaluate their appearance, which is why celebrity endorsement for fashion brands is still an effective marketing communication strategy in terms of managing brand identity by association and in generating admiring followers. This led to the emergence of the celebrity-fuelled magazines from the 1990s as Pamela Church Gibson's piece, "The changing face(s) of the fashion magazine and the new media landscape" in this section explains, "a whole new group of celebrity magazines joined the successful gossip-driven *Heat*. The titles themselves are interesting and indicative—*Closer, Reveal, Look, Now, More*" (Church Gibson, 2011: 130). The importance of affiliation for social belonging and development also led to the popularity of celebrity driven publications filled with endorsed fashion and lifestyles. As Church Gibson in this section also notes, "the habit of reading celebrity magazines in pairs or in groups, and of invariably discussing the latest images with other female readers" is fundamentally a social practice that parallels the homosocial grooming behaviors of young women across time.

As fashion is a visual product it has the capacity to openly communicate and generate a response from the viewer. It can also be regulated by social and cultural norms that may influence both wearer and viewer, in addition to the need for social congruence. Groups also vary according to their demographic profile in terms of how they process and evaluate fashion, with the younger generations relying more on peer feedback, whilst women in general also tend to depend on others judgments both pre- and post- purchase. This empirical observation also suggests that individuals use fashion and clothing to construct their identity and to signify allegiance to cultural, social or demographic groups based on prevailing meanings, but at the same time, are constructed by cultural structures that often provide new and dynamic interpretations of sartorial identities. In this section, Julia Twigg in "Magazines, the Media and Mrs. Exeter" (2013), explores the representation of the older woman in fashion magazines that revealing the deeply held cultural beliefs about the horrors of ageing and the consequent for eternal youth that are endlessly promoted these by magazines and their fashion and product pages. In this way, fashion communicates by symbolically and socially by creating and developing self-identity as an entry to acquiring social status or approval, which may of course be accepted or rejected.

The fashion item or outfit is open to social interpretation and subject to shifting meanings. Barthes in *The Fashion System* (Barthes, 2006) made the distinction between 'written and image clothing' by focusing on how fashion is constructed verbally and visually. According to this dual schema, image clothing concerns the presentation of a garment, accessory or outfit in a photographic or illustrative format that is typically found in fashion magazines constituting its own coded language. Written clothing verbalizes the image-clothing item and gives it meaning through language in two ways. Firstly, fashion writing as editorial, fashion photograph or as photographic caption in a fashion magazine or article grounds meaning by connecting the clothing in the image to the real world. Barthes labels these as Type A statements, including descriptions of fabrics and colors (raw silk + summer; blue is in fashion this year). Equally, fashion written about in this mediated context can be associated with structural phenomena such as professions or situated scenarios (e.g. prints are winning at the races). On the other hand, Type B fashion statements involve writing about fashion or referring to its specific mechanisms without referring out to the wider world (for example, in the shape of a neckline, the sleeve length, the styling detail). This type of described fashion by supplying meaning or signifiers for the fashion object or outfit as signifier has three functions in terms of anchoring the meaning of the image; in providing information about the image content and by making sense of the image in terms of what it contains, in addition to what is missing from the fashion image (e.g. no zippers or buttons). By way of contrast, image clothing represents the real garment and, as such, the meaning of the fashion garments are represented in the photograph as relating to real scenarios that operate as the backdrop in a theatrical sense providing the context for the scene, such as futuristic (hi-tech surfaces, minimalistic), or exotic scenarios (rickshaws or white beaches). These fashion descriptions can also be represented, according to Barthes, in three ways as literal (travel scenes on location), romantic (doves, roses) or mockery (hyperbolic scenes of oversized clothes and accessories or in the use of models with exaggerated makeup).

FASHION WRITING VERSUS FASHION IMAGE

Applying diffusion theories to explain how fashion is defined and marked out as fashionable from an individual and institutional perspective, Kawamura identifies two forms of agent who influence fashionable taste based on interpersonal connections and structural networks. These taste making agents consist of designers based on their aesthetic prowess and recognized taste inducing skills, in addition to "fashion journalists, editors, advertisers, marketers/merchandisers and publicists" who actively form trends based on their edited pronouncements on fashion (Kawamura, 2012).

Interpretations of fashion covering designers, collections mediated fashion show events are constructed by fashion commentators and cultural intermediaries such as editors, journalists and marketers (Blaszczyk, 2002) in the process of knowledge transfer. They are based on the premise that humans are drawn to verbalize and visualize fashion as a signifying system in order to make sense of its existence within their own lived and social experiences. Fashion has to be adopted by the majority for it to exist and involves a network of actors across the consumption chain. Cultural intermediaries in the fashion system are responsible for shaping consumer taste (Bourdieu 1993) and for earmarking what is in and trending, or what is out and old fashioned by using carefully crafted words and images featuring and critiquing fashion as their subject matter. Yet, fashion commentary both in visual and verbal form is not a purely modern preserve as Barthes noted,

> In the eighteenth century many books were written on clothing. They were descriptive works but were based explicitly, and very consciously, on the coding of clothes, that is on the link between certain types of dressing with certain professions, with certain social classes, certain towns and certain regions. (Barthes, 2006: 90)

Other commentators have mapped out the origin of the fashion magazine in particular to the 17th century arts and culture publication, *Le Mercure Gallant*, for example. This form of fashion media appears to have functioned across time to present day as markers of the zeitgeist influencing tastemakers and style setters. As Miller observes, fashion magazines from their early inception "have functioned not only as repositories of the progress of sartorial fashion and the most up-to-date social, cultural and artistic developments, but also as self styled barometers of taste" (Miller, 2013: 13). Their educative and informative function, in using images and words to update their female readers on the latest styles and future seasonal trends, has remained a constant since their inception although the cover photographs, content, angle and intended demographic have changed alongside the evolving social mores, as Church Gibson explains further in this section. This observation is also true of lifestyle magazine content that is targeted at a range of age groups, including the older woman, which operate not just as information sources, but also as a cultural mirror reflecting contemporary beauty standards. As Twigg notes in this section,

> Magazines need to be understood not simply as reflectors of the culture, but creators of it. As such, they contribute to a particular discursive construction of later years…it is one that emphasizes being positive, remaining part of the mainstream, presenting yourself well and engaging in beauty practices and anti-ageing strategies (Twigg, 2013: 117).

At the same time, while older readers might recognize the unreality of the youthful fashion images being presented in these magazines, where the signs of getting old as covered in editorial content are something to be avoided other than in the ability of fashion and cosmetics to provide the desired eternal youth, other discursive frames such as embracing ageing and grey hair are always absent.

This construction and dissemination of professional knowledge is critical in activating the global production and flow of fashion often founded on an inexact scientific approach to trend forecasting in the now and the future forming mediated fashion content both in print and online. As Skov points out,

> It is ironic that even though fashion intermediaries can be said to be in the business of novelty, their practical theory of change is based on intuitive leaps rather than on action an causation […] Fashion intermediaries can observe these changes in a neutral and objective manner in order to turn them into commercial products (Skov, 2014:121).

Fashion intermediaries frame and promote clothing collections within relatable fashion brand stories (Hancock, 2016) laden with aspirational values and ideals. In essence, the fact that fashion is in a constant state of renewal quickly requires intermediaries to provide guiding information about and justification for, these changes in order to drive sales. Some commentators claim that fashion communication and branding have become the key driving force behind the industry (Agins, 1999). Yuniya Kawamura (2012) in a piece entitled, "Production, Gatekeeping and Diffusion of Fashion" notes that,

> Other producers of fashion besides designers, such as advertisers and marketers, also make a major contribution in fashion culture. Fashion is about change and the illusion of novelty. Those who take part in the production of

fashion help create the ideology of fashion and determine which items of clothing will be defined as fashion and fashionable. (Kawamura, 2012: 73)

One of the main drivers of fashion advertising is "to stimulate a desire for the same thing at the same time in a large number of people to build collective belief among consumers" (Kawamura, 2012: 86). Traditionally, fashion advertising from the late 18th and early 19th centuries onwards featured the image-written format conveying functional information and the reasons why consumers should purchase branded garments. The forerunner of modern mood-based advertising emerged in the late 19th and early twentieth centuries. Yet, it appeared more in the form that would be recognized today in the inter-war period, given the rise of a professionalized and systematized industry commissioned not just to convey product information, but also to persuade consumers to make one choice above another given the proliferation of ready to wear, branded fashion goods. The advertising copywriters and art directors responsible for fashion advertising in this mid-century period largely applied the normative aesthetics of the masculine gaze (Mulvey, 1975) depicting the female form for pleasure, as had been the case across the history of art (Berger, 1972). Even then, this was often problematized in advertising for male underwear and clothing products as both Bruce H. Joffe in "Skivvies with the Givvies: Vintage American Underwear Ads Feature Sexual Innuendo between "Boys" in the Brands" (2008), and Paul Jobling in "'Nice Stuff Against the Skin' Pleasure and Spectatorship in Men's Underwear Advertising" (2005) respectively argue in this section. Hence, male underwear advertising from the late 19th century pre-empted Calvin Klein's eroticized aesthetic approach, for example, appearing later in the 20th century. As Bruce Joffe observes these early advertisements played with the 'sex sells' mantra in their verbal and visual discourse. In doing so, they consistently "incorporated themes such as vanity, virility and pleasure in their ads" in an implied or overt manner using "homoerotic overtures, themes and subtexts embedded within their messages" (Joffe, 2008: 4) depending on the aesthetic interpretation of the advertising art director. In addition, the persuasive message underlying the promotion of men's underwear, in contrast to its female equivalent, associated this apparel with comfort and health in the context of sporting prowess that was imbued the with the haptic pleasures of touch and feel, plus the pleasure of a snug fit (Jobling, 2005).

Equally, the active female spectatorship of contemporary fashion magazines challenges the normative gaze associated with 'image fashion', as Church Gibson posits. Designers and their brands have also actively used intertextual and indexical associations with fine art or celebrity as a form of public relations strategy or borrowed interest in their brand storytelling (Hancock, 2012). This approach to fashion branding is arguably more cost effective and socially impactful than traditional advertising (Peirson-Smith, 2014) and challenges the notion of personalized, unique identity by destabilizing the link between the real and representational in the dynamic world of fashion.

In contemporary terms, the multi-modal and multi-channel nature of fashion communication is a hallmark of the 21st century; having moved beyond its origins in the printed word, static illustrated or photographic image to a virtual, abstract state. As Shinkle points out,

> The dissemination of fashion has grown to encompass much more diffusion agents than still images: it now includes films, podcasts, Web sites, sound works, online magazines and other forms – all increasingly articulated around virtual bodies and located in virtual places (Shinkle 2013: 174).

A good example of this is the increasing use of short fashion films to tell the brand story in an experiential way using new technology "to set a new and revolutionary paradigm in terms of knowledge access. But also prepare us for a new relationship with brands since consumers are, more than ever, ready to listen and to collaborate with them" (Díaz Soloaga and García Guerrero 2016: 58).

The interest in described and captured fashion appearing in verbal and visual form have operated as constant aspects of the fashion story across modern life aiding the mediated production, flow and accessibility of fashion to end consumers. But, the fashion world is also currently experiencing challenges in its forced response to rapid technological changes that impinge on every aspect of life across a range of communication platforms and that decenter the traditional fashion communication process. Also, as Rocamora asks, "How new are new media?" (Rocamora, 2013: 157) as old and new media come to "represent and refashion" each other in the process of remediation within the production and consumption cycle (Rocamora, 2013:160). Indeed, the non-linear, hyperlinked structure and image/textual content of blogs is often taken from linear formatted static print media, for example. In this process of remediation fashion bloggers display their fashion wares or cosmetics and often emulate the traditional frozen framed poses found in fashion magazines (Luvaas, 2012). In the same way, fashion print media have remediated street fashion blog visuals in their content, thereby mirroring the digital communication format.

The endorsement of fashion has always relied on word of mouth reinforcement, non-verbal cues and observation skills within social networks, given that fashion enables wearers to gain access to and recognition in social environment based on the social, cultural and knowledge capital that is affords. Whether face-to-face, in situ or online, blogs and bloggers also provide a source of information, social support, advice and judgments on fashion. As Church Gibson explains, "blogs have more in common with the spirit of the earlier women's magazines, who see their function as giving helpful and financially sound fashion advice and information across a range of topics." Yet, while the tone adopted in blogs is often more conversational than traditional fashion magazine editorial content, fashion discourse online or offline still takes its place in the evolution from dispensing beauty and style information in a maternal voice (Barthes, 2006) from the mid 20th century to the more friendly, sassy voice adopted in the 21st century magazine formats based on "ideal and emotive novelisation" (Ballaster et al., 1991: 48) creating mythic worlds that can only be accessed by purchasing the featured fashion brands.

There has also been a decentering of fashion commentary in word and image format. This manifests itself, not only geographically with non-traditional fashion cities being represented as blog content, but also through the curated images and words of traditional fashion media tastemakers operating as "the sole, influential fashion media intermediaries […] fashion journalists, stylists and photographers linked to established titles" (Rocamora, 2013: 159). Fashion journalists, editors and publicists now have to share the role of fashion expert with amateur turned professional blogger, despite the latter's lack of professional training and possible lack of objectivity, given their increasing sponsorship support from major fashion, lifestyle and cosmetic brands Pedroni, 2015).

To contextualize the topic of fashion communication, the following edited pieces in this section yield insights into the various aspects of how fashion information in visual and verbal form, image and text, print and digital is constructed and conveyed to fashion consumers. These essays highlight the notion that the fashion system operates beyond material production being founded on ideological constructions that are embedded in persuasive, communicated messages by a range of fashion intermediaries, both old and new, such as journalists, advertisers, publicists and bloggers that increasingly impact on consumer awareness and ultimately define the business of fashion.

References

Agins, Teri (1999), *The End of Fashion: How marketing changed the clothes business forever*, New York: William Morrow & Co. Inc.
Ballaster, Ros, Margaret Beetham, Elizabeth Frazer and Sandra Hebron eds. (1991), *Women's Worlds: Ideology, Femininity and the Woman's Magazine*. London: Macmillan.
Barnard, Malcolm. (2007), "Fashion Statements: Communication and Culture." In Malcolm Barnard (ed.), *Fashion Theory: A Reader*, pp. 170–181. London: Routledge.
Barthes, Roland (2006), *The Language of Fashion*. Andy Stafford Transl., Andy Staffird and Michael Carter (eds.) London: Bloomsbury Books.
Berger, John (1972), *Ways of Seeing*, London: Penguin.

Blaszczyk, Regina Lee (2002), *Imagining Consumers: Design and Innovation from Wedgwood to Corning*. Baltimore, MD: Johns Hopkins University Press.
Borrelli, Laird O'shea (1997), *Dressing Up and Talking about It: Fashion Writing*. In: Vogue from 1968 to 1993, *Fashion Theory*, 1:3, 247–259.
Bourdieu, Pierre (1993), *The Field of Cultural Production: Essays on Art and Literature*. Cambridge: Polity Press.
Breward, Christopher, (1995) *The Culture of Fashion*, Manchester: Manchester University Press.
Church Gibson, Pamela (2011), *Fashion and Celebrity Culture*. London: Berg.
Craik, Jennifer (1994), *The Face of Fashion: Cultural Studies of Fashion*, London: Routledge.
Díaz Soloaga, P. and L. García Guerrero. (2016), "Fashion Films as a New Communication Format to Build Fashion Brands." *Communication & Society*, 29(2), 45–61.
Entwistle, Joanne. (2015), *The Fashioned Body: Fashion, Dress and Modern Social Theory*. Cambridge: Polity Press.
Hancock II, Joseph, H. (2016), *Brand/Story: Cases and Explorations in Fashion Branding*, 2nd ed. New York, NY: Fairchild Books.
Jobling, Paul. (1999), *Fashion Spreads: Word and Image in Fashion Photography since 1980*. Oxford: Berg.
Jobling, Paul. (2005), *Man Appeal: Advertising, Modernism and Menswear*. Oxford: Berg.
Joffe, Bruce H. (2008), *Textile: The Journal of Cloth & Culture*, 6, (1): 4–17.
Kawamura, Yuniya. (2012), *Fashionology*. Oxford: Berg.
Lipovetsky, Gilles. (2002), *The Empire of Fashion: Dressing Modern Democracy*. Princeton, NJ and Oxford: Princeton University Press.
Lurie, Alison. (1981), *The Language of Clothes*. New York, NY: Random House.
Luvaas, Brent. (2012), *DIY Style: Fashion, Music, and Global Digital Cultures*. London and New York, NY: Berg.
Miller, Sandra. (2013), Taste, Fashion and the French Fashion Magazine. In Djurdja Bartlett, Shaun Cole and Agnes Rocamora (eds.), *Fashion Media: Past and Present*, 13–21. London: Bloomsbury.
Mulvey, Laura (1975), Visual Pleasure and Cinema. *Screen*. Oxford Journals. Autumn, 16 (3): 6–18.
Pedroni, Marco (2015), "Stumbling on the Heels of my Blog": Career Forms of Capital and Strategies in the (sub) Field of Fashion Blogging. *Fashion Theory*. 19(2): 179–200.
Peirson-Smith, Anne (2014), 'Comme on Down and Choos your Shoes: A study of consumer response to the use of guest designers by H&M as a co-branded fashion strategy', Joseph H. Hancock II, Veronica Manlow, Gjoko Muratovski and Anne Peirson-Smith (eds.), *Global Fashion Brands: Style, Luxury & History*, 57–81. Bristol: Intellect.
Peirson-Smith, A. and J.H. Hancock. (2018). Introduction, *Transglobal Fashion Narratives: clothing communication, style statements and brand storytelling*. Bristol: Intellect Books.
Rocamora, Agnes (2009), Fashioning the City: Paris, Fashion and the Media. London: I.B. Taurus.
Rocamora, Agnes (2013), How New are New Media?: The Case of Fashion Blogs. In Djurdja Bartlett, Shaun Cole and Agnes Rocamora (eds.), 155–159. *Fashion Media: Past and Present*, London: Bloomsbury.
Shinkle, Eugenie (2013), Fashion's Digital Body: Seeing and Feeling in Fashion Interactives. In Djurdja Bartlett, Shaun Cole and Agnes Rocamora (eds.), *Fashion Media: Past and Present*, 175–83. London: Bloomsbury.
Skov, Lise (2014), Fashion, In *The Cultural Intermediaries Reader*, Jennifer Smith Maguire and Julian Matthews (eds.) 113–24. Los Angeles, CA: Sage.
Twigg, Julia. (2013), *Fashion and Age: Dress, Body and Later Life*. London: Bloomsbury Academic.

Further Reading

Bartlett, Djurdja. (2013), *Fashion Media: Past as Present*. eds. Djurdja Bartlett, Shaun Cole and Agnes Rocamora. London: Bloomsbury.
Davis, Fred. (1992), *Fashion, Culture and Identity*. Chicago, IL and London: University of Chicago Press.
Crane, Diana. (2000), *Fashion and Its Social Agendas: Class, Gender and Identity in Clothing*. Chicago, IL: University of Chicago Press.
Hollander, Anne. (1993), *Seeing through Clothes*. Berkeley Los Angeles, CA: University of California Press.
McNeil, Peter and Sandra Miller. (2014), *Fashion Writing and Criticism: History, Theory. Practice*. London: Bloomsbury.
Rocamora, Agnès. (2012), 'Hypertextuality and Remediation in the Fashion Media.' *Journalism Practice*, 6(1): 92-106.
Wilson, Elizabeth (2007), *Adorned in Dreams: Fashion and Modernity*, New Brunswick, New Jersey: Rutgers University Press.

34

SKIVVIES WITH THE GIVVIES:
Vintage American underwear ads feature sexual innuendo between "Boys" in the brands

Bruce H. Joffe[1]

"Over the years, underwear has been associated with modesty—or with the lack of it," according to Vintageskivvies.com. "Underclothes are inextricably associated with morality, sensuousness, cleanliness, sexuality, hygiene and—sometimes—even social status," claimed the underwear retailer on the archival pages of its website.

This online retailer had a twist: in addition to its virtual store selling products with a sizing chart and posting its sales, return and shipping policies, along with a clickable list of brick-and-mortar underwear retailers, Vintageskivvies.com featured an archives section with articles, blogs, a glossary, history, and ad gallery all about underwear. It was the world's first e-museum to focus on what men have worn under their trousers.

It is a complex topic, further complicated by the whims of fashion. Then as now, advertising attempted to fulfill its *raison d'être* by communicating the changes in underwear to consumers. But in the process, it succeeded in doing more: explicit or implied, advertising incorporated homoerotic overtures, themes and subtexts within its messages. Take the saga of BVD, for instance.

A BETTER VIEW DESIGNED

Founded in 1876 by three businessmen—surnamed Bradley, Voorhees and Day—BVD was first known for its men's "spiral bustle" with long sleeves and legs made of a heavy knitted fabric. In 1908, that bulky and tight-fitting garment was turned into a new, looser line of underwear. BVD then added a two-piece number and the popular "union suit" to its offerings. With the ever-popular advertising slogan "Next to Myself I Like BVD Best," the company introduced a lightweight, waffle-like fabric, notes *Esquire* contributor John Berendt (1987).[1]

Intrinsic to almost every BVD ad produced between 1913 and 1926 is a pair of book-ended boys who seem to become increasingly involved with each other as their advertising adventures unfold.

"The Fag-Free 'Fans' Wear BVD" (Figure 1) published in 1913 features a crowd of people illustrated in cartoon-like fashion. Headline and copy literally flow below the illustration to form a T-format layout with the two buddies in their BVDs placed symmetrically in ovals aligning the copy as somewhat mirror images. Though obviously interested in each other, the BVD boys are young, fresh and still relatively innocent.

Following their fag-free outing, the buddies are back in 1914 with another ad that, again, fits them to a "T." This time they appear cool, calm and collected below a bunch of chums struggling to enjoy their vacation in the stifling summer heat. "No Fun," Says He, "Unless You Wear BVD." It is not precisely clear who the speaker is in the headline here, but, for argument's sake, let us assume it is one of the smiling guys lifting the boat out of the water. If so, he is facing

---

[1] From Bruce H. Joffe, 2008 Skivvies with Givvies: Vintage American Underwear Ads Feature Sexual Innuendo Between "Boys" in the Brands, Textile, Volume 6, Issue 1, pp. 4–17, Taylor & Francis.

the seated lad who is uncomfortably wiping sweat off his brow, tie undone and hat on his knee.

The loose-fitting, light woven BVD underwear teaches them the fine art of "Take-It-Easy," as in a 1916 ad where they are admiring each other while holiday travelers hustle and bustle about in an illustration above them. Wherever they are and whatever they are doing, there is one thing they both agree upon—the BVD slogan, "Next to myself I like 'BVD' best." To BVD, they are obviously worth the words and congenial compliment.

The graphic "T" layout returns in a 1917 ad in which the BVD boys continue to enjoy each other's company (at the bottom of the ad) while a baseball game is played above. Any question about the appropriateness of the appreciation the BVD boys may share for each other is overshadowed by the ad's striking athleticism, in which a batter and catcher face a crowd full of fans.

Recreation is also the theme of a 1917 ad where our buddies, crisp as cucumbers, relax in their underwear. Above them, a park filled with people swelter wearing parasols and hats. Whatever the temperature might be outside (or in), the relationship between the BVD boys has heated up by the time they appear in a 1919 ad. While still separated by the copy between them (below), their thoughts are on the two men pictured (above) who would be too close for comfort in other circumstances or surroundings. Here, however, they're quite at home . . . ready to turn in and spend the night together.

As the First World War raged, a 1918 BVD ad reminds us that "the comfort of the individual must come second to the need of the nation." Back then, even government requirements urged all citizens to "please be tolerant," as undergarments were not as freely available as previously. The consequences of such a shortage surely must have created a challenge, as well as untold possibilities. Even though the BVD boys by now have been liberated from their chaperones, spectators and companions—they appear alone (without even a "double-date") from this point on in BVD ads—it is comforting to know, especially given the circumstances, that their undergarments have not been sacrificed to the war efforts.

Somewhat older and a bit more mature in a 1920 ad, red as color is added to the BVD advertisement. Perhaps it is a registration problem with the printing press or process, but our protagonists appear to have rouge on their cheeks, while the man on the left has obvious traces of red lipstick on his mouth. One is holding onto the Victrola, the other has a vinyl record in his right hand with his left hand resting atop a nearby chair. Smiling, both seem to be happy in their underwear—alone yet together. The man with darker hair (on the left) has his undershirt unbuttoned from top to bottom, although the buttons fastening his bottoms are completely closed.

In this continuing BVD soap opera can a later (1921) ad showing them in the same underwear as the earlier (1920) ad be an allusion to the morning after? It looks like the one on the left is holding a note in his hand as his line of vision heads directly towards his partner's crotch. What is more, a small inset of his posterior may hint at another view they have shared together. His undershirt still unbuttoned, feet sheathed in slippers, one of the boys holds onto a bathrobe. Has he just taken it off, or is he about to put it on?

Two other 1920 advertisements for BVD merit a mention. In both, the boys again are alone in their underwear.

In "Longwear," the man on the left holds out what looks like a tennis ball, inches from his buddy's lips. It is a gesture reminiscent of Eve tempting Adam with an apple and one almost expects to hear that "the serpent beguiled me and I did eat." Copy in this ad seems rather defensive or competitive, making the point that you get a lot for your money with the BVD brand: "Materials of enduring strength and workmanship of scrupulous care make BVD wear far beyond what it is fair to expect."

The second 1920 ad, "Quality," refers to it being a "tradition with its makers and a proverb with its wearers." While it might be a proverb for other wearers, our boys here seem to be scanning the morning newspaper instead of reflecting on their Bibles.

Looking almost angelic and cherubic, the BVD boys pose in front of a Christmas tree inside a home parlor in a 1924 ad. Despite any pretense about what they've been doing together, undressed except for their undies, they're obviously comfortable and at ease.

Modeling their starchly pressed union suits, our own Betty (blond) and Veronica (brunette) are warned to "Look before you leap!" in a 1925 ad. To their right, sketchy cartoonish characters incautiously jump off a diving board onto the beach below. But they hold little interest for the BVD boys, who are immaculately attuned to each other. The "'Looking for the label' *after* you're sorry won't change it to 'BVD'" subhead is a curious reminder during our current era of sexually transmitted diseases, HIV and AIDS to use protection and practice safe sex rather than suffering the potential consequences later.

In 1926, the BVD ads took on a new look with illustrator Walter Jardin. Artwork is sketchier, with less emphasis on the earlier style of portraiture or classical realism. The ads, here one-third instead of full-page, are smaller but contain almost the same wording and copy in their texts and headlines. To be sure, the type and font are similar, but the focus remains on both BVD boys.

In one 1926 ad they are in a park or forest, again spinning records and enjoying music. Flies, ants, bugs and bees don't bother these two, even though dressed only in their underwear. "The test of underwear comfort is to be able to forget you have underwear on," advises the ad copy. Somehow, that seems not to be an issue for these buddies in their BVDs.

A second 1926 ad places the boys inside a house, maybe in a parlor, living room or sitting room adjoining a bedroom. "Every Time You Dress give yourself the delight of slipping into cool, fresh BVD!" headlines the copy. Given the implications of the illustration, however, a slight variation might make for a more appropriate title and lead copy: "Every Time You *Un*dress, give yourself the delight of slipping *out of* cool, fresh BVD!"

BATTLES AMONG THE BRANDS

BVD was not the only brand courting the male underwear market in the 1920s. Other makers included Duofold, Hanes, Hatch, Madewell, Munsingwear, Navicloth, Superior Underwear and Topkis. Unlike today's sensual poster boy exhibitionists in their Calvin Kleins, underwear was not always attire for the fashion-conscious male. Instead, men sought comfort and value from the clothing that came closest to their skin, and, maybe, a psychological pick-me-up from their advertising, too.

"All a man used to seek was some sort of underwear that would not bulge, bind, gap, chafe, or sag," said Vintageskivvies, "something that—when hung out to dry—would not attract enemy fire."[2]

A cute 1915 Wilson Bros. ad, for example, advances the company's undergarments with two men in their athletic union suits out on a dock of the bay casually shooting the breeze and smoking pipes. Neither appears to be embarrassed or self-conscious about doing something out of the ordinary as they chat and relax outside dressed only in their underwear.

"Sold in a Cleaner Way" was the distinguishing characteristic of Sealpax Athletic Underwear for Men. Surrounded by admiring male fans in the bleachers, an athletic underwear champion jumps over the Cool and Clean sidelines holding honors in hand in a 1921 Sealpax ad loaded with homoerotic innuendo:

> "Boy, oh Boy," you appreciate Sealpax when you're mixed up in a crowd, when it is hot—and stuffy—and everybody 'round you is sweltering. Sealpax keeps you cool as a cucumber. It's that kind of underwear—built for man-sized comfort. Cool because the fine nainsook fabric is cool—comfortable because it is cut to follow the movements of your body—no chafe—no irritation—the coolest, finest underwear a man can slip into.

But the best thing about the underwear is the brand's package: "Sealtex is better athletic underwear and it is sold in a cleaner way—packed in the individual Sealpax envelope which keeps it as fresh and clean as the day it was made and laundered." Not unlike today's prophylactics, that sanitary covering was salutary and undoubtedly appealed to health-conscious men.

That same year (1921), Hatch advertised its one button union suit with a two-thirds page black-and-white ad. Two pretty men standing very close to each other draw all eyes to their interaction. With an hourglass body, the one on the left has his right hand on his hip in a most unmanly manner. Meanwhile, the man on the right has his right hand on the other's shoulder and his left touching the man's chest. The way they're drooling over each other as caught at this snapshot in time leaves little question about what's on their minds and what they intend to do about it.

THE FOCUS SHIFTS

As the industry turned the corner, making inroads through the 1920s, its emphasis began to shift towards convenience, comfort, and value. Perhaps no other company better synthesized these concepts in its market positioning as Topkis Athletic Underwear.

If BVD had its boys preening and admiring each other as the company's advertising developed, Topkis—whose very name conjures up a talisman capable of girding one's loins—distinguished the different men pictured in each of its ads not as playful, peek-a-boo boys, but more mature and fully functional men capable of carrying on life's affairs and, perhaps even, a relationship with each other.

Moreover, BVD may have been the market leader in men's underwear back then, but Topkis had its own marketing strategy and unique selling proposition: value. In fact, nearly all Topkis ads emphasized how much quality you got for just a dollar.

A young man formally dressed in a suit, white shirt and tie sits backwards on a chair ogling another youthful gentleman wearing only his underwear in a half-page, black-and-white Topkis ad published in 1921. Even though it is only early fall, the headline warns, "Your skin must breathe in winter, too." Midway through the copy, however, we find out that "The way to let your skin breathe properly is to wear the Topkis Athletic Union Suit *all year 'round.*'" Soon, the brand's positioning statement appears: "It's the biggest underwear value your dollar ever bought." That said, a rationale for the graphics still must be questioned: Why are two young men—one fully attired, the other only in his underwear—sitting that closely together and smiling so playfully at each other?

Unlike the iconic BVD boys who appear in each of the brand's advertisements seen here, different men participate in the action of Topkis.

Once again, a fully and formally clad gentleman is seated backwards on a chair and seriously contemplating a young man—this time standing with a brush in his right hand, his left hand ruffling through his hair—in a 1923 ad of the same size and graphics. The Topkis positioning statement is prominently articulated in the headline: "You can't beat Topkis at double the price." The copy is convincing and market-driven. But what is the story of the two men in the picture? Why does it seem that one is standing in the footlights, "auditioning" for the other?

"Topkis is worth lots more than a dollar," insists the headline of another Topkis ad, also published in 1923. Evidently, the handsome man looking intently at the binoculars he is holding—possibly a gift from the chap dressed to the nines in a sailor's jacket, cuffed slacks, cap, white shirt and bowtie who is seated in front of a ship's porthole—is worth lots more than a dollar, too. From the following copy, it is obvious that the clotheshorse is used to paying the price for what he wants and that is used to having his way: "An athletic union suit has to be a good bit above the average to satisfy me," he says. "It must fit me without either skimpiness or bagginess—the material must be of good quality—and I insist on long service." We learn a bit more about him, too, in his following revelation: "I've been accustomed to paying fairly stiff prices to get the kind of underwear I want. But no more! Topkis gives me everything I could ask for—and at One Dollar!" Are the binoculars a gimmick or prop—or are they a bribe, a teasingly tempestuous toy that will figure more prominently into whatever may happen next between these two swains?

The beat goes on as another debonair young man, hat in hand, admires the virgin-white Topkis athletic underwear exposed when his cute friend removes his bathrobe. Unlike the previous ads, both men are standing here. This half-page ad, which ran in 1924, bears the headline: "Dollar Topkis worth more say the men who wear it." Why, just ask any man who wears it and he'll tell you "the way to be sure of getting the most for your money when you buy underwear is to look for the famous Topkis label." But where, exactly, is that label? Following the gentleman's line of vision, the label must be directly below the belly button, somewhere above the crack in the shorts!

Two months later, Topkis ran a half-page ad featuring two other men. A hunky stud in all-white undies begins to unbutton his athletic underwear in the April 1924 ad's foreground, as a shorter and somewhat stoical cohort—maybe his butler or valet?—is standing nearby. Dressed in dark colors, he uses a brush to remove any lint from the jacket he is holding. For some reason, the guy appears subservient and not too happy. Maybe it has something to do with the book on the bench between them with its pages open to a particular passage? Though the darker man's face has turned in the direction of his client or patron, he stands with an arched back angled away from him. "One dollar—and a dollar never bought more value," heralds the headline.

AND THE BOYS IN THE BRANDS PLAYED ON . . .

As the underwear battles continued throughout the 1920s, one maker's attributes and the qualities that set it apart from another manufacturer's jockeyed for market position. Whether it was Wilson's, Hanes, BVD or Topkis, the boys in the brands played on.

Hanes had the anti-squirm shorts with the seamless seat, but Topkis underwear boosted the roominess, allowing men to move in comfort: "Why, man, Topkis lets you forget you have underwear on! Fit? It sure does! Roomy, easy—never a hint of skimpiness *anywhere*," claimed a company ad published in 1921.

About a decade later, in a statement to fashion-conscious men of the time, an Arrow underwear ad appearing in the Spring 1933 issue of *Apparel Arts: Fabric & Fashions* skirted the delicate line between being gay . . . but not *too* gay: Two handsome jocks in a locker room (either dressing or undressing) evidently are pleased with the virtues of their underwear. "And now the Shorts with the Seamless Crotch go Gay! (BUT NOT TOO GAY)," we are happy to learn from the headline, as the text's message extols the "greatest contribution ever put in shorts—the *seamless* crotch."

HOMOEROTIC OR SIMPLY A "GAY" *TROMPE L'OEIL*?

Advertising is typically designed to convince us to buy a specific product or service, whether for the first time or by switching brands. In pursuit of consumers, themes such as vanity, vitality and pleasure are strategically communicated.

What can we conclude from these early years of underwear advertising, before gay-specific images became so prolific? That ads infused with same-sex imagery and intimacy simply stood out and caught the readers' attention because they were oddly dramatic or hinted at homoerotic themes?

Or is it all but a devotion to smoke and mirrors, a razzle-dazzle gay *trompe l'oeil*? Exploring, explaining and extolling the homo-eccentricities of these ads, perhaps what we see here is just a curious by-product of the author's misguided imagination?

No—the trail of evidence is quite clear. Discount, if you will, some of these ads as funny fabrications and fantastic stretches of the imagination. Remaining is a large number of advertisements that, without question, are indicative of sexual and/or emotional intimacy and contact.

Obviously, the time was not right for Madison Avenue to launch a concerted effort to court the homosexual consumer, for this market and constituency did not yet dare to speak its name. It was not defined or measured and the power of its purse strings had not been imagined—qualitatively or quantitatively. Nor were the media yet in place to target the community of gay consumers efficiently, effectively—or even legally.

Looking at them now through the trajectory of time and prism of exposure, we are tempted to presume that some of the people or activities depicted were indeed gay, or, at least, given the circumstances, that they found themselves involved in actions, activities, situations and/or environments we would label today as "gay."

"Even in ads intended to appeal primarily to heterosexuals, there may be a homosexual subtext," opines journalist Georgia Dullea (1992).

Now *that's* the real giwies on the skivvies!

Notes

1 Background on BVD can be found on the company's website (http://www.bvd.com), in Wikipedia (http://en.wikipedia.org/wiki/BVD), and in *Time* (1951).

2 At the time of writing, Vintageskivvies had a series of archival pages at http://www.vintageskivvies.com/pages/archives/history (accessed November 18, 2006). As of this issue's press date,

however, it appears that these archive pages are no longer posted online.

References

Berendt, John. 1987. "Boxer Shorts." *Esquire* 108 (September): 44–5.

Dullea, Georgia. 1992. "With Varying Degrees of Openness, More Companies Lure Gay Dollars." *The New York Times*, March 2, D9.

Time (1951) "Undercover Artists." *Time*, August 13. Available from: http://www.time.com/time/magazine/article/0,9171,889224,00.html?id=chix-sphere (accessed November 18, 2006).

35

MAGAZINES, THE MEDIA, AND MRS EXETER

Julia Twigg[1]

The chapter draws on four magazines, aimed at different sectors of the market: *Woman & Home,* a classic women's magazine primarily read by middle- and lower-middle-class women in their forties to sixties; *SAGA,* a proponent of Third Age lifestyles read by slightly older and more affluent women (and men); and *Yours,* a mass market magazine read by working-class women in their sixties and seventies. The aim was to understand how fashion operated in magazines aimed at older women. The fourth magazine was *Vogue,* chosen to represent the premier UK fashion magazine. Here the task was slightly different: to understand how age was presented, but also effaced, in a magazine focussed on high fashion. This was achieved primarily through a concept of 'ageless style', and this forms the basis of its current approach. But this was not always the case. Age has been managed differently by *Vogue* in the past, and in the last section of the chapter I explore the lost world of Mrs Exeter.

MAGAZINES AND THE CONSTITUTION OF IDENTITY

Since the 1970s women's magazines have been the focus of extensive sociological analysis exploring their role in the constitution of women's identities under late capitalism.

There has, however, been relatively little work that extended these understandings to the constitution of aged identities. New work around identity and age, however, suggests this may not be the case, resting as it does on a concept of identity as something formed in youth and carried forward into later life, as opposed to developing over time, unfolding and changing through the life course in interaction with cultural structures, including in relation to age.

Magazines need to be seen as sites of contestation over cultural meanings, primarily of gender, but increasingly of age. Given the economic and cultural location of most media these will reinforce the dominant values of a society. In relation to women's magazines, this means the dominant values of femininity and the importance of maintaining these as one ages through practices like beauty regimes and engagement with fashion (Dinnerstein and Weitz 1994).

WOMEN'S MAGAZINES, FASHION AND AGE

Though it is sometimes asserted that there are no magazines for older women, this is not in fact the case. Perusal of UK market data sources such as British Rate and Data (BRAD), which lists all UK magazines with brief information about their characters and readership, throws up a significant number of classic women's magazines aimed at the over fifties. One of the features of the magazine sector since the 1980s has been the way it has pursued finer market segmentation. Magazines are much more narrowly targeted now, with life-styles as the key determinant. But underlying lifestyle is nearly always a concept of age; significantly,

---

[1] In Julia Twigg (2013) Magazines, the Media and Mrs Exeter In: Fashion and Age: Dress, The Body, and Later Life. London: Bloomsbury, 97–117.

the two parameters on which BRAD provides readership data are age and socioeconomic status.

THE MAGAZINES AIMED AT THE OLDER MARKET

Woman & Home (see Table 8) is a classic women's magazine with a typically strong emphasis on beauty and fashion, which occupies about a fifth of the editorial space. There is a strong emphasis on being positive, on new beginnings and the potential role of clothes in this. Fashion is seen as a central part of the 'treat' of the magazine. Printed on glossy paper with a spine, it is produced by IPC from its main London office in conjunction with a range of fashion and other titles. The readership centres on those in their late forties to sixties, predominantly middle class. The circulation data is taken from British Rate and Data (BRAD 2008) for the period when the main interviews were undertaken. A value of 100 represents the population norm for the subgroup, and figures above and below display a bias towards or against the category.

SAGA Magazine (see Table 9) is a general lifestyle magazine aimed at the affluent retired, promoting consumption lifestyles. It is an offshoot of the travel and insurance corporation. Fashion only developed significantly in the magazine in the early twenty-first century, and it provided a relatively small and varying part of the offer, partly because the magazine is aimed at both men and women. It has relatively high production values with glossy paper and a spine, and at the time of the fieldwork it included fashion shoots mirroring those in mainstream fashion magazines. In general the coverage reflected that of newspaper colour supplements and other lifestyle magazines.

Yours (see Table 10) is a mass-market publication aimed at older and less affluent women. It is a fortnightly,

Table 8 *Woman and Home*: Readership by age and socio-economic status

15–24	25–34	35–44	45–54	55–64	65+
17	47	67	141	207	128
A	B	C1	C2	D	E
167	132	120	79	46	64

Table 9 *SAGA Magazine*: Readership by age and socio-economic status

15–24	25–34	35–44	45–54	55–64	65+
2	4	8	47	206	308
A	B	C1	C2	D	E
225	145	113	67	44	60

Table 10 *Yours*: Readership by age and socio-economic data

15–24	25–34	35–44	45–54	55–64	65+
7	10	24	48	125	342
A	B	C1	C2	D	E
31	58	110	128	94	153

printed on cheaper, nonglossy paper and stapled. It is published by Bauer, who own *Heat* and *Grazia*, but significantly it is edited from its Peterborough office in conjunction with other special interest magazines, not from London where the more directly fashion-oriented magazines are produced. Clothes tend to be cheaper, concentrated on high street staples like M&S and the value retailers. There is a warm, homely tone, and the magazine has a particularly close relationship with its readers who regard it as a 'friend': the editor receives over 750 letters and e-mails per issue. Circulation data confirms that it is heavily read by women over sixty-five, and that it has a socioeconomic profile weighted towards lower-middle- and working-class readers.

TENSIONS IN VISUAL CULTURE

Magazines operate in a visual culture that systemically devalues and erases age. In the late twentieth and early twenty-first centuries, however, this visual culture has taken on new significance with the exponential growth of the modern media. As a result culture has become saturated with images of bodily perfection, supporting a growing reflexive preoccupation with appearance in which individuals—typically women—measure themselves up against unattainable standards, pursuing self-worth and status through work on their bodies (Shilling 2003). These processes increasingly affect older women, who find themselves in a visual culture that systemically erases the signs of age, regarding them as a disruption in the visual field.

MODELS, MAKEOVERS AND CELEBRITIES

Yours, aimed at a distinctly older market, gets round the issue of older models by avoiding fashion shoots altogether. They are expensive and produce images readers find difficult to relate to. Instead the magazine shows fashion through spreads that illustrate garments and accessories, but without the bodies containing them. It is an approach widely used in magazines generally.

The most prominent way the magazines address the visual presentation of age is through makeovers. These allow magazines to relate directly to the lives of readers, getting round the difficulties posed by classic fashion shoots. They are a particularly important element in *Woman & Home.*

The magazines also relate to their readers through the use of celebrities who are themselves older. Over the last decade all magazines have increasingly featured celebrities on the covers and inside. In particular they are there to present a successful version of the older woman: looking good (and part of this means younger) and at the centre of attention. They assert the continued value and status of the older woman, placing her fully in the public eye, styled up in glamorous clothes and make-up, fully integrated with younger celebrity culture. The image is designed to draw the reader in and confirm her—idealized—identification with the magazine through its image of the older woman.

NEGOTIATING AGE

Much of the presentation of fashion in magazines takes the form of guidance and support in relation to the difficult matter of self-presentation, something all three editors recognized was increasingly important. Even the editor of *Yours,* which is read by working-class women in their seventies and over, comments: 'We've all got so much more conscious of what we should be wearing and what we shouldn't be wearing.' It is much less clear today how to be older. As a result women often lack confidence. Clarke and Miller (2002) argue that dress, though a realm of pleasure, is also one of anxiety with, in Simmel's (1904/1971) terms, the competing desires to stand out and to fit in weighted significantly towards the latter. In relation to older women, there are added pressures of dressing in an age-appropriate way, in which the fear of being inappropriately dressed is strong. Many older women lose confidence in how to dress as their bodies change and as cultural expectations in relation to age bear in on them. As the fashion editor of *Woman & Home* commented: 'I've seen a lot of women who. . .have lost their way.'

Offering guidance on how to negotiate the difficult cultural territory of being older was thus a central part of what the magazines do. As the fashion editor of *Woman & Home* explained: 'It's our job to edit for people. That's what we do.'

For these fashion editors, it is axiomatic that there is always a way for older women to wear the latest styles—though the fashion editor of *SAGA* concedes that certain trends, for example, 'Neon, Boudoir', were very difficult. The purpose of the fashion sections is to concentrate on what can be worn by older women and to show readers how to do it.

Fashion—or rather dress—also performs an additional distinctive function in *Yours.* The magazine often runs features in which readers send in pictures of themselves in the past wearing glamorous clothes. Or it takes a current look—for example, bubble skirts—and shows how 'we' did it first, and by implication better, in the 1950s. These strategies allow the reader to imagine herself back in her youth and to assert her value as someone who did once look different and better. They draw on the evocative nature of remembered clothes and the power that lies in such material artefacts of the past with their intimate, embodied connections (Weber and Mitchell 2004). The magazine thus offers an opportunity to assert the memories and values of the group in the face of the cultural erosions of age, of what Vincent (2003) has described as the sense of becoming exiled in one's own culture.

Not all women, however, welcome this renewed emphasis on fashion and appearance. *Woman & Home* is largely bought by women who do still want to engage with these fields; and they form a prominent part of its appeal. But both *Yours* and *SAGA*, possibly because of their older age groups, have experienced more ambivalent responses from readers.

AGEISM AND AGE SLIPPAGE

Across the adult magazine sector is a systemic pattern of age slippage in which target readership is described as significantly younger than the actual age profile. This reflects the desire to maintain the status of the magazine in a commercial culture in which younger represents better. It allows the magazine to position itself in an aspirational space, presenting the reader with a visual world younger than the one they inhabit, allowing them to identify with a younger, generally more successful self. This pattern was evident in the magazines analysed here, all of which described themselves as targeted on significantly younger age groups than the ones reported by the readership data. For example *Yours* describes itself as 'targeted on the over 50s', whereas as the readership data shows, it is predominantly bought by those in their late sixties and older. Partly this is about lifting the status of the magazine in ways complicit with the desires of readers, reflecting back a significantly younger world. The fashion editor of *SAGA*, for example, divided readers into the 'new old' and the 'war old'; and saw her task when appointed to respond to the interests of the first through the use of mainstream fashion shoots as part of a process of lifting the magazine visually.

The tensions are also reflected in the responses of manufacturers and advertisers who are reluctant to be associated with this sector of the media. To cover fashion, editors need to borrow samples. All three editors, however, had had difficulties doing this. Initially when the fashion editor of *SAGA* attempted to include fashion, she found manufacturers would not lend, and she was forced to buy the clothes on a credit card and return them the next day.

The other editors experienced similar problems. The editor of *Yours* believed that retailers have 'delusions of grandeur about who is buying their clothes'. All three reported they had had some success in bringing round some retailers through their capacity to show how the magazine could deliver sales. This is a market often neglected by retailers, and as a result featured items were often taken up very strongly. The editor of *Yours* noted that the magazine had a 'response level that other magazines would kill for. . .there's an awful lot of money out there from these people.'

A similar dynamic works in relation to advertising. None of the magazines secured high status or even extensive fashion advertising. They attributed this partly to the fact that the British fashion industry did not spend much on advertising, expecting to get its coverage free; but more strongly to systematic biases in the advertising industry which is dominated by the young, who do not want to deal with magazines aimed at older readers (Lee 1997; Long 1998; Carrigan and Szmigin 2000). Status for the brand and the brand manager lies in securing space in magazines like *Vogue*, even though these might not sell the goods in the way an advert in one of their magazines might. As a result the advertising the three magazines did secure was noticeably older and less fashionable than the image presented in the editorial pages. Adverts were often for garments that were strongly age coded: in *SAGA* for example, leisure suits in pastel colours, with machine-embroidered floral detail. These were typically shown on very young models, again contrasting with the editorial policy, who would not conceivably wear such garments. As a result they struck a discordant note, but clearly one that did not disturb advertisers. There is thus a notable disjunction between the message about age conveyed in the editorial pages and the advertising.

THE HIGH FASHION MAGAZINE: *VOGUE*

We now turn to a very different magazine, *Vogue*, to explore how a high fashion magazine negotiates the issue of age. *Vogue* is the premier British fashion magazine (together with the trade paper *Draper's Record*), though it is also a lifestyle magazine aimed at well-off women. One of a stable of glossy journals produced by Conde Nast, it is part of an international publishing empire, with editions in fifteen countries. Each is distinctive and reflects local commercial and visual culture, though in recent decades they have together become carriers of a globalized style that supports international branding (Moeran 2004; David 2006; Borelli 1997; Kopina 2007). *Vogue* is notable for an almost perfect match between editorial and advertising, with the high production values of its fashion spreads reflected in the adverts for major perfume and garment houses. Its high advertising revenue means it is one of the most profitable women's magazines. The current UK circulation is around two hundred twenty thousand, with an attributed readership of 1.2 million. Its target readership is described as 'concentrated in the ABC1 20–44 demographic group. A high proportion are in some kind of job or profession and are in the higher income groups.' The sociodemographic profile confirms this, with a preponderance of As (BRAD 2008). In terms of age, the profile is heavily biased towards those in their twenties and thirties, with a clear falling off from the mid-fifties.

HOW DOES *VOGUE* NEGOTIATE AGE?

Vogue is not aimed at older women (see Table 11). As the marketing data shows, its readership is heavily biased towards those in their twenties and thirties. In recent years, however, it has made attempts to relate to the older market. This partly arose, as the editor explained in the interview, from the realization that older women represented a growing and affluent part of the market. Women in their fifties and sixties have particularly high disposable incomes, and *Vogue* is interested in capturing these for the fashion industry. It also resulted from comments from readers, for, though *Vogue* does not normally attract reader's letters, on the issue of the absence of clothes for older women, it does. Lastly, the editor herself, like many senior journalists, is encountering dilemmas of growing older while still retaining an active interest in dress and fashion.

Table 11 *Vogue*: Readership by age and socio-economic status

15–24	23–34	35–44	45–54	55–64	65+
215	124	92	88	52	39
A	B	C1	C2	D	E
201	136	110	70	68	52

In relation to fashion shoots there is an additional problem in using older models that arises from the visual values of the photographic community which are strongly influenced by wider movements in art and photography. This is most noticeable in magazines like *Vogue* where fashion shoots over the last two decades have increasingly deployed highly sexualized, edgy noir imagery (Jobling 1999). Ruggerone (2006) argues this reflects a masculine hegemony in which women are constructed as if intended for a young male spectator's gaze, embodying his expectations of women and male-female relationships. This aesthetic culture presents difficulties for the depiction of fashion in relation to older women who by and large do not respond positively to such images. They would indeed be transgressive if presented in these terms, but not in a way that chimes with current visual values.

Up until 2007, age only featured sporadically in *Vogue*; and it was wholly absent from its covers. The pattern was broken in July 2007 with an issue that addressed 'Ageless Style'; which has been repeated in subsequent years. The cover of the 2007 edition featured eight models integrated into unity through being dressed in white. None showed any visible signs of age, though close scrutiny of one slightly blank face might suggest cosmetic enhancement. Inside, however, their ages are revealed as nineteen to fifty-three. The cover conveys lightness (white with touches of red), glamour and youth. There are no visible signs of age.

The covers that followed in 2009–12 continued this evolution away from the initial use of multiple images, with its diffusionary effect, towards a more classic approach focussing on a single individual, though always a celebrity, reinforcing the way age is dealt with through actual women not models.

Vogue had on occasion addressed age before 2007, though not on the cover. Notably in 1998 it was the topic of a *Vogue* Debate. There were four such, which took the form of round table discussions by eight or so invited guests. The subjects were ultra-slim models; appropriate dress for professional women; the absence of black models; and ageing. Each carried a sense that it was a topic where *Vogue* was under fire for promoting malign versions of the female body that supported the culture of anorexia; for failing to acknowledge the changes in women's lives resulting from entry into work where ultra-fashionable, frivolous or overtly sexual dress was inappropriate; for endorsing implicit racism through its promotion of an exclusively white model of beauty; and for excluding older women from view. The model and work debates were mentioned on the cover; the ageing one was not. The panel for the ageing debate included the deputy editor of *Vogue* (42), the beauty director (age not given), a novelist (Fay Weldon, 66), the director of a model agency (54), a property administrator (66), a retailing director (48), a designer (Edina Ronay, age not given) and a private GP (50). The discussion mostly turned around appearance rather than dress, with particular attention paid to cosmetic surgery and HRT. The tone was largely upbeat, with a characteristic magazine emphasis on feeling good and the importance of positive thinking and inner beauty. This last note was somewhat punctured, however, by the intervention of the beauty editor: 'I have to say that it's an irony to listen to us all sitting around saying it's great to be older, when I know that the phones are ringing in the beauty department with women our age asking "Where can I get Botox injections?"' (266). The discussion ended with an editorial note that explained that, unlike the other three debates, this one produced 'no clear conclusions', and it was described as 'not an easy topic'.

In the 2008 special issue she wrote more directly on the experience of becoming fifty. She states that she is unwilling to get involved in battles that she is going to lose: 'You can't win a battle against time.' She notes how it is easier to face age if one has been nice looking but never beautiful: 'For those whose identities are completely bound up in their good looks, the diminution is terrifying' (143).

LOCALIZATION, DILUTION AND PERSONALIZATION

A systematic examination of the editorial pages of the magazine reveals three main strategies deployed by *Vogue* to finesse the difficulties of representing age: localization, dilution and personalization. *Localization* refers to the strategy whereby older women are confined to certain parts of the magazine. Typically, and most strongly, they feature in the beauty pages where anti-ageing strategies are a central concern. They are never represented visually here.

Dilution strategies are pursued through a number of classic journalistic techniques. The first of these, widely used across the magazine sector, is the decades approach, in which fashions are illustrated on women in their twenties, thirties, forties and so forth. Until recently such decades tended to stop at the forties, with the fifties being a daring extension. The 'endpoint' of fashionability is, however, being pushed later in *Vogue* and in other magazines. From 2005 *Vogue* included— exceptionally—a woman in her seventies. The article illustrated key trends, showing how these could be worn by all ages; the woman in her seventies featured 'white'. She did, however, look somewhat different from the earlier decades—more distinctly old. By the time the format was repeated in 2008, *Vogue* managed to illustrate a woman in her seventies who, presumably through cosmetic surgery and airbrushing, was fully integrated with other images, almost wholly devoid of any appearance of age.

Another classic dilution technique is that of generations. It is a strategy often used by advertisers who want to show their clothes as relevant and sellable to all ages without compromising their fashionability, and so illustrate them in family groups. These contrast with the full-page fashion spreads. Here the images of older women are diluted by small images and a predominance of younger women. Such pages enable the magazine to reach out to and relate to older readers by showing something of their lives, but without defining the magazine as aimed at this group.

The third strategy is that of *personalization*. In every case where an older woman is featured in *Vogue*, she is a named individual. These are always real women, not models, living real lives, though with the proviso that these are *Vogue* lives and, as a result, far from the lived reality of most people, even most readers. There are parallels here in the emphasis on actual older women in less elite magazines through the use of makeovers and celebrities, though *Vogue* does also use the latter. The editor noted, however, that it has proved difficult to find powerful or senior women prepared to be photographed in *Vogue* because they see it as threatening to their standing: 'They think that it will be seen as trivial.'

This account of the treatment of age and ageing should not lead us to think that these are central themes for UK *Vogue*. They are not. They are marginal and sporadic. We noted how age-themed issues are always published in July, a dead period for fashion magazines; though the editor in the research interview confirmed that these put on readership. Otherwise features on older women are infrequent and older women only appear occasionally. But this was not always so. During the 1950s, older women had a regular slot in *Vogue* in the guise of Mrs Exeter.

THE LOST WORLD OF MRS EXETER

Mrs Exeter was a character developed by *Vogue* in the late 1940s to represent the older woman (Halls 2000). In 1949 she was described as 'approaching sixty' (March 1949). She appeared twice on the cover of *Vogue* (1948 and 1951), including in a glamorous shot by Cecil Beaton, and was a regular and successful feature through the 1950s. Initially represented by drawings, including by the artist John Ward, she developed a distinctive photographic image in the 1950s. By the end of the decade, however, Halls notes that she was getting steadily younger; and she eventually disappeared in the mid 1960s, killed off by the rise of youth fashion

The phenomenon of Mrs Exeter is an interesting one; and we can ask why, despite remaining something of a memory in *Vogue*'s collective consciousness (she features from time to time in articles), she has not been—and indeed could not be—revived. Part of the reason is that she is so much a figure of her times, the 1950s, and she remains confined by that period. Her identity is heavily inflected with class and gender. With her elegant, restrained clothes, she epitomizes the bourgeois lady of the period. Always referred to by her married name, she remains encased within her marriage. It is inconceivable that she could have a job. She thus represents a way of life that has ceased to exist for the majority of middle- and upper-middle-class women who are the main audience for the magazine.

Vogue now promotes an ideal of ageless style in which seamless integration is the goal and in which older women—if they pursue the ideal of fashionability—can remain part of the mainstream. And yet this integration is based in significant ways on an effacement of age. The covers that featured ageless style show no signs of age at all. *Vogue* consistently features older women who look decades younger than their age, and achieving that state is valorized as the ideal. Here the aim is not to move graciously on to the next stage of life like Mrs Exeter, but to look ten years younger and to remain actively integrated into the world of appearance and consumption, reflecting a cultural ideal in which success is ageing without showing the visual signs of doing so.

CONCLUSION

Magazines for older women—as for younger—are a deeply ambivalent cultural phenomena, reflecting the wider cultural of ageism, and to that degree endorsing its meanings, at the same time as offering forms of escape from and resistance to it. The wider culture prizes youth, and it is not surprising that magazines present themselves in ways that reflect that valuation.

The upbeat character of the magazines is particularly evident in the makeover pages which include a prominent part of the fashion coverage, and the place where the magazines connect very directly with the readers and their aspirations for themselves. These features centre on making the best of yourself and on being positive. They are about countering the pervasive negativities of later years and the erosion of confidence that can come with these. All three magazines aimed at the older market emphasized this, though in the contexts of their different demographics.

At the same time, like most women's magazines, they contain strongly escapist elements, presenting an idealized, aspirational world that allows older women to escape from the day-to-day limitations of their lives. Magazines can also offer other forms of escape in relation to age. *Yours* makes a point of taking readers into spaces where their values are endorsed and shared by a community of others and where, despite the cultural erosions around them, their memories are shared and appreciated.

Magazines need to be understood not simply as reflectors of the culture, but creators of it. As such, they contribute to a particular discursive construction of later years. As we have seen, it is one that emphasizes being positive, remaining part of the mainstream, presenting yourself well and engaging in beauty practices and anti-ageing strategies. It rests on an active engagement with consumption. It is clearly attractive to readers—and advertisers. But in doing so, other discursive constructions are implicitly silenced—those, for example, of giving up, of not bothering to keep up appearance or 'making the best of yourself', of radical disassociation from material possessions or concerns with appearance, not trying to look younger, but accepting being and looking old. These are absent from their pages.

References

BRAD (2008), *British Rate and Data* (October), London: Emap Media, 559.

Carrigan M. and I. Szmigin (2000), "'Advertising in an ageing society'", *Ageing and Society*, 20: 217–33.

Clarke A. and D. Miller. (2002), "'Fashion and anxiety'", *Fashion Theory*, 6, 2: 191–214.

Dinnerstein M. and R. Weitz (1994), "'Jane Fonda, Barbara Bush and other aging bodies: femininity and the limits of resistance'", *Feminist Issues*, 14, 1: 3–24.

Shilling C. (2003), The *Body and Social Theory*, second edition, London: Sage Publications.

Halls, Z. (2000), "Mrs Exeter—The Rise and Fall of the Older Woman." *Costume*, 34: 105–12.

Jobling, P. (1999), *Fashion Spreads: Word and Image in Fashion Photography since 1980*. Oxford: Berg.

Lee, R. A. (1997), "The Youth Bias in Advertising." *American Demographics*, 19(1): 47–52.

Long, N. (1998), "Broken Down by Age and Sex—Exploring the Ways We Approach the Elderly Consumer." *Journal of Market Research Society*, 40(1): 73–92.

Ruggerone, L. (2006), "The Simulated (fictitious) Body: The Production of Women's Images in Fashion Photography." *Poetics*, 34: 354–69.

Simmel, G. (1904/1971), "Fashion." In *On Individuality and Social Forms: Selected Writings*, trans. D. C. Levine. Chicago, IL: University of Chicago Press.

Vincent, J. (2003), *Old Age*. London: Routledge.

36

'NICE STUFF AGAINST THE SKIN':
Pleasure and spectatorship in men's underwear advertising

Paul Jobling[1]

Most histories of fashion, including those devoted specifically to undergarments, tend either to marginalise the development of men's underclothing or ignore it altogether. One of the chief reasons for this relegation lies in the comparative simplicity and utilitarian aspect of men's underwear itself, a point which is expressed by Willett and Cunnington (1981: 41) in *The History of Underclothes*: 'Man has never used provocative underclothing; its plain prose has been singular in contrast to the poetic allurements worn by women'… Moreover, while men's underwear may often be regarded as prosaic, when we examine the various ways that it has been codified in advertising during the twentieth century, more than a certain 'poetic allure' becomes apparent. This is probably most evident in the erotic appeal of advertisements for men's underwear produced since the early 1970s, such as those for Hom and, most notably, in various campaigns for Calvin Klein. The first of these tantalisingly voyeuristic promotions, produced by the In-House agency, appeared as a traffic-stopping bill-board in New York's Times Square in 1982, and subsequently in magazines like American *GQ*.

But it would be erroneous to regard this type of display of men's bodies as the underwear advertising in Britain as well as the United States earlier in the twentieth century reveal. Indeed, such promotions were ubiquitous, appearing in most daily newspapers as well as an eclectic spread of periodicals, including *Punch* and the *Radio Times*. Accordingly, in this chapter I want to uncover the mythology that it is only since the 1980s that men's underwear advertising in Britain became an economically potent force as well as visually provocative and erotic (as we shall see, many promotions of the interwar period were artfully executed). In this regard the visual and verbal rhetoric in publicity for several manufacturers during the 1920s and 1930s underscored the fetishistic nature of underwear, the feel of 'nice stuff against the skin' as an advertisement for Courtaulds in the *Radio Times* on 19 March 1937 proclaimed, while in their imbrication of pleasure, spectatorship and gender many advertisements also resorted to strategies of camp and sexual ambiguity. But first, it is necessary to raise once more the issue of advertising style to see how it related to the promotion of new materials and styles of underwear.

A FITTING FOUNDATION: UNDERWEAR AND ADVERTISING STYLE

On both sides of the Atlantic the interwar period was crucial in the technological and stylistic development of both the men's underwear and advertising industries. Consequently, men's underwear was bound up in the debates concerning a new discourse for a modern, democratic form of advertising and its importance in attracting the most suitable target audience. During the first ten years of the twentieth century, for example, Mather & Crowther's advertisements

---

[1] From Paul Jobling (2005) 'Nice Stuff Against the Skin' Pleasure and Spectatorship in Men's Underwear Advertising In: Man Appeal: Advertising, Modernism and Menswear. Oxford: Berg, 121–34.

for Wolsey underwear, which usually foregrounded the manufacturer's symbolic trademark of Cardinal Wolsey's head, were frequently praised for their boldness in design, directness in wording, and . . . striking pictorial quality. By contrast, promotions for Pesco tended to incorporate photographic imagery and copy in imaginative configurations, such as the press campaign for the autumn of 1907 which reproduced an aerial photograph of grazing sheep penetrated by a wedge-shaped space containing text that drew attention to the lightness and warmth afforded by woollen underwear. At the same time, it was realised that the evolution of striking publicity could contribute significantly to a company's financial success. Thus advertisements for Pesco underwear were distributed at the entrance to the National Scottish Exhibition in Edinburgh, held in the summer of 1908, in order to get people to visit its stall, and Peter Scott & Co. claimed that sales of the brand in 1909 had increased sixfold after nearly ten years of advertising in the general and trade press (*Advertising World* 1910).

Along with promotions for Horne Brothers' Cutuna brand of underwear, therefore, both and Wolsey and Scott were generally commended by the *Advertising World* for the standard of their publicity before the First World War. Nonetheless the magazine did conclude that British underwear advertising lagged behind promotions for American brands such as B.V.D. in terms of quality, character, form and symbolism (*Advertising World* 1913c). In 1930, for instance, W.S. Crawford took over the Jaeger account, which they rejuvenated with figures drawn by Prentis of robotic men performing various movements and type set in Gill Sans. During the 1930s also promotions for I.R. Morley's Theta brand that were handled by Pritchard, Wood and Partners used Kabel light typography for the headlines alongside a contrasting Ambassador serif face for the main copy and illustrations with a strong sense of linear and tonal values, while under the art direction of Marjorie Marene (alias Marjorie Janko) several promotions for British Celanese were designed by Traus of Carlton Studios in a fashionably monumental *moderne* style.

But it was probably the interwar publicity for Wolsey underwear, which was in the hands of several different agencies at this time, that was the most stylistically varied. During the 1930s full-page promotions for Wolsey's goods could he found in the *Daily Mail* and *Daily Express,* and half-page advertisements in the *Daily Mirror* and *Daily Herald*. Under Pritchard, Wood and Partners, the hallmark of Wolsey advertising between 1930 and 1932 was a clean layout, usually incorporating the company's trademark alongside an illustration of a male figure, with headlines set in Erbar bold, one of the new German sans serif typefaces designed in the early 1920s (Harrison 1930a: 280). By contrast, in the spring of 1934 the London Press Exchange introduced a sense of humour to Wolsey advertising with the Walrus-moustached and monocled character of Colonel Blimp. Conceived by the cartoonist David Low, who worked principally for Lord Beaverbrook's *Evening Standard* between 1927 and 1950, and first introduced on 21 April 1934, Blimp was the corpulent militaristic gas-bag who Low used to symbolise both right- and left-wing political incompetence. It must be noted, however, that photographic advertising for underwear was the exception at this time in Britain and did not become the norm until the 1960s. Only three further advertisements using photographs were found, for instance, in the research conducted for this chapter and, probably on the grounds of decorum, they appeared in the trade journal *MAN and his Clothes* rather than the general press. Furthermore, according to an anonymous reviewer in *Advertiser's Weekly* on 5 November 1936, hand-drawn illustrations of undergarments were favourable to the realism of photographs.

In common with other men's wear retailers and manufacturers, therefore, the advertisers of male underwear faced a twofold challenge at this time – how to transcend the apathy or resistance of the male customer, and how to combat the idea that men don't care what underwear looks like as long as it keeps them comfortable.

A MATERIAL WORLD: UNDERWEAR, HEALTH AND SPORT

One of the most common ways that this double impetus was codified in men's wear advertisements for several manufacturers during the first half of the twentieth century was by framing health and comfort in terms of sporting ability. In 1927, for example, promotions for both British Celanese and Aertex emphasised respectively the versatility of their rayon and cellular cotton underwear to keep you cool or warm, depending on the weather, by representing men at the top of their game in sports as diverse as golf, cricket and tennis.

Hence, on one level the rhetoric of these promotions clearly overlapped with the discourse of reform for better hygiene and living conditions that had grown apace in Britain, Europe and the United States since the late nineteenth century. By the 1920s and 1930s the culture of the fit and healthy body was central to such debates and, as we have already seen, organisations such as the British Men's Dress Reform Party (1929–37), in which J.C. Flugel was a leading figure, began to address the issue of restrictive clothing. In this respect, research was also undertaken into the efficacy of different materials for underwear, and usually centred on the relative merits of wool and cotton. In 1893, for example, a series of articles by Dr Gustav Jaeger, Professor of Zoology and Physiology at the University of Stuttgart, in *Aglaia* (published by the Healthy and Artistic Dress Association, which had been founded in 1890) had extolled the virtues of wool, since its porous nature would allow 'noxious inhalations to disperse' (Wilson 1985: 213–14). This point of view had been compounded after the experiences of army personnel during the First World War, when woollen underwear by the likes of Pesco had been issued to conscripts from October 1917 onwards (Currington 1919: 357). By contrast, Dr Lahmann, who ran a sanatorium in Dresden, insisted in 1938 that cotton mesh underwear was the most versatile since it was warm in winter and cool in summer (*MAN and his Clothes,* November 1938: 25). And in 1935 George Spencer of Cheapside devised a *juste milieu* in male underwear that pandered to both tastes, producing a range called Tuplex, which was made of botany wool but had an internal lining of superfine cotton. A contemporaneous advertisement in the national press claimed that the product had been widely tested among a range of professional types including doctors, actors, army officers and school teachers, and that over 99 per cent of them had liked wearing it (*MAN and his Clothes,* January 1935:10).

The question as to which material was the most suitable for underwear for the modern man was likewise analysed in articles in *MAN and his Clothes,* where support was given to the idea that lighter-weight fabrics and closer-fitting garments could be worn the whole year round on the grounds of style and health, witness this comment: 'When we take into consideration the fact that fully half the autumn underwear sold today is cut on athletic lines, there seems to be a plain indication that men in this country are getting healthier' (*MAN and his Clothes* 1937:26). In fact, the first half of the twentieth century witnessed considerable experimentation and ingenuity in the design and manufacture of more athletic and minimal forms of underclothing for men, such that many of the prototypes we are used to buying today were established. B.V.D. was one of the first companies to pioneer popular athletic styles of underwear in the United States and Britain with the introduction of the one-piece union suit in 1914. Modelled on an athlete's outfit, this was a loose-fitting combination of shorts and a sleeveless vest with an adjustable waistband that was initially made from lightweight cottons such as nainsook but by the 1920s was available in knitted cotton, silk, rayon and poplin. By the early 1920s, individual boxer shorts and vests had begun to supplant the one-piece union suit. The T-shirt had been available in North America since 1909, while boxer shorts had been issued to US servicemen during the First World War as summer attire and proved to be so popular that many men continued to wear them afterwards. Boxer shorts and vests with 'v' or round necks also became available in Britain during the late 1920s, alongside French and American shorts in ribbed cotton or cashmere with fancy patterns and elasticated waistbands or adjustable side straps (Albemarle 1932). Styles of vests and trunks by Meridian in lightweight knitted lastex yarn, a mixture of wool and elastic originated in 1933–34, retailed in the region of 3s to 5s between 1927 and 1935, which meant that they would also have been within the pocket of the average working-class man, who earned typically £3 10s per week during the early 1930s. More expensive at this time was underwear by Aertex in knitted cellular cotton, which cost between 5s and 8s 6d, and underwear by British Celanese in rayon, an artificial cellulose silk first developed in 1905, which cost between 10s 6d and 15s 6d.

After 1935, the Union Suit and boxer shorts were both largely superseded by the advent of Y-fronts, pioneered by Coopers Inc. of Kenosha, Wisconsin. In 1911 Coopers had devised the KKK (Kenosha Klosed Krotch) brand of underpants, which had two flaps of fabric at the front overlapping in a X-formation – a prototype that was modified by Wolsey in Britain with their X-fold underpants in 1951. The first experimental Y-front briefs, called Model 1001, were patented in August 1935 in knitted mesh fabric and based on the swimming trunks with a front pouch as worn by men on the French Riviera. Initially these were viewed with great scepticism by the underwear industry and men's wear retailers alike but became an immediate success with the buying public – 12,000 pairs were purchased during the first week of promotion alone. At the same time *MAN and his Clothes* (August 1935: 46) commented that the new jockey shorts had been inspired by the 'spell of Tarzan and the Apes' and predicted that the style would also revolutionise the underwear market in Britain and Europe. Indeed, Lyle and Scott became the main franchiser of the brand for Britain, France and Denmark in 1938, manufacturing an average of 60,000 garments per week in their purpose-built factory in Hawick, Scotland from June 1939 onwards. The name 'Y-front' went on to become a generic term for other brands of men's underwear and greatly democratised the market.

Significantly, the promotion of athletic underwear as a desirable garment was achieved not just in terms of class or income but of age as well, and *MAN and his Clothes* noted considerable polarisation in the British market for the new underwear styles on this level. Sales surveys were revealing that colourful boxer shorts, for instance, were mostly being bought by a 'younger set of men', with brands in pale blue, silver grey, pale pink and green being much in demand (Albemarle 1931). The association of these kinds of shorts with fashionable young males is evident in an advertisement that appeared in *Punch* on 29 May 1929. This comprised an illustration of a man wearing a button-top vest with coloured stripe trunks and a tagline affirming: 'Aertex in colour adds to the gaiety of nations'. While the word 'gay' had probably come into currency in the United States by the 1920s to refer to homosexuals, it is unclear whether the term was being used simultaneously in Britain in entirely the same way (Dynes 1990:456). Nonetheless, it is interesting to note that by this time pale blue had been designated the 'trade mark' of gay men according to the recollections of several correspondents in a Mass-Observation survey into sexual behaviour conducted in 1949, and to discern also the way that the male figure illustrated in the Aertex promotion crooks his wrist limply on his hips.

PLEASURE, FETISHISM AND SEXUALITY

The advertisements from the interwar period are not just instructive in the way they reveal the considerable variation that was available in cut, materials and styles, for they also connote the psychological momentum to be had in purchasing and wearing underwear. The haptic and sensory pleasures that could be attained from the touch and feel of soft, contour-revealing fabric, for example, is connoted in both the verbal and visual rhetoric of several of the underwear promotions reproduced here. Thus, the copy in the advertisements for 'Celanese' and Courtaulds stress the comfort and luxury of rayon underwear in terms of the 'clean, fresh feel of the fabric' and feel of 'nice stuff against the skin' respectively, while the texture of knitted wool is described as 'smooth and soft' in the publicity for Meridian, and 'silky smoothness' in that for Morley. At the same time, the fact that the new styles of garments cling to and caress the skin – the idea of being 'snug inside' expressed in one Morley Theta campaign in 1935 – is represented in the way that the underpants fit snugly around the buttocks of the man viewed from behind. Such a fetishistic desire for soft, figure-hugging fabric is also expressed in an article that appeared in *MAN and his Clothes,* which stated: 'Once a man has experienced the psychological stimulus of fine underwear, he will never go back to an inferior quality' ('Stylus' 1927:14).

Accordingly, underclothing has a special place in this economy of pain and pleasure since it crystallises 'the moment of undressing, the last moment in which the woman could still be regarded as phallic' (Freud 1977b: 354–5). By extension, men's underwear could be regarded in parallel terms, both as a way of concealing the phallic power of the male subject, and as a form of protection from his own (potential) unveiling and castration. It is interesting in this regard that the male in the advertisement for 'Celanese' does not even model the advertised brands of underwear but is represented playing tennis fully c. Moreover, the figure-hugging underpants represented in the Morley advertisement appear to align with the scopophilie drive and the play on concealing and revealing that is also evinced by Freud. In the 'Three Essays' he maintains: 'The progressive concealment of the body which goes along with civilisation keeps sexual curiosity awake. This curiosity seeks to complete the sexual object by revealing its hidden parts' (1977a: 69).

A HAZE OF SMOKE: THE AMBIGUITIES OF PLEASURE AND SPECTATORSHIP

Rather than being portrayed as something that should be kept out of sight, then, the undergarments in the majority of British advertisements in the twentieth century are implicated in a double-edged act of conspicuous consumption. Given that women were the largest purchasers of men's underwear – a survey by George Smith & Co. revealed that by the early 1950s they were buying 85 per cent of men's socks and underclothing – it is hardly surprising to find some advertisers making an overt appeal to them. The 1937 Courtaulds advertisement 'Confidential – To Wives and Mothers' is one such that interpellates women as active agents in the consumption of men's undergarments, but it does so in patriarchal terms. Thus the copy objectifies women not only as the natural purchasers but also as the launderers of men's underwear. By contrast, the illustration by Tisdall Carter of two men in their shorts and vests sharing a drink, ostensibly in a ship's cabin, portrays an exclusive homosocial atmosphere, something which appears to be the norm in publicity for men's underwear until after the Second World War, by which time women were not just referred to but sometimes actually or symbolically included in certain advertisements. During the interwar period, therefore, the males in such advertisements were frequently represented as solipsistic narcissists, while their bodies were also put forward for the spectatorial pleasure of others, by which I mean men as well as women. Furthermore, as the campaign for Aertex in 1929 reveals, male sexuality and masculine identity could be connoted in somewhat transgressive and queer terms, a suggestion that is amplified in underwear promotions for the likes of 'Celanese', Chilprufe, Irmo and Meridian, all of which represent men in their underwear and smoking cigarettes in intimate surroundings such as the bedroom or dressing room.

Of course, one would not want to overdetermine the gayness of some of these texts … could be regarded as innocently homosocial. But, the camp gestures and poses portrayed in them also nod in the direction of queer desire, and trade on the irony that those in the know will recognise such codes while those on the outside will remain oblivious to them. Particularly suggestive in these promotions is the trope of smoking. Once again, an idea from Freud's 'Three Essays' (1977a: 98–9) springs to mind here, inasmuch as he argues that smoking can signify a deep-seated desire to recuperate the pleasure of contact with the mother's breast, encountered as an erotogenie zone during breastfeeding. But Freud is speaking of obsessive smoking rather than the social activity that appears to take place in the advertisements. Nor can or should we regard the communal act of smoking in these advertisements as being as straightforward in terms of normative masculine identities as the solitary act of smoking connoted, for instance, in many tobacco campaigns of the period.

In fact, the 'in' codes of such advertising could have been intentional. Boyce, for example, in assessing the iconography of J.C. Leyendecker (who had been employed by Calkins & Holden and was reputed to be gay) and other advertising artists working in the United States during the early twentieth century, attests: 'What is clear is that a number of artists and admen of the day were homosexual, so it would not be unexpected for their affectional desires to have seeped into their ads' (Boyce 2000: 26). Judging from many of the advertisements for underwear and other items of clothing that appeared during the same period in Britain, it is probably safe to argue that there must also have been a parallel – though clandestine – gay presence in the British advertising industry., in common with other cultural producers in Britain during the interwar period, advertising artists and agencies were made to tread a fine line in dealing candidly with gay desire and queer identities.

By extension, the 1935 press promotion for Morley objectifies the male body in an entirely different way, representing a man from the rear. This was not the first advertisement to depict men's underwear from such a perspective. In 1914, for example, J.C. Leyendecker coined the emblematic 'Man on the Bag' illustration for S.T. Cooper & Sons (now Jockey International), representing a man in a KKK union suit from the back. At the same time, however, he is depicted pressing the weight of one leg on top of a leather bag as he tightens the strap with his hands. The pose is deliberate since it enables the spectator to see the way that the KKK garment had been engineered to enable freedom of movement with its asymmetrical closing and single button, positioned for comfort high up on the right buttock. The male figure drawing the curtains in the Morley advertisement has likewise been placed in a situational context, yet the way that we see underwear not only worn from behind but also clinging to and defining his own behind is exceptional for the period and seems to register anal desire on a completely different level to Leyendecker.

The Morley advertisement, however, can be seen to transgress and transmute these binary codes. Here, the body part that is regarded in social terms as the most private and most unclean is made visible, and veiled in tight-fitting underpants and bathed in seductive lighting that emphasises its pert and rounded contours, it is elevated to the status of fetishistic desirability and spectatorial pleasure, for women and men, and straights and gays alike. Thus the advertisement certainly appears to be more daring and deviant than other underwear promotions during the interwar period in the way it encodes feelings of comfort and pleasure. Yet like many of them, it also highlights the ambiguities of putting the male body on display and the way that such publicity intersects with both commodity and corporeal fetishism. It is in this respect, then, that the rhetoric of underwear advertising exceeds the advertising of the garment itself, just as much as the publicity addressed in the previous chapters is more than merely advertising for suits, shirts and shoes.

References

Advertising World (1910), 'The "Pesco Campaign", *Advertising World*, August: 149-52.
Advertising World (1913c), 'In the Magazines', *Advertising World*, July: 100 and 102.
Albemarle, G. (1931), 'Flashes of Fashion', *Man and his Clothes*, February: 29.
Boyce, D.B. (2000), 'Coded Desire in 1920's Advertising', *Gay and Lesbian Review*, Winter: 26-9.
Currington, R.H. (1919), 'Scientific Selling of Branded Underwear, *Advertiser's Weekly*, 16 May: 357-8.
Dynes, W.R. (ed.) (1990), *Encyclopedia of Homosexuality*, 1, Chicago: St. James Press.
Freud, S. (1977a[1905]), 'Three Essays on the Theory of Sexuality' in *On Sexuality*, trans, J. Stachey, Peguin Freud Library, vol. 7, pp. 31–169, Harmondsworth: Penguin.
Freud, S. (1977b[1927]), 'Fetishism' in *On Sexuality*, trans. J. Strachey, Penguin Freud Library, vol. 7, pp. 345–57, Harmondsworth: Penguin.
Harrison, J. (1930a), 'The New Simplicity in Press Advertising', *Commercial Art*, December: 276–80.
'Stylus' (1927), 'Sell Better Underwear', *Man and His Clothes*, May: 13–14.
Willet, C. and P. Cunningham. (1981), *The History of Underclothes*, London: Faber & Faber.
Wilson, E. (1985), *Adorned in Dreams: Fashion and Modernity*, London: Virago.

Archives, Annuals and Periodicals

Advertising World, 1901–1940
Man and his Clothes, 1926–59.
Punch, 1902–45.

37

THE CHANGING FACE(S) OF THE FASHION MAGAZINE AND THE NEW MEDIA LANDSCAPE

Pamela Church Gibson[1]

Traditional fashion magazines and women's magazines still exist, though they have changed their appearance and their format quite drastically in this new era of celebrity. But they now depend increasingly on television for their content, together with their longstanding reliance on cinema, and, more significantly, they have their own websites. With the increasing proliferation and power of fashion blogs over the past few years, whose authors can challenge, compete or corroborate, fashion journalism has been forced to cooperate with the bloggers. Overall, there is an interdependence in the presentation of contemporary fashion which is very new; a recognition of mutual needs has helped to create this reconfigured media landscape.

This shows quite clearly a recognition right across the media of the changes, their significance—and their potential. Many of the best-known fashion bloggers display on their sites a border that lists their powerful sponsors, who might include, say, *Vogue* magazine and a number of leading luxury brands. Susie Lau, who as Susie Bubble writes the leading blog Style Bubble (stylebubble.typepad.com), is among those most assiduously courted…Although she is employed full-time at the magazine *Dazed and Confused,* founded by Jefferson Hack in collaboration with photographer Rankin, the blog, she explains, gives her the chance to 'write about stuff I like' (Uhlirova 2009: 60). Since 2009, Lau has been invited to the more traditional fashion shows rather than bloggers-only previews and photographed sitting in the front row as befits her new celebrity status (also see Stebbins 2010b). Another celebrity blogger, Bryanboy, is a regular feature there; he has his blog sponsored by Chanel, while Marc Jacobs has named an ostrich-leather bag after him. However, many fashion bloggers keep their amateur status and the independence it brings. Many of them are also preoccupied with celebrity style, and we will return to the blogosphere at the close of this chapter.

In this new mixed-media climate, shaped and even inspired by the new culture of celebrity and its close links with fashion, all magazines where fashion is a key element have completely changed, chameleon-like, to adapt to and reflect the world of celebrity dominance. If, once again, we look back across the years, we will find that there was a time when the 'woman's magazine' saw its role as that of straightforward everyday helpmeet (see Ferguson 1983; Gouah-Yates 2003); it is significant that certain very successful blogs have now taken on this particular role (see Make Do Style, makedostyle.com; Economy of Style, economyofstyle.blogspot.com; The Budget Babe, thebudgetbabe.com).

Perhaps it is here, in this chapter, that we might try to investigate the question of 'looking'. For, in an era of endlessly circulating images of young women, largely presented directly *to* and *looked at* by other young women, the traditional theoretical arguments around 'the gaze' (Berger 1972; Mulvey 1975; Doane 1982) are no longer relevant; they depend upon the presumed dominance of the male gaze behind a camera, the idea of scopophilia and on different modes of address.

---

[1] From Pamela Church Gibson (2012) The Changing Face(s) of the Fashion Magazine and the New Media Landscape. In Fashion and Celebrity Culture: London: Berg 125–38.

I would contend that the changes within the world of fashion have rendered this argument increasingly problematic, dominated as it now is by *women* looking—and looking in new ways, perhaps. The anthology *The Female Gaze* (Gamman and Marshment 1988) is also rendered superfluous, for there is nothing in its pages which can help us to disentangle the difficulties around today's proliferating images of women, celebrity and fashion, addressed to a largely female audience.

I would venture to suggest that the gaze in the changed world of fashion is, in fact, *homosocial* (see Sedgwick 1985, 1990, 1993), as is so much of the dedicated space within the new world, not only of fashion but of the fashion-celebrity alliance. In Western societies of the past, the sexes in the upper echelons of society were segregated for the greater part of the day, just as they still are in other cultures, and only permitted to meet under the watchful eye of their elders. Young women, corralled together for long periods of time, would often engage in what anthropologists call 'homosocial grooming behaviour' (see Castle 1993): combing, brushing and dressing each other's hair; assisting each other in their toilettes; trying on each other's clothes, necklaces, earrings.

I would put forward the viewing of these new images as a modern variant on such activity. The habit of reading celebrity magazines in pairs or in groups, and of invariably discussing the latest images with other female readers, would seem to validate this suggestion (interviews, Church Gibson 2008–2010). The magazine *Grazia*, which has so successfully addressed the new twinned interest in fashion and celebrity, did so after a good deal of research prior to its launch in 2003. This involved the use of numerous focus groups within the targeted demographic of the new publication (interviews, Church Gibson 2008–2010). This focus group work showed that the prospective readers wanted these two ingredients alone, fashion and celebrity, within the proposed new magazine; the other traditional staples of a magazine for women were of far less interest and were, indeed, best avoided. Since the launch, the magazine has primarily addressed these two areas, and its sales reflect the validity of its new editorial policy.

MAGAZINES CHANGE SHAPE

Magazines directed at women alone first appeared in the eighteenth century: the purveying of information about the latest fashions was part of their remit, but they had other tasks to perform. The earliest magazines on both sides of the Atlantic were serious publications, often with an educational element (Ferguson 1983; Gough-Yates 2003)….The idea that the function of the magazine included the provision of both information and pictures to show and explain changes and new trends in fashion has remained a constant ever since.

The early magazines were targeted at women in the upper middle classes; so too were *Vogue, Harper's Bazaar* and similar fashion-led publications which appeared at the end of the nineteenth century (Hughes 2008). More down-to-earth magazines, created for middle- and working-class housewives, were launched in the 1920s and 1930s—titles such as *Good Housekeeping* and *Woman and Home* are self-explanatory. However, the information about running a home was nevertheless accompanied by that concerning the personal appearance of the 'homemaker', telling her how to look her best, often on a limited budget, and providing information on the latest trends in dress, hair and makeup….film stars rather than fashion models were of most interest to those of more modest means, and the new magazines of the 1920s and 1930s—including *Woman,* still on the market in 2010—responded to this fact by purveying information and images of the stars (see Ferguson 1983; Berry 2000a,b). Magazines for *young* women—for teenagers—in fact did not appear until the late 1950s and early 1960s, when the 'teenager', first identified and named in 1945 (Savage 2007), was suddenly targeted. As the demographic patterning of society changed radically and the effect of the baby boom phenomenon began to be understood, so the new spending power of the young was now pursued (Lewis 1978).

Before the watershed of the supposed sexual revolution, the more domestic, middle-market magazines traditionally told their readers that this involved maintaining a slim figure and youthful look, dressing as well as possible on whatever budget might be available, creating a pleasant, comfortable home and cooking the best possible meals using ingredients within the means of the reader. The magazines targeted at the young tended to ignore homemaking; more significantly, the changed mores of the 1960s and 1970s meant that there were other ways to please a man.

Cosmopolitan, often parodied but widely imitated, took the notion of pleasing a man into the bedroom and made it quite clear that here women could not rely on their skilled wielding of furniture polish, duster and vacuum cleaner alone. There must be more varied activity in this domain, not merely the weekly changing of the sheets and the daily plumping up of the pillows (see Radner 1995; Radner and Luckett 1999).

If the new magazines of the 1920s and 1930s took the new interest in Hollywood stardom and built it into the world they were carefully creating, that world has changed once more, so radically that existing magazines across all market levels have had to adjust if they are to survive. Interestingly, some of the less glossy publications first began to modify their approach in the late 1980s and early 1990s; they used popular soap operas and their stars, often for their covers and usually for one or two of their main stories (*Bella, Best,* et al.).

However, with the dominance of celebrity culture, what is significant within magazine journalism is not just the way in which existing publications have now utilized the celebrity factor to ensure that they remain in print. More significant is the raft of completely new publications, created to reflect a new and radically changed world order. These changes, incidentally, are not confined to women's magazines; men's magazines now feature near-naked celebrities on their covers rather than using anonymous glamour models. This state of undress is not always deployed to satisfy the presumed male heterosexual gaze.

Things started to change and to reflect the new interest in celebrity with the launch and success of *Hello* in 1993 and the similar magazines that followed it into print, all of which combined celebrity coverage with fashion. It is interesting now to look at the early issues of *Hello,* for there was a clear attempt to focus on the higher end of the social spectrum. Its photo spreads featured the homes and lifestyles of the rich, famous and well connected. As celebrity culture took hold, these extended to the homes of footballers, musicians and television stars. However, *Hello* now covers the weddings of lesser soap stars while showing off the homes of those in manufactured boy or girl bands.

The US fashion magazine *In Style* was originally unique in that it offered the usual mix of fashion, beauty and interior decor, but here all of these features were celebrity-driven from its first appearance. Appearing in England in 1999 with Julia Roberts on its cover, its sales were spectacular, and other magazines swiftly adopted its formula. At the lower end of the market, a whole new group of celebrity magazines joined the successful gossip-driven *Heat.* The titles themselves are interesting and indicative—*Closer, Reveal, Look, Now, More.* There is some very interesting work on 'gossip magazines' as female domain by Joke Hermes (1995) and Rebecca Feasey (2006, 2008), but these modes of exploration cannot be used to analyse shopping-driven, luxury brand–showcasing magazines like *Grazia.*

As the new magazines increased in number and popularity, so the paparazzi photographs which formed their content were invariably accompanied by often uncharitable comments on their new staple ingredient, the celebrity body. Relentlessly scrutinized in their pages, it obviously affected readers in their own endless quest for perfection and fuelled their feelings of dissatisfaction. *Heat* magazine was originally intended as a weekly publication which would provide television listings and act in a 'what's on' capacity. However, its first editor, Mark Frith, had the idea of making it into a forum for a particular mode of celebrity gossip and pictures. As it became more successful, some of its features were copied by other new publications.

One interesting characteristic of *Grazia* was its very *glossiness.* Traditionally, weekly magazines have been matt in appearance; the cost of producing a glossy magazine weekly was seen as prohibitive (interviews, Church Gibson 2008–2010). The glossiness, closer to the appearance and appeal of *Vogue* and *Harper's Bazaar,* helped to set it apart from the gossip magazines.

Not only the 'face' but also the faces featured within the glossy magazines have changed. In the 1980s, of course, fashion models were automatically used on most magazine covers and for the large-scale advertising campaigns of luxury brands and fashion-related products. But the first *Vogue* of the new decade was in some ways a portent. Normally *Vogue* has one single female face on its cover, but on the front of the January 1990 issue, it was felt that there was a need for five. They were selected from among the supermodels, created and then lionized as celebrities in the 1980s....The cover featured Linda Evangelista, Cindy Crawford, Tatjana Patitz, Naomi Campbell and Christy Turlington, all dressed alike in Levis and body hugging jersey tops, clustered on a grainy New York street...But magazine covers and fashion advertising campaigns now depend for their success upon their exploitation of the celebrity factor and have recently tended to feature a fashionable celebrity in preference to an anonymous model.

Magazine covers have now moved on beyond the heroines of the screen. US *Vogue* has featured Hilary Clinton, Oprah Winfrey and Michelle Obama on its covers. Anna Wintour, fashion celebrity, has yet to choose a solo shot of Victoria Beckham for her cover; however, in January 1998, Victoria was featured together with her fellow band members, the Spice Girls. She has now been seen on various different international fashion magazine covers; she has graced the covers of British, Indian, Russian, Spanish and German *Vogue*, also appearing with husband David in a special issue of *Italian Sport Vogue*, photographed by Steven Klein (July 2003). In addition, Ellen von Unwerth chose to photograph her for the cover of Turkish *Vogue* (August 2010) in a provocative manner. Although Beckham is fully dressed, she is nevertheless conspicuously holding both a cocktail and a lighted cigarette. Given that Turkey is a predominantly Muslim country, this is insensitive or, perhaps, given some of von Unwerth's past images, was in fact intended to provoke maximum controversy.

This leads us into an examination of the extraordinary symbolic power of *Vogue*, and US *Vogue* in particular, which has little to do with its sales figures but has given unquestioned celebrity status to its current editor, Anna Wintour.

ANNA AND THE NEW CELEBRITY: THE BIBLE ON SCREEN?

In the 1980s and even the 1990s, whilst a few photographers might be recognized within the public domain, the editors of glossy fashion magazines were not exactly household names, nor were they the subject of tabloid gossip and documentary film-making. In the past, even editors as well known as Diana Vreeland and Carmel Snow were not familiar, except of course to those especially interested in fashion. Most of those who saw the film *Funny Face*—now such a favourite with fashion cognoscenti—when it was released in 1955 would not have known that the overbearing fashion editor played by Kaye Thompson was intended to illustrate certain characteristics of both these women. One line of dialogue, 'My message to the women of America is—think pink!' used as the basis for a song-and-dance number, was apparently inspired by something Vreeland herself had once written, that 'pink is the navy blue of India'. And the fashion editor portrayed here never follows her own diktats; she has evolved her own unchanging style, a kind of uniform. This, too, is true of Vreeland herself (see Vreeland's advice throughout *D.V.*, her autobiography, 1984/2003).

The audiences who enjoyed *Funny Face* in 1955 had perhaps gone to the cinema to see Audrey Hepburn; some might have been aware that she had now formed a famous collaboration for Givenchy, who designed the 'Spring Collection' seen in the film. But very few would have automatically recognized the visual style of Richard Avedon, who not only took the photographs we see in the film but acted as overall visual consultant and who is named as such in the film's credit sequence.

Now, it seems, we are all much more aware not only of designers and of brands, but of key personnel within the industry. Anna Wintour is understood to have been at least partly the inspiration for a fictional cinematic narrative; she has also figured conspicuously within a successful documentary.

Initially, she appeared as the purported inspiration for Miranda in *The Devil Wears Prada,* discussed in the earlier section on the new fashion films. However, in *The September Issue* (US, 2009), she appeared as herself. This documentary, filmed over a number of weeks, showed the creation of an issue of US *Vogue,* foregrounding not only Wintour herself but also the creative director, Grace Coddington....such a film would not have met with much success ten years earlier, and might not even have been made. As we saw earlier, the film not only cemented the status of Wintour as celebrity, but also made a star of Coddington. *Grazia* magazine actually asked its readers, 'How cool can a sixty-eight year old woman BE?' (*Grazia,* April 2009).

The most interesting thing in this film is perhaps the relationship between these women, and the extraordinary contrast between them. Wintour is impeccably groomed throughout, even while 'relaxing' at home in Lacoste polo shirt and slacks; at work, she seems to wear a uniform of designer dress, cardigan, heavy necklace and slingback Manolo Blahnik shoes. Her hair, however, is never off-duty; it seems to be blow-dried into her trademark angular bob even for a day at home in the Hamptons. Coddington, by contrast, is always casually dressed, her long red hair loose over her shoulders in a much simpler uniform of long white shirts or loose black linen dresses, always worn with flat sandals.

Coddington's beautifully styled, even painterly fashion spreads provide aesthetic pleasure and showcase *clothes,* not celebrity bodies. But the cover girl for this issue and for the central shoot, not styled by Coddington, is the celebrity Sienna Miller, taken to Rome to be photographed by Mario Testino. She has a hard time. Her hair is deemed unsatisfactory and so a wig is specially made but then discarded because it's 'not working out'. Finally, the offending hair, described on screen as 'lank and lifeless', is tied up in a knot on top of her head. Even then, the cover image, when presented, is met with criticism: 'Look at her teeth,' murmurs Wintour.

These films perhaps make good the deficiencies of television outlined in a later chapter. Here, we see Demarchelier at work, as in Sex *and the City: The Movie,* while we once more meet André Leon Talley. This time, he is seen learning tennis at Wntour's behest, he explains, as part of an effort to get him fit and perhaps a tad slimmer; there's no one to protect him, no airbrushing possible and no chance of Grace intervening. He mops his sweating brow with—what else?—a Louis Vuitton towel. There are, too, special Vuitton boxes, presumably customized, which contain tennis balls, while still others hold his supplies of Evian water.

BLOGGERS, FASHION AND CELEBRITY

The Internet was once conceived of as an information superhighway; however, the information it carries today is not quite that implicit in the phrase coined by former British Prime Minister Tony Blair. Much of the Internet is now used for hardcore pornography, and the rest for different forms of selling and gazing; just as there is no policing in cyberspace, there is no editing, no deferring to superiors, no worries around copyright. Anyone can access images; anyone can create a site or set up a blog…Part of the appeal of blogs, perhaps, is the fact that they are interactive; with a few clicks, a reader can become a part of the fashion text and a participant in the dialogue.

There are now very different modes of fashion blogging, though most follow the visual-diary format. Some simply focus on the blogger's own purchases and activities, but others see it as their task to comment daily on celebrity fashions, while still others are what Rocamora and O'Neill describe as the 'straight-up street fashion blogs' (2008). Here, the term 'street fashion' is open to different modes of interpretation, as we will see.

Where once bloggers bypassed the official system and short-circuited it, and while many still try to work independently, the industry has noted their extraordinary appeal and, particularly with the luxury brands, adapted accordingly. There are the bloggers-only previews and other events mentioned earlier (interviews, Church Gibson 2008–2010) …, some bloggers have themselves become celebrities. The youngest to have a high profile, the thirteen-year-old American girl Tavi, was invited to all the couture shows in the winter of 2009, and also to the Prada–Vezzoli–Lady Gaga installation in Los Angeles…in the press coverage of the Paris collections in the spring of 2010, Tavi was given a front-row seat at Dior and appeared in more photographs of the show than did the clothes paraded down the catwalk.

The bloggers who evaluate celebrity style are now multitudinous; but because there is no redress, they can say whatever they wish, as can those who respond to their posts. The pictures they upload may be those seen in the press; the comments may be more blunt. Some, like the two women who write the blog Go Fug Yourself (gofugyourself.com), write only on celebrity, but do so critically. Other bloggers, for example Disney Roller Girl, disneyrollergirl.net, and Coco's Tea Party, cocosteaparty.com, combine comprehensive coverage of fashion shows and new ranges mixed with celebrity photographs and commentary, sometimes critical, sometimes not.

However, there are those whose blogs have more in common with the spirit of the earlier women's magazines, who see their function as giving helpful and financially sound fashion advice and information across a range of topics. They link up with like-minded bloggers and create a virtual community; they can then refer their readers to other helpful blogs….There are, too, blogs and sites to provide alternative eco-friendly information for those who want to be fashionable (for example, www.ecofashion.com) and are mindful of waste. Bloggers swap information and images, undercutting the official voices of the fashion journalists and creating a subversive subtext for fashion that arguably influences buying habits more than anything else. Fabulously Broke in the City (fabulouslybrokeinthecity.com) is actually written by a young woman whose former spending habits drove her to declare herself bankrupt, and who is now managing to be stylish with very little outlay.

NOTASTREETBLOGGER.COM? THE SUCCESS OF THE SARTORIALIST

The street bloggers can and do make passing fashion celebrities of the stylish unknowns who people their posts. What is rather disconcerting is when something that masquerades as a street blog not only makes a celebrity of the blogger involved, but also goes beyond the pleasure of what he or she sees and captures as stylish into very rigorous judgments about the taste of others. Schuman has a background in the fashion industry, and this is apparent in the cityscapes of his blog; many of his apparently random photographs are taken on streets near the sites of the major fashion shows, and he also positions himself carefully on the Rue St Honoré very near Colette, one of the most exclusive shops in Paris. There is nevertheless a deep-rooted belief that he takes photographs of 'ordinary people' (Stebbins 2010a; Olins 2009). In fact, he takes photographs of those who fit his particular ideas around style, which are curiously rigid.

He does indeed have a clear typology; on 7 July 2010, his post, headlined 'Italian men and the "back-dart" in their shirts', asked us to examine exactly that, to see how beautifully their shirts fit as a result. This may be a very accurate observation, but his tone can become waspish, or perhaps more accurately WASP-y….It is clear that, for him, most celebrities in the 'media parade' are automatically *without* style.

References

Berger John (1972), *Ways of Seeing*, London: Penguin Books.
Berry Sarah (2000a), '*Hollywood Exoticism*: Cosmetics and Colour in the 1930s', in David Desser and Garth Jowett (eds), *Hollywood Goes Shopping*, Minneapolis: University of Minnesota Press.
Berry Sarah (2000b), *Screen Style*: Fashion *and Femininity in 1930s Hollywood*, Minneapolis: University of Minnesota Press.
Castle Terry (1993), The *Apparitional Lesbian: Female Homosexuality and Modern Culture*, New York: Columbia University Press.
Church Gibson Pampela (2008–2010), *Interviews: Celebrity*, Fashion *and Consumption*, based at London College of Fashion.
Doane Ann (1982), '*Film and* the *Masquerade*: Theorising the Female Spectator', reprinted in Thornham Sue (ed.) (1999), *Feminist Film Theory: A Reader*, Edinburgh: Edinburgh University Press.
Feasey Rebecca (2008), '"Reading Heat": The Meanings and Pleasures of Star Fashions and Celebrity Gossip', *Continuum: Journal of Media and Cultural Studies*, 22/5 (October): 687–99.
Feasey Rebecca (2006), '*Get a Famous Body*: Star Styles and Celebrity Gossip in Heat Magazine', in Su Holmes and Sean Redmond (eds.), *Framing Celebrity: New Directions in Celebrity Culture*, London and New York: Routledge.
Ferguson Marjorie (1983), Forever Feminine: *Women's Magazines and* the *Cult of Femininity*, London: Heinemann.
Gamman Lorraine, and Margaret Marshment. (1988), *The Female Gaze: Women as Viewers of Popular Culture*, London: Women's Press.

Gough-Yates Anna (2003), *Understanding Women's Magazines: Publishing, Markets and Readerships*, London and New York: Routledge.

Hermes Joke (1995), *Reading Women's Magazines: An Analysis of Everyday Media Use*, London: Polity Press.

Hughes Kathryn (2008), 'Zeal and Softness', *Guardian* (20 December), <www.guardian.co.uk/books/2008/dec/20/women-pressandpublishing> accessed 27 September 2010.

Lewis Peter (1978), *The Fifties*, London: Lippincott, Williams and Wilkins.

Mulvey Laura (1975), '"Visual Pleasure and Narrative Cinema"', *Screen* 16/3: 6–18.

Olins Alice (2009), 'The Sartorialist Scott Schuman: What Makes Someone Stylish', *Times* (14 October), <women.timesonline.co.uk/tol/life_and_style/women/fashion/article6873270.ece> accessed 28 September 2010.

Radner Hilary (1995), *Shopping Around: Feminine Culture and the Pursuit of Pleasure*, London: Routledge.

Radner Hilary, and Moya Luckett (1999), *Swinging Single: Representing Sexuality in the 1960s*, Minneapolis: University of Minnesota Press.

Savage J. (2007), *Teenage: The Creation of Youth Culture*, London: Chatto and Windus.

Sedgwick Kosofsky (1985), *Between Men: English Literature and Male Homosocial Desire*, New York: Columbia University Press.

Sedgwick Kosofsky (1990), *Epistemology of the Closet* Berkeley: University of California Press

Sedgwick Kosofsky (1993), *Tendencies* London: Routledge

Stebbins Meredith (2010a), 'Speaking with The Sartorialist', *Vanity Fair Daily* (20 February), <www.vanityfair.com/online/daily/2010/02/speaking-with-the-sartorialist.html> accessed 29 September 2010.

Stebbins Meredith (2010b), 'Who Sits Where at Fashion Week and Why', *Vanity Fair Daily* (10 February), <www.vanityfair.com/online/daily/2010/02/who-sits-where-at-fashion-week-and-why.html> accessed 9 August 2010.

Uhlirova Marketa (2009), '"In The Bubble"', *City*, 63 (April/May): 60.

38

PRODUCTION, GATEKEEPING, AND DIFFUSION OF FASHION

Yuniya Kawamura[1]

The fashion system creates symbolic boundaries between what is fashion and what is not fashion and also determines what the legitimate aesthetic taste is. Producers of fashion, including designers and other fashion professionals who are agents of fashion, make a contribution in defining a taste that is represented as items of fashionable clothing. After clothes are manufactured, they go through the transformation process and the mechanism of fashion production passing through different institutions. Individuals involved in the production of clothing manufacture items of garments, and then those items must go through the legitimation process and pass the criteria set by gatekeepers[1] of fashion before they are disseminated to the public….designers are involved in both clothing as well as fashion production processes, and without the designers, there would be no fashion to start with. However, the designers alone cannot produce fashion, nor can they sustain the fashion system that leads to the making of fashion culture. Other producers of fashion besides designers, such as advertisers and marketers, also make a major contribution in fashion culture. Fashion is about change and the illusion of novelty. Those who take part in the production of fashion help create the ideology of fashion and determine which items of clothing will be defined as fashion and fashionable.

The fashion system has two types of diffusion agents: 1) designers who take part in seasonal fashion shows in Paris, London, Milan and New York, and are frequently the very conspicuous individuals who establish themselves as arbiters of good taste and surround themselves with a cult of personality, and 2) fashion journalists, editors, advertisers, marketers/merchandisers and publicists. We must find out the actual agencies through which fashion works so that we can review concrete ways in which fashion is formed and felt.

This chapter explores diffusion theories of fashion from individual and institutional perspectives, aesthetic judgments of fashion, diffusion strategies, such as fashion dolls in the past and fashion shows today, fashion propaganda through the use of advertising, and technological influences on fashion diffusion.

DIFFUSION THEORIES OF FASHION

Diffusion theories of fashion seek to explain how fashion is spread through interpersonal communication and institutional networks, and they assume that the fashion phenomenon is not ambiguous nor unpredictable.

Diffusion is the spread of fashion within and across social systems. Whereas the adoption process focuses on individual decision-making, the diffusion process centers on the decision of many people to adopt an innovation. How fast and how far an innovation diffuses are influenced by several factors: formal communications from the mass media, personal communications among current adopters and potential adopters, the persuasive influence of consumer leaders

---

[1] From Kawamura, Yuniya (2005) Production, Gatekeeping and Diffusion of Fashion. In Fashion-ology: An Introduction to Fashion Studies. Oxford: Berg, 73-93.

and other agents, and the degree to which the innovation is communicated and transferred from one social system to another. It is often believed that it is the designers who impose a new fashion upon the public in order to stimulate the market and the economy. But clothing manufacturers are necessary because they work with fashion producers who produce the idea of fashion.

INFLUENTIAL LEADERS OF FASHION DIFFUSION

In the context of clothing fashion adoption, innovativeness and opinion leadership are highly related. Diffusion theories of fashion seek to explain how fashion is adopted by many people within a social system.

According to Katz and Lazarsfeld (1955), informal person-to-person communication influences everyday situations, and their study showed that verbal personal influence was the most effective type of communication in fashion situations. It was the reaction of friends and acquaintances or salespeople on seeing a woman's hairdo or dress that counted, and in most cases, women influence other women like themselves. Approval and admiration will encourage behavior of the same kind; disapproval or disdain will tend to bring about a change in dress. In this way, fashion diffusion can first be explained from a micro-scale interpersonal perspective. Communications can also enter a social system from other social systems. Ultimately, awareness of the innovation is diffused to most members of the social system through the combined influence of external sources and interpersonal communications within the system. Then the innovation is recognized as fashion, and for that, legitimation is indispensable.

The fashion system invents new cultural meanings, and this invention is undertaken by opinion leaders who help shape and refine existing cultural meaning, encouraging the reform of cultural categories and principles. These groups and individuals are sources of meaning for the masses, and they invent and deliver symbolic meanings that are largely constructed by prevailing cultural co-ordinates established by cultural categories and cultural principles. These groups are also permeable to cultural innovations, changes in style, value and attitudes which they then pass along to the subordinate parties who imitate them (McCracken 1988: 80). Therefore, in order to understand the diffusion of fashion, we must first consider the roles played by those social groups most directly connected with its propagation. It does not matter who plays the roles, but it is very important that the roles are played.

In the aristocratic society of seventeenth- and eighteenth-century Europe, the fashion leaders were members of royalty. Their showcases were the royal courts. The best artisans were called upon to adorn the sumptuously elegant costumes that were paraded in the splendid setting of the French court (Brenninkmeyer, 1963). This policy continued in France until the Revolution, when actresses began creating their own costumes for the stage. Then a period of deterioration followed, and it was not until the years 1875 to 1918 that the theater again became the center for fashion inspiration. Fashions began to emerge from stage costumes and hairstyles often acquired the name of the actress who wore them.

In democratic societies where there are no royals, politicians' wives, such as Jackie Kennedy, and celebrities, like Madonna, have become the leaders of fashion. Fashion cannot be entirely accounted for in terms of individuals, either on the side of the producers or the wearers. For a new style to become fashionable, it must in some way appeal to a large number of people. The clothing habits of an individual are the result of group life.

INSTITUTIONAL DIFFUSION

In the 1960s and 1970s, when much of the work on fashion using diffusion models was done, diffusion models were conceptualized as relatively unorganized interpersonal processes, but today, fashion diffusion is highly organized and managed within cultural production systems that are intended to maximize the extent of diffusion (Crane 1999: 15).

The source of fashion diffusion used to be a highly centralized system, initially started in Paris. Innovators belonged to a community that could be understood in terms of Becker's concept of art world, a cluster of individuals and organizations involved in the production, evaluation, and dissemination of a specific form of culture (1982). Fashion worlds comprised designers, publicists, owners of trendy fashion boutiques and local fashion publics, consisting of fashion-conscious individuals. Opinion leaders included editors of leading fashion magazines and highly visible fashion consumers, such as society women, movie stars, and popular music stars (Crane 1999: 16). Awareness of fashion innovations was stimulated by fashion printed in fashion magazines and periodicals.

There is a view that the centralized fashion system has been replaced by another system, and according to Crane (1999) fashion designers in several countries create designs for small publics in global markets. Trends are now set by fashion forecasters, fashion editors, and department store buyers. Industrial manufacturers are consumer driven, and market trends originate in many types of social groups, including adolescent urban subcultures, and consequently, fashion emanates from many sources and diffuses in various ways to different publics (Crane 1999: 13). At the same time, the distinction between production and consumption is becoming increasingly hazy and blurry. The diffusion of fashion has become more difficult to study because the creation of fashion has become less centralized. The increasing decentralization and complexity of the fashion system has necessitated the development of fashion forecasting, which began in 1969. Forecasters consult with fabric designers to predict colors and fabrics a few years before a particular style is marketed.

SOCIOLOGICAL THEORIES OF FASHION DIFFUSION

Diffusion studies point out that they are addressing the spread of an item, idea, or practice over time to adopting individuals, groups, or corporate units that are embedded in channels of communication, social structures, such as networks, communities or classes, and social values or culture (Katz, Levin and Hamilton 1963: 147).

Two sociological models of diffusion have generally been applied to fashion. First, the classical model of the diffusion of fashion, exemplified by Simmel's theory that new styles are first adopted by upper-class elites and then the working class. The social processes underlying this model are imitation, social contagion, and differentiation (McCracken 1985). Second, the alternative to this top-down model is a bottom-up model in which new styles emerge in lower-status groups and are later adopted by higher-status groups. Both models assume widespread adoption of a particular fashion and a process of 'social saturation' in which the style or fad eventually becomes overused (Sproles 1985). In the second model, the innovators generally emerge from communities in urban areas that are seedbeds for other types of innovation, such as popular music and the arts. To be disseminated to a larger audience, innovations have to be discovered and promoted. According to Crane (1999: 16), innovators tend to be small firms that are created by individuals who belong to the communities in which the innovations originate. If the style or fad shows signs of becoming popular, large firms begin to produce their versions of it and to market it aggressively.

GATEKEEPERS: MAKING AESTHETIC JUDGMENTS

Despite its high profile in the media, fashion is not generally regarded as a topic serious enough to appear on the 'real news' pages. Fashion is a luxury and is considered trivial, frivolous and fun. However, fashion writings in the print media have important functions for fashion diffusion. In order for designers to be known and become world famous, they need to be legitimated by those who have the power and authority to influence, such as editors from major fashion magazines. Recognition by them gives the designers the prestige and confirmation that they are talented.

Fresh ideas in fashion design or any field of creative endeavor are news, and new styles attract attention, especially in a culture where people tend to believe that everything new is admirable. The creative couture designer and his or her high fashion models are widely reported in the mass media which confers status. A rise in the social standing of individuals and/or things commands favorable attention in print or on the air. Every fashion periodical, whether it caters to the fashion professionals, the high fashion world, women in general or the younger population, enjoys the trust of and acceptance by a large portion of the audience it serves. The items it reports are accepted as 'superior' pieces and the magazine is considered an important source of information to its readers.

Most participants in the system make aesthetic judgments frequently. The judgments produce reputations for the designers and their works. Thus, the participation becomes crucial. The value of fashion arises from the consensus of the participants in the fashion system, and those participants who control access to distribution channels become influential. People search for fashionable items because they are made to believe that fashion is better and more aesthetic than non-fashion.

Writers and reporters of fashion can be divided into two groups (Kawamura 2004): journalists and editors. Both play a large part in making a style the fashion, for they can interpret a designer's ideas to a public that is not comprised of fashion professionals and give them immense publicity. Their choice is of great significance to designers and buyers alike. Journalists and editors are gatekeepers, and they review aesthetic, social and cultural innovations as they first emerge and judge some as important and others as trivial. They, along with consumers, have the power of discovering interesting new designers. Fashion is an important influence on what we wear and what we think. Consumers are informed of fashionable clothes, fashionable shapes of colors, fashionable bodies, fashionable faces and fashionable people.

Above all, fashion magazines have an important function to fulfill because they directly serve the interests of the fashion industry. They diffuse ideas to encourage the selling of latest styles. These magazines appeared prior to and after the First World War and have since profited immensely from the improvements in the techniques of photography and illustration (Brenninkmeyer 1963: 82). The art of fashion photography that began in the 1920s steadily improved over the years and can be used as important visual record. It has, at the same time, accelerated fashion promotion. It has now become one of the most important means of fashion propaganda to be seen in magazines and newspapers.

FASHION JOURNALISTS

Fashion journalists write for daily papers whose reports reach a large public. The fashion journalist is usually only a reporter and not a critic. Architects, painters, writers or musicians expect their work to be severely criticized by critics and must brace themselves to receive critical remarks but not the fashion designer. In order to create a mystique, and possibly because fashion is too ephemeral for a standard of comparison to be established, harsh criticism is more often the exception than the rule. This creates a very different climate from the conventional art criticisms and reportage and is largely responsible for the vast amount of descriptive writings about fashion.

One of the most controversial issues in mass media reporting is the conflict between the advertising department and editorial comment. Because the mass media are mainly supported by investments from advertisers rather than from subscribers, it is difficult for the journalists to report fashion news impartially.

FASHION MAGAZINE EDITORS

Fashion editors write for fashion magazines, where the role of writer merges into the role of merchandiser/stylist. While the journalists' major task is fashion reportage, fashion editors are directly connected to retail stores and indirectly to manufacturers. They together play a major role in producing fashion as an image and maintaining and continuing the belief in fashion. Fashion is portrayed in such a way that it is desirable and highly valued in society. Fashion editors and buyers both from stores and the wholesale trade frequently confer together, for one wants to tell her readers where the new fashions can be found, and the other knows that magazines mold public opinion and can help to sell their goods. This is collaboration between press and trade.

A good fashion editor can be the pivot around which revolves the whole complicated apparatus of launching a new idea, all parts of which must be carefully coordinated if it is to be successful. Once a decision is made to promote a certain line or color, all the selected manufacturers of garments, fabrics and accessories must be approached and agree to cooperate in order to produce the required goods at the right time. The advertising managers of the various firms, in addition to those of the shops who will eventually retail the goods, arrange publicity and possibly take space in the editor's paper; the store buyers agree to carry sufficient goods to back the advertising campaigning, the manufacturers to deliver at a given date, and the stores to devote window displays to the new idea, in which enlargements of the magazine's pages will probably feature. All these phases must coincide with each other and with the date of publication. Thus an editor's selection of just one style from a couture house in Paris may ultimately result in a series of window displays throughout the country, the sale of many thousands of dresses, and the boosting of a new fashion.

The fashion editor, however, has two potent weapons: silence and space. She can ignore collections she considers bad, and she can give the largest possible amount of space to those she thinks are good, with priority in placing and the preference, if any, of color reproductions. Like fashion reporters, few editors can totally ignore advertisers and their demands, for it is on advertising revenue that a fashion paper depends.

DIFFUSION STRATEGIES FROM FASHION DOLLS TO FASHION SHOWS

Fashion Dolls

At one time new styles were suggested to clients by sketches accompanied with bolts of material or if a complete dress was produced, it was shown on a wooden dummy, not worn by a living woman. Long before life-size models had been thought of, fashion dolls, or milliner's mannequins as they were called, were used to spread the knowledge of new fashions. Fashion dolls were said to be the first means of circulating the latest styles of dress. It became the practice in Paris to display two life-size dolls dressed in the current fashions. 'La Grande Pandora' was fitted out from head to toe each time the fashions changed. The smaller of the dolls, 'La Petite Pandora,' even wore the appropriate underclothes. As early as 1391, Charles VI of France sent the Queen of England full-sized dolls wearing the latest styles made to the Queen's measurements (Diehl 1976: 1).

French fashion dolls became popular in the seventeenth and eighteenth centuries and were sent to all parts of Europe, and as far away as Russia, by milliners, dressmakers and hairdressers. They were considered indispensable to the general export of French fashion novelties. These dolls illustrated current styles in real jewelry as well as hair and dress styles. As France and the French court became politically powerful, the European capitals became very dependent on the flow of dolls from France for fashion news. Rose Bertin, the best-known French dressmaker of her day, also used the dolls as advertisements for her services. She outfitted Marie-Antoinette and her model dolls in her creations.

A woman selected a pattern or a style from a fashion doll. She would next select fabric and trimmings, and her final stop would be the dressmaker's shop where the garment was made according to specifications. The popularity of fashion dolls lasted well into the nineteenth century when they were gradually superseded by French fashion plates and, later, fashion magazines (Diehl 1976: 2).

FASHION SHOWS

What is a fashion show? By definition, a fashion show is a presentation of merchandise on live models. A good show makes one or more general statements about fashion while at the same time showing individual and specific items to support or illustrate these comments. The items must be authoritative, pulled together, edited by the store for the customer (Diehl 1976: 16). Fashion shows as we have today began in France after the institutionalization of fashion.

The living mannequin was the invention of the British couturier in Paris Charles Worth. When he opened his own store in 1858, he not only revolutionalized the couture by designing for an individual woman's type and personality, but he used his wife, Marie, to model his creations in his salon. As he became more successful, he employed a number of mannequins to show his collections to consumers, and those mannequins walked about in the salon or down the runway. By the early 1900s, the use of live models to show fashions to private customers and the press was well established, both inside the couture houses and outside, at special galas and social events (Diehl 1976: 7). By 1911, even in the US, living models were used as a regular part of fashion promotions for retailers as well as manufacturers.

The fashion show owes a great deal of its development to the inventiveness of Worth and to the showmanship of Paul Poiret. While Worth created the modern couture, Poiret extended its range. Poiret radically changed the feminine silhouette and, in the process, developed techniques of fashion promotion that we continue to use. He used his promotional instincts to generate free publicity. He toured chic resorts, Russia and various other countries, making personal appearances and giving fashion showings which were tremendous successes. He was among the first couturiers to parade mannequins at the races, showing pieces from his latest collection to great effect. Throughout his career, he entertained on a lavish scale, throwing huge parties, theatrical presentations and costume balls. They were colorful extravaganzas, well covered in the press (De Marly 1980).

THE SIGNIFICANCE OF FASHION SHOWS

The fashion show is a tool of retailing with one basic purpose, that is to sell merchandise. The show must have entertainment value to hold the audience's attention. Another reason for a show might be public relations.

Clothes are sold via a 'merchandising' approach. A fashion is created and promoted to the retailer who stocks it. It is touted in the fashion publications and appears so irresistible that the consumer goes to their favorite store and buys it. The primary thrust in fashionable items is toward the trade. The retailer is critical because the consumer must be able to see, feel and try on the article for a sale to be made in the store they shop at. Conversely, the sale cannot be made if the article is not accessible to the consumer. Clothes are merchandised and marketed as fashion, and they are pushed through the distribution pipeline from manufacturer to retailer to consumer.

The marketing approach requires for the needs of the consumer to be identified specifically and a new product is created to satisfy a need, or an existing product is repositioned or remarketed in line with that need. Advertising to the consumer has concentrated on creating desire for fashion while it is clothing that satisfies the need. Fashion has been the ingredient that sells clothing. Clothing is a basic human need while fashion is not. This is one way to differentiate fashion from clothing. Authoritative fashion statements made by journalists and editors must go beyond the clothing to include accessories and beauty hints included in the broad area covered by the word 'fashion,' and in presenting the fashion story, they must include all the elements of a good, newsworthy story.

TECHNOLOGICAL INFLUENCES ON FASHION DIFFUSION

It is also important to remember that fashionable clothes became widely available due to technological advances in clothing manufacturing. Fashion was democratized at a fast pace after the invention of sewing and embroidery machines. Worth's big business was helped a great deal by technology.

Technological advances started a chain reaction throughout interrelated industries. For instance, sheer wool did not become fashionable until the mechanization of the combing operation made the worsted industry possible. Form-fitting knitted underwear and thin stockings followed the invention of suitable knitting machinery.

The enormous expansion of the women's garment and fashion industries was the result of technical and industrial interrelationships. A shift from production of garments in the home to large-scale production in the factory is dependent upon a ready supply of cloth, which is dependent on the availability of yarn. Lower costs, which increase consumption and enlarge production, are dependent upon the invention of suitable stitching machinery which, in turn, is dependent on the availability on suitable sewing thread, which is dependent on the development of mechanical combs.

Furthermore, modern society resulted in mass production and improved methods of transport, and distribution have made it possible to supply copies of all the newest and exclusive models rapidly, in great numbers, and at relatively low prices, so that women of moderate means in small provincial towns can wear clothes of practically the same design as those that were introduced by the leaders of fashion.

FASHION PROPAGANDA THROUGH ADVERTISING

Ideas about fashion are spread through the population by organized means of mass propaganda. One function of fashion propaganda through advertising is to stimulate a desire for the same thing at the same time in a large number of people to build collective belief among consumers. In the technical and industrial age in which we live, the possibilities of influencing masses of people are innumerable. Individuals are always on the outlook for what they should have, do or look like, to fit into the appropriate group structure because the majority of modern people no longer live under the influence of ancestral traditions. People in modern society are susceptible to all kinds of propaganda. They read newspapers, current periodicals, advertisements and films to discover what the latest fashion trends are. They wear what other people would like to see them in and thus it becomes important for them to know what is fashionable and what may fit into the framework of social life.

According to Millerson (1985: 102), to a greater or lesser extent, all fashion products tend to be aspirational: the product is positioned substantially or slightly above consumer reality toward the kind of person the target group would like to be, and society creates people's desire to purchase and willingness to wear new as opposed to past fashion looks.

This is why a great deal of investment goes into national brand advertising. If the consumer can be made brand conscious and brand loyal, even in an unimportant area, it can mean financial success for a company or a designer. The purpose of using brands is to build a market. A brand is a device, sign or symbol which is used to identify products so the advertiser can reap the benefits of any demand created. Through a brand name the manufacturer hopes to build prestige for their product, to differentiate it from others in the consumer's mind, and lessen price competition by creating loyal customers who are reluctant to accept other brands. Brand names help consumers repeat a purchase found satisfactory or avoid one that is unsatisfactory. Where fashion companies specialize in one area of design, fashion goods labels become identified with a design style and occasion-type of garment, offering certain quality at a certain price. As long as the designer is consistent with the image that is provided, the brand is a guide for the consumer. The use of brand names is a form of persuasive advertising, a type of propaganda.

CONCLUSION

The fashion system is about fashion production and not clothing production. Individuals, such as influential leaders of fashion, and institutions that help create and spread fashion, such as fashion magazines and newspaper periodicals, are participants in the system. When we separate clothing production from fashion production, the difference between clothing and fashion become even more succinct. Fashion is produced as a belief and an ideology. People wear clothes believing that they are wearing fashion because it is something considered to be desirable. Clothing production involves the actual manufacturing of fabric and shaping it into a garment. The ideology of fashion needs to be sustained so that consumers return to purchase the items of clothing which are labeled as 'fashion.' The contents of fashion trends, that is particular items of clothing, may be abandoned and replaced with new styles, but the form of fashion remains and is always considered desirable in modern, industrialized nations.

References

Becker S. (1982), *Art Worlds*, Berkeley: University of California Press.

Brenninkmeyer Ingrid (1963), *The Sociology of Fashion*, Koln-Opladen: Westdeutscher Verlag.

Crane Diana (1999), '"Diffusion Models and Fashion: A Reassessment, in The Social Diffusion of Ideas and Things"', *The Annals of The Academy of Political and Social Science*, 566, November: 13–24.

De Marly Diana (1980), *The History of Haute Couture: 1850-1950*, New York: Holmes and Meier.

Diehl Ellen (1976), *How to Produce a Fashion Show*, New York: Fairchild Publications, Inc.

Hamilton (1963), '"Traditions of Research on the Diffusion of Innovation"', *American Sociological Review*, 28: 237–52.

Katz Elihu and Paul Lazarsfeld (1955), *Personal Influence*, New York: Free Press.

Kawamura Yuniya (2004), *The Japanese Revolution in Paris Fashion*, Oxford: Berg.

McCracken D. (1985), 'The Trickle-Down Theory Rehabilitated,' in Michael R. Solomon (ed.), *The Psychology of Fashion*, Lexington, MA: D.C. Heath Lexington Books.

McCracken D. (1988), *Culture and Consumption: New Approaches to the Symbolic Character of Consumer Goods and Activities*, Bloomington, IN: Indiana University Press.

Millerson S. (1985), 'Psychosocial Strategies for Fashion Advertising,' in Michael R. Solomon (ed.), *The Psychology of Fashion*, Lexington, MA: Lexington Books.

FURTHER READING

Bartlett, Djurdja (2013), *Fashion Media: Past as Present* Djurdja Bartlett, Shaun Cole and Agnes Rocamora (eds.), London: Bloomsbury.

Davis, Fred (1992), *Fashion, culture and Identity*, Chicago and London: University of Chicago Press.

Crane, Diana (2000), *Fashion and Its Social Agendas: class, gender and identity in clothing.* Chicago: University of Chicago Press.

Hollander, Anne (1993), *Seeing Through Clothes*, Berkeley Los Angles, California: University of California Press.

Peirson-Smith, Anne and Joseph H. Hancock II, (2018) *Transglobal Fashion Narratives: Clothing Communication, Style Statements and Brand Storytelling*, Bristol: Intellect.

Rocamora, Agnès. (2012), "Hypertextuality and Remediation in the Fashion Media." *Journalism Practice*, 6(1): 92-106.

Werner, Thomas (2018), *The Fashion Image, Planning and Producing Photographs and Films*, London: Berg

Wilson, Elizabeth (2007), *Adorned in Dreams: Fashion and Modernity*, New Brunswick, New Jersey: Rutgers University Press.

Wolbers, Marian Frances (2009) *Uncovering Fashion: Fashion Communications and the Media*, New York: Fairchild.

Figure 28 Lawrence Connor, Photo Courtesy of Brent Luvaas.
Source: Brent Luvaas

PART IX
Consumption and Identity

Figure 29 Jillian Mercado, Photo Courtesy of Brent Luvaas.
Source: Brent Luvaas

INTRODUCTION

Srikant Manchiraju

One of the main questions underpinning the related topics of consumption and identity is: *are we what we consume*? In other words, in contemporary society we buy goods to express who we are or who we want to be, or who we do not want to be. Part of the answer to this question resides in the history and philosophy behind the act of consumption itself and its rationale. These notions about are founded in the of origins of 17th consumerism which emerged in the face of a growing middle class in society intent on displaying their wealth through luxury good, including fashion, that they could afford as a sign of their social status and taste based on modern cultural values (Lipovetsky, 1994). The availability of mechanized, mass-produced goods in the 19th century and an increase in disposable incomes laid the foundations for modern forms of extended consumerism in terms of creating an unending (over) production alongside the evolution of mass mediated channels to market and promote the supply and consumption of goods such as fashion and clothing.

Consumption refers to the search for, choice, acquisition, possession, disposal of goods and services (Hogg & Mitchell, 1996) and "both personal and social characteristics of people as understood by themselves and others" (Dittmar, 1992: 72). This view of life suggests that meaning, accomplishment and fulfillment are founded on the material goods that we own and acquire (Belk, 1985; Richins, 1994). Put simply – to have is to exist and people define themselves and others by their acquired possessions (Swagler, 1994). Despite the social context in which consumption occurs, it is located at individual-society interface (Dittmar, 2008; Hogg and Mitchell, 1996; Kleine III, et al. 1992), with some scholars (Shrum et al., 2013) noting that identity drives consumption. The contradiction here is that individuals seek social acceptance in terms of their uniqueness, yet individually consume goods and services based on collectively shared aspirations (McCracken 1998).

CONSUMPTION/MATERIALISM AND SELF

To understand consumer behavior, it is imperative to address the meanings that consumers assign to possessions (Belk, 1985). Tuan (1980: 472) posited, "our fragile sense of self needs support, and this we get by having and possessing things because, to a large degree, we are what we have and possess." The premise that we are what we possess is not new (see James, 1890). For instance, Belk (1988:139) echoed James (1890) sentiment by noting, "if we define possessions as the things we call ours," then "we are the sum of our possessions". Thus, Belk proposed the concept of *extended self* which refers to external objects and possessions, including persons, places, and group possessions such as clothing, as well as personal possessions such as body parts and vital organs (Belk, 1984). In Belk's terms, "The notion of the extended self is a superficially masculine and western metaphor comprising not only that which is seen as 'me' (the self), but also that which is seen as 'mine'" (Belk: 1988: 140), given that there will be cultural differences (Ger and Belk, 1996).

Consumption habits are very much based on value systems. Materialism is a value based consumption pattern, in which people assign a high priority to material possessions and monetary gain (McClelland, 1951; Perlinger, 1959). As O'Cass and Julian observed of the confluence between the growing link between fashion consumption and materialism in post-industrial societies, a growing preoccupation with possessions is reflected in such consumption values as "shop till you drop" and "he who dies with the most toys, wins" and the rise in credit card usage and consumer debt. Such approaches to life are the basis of materialism. This does not imply that every consumer is materialistic, as there is significant variance between individuals' prioritisation of and attachment to materialistic values...more materialistic values has been associated with using possessions for portraying and managing impressions (O'Cass and Julian, 2001)

According to Belk "besides control over objects, control by objects may also contribute to an item being viewed as part of self" (1988: 141). In other words, the very idea of consumption, imperative to all humans is part of one's extended self or identity. So materialistic habits are linked with an understanding that individual possessions operate symbolically to signal an individual's interests and identity (Douglas & Isherwood 1979).

Allport (1937) posited that the process of establishing one's identity, and thereby gaining self-esteem, from infancy to mature adulthood happens by extending the self by continuously expanding the set of things that we own. In other words, our possessions define various dimensions of one's self, true for materialists as well as non-materialists. George Simmel (1950: 322) echoed similar sentiments by noting, "material property is, so to speak, an extension of the ego, and any interference with our property is, for this reason, felt to be a violation of the person." Likewise, Niederland and Sholevar (1981) suggested that for many young American males, the automobiles that they own are part of their extended selves and their ego ideals, while Craik (1994) observed that people take great offence if their material appearance is criticized indicating the significance placed on possessions and how they are received.

Belk also noted that by making things part of our self, by creating or altering them, appears to be a universal human trait. Csikszentmihalyi and Rochberg-Halton (1981) provided a more precise psychological explanation to why we assign importance to possessions, and their relationship to self by suggesting that we invest a "psychic energy" in an object in which we have directed our effort, time, and attention. Therefore, this energy and its by products are regarded as being part of one's self because they have organically grown from within. Jean-Paul Sartre also commented on the importance of possessions in defining identity in his seminal work, *Being and Nothingness*, (Sartre, 1943) where he admitted, "that the only reason we want to have something is to enlarge our sense of self and that the only way we can know who we are is by observing what we have" (Belk, 1988: 146). Put differently, having and being are distinct, but inseparable as Sartre noted. In short, several scholars (Belk, 1985) and social philosophers (Marx, 1978) acknowledge that having possessions functions to create and to maintain a sense of self-definition and that having, doing, and being are all interrelated.

THE SEARCH FOR IDENTITY THOUGH FASHION AND CLOTHING

Identity as a serious topic of study evolved in western cultures from a more historical interest in notions of the self, subjectivity and personality. The origins of identity can be located in the rise of more self-aware notions from the 16th century onwards about the existence of the fashioned individual (Breward, 2003). Identity based sartorial trends continued across centuries as consumers continued to personalize their clothing relationships so that by the 19th century identity was firmly connected to possessions especially in urban centers where the opportunities for retail and personal display or conspicuous consumption (Veblen, 1964) both enabled and encouraged this tendency.

The seismic shift from class based to consumer fashion was complete by the 20th century as an expression of urbanized modernity (Gilloch, 2013). Yet, the dissonance of the modern city and the challenges of modern industrial capitalism was often manifested in the 'hysteria and exaggerations of fashion; (Wilson, 2003:10) whereby ambiguous fears of individual expression were assuaged in fashion given the option of dressing like others in mass produced garments. Yet, in counter opposition to this system of top down style influence, across the past 20th century has emerged a proliferation of style tribes expressing various identities in opposition to the dominant discourse (Polhemus, 1997). This trend also accords with Gregory Stone's ideas about identity founded on personal appearance as an interpretation of the self negotiated through social interactions and based on recognized identification with, and differentiation from others (Stone, 1965). Hence, racial, ethnic, gender, generational and sexual identities can be expressed, negotiated and challenged through deliberate fashion and style choices to conform with the system – think school or office uniforms (Craik, 2006), or for confrontation as with youth style (Hebdige, 2012) or to transgress social norms as with the feminist and LGBT movements.

POSSESSING FASHION AS IDENTITY

The ownership and fashion and clothing is considered by some theorists to reflect at the macro-level social, cultural, political economic fluctuations across time, space and place, while at the same time communicating modernity, progress and the zeitgeist (Blumer, 1969; Laver, 1937) so it is a mirror, but also a definer of historical change and societal trends. Essential to this understanding is the notion of constant change and renewal based on a fashion cycle involving the constant production and distribution and consumption of designed products that are collectively selected and purchased by groups of people responding to clothing trends which has accelerated with the advent of fast fashion (Bhardwaj and Fairhurst, 2010). On a micro level, the fashion consumer taps into this larger fashion system reflecting the duality of individualism and collectivism given that fashion is a "cultural practice that is bound up with the specification of our sense of self both as individuals and members of groups. But, as identity means creating distinctiveness, fashion always has to balance reflecting the contemporary consensus about fashion with specific arrangements of signs an symbols that mark out an individual as appearing to be unique." (Craik, 2009: 2).

So, fashion can be used to identity an individual with a group or style tribe – such as punks or Goths – while at the same time emphasizing their unique personality. This dual expression of collectivism and individualism for some is based on the intrinsic pleasures that humans experience from this act of dressing in and dressing out (Simmel 1950). Others saw this conundrum in terms of elitist tendencies so that fashion for the individual can be used to emulate those who are considered superior - think celebrities - while at the same time dressing differently from those who are considered to be inferior - think luxury fashion brands as opposed to fast fashion labels or early adopters of fashion trends versus laggards who acquire the 'look' at the end of the trend cycle (Rogers, 1974).

Hence, appearance matters and fashion and accessories project the identity of the wearer and their aspirational social role. This is made possible because fashion and clothing styles represent a dynamic, constantly shifting coded system (Davis, 1994) as opposed to being a fixed "language" visual and verbal linguistic system (Barthes, 1983). The codes of fashion are able to express basic demographic characteristics of an individual wearer such as their age, sex, status, occupation, in addition to more nuanced aspects of their persona – such as their interests and lifestyles.

While clothing an fashion have historically been used to express status and wealth in terms of materiality and social order (Entwistle, 2015), the changing interpretations and performances on 18th century notions linking beauty and fashionable dress with submissiveness in contrast to the serious nature of men's dress equated with power that found its ultimate expression in the 20th century male business suit (Breward, 1995). Equally, these expressions of assumed identity also encapsulate a political dimension in the sense that they can reflect power relations in a given place and time by privileging some sections of society over others because of their economic status, ethnicity or gender. Hence, fashion can normalize and project certain dominant interests over others based on binary meanings - masculinity or femininity, western versus non-western, for example. Yet, the expressions of identities using fashion and clothing are essentially ambiguous and ambivalent (Davis, 1994), and are not clear-cut if we think of the complexities of gender versus sexuality, for example. In essence, fashion expresses but also complicates and plays with meanings underlying the binary dualities of identity categories such as male versus female; old versus young; new versus old; urban versus non-urban; elite versus non-elite etc. Some believe that this is where the creative expression of fashion and its innovative potential and ever changing nature resides

The 'massification' of fashion across the 20th century fuelled by industrialization and the arrival of a working class with disposable income co-joined with the availability of clothing items and accessories at all price points for a wide demographic range, also allowed it to become widely available across all sectors of society and a way of expressing identity, status, difference and belonging. In a postmodern sense, fashion in its most fluid state, has enabled expressions of alternative or new identities as challenges to older ways of being and thinking. Arguably, this started when women wore trousers in the 1960s, courtesy of Yves Saint Laurent – and has evolved through cross-dressing to the current trend for gender-neutral, inclusive clothing that offer a liberating, boundryless opportunity for the consumer to express themselves beyond traditional social constraints (Peter, 2017).

The style influences of fashion within its system of production and consumption have also changed direction as the traditional top-down influence of elite fashion system from catwalk to consumer has been upended as we see urban-wear dominating the aesthetic inspiration for all levels of fashion, including couture and 'catwalk chic' based on expressions of authenticity (Fury, 2016).

The active communication of identity through body modification and the clothed body today can either manifest itself as a way of locating identity in recognized, yet ambiguous categories of ethnicity, gender, age, religion or occupation or in the reinterpretation of the real individual self.

As Craik suggests,

The combination of roles and performances compose our sense of self and identity…Individuality, then is a specific contingent social construction unique to our culture and our repository of social performance…in history and in other cultures identity has been and is composed by family membership, regional belonging, class position or gendered performances, in our culture we struggle to project a unique sense of self…we have greater freedom of choice to fashion our identity and our identity becomes a social entity in itself. Maintaining individuality requires content maintenance and fashioning (Craik, 2009: 138).

The readings in this section reflect the evolution of expressing identity through fashion consumption across history. The chapter entitled, "Fashion as collective and consumer behavior" contains a sampling of work by authors from various disciplines who have examined fashion as a form of collective consumer behavior. From a sociological perspective Herbert Blumer (1939) draws the boundaries of fashion wider than considerations of dress and apparel to encompass the influential fields of the arts and sciences. Blumer mirrors the views of Simmel (1904) and Laver (1937) about fashion's unique role as a way of social differentiation through emulation of the elite order and as a way of fulfilling subjective needs, while tapping into collective taste and knowledge. The economic angle is explored by Adam Smith (1789) who reflects the elitist mores of the time comments on the trickle down effect of fashion styles from high to low rank as a dilution of beauty. Extending the analysis of fashion through the lens of consumer behavior, Thorstein Veblen (1894, 1899) traces the evolution of fashion from aesthetic to economic concerns, given that clothing and adornment signifies the wealth of the wearer or owner, with male dress expressing utility and women's dress their pecuniary ownership, often considered as wasteful in its excesses. Finally, Estelle De Young Barr (1934) scientifically and theoretically analyses the motivations of female consumer behavior beyond its economic and communicative social functions, including broader options of aesthetics, functionality and psychology. A systemic approach to fashion cycles is covered in the next reading, "Changing Fashion" where the author typifies fashion as a cycle across various classifications from long term to short term circular forms. A range of theories and work is examined including 'style-based fashion cycle theory; diffusion of innovation theory; status signaling theory; fashion as a positional status-marker theory; status conferred by the purchaser theory; artificial obsolescence theory; super organic long-term fashion cycle theory; and fashion as a function of reproductive strategy. Each of these theories contributes to the ever-changing dynamics of fashion and consumption. A generational focus on the fashion needs of older female consumer in a contemporary cultural economy is adopted by Julia Twigg in "The High Street Responds: Designing for the Older Market". Based on ethnographic interviews with consumers and the cultural intermediaries responsible for the design and promotion of fashion for an aging demographic reveal on the one hand, that the changing needs and outlooks of the consumer are being accommodated and are well received. On the other hand, industry assumptions about the universality of the progressive needs of this consumer group to be fashionable and youthful are causing tension among those who would prefer to dress and age outside of those expectations. The spotlight shifts to the male consumer, Kevin Matthews, Joseph Hancock II and Zhaohui GU in "*Re*branding American men's heritage fashions through the use of visual merchandising, symbolic props and masculine iconic memes historically found in popular culture." This interpretive study reveals how with the increased attention being played out by fashion brands on the male retail market that brand narratives need to be tailored to make them more relatable using props and memes from popular culture and popular history both in symbolic promotional campaigns and in branded retail environments to convey compelling notions of authenticity and masculinity.

Extending the male gaze, Benjamin L. Wild in "To have and to hold: Masculinity and the clutch bag" examines how the contemporary male consumer is increasingly expressing their identity though clothing and accessories. This reading specifically focuses on the ubiquitous, strapless leather clutch bag trend for men as featured in style magazines and on the streets. The author locates the reason behind the popularity of this impractical, sartorial statement in terms of its role as a safety blanket, a reassertion of male spending power, or as a response to the female oriented top handle bag equivalent, in view of changing male self-perceptions in post-industrial societies.

References

Allport, G. W. (1937), *Personality: A psychological interpretation*. New York: Henry Holt.
Barthes, R. (1983), *The Fashion System*, transl. Matthew Ward and Richard Howard, New York: Hill and Wang, New York.
Belk, R. W. (1985), Materialism: Trait aspects of living in the material world. *Journal of Consumer Research*, *12*(3), 265–280.
Belk, R. W. (1984), Three scales to measure constructs related to materialism: Reliability, validity, and relationships to measures of happiness. *Advances in Consumer Research*, 11, 291–297.
Belk, R. W. (1988), Possessions and the extended self. *Journal of Consumer Research*, *15*, 139–168.
Bhardwaj, V. and A. Fairhurst. (2010), "Fast fashion: response to changes in the fashion industry. *The International Review of Retail, Distribution and Consumer Research*, *20*(1), 165–173.
Blumer, H. (1969), Fashion: From class differentiation to collective selection. *The Sociological Quarterly*, *10*(3), 275–291.
Breward, C. (2003), *Fashion*. Oxford: Oxford University Press.
Breward, C. (1995), *The Culture of Fashion*, Manchester: Manchester University Press.
Craik, J. (1994), *The face of fashion: Cultural studies in fashion*. London: Routledge.
Craik, J. (2005). *Uniforms Exposed: From Conformity to Transgression*. Oxford: Berg.
Craik J. (2009), *The Face of Fashion: the key concepts*. Oxford: Berg
Csikszentmihalyi, M., and E. Rochberg-Halton. (1981), *The meaning of things: Domestic symbols and the self*. Cambridge, MA: Cambridge University Press.
Davis, F. (1994), *Fashion, Culture, and Identity*. Chicago: University of Chicago Press.
Dittmar, H. (2008), Consumer society, identity, and well-being: The search for the 'Good Life' and the 'Body Perfect'. *European monographs in social psychology series*.
Dittmar, H. (1992), *The social psychology of material possessions: To have is to be*. Hemmel Hempstead, UK: Harvester Wheatsheaf.
Douglas, M., & Isherwood, B. (2002), *The world of goods*. London: Routledge.
Entwistle, J. (2015), *The Fashioned Body: Fashion, dress and social theory*. London: John Wiley & Sons.
Fury, A. (2016), How Streetwear Crossed Over from Urban Cool to Catwalk Chic: the triumph of aesthetic honesty, *The Independent*, 21 March, https://www.independent.co.uk/life-style/fashion/features/how-streetwear-crossed-over-from-urban-cool-to-catwalk-chic-the-triumph-of-aesthetic-honesty-a6944721.html
Ger, G., & R. W. Belk. (1996), Cross-cultural differences in materialism. *Journal of Economic Psychology*, *17*(1), 55–77.

Gilloch, G. (2013), *Myth and metropolis: Walter Benjamin and the city*. London: John Wiley & Sons.

Hebdige, D. (2012), *Subculture: The meaning of style*. London: Routledge.

Hogg, M.K. & P. C. N. Mitchell. (1996). Identity, self and consumption: A conceptual framework. *Journal of Marketing Management*, 12(7), 629–44.

Kleine III, R. E., S. S. Kleine, & J. B. Kernan (1992). Mundane Everyday Consumption and the Self: A Conceptual Orientation and Prospects for Consumer Research. *Advances in Consumer Research*, 19(1), 411–15.

Laver, J. (1937), *Taste and Fashion-From the French Revolution to the Present Day*. London: Read Books Ltd.

Lipovetsky, G. (1994), *The Empire of Fashion: Dressing Modern Democracy*. Princeton, NJ and New York: Princeton University Press.

McCracken, G. (1986), "Culture and Consumption: A Theoretical Account of the Structure and Movement of the Cultural Meaning of Consumer Goods." *Journal of Consumer Research*, 13(1), 71–84.

Marx, K. (1978 original 1867). *Capital: A Critique of Political Economy*, vol.1, trans. Ben Fawkes).Harmondsworth: Penguin.

Niederland, W. G. and B. Sholevar (1981), "The Creative Process—A Psychoanalytic Discussion." *Arts in Psychotherapy*, 8(1), 71–101.

O'Cass, A. and C. C. Julian (2001), "Fashion clothing consumption: studying the effects of materialistic values, self-image/product-image congruency relationships, gender and age on fashion clothing involvement", in S. Chetty & B. Collins (eds.), Bridging marketing theory and practice: Proceedings of the Australian and New Zealand Marketing Academy (ANZMAC) Conference, Auckland, New Zealand, 1-5 December, Massey University Press, Auckland, New Zealand. Retrieved 2017 from: https://epubs.scu.edu.au/cgi/viewcontent.cgi?article=1388&context=comm_pubs

Perlinager, E. (1959), Extension and structure of the self. *Journal of Psychology*, 47, 13–23.

Peter, O. (2017), Is gender-neutral clothing the future of fashion. *The Independent*. https://www.independent.co.uk/life-style/fashion/gender-neutral-clothing-fashion-future-male-female-women-wildfang-hm-a8017446.html

Polhemus, T. (2010), *Streetstyle*. London: Pymca.

Richins, M. L. (1987). Media, materialism, and human happiness. *Advances in Consumer Research*, 14.

Rogers, E. M. (2010), *Diffusion of innovations*. New York: Simon and Schuster.

Sartre, J. P. (1943). *Being and nothingness: A phenomenological essay on ontology*. New York: Philosophical Society.

Shrum, L. J., N. Wong, F. Arif, S. K. Chugani, A. Gunz, T. M. Lowrey and K. Scott. (2013), Reconceptualizing materialism as identity goal pursuits: Functions, processes, and consequences. *Journal of Business Research*, 66(8), 1179–1185.

Simmel, G. (1950). *The Sociology of Georg Simmel*,. Kurt H. Wolff. (transl.) Glencoe, IL: Free Press.

Swagler, R. (1994), "Evolution and Applications of the Term Consumerism: Theme and Variations". *Journal of Consumer Affairs*. **28**(2): 347–360.

Tuan, Yi-Fu. (1980). The significance of the artifact. *Geographical Review*, 70(4), 462–472.

Twitchell, J. B. (1999). *Lead us into temptation: The triumph of American materialism*. New York: Columbia University Press.

Veblen T. (1964), "The Economic Theory of Women's Dress." In: *Essays in Our Changing Order*. Leon Ardzrooni (ed.). New York: Viking Press.

Wilson, E. (2003), *Adorned in dreams: Fashion and modernity*. London and New York: I B Tauris.

FASHION AS COLLECTIVE AND CONSUMER BEHAVIOR

Herbert Blumer, Adam Smith, and Thorstein B. Veblen[1]

FASHION MOVEMENTS *HERBERT BLUMER*

While fashion is thought of usually in relation to clothing, it is important to realize that it covers a much wider domain. It is to be found in manners, the arts, literature, and philosophy, and may even reach into certain areas of science. In fact, it may operate in any field of group life, apart from the technological and utilitarian area and the area of the sacred. Its operation requires a class society, for in its essential character it does not occur either in a homogenous society like a primitive group, nor in a caste society.

Fashion behaves as a movement, and on this basis it is different from custom which, by comparison, is static. This is due to the fact that fashion is based fundamentally on differentiation and emulation. In a class society, the upper classes or so-called social elite, are not able to differentiate themselves by *fixed* symbols or badges. Hence the more external features of their life and behavior are likely to be imitated by classes immediately subjacent to them, who, in turn, are initiated by groups immediately below them in the social structure. This process gives to fashion a vertical descent. However, the elite class finds that it is no longer distinguishable, by reason of the imitation made by others, and hence is led to adopt new differentiating criteria, only to displace these as they in turn are imitated. It is primarily this feature that makes fashion into a movement and which has led one writer to remark that a fashion, once launched, marches to its doom.

Source Excerpted from Blumer H. (1939). *Fashion Movements*. In R. E. Park (ed.), *An Outline of the Principles of Sociology*, 275–7. New York, NY: Barnes and Noble.

OF THE INFLUENCE OF CUSTOM AND FASHION UPON OUR NOTIONS OF BEAUTY AND DEFORMITY *ADAM SMITH*

. . . Fashion is different from custom, or rather is a particular species of it. That is not the fashion which every body wears, but which those wear who are of a high rank or character. The graceful, the easy, and commanding manners of the great, joined to the usual richness and magnificence of their dress, give a grace to the very form which they happen to bestow upon it. As long as they continue to use this form, it is connected in our imaginations with the idea of something that is genteel and magnificent, and though in itself it should be indifferent, it seems, on account of this relation, to have something about it that is genteel and magnificent too. As soon as they drop it, it loses all the grace which it had appeared to possess before, and being now used only by the inferior ranks of people, seems to have something of their meanness and awkwardness.

Source Excerpted from Smith, A. (1966). *The Theory of Moral Sentiments.* New York, NY: Augustus M. Kelley. (Original work published 1759)

THE ECONOMIC THEORY OF WOMAN'S DRESS *THORSTEIN B. VEBLEN*

Under the patriarchal organization of society, where the social unit was the man (with his dependents), the dress of the women was an exponent of the wealth of the man whose chattels they were. In modern society, where the

---

[1] From Herbert Blumer Adam Smith Thorstein Veblen Fashion as Collective and Consumer Behavior Berg Fashion Library.

unit is the household, the woman's dress sets forth the wealth of the household to which she belongs. Still, even to-day, in spite of the nominal and somewhat celebrated demise of the patriarchal idea, there is that about the dress of women which suggests that the wearer is something in the nature of a chattel; indeed, the theory of woman's dress quite plainly involves the implication that the woman is a chattel. In this respect the dress of women differs from that of men. With this exception, which is not of first-rate importance, the essential principles of woman's dress are not different from those which govern the dress of men; but even apart from this added characteristic the element of dress is to be seen in a more unhampered development in the apparel of women. A discussion of the theory of dress in general will gain in brevity and conciseness by keeping in view the concrete facts of the highest manifestation of the principles with which it has to deal, and this highest manifestation of dress is unquestionably seen in the apparel of the women of the most advanced modern communities.

. . . Woman, primarily, originally because she was herself a pecuniary possession, has become in a peculiar way the exponent of the pecuniary strength of her social group; and with the progress of specialization of functions in the social organism this duty tends to devolve more and more entirely upon the woman. The best, most advanced, most highly developed societies of our time have reached the point in their evolution where it has (ideally) become the great, peculiar, and almost the sole function of woman in the social system to put in evidence her economic unit's ability to pay. That is to say, woman's place (according to the ideal scheme of our social system) has come to be that of a means of conspicuously unproductive expenditure.

Source Excerpted from Veblen, T. B. (1894). "The Economic Theory of Women's Dress." *Popular Science Monthly,* 46: 198–205.

DRESS AS AN EXPRESSION OF THE PECUNIARY CULTURE **THORSTEIN B. VEBLEN**

The dress of women goes even farther than that of men in the way of demonstrating the wearer's abstinence from productive employment. It needs no argument to enforce the generalization that the more elegant styles of feminine bonnets go even farther towards making work impossible than does the man's high hat. The woman's shoe adds the so-called French heel to the evidence of enforced leisure afforded by its polish, because this high heel obviously makes any, even the simplest and most necessary manual work extremely difficult. The like is true even in a higher degree of the skirt and the rest of the drapery which characterizes woman's dress. The substantial reason for our tenacious attachment to the skirt is just this: it is expensive and it hampers the wearer at every turn and incapacitates her for all useful exertion. The like is true of the feminine custom of wearing the hair excessively long.

But the woman's apparel not only goes beyond that of the modern man in the degree in which it argues exemption from labor; it also adds a peculiar and highly characteristic feature which differs in kind from anything habitually practised by the men. This feature is the class of contrivances of which the corset is the typical example. The corset is, in economic theory, substantially a mutilation, undergone for the purpose of lowering the subject's vitality and rendering her permanently and obviously unfit for work. It is true, the corset impairs the personal attractions of the wearer, but the loss suffered on that score is offset by the gain in reputability which comes of her visibly increased expensiveness and infirmity. It may broadly be set down that the womanliness of woman's apparel resolves itself, in point of substantial fact, into the more effective hindrance to useful exertion offered by the garments peculiar to women. This difference between masculine and feminine apparel is here simply pointed out as a characteristic feature. The ground of its occurrence will be discussed presently.

So far, then, we have, as the great and dominant norm of dress, the broad principle of conspicuous waste. Subsidiary to this principle, and as a corollary under it, we get as a second norm the principle of conspicuous leisure. In dress construction this norm works out in the shape of divers contrivances going to show that the wearer does not and, as far as it may conveniently be shown, cannot engage in productive labor. Beyond these two principles there is a third of scarcely less constraining force, which will occur to anyone who reflects at all on the subject. Dress must not only be conspicuously expensive and inconvenient; it must at the same time be up to date. No explanation at all satisfactory has hitherto been offered of the phenomenon of changing fashions. The imperative requirement of dressing in the latest accredited manner, as well as the fact that this accredited fashion constantly changes from season to season, is sufficiently familiar to everyone, but the theory of this flux and change has not been worked out. We may of course say, with perfect consistency and truthfulness, that this principle of novelty is another corollary under the law of conspicuous waste. Obviously, if each garment is permitted to serve for but a brief term, and if none of last season's apparel is carried over and made further use of during the present season, the wasteful expenditure on dress is greatly increased. This is good as far as it goes, but it is negative only. Pretty much all that this consideration warrants us in saying is that the norm of conspicuous waste exercises a controlling surveillance in all matters of dress, so that any change in the fashions must conform to the requirement of wastefulness; it leaves unanswered the question as to the motive for making and accepting a change in the prevailing styles, and it also fails to explain why conformity to a given style at a given time is so imperatively necessary as we know it to be . . .

Source Excerpted from Veblen, T. B. (1899). *The Theory of the Leisure Class.* New York, NY: Macmillan.

A PSYCHOLOGICAL ANALYSIS OF FASHION MOTIVATION *ESTELLE DE YOUNG BARR*

Overview of the general problem

The psychology of choice is one of the most fundamental problems in applied social psychology. It is essentially the study of motivation, of attitudes and desires functioning as "coercive" and directive energies leading to acceptance-rejection responses.

It is the purpose of this investigation to study the practical problems of choice in the selection of women's clothes. For the sake of concreteness and comparability of data only the selection of the "daytime frock," a garment of general utility, is considered. This study is concerned with the complex of numerous varied factors in such selection, their relative potencies, their interrelationships and their conflicting and congruent effects on the resultant activity of choice.

The choice of a dress is a major social activity. A study of this selective activity involves not only a consideration of the cultural pattern but of the individual as an element in the pattern. It involves also a consideration of the individual's awareness of the self as an entity, a Gestalt, within the total configuration.

The problem is concerned with such questions as: To what extent does the awareness of self involve self-analysis? How cognizant is the individual of the qualities and characteristics of the physical I and the I that is called personality? If self-analysis leads to awareness of the qualities that contribute to the total Gestalt, the prevalent mode determines the standard of beauty by which these qualities are judged acceptable or unacceptable. Clothes attitudes may be analyzed down to awareness of self, self-analysis, recognition of defects and the creation of an "ideal" self. Clothes are not only part of the self, but they are the means for expressing those traits which seem desirable. They are at once the instrument of self-expression and of conformity to an ideal. If a woman chooses clothes to present a certain picture of herself, the choice depends not only on a knowledge of self, but also on the perception of certain basic elements of design of the garment. Thus the desire for conformity, desire for self-expression and aesthetic preferences and judgements exert their influences on the selection of the dress, which is both an end and a means . . .

Fashion is sometimes compared to or contrasted with "custom" which, of course, has greater stability as well as wider scope. In general, fashion is defined as the "mode" in choices within a group; mode in a statistical sense. But, besides its connotations of conformity, popularity, prevalence and majority opinion, it is also recognized as being characterized by change often described as "cyclic," but not necessarily associated with progress. The modal elements might be considered centripetal and the cyclic elements centrifugal in their influences.

Suggestibility, imitativeness, desire to conform, desire for companionship and fear of social disapproval are some of the individual tendencies most often mentioned to account for this group modality in choices. Desire for the new, progress, desire for economic and social prestige and desire for leadership and self-assertion are some of the urges usually associated with change in fashion. Commercial interests and fashion experts are included among the factors which make for style change and style adoption.

RELATIVE IMPORTANCE OF GROUP ATTITUDES

Of the fundamental attitudes involved in the psychology of choice of dress, the following are found to be among the more significant:

1 Desire to conform is the most diffuse of the desires measured; is more effective as a motive in determining the time of buying than desire for economy, and varies in intensity with the technical or professional interest of the group.
2 Desire for comfort with respect to temperature and tactual sensations is very important.
3 Modesty, though a significant factor, is not a very important motive for resisting a new fashion (brassiere bathing suit). Desire for comfort (freedom of movement), aesthetic standards, awareness of physical style defects, desire for conformity, are other factors creating resistance.
4 Desire for economy is very widespread as an attitude but as a motive in determining time of buying is less effective than the desire to conform
5 The aesthetic impulse is very important in the choice of a dress and functions in conjunction with the desire to be beautiful and the desire for conformity.

Of the constellation of fundamental attitudes related to the desire for self-expression:

1 Awareness of the physical self is very important in the choice of clothes.
2 Desire to be beautiful is important and operates in conjunction with the desire to conform.
3 The expression of different personality traits through the choice of a dress is of variable importance:
Desire to express "personality" is of more than moderate importance.
Desire to appear distinctive is of moderate importance.
Desire to appear dignified or youthful is of barely moderate importance.
Desire to appear competent is of less than moderate importance.
Desire to appear prosperous is of very little importance.

The most important factor determining the place of purchase is direct experience or experimental investigation rather than advertisements or recommendation.

Sources of style knowledge are of variable importance to the different groups. Reading sources are on the average, among the more important; social sources are among the less important.

Fashion knowledge is approximately commensurate with reading habits and technical interest in fashion.

CONCLUSIONS

The following conclusions are drawn from the results of this investigation: The really fundamental attitudes in the choice of clothes – those associated with the desire to conform, desire for comfort, desire for economy, the artistic impulse, and with self-expression through sex and femininity – occur so positively and so widely diffused as to seem to be "universal." They cut across differences in educational backgrounds, in economic status, in reading habits, in amount of technical fashion knowledge and in professional interest in fashion.

Most differences in attitudes involve differences in the intensity of the desire to be in fashion and in the more specific and practical expression of the fundamental attitudes.

Awareness of the physical Gestalt and a definite desire to attain to ideals of slenderness and tallness, particularly by those who deviate most from the standards of beauty set by fashion, are keen. Attitudes are naturally very closely interwoven and interact functionally on each other. The choice of particular design elements in a dress may at once express the individual's ideas of what is beautiful, the desire to conform to the prevailing mode and the desire to be beautiful through creating the illusion of beauty of form and through enhancing personal coloring with clothes colors.

The desire to be beautiful is evidenced by the choice of design elements of dress effective in creating the illusion of beauty of form and by the choice of colors to enhance the tones of the physical self.

The desire to express personality is very widely diffused, although such individual personality characteristics as distinctiveness, youthfulness and dignity seem to be of barely moderate importance as objectives in the choice of a dress. Expression of the economic or social traits – the desire to appear competent or affluent – seems to be definitely negative as motivating factors.

The attitudes involved in the expression of the self do not differ significantly as between different groups.

An index of the importance which the choice of a dress assumes in the mind of the consumer is the amount of time and effort expended in window-shopping and shopping around, which more often than advertisements or recommendation directly determine the place where to buy.

Advertising seems to be more potent as a source of fashion ideas than as a direct stimulus to buying. Discrepancies in advertising practice and consumer attitudes may account in part, though not entirely, for this loss in effectiveness.

Source Excerpted from Barr, E. (1934). "A Psychological Analysis of Fashion Motivation." *Archives of Psychology,* 26: 1–100.

40

FASHION AS CYCLE

Annette Lynch and Michael Strauss D.[1]

The only consistent behavior about fashion is its ephemeral nature. Despite its cyclical nature, theorists and scholars have developed models and theories, which increase our understanding or predictability of fashion's flow, as a function of time. A Fashion cycle refers to fashion diffusion among the population, their rate of acceptance or rejection by the general public, and duration of, or interest in it. Sproles (1981) noted that theories and models of fashion cycles typically fall into two categories—*short-term* and *long-term* contexts. Short-term fashion cycles refers to life of a product, which can last for few months to perhaps a year or two. On the contrary, long-term fashion cycles follow evolutionary style movement that lasts up to a century, far exceeding the life span of most humans. In this chapter, emphasis is placed on fashion-change theories, which focus on short-term and long-term cyclic periods.

SHORT-TERM FASHION CYCLES

Style-based short-term cycles. Nystrom (1928) posited that fashion *style* and the frequency of its acceptance among the general public was crucial to understanding the fashion's cyclical behavior. Style can be defined as a, "Characteristic or distinctive mode or method of expression, presentation or conception in the field of some art" (Nystrom, 1928, p. 3). In the case of dress, for example, style can be seen as constellation of features that sets the garment apart from its generic form. For instance, a men's blazer has stylistic elements, which include body shape, fabric structure, lapel form, location of pockets and vents, among others that sets it apart from other men's apparel. From Nystrom's perspective, style is important since it defines the prevalence of a particular fashion in the marketplace. In other words, fashion can be quite essentially defined as the prevailing or normative style in a given period of time. Hailing from a business and marketing background, Nystrom believed that fashion should be opinion free, which is too subjective. Instead, he recommended that fashion should be documented in quantitative terms; by actually counting the populations of people wearing particular styles.

Typically, fashion styles are bell-shaped curves. Although they differ in slope steepness at both—inception as well as completion of the life cycle, which in turn is a function of—acceptance and rejection of a particular style in question. Furthermore, the curve height can vary; depending up on the quantitative number of consumers who adopt that particular fashion style at the peak of its popularity. Additionally, fashion is a function of duration too, which also dictates the shape of the curve. For example, a fad, typically rises and falls sharply, leaving a sharp-peaked curve. On the other hand, a classic, a style favored by consumers for a long time will have a broad and lengthy positioned center portion of the bell curve. Sproles and Burns (1994) illustrated Nystrom's fashion life cycles—a fad, classic and normal fashion cycle.

As noted above, Nystrom believed in quantitatively measuring fashion life cycles, he did not present any

---

[1] From Annette Lynch and Michael Strauss D, (2007) Fashion as Cycle: in Changing Fashion: A Critical Introduction to Trend Analysis and Meaning. Oxford: Berg 127–50.

form concrete, research-developed, fashion cycle in his work. Nevertheless, it is important to note that Nystrom's propositions related to fashion cycles is significant in that it provided fashion professionals with a theoretical shape from which life times of fashion products could be considered. In similar vein, his propositions help determine fashion styles, and for distinguishing fashion subsets (e.g. fad vs. classic).

In essence, a fashion cycle represents how fashion spreads and diffuses among the population. Myriad fashion style exists; however, to belong to a particular group, one has to adopt a specific fashion style. Therefore, Nystrom fundamentally assumed that imitation was the primary motivation that drove fashion diffusion among the general public. Not only Nystrom focused on imitation, but also underscored the importance of other macro-factors that influenced the rate of fashion adoption (e.g. leisure time, consumer education levels, and relative prosperity).

Diffusion of innovation. Fashion analysts have also sought to understand short-term fashion cycles, by focusing on variations of consumers than just style per se. From this perspective, the focus is on the human adoption and spread of fashion trend. It is important to note that this perspective was built up on research principles related to agriculture, with regards to adoption of innovation diffusion studied by Everett Rogers (2004). Rogers also focused on fashion and other varied fields. Per Roger's diffusion of innovation, the basic assumption is that humans vary in degrees of receptiveness when it comes to embracing innovation. If anything, receptiveness to innovation when equated to fashion, then Roger's work is critical in understanding fashion-change theory.

Per Rogers' research, the tendency of people to adopt or resist innovations is a continuous variable that can be plotted as frequency distribution over time, which yielded the familiar bell-shaped curve. His research noted that human behaviors, including a propensity to adopt innovation, were normally distributed. In the case of diffusion of innovation curve, the bell curve commences with small proportion of population, who are early adopters of innovation. As time passes, more and more people entertain the innovation at an increasing rate, which has been labelled as "binomial expansion." Subsequently, the curve reaches its peak, when the innovation is in vogues, and maximum number of people have adopted the innovation, before it starts to dwindle and ultimately dip, completing the path of a normal distribution.

Rogers classified fashion or innovation adopters into five different categories, using two key statistics— mean (i.e., representing the average proclivity for innovation adoption) and standard deviation (i.e., average variability of in innovation adoption). The five segments have been labelled as: innovators (2.5%), early adopters (13.5%), early majority (34%), late majority (34%), and laggards (16%). He also proposed a sixth category, which refers to the people who fall outside Rogers' statistical analyses (i.e., who refuse to adopt an innovation; for more information, see Lynch and Strauss, 2007). Rogers used "social system" to describe the context within which individuals choose to adopt innovations. The defining characteristics he found clustered around socioeconomic status, personality values, and communication behavior. For instance, earlier adopters were mostly educated, upper-class, and upwardly mobile from an economic standpoint.

Status-driven models of fashion cycles. Collective behavior theories based on the principle that people use consumer products to express and maintain status have also been used as a foundation to understand fashion cycles. Several mathematical models, chiefly developed by economists (e.g., Frijters, 1998) have been developed to account for fashion-change behavior, which was built on sociological assumption of status acquisition. In this sub-section, three models based on different assumptions are briefly explained:

1 Wolfgang Pesendorfer's (1995, 2004) status-signaling theory: Pesendorfer's economic models considered various aspects: collective behavior, product design, product availability, and pricing structure as additional variables in understanding fashion cycles. Two assumptions are noteworthy: (1) fashion items serve as signaling device (e.g., social status) and (2) fashion item typically has a finite lifetime, being cyclically replaced by other

fashion items. Pesendorfer's economic models considered fashion cycles in both equilibrium and dynamic contexts. In equilibrium context, people participating in fashion process are basically of two types—*high* or *low*. High types are located in upper strata of social structure, whereas low types were the lower strata member—purely, a function of wealth, family, and education. The high types wish to commune with other high types, at the same time try to stay away from the low types. He further assumed that social status was unobservable without the benefit of dress. Per Pesendorfer, fashion items are devoid of any intrinsic value, other than offer a means to signal one's status. Thus, in equilibrium context, high types try to match other high types, and low types with low types, thus, reaching equilibrium. But, once the fashion degrades, it suffers its signaling value and eventually adopted by the low types. On the other hand, in a dynamic system, fashion producers offer expensive items in the marketplace, which high types sought. On the contrary, due to its prohibitive cost, low types are unable to purchase the item in question. According to the latter model, fashion maintains its signaling integrity, prices will remain high, and high types continue to buy the fashion item. Thus, rendering a longer life cycle. But, if the high types are bored, the producers will manufacture at lower cost to cater to the low types. He referred to this circumstance as "status-signaling degradation." It refers to a situation where a fashion style is simultaneously adopted by high and low types. Therefore, at this point, we see the end of the fashion cycle. Even if producers do not lower the cost of a fashion, the item is likely to suffer status degradation because high types seek novelty in order to confirm their social standing; thus, initiating a new fashion cycle.

2. Coelho and McClure (1993) developed economic models associated with fashion cycles. They approached their model development from evolutionary theory perspective, which supported the notion that pursuit of social status was a socio-biological drive that humans as well as other animals, motivated by the biological urge to pass their genetic material. Therefore, higher the social status, the higher the chances of genetic propagation. Wearing fashionable dress is an important social status construction means. Thus, Coelho and McClure's fashion cycle begins with seeking status, as a primary goal. At inception of fashion item, it is highly priced. Thereby, status-seekers procure pricey and scarce fashion items to secure social distinction (also see snob effect, Leibenstein, 1950). Taking advantage of the situation, the producers seeks this target market for their highly priced fashion merchandise—a practice referred to as prestige-pricing—creating snob effect. Eventually, the snob effect devolves, and the item is widespread among the general populace. When the fashion cycle sees its demise (see Lynch & Strauss, 2007; Coelho, Klein, & McClure, 2005).

3. Paul Frijters' (1998) studied fashion cycles too. Per Frijters, his model was built upon the proposition that early adopters were wealthy, high-status individuals who were willing to pay a premium price for fashion products and thus confer status to the purchased product. Thus, making the lofty priced fashion item as desirous and status-seeking. It is important to note that the Frijters model did not work on the assumption that all highly priced items were sought after by the wealthy. Only items that showed the potential to be highly priced for probable future were accrued. Thus, wealthy people viewed fashion as an investing in the future. Frijters maintained that price sensitivity can be used as a pricing strategy.

Fashion cycles driven by purposeful obsolescence. Sproles (1981) proposed that constant introduction of new styles is in the very nature of fashion industry. Recall that fashion is cyclical in nature, which does not necessarily equate to simple procedure. In fact, developing new fashion item is a complex procedure. Occasionally, there are fashion items that are rejected by the masses (e.g., midi dresses rejection in the late 1970s, Reynolds & Darden, 1972). Although occasional rejections exists, the fashion industry continues to produce new styles. Paul Gregory (1947) studied the rate at which fashion styles were being introduced in the marketplace. He noticed that the producers produced far more styles than needed. Thus, Gregory attributed fashion to economic inefficacy, by artificially increasing the rate of fashion cycles. "Purposeful obsolescence" was the term coined by Gregory to describe the behavior when manufacturer conspires to shorten the lifetime of a product; a phenomenon common in many consumer goods sector. Gregory defined two specific types of purposeful obsolescence; namely, deliberate under-engineering of the product (thereby, product fails faster) and calculated destruction of psychological utility of the product (for more information, see Gregory, 1947).

LONG-TERM FASHION CYCLES

Super organic long-term fashion cycle theory. Alfred Kroeber (1919, 1940), an anthropologist, was the one to uncover long term fashion cycles. Especially, in the context of understanding civilizations. His work has been appreciated and adopted by fashion scholars to understand long term fashion cycles, noted Carter (2003). Kroeber observed that copious anecdotal evidence exists that demonstrates the cyclical nature of the rise and fall of nations, empires, arts, and culture. Since the topic are macro in scope, in order to understand fashion cycles he chose to analyze women's dress styles. Per Kroeber, argued that long term fashion style cycles are a result of complex "super organic" forces, which lies beyond the range of human perception. Whereas, short-term fashion cycles, which occur within the long-term cycles could be attributed to unsettling times caused by political conflict or social upheaval. Unfortunately, Kroeber, who suggested a super organic force, never explained its nature.

Kroeber's original work inspired some researchers (e.g., Lowe & Lowe, 1982) to study long-term fashion cycles. For example, Robinson (1958, 1961) noted that fashion fluctuated cyclically over long period of time; and, compared it to pendulum movement. Furthermore, Robinson explained that when an extreme in dress design was reached, the fashion suddenly collapses under its own weight, and it gravitates back to the center point—the golden mean (or the equilibrium point, Lowe & Lowe, 1982). Loops and bustles fashion during the Victorian age was cited as an example. Lowe and Lowe (1982) revisited prior works on long-term fashion cycles (e.g., Kroeber, 1940). They commented up on Kroeber's "golden mean," which referred to a point from which the fashion changes cyclically; usually emanating and then returning back to the point. Lowe and Lowe (1982, p. 540) explained that the equilibrium point represented "intersection of esthetic constraints." Additionally, they noted that two forms of stylistic perturbations occurred: (1) random disturbances around the golden mean and (2) replacement of the golden mean of a fashion style by new one (e.g., traditional gowns to pants).

Women's dress fashions as a function of reproductive strategy. Barber (1999) refocused on previous literature related to long-term fashion cycles (Kroeber, 1940; Lowe & Lowe, 1982; Weeden, 1977), which correlated with economic and social changes to long-term fashion. Barber proposed that long-term fluctuations of women's evening wear around the golden mean were directly associated with women's reproductive strategies. Barber elucidated that as women become more financially stable, their dress reflects less dependence on marriage. He found that when marriage was an economic necessity, women's style became modest; thus, making women seem less sexually accessible. On the other hand, when marriage was not an economic necessity, women dressed in more revealing manner. A conclusion also reached by Lowe and Lowe (1982), who suggested that cultural construction of women's sexuality might be the underlying cause of long-term fashion cycles. The aforementioned view is consistent with Flugel's (1930) shifting erogenous zones theory, which states that fashion is primarily dictated by sexual competition.

CONCLUSION

In sum, this chapter reviewed cyclical fashion and its nature. Furthermore, various theories related to changing fashion were discussed. Both focusing on short-term as well as long-term fashion cycles. The theories include: style-based fashion cycle theory; diffusion of innovation theory; status signaling theory; fashion as a positional status-marker theory; status conferred by the purchaser theory; artificial obsolescence theory; super organic long-term fashion cycle theory; and fashion as a function of reproductive strategy. It is important to note that the aforementioned fashion cycle theories are by no means exhaustive (e.g., Flugel, 1930; see Lynch & Strauss, 2007; Sproles, 1981).

References

Barber, N. (1999). "Women's Dress Fashions as a Function of Reproductive Strategy." *Sex Roles*, 40(5/6): 459–71.

Carter, M. (2003). *Fashion classics from Carlyle to Barthes*. Oxford, UK: Berg

Coelho, P. R. P., Klein, D. B., & McClure, J. E. (2005). Rejoinder to Pesendorfer. *Economic Journal Watch*, 2(1), 32–41.

Coelho, P. R. P., & McClure, J. E. (1993). Towards an economic theory of fashion. *Economics Enquiry*, 31, 595–608.

Flugel, J. C. (1930). *The psychology of clothes*. London, UK: Hogarth Press.

Frijters, P. (1998). A model of fashion and status. *Economic Modeling*, 15(4), 501–517.

Gregory. P. M. (1947). An economic interpretation of women's fashions. *Southern Economic Journal*, 14(2), 148–162.

Kroeber, A. L. (1919). On the principle of order in civilization as exemplified by changes of fashion. *American Anthropologist*, 21(3), 235–263.

Lowe, J. W. G., & Lowe, E. D. (1982). Cultural pattern and process: A study of stylistic change in women's dress. *American Anthropologist*, 84(3), 521–544.

Nystrom, P. H. (1928). *Economics of fashion*. New York: Ronald Press.

Pesendorfer, W. (2004). Response to 'fashion cycles in economics.' *Economic Journal Watch*, 1(3), 455–464.

Pesendorfer, W. (1995). Design innovations and fashion cycles. *American Economic Review*, 85(4), 771–792.

Reynolds, F. D., & Darden, W. R. (1972). An Analysis of Selected Factors Associated with the Adoption of New Products. *Review of Financial Economics*, 8(2), 31.

Robinson, D. E. (1958). Fashion theory and product design. *Harvard Business Review*, 53, 121–131.

Robinson, D. E. (1961). The economics of fashion demand. *Quarterly Journal of Economics*, 75, 376–398.

Rogers, E. M. (2004). A prospective and retrospective look at the diffusion model. *Journal of Health Communication*, 9(1), 13–19.

Sproles, G. B. (1981). Analyzing fashion life cycles: Principles and perspectives. *Journal of Marketing*, 45(4), 116–124.

Sproles, G. B., & L. D. Burns. (1994). *Changing appearances: Understanding dress in contemporary society*. New York: Fairchild Publications.

Weeden, P. (1977). Study patterned on Kroeber's investigation of style. *Dress*, 3, 9–19.

41

THE HIGH STREET RESPONDS:
Designing for the older market

Julia Twigg[1]

The fashion industry is a schizophrenic trade: at one end imbued with the values of high fashion and with the glamour and froth of an industry based on fast-moving styles of cultural elites; at the other pursuing the day-to-day task of providing clothing for the population as a whole. This tension lies at the heart of many of the difficulties the industry faces in responding to the older market. In this chapter I explore how the high street conceptualizes or imagines the older customer, and how it designs and markets specifically for her. I focus in particular on the ways it adjusts the cut and style of its offer to respond to the ways the body alters with age and the challenges this presents for fashionability. I also explore the use of colour and the wider significance of this in relation to the changing cultural location of older people. But first I need to explore briefly the nature of the Fashion System and some of the changes that have occurred in it over the last twenty years.

CHANGES IN THE FASHION SYSTEM

In the past, large sectors of the clothing market took the form of stable, little-changing lines, relatively unaffected by fashion. But with the new world of short production runs, quicker time scales and flexible batch production, more of the market has been drawn into the orbit of fashion (Braham 1997). Clothes have shifted from being durables, expensive items required by everyone and bought infrequently, to consumables, cheap items bought frequently as part of active engagement with consumption (Majima 2006). In this period, consumers move from a world when a coat in the 1960s was a major item of expenditure expected to last several years, to one in the 2000s where single-season coats of fashionable cut and colour became widely available in supermarkets and other low-cost retailers.

Older women have also been drawn into the faster shopping cycle. These women are not, however, spending a larger proportion of their income on clothes. This is largely because of the reducing cost of clothes, which have become significantly cheaper over the period. There is thus evidence to support the view that the behaviour of older women has been affected by the general climate; and that they have been drawn into the faster shopping cycle that marks the period.

FRAMING THIS MARKET

Fashion marketing to older women rests on an essential tension: that of building a market centred around a negative identity. The editor of *Vogue* expressed this starkly.

> I think at some level nobody wants to be older. Nobody wants to be fat and nobody wants to be old. You don't want to be poor either. There's lots of things that nobody wants to be, and actually older is just, in general, one of them. So to sort of create a kind of niche whereby if you buy it you're saying, 'I am older,' you can kind of see why people don't necessarily want to do that.

---

[1] From Julia Twigg (2013) The High Street Responds: Designing for the Older Market. Fashion and Age: Dress, The Body and After Life. London: Bloomsbury, 119–42.

These ambivalences set up problems for brands in signalling that they are relevant to older customers—that they have garments designed for them and their bodies—at the same time as avoiding the negative connotations of being directly labelled as for the old. Fashion is profoundly—perhaps inherently—youth-oriented. At its high fashion core, the system is centred on youthfulness. These values are to a significant degree shared by the customers who have internalized ageist standards, seeking youthful fashions in the attempt to look more youthful themselves. This, however, presents a dilemma. Many women want styles associated with youthfulness, and with this, attractiveness, success and fashionability, but in forms adjusted to their bodies and to the social and cultural interpretation of these. I return to this issue when I discuss adjusting the cut.

CONCEPTUALIZING THE MARKET: AGE OR LIFESTYLE?

The grey market is, as we have noted, far from unitary; older people are as diverse in their circumstances, values and lives as younger people, and in some circumstances more so (Metz and Underwood 2005). As a result marketing literature frequently raises the issue of whether lifestyle rather than age is a more appropriate category on which to base market segmentation.

Clothing companies in the study clearly drew on lifestyles in thinking about their collections. Age was, however, clearly part of this process of 'imagining'—as indeed was class, as this quotation with its references to 'professional' makes clear.

Lifestyle is clearly important in their thinking and in the wider culture, but as this comment makes clear, this cannot be separated wholly from age because lifestyles themselves reflect age: what people do, how they live their lives, their values and attitudes, in part derive from their age and their position within an age-ordered social structure.

'MOVING YOUNGER'

Across this field there is a pervasive language of 'moving younger'. Partly this reflects the aspirational nature of consumption itself. Clothes are part of consumption culture, goods promoted in terms of a dream of an idealized self. This is the central dynamic that fuels the constant pursuit of goods, and it is of particular significance in the case of clothing where retailers are selling in a saturated market.

But companies also want to move younger because they perceive that the market itself has changed and that people in their sixties and over no longer want the sorts of clothing they once did. They believe the current generation of older people is in some sense different, wanting younger-looking styles that no longer label them as old.

The testimony of retailers, including some who had worked in the field for many decades, clearly endorsed the reconstitution of age thesis, believing that this generation is in some sense different, younger in spirit and expectations. As a result, they recognize that they need to adjust their responses, learning to imagine the customer differently.

ADJUSTING THE CUT

In designing for the older market manufacturers need to adjust the cut of their clothes to respond to changes in the body that occur with age. Clothes lie on the interface between the physiological body and its cultural presentation. They directly reflect the materiality of the body, although always within a cultural context. Adjusting the cut, therefore, is a complex process that encompasses both the literal fit of the garment and its capacity to reflect norms about the older body and its presentation.

The female body, as it ages, changes: waists thicken, busts lower, stomachs expand, shoulders move forward (Goldsberry et al. 1996; Birtwistle and Tsim 2005). Typically there is some loss of height and a reduction of length between neck and waist. This process sets in by the middle years, and over time acts to change the body in ways characteristic of age. The body at sixty or eighty is different from at forty, and this has implications for the design of dress.

Clothes do more than just fit the body, they aim to enhance it, presenting it in ways that accord with the body ideal of the period. Part of adjusting the cut is, therefore, about producing garments that assist the wearer to appear nearer the current fashionable norm; in the case of women, nearer the body of a slim, young woman. Clothes have always performed this function, enabling individual bodies with their idiosyncrasies to be presented in a form nearer the current norm. Such adjustments reflect systematic ideals about the body.

Adjusting the cut to make it fit better can, however, have the effect of ageing the garment, writing into its very structure information about the sort of body meant to inhabit it.

One way retailers can attempt to get round the issue is by featuring softer and looser styling. Some of the more successful and modern-looking ranges for older market use this approach, with companies like Oska or Masai Company managing to cross the age barrier by deploying loosely cut modern styles influenced by a Scandinavian aesthetic.

Fabric can also have a role to play. Jaeger, for example, avoids sheer or light fabrics that offer little in the way of coverage for the older body

> because a woman when she reaches those more mature years, can't wear sheer clothes. She can't wear very, very fine—if we buy a very, very fine wool, then it's too lightweight to give her the coverage and the confidence, because as you get more mature you want a bit more coverage. So we're very mindful of the weights of our fabrics, of lining things in beautiful linings, so again she feels confident in how she's dressing. . .If you wear a very fine wool trouser, you know, women do have sort of cellulite and they—you know, and if you start seeing the ripples through this very sheer wool, there's nothing worse. So that's why for us, we believe a good weight of fabric—as long as it's not heavy—the weight gives you the coverage and the confidence.

The repeated emphasis on confidence in this passage is significant. Here the older body is seen as something that can potentially embarrass or betray the customer. Well-designed clothes aim to avoid this.

Adjusting the cut can also be about preventing the exposure of the body in ways that may violate norms about the visibility of older bodies, in particular where this is linked to expressed sexuality. All the retailers were conscious of these issues and the significance of avoiding low necks, exposed upper arms and excessive flesh in general. The design director at Viyella noted how if necklines are too low, husbands comment.

> But I've actually seen a lot of husbands say, 'That's too low'. Because I think this area can get a little bit—I think it can get a bit too thin can't it, so you don't want to show it?

Many women put on weight as they grow older; and one of the marked features of ranges aimed at older customers is that they have 'generous' cut. Indeed one of the ways one can recognize such ranges is through sizing: shops aimed at the teen or young market cut to a smaller size, though all use the standard UK terminology of 10, 12 and so forth. Ranges thus aim to flatter older women and confirm them in their identities by allowing them to believe they still fit into size 12 or whatever their size had been.

COLOUR AND AGE

Designers also adjust their designs in term of the colours they choose, once again responding to the interplay between physiological and cultural ageing. In particular they emphasized the need to move away from strong, hard, high-saturation colours, which were deemed unflattering for white complexions as they age. As the design team at Asda explained:

> Design manager: People's skin tone and hair colour, they do naturally get lighter as you age, you know it's a natural process, so we always take that into consideration. But what we do do is still try and give her the colour palette or elements of the colour palette of the season.
>
> Buying manager: We can soften it, it's more like what we would call mid tones rather than full tones, because full tones are very harsh. So it would be like what we call a mid tone which actually is more flattering, but also is more sophisticated. But the ranges are colourful.

They aimed to provide clothes in positive colours that were flattering for this group while still reflecting the dominant fashion mood.

Fashion in colour changes with the fashion cycle. Trends are set up to two years in advance, led by the yarn and fabric manufactures and defined by the cycle of trade fairs and coordinating meetings (Diane and Cassidy 2005). The International Inter-color Committee analyses colour trends every six weeks (Aspers 2010). Some trends are long term; others involve accent colours for just one season. In designing for the older market, retailers aim to pick up these trends, thus integrating older people with the mainstream, but in ways adjusted to be flattering. The team at Asda explained how they did this:

> Buying manager: For example on G21 [the younger range] if red is the colour of the season, we might have red with cobalt blue, with bright green. You know, really poppy colours and lots of poppy colours. Whereas with Moda [aimed at women over forty-five] we will take the red. . .
>
> Design manager: And go more spicy with it, you know, because she likes the spice. So we put it with like a burnt orange. The red might not have so much orange in it, you know, it might be slightly kind of softer, although she would wear black, white and red. But it's about the tone of the red. It's quite a difficult thing to explain without a colour wheel, but it's just like a softened palette, less brash.
>
> Buying manager: Not dowdy, because that's the whole thing, she does like colour. But just softer tones with it as well.

The key terms in this passage are 'softer, 'less brash' and 'not dowdy'.

All the respondents emphasized that these customers embrace colour: 'This is a customer who likes colour' (Asda); 'We can sell bright colours really well' (EWM); 'She likes colour' (M&S referring to Classic range). These views were echoed in the interviews with older women. The liking of colour was thus presented as part of the positive upbeat discourse of the retailers in relation to this group, a repudiation of drab, self-effacing colours that seemed to embody cultural exclusion and depression.

THE MEANINGS OF COLOUR

Such comments need to read against the traditional meanings of colour in dress in relation to older people. There is a long history that associates age with the adoption of darker, drab colours.

However the avoidance of strong colour is still a significant part of people's ideas about age. These associations can be interpreted as part of the wider process of toning down in dress, the adoption of self-effacing, don't-look-at-me clothes that reflect the imposed cultural invisibility of older people, particularly women. These are colours that make no bid to be noticed, that have retreated from public view.

Black is an exception here. In the historical past, black was associated with age, particularly through its connection with mourning; and many women adopted black as standard wear from their middle years onwards. The meaning of black in dress, however, was never confined to this; and black also has connotations of drama, romanticism, eroticism and elegance (Lurie 1992; Harvey 1995; Pastoureau 2008). Today the connection with mourning has faded and for the generation discussed here is no longer significant.

The emphasis on colour is, however, open to an additional interpretation, one that sees it in terms of a retreat from cut. As the body changes, particularly in later old age, it becomes less amenable to the imposition of the normative feminine figure that much cut in dress is designed to display.

CONCLUSION

Fashion is part of the cultural economy in which meanings circulate in and through material production. In this, design directors, like journalists and advertisers, operate as cultural mediators, shaping the aspirations of customers, proposing new ways of being and providing the material means of achieving these at a directly bodily level. Increasingly such activities encompass older people. Clothing retail companies, therefore, need to be understood as part of the wider set of cultural influences shaping the ways ageing is imagined, performed and experienced in contemporary culture.

Design directors, of course, respond to the market. Their task is to provide goods people want to buy; and a central part of their skill lies in sensing what these will be. They do this through imagining the lives, wishes, aspirations—and to some degree anxieties—of their customers. But they are not simply responding to demand, but also shaping and creating it, stimulating the market for new goods. This is especially so in relation to fashion, whose nature is that it evolves and develops beyond the reach of customers, constantly presenting to them new ways of dressing, new ways of being. Older people are increasingly integrated into this aspirational culture.

Clothing retailers are interested in the older market. The massive growth in productivity, the reduction in the cost of clothes and the speeding up of the fashion cycle have produced a situation where the youth market is, to some degree, saturated. As a result retailers have sought to develop new markets, including those for older people. This has meant extending the idea of fashionability beyond its traditional reach, to older people.

Though clothes are wholly cultural artefacts, their design intersects with the materiality of the body. There is an inevitable interplay between elements of cultural and bodily ageing, and this is carried through into the design—and wearing—of clothes. We have seen how the designers adjust the cut of clothes so that they fit and flatter; how they select colours that enhance the skin as it ages; how they avoid forms of bodily exposure deemed culturally shameful or that expose the body as failing to meet the cultural norms of youthfulness. But they are also increasingly using positive colour for this group, which is no longer confined to the low, drab tones of the past; and they have moved designs towards a younger, more relaxed body style that reflects the norm pertaining in the mainstream market. All the respondents in the study recognized the pervasive cultural aspiration of looking younger. Clothes have become part of the wider culture of anti-ageing. 'Moving younger' is a central part of what design directors, particularly for ranges aimed at women in later middle age, are doing. But they have to balance this against the realities of bodily ageing. Extremely youthful styles do not necessarily make the wearer look younger; they can point up the mismatch in expectations, the discrepancy between the ageing body and the youthful style.

Evidence from the study does support the idea that the lives and experiences of older people are changing and that spheres like consumption and the wider cultural economy are playing a part in this. Design directors clearly believed, on the basis of their commercial experience, that current generations of older people are 'different', and have aspirations that mark them apart from earlier ones; though I also noted reasons to be cautious in accepting these views uncritically, registering in particular the danger of confusing the processes of 'moving younger' with processes of style diffusion itself. The design directors presented these developments in positive terms; and the interviews were imbued with an upbeat, celebratory tone that lauded the new cultural opportunities opening for older women. This is unsurprising. Like other actors in the sphere of consumption, they are in the business of selling goods and this means selling attractive lifestyles. But these cultural developments, like many others in relation to older people, are Janus-faced. The spread of fashion opportunities to older women also entails the colonization of their bodies by new expectations, new requirements—ones that demand that they be fashionable or well-dressed, and present the body in such a way that age is—as far as possible—effaced.

References

Aspers P. (2010), *Orderly Fashion: A Sociology of Markets*, Princeton, NJ: Princeton University Press.

Birtwistle G. and C. Tsim (2005), '"Consumer purchasing behaviour: an investigation of the UK mature women's clothing market"', *Journal of Consumer Behaviour*, 4, 1: 453–64.

Braham P. (1997), 'Fashion: unpacking a cultural production', in P. du Gay (ed.), Production of Culture/Cultures of Production, 119–76. London: Sage Publications.

Diane T. and T. Cassidy. (2005), *Colour Forecasting*, Oxford: Blackwell.

Goldsberry E., S. Shim and N. Reich. (1996), "'Women 55 years and older: Part I current body measurements as contrasted to the PS 42-70 data'", *Clothing and Textiles Research Journal*, 14, 1: 108–20.

Harvey J. (1995), *Men in Black*, London; Reaktion Books.

Lurie A. (1992), *The Language of Clothes*, London: Bloomsbury.

Majima S. (2006), 'Fashion and the Mass Consumer Society in Britain, c. 1951–2005', unpublished D. Phil. thesis, University of Oxford.

Metz D. and M. Underwood (2005), Older, Richer, Fitter: Identifying the Customer Needs of Britain's Ageing Population, London: Age Concern.

Pastoureau M. (2008), *Black: The History of a Colour*, Princeton, NJ: Princeton University Press.

42

REBRANDING AMERICAN MEN'S HERITAGE FASHIONS THROUGH THE USE OF VISUAL MERCHANDISING, SYMBOLIC PROPS AND MASCULINE ICONIC MEMES HISTORICALLY FOUND IN POPULAR CULTURE

Kevin Matthews, Joseph H. Hancock II, and Zhaohui Gu[1]

Men's fashion styles are influenced by, and have inspired, American culture. Throughout history, men's clothing has teetered between ostentatious as well as conservative styles (López-Gydosh and Hancock, 2009). During the early twenty-first century, men's mass-fashion sportswear has been stylized by social constructions of work- and sports-influenced principles in order for contemporary men to appear culturally accepted as masculine (Edwards 2006: 99–115). Retailers selling these garments have realized men are important consumers to pursue; and, by doing so, successful retailers gain dollars and market share (Pellegrin 2009: xv–xxii).

As competition among men's mass-fashion retailers grows, branding becomes an essential component in the retailing strategy (Hameide 2011: 178). One method of a branding strategy utilized to enhance mass fashion in the retailing context is visual merchandising and display. One goal of visual display is to convey a cohesive story-like theme to the consumer in order to gain his attention. Through the use of various types of props, found objects, furniture, and other such items, a visual merchandiser can create a selling context for mass-fashion garments giving them a centralized meaning (Diamond and Litt 2009: 361–64). A brand-like storytelling context and association to pop-cultural meanings often overshadows the actual product consumers are purchasing (Hancock 2009a: 28–31).

Because the men's mass-fashion retail industry provides similar products such as T-shirts, jeans, khaki pants, woven shirts, sweaters, shorts, etc. to consumers, a branding technique such as visual display becomes the primary means used to sell these products to the consumer (Hancock 2009a). With differences in the logo, style, price or colour as negotiable to some consumers, a men's 100% cotton piqué polo shirt may look quite similar at Rugby, Club Monaco, Abercrombie & Fitch, American Eagle, Polo Ralph Lauren, or even Tommy Hilfiger. Devoid of retailing or visual-selling context, a product as ostensibly basic as a cotton piqué polo shirt does not convey the brand message or meaning (Barthes 1967: 3–18). Yet the brand insignia or label may conjure images of fashion hierarchy or associations in a consumer's mind; thus influencing his purchase decision (Hancock 2009a). The process of contextual display, such as visual merchandising, allows for mass-fashion garments to establish, change and reorganize their position in relation to other clothing items.

By discerning the various intended visual themes created through artistic display, story-like brand narratives often reflect contemporary cultural markers of what appears to be acceptable masculine dress (Pellegrin 2009: 38–56).

---

[1] From Kevin Matthews Joseph H. Hancock II and Zhaohui Gu Rebranding American Men's Heritage Fashion Through The Use of Visual Merchandising Symbolic Props and Masculine Iconic Memes Historically Found In Popular Culture in Critical Studies in Men's Fashion Volume 1 Issue 1 (2014) pp. 39–58.

Figure 30 Ralph Lauren Double RL store in New York City's Nolita Area. Note the various icons associated with Western wear and the blatant use of the cowboy as a marker for acceptable men's fashion. Photo courtesy of Kevin Matthews and Joseph Hancock, 2012, All Rights Reserved.

In recent years, greater numbers of men's fashion focused clothiers have been opening across the nation. With the rise of these stores, a return to what has been referred to as vintage; clothes associated with 'Made in the USA' authentic, legendary and retro-American fashion have risen among male shoppers. The metrosexual has vanished and a new image of a more hunky masculine man has taken his place in such magazines as *Fantastic Man*, *V-Man* and *Hercules*. In his *New York Times* article, 'From Boys to Men', author Guy Trebay (2010) states:

> On catwalks and in advertising campaigns the prevalent male image has long been that of skinny-rat, a juvenile with pipe-cleaner proportions [...]
> Suddenly evidence of a new phase in the cycle of evolving masculinity imagery was all over the catwalks in the runway season [...] where the boys of recent memory have been transformed overnight into men.

In the height of a recession and in a current labour market where most work is digital, a return to an era when labour actually produced goods and services is becoming desirable and men want to be reminded of what labour used to be like through images and icons of popular culture. In Trebay's article Jim Nelson, editor of *GQ* Magazine, states, 'that we as men do work, we do labour, we do still make things' (2010).

Designers have been inspired by these ideas of retro-branding 'heritage' labels and workwear where the models for these garments are manly men, with hairy bodies, hunky builds and mature looks – men who do not appear to have been waxed and manicured (Trebay 2010). It is a rugged, masculine return to a work and labour era gone by that is influencing fashion, when men went hunting, joined a bowling league, and learned to play the guitar under the night sky.

PURPOSE OF THIS STUDY

This article takes a critical examination of how merchandising inspired by popular culture communicates various notions of history, and in this case, to display and sell heritage fashion lines. In specific retail locations popular and historically cultural-influenced visual display and aesthetic merchandising strategies are studied to ascertain and interpret the importance of visual display as one vehicle of *fashion branding*. A careful interpretive analysis determines that retailers associate cultural-influenced thematic props and icons reflective of America culture to sell men's mass-fashion garments and give them an aura of authenticity and American heritage. These displays and the branding stories convey conceptual (pop) cultural masculine icons or noted historical *memes* of US historical masculine imagery that include such male icons as the rebel, the cowboy, the Ivy Leaguer, jocks and blue-collar workers, revealing how these worn styles have infused into American culture and men's mass fashion as contemporary street style.

FASHION BRANDING

Consumer brand knowledge relates to cognitive representation of the brand. Interpretations of fashion-branding strategies are necessary to understand a company's advertisements and their relationships to consumers (Heding, Knudtzen and Bjerre 2009: 205). The cultural approach to branding relies on interpreting how brand meaning impacts consumers and how, in turn, consumers influence future meaning and branding techniques (Heding, Knudtzen and Bjerre 2009: 215). Increasingly competitive marketplaces demand that companies associate their brands with other people, places, things or brands as a means of building or leveraging knowledge that might otherwise be difficult to achieve through product marketing programs (Keller, 2003: 597). Linking the brand to another person, place, thing or cultural movement affects how consumers view the brand or 'primary brand knowledge'. A deeper understanding of how knowledge of a brand and other linked entities interact is of paramount importance. The linkages to the originating or primary brand become 'secondary' brand associations such as other brands, people, events, places, social causes and/or other companies. To provide comparable insight and guidance, a conceptually visual model demonstrates this leveraging process (Figure 31).

Linking the brand (primary source) to various parts of culture (secondary source) creates new primary brand knowledge (Keller 2003: 598). The linking of brand-A to other aspects of popular culture creates recognition and association with other causes and meanings thereby creating new narratives (primary brand + secondary brand = new meanings). While a consumer may know nothing about the retailer where they are shopping, they may be aware of secondary branding sources associated with the retailer, such as props and display design, and this could entice them to become more knowledgeable about the store and what they are about to purchase.

VISUAL RETAIL SPACES AND MEMES

Visual merchandising can be defined as the features and characteristics of a retail space that create an inviting and exciting environment for the consumer (Diamond and Litt 2009: 213–14). Elements of store design and display such as colour, furnishings, props, artwork, signage, and more all contribute to visual merchandising. Stores may have an in-house design team, corporate visual-merchandising branch, or can employ freelance merchandisers to positively impact sales. Balance is of utmost importance in all aspects of visual merchandising, as the proper message and story must be conveyed at all levels of brand communication. Without visual merchandising, stores might look unappealing or find it difficult to compete with other retailers carrying similar products (Diamond and Litt 2009: 214).

Establishing a retail store using visual display is imperative to discuss the system for understanding how consumers create associations for brand meaning (Hancock 2009b). Utilizing certain props in a store is shown to be effective to explain the phenomenon of how a brand can become associated with notions of authenticity or masculinity. For example, a trade-magazine article exploring the use of props in retail stores found that bikes and motorcycles were a common theme in several successful fashion retail brands in London (Anon. 2012), directly linking the display of a non-fashion object to successful visual merchandising.

USING MEMES IN RETAIL BRANDING SCHEMES

One theory in marketing research is *memetics,* or the study of memes. In business and marketing application, meme theory has been used to explain the success of certain management strategies, advertising campaigns and brand identities (Pech 2003; Marsden 2002; Williams 2000; Wu and Ardley 2007). Russell Williams, in his exploration of memes involved in

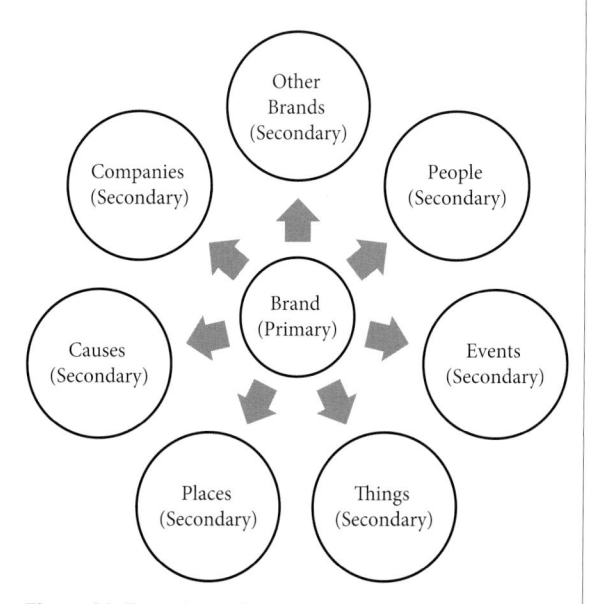

Figure 31 Examples of Brand Linkages to Popular Culture. Modified from Keller (2003: 598).

each of these categories, inadvertently integrates the concept of brand icons and the proliferation of a meme by referencing the 'Marlboro Man' (2000: 276). The Marlboro Man was created in the 1950s to advertise filtered cigarettes and give them a masculine identity by using a cowboy. The iconic image resonates with Americans in a far different, but no less pleasing, way than it does with West Africans. However, though the cultural digestion of this meme is associated with different notions, the brand is successful in both markets. This is a positive example of an accidental brand evolution: much like genes, memes can mutate through their dissemination.

Brand meme creation and mutation can occur from the actions of the producer or the consumer. Yufan Wu and Barry Ardley discuss the difficulty and importance of recognizing the power of the meme, noting that its memetic transmission must be carefully followed if the brand is to maintain an appropriate identity (2007: 307). In this case, it is important to note that the vehicles for meme transmission can be auditory, visual and linguistic (Pech 2003: 173–74). In the context of the retail store, all three sensory types are engaged. Thus, brand meme creation, mutation and even confusion can occur at a much higher rate through a customer's interaction in a store.

Joseph Hancock's study of Abercrombie & Fitch (2009b) highlights this concept. His exploration of the flagship store on 5th Avenue in New York City describes the dance music and erotic imagery set amongst rugged preppy clothing and other signs of the great outdoors (2009b: 79–80). Because the Abercrombie brand focuses on notions of masculinity and sex, these seemingly conflicting memes serve to bombard the customer with enticing brand messages.

Another crucial element of Hancock's study was the comparison of gay clone culture to the *hypermasculine* imagery of the Abercrombie store (2009b: 76–83). In Martin Levine's landmark study on gay clone culture in the 1970s, several archetypes of masculinity are identified with accompanying clothing styles (1998: 60; see Table 12). Levine notes that gay men in clone culture overemphasize masculine images to create sexual appeal, and refers to this concept as hypermasculinity (1998: 56–60). These cultural markers of masculinity, or memes of masculinity, are not new; many are historical references to various aspects of American history. Another book, *Jocks and Nerds*, by Richard Martin and Harold Koda, also details these masculine style tropes (1989: 7–9). Using the work of Martin and Koda alongside Levine proves the cultural importance and longevity of these memes. Levine's study, conducted in the 1970s, and Martin and Koda's work, published in 1989, provide a continuity in the study of cultural masculinity as it relates to fashion and the use of repetitive archetypes.

Levine uses the terms *Western, Leather, Military, Labourer* and *Athlete*. The roughly corresponding chapters in *Jocks and Nerds* are 'The Cowboy', 'The Rebel', 'The Military Man', 'The Worker' and 'Joe College'. Each meme has associated signposts that serve to conjure notions of masculinity, authenticity and

Table 12 Butch Sign Vehicles in Clone Fashion. Taken from Martin Levine (1998: 60).

Butch image	Sign vehicles
Western	Cowboy hat, denim jacket, cowboy shirt, Western belt, leather chaps, Frye or cowboy boots, farmer bandanas, rawhide thongs
Leather	Black leather motorcycle cap, jacket, pants and boots. Black or white T-shirts, studded black leather belt and wrist band, chains, tattoos
Military	Green army cap, flight jacket, red belt and fatigues. Brown leather bomber jacket, khaki army shirt, combat boots
Labourer	Hardhat, denim jacket, plaid flannel shirt, painter's pants, construction boots, keys
Athlete	Team jacket, sweatshirt, Lacoste shirt, tank top, sweatpants, gym shorts, jock straps, white crew socks and running shoes

heritage. Though multiple memes can be referenced while creating a visual-merchandising strategy, these five have a storied cultural history that is associated with American heritage and masculinity.

MEME ONE: THE REBEL

The iconic appearance of the rebel, though inextricably linked, in some cultural references, to the motorcycle, can also stand alone as fashion inspiration for an entire subculture. The coiffed hair, leather jacket, plain white T-shirt, cuffed jeans and black boots ensemble has clothed bikers, punks, skinheads and even Fonzie on ABC's television show *Happy Days* (Garry Marshall, 1974–84). Because each of these groups has adopted and altered this basic palette, it is important to reference the icon of the rebel more generally. Even when using a motorcycle to evoke the entire look and feel of the rebel, a merchandiser must be conscious not to place a heavily embellished leather jacket nearby that could suggest the uniform of a Hell's Angels member. The rebel, being far less distinct in apparel choices than the cowboy, has significant symbols in his own right; however, image management and discretion can provide the best allure for consumers.

By committing strongly to the iconic image of the leather-clad motorcycle rider, the Isle of Man (Figure 32) evokes notions of masculinity and authenticity from both the jacket and the motorcycle that a male customer might be seeking. Especially considering the price point of the store, the quote above might accurately represent its clientele. In this case, these men who have worked diligently to create comfortable lives for themselves can purchase the identity of the rebel through the items at the store. In doing so, they are solidifying the process that began when the first motorcycle picture was hung on the store's wall: these men are validating the notions of freedom that are assigned from the visual display and store signage onto the goods.

As an icon, the rebel stands inherently opposed to the consumerism that drives the world of fashion. However, by referencing symbols such as the motorcycle and the leather jacket, retailers can retro-brand a store's visual display to highlight distinctly

Figure 32 Isle of Man, a boutique in Chicago, features a motorcycle prominently in the store, creating notions of masculinity and authenticity linked with the icon of the rebel. Photo courtesy of Kevin Matthews and Joseph Hancock, 2012, All Rights Reserved.

masculine attributes. By showcasing a worn biker jacket haphazardly strewn on a vintage motorcycle, the message is not a disdain for the world. Rather, this image would underscore the rugged outsider aspect of the rebel, encapsulating it in the essence of cool. The themes of ruggedness and the appeal of the outsider are also consistent in other iconographic memes of masculinity, such as the cowboy.

MEME TWO: THE COWBOY

Ever present in American culture since the first few rode out in the late nineteenth century, the cowboy has become an iconic image that is easy to reference in visual display (Martin and Koda 1989: 77). A simple touch of a red paisley-print cotton bandana can evoke images from pop culture of the brave pioneers who travelled out to conquer the West. Though photographic accounts throughout the cowboy's history have shown considerable changes in dress, there are some garment styles and details that will always be attributed to Western wear: snap-front shirts, fringe jackets, ten-gallon hats and leather chaps. No matter which cultural groups have adopted these into their uniform, they still ring true to the nostalgic image of the cowboy. Just as the Marlboro Man was a successful branding tool to make cigarettes appear masculine, other brands can also use aspects of the cowboy to create notions of masculinity and authenticity.

As suggested by the visual display of several key men's fashion retailers, however, the *image* of cowboy is far from obsolete. In the conclusion of her article, Wilson notes that the cowboy style tends to have resurgences when Americans need a solemn, nostalgic, heroic figure (2009: 476). Because the profession of a working cowboy is no longer part of our cultural landscape, the image of the cowboy is the perfect locus for retro-branding a retail experience. Men who purchase Western wear in New York City at Ralph Lauren's Double RL store are not going to herd cattle in Wyoming (Figure 30). Therefore there is safety in this fantasy and illusion showcasing aspects of how the icon of the cowboy is conjured by visual merchandising.

Much of the definitive aspects of cowboy dress are rooted in function – namely protection. The cowboy is, of course, a lone ranger. In a retail marketplace saturated with identical styles from different makers, utilizing Western themes in visual display creates the perfect attraction for the consumer that he feels he needs to stand out. In doing so, he is also protecting his masculinity by adopting that of a cowboy.

MEME THREE: JOE COLLEGE

When describing the origin of the term 'Joe College', Martin and Koda refrain from precise historical placement (1989: 137). Instead, they focus on the defining cultural characteristics of collegiate men's style and the iconic symbols they produced. While fashion dictates change in acceptable dress, collegiate style has focused on, and created, classic styles that speak to the irreverence of youth. Even styles that transcend generations, such as the button-down shirt, are worn and styled in a way to defy conventional modes of dress. Thus, Joe College has been symbolized through several college symbols, including sports, books and typewriters.

Unlike other men's fashion icons, which begin from functional garments and become associated with the masculine traits of their usage, Joe College represents a lifestyle that is seeped in tradition, elitism and knowledge. As lifestyle branding has taken off in the fashion world in recent years, preppy has gone from a

Figure 33 The Brooklyn Circus boutique in New York uses a typewriter and antique desk to convey the image of Joe College. Photo Courtesy of Kevin Matthews and Joseph Hancock, 2012, All Rights Reserved.

singular garment, such as a sweater vest, to an entire brand, such as a menswear store designed like a lavish study. Wall shelves that display shoes can be filled with encyclopedic books, such as in the Brooklyn Circus flagship store in New York City. Directly opposite the shelves is an antique leather couch. This playful interior juxtaposition can easily allude to the Ivy League frat house, or perhaps a campus library. In the college context, this creates a notion of authenticity very different from the cowboy or military man.

MEMES FOUR AND FIVE: MILITARY AND BLUE-COLLAR WORKER

Two of the strongest memes that are associated together are military and blue-collar. They are symbolized through such items as work wear styles and primarily jeans. These garments are now available at every tier of fashion and this garment has a long history that is inextricably linked to America's working class (Sauro, 2005). Pioneered by Levi Strauss in 1873 for use in mining and other labour-intensive industries, denim jeans have evolved into a ubiquitous garment throughout most of the world. Styles used in blue-collar industries are still produced and worn today; alongside the various denim boutiques showcasing different levels of distressing in denim, however, the mark of an authentic pair of jeans may vary completely depending on the viewer.

Another symbolic garment of blue-collar labour is the apron (Gau n.d.). Used in a variety of labour-intensive jobs, the apron has several important similarities to jeans: both garments are generally constructed of a thick-weight fabric, such as canvas or twill; both are of utmost importance in function and protection; both will show signs of wear due to regular use. Unlike fine suiting that white-collar labour calls for, aprons and jeans are not meant to stay pressed or clean. Though the apron is less likely to make a strong revival as a fashion item, its use as a tool for branding and retro-branding is eminent. As men's fashion retail branding begins to adopt these and other staples of workwear, it is important to evaluate the shift in American culture that occurs alongside these trends.

The prevalence of men's fashion retailers celebrating the working class seems to coincide with a rapidly shrinking manufacturing sector and an increasingly virtual globalized economy. By presenting objects from labour-intensive industries as antiques, and by using them as part of a retro-branding motif, it seems as if men's fashion retailers believe the remaining textile and apparel manufacturers to be novel. Instead of truly celebrating the working class of America, men's fashion retailers are idolizing the 'blue-collar heroes' of times past.

CONCLUSION

The concepts and fieldwork conducted in this study conclude that strong visual merchandising can aid men's fashion retailers in creating a solid brand identity by conjuring cultural memes. These iconic memes convey notions of authenticity and masculinity for the retail brands in which they are presented. If referenced properly by way of visual display, a men's fashion brand can build a strong identity and create multiple meanings and associations for the consumer. In a competitive marketplace, this type of branding will help to set a retailer apart from its peers. As men continue to engage in fashion consumption, narrative branding will not only ensure higher profits, but also reflect and inspire cultural standards of masculinity and authenticity.

References

Anon. (2012), 'What are 2012's visual merchandising trends?', *Retail Week*, http://www.retail-week.com/stores/what-are-2012s-visual-merchandising-trends/5033405.article. Accessed 9 August 2013.

Barthes, Roland (1967), *The Fashion System*, New York: Columbia University Press.

Diamond, Jay and Sheri Litt. (2009), *Retailing in the Twenty-First Century*, New York: Fairchild.

Edwards, Tim (2006), *Cultures of Masculinity*, London: Routledge.

Gau, Colleen (n.d.), "Conventional Work Dress and Casual Work Dress." *Berg Encyclopedia of World Dress and Fashion: Volume 3 – The United States and Canada*, http://www.bergfashionlibrary.com/view/bewdf/BEWDF-v3/EDch3042.xml, Accessed 18 November 2012.

Hameide, M. Kaled. (2011), *Fashion Branding Unraveled*. New York: Fairchild.

Hancock, Joseph H (2009a), *Brand/Story: Ralph, Vera, Johnny, Billy, and Other Adventures in Fashion Branding*, New York: Fairchild.

Hancock, Joseph H. (2009b), 'Chelsea on 5th Avenue: Hypermasculinity and Gay Clone Culture in the Retail Branding Practices of Abercrombie & Fitch', *Fashion Practice*, 1: 1, pp. 63–86.

Heding, Tilde, Charolette F. Knudtzen and Mogens Bjerre (2009), *Brand Management: Research, Theory and Practice*, London: Routledge.

Keller, Kevin L. (2003), 'Brand Synthesis: The Multidimensionality of Brand Knowledge', *Journal of Consumer Research*, 29: 4, pp. 595–600.

Levine, Martin P. (1998), *Gay Macho: The Life and Death of the Homosexual Clone*, New York: NYUP.

López-Gydosh, Dilia and Joseph Hancock (2009), 'American Men and Identity: Contemporary African American and Latino Style', 32: 1, pp. 16–28.

Marsden, Paul (2002), 'Brand positioning: Meme's the word', *Marketing Intelligence & Planning*, 20: 5, pp. 307–12.

Martin, Richard and Harold Koda (1989), *Jocks and Nerds: Men's Style in the Twentieth Century*, New York: Rizzoli.

Pech, Richard J. (2003), 'Memes and Cognitive Hardwiring: Why are Some Memes More Successful Than Others?', *European Journal of Innovation Management*, 6: 3, pp. 173–81.

Pellegrin, Bertrand (2009), *Branding the Man*, New York: Allworth Press.

Sauro, Clare (2005), 'Jeans', A-Z of Fashion', *Berg Fashion Library*, http://www.bergfashionlibrary/view/bazf/bazf00329.xml. Accessed 18 November 2012.

Trebay, Guy (2010), 'From Boys to Men', *New York Times*, 15 October, http://www.nytimes.com/2010/10/17/fashion/17MANLY.html?pagewanted=all&_r=0. Accessed 4 August 2013.

Williams, Russell (2000), 'The Business of Memes: Memetic Possibilities for Marketing and Management', *Management Decision*, 38: 4, pp. 272–79.

Wu, Yufan and Barry Ardley (2007), 'Brand Strategy and Brand Evolution: Welcome to the World of the Meme', *The Marketing Review*, 7: 3, pp. 301–10.

TO HAVE AND TO HOLD:
Masculinity and the clutch bag

Benjamin L. Wild[1]

Fashion commentators have made much of men's increasing willingness to express their personality through appearance. They suggest men are more cognisant of how their dressed body conveys status and are becoming adept at making effective sartorial choices. Discussion of men's relationship with fashion has been framed by more general reflections on their changing role within society, which economic malaise and civil unrest in several European cities has led some people to suggest is in terminal decline (Bekiempis, 2011; Cohen, 2012; Armstrong, 2013a). Focusing on one of men's latest sartorial accessories, the clutch bag, this article analyses men's clothing in the context of his social and gendered role. The clutch bag stands out, for unlike other clothing innovations that men are presently adopting, or being encouraged to adopt, this accessory is not cheap or especially practical.

MALE ACCESSORIZING

Generally, there are typically two factors in men's acquisition of adornments, which can be defined in this context as items of apparel or ornamental detailing, possessing of no inherent utility, that are purchased and worn to convey some element of the wearer's character: price and utility (Tungate, 2008: 37, 61). From pocket squares to jackets with contrasting elbow patches, the majority of items worn by street-styled men (a diverse, if predominantly urban, cross-section of their gender) are practical or, if more decorative, relatively inexpensive. A pocket square has limited utility, but can be acquired for around £20 ($33). A jacket with contrasting elbow patches is a more practical item of clothing and does not necessarily cost more than a plainer variant, although this will depend on the label it carries and where it is bought. Reflecting on the multiplicity of male accessories and appearance-enhancing procedures that have been showcased in magazines and photographed for social media, in recent years many have been inexpensive or practical; the majority have been both.

But then the clutch bag appeared. This small, typically strap-less, usually leather pouch, measuring in the region of 250×205×10mm made its debut in the autumn/winter catwalk shows of Valentino and Gucci in 2012. Several high-street retailers, including Reiss, Zara and Ted Baker, marketed the clutch bag almost immediately, but it is only now becoming ubiquitous. Prima facie, it seems hard to explain why, for the majority of clutches do not compare favourably with other styles of bag when it comes to price and utility. First, they are not inexpensive. One of the cheapest clutches available for autumn/ winter 2013 was by Commes des Garçons for £75 ($123). The majority of clutch bags, by the likes of Balenciaga, Pierre Hardy, La Portegna and Reiss cost over £100 ($165); styles by Gucci and Smythson were in excess of £600 ($990). More fundamentally, none of these bags are particularly practical because they deprive owners of the use of one of their hands. But this could be the point. Paradoxically, the fact that the clutch significantly reduces a man's manual dexterity and costs as much as a larger and

---

[1] From Benjamin L. Wild (2015). To Have and To Hold: Masculinity and the Clutch Bag, Critical Studies in Men's Fashion, Volume 2, Number 1, pp. 43–54, Intellect.

more practical bag is probably what accounts for its commercial success.

HANDICAPPED PEACOCKS

According to Charles Darwin's theory of sexual selection, the peacock grows bright and large tail feathers to attract female mates. His beauty is a biological trick to improve his chances of leaving more offspring and spreading his genes. This straightforward logic may convince, but Darwin neglected to explain why peahens should be attracted to large, bright plumage in the first place. A possible answer is that the peacock's tail is a deliberate 'handicap', a term coined by Amotz Zahavi, who suggested that 'the peacock uses his large tail to advertise to the peahens that his genes are of such quality he can afford to drag his long, ungainly, costly tail around behind him and still survive' (Pagel, 2012: 154). As Mark Pagel explains:

> [T]he females' aesthetic preferences now evolve for a good reason: the 'medium is the message' in Marshall McLuhan's memorable phrase. Here the medium is a wasteful display whose message is, 'you can believe me'. It is a symbol of something greater lurking underneath, and this is why the peahens prefer it. (2012: 155)

The biological traits of the peacock are relevant to our query about the clutch bag because humans have long exhibited 'handicaps' to gain social recognition. Pagel continues his discussion with reference to Thorstein Veblen, whose nineteenth-century study of the American Leisure Class profoundly influenced discussions about status expenditure by enunciating the concept of conspicuous consumption, a spectacular form of 'handicapping'. By actively pursuing costly pursuits and conspicuously squandering key resources, not least time and manual labour, the wealthy revealed their formidable financial resources and unassailable position at the apex of the social pyramid. Veblen was critical of the Leisure Class' behaviour, particularly because their motive for acquiring opulent and expensive clothing was fictive; possessing limited utility, their garments were inherently ugly and became only more so as larger sums were lavished on them (1899: 116–18). But beautification was never the principle reason for such prolific expenditure; the point was to proclaim that even with such expensive, impractical and uncomfortable raiment, the elite retained their privileged position.

Sartorial analysis now downplays the role of dress in demarcating social hierarchies (Davis, 1992: 9, 59–60, 110–11), but Veblen's observations remain apposite because studies of diverse cultures, from the eighteenth-century court of Louis XIV of France to the nineteenth-century archipelagos of Melanesian New Guinea, reveal that penurious status expenditure has been necessary to maintain public authority throughout human history (Malinowski, 1961; Elias, 1969: 44–65). The clamour for branded fashion accessories in China reveals that status expenditure remains prevalent today (Soames, 2013). Highlighting the importance of status expenditure, cultural studies also show how the profligate wastage of resources has been demonstrated in a consistent manner across cultures. A common 'handicap' adopted by human males is a practically useless prop carried in one hand to symbolize singular authority. The ruler's sceptre, Field Marshall's baton and walking cane are perhaps the most iconic examples of such objects in the west. These items are uncommon today, possibly because the expansion of the Leisure Class renders 'loud' dress accessories unnecessary; subtler signifiers – or what is frequently termed 'stealth wealth' (Asome, 2014) – can serve the same function within a society cognisant of 'delicate variations in the evidences of wealth and leisure' (Veblen, 1899: 122–3), although royalty and the military still make use of them. The significance of the human hand remains, however, and has arguably increased with the advent of technology and the design of smaller handheld applications that rely on expert manual manipulation.

HAND (UN)FREE

Throughout history and across many cultures human hands have been subject to special treatment and belief because of their singular role in giving people's thoughts material form, chiefly through the evolution of the opposable thumb. At various times it was thought that washed hands conveyed moral and judicial purity; royal hands cured sickness (Bloch, 1973) and amputated limbs signified criminality; curiously, the hands of hanged felons were considered to furnish good fortune (Harris et al., 2013: 175). Gloved hands have particular associations and express temporal authority, effeminacy and formality (McDowell, 2013: 90–3). To hold something in the hands is to signify intent. Objects are carried for specific purposes and in the majority of situations this involves doing something active. The object thereby references the power of human agency, a person's labour and thought. To hold a practically useless object, therefore, is to claim a higher social position because of the immediate implication that other people are labouring, even thinking, on behalf of the object holder, whose labour and thought is being reserved for something else, something that is supposedly more significant.

During the eighteenth century, no well-heeled gentleman would have ventured out of doors without a cane. Some men would have needed support for their daily perambulations, but the vast majority carried their highly polished, intricately carved and exquisitely embellished stick as a status symbol. Held insouciantly, and rendering one hand useless, the cane suggested its owner enjoyed a surfeit of time. Depending on quality, the cane also indicated that its owner possessed sufficient disposable income. The cane, unless genuinely needed as a walking aid, has become a historical curiosity, much like the sceptre – although in 1967 Mohammad Reza Pahlavi carried a gold gem-studded sceptre during his lavish coronation (Gaulme and Gaulme, 2012: 240–1). His western-style regalia and subsequent clothing reforms were an attempt to demonstrate the legitimacy and modernity of Iran (Chehabi, 1993). Whilst sceptres and canes are no longer de rigueur, men reveal a lingering preference for hand-occupying items through their choice of luggage. The tote, messenger and rucksack all have shoulder straps and have enjoyed moments of wide popularity. The rucksack is presently in vogue along with other aspects of 1990s popular culture, but the briefcase or satchel is the most common form of holdall used by men and they are almost invariably carried by hand.

The briefcase, a rigid, box-shaped case carried by means of a single handle and typically measuring 340×470×130mm, alludes to a man's social seniority, for he does not need to use his hands to make his living. It signifies a life of comfort and, depending on its quality, affluence. In his best-selling book, 'wardrobe engineer' John T. Molloy suggested:

> Attaché cases are always positive symbols of success, regardless of what they carry, a lot more of them than you think are used only to carry lunch. (1975: 157)

These sartorial significations are hard to demonstrate empirically although recent advertising research has emphasized men's sensitivity to financial messages and inclination to compare their earnings with the people around them (Gulas and McKeage, 2000: 20; Tungate, 2008: 219); sartorial props, the significance of which has been discussed by Erving Goffman (1959), therefore play an important role in framing men's public profile. This could elucidate the commercial success of the men's luxury luggage sector. Between 2009 and 2013, the global market for men's luxury luggage increased 25.4 per cent; over the same period, the total market for menswear products increased 15.6 per cent (Crompton, 2013). Correlatively, retailers from Dunhill to Mulberry are now investing more money to expand their lines in male luggage; one such item is the clutch bag. If the briefcase is a sartorial handicap signifying social distinction, the more expensive and impractical clutch potentially makes a more clamorous statement about the wealth and social confidence of its owner.

THE END OF MEN

There are two likely reasons why the clutch bag is becoming ubiquitous in *Style* magazines and on the street at this particular moment in time (Brooks and Hayward, 2013): first, the long-running discussion about men's societal role in our post-industrial society, which has become increasingly critical following the banking crisis of 2008, and second, the recent popularity of the top-handle bag among women.

Sociological models, not least Norbert Elias' civilizing process, have long noted that developments within society engender changes in people's self-perception (1987: 167–8). Sartorial studies, in particular, have suggested that the advent of a post-industrial society has acutely affected men's self-perception and presentation (Craik, 1993: 177–8; Crane, 2000: 171). The banking crisis has given discussions about men's role and appearance a greater significance and an increasingly fatalistic slant. The argument that men will become redundant in a society that lauds cooperation over competition, brains over brawn and empathy over egotism, was initiated by Hanna Rosin (2010). Following her lead, commentators and politicians have cited the increased frequency of diet-related illness (Cohen, 2012), the preponderance of adolescents turning to crime (Abbott, 2013), and the wistful longing for maverick leaders (Bekiempis, 2011), as symptoms of men's societal displacement and deepening disillusionment. With regard to dress, Fred Davis is right to stress the difficulty of connecting 'great political and economic developments' and fashion trends (1992: 133), but Charles Baudelaire's pithy observation that innovations in clothing and avant-garde styles of dress become prevalent during moments of confusion and transition rings anecdotally true (Irvin and Brewer, 2013: 16); presently, men's clothing is becoming increasingly expressive with its cut, colour and texture and dandical dress is attracting new adherents (Adams, 2013; Irvin and Brewer, 2013).

The emergence of the postmodern dandy is of particular note because it highlights the fact that recent influences for menswear collections have been conspicuously time bound and reference historic periods when men appeared prosperous and their social position commensurately secure. It seems hardly coincidental that many of the accessories that men have recently adopted, from braces, boutonnières, pocket squares and tie pins, to monk shoes, moustaches and slicked hairstyles, hark back to the 1930s and 1980s, two decades when men's fortunes were ascendant and the basic shape of their wardrobe became fixed (Crane, 2000: 173–4).

The displacement that men are said to be feeling is correlative with the sense of loneliness that all people can encounter as society develops and becomes increasingly complex (Elias, 1987: 105–6). Feeling isolated in the present, and uncertain about their future, it is explicable that men would seek reassurance in the past. The clutch bag, which is a conspicuous form of sartorial handicapping because it is pricey and impractical, references, akin to the other accessories that are currently available for them, a time when their financial, political and social position seemed unassailable. Materially, the clutch bag confers a confidence on its owner that present circumstances have denuded him of. But the clutch bag is more than a figurative security blanket. In light of women's renewed interest in the top-handle bag, it could also be seen as an aggressive reassertion of men's traditional gendered role as provider.

WOMEN DOING IT FOR THEMSELVES

The top-handle bag, which Harrods reported to be one of the most popular styles for autumn/winter 2013 (Shi, 2013), has a similar signification for women as the briefcase does for men because it is similarly restrictive and expensive; the same is true of the midi bag (Asome, 2014). It signifies the disposable income, leisure and luxury that professional women can now access and enjoy (cf. Boyd, 2014). Serena Boardman, senior global real estate adviser and associate broker at Sotheby's Realty owns a Hermès Bolide Bugatti and opines:

> A handheld bag has something special about it – it evokes memories of a kinder, less harried, gentler, more ladylike time. (Shi, 2013)

The top-handle bag is also capable of making an assertive statement about women's ability to challenge men, chiefly because of its association with former British Prime Minister Margaret Thatcher and her inimitable approach to political discourse. The verb to 'hand-bag' – 'to verbally attack or crush (a person or idea) ruthlessly and forcefully' – entered the Oxford English Dictionary because of Thatcher's combative approach to chairing ministerial meetings and her iconic Launer handbag, sales of which increased 53 per cent after her death (Bergin, 2013).

The present popularity of the top-handle bag is significant because whilst women use sartorial props to demonstrate their social standing – when they wave a fan, carry a clutch bag to an evening event or, like men, use a mobile telephone – they have rarely limited their manual dexterity by carrying a practically useless prop. This is possibly because they wish to distance themselves from the dominant clothing discourse of the nineteenth century that had made mannequins of them to demonstrate the social prosperity of their significant male relatives, to whom they were supposedly subordinate (Crane, 2000: 100). However, as Diana Crane has argued, whilst many women conformed to Victorian sartorial mores, a significant minority wore 'alternative dress', clothes that 'incorporated items from men's clothing, such as ties, men's hats, suit jackets, waistcoats, and men's shirts, sometimes singly, sometimes in combination with one another, but always associated with items of fashionable female clothing' (2000: 101). Through non-verbal communication and symbolic inversion, women attempted to show that their gendered role and power could, and should, be coequal with men's (2000: 128).

The present popularity of the top-handle bag among women could be viewed in a similar light; namely, as the adoption of a characteristically male sartorial trait to demonstrate socio-economic parity. In the context of recent discussions about the redundancy of men's societal role in political forums (Abbott, 2013), newspapers (Armstrong, 2013b; Mills, 2013; Gratton, 2013) and books (Rosin, 2012; Gerzema and D'Antonio, 2013), the prevalence of the top-handle bag could signify more. It could suggest that women are now able to surpass men. The adoption of the clutch bag by men, therefore, could be an attempt to reassert their social hegemony, or at least gain equality. Whilst this battle of the bags is inevitably difficult to determine empirically, innovations within the design and distribution of clothing worn by one of the sexes rarely occurs without parallel changes in the other, chiefly because societal changes typically affect both sexes simultaneously (Craik, 1993: 198–9).

CONCLUSION

Prima facie, the appeal of the male clutch bag is difficult to determine because it is impractical and expensive when compared with similar forms of male luggage. The bag's popularity becomes more explicable in the context of the present socio-economic climate and the historic significance of social handicapping to demonstrate status. By virtue of its cost and impracticality, the clutch bag is a sartorial handicap that seeks to demonstrate the continued strength of men's socio-economic status. In so doing, the bag follows recent trends in menswear accessories that have referenced periods, chiefly the 1930s and 1980s, when men's social position seemed unassailable. The implication is that through the acquisition of objects signifying disposable income, and thus demonstrating socio-economic worth, men can regain their societal footing, or at least peace of mind. The clutch bag seems to be a more assertive, perhaps even aggressive, example of this trend, however, because its emergence coincides with the popularity of the top-handle bag among women. If the top-handle bag is a material manifestation of women's ability to challenge men's societal role – ably amplified by its association with Margaret Thatcher – the male clutch bag could be a countervailing sartorial response. This conclusion is theoretical, but it has significant implications for sartorial studies that consider the connections between men and women's fashions, the communicative ability of clothes and, perhaps above all, the extent to which disparate designers and consumers can foster a coherent discourse through dress.

References

Abbott, Dianne. (2013). "Britain's Crisis of Masculinity." A Demos Twentieth Birthday Lecture, Magdalen House, London, May 16.

Adams, Nathaniel. (2013). *I Am A Dandy: The Return Of The Elegant Gentleman*. Berlin: Gestalten.

Armstrong, Stephen (2013a). "Bronze Age Man." *The Sunday Times: Style*, March 17, 62.

Armstrong, Stephen. (2013b). "How to Make Men a Laughing Stock." *The Sunday Times: Culture Magazine*, May 19, 14–15.

Asome, Carolyn (2014). "The Rise of the Midi Bag." *The Times*, February 5, 6.

Bekiempis, Victoria. (2011). "The Cowboy in Crisis, or Male Anxiety in American Politics." *The Guardian*, June 28. http://www.theguardian.com/commentisfree/cifamerica/2011/oct/25/cowboy-crisis-male-anxiety. Accessed January 2014.

Bergin, Olivia. (2013). "Sales of Margaret Thatcher's Handbag Double." *T Fashion*, April 17. http://fashion.

telegraph.co.uk/article/TMG10001436/Sales-of-Margaret-Thatchers-handbag-double.html. Accessed April 2013.

Bloch, Marc. (1973). *The Royal Touch: Sacred Monarchy and Scrofula in England and France*. Trans. J. E. Anderson. London: Routledge & Kegan Paul.

Boyd, Annita. (2014). "Oh, Honey! It's Not So Much the Style, It's What Carrying It Means: Hermès Bags and the Transformative Process." *Fashion, Style & Popular Culture*, 1(1): 81–96.

Brooks, Chris and Catherine Hayward. (2013). "Thursday afternoon." *Esquire: The Big Black Book*, Spring/Summer, pp. 144–53.

Chehabi, Houchang E. (1993). "Staging the Emperor's new clothes: Dress codes and nation-building under Reza Shah." *Iranian Studies*, 26: 3–4, pp. 209–33.

Cohen, Richard (2012). "James Bond and the new sex appeal." *The Washington Post*, 26 November, http://www.washingtonpost.com/opinions/richard-cohen-james-bond-and-the-new-sex-appeal/2012/11/26/098813e6-37f4-11e2-8a97-363b0f9a0ab3_story.html. Accessed January 2013.

Craik, Jennifer (1993). *The Face of Fashion: Cultural Studies in Fashion*, London: Routledge.

Crane, Diana (2000). *Fashion and Its Social Agendas: Class, Gender, and Identity in Clothing*, Chicago: The University of Chicago Press.

Crompton, Simon (2013). "The big bag theory." *Financial Times: Life & Arts*, 12/13 October, p. 4.

Davis, Fred (1992). *Fashion, Culture, and Identity*, Chicago: The University of Chicago Press.

Elias, Norbert (1969). *The Court Society* (trans. E. Jephcott), New York: Pantheon Books.

Elias, Norbert (1987). *The Society of Individuals* (ed. Michael Schröter and trans. E. Jephcott). London: Basil Blackwell.

Gaulme, Dominique and François Gaulme. (2012). *Power & Style: A World History of Politics and Dress*. Paris: Flammarion.

Gerzema, John and Michael D'Antonio. (2013). *The Athena Doctrine: How Women (And Men Who Think Like Them) Will Rule The Future*, San Francisco: Josse-Bass.

Goffman, Erving (1959). *The Presentation of the Self in Everyday Life*, London: Penguin.

Gratton, Lynda (2013). "Make room at the top." *Financial Times: Life & Arts*, May 4/5, p. 8.

Gulas, Charles S. and Kim McKeage. (2000). "Extending social comparison: An examination of the unintended consequences of idealized advertising imagery." *Journal of Advertising*, 29: 2, pp. 17–28.

Harris, Oliver J. T., John Robb and Sarah Tarlow. (2013). "The body in the age of knowledge." in John Robb and Oliver J. T. Harris (eds.), *The Body in History: Europe from the Palaeolithic to the Future*, pp. 164–95. Cambridge: Cambridge University Press.

Irvin, Kate and Laurie Anne Brewer (2013). *Artist, Rebel, Dandy: Men of Fashion*, Museum of Art, Rhode Island School of Design: Yale University Press.

Malinowski, Bronislaw (1961). *Argonauts of the Western Pacific: An Account of Native Enterprise and Adventure in the Archipelagoes of Melanesian New Guinea*, Illinois: Waveland Press Inc.

McDowell, Colin (2013). *The Anatomy of Fashion: Why We Dress The Way We Do*, London: Phaidon.

Mills, Eleanor (2013). "We don't make men like we used to." *The Sunday Times*, May 19, p. 4.

Molloy, John T. (1975). *Dress For Success*, New York: Warner Books.

Pagel, Mark (2012). *Wired for Culture: The Natural History of Human Cooperation*, London: Allen Lane.

Rosin, Hanna (2010). "The end of men." *The Atlantic*, 8 June, http://www.theatlantic.com/magazine/archive/2010/07/the-end-of-men/308135/. Accessed December 2012.

Rosin, Hanna (2012). *The End Of Men: And The Rise of Women*, London: Viking.

Shi, Jim (2013). "It's all in your hands." *Financial Times: Life & Arts*, September 28/29, 6.

Soames, Gemma (2013). "Orient express." *The Sunday Times: Style*, November 18, p. 35.

Tungate, Mark (2008). *The Branded Male: Marketing to Men*, London: Koran Page.

Veblen, Thorstein (1899). *The Theory of the Leisure Class*, Oxford: Oxford University Press.

FURTHER READING

Barry, Ben and Martin Dylan, (2015), "Dapper Dudes: Young Men's Fashion Consumption and Expressions of Masculinity, *Critical Studies in Men's Fashion*, Volume 2, Number 1, pp 5–21, Intellect.

Crane, D. (2012), *Fashion and its social agendas: Class, gender, and identity in clothing*. Chicago University of Chicago Press.

Gale, Colin and Jasbir Kaur (2004), *Fashion and Textiles: An Overview*, Oxford: Berg.

Lynch, Annette and Michael D. Strauss, (2007) *Changing Fashion: A Critical Introduction to Trend Analysis and Meaning*, Oxford: Berg.

Mackinney-Valentin, M. (2017), *Fashioning Identity: Status Ambivalence in Contemporary Fashion*. London: Bloomsbury Publishing.

Robbins, R. H. (1973), Identity, Culture, and Behavior. In: J. J. Honigmann (ed.). *Handbook of Social and Cultural Anthropology*, 1199–1222. Chicago, IL: Rand McNally.

Sweetman, P. (1999). Anchoring the (postmodern) self? Body modification, fashion and identity. *Body & society*, 5(2–3), 51–76.

Figure 34 Nick Wooster, Photo Courtesy of Brent Luvaas.
Source: Brent Luvaas

PART X

Global Fashion and Reinvention

Figure 35 Fashion Diva Photo Courtesy of Brent Luvaas.
Source: Brent Luvaas

INTRODUCTION

Brent Luvaas

Waiting in line for the runway shows at Jakarta Fashion Week (JFW) in late October of 2016, it was almost impossible to avoid appearing in other peoples' selfies. Packs of hijab and sneaker-clad twenty-somethings continuously snapped shots of each other on their widescreen smart phones, while I sipped my sugar-saturated, sponsor-provided "flat white" coffee and attempted to disappear into the background. I kept seeing my black baseball cap, pulled down over my eyes like the world's least subtle special agent, popping up behind a shoulder or between a pair of heads on small shiny plastic screens in front of me. *Selfie collateral damage*, I called it in a tweet that I posted while queuing.

These were not my first fashion events in Indonesia. I had been coming to the Southeast Asian archipelago for study and research for some twenty years prior to this, and much of my earlier work had focused on independent streetwear brands like Invictus and Unkl347 (Luvaas, 2012). Indonesia has hundreds of those, each with its own distinctive logo and aesthetic, each staking its local claim on a set of global urban trends. But these were my first fashion events since the advent of the smart phone, and the smart phone—or at least it felt like, waiting in line at JFW—changes everything. Fashion shows aren't just an advertisement for upcoming collections anymore. They are a mass smart phone simulcast.

When the lights went out at the start of each event, the candle-like glow of the audience's phones went on. It created a ghostly effect, like a graveyard swarming with fireflies. Nearly everyone in the audience seemed to be recording the shows, posting them to Instagram, streaming them on Snapchat. No wonder JFW's sponsors saw them as such a great opportunity for exposure. Each show was preceded by at least 15 minutes of commercials: Batik Air airlines, Bakmi Mewah "gourmet" instant noodles, some local brand of sensitive teeth toothpaste. I couldn't imagine such blatant commercialism being tolerated at New York Fashion Week. New York's fashion crowd is too determined to mask the marketing function of their events. Fashion masquerades as art. JFW is less concerned with maintaining that pretense. Commercialism is worn like a shiny badge of honor. Many of the most prominent shows at JFW were even sponsored by government bodies, eager to connect themselves with the commercial splendor: "The Embassy of India Presents Eka," "Council of Fashion Designers of Korea Presents Toton," "Indonesia Fashion Forward Presents Bateeq, Byo, and Etu by Restu Anggraini."

Jakarta Fashion Week, in short, was a cross promotional free for all. After each show, a stream of fashion bloggers and other would-be social media influencers would meander over to the broad concrete walkway before Senayan City, the luxury, high-rise shopping center where Jakarta Fashion Week is held, to snap outfit-of-the-day (OOTD) posts for their social media feeds. Some of Southeast Asia's most prominent bloggers attend these events: Diana Rikasari (Indonesia, 219,000 Instagram followers), Raja Nadia Sabrina (Malaysia, 117,000 Instagram followers), and Dian Pelangi (Indonesia, 4.4 million Instagram followers), and each of them does their own personal reporting on the proceedings. Indonesian movie and music stars do too, serving as their own PR agents and marketing companies. And to catch the whole self-promotional extravaganza (for their own blogs, Instagram, and Snapchat feeds, no less), a few, lonely street style photographers hunch near the crosswalk that connects the shopping center to the tent, snapping 'candids' of the celebrities and influencers as they trickle past. At JFW, this is a relatively slow and boring thing to do. The shows start only once an hour, and there is generally only one going on at a time. Most people hang out in the waiting lounge before each show. The photographers, absent a crowd to shoot, mainly just sit on the curb, staring at their sneakers and smart phones, until security guards tell them to wander elsewhere.

To keep themselves occupied, the street style photographers turn to the models, lanky and leggy, and still made up according to the distinctive, exaggerated visions of whatever designer they were recently walking for, as they head over to the mall to get food and window-shop. At least half of the models are Indonesian, stars of local magazine editorials and cosmetic campaigns. The other half are white Europeans, mostly temporary immigrants from Eastern bloc countries. They hit Southeast Asia on route to bigger fashion destinations. Here, they work with local photographers and designers to gain experience and build their portfolios in the hopes that they can someday use those portfolios to attract agencies in New York, Paris, and London. For Indonesian fashion brands, the Eastern European models are a mark of transnational sophistication. For the models, however, Indonesia is just a cultural backwater, some place they pass through on their way to somewhere else. It is a layover, not a destination.

Jakarta Fashion Week, like dozens of similar fashion weeks happening in cities around the world, is at once a profoundly global event and a spectacular display of local insularity. Featuring some 250 designers in its most recent iteration, it is a grand, national pageant, an effort, by the government, local brands, and various invested parties, to reinvent Indonesian fashion for an imagined global audience. It is also a continual nagging reminder that no matter how big and grandiose it has become, how diverse and refined its apparel, it still pales in importance to the fashion weeks happening elsewhere. Outside Southeast Asia, few people are paying attention to JFW. It is not on the itineraries of international fashion journalists. It is skipped over by leading industry buyers and trend watchers. Jakarta remains stuck in fashion's third world (Luvaas, 2013), a peripheral city in an increasingly global industry.

THE STRUGGLE FOR REINVENTION IN GLOBAL FASHION

The global circuits of fashion, the chapters in this section remind us, are not creating a level playing field between fashion's disparate centers. They are, instead, concentrating money and influence in a few urban hubs (Sassen, 1996), "fashion's world cities" as David Gilbert (2006) has referred to them. These include, most notably, New York, London, Paris, and Milan (see Reinach, this volume). New York remains the center of commercial mass-produced fashion (Moon, 2009), Paris of couture (Gilbert, 2006), London of avant garde (Breward, 2004), and Milan of ready-to-wear (see Reinach, this volume), even as growing economic powers, particularly in China (see Tsui, this volume), inject hundreds of millions of dollars in the effort to shift the centers of creative production to their own home terrain. In the globalized fashion industry today, there are two kinds of fashion cities: the ones where fashion is dreamed up, designed, and marketed, and the ones where the actual manufacturing of apparel takes place. It doesn't take a lot to recognize which type of city receives the bulk of prestige. The globalization of fashion is thus a hierarchical process of simultaneous *de-materialization* (Hardt and Negri, 2001; Lazzarato, 1996), the replacement of material production with less material, more intellectual labor, and *proletarianization* (Harvey, 2005), the conversion of a country's workforce into the manufacturers of other peoples' products. Indonesia, despite its best efforts at reinvention, remains firmly entrenched in the latter process.

Indonesia may be home to many of the factories where brands like Ralph Lauren, Ben Sherman, and the Gap produce their clothes. It may also be home to hundreds of talented designers, often trained in the West, who fuse cutting edge aesthetics with traditional dying and weaving techniques. And it may even have become a major shopping destination for people in neighboring countries, with luxury brands like Gucci, Saint Laurent, and Burberry readily available in Jakarta's innumerable upscale malls. But it is barely a blip on the fashion world map. The places that actually matter to fashion—New York, Paris, London, Milan, and increasingly Tokyo, Seoul, and Shanghai—are thousands of miles away.

The chapters in this section also remind us, however, that despite the structural inequity of the global fashion industry, despite the near unidirectional influence of west to east, north to south, it remains premature—if not outright incorrect—to see the cultural product of the global fashion industry as a transnational uniformity of dress and taste. Global fashion, to be sure, has its clothing staples (see Maynard, this volume): T-shirts (Carbone and Johnson, 2011), sneakers (Kawamura, 2016), jeans (Miller and Woodward, 2012). But, it also becomes localized in various and often in unpredictable ways as it travels from place to place (see Maynard, this volume). Business button downs are printed over with batik in urban Java; American workwear is re-imagined, even in its meticulous recreation, by denim enthusiasts in Japan (Keet, 2015). Moreover, the globalization of fashion puts greater emphasis on the distinctiveness of national costume (see Maynard, this volume). Chinese designers take pains to inject something of their own cultural legacy in the clothes they produce (see Tsui, this volume). Australians deliberate at length on the proper way to include indigenous motifs on board shorts and t-shirts (see Craik, this volume).

Globalization, then, is not a simple, one-way process. It is not a flattening out of fashion terrain. It is complex and contradictory, producing meaningful local and national hybrids, even as it sweeps up the most remote provinces into its massive, transnational web.

Lastly, the chapters in this section remind us that the globalization of fashion is neither new nor final. There is, indeed, something almost preposterous about applying the term "globalization" to fashion, as if the apparel industry in the west were breaking new ground by engaging in international trade. Fashion, at least if we are using the broadest possible definition, as simply a synonym for "dress" (Eicher, 1999), has already been global for centuries (see Maynard, this volume). Textiles, inks, dyes, and fully realized items of clothing have been among the most traded items between disparate peoples as far as back as the historical and archeological records can go. The broad circulation of second-hand clothing, as Hansen discusses at length in her chapter in this section, may be new, but the circulation of clothing itself is as old as trade.

Even, however, if we are using a narrower definition of "fashion," as, that is, a historically specific process of artificially generating novelty in clothing and style (Lipovetsky, 2002), globalization is nothing new to fashion. Paul Poiret, often credited with being Paris' first master couturier, drew heavily from "Oriental" motifs, which, in his day and age, largely meant an exaggerated, fetishized version of what women were wearing in the Middle East. Contemporary fashion designers in the United States and Europe, likewise, find continual inspiration from China, India, Southeast Asia, South America, and Africa. And despite a much more pronounced flow from west to east, it is also important to point out that this isn't the only way fashion moves. As the work of Dorine Kondo (1997) reminds us, Japanese designers like Rei Kawakubo and Yohji Yamamoto played a significant role in defining the look and feel of Parisian couture in the mid-1990s.

Yet, it is evident to even the most casual observer that fashion today is *more* global than ever before—more caught up in the currents and frictions (Tsing, 2005) of global capital, more accelerated in its pace and flow (Harvey, 1989). Motifs and silhouettes circulate with an unprecedented speed. New collections are visible throughout the world through their simultaneous broadcast on social media and websites. Transnational fast fashion brands like Uniqlo, H&M, and Zara are now even more transnational, with stores in urban, and suburban, centers in countries around the world. We need some way of talking about and theorizing these transformations. The chapters in this section go some distance towards doing so.

Perhaps another snapshot from my recent excursion to Southeast Asia helps illustrate what is at stake in this conversation. On the final day of Jakarta Fashion Week 2016, I picked up and took off for Singapore. The small island city state, just an hour and a half by plane from Jakarta, was in the midst of its own fashion week. I was curious to compare it to Jakarta's. In many ways, there was no comparison. Jakarta's fashion week featured more than 250 brands, while Singapore's came just shy of 20. Jakarta Fashion Week was jam packed with events, while Singapore Fashion Week could barely fill a few afternoons and evenings. And Jakarta Fashion Week spilled out into the shopping area around it, drawing in onlookers and would-be influencers determined to use the event for their own self-promotion, while Singapore Fashion Week took place inside the stately National Gallery, an elite crowd in high-end couture sipping Absolute Elyx cocktails on a balcony overlooking the city. Singapore Fashion Week felt like a vanity event for the city's idle rich. Yet, there I was, sipping free cocktails along with the rest of them.

I should have been sad to leave the relatively ethnographically rich field site of JFW for SFW. But I was doing research on social media influencers in Jakarta, and many of the biggest social media influencers I had been researching had already left for Singapore. I knew this from following their Instagram feeds. Olivia Lazuardy (207,000 Instagram followers), Anastasia Siantar (304,000 Instagram followers), and others were posing for photos at swanky Swarovski Crystal events, while their countrymen's designs were parading down the Jakarta runway. Why? It's pretty simple really. Singapore has money, lots of it, and its companies pay Indonesian social media stars to come to their events. Plus, far more people in the global fashion industry are paying attention to these events than Jakarta Fashion Week. Indonesia's social media influencers know that it pays—both financially and in terms of the reach of their influence—to go to SFW.

Despite its diminutive size, Singapore is already the finance and trade capital of Southeast Asia. Its deep-pocketed government and businesses are now determined to reinvent it as a fashion capital as well. As the chapters in this section demonstrate, fashion is deeply wound up in larger projects of nation-building and economic development. It is never *just fashion*. Singapore knows that. It is eager to exploit the fashion mystique to enhance other sectors of the Singapore economy. Unfortunately, they do not have much of a local pool of designers to draw from in order to do so. What they do have are the clout and financial resources to import designers from elsewhere to help draw the fashion world's eyes to the city. This year's "headliners" were Naeem Khan and Self Portrait, both based in New York City.

The global circulation of fashion is not just about the circulation of goods and services, then; it is also about the circulation of people. With Raf Simons from Belgium to Paris to New York. Naeem Khan from India to New York to Singapore, and Olivia Lazuardy from Jakarta to Singapore (I also, by the way, once ran into her at New York Fashion Week). Would-be industry insiders follow the flow of opportunity, and a fashion "brain drain" draws talent from south to north, east to west. The legacy of colonialism lives on.

Singapore, like Jakarta, would like to change that directional flow. Both cities hope to challenge the entrenched hierarchies that continue to animate global fashion today and to reinvent themselves as fashion world cities. They have quite a struggle ahead of them, one that social media "democratization" has yet to neutralize. It is this struggle, above all, that defines the circulation of fashion today: the struggle between hubs of design, manufacture, and consumption; the struggle to matter on a global scale; the struggle to redefine and reinvent one's place within a rapidly shifting—yet stubbornly persistent—transnational fashion landscape.

The following chapters address aspects of that struggle for reinvention in different national contexts. Maynard provides an overview of processes of globalization in fashion, with particular attention on the processes of reinvention that happen at the local level. Hansen traces the transnational pathways of clothing once they have left their traditional life cycle, how second-hand clothes become reinvented in new contexts. Tsui and Craik both chronicle the efforts of national fashion scenes to redefine themselves in the wake of globalization. Also, Reinach outlines the shifting terrain of ready-to-wear in its historic global center, showing how Milan became a fashion city in the first place and questioning how it moves forward from here.

References

Breward, Christopher. (2004). *The London Look: Fashion from Street to Catwalk*. New Haven: Yale University Press.
Carbone, Bradley and Noah Johnson. (2011). "An Oral History of the Graphic T-Shirt." *Complex*, Vol. 2011: http://www.complex.com/.
Eicher, Joanne. (1999). *Dress and Ethnicity: Change Across Space and Time*. Oxford Berg.
Gilbert, David. (2006). Fr*om Paris to Shanghai: The Changing Geography of Fashion's World Cities*. In: C. Breward and D. Gilbert (eds.), Fashion's World Cities, 3–32. Oxford: Berg.
Hardt, Michael and Antonio Negri. (2001). *Empire*. Cambridge: Harvard University Press.

Harvey, David. (1989). *The Condition of Postmodernity: An Enquiry into the Origins of Cultural Change.* Malden and Oxford: Blackwell Publishers.
Harvey, David. (2005). *A Brief History of Neoliberalism.* Oxford and New York: Oxford University Press.
Kawamura, Yuniya. (2016). *Sneakers: Fashion, Gender, and Subculture.* London: Bloomsbury.
Keet, Philomena. (2015). Making New Vintage Jeans in Japan: Relocating Authenticity. Textile: *The Journal of Cloth and Culture,* 9(1):44–61.
Lazzarato, Maurizio. (1996). Immaterial Labor. In: P. Virno and M. Hardt, (eds.). *Radical Thought in Italy: A Potential Politics,* 133–50. Minneapolis, MN: University of Minnesota Press.
Lipovetsky, Gilles. (2002). *The Empire of Fashion: Dressing Modern Democracy.* Princeton and Oxford: Princeton University Press.
Luvaas, Brent. (2012). *DIY Style: Fashion, Music, and Global Digital Cultures.* London and New York: Berg.
Brent, Luuvas. (2013). Third World No More: Re-Branding Indonesian Streetwear. *Fashion Practice* 5(2):203–228.
Miller, Daniel, and Sophie Woodward. (2012). *Blue Jeans: The Art of the Ordinary.* Berkeley: University of California Press.
Moon, Christina H. (2009). From Factories to Fashion: An Intern's Experience of New York as a Global Fashion Capital. In: E. Paulicelli and H. Clark, (eds.), *The Fabric of Cultures: Fashion, Identity, and Globalization,* 194–210. London and New York, NY: Routledge.
Sassen, Saskia. (1996). A New Geography of Centers and Margins: Summary and Implications. In: R. T. LeGates and F. Stout (eds.), *The City Reader,* 69–74. London and New York, NY: Routledge.
Tsing, Anna Lowenhaupt. (2005). *Fiction: An Ethnography of Global Connection.* Princeton, NJ and Oxford: Princeton University Press

44

IS AUSTRALIAN FASHION AND DRESS DISTINCTIVELY AUSTRALIAN?

Jennifer Craik[1]

INTRODUCTION: THE PROBLEM OF DEFINING NATIONAL DRESS

How do we define a style of dress or particular garments as distinctively national in character? There are some forms of dress that are automatically identified as a form of national dress: kimonos as Japanese, Aloha floral shirts as Hawaiian, berets as French, clogs as Dutch, saris as Indian, Mao jackets as Chinese, ponchos as Tibetan, sombreros as Mexican, "plus fours" as Scottish, batik shirts as Indonesian, and Mother Hubbard dresses as South Pacific Islander, and so on. Many of these forms of national dress are customary or anthropological forms of dress that may be traditional or reinvented as forms of national dress. More often than not, they are *not* worn as everyday dress in contemporary societies. Even so, they may be recognized as distinctively emblematic of a particular culture or nation.

But some forms of clothes and dress styles are not so easily assigned to a particular culture, for example, T-shirts, cargo pants, runners or trainers, parkas, business shirts or stilettos. These are regarded as "global" items of clothing that might be worn anywhere. This is despite the fact that they may have emerged from particular cultures (such as "baseball" caps from North America that are now worn everywhere and often worn in that culturally specific but irritating back-to-front manner of baseball stars, elite tennis players, and rappers).

This article explores the succession of ways in which the Australianness of fashion has been defined and articulated. Three version of "Australianness" are examined: first, the transformation of traditional *"bush wear"* from practical everyday dress worn in the rugged outback into high-street fashion popular not just in Australian cities but globally; second, the centrality of *swimwear and surfwear* in iconic representations of the outdoors and casual Australian way of life as well as a central motif of generations of Australian fashion; and third, the incorporation of, on the one hand, *Australiana* imagery and, on the other, appropriation of *indigenous motifs* in the fabric and surface design of clothes as part of periodic obsessions with defining national identity and the associated symbols of national culture. In cycles of transforming dress into fashion (and sometimes anti-fashion), these three forms of "Australianness" have dominated the sense of distinctive codes of dress that have underpinned the idea of Australian style.

These three modalities address respectively: a sense of *place*; a sense of *body*; and a sense of *cultural heritage*. By oscillating between these modalities, they have become the rationale for an emergent sense of Australian style that encapsulates post-colonial heritage and contemporary themes of national identity.

Australia is not the only place where an obsession with the components and rules of national dress has occurred. Similar trends have been observed in other former British colonies and dominions such as New Zealand (Wolfe, 2001) and Canada (Palmer, 2004; Routh, 1993). In each place, derivative European dress codes competed with embryonic local modes of dress

---

[1] From Jennifer Craik, Is Australian Fashion and Dress Distinctively Australian? Fashion Theory, Volume 13, Issue 4, 2009, Taylor & Francis.

as well as incorporating—at different moments—aspects of "indigenous" design and culture; in the case of Canada, the stylistic forms of Inuit and First Peoples, while, in New Zealand, Maori and Polynesian motifs and decorative traditions (such as tattooing). In each case, distinctive dress codes emerged in response to climate and lifestyle as well as reflecting changing ideas about national character (Craik, 2002).

In all three countries, early settlers faced the challenges of surviving in severe and isolated communities necessitating a preoccupation with the practicalities of providing food and shelter. Yet, clothing was also a preoccupation. Sourcing fabric and garments was essential and industries were quickly established in each country to import, manufacture, and sell clothing. Some of these clothes were intended for the farmers and remote subsistence communities in rugged landscapes and extreme climates, while other clothes were aimed at the city and town communities of administrators, trades people, blue-collar workers, and professionals. From the outset, then, there were competing and very different clothing genres in these colonies and dominions.

In Australia, clothing history has been preoccupied with the convict beginnings and settlement of the bush. Margaret Maynard (2001), for example, identifies the following themes: the stranglehold of the "bush" myth and obsession with the rugged landscape; a preoccupation with leisure; an ongoing tussle with moral conservatism and exhibitionism; a predilection for outdoor pursuits such as swimming, surfing, and tanning the body; the centrality of Australian fauna and flora in national identity; and the appropriation of indigenous and migrant stylistic traditions. These themes have shaped the development of distinctive Australian fashion and dress, and how its history has been written.

In many other countries and cultures, however, debates about national dress are a vibrant and recurring feature. I have argued elsewhere (Craik, 2002: 460) that a national sense of style or fashion is the expressive encapsulation of the cultural psyche or *zeitgeist* of a place through its people that occurs when three realms are synchronized: *aesthetics, cultural practice,* and *cultural articulation.*

The *aesthetic dimension* refers to the distinctiveness and recognizability of clothing styles, including the choice and habitual preference for certain motifs (surface expression of identity); particular choices of garments, cut, and composition; distinctive ways of wearing clothes and combining different garments to create a particular "look"; and the cultural preference for certain fabrics and materials in the manufacture of clothes (such as cotton, wool, synthetics or silk). An Australian sense of dress, then, might be parodied as a slightly unkempt combination of informal colorful ("loud") shirt or T-shirt probably in cotton, khaki shorts or trousers, boots, wide-brimmed hat, and suntan. These may come from Country Road, Colorado, Rivers or Jeans West rather than R. M. Williams but these garments still retain their "bush" wear symbolism.

Cultural practice refers to the uptake and consumption of clothing as either everyday wear or niche wear in ways that signal specific relations between the body and the cultural domain. While local adoption is the central element, this specificity must be recognizable to those from elsewhere who may, in turn, adopt elements of the style to emulate "localness" (for example, tourist purchases of Akubra hats, Billabong surfwear, Mambo shirts, elastic-sided boots, and Okanui board shorts). Accordingly, there must be some continuity of these cultural practices reflected in effective supply, distribution, marketing, and representation.

The third dimension, *cultural articulation,* refers to the ability of the style or fashion to be projected with confidence to the point where it becomes taken-for-granted or "naturalised," such that internal and external perceptions of the essence of national stylistic identity overlap. Beachwear, for example, with logo-printed singlet (e.g. Quiksilver or Brothers Nielsen), microfiber board shorts, and thongs as footwear, is one example where internal and external perceptions coincide.

As well as considering how these shifting, competing, yet interconnected versions of Australianness came about, it is equally important to consider what happens when these fashions become old fashioned, anti-fashion or unfashionable ("dorky," crass, "folksy" or frumpy such as Bri-nylon shirts, Crimplene dresses, "terry" toweling hats or "Jesus" sandals). What are the implications of these shifting versions of Australianness and will the impetus to produce distinctively Australian fashion recede if Australia establishes a foothold in the global fashion and design arena? If so, will un-Australian fashion become the linchpin of Australian fashion culture and dress codes?

MAPPING THE RELATIONSHIP BETWEEN BODIES, CLOTHES, IDENTITIES

Australian bodies have been produced in a succession of ways that retrospectively have been identified as the true Aussie body—the stockman, the squatter, the surfer, the digger, the larrikin, and so on. My interest is the ways in which relations between the body, clothing, body decoration, and gesture interrelate and thereby produce a range of social bodies. Each body type or image is a component of clothing, accoutrement, posture, and conduct gelled into a single iconic moment (see Craik, 1984, 1994). From this range of possible Aussie looks, at any one time, one is deemed to be quintessential.

Adopting this theme, Australia's entrant in the Miss Universe 2007 contest, Kimberley Busteed, wore a red one-piece swim costume and yellow surf lifesaver's cap for the national costume parade, a choice that attracted widespread criticism for being "frumpy" (AAP, 2007; Agencies, 2007). For the 2008 competition, Australia's entrant, Laura Dundovic wore a layered chiffon gown of frills in shades that, according to its designer, "reflected the Australian landscape" in an "abstract" way—"ivories to reef blues to sky blues to really rich rust browns"—a confection that was criticized because it "didn't reflect true Aussie dress" (Melocco, 2008). This is not the only time that the problem of defining a national costume has haunted international beauty competitions. Yet, although this is a dominant stereotype of national dress, it is not the *only* image of Australianness in fashion. The three examples cited above illustrate interrelated aspects of body-clothing relations:

- revelation and concealment;
- the embodiment of national identity through surface markings of iconic representations; and
- the embodiment of national identity through clothing associated with traditional Australian body–space relations.

Considered together, they incorporate competing yet overlapping narratives of Australianness. This array of genres of "distinctive" Australian dress may have relevance for debates about national dress more generally since it suggests that there is never a single emblematic genre but successive and competing versions that play out in changing contextual circumstances.

Defining the "essence" of Australian fashion has been a constant preoccupation. In the 1980s, an Australian sense of style was defined as a combination of distinctive uses of "colour, texture and fabric and the dictates of lifestyle," namely an outdoors life which has given people "greater freedom" to choose and express themselves. Together, "the national psyche, the way of life, the particular Australian light, have helped consolidate the Australian essence" (Symons, 1983).

Yet, if these characteristics define Australianness, what does it mean to speak of un-Australianness? A term that has punctuated Australian cultural history, it has gained considerable attention and notoriety during the tenure of John Howard's conservative coalition government in Australia (1996–2007). It is difficult, nonetheless, to locate a clear definition or discussion of what the term means. In 2003, a feature article in the *Sydney Morning Herald Good Weekend Magazine* was devoted to exploring the idea of "UnAustralian-ness." One commentator defined it as a term used to "scapegoat individuals, ideas and groups with a different perspective" (Jesse Hooper, guitarist in the popular band Killing Heidi, quoted by Dapin, 2003: 20).

Often the very attempt to define Australian or national dress evokes a sense of un-Australianness, especially if the chosen image contradicts popular perceptions or embedded though perhaps not articulated ideas of Australianness. Above all, rules about national dress are contextual, applauded or tolerated in some contexts but not in others. Another example concerned reactions to the coverage of the death of wildlife adventurer, Steve Irwin, in 2006 when he was killed by a stingray while filming on the Great Barrier Reef. He had become an international icon of "Australianness" through his Australia Zoo and larger-than-life television programs (such as *The Crocodile Hunter*), and synonymous with his choice of military-style khaki shirt and shorts (also favored by his wife and children) as a quasi-uniform worn on all public occasions (even at a "formal" barbeque hosted by Australian Prime Minister, John Howard, for United States President, George Bush). Although Australians were somewhat skeptical of this sartorial statement during his life, after death, khaki became an almost mandatory way to mourn his passing with crowds outside Australia Zoo creating a khaki army.

Similar debates occur during every Commonwealth and Olympic Games over the choice of the official team uniform for the Australian team. The choice of a blue tie-dyed bomber jacket with silver lining and matching cargo pants for the Beijing 2008 Olympics once again split the nation. Arguably, there has not been a single instance where public opinion has endorsed unanimously the chosen design. As with the choice of national costume for Australian entrants in Miss World and Miss Universe competitions, there is always controversy about whether this is *really* Australian and authentically reflects Australian culture and mode of dress.

Like the aforementioned Kimberley Busteed, Australia's entrant in Miss Universe 2006, Erin McNaught, was highly favored by bookies but unplaced. Yet she made her mark in other ways, in particular by her choice of national dress (AAP, 2006). McNaught wore a sexualized version of "bush" wear and "Aussie digger" (military) uniforms, namely a slouch hat, denim jacket redolent of military dress, "indigenous" patterned singlet, mini denim "cargo style" shorts with low-slung leather belt, and stilettos with puttees and leather straps. Through her belt, was a nonchalantly slung stock whip. This was a controversial take on "bush" wear (also the icon of the Aussie "digger") ostensibly more suitable for a nightclub or Mardi Gras. While it had its roots in traditional Australian dress, it was arguable un-Australian in its sexualization and juxtaposition of items of dress.

OUTBACK GEAR: DRESSING UP BODY-SPACE RELATIONS

The first example of distinctive Australian style considered here is the legacy of "bush wear" in contemporary fashion. "Bush wear" evolved informally as the Australian outback was settled and settlers had to make do with uncertain supplies of clothes, fabric, harsh climatic and working conditions, and limited opportunities for dressing up in their finery. Clothes had to be practical and hardwearing. Over time, a distinctive mode of dress evolved, one that was intimately connected with the remoteness and mateship of outback life.

While motifs of Australia form one set of representations about Australianness, another register derives from the mythology of the Australian outback as conveyed through cultural re-workings of the figure of the pioneer settler in the bush. These are of course related but the latter puts the emphasis on the survival of settlers in a hostile environment—living with and overcoming adversity. Many commentators have noted that the bush is a foreign land to most Australians—Australia is one of the most urbanized countries in the world with its population concentrated in coastal nodes. Yet, the bush continues to occupy a central place in the national imaginary and constructions of national identity and character.

Central, too, is the notion of a lifestyle that is casual and informal. It is increasingly this element that has come to characterize ideas about Australian style and fashion sense as a generic category. As the former editor of *Vogue Australia,* Nancy Pilcher, put it: "this relaxed air is the very essence of Australian style" (quoted by Alderson, 2000). She continued:

> I do think Australian people have a specific style. And the way they interpret the fashion that is presented to them is often more interesting than the fashion itself.

The look is relaxed and the attitude is of taking quite dressed-up things and making them relaxed . . . here you can combine different looks without going head to toe in something (Quoted by Alderson, 2000). Added to this, says Alderson, is the centrality of the climate and outdoor sporting life in Australian culture:

Surf culture is responsible for a large part of our international style ... We're an outdoor society who are [sic] really comfortable with our bodies. We're not scared to show them off, we're not scared of colour—in fact, we embrace all those things, and if that translates into Australian style then we have one. (Belinda Seper, Sydney boutique owner, quoted by Alderson, 2000)

But while surfwear and swimwear may be the most spectacular images of Australian style, outback wear has also had a strong impact on the emergence of a broadly based idea of Australian dress sense and style. The combination of the two influences (outback and informal) has given the freshness and vitality to what are in reality a language of mundane garments and combinations. Lines such as Scanlan and Theodore that are said to typify this casual yet smart fashion have been described as "urban, intelligent, easy and clean sportswear you'd feel good wearing. It didn't say particularly 'Australia' to me, it has an international look" (Mary Gallagher, London fashion store consultant, quoted by Alderson, 2000). In other words, a distinctively Australian sense of style has evolved from dominant cultural influences, climatic pressures and lifestyles (cf. Symons, 1983).

In the early 2000s, R. M. catalogs dropped the bush imagery and accessories in favor of a softer rural image (for example, one catalog was shot in the wine-growing Hunter Valley and another at the Windsor Polo Club) and featured a more urban-oriented range of clothes. The change has been particularly noticeable in the women's range, which features more fashionable "softer" cuts and pastel shades with names like Grevillea, Frangipani, and Sweet Pea borrowed from Australian flora. The result was a catalog and outfits more in keeping with the Country Road look than a bush dance or the Wild West.

However, the catalogs for 2007 and 2008 revived the "longhorn" legacy by shooting in remote spots in the outback of the Northern Territory and interspersing a broad array of women's fashions (from traditional "bush" clothes to feminine "urban" ones) throughout the catalog—even including action shots of women mustering and horse riding: the past and the present are fused together. This may reflect the reality of the bush today, namely, that women are often managing properties while men work in jobs in town. Either way, the R. M. Williams representation of "bush wear" for women is a long way from McNaught's provocative outfit.

As the marketing reveals, the continuation of traditional approaches to manufacturing, design, and production—preferably within a family or at least Australian-owned company—is part of this appeal to an essential sense of Australianness and sense of national identification and belonging. Sure it is a form of simulacra that draws on an imaginary and nostalgic idea of the Australian outback, but here the bush comes to the city—and other global spaces.

FROM NECK-TO-KNEES TO BIKINIS TO "FASTSKINS": THE PLAY BETWEEN REVELATION AND CONCEALMENT IN NATIONAL DRESS

The history of swimming culture in Australia is tied up with successive controversies about the design of garments for swimming. The most recent controversy concerned with launch in 1999 by Adidas of a bodysuit for competitive swimming. It was called the Equipment Bodysuit and consisted of a Teflon-coated long-john suit that went from neck to ankle (Rushell, 2000). In March 2000, Speedo launched its full-body silhouette Fastskin, which it promoted as "the fastest swim suit ever made" (Speedo, 2000). Made from a "new fabric and revolutionary design," the swimsuit was heralded as improving performances by 3%. The Fastskin was the successor to the Aquablade, the suit worn by 77% of winners at the Atlanta Olympic Games in 1996. Other companies such as Arena also introduced similar suits (Malone, 2000).

The aim of these innovations in swimwear design was to streamline the body and cut down resistance as the body was propelled through the water. While the public had become used to hyperbolic claims about new approaches to swimwear, these developments were criticized as creating "a different era and a different sport" (swimmer Kieran Perkins, quoted in Malone, 2000; cf. le Grand, 2000; Smith, 2000; Dixon, 2000a, 2000b). The full bodysuits were alleged to be equipment—not costumes or uniforms—and as such created an artificial advantage for swimmers who wore them. These swimsuits were, then, of a different order than the shift from wool to cotton to nylon and then to Lycra. They were arguably creating a new body technique.

The new suits were approved by the Federation Internationale de Natation Amateur (FINA—the international ruling body on swimming) in November 1999 and first worn *en masse* at the 2000 Sydney Olympic Games. Despite huge controversy in the lead up to the Games, once their benefits became clear (even if they were technically "equipment" not swimsuits), the Fastskins quickly became accepted racing wear, and were adopted by competitive amateur swimmers internationally. The new look has become the norm and subsequent modifications have explicitly acknowledged that the new suits constitute equipment…Implicit in this discussion was an assumption about how swimmers and bodies should look as much as the rules of how the body should work as a swimming device. In particular, the suits once again highlighted the debate about the play between concealment and revelation that has been central to the development of public swimming and swimming costumes. While the twentieth-century history of swimsuits and bikinis has been towards revealing more and more flesh as attractive and aiding speed, the new suit is based on the reverse logic, namely that the new fast fabrics should cover as much skin as possible.

As American swimmer, Jenny Thompson, observed: "People thought that the less material the better, the skimpier the swimsuit the faster. Now it's the opposite. Now because the material is so fast, it's the more material the better" (quoted by Brooks, 2000). Although this does not appeal to some spectators, others find the cover-up all the more appealing. As one spectator put it: "They still enhance all their bits . . . These are completely full on. They're as tight as can be, really" (quoted by Harari, 2000).

The new look is androgynous at one level because it compresses the lumps and bumps of the body but, because it is so tight, it also signals the imprisoned attributes of gender rather like S & M gear or transvestite costumes. This shift inevitably provoked a revised set of guidelines about swimwear design and its relation with the body. These guidelines specified in minute detail codes of modesty to ensure that the pubic area and upper body were covered. Such guidelines stem from assumptions about the body–space relation in the act of swimming and the role of fabric and clothing in that activity.

But there is more to the debate than questions of technical advantages and images of bodies. In Australia, the debate was transformed into issues of national identity. Although the new suits were an international issue for all competitive swimmers, the centrality of champion swimmers in the Australian pantheon of national heroes meant that the Fastskin challenged accepted ideas about the swimming Aussie body. In other words, the new body undermined the narrative of the beautiful swimming and surfing Aussie body epitomized in popular culture by the 1937 Max Dupain photo "The Sunbaker," a black and white photo of the head and torso of a sunbather lying on the white sand of a beach, his bronzed skin glistening with suntan oil.

CONCLUSION: RECONCILING AUSTRALIANNESS AND UN-AUSTRALIANNESS IN THE MODALITIES OF AUSSIE BODIES

These examples of different ways in which body–clothes relations in Australia have been produced each depend on explicit narratives about the peculiarities of the Aussie body. While these narratives intersect and overlap, there are distinct elements that are picked up in each version reflecting specific preoccupations. While the *swimming body* continually ignites issues of modesty in the process of revelation and concealment, the *Australiana body* reflects the debate about the fit between settler bodies, the environment, and Australia's first inhabitants. Finally, the *outback body* reworks concepts of the bush, hard yakka, and the battler in a narrative about adversity and survival. Oddest of all is the fact that although these bodies are insistently—even stridently—nationalistic in tone, their appeal has not only grown domestically but internationally. Perhaps these bodies are working as counterpoints to other narratives or perhaps they are together devising a body habitus for the truly global body.

Images of "the national" continue to be constructed through clothes and modes of representation. Distinctive fashions in clothing and how they are depicted have changed with the globalization of Australian culture. Australia and culture were traditionally seen as contradictory yet in recent years, diverse forms of Australian culture have been exported and re-imported. Australians now have an internationalized and cosmopolitan image of themselves that has been reflected in trends in fashion and clothing. The dominant types of dress that have been explored here, namely "bush" wear, swim and surfwear, and Australiana and indigenous design, remain the foundations of national dress and an Australian sense of style. But, as these modes are embedded in their own cultural politics, any sense of Australianness equally evokes an allusion to un-Australianness. National dress is the most vexed arena in which such debates are played out.

Meanwhile, Australia has become a multicultural society with many other cultural forms of dress and fashion molding national culture. It is not yet clear to what extent these new cultural influences have changed the *zeitgeist* of national identity or shaped the way it is represented in the fashion media and popular culture. These remain research issues for the future.

References

AAP. (2006). "Aussie Hot with the Bookies and the Trump for Donald." *The Australian*, July 24: 13.

AAP. (2007). "Miss Australia Defends her Togs." *Herald Sun Mobile/PDA Edition* May 24. http://www.news.com.au/heraldsun/wirless/story/0,22282,661-21784518,00.html.

Agencies. (2007). "Memoir of a Grandma Inspires Miss Japan." *The Australian*, May 30: 3.

Alderson, Maggie. (2000). "Relax, It's Australian." *Sydney Morning Herald*, May 2.

Brooks, Janet Rae. (2000). "Sleek Swimsuit Makes Waves with Olympians." *The Salt Lake Tribune*, April 13.

Craik, Jennifer. (1984). "Fashion, Clothes, Sexuality." *Australian Journal of Cultural Studies*, 2(1): 67–83.

Craik, Jennifer. (2002). "Book Review. *Out of Line: Australian Women and Style* by Margaret Maynard (UNSW Press, 2001)". *Fashion Theory*, 6(4): 457–62.

Dapin, Mark. (2003). "Aussie Rules." *The Sydney Morning Herald Good Weekend Magazine,* February 22: 16–20.

Dixon, Catriona. (2000a). "New-age Costume Designed for Gold. Pads, Seams, Nodules Set Suit Apart." *The Advertiser*, March 15.

Dixon, Catriona. (2000b). "New-age Swimsuit Unveiled. Aussies Go Back to the Future." *The Advertiser*, April 18.

Harari, Fiona. (2000). "Suits Take the Perve out of the Pool." *The Australian*, May 17: 28–31.

Le Grand, Chip. (2000). "Costume Drama." *The Australian*, April 15.

Malone, Paul. (2000). "Jury Still out on Suit's Worth." *The Courier-Mail*, May 5.

Maynard, Margaret. (2001). *Out of Line: Australian Women and Style.* Sydney: UNSW Press.

Melocco, Jen. (2008). "Miss Universe Clamour over 'Aussie' Glamour." *The Daily Telegraph*, June 17. http://www.news.com.au/dailytelegraph/story/0,22049,23879148-5001021,00.html.

Palmer, Alexandra (ed.). (2004). *Fashion. A Canadian Perspective*. Toronto, Buffalo and London: University of Toronto Press.

Routh, Caroline. (1993). *In Style: 100 Years of Canadian Women's Fashion.* Toronto: Stoddart.

Rushell, Brent. (2000). "A Serious Threat to the Very Nature of Competitive Swimming or Not?" www-rohan.sdsu.edu/dept/coachsci/swimming.htm.

Smith, Wayne. (2000). "Speeding Frenzy." *The Courier-Mail*, April 1.

Speedo. (2000). "SPEEDO introduces Fastskin—the Fastest Swimsuit." Company Press Release, March 16.

Symons, Sandra. (1983). "Australian Essence." *Mode*, August/September: n.p.

Wolfe, Richard. (2001). *The Way We Wore: The Clothes New Zealanders Have Loved.* Auckland: Penguin Books.

45

SECONDHAND CLOTHING

Karen Tranberg Hansen[1]

CHARITY AND COMMERCE

Established charitable organizations are the single largest source of the twenty-first-century global trade in secondhand clothing, supplying both domestic and foreign secondhand-clothing markets through their collection efforts. Since the end of the nineteenth century in both Europe and the United States, philanthropic groups have been involved in collecting and donating clothes to the poor. In the late 1950s, many charitable organizations introduced store sales, among them the Salvation Army, whose income in the United States primarily came from the sale of used clothing. The major charitable organizations in the twenty-first century include, in the United States, the Salvation Army, Goodwill Industries, St. Vincent de Paul, and Amvets and, in Europe, Humana, Oxfam, Terre, and Abbey Pierre, among many others. When post–World War II shifts in income distribution and growing purchasing power enabled more consumers than ever before to buy not only new but also more clothes, specific garment niches emerged, including fashions and styles oriented toward, for example, teenage clothing, corporate and career dressing, and sports and leisure wear. Such dress practices produced an enormous yield of used but still wearable clothes, some of which ended up as donations to charity.

Charitable organizations dominated the domestic secondhand-clothing retail scene in the 1960s and 1970s. They were joined during the 1980s by a variety of specialist stores operating on a for-profit basis with names that rarely feature words like *used*, *secondhand*, or *thrift*. Most of these specialty stores cater to women, yet some stock garments for both sexes; there are children's apparel shops, and men's boutiques have appeared as well. Menswear and children's wear take up far less space in secondhand-clothing retailing than women's apparel. The clientele also includes far more women than men. Some of these stores target specific consumers, among them young professionals who want high-quality clothing at modest prices or young people keen on retro (revival of past styles) and period fashion, punk, and rave styles. Some customers collect garments with investment in view. Some of these stores operate on a consignment basis; others source in bulk from secondhand-clothing vendors; and some do both. And some of these businesses donate garments that do not sell well to "charity," while others dispose of their surplus at bulk prices to commercial secondhand-clothing dealers.

The relationship between charitable organizations and textile recyclers and graders adds a business angle, concerning its profitability there is considerable anecdotal but little substantive information. Because consumers in the West donate much more clothing than the charitable organizations can possibly sell in their retail shops, they in turn dispose of their massive overstock at bulk prices to commercial secondhand-clothing dealers. The media routinely fault the charitable organizations for making money from the sale of donated clothing and criticize the textile graders for turning surplus donated clothing into a profitable economic niche. At the same time, growing environmental concerns in the West have enhanced

---

[1] From Karen Tranberg Hanson, Secondhand Clothing, in Joanne Eicher and Phyllis Tortora (eds), Berg Encyclopedia of World Dress and Fashion (Bloomsbury).

both the profitability and respectability of this trade, giving its practitioners a new cachet as textile salvagers and waste recyclers. As the last but not the least ironic twist in this process, used clothing has become the latest "new" trend as consumers across the globe eagerly purchase secondhand garments in local market stalls, stores, boutiques, and online. The trade universe for the sourcing of secondhand clothing includes informal sites like garage sales and flea markets as well as estate sales and high-end auction houses such as Sotheby's and Christie's.

The textile-recycling industry is made up of salvagers and graders, fiber recyclers, and used-clothing dealers, brokers, and exporters. "Used clothing" comprises not only garments but also shoes, handbags, hats, belts, draperies, and linens. Soft toys—for example, teddy bears—have found their way into this export. The textile recyclers sort and grade clothing and apparel into many categories, some for the domestic retro or upscale market and others for export; some for industrial use as rags, and others for fiber. In the twenty-first century, wool garments that used to be exported to Italy for the wool-regeneration industry in Prato near Florence are shipped in bulk to northern India for reprocessing. Blue jeans, especially Levi Strauss 501, the original button-fly jeans created in 1853 for miners and cowboys in the American West, are popular in Japan. Intermediaries called "pickers" and expert buyers, among them foreign nationals, lessen the hard work of sourcing by traveling between the large textile-recycling warehouses and selecting garments with particular appeal to, for example, domestic youth markets, special period markets such as retro and vintage, and niche markets in Japan.

Once sorted, the better grades of secondhand clothing are exported to Central American countries such as Costa Rica, Honduras, and Guatemala and also to Chile in South America. The lowest grade goes to African and Asian countries. Most recyclers compress sorted garments into bales of fifty kilograms (110 pounds), while some press unsorted bulk clothing into bales weighing five hundred or even one thousand kilograms (1,100 or 2,200 pounds). The bales are wrapped in waterproof plastic, tied with metal or plastic straps, placed in containers, and shipped. Most of the large textile recyclers in the United States that are involved in buying and reselling for export are located near port cities along the Atlantic and Pacific coasts and on the Great Lakes. Many of the large firms are family owned. Since the turn of the millennium, the focus of the trade has shifted to Canada, where many now consider Toronto to be the world's used-clothing capital. Several of the new operators originate from South Asia, some of them coming from families with experience living in Africa, and they know the overseas markets through personal connections. In Europe, for historical and geographic reasons, the hubs of commercial sorting were the Netherlands and Belgium, with easy access to the world's major ports. In efforts to save labor costs, some of these firms have moved their sorting operations to countries in eastern Europe, among them Hungary.

Because secondhand clothing is a potentially profitable commodity, its charitable collection is challenged by fraudulent practices. Many parking lots and strip malls are dotted with gaily colored collection bins, put up by established charities as well as by for-profit groups with the permission of adjacent business owners or, in some states in the United States, after receiving permission from the local authorities. The logos on some of these bins advocate third-world relief, while others focus on environmental protection. Collection bins appealing for urgently needed clothing sometimes feature names of nonexistent charities, and flyers inviting householders to fill bags with unwanted clothing have been known to give the impression that the collected garments would be donated to the poor in third-world countries. The mostly voluntary workforce of charitable organizations makes it difficult to supervise activities related to collection bins; therefore, some of them have phased out collection bins entirely. The items that are collected through fraudulent advertising or outright theft may enter the export circuit through brokers. Truckloads of used clothing collected as a result of such scams eventually reach markets in eastern Europe, Africa, South America, and the Indian subcontinent. In Great Britain and Ireland, for example, leading charitable organizations have experienced massive losses to organized gangs from Latvia, Lithuania, and Poland who battle with groups from Northern Ireland, Scotland, and England for control of the market in secondhand clothes stolen from charity bins.

FROM THRIFT TO FASHION, FROM WASTE TO RECYCLING

Toward the end of the twentieth century, growing consumer concerns with self-styled uniqueness and rising preoccupations with recycling in the West have complicated the long-standing association between secondhand clothing and thrift. The world of secondhand clothing has become a flourishing fashion scene. In fact, since the turn of the millennium, used clothing has drawn a bigger spotlight than ever—not as secondhand but as vintage, thanks in part to rich and famous people who have worn vintage garments at celebrity events. At the Oscar Awards ceremony in 2001, Julia Roberts wore a vintage Valentino dress. Nicole Kidman, Reese Witherspoon, Kirsten Dunst, and many others have been spotted in vintage couture at red-carpet events that draw both media and widespread public attention to dress.

The range of previously used dress options has expanded as thrift has become associated with charity and period clothing with an assortment of apparel in which "real" vintage dates to before the 1970s. These developments have been accompanied by the emergence of specialized points of purchase. The quality of the merchandise varies with the selling environment and the ambience. And the clientele tends to differ. Many thrift stores have a warehouse feel and are crowded with clothing, accessories, and garments hung on racks loosely classified by type. Teenage shoppers who do not actually need clothing search such racks for garments that make a fashion statement. In twenty-first-century Germany, for example, the 1960s-style scene of movies, music, and material culture is popular with young people, who dress in garments from the 1960s or make their own clothes constructed from old patterns. This retro style attributes history and authenticity to garments that wearers experience as unique and personal. Style-conscious shoppers rummage, browse, and look for clothes in various places with dedication and zeal.

Secondhand-clothing shopping offers the thrill of the chase, the bargain, and the pleasure of making a find or discovery. The interiors of many consignment stores and upscale resale boutiques are strategically designed with visual stimulation and dazzling displays to create a fun and eclectic ambience. Offering a mixture of old and new, many of these stores combine vintage and modern garments with retro appliances, memorabilia, and furniture. Such stores are both about the shopping experience and about finding unusual pre-owned apparel.

Vintage has different meanings for everyone, and the clientele varies widely in the twenty-first century. For a baby boomer, vintage means clothes from the 1930s and 1940s, whereas for the twenty-first-century high-school cohort, vintage garments are from the 1970s and 1980s. Teenage shoppers are attracted to vintage because it adds glamour to their everyday wardrobe and shopping at vintage stores offers an experience of playing dress-up. Other customers search for period dress or costumes for decade-specific parties; college students purchase items for themed events, among them, dance marathons. Top celebrities wear vintage, high-street shops are copying it, and upwardly mobile consumers are purchasing it as an investment as the auctions of garments owned by Princess Diana and Jacqueline Kennedy demonstrate. The blending of fashion with celebrity obsession is evident also at VIP events that raise money to support selected charities through the sale of tickets and designer clothes donated by socialites. Whatever the occasion, people who are keen on style purchase used designer labels as they do all secondhand garments, because they follow their own tastes and like to purchase something that is unique.

The development of the World Wide Web has enhanced the secondhand-clothing market, especially its designer-trading aspect. In effect, the Internet, auction sites, and specific Web-based sites have expanded the previously worn clothing business vastly. Hard-to-come-by, limited-edition branded items appear on auction sites, which makes high-end clothing affordable. On eBay, the global online marketplace, consumers are able to buy just about anything at auction or through fixed-price arrangements. In fact, sellers receive a larger part of the profit from eBay transactions than they do in most consignment stores. And because most garments offered for sale at eBay end up being purchased, concerns about the disposal of excess clothing are limited. Shopping from home for gently used or pre-owned quality garments, eBay customers have access to designer items that may not even be available where they live.

Several trends converge in contemporary preoccupations with clothing recycling. For one, the secondhand-clothing trade keeps garments out of landfills, reducing or temporarily postponing environmental degradation. What is more, alteration personalizes garments, customizing makes them fit, and repair extends the life span of used clothing whereas a variety of transformations give it new leases on life. Quality- and style-savvy consumers recognize the potential that may not be immediately apparent in garments, and some possess skills to effect transformations by taking apart, reshaping, and turning used clothing into something else by means of embellishment, patchwork, buttons, and trim, among many other practices. Last but not least, since the early 1990s, established designers such as Rei Kawakubo of Comme des Garçons in Paris and Dolce & Gabbana in Milan have featured garments that look recycled on the fashion runway, while in Paris, Roland Simmons incorporated what the French colloquially call *fripes* (from *friperie,* meaning "used clothing") among the designer labels in his boutique. Also in Paris, Mali-born avant-garde designer Lamine Kouyaté has taken a couture-like approach to recovered clothes in his designer label Xuly-Bët, deconstructing them into reconfigured one-of-a-kind garments. Then there is Martin Margiela, known as "fashion's founding father of recycling, the 1970s revival and thrift-shop style" (Menkes 1993), who in his Paris studio showcased the recycling of clothes by giving them new life.

While the recycling of clothing constitutes a creative component of the work of some fashion designers, some consumer groups have returned to thrifting but with a twist. Changing from pursuing bargain hunting to a "green" position, some consumers concerned with sustainability focus on the recycling aspect of the trade. Eco-conscious parents, for example, may seek out secondhand items made from conventionally grown cotton for their infants because frequent washing has removed the pesticides. Infants outgrow their clothes quickly, most certainly before they wear them out, so returning such garments to consignment shops reduces their environmental impact even further. Such positions may be enmeshed with other forms of provisioning practices, including the purchase of fair trade products, that, when taken together, represent an ethical rather than merely a prorecycling consumption position.

GLOBAL CONTEXTS

The secondhand clothing trade has expanded hugely in both its economic power and global scope, more than doubling worldwide between 1991 and 2004, in the wake of the liberalization of many third-world economies and following the sudden rise in demand from former Eastern Bloc countries in the early 1990s. In the twenty-first century, secondhand clothing makes up a specialty or niche market in much of the West, whereas in many third-world countries, secondhand clothing imported from the West is an important clothing source. The United States is the world's largest exporter in terms of both volume and value, followed in 2004 by the United Kingdom, Germany, and the Netherlands (United Nations 1996, 20; 2006, 120–121).

The countries of sub-Saharan Africa are the world's largest secondhand-clothing destination, receiving close to 26 percent of total world exports in 2004. Close to 20 percent of world exports in 2004 went to Asia, where Japan, Malaysia, India, Cambodia, Singapore, and Pakistan (in this order) are large net importers. Other large importers include Tunisia in North Africa and Guatemala in Central America. The export does not target the third world exclusively. Sizable exports are destined for Japan, Belgium-Luxembourg, and the Netherlands, which all import and reexport this commodity. In fact, in 2004, Europe, including eastern Europe and the former Soviet Union, imported about 25 percent of the total of secondhand clothing traded, almost the same amount as Africa (United Nations 1996, 20; 2006, 120–121).

The global secondhand-clothing trade shows some striking trends. Many large importers of secondhand clothing in South Asia, such as India and Pakistan, are themselves textile and garment exporters, which puts an interesting spin on arguments about the negative effects of used-clothing imports on domestic textile and garment industries. This is also the case for some African countries, for example, Kenya and Uganda: Both are large importers of secondhand clothing but have textile- and garment-manufacturing firms that export to the United States under the duty- and quota-free provisions of the African Growth and Opportunity Act.

Although the Philippines bans the import of secondhand clothing, trade in it has grown in the wake of the opening up of the economy in the mid-1980s. Secondhand clothing only recently became readily available, illegally shipped to Philippine ports or arriving via Hong Kong. In Ifugao, a town in northern Luzon, this trade circulates through channels that are rooted in local cultural traditions and guided by notions of personalized contacts that women traders make use of in their business activities. When retailers, vendors, and consumers talk about secondhand clothing, they draw connections between people and clothes that constantly change. Such accounts domesticate the logic of the market and the meaning of this global commodity in terms of local norms of status and value; in the process, they transform them. Combining secondhand garments into styles that display knowledge of wider clothing practices or subvert their received meaning, traders and consumers refashion this imported commodity to serve their personal and community identities.

India prohibits the import of secondhand clothing yet permits the import of woolen fibers called *mutilated hosiery,* a trade term for wool garments shredded by machines in the West prior to export. Imported "mutilated" fabrics are sorted into color ranges, then shredded, carded, and spun, to reappear as threads used for blankets, knitting yarn, and wool fabrics for local consumption and export in the Indian shoddy industry (the reclamation of fabric fibers). Domestic recycling of Indian clothing also occurs through barter, hand-me-downs, donations, and resale. Some Indian consumers donate their still-wearable clothing to the poor or barter it for household goods. Other practices involve saris with intricate borders that are transformed into new garments and household items for niche markets in the West, while the remains of cotton cloth are shipped abroad as industrial wiping rags. This recycling of imported and domestic secondhand clothing creates employment at many levels of the Indian economy. In the process, an export supply chain formalizes what began as an informal trade.

AFRICAN SECONDHAND CLOTHING MARKETS

Secondhand-clothing consumption practices in Africa are shaped by the politics that regulate these imports and by distinct regional conventions concerning bodies and dress. Some African countries have at one point or another banned the import of secondhand clothing—for instance, Côte d'Ivoire, Nigeria, Kenya, and Malawi. Some countries have restrictive policies—for example, South Africa, which allows import of secondhand clothing only for charitable purposes and not for resale. African secondhand-clothing markets undergo changes not only because of the legal rules that guide or prohibit secondhand-clothing imports but also because of civil strife and war. Some small countries like Benin, Togo, and Rwanda before its civil wars have been large importers and active in transshipment and reexport. Although secondhand-clothing imports are banned in some countries, a brisk trade moves this popular commodity across Africa's highly penetrable borders.

There is considerable regional variation in Africa's clothing markets. In Muslim-dominated North Africa, for example, secondhand clothing constitutes a much smaller percentage of total garment imports than in sub-Saharan Africa. The North African imports consist largely of men's work and everyday garments like trousers, jackets, and shirts and of children's clothes. Dress conventions differ throughout the continent, not only in terms of religious norms (for instance, whether people are Muslim or Christian), but also by gender, age, class, and region or ethnicity Taken together, these factors inform the cultural norms of dress practice, influencing what types of garments which people will wear and when.

In several countries in West Africa, distinct regional dress styles that are the products of long-standing textile crafts in weaving, dyeing, and printing coexist in the twenty-first century with dress styles that were introduced during the Colonial period and after. In Nigeria and Senegal, for example, secondhand clothing has entered a specific niche. Although people from different socioeconomic groups, not only the very poor, purchase imported secondhand clothing and use it widely for everyday wear, Senegalese and Nigerians commonly follow long-established style conventions, dressing with pride for purposes of displaying specialty cloth in "African" styles, some of it locally produced, since the late 1990s, however, much of the printed fabrics are manufactured in China. This stands in contrast to Zambia, where such textile crafts hardly existed in the pre-Colonial period and where in the twenty-first century people across the socioeconomic spectrum, except those at the top, are dressing in the West's used clothing. Secondhand clothing flows from the point of donation in the West through sorting centers for export from where it is shipped by container and arrives by overland transport in Zambia. There, distribution and consumption practices incorporate secondhand clothes as desirable apparel into a gendered dress universe that is informed by a local cultural economy of judgment and style. Far from emulating the West's fashions, secondhand-clothing practices in Africa involve clothing-conscious consumers in efforts to reconstruct these garments culturally and materially and in the process change their lives for the better.

Last but not least, dress, both new and used, is a dynamic resource in young people's identity constructions in Africa's rapidly growing urban areas. Young male street vendors in Zambia buy oversized secondhand garments, while secondary school students search for items that create a suitable look to signal their upwardly mobile status. Youth in Dakar, Senegal, a city rich in historical exchanges with the rest of the world, search for *feggy jaay* garments (a Wolof term meaning "shake and sell," or secondhand clothing), brand-name imports, and Chinese knockoffs to represent their aspired status: as "Boy Town," someone who is indigenous to Dakar; "Coming Town," the rural migrant; or the "Venant," a returned transnational migrant. Engaging with local views of fashion trends, the rich knowledge youth possess about the specifics of style enables them to read clothing and to identify the position of others, in this way navigating their way in the city, shaping both themselves and the urban scene.

CONCLUSION: WHEN OLD TURNS NEW

The process of recycling clothing never rests. Because every piece of garment has many potential future lives, the trade in secondhand clothing and textile recycling is lucrative. Garments that sit on the rack unsold for too long in the consignment store are either retrieved by their owners or donated to charity—for example, a shelter for the homeless, where in fact they may wear out their life. Alternatively, unsold garments are disposed of in bulk to textile recyclers who sort and grade them, some for the industrial cleaning-rag market and more for the secondhand-clothing export market. Once they have arrived abroad, the West's discarded clothing in turn assumes new life as such garments become part of the biographies of their next owners; for example, in Africa, they not only cover basic clothing needs but also fulfill desires about bodies dressed in "the latest" as locally defined. Secondhand clothing provides a dress practice through which people construct gender, appearance, and identity. In secondhand-clothing consumption, desire confronts emulation. What goes around in this global process does indeed come around locally, yet with creatively changed meanings. Finally, the online secondhand-clothing market on the World Wide Web has redrawn the global map of clothing by opening access to it to all.

Reference

United Nations. (2006). *International Trade Statistic Yearbook*. New York, NY: United Nations.

46

GLOBALIZATION AND DRESS

Margaret Maynard[1]

The trading of articles of dress, cloth, body adornments, precious stones, oils, and perfumes across wide areas of the globe, whether by sea, river, or overland routes, has taken place for centuries. All manner of cultural transfers and modifications of dress have eventuated because of migrations, diasporic movements, and subjugation of peoples. Something very different, though, is the globalization of dress, the increasing dominance of mass-produced standardized clothing across the world, which some would call the general modernization of dress. As large-scale international trade agreements and transnational corporate networks override the discrete nation-state, so industrialized apparel making has seemingly engulfed the individuality of the clothing products of small-scale agrarian cultures.

The explosion of advertising from the start of the twentieth century began the process of creating mass markets for relatively similar dress types and cosmetics across Europe, the United States, Asia, Africa, the Pacific, and elsewhere; during the latter part of the century, style uniformity in clothing intensified. As became especially evident after the 1970s, mass-produced clothing offers many cultures more advantages than did former slower methods of making traditional dress. Making by hand specialized body wear, often invested with spiritual or ritualized meanings, from the flora and fauna found in the immediate environment or from materials traded from elsewhere was time consuming, compared to the convenience of store-bought clothing.

Dress and fashion scholar Joanne Eicher in important collaborative work, has coined the term *world dress* for commonly worn high-volume clothing for both sexes (some of which is gender and age neutral), including business suits, jeans, athletic trainers, sandals, baseball caps, long-sleeved shirts and T-shirts, anoraks, overalls, and trousers. Much of this is based on standardized sizing, although there are disparities, for example, between Chinese and Australian clothing sizes. International firms like Lands' End are, in fact, creating company-specific standards. Despite the acceptance of similar kinds of dress across the world, a picture of global attire must acknowledge the crucial place of differing ethnic and personal preferences, philosophies (cosmological beliefs about garments, cloth, and body modifications), and religious and moral attitudes. The sheer prevalence of universalized attire has brought with it serious ethical issues relating to excess consumption, overuse of resources, and land degradation. The constant replacement of fashionable and everyday dress, as opposed to reused clothing, comes at an environmental cost.

The globalizing of dress would not have occurred without improved transport, free trade agreements, accessibility of goods all over the world, and the phenomenon of branding. Nor could this process have happened without the penetration of capitalist practices and sophisticated marketing systems into areas formerly remote from Western influence. The result is that adults and children in the remote province of Xiahe in Little Tibet, China, can wear clothes identical to those of any Australian, North American, or European. The textile and apparel industries were

---

[1] From Margaret Maynard, Globalization and Dress in Joanne Eicher and Phyllis Tortora, Berg Encyclopedia of World Dress and Fashion (Bloomsbury).

the first to upgrade to global trading, allowing developing countries into the world marketplace. Shifts in production away from high-cost economies like the United States to China, India, and lately Indonesia and Fiji have been a major factor enabling the volume manufacturing of low-cost, generic clothing, although there are signs that this outsourcing practice is changing. At the same time, new technologies and targeted business methods have made it possible for mass-produced international brands such as Zara (Inditex group) to be demand-driven. With about half of its garments produced in Spain, Zara provides a speedy and direct response to consumer tastes, with stock perhaps differing from store to store, indicating the global market is both standardized and segmented.

Without question, globalization is a far more complex phenomenon than it appears. Some regard it as hegemonic and standardizing, while others take a more subtle approach and see it as a sign of advanced interlinking techniques and marketing practices. At the same time, the pervasive trend toward the similarity of products is matched by marketing attempts to differentiate commodities in such a way that customers will be led to believe they are constantly being offered something new. Convergence as well as increasing divergence exists within the global market. An example is the intense promotion of familiar brands like Burberry, which need to be constantly reconceptualized to maintain exclusivity, as their logos become subject to faking or overuse. While basic clothing is remarkably similar in cut and overall style, this is disguised by ever-changing modifications to brands, however small, and changing techniques of concept selling.

Eicher and her colleagues correctly recognize that total uniformity of clothing cannot exist. They qualify the concept of world dress with a process they call "cultural authentication," whereby small-scale cultures assert their identity by individualizing Western dress and vice versa. They offer the example of a Western shirt modified for wear in a non-Western culture—for example, as a chief's knee-length tunic in coastal Nigeria or combined with other garments specific to a particular ethnic group. The resulting outfit might partake of global attire but not fall within the definition of standardization. Tactical dressing also occurs. In Indonesia, a man may wear a Western-style suit for work, tour the country in a so-called safari suit, attend a reception in a modern batik shirt, and wear a regional outfit for a wedding celebration. A montage of Western and multifarious other kinds of dress—subtle adaptations with nuanced meanings, ethnic specificities, or the use of generic-style dress for some, perhaps most, occasions but not others—is a prominent characteristic of the global landscape of appearance.

The strategic nature of clothing choice, whether for uniformity or difference, inevitably works against any sense that global dress is uniform or generic. Global consumers, even those who rely on secondhand dress, are keenly tuned to subtleties of self-presentation and exercise choice where they can. Clothing can be a sign of power relations, a choice between "traditionalist" and modern, a religious or economic indicator, or a political gesture. Or it can be a demonstration of national pride or grassroots resistance. Yet dress choice can never be fully divorced from the frameworks that surround it, for it is inextricable from the cultural and socioeconomic environment in which it occurs.

It is a mistake to imagine anything like a one-way traffic of style emanating from the West within the phenomenon of globalized dress. Asian dress has made strong inroads into Western fashion including the catwalk. Conversely, expressions of ethnicity and use of modified clothing practices of the past to express nationhood are often inflected by modern adaptations. Selectivity is as important a part of worldwide dress at every level as is uniformity. The universalizing of consumption has occurred and does occur simultaneously with the interweaving of global and local patterns of wearing and also with individual expressions of identity, as in the Pacific, where women regularly sew and weave, or in India, where Muslim women seek out fabrics to be custom-stitched, not ready-made garments. Concurrently, in Western cultures, there is increasing interest, even value, placed on "handcraft" and the handmade as an antidote to mass clothing. The popular engagement with personal sewing, beading, embroidery, and knitting as well as tourists' interest in supposedly handmade items sold in street markets are examples. Sometimes simply conveying the illusion of being handcrafted or individualized is sufficient. Customizing T-shirts, using them as a vehicle for political slogans, or placing a unique imprint on a garment gives individual value in a world where there is little personal control.

GLOBALIZED STYLES

Global dressing is a competitive phenomenon driven by corporations, which offer mass availability of desirable goods using the media as a tool of dissemination. Market-driven globalization does not necessarily favor diversity. Instead, it finds profit in uniformity or in minutely targeting markets believed to demand some minor difference of cut or color. Ironically, at the bulk marketing level, lack of variety is the fundamental imperative, a curious paradox in an industry (especially fashion) historically based on regular changes of style.

A great many people in Asia, South America, Africa, Europe, and the United States wear dress inflected by a kind of "sameness," either most or part of the time. However, a distinction must be made between generic forms of everyday dress and a host of other levels of dressing, including pan-Indian, pan-Pacific, pan-Islamic, and pan-African forms of dress. In Western dress, too, there are variations between specialist lines produced by higher-status brands, aware of the latest trend forecasts (likely informed by Worth Global Style Network); the styles of mass merchandisers and chains; and secondhand economies. Elite designer-fashion originals seen on major catwalks in Europe (especially Paris), the United States, the United Kingdom, and increasingly Asia, Australia, and New Zealand are beamed around the world, supported by the press and local fashion weeks outside major centers (for instance, Fashion Week India commenced in 2000), increasing the knowledge about and availability of high fashion among different groups of customers. Versions of elite designer ready-to-wear garments eventually find their way downstream to chain stores. Garment designs are digitally, and thus instantaneously, transmitted for immediate reproduction in China or elsewhere. It can be a remarkably rapid process, aptly termed *fast fashion*. According to the British journalist Mark Tungate, some companies like H&M have a lead-time of two to three weeks for high fashion, but for basic products it is a good deal longer.

Huge branded multinational corporations, mainly based in Europe and the United States, design, produce, and market their clothes all over the world by exploiting decentralization and using low-paid workers located far from their corporate headquarters. A key feature of global dress is the very fact of how and where it is manufactured. Free trade agreements mean transnational companies can have garments made anywhere, as they find sites offering lower and lower wages, whether in Central America, the Caribbean, Mexico, Eastern Europe, sub-Saharan Africa, China, Bangladesh, Samoa, or Southeast Asia including Vietnam.

Conditions in work-processing "zones," some surrounded by barbed wire or other fences, are almost like indentured slavery, although most major cities in the West harbor hidden sweatshops. Tony Hines (a professor of marketing) and Margaret Bruce (a professor of design management and marketing) have estimated that in 2007 there were about forty million jobs in the global textile and clothing industries, over 70 percent of which were filled by women working for the lowest wages in their respective countries.

China, India, and Pakistan have the largest numbers employed in the textile sector both by count and percentage. In 2002, the expanding garment industry in China reported the output of twenty billion garments. While conditions for workers are without doubt poor, one could argue that the alternative for developing nations might be worse. In these kinds of conditions, mass-produced clothing provides much-needed employment, without which people would be even further impoverished. As companies seek cheaper and cheaper manufacturing locations in less-developed areas, the clothing industries of the developed nations have mostly declined. Garment manufacturing in Australia began to lose market share in the 1970s, as trade barriers fell. While local everyday footwear and clothing manufacturers continue to be forced out of the market, designer Australian-made dress, like high-end imports, has become more highly priced. At the same time, the mass production of clothes has generated new value-added services and a related new business-services sector to assist with benchmarking, product finishing, design, advanced retail, and stock-control technologies.

A feature of the global market is that one cannot determine with confidence that garments are necessarily characteristic of any particular location, even if they are supposedly "local" or "ethnic" in style. Garments may pass through many locations, being designed in one country, assembled elsewhere, and sold in a third country. Unlike premodern dressmakers and tailors, workers in clothing factories are likely to be disassociated from those who make the textiles and those who wear the finished garments. In the twenty-first century, an article of dress such as the woman's *sa/war kameez* (tunic and trousers), originally from North India and Pakistan, is widely used by other women living in Western countries who enjoy the pseudoexotic nature of Indian and Asian clothing. Yet these garments may have been designed and made by people who have never visited or lived in Asia, and their place of origin may be indeterminable. Mexicans feel that Mexican-made Nike garments are U.S. clothes. The Nike "Swoosh" logo is so schematic and reproducible that dress bearing the sign could have been made anywhere.

Paradoxically, even if faked, the logo still works as free advertising for the corporation. It even survives the process of being resold in secondhand markets. China is the country most notorious for copying designs. In 2000, at least twenty-six fake Valentino brands were made in China, some sold in original Valentino boxes, mostly for sale abroad or to the tourist market. In fact, the label "made in Italy" may well disguise the fact that the clothes are actually made in China. Certain designs like those found on traditional Tongan barkcloth, even dot motifs (which have become popularized as a signature style of Aboriginal people in Australia), are not necessarily authentic to the original culture. When transposed onto mass-made T-shirts, they become clichéd signs of the Pacific; in Australia, these designs may not only be clichéd but at times violate artistic copyright.

Consumers of both sexes and all ages on every continent of the world, whether in major cities, towns, or rural areas, wear quite similar low-key generic forms of dress for many occasions. These include jeans, tracksuits, shorts and trousers, long- or short-sleeved shirts, skirts, sweaters, underwear, trainers, T-shirts, and baseball caps. Since the early twenty-first century, supermarkets have increasingly involved themselves in selling such basic garments, sometimes with a veneer of "fashion." Corporations like Walmart, with 3,500 stores in the United States alone in 2007, and food companies like Tesco are leading the way. But as noted, one cannot regard global dress as undifferentiated. For example, there are various grades of homogeneous clothing. China in the twenty-first century has a reputation for producing vast quantities of same-looking clothing at extraordinarily cheap rates, dominating the lowest end of the market, but also "fast fashion" copies of ready-to-wear collections. Some generic garments like tracksuits or athletic shoes, originally conceived as nonspecific everyday wear, have been co-opted and redesigned as semifashionable items or as elite sportswear, bearing branded logos and sold in higher-class outlets. Gap, a firm that pitches to the middle range, has a more exclusive subbrand called Banana Republic. Lands' End, a middle-of-the-road company, offers Lands' End Custom so that customers can order jeans, pants for men and women, and dress shirts with personally chosen fabric and features.

While people want to feel part of a group, such as supporters of a football club or perhaps users of a certain brand, global clothing companies are finding that attempting to define buyers of particular discrete clothing categories is less productive than constructing links with particular lifestyles or occupations, as with CAT footwear, which seeks to invoke an association with the honesty and strength of Caterpillar company. The way sports, fashion, and music can overlap in terms of buyers' tastes is a case in point. While on one level manufacturers reduce product choice, they are more frequently formulating complex marketing strategies that coalesce around notional consumers, using all kinds of packaging, free offers, and "piggybacking" of products in their attempts to increase profits.

One of the most universalized forms of dress across the world is the business suit, which is worn by both genders. The two-piece suit, usually brown, gray, or black, worn by men with a shirt and tie and by women (with either pants or skirt) with a blouse, is a global, though not a static generic, style; it is used by the managerial classes, or those who aspire to these classes, to signify acceptance of Western values. It has become a symbol of professional credibility, authority, success, and corporate trust, although some, such as Australian rural dwellers, may regard suits with suspicion. Since the 1980s, women in Western businesses have been encouraged to wear suits as part of corporate wear. This uniform style supposedly allows women to participate with greater self-assurance in what is a male-dominated environment. The allegedly nonsexual so-called power suit of the 1980s with wide shoulder pads sends the opposite message when suits are worn with very short skirts and feminine articles like high-heeled shoes and low-cut blouses. The softly draped head covering worn with the suit by women in Muslim countries, for reasons of modesty, complicates the corporate message of the suit.

Despite their use across the world, the meanings of suits are by no means absolute. The Mao suit, seldom seen in the twenty-first century except in rural areas, was one example that had intense political significance in the totalitarian regime of China. More generally, Western suits vary in cut, fabric, and price, thus signaling differences related to the wearer's degree of affluence and occupation. Subcultural groups in Europe and the United States have also used suits to parody the status quo, and they are regularly worn with regional or religious accessories such as the Jewish yarmulke or skullcap.

Denim jeans are another form of attire worn by men, women, and children, rich and poor, all over the world, an archetypal product originating in the United States during the nineteenth century, popularized by movie stars like James Dean. Durable and adaptable, they seem to be a classless, ageless garment, outside fashion, perhaps because of their working-class origins. Indian Muslim men striving for a "decent" appearance, even if reformist, do not wear jeans, but Hindus and Christians find them highly desirable. Mostly but not entirely used for everyday casual wear, jeans appear on every street corner but are not universally the same. Jeans can be mass or custom made; light blue, navy, or other colors; baggy with straight legs or bell-bottomed, showing fashionable changes over time. They also vary in value. Although jeans are cheap in mass-market stores, high-end designers may style these garments and sell them for exorbitant prices, or they can be valued as rarities and auctioned as antiques.

DRESS, MATERIALS, AND THE ENVIRONMENT

Consumption of fashion, everyday dress, and all forms of body modification are key elements of modern life. They include an alternative form: the consumption of secondhand clothing in all parts of the world, primarily but not entirely by those of limited means. Consumption of dress is part of endlessly changing sets of interrelationships and networks of buyers and sellers. Dress is a resource used, reused, bartered, or sold, altering its status and meaning as it moves from marketplace to marketplace. Gilles Lipovetsky (writing from his Western point of view) has gone so far as to say that preoccupation with fashion—that is, fashionable style in the wider definition of the word—is so pervasive and so intense that style has become the organizing principle of modern life. Consumption of style, in his view, discourages ideology and extremism. The more is purchased, he has said, the less time people have to engage in aggressive and antisocial behavior. Nonetheless, consumption may not be that benign. The explosion of the world population, the acceleration of clothing manufacture, the making of synthetic fabrics, and the widespread farming of cotton have all contributed to the denuding of agricultural land and massive environmental problems.

As fears of global warming grow, the issue of excessive consumption is coming under scrutiny. For some reason, dress seldom features in the dire predictions of earth watchers. While morality in dress has been an issue for a long time, questions of ethical consumption and pressing concerns for workers' lives and conditions are coming to the fore, with many mainstream branded companies promoting themselves as environmentally responsible and setting out positions on ethical practices, something of increasing concern to shareholders. Yet codes of practice cannot be enforced, resulting in widespread cynicism. Concerns have also been raised about outsourced labor practices and the use of fabrics that degrade the environment. Antifur campaigners and antisweatshop protestors are merely some of the groups of people who speak out against unethical fashion practices. They have done so with some success but overlook the harm that ending outsourced manufacturing could cause to the livelihoods of thousands in third-world countries. More recently, it has been argued that making fake fur is more polluting than farming animal fur, a curious reversal of viewpoint.

Virtual consumption has both a positive and negative role to play. It creates cultures of envy, while at the same time the Internet offers endless opportunities to purchase so-called green or naturally produced clothing. Yet natural products, if not made of organic fibers, are some of the most troubling environmental offenders. Cotton is possibly the worst water-dependent plant, denuding the soil of nutrients and requiring large amounts of pesticides and fungicides. Cotton is not the benign product that promoters constantly depict it as but, ironically, is one of the key materials used in the making of jeans, the most widely used of global clothes. Moreover, the stonewashing of jeans actually causes the indigo to run off in rivers, damaging plants and fish.

Textile manufacturing uses thousands of polluting chemicals, whether for growing natural fibers or for making synthetics. Pollution occurs at every point of manufacturing, from cultivation to processing, bleaching, and finishing, to washing and even dry cleaning. Some changes have occurred since the 1990s. Corporations are responding to the concept of "green" consumption. Many ecofriendly and alternative Internet sites are selling supposedly responsible clothing made of organic fibers. One of the difficulties is that these so-called green clothes are not necessarily fashionable or designed in tempting ways. Many lack the stylishness and high finish of clothing on display in shops and malls all over the world. The answer to this environmental dilemma may lie in part in "smart" clothing, that is, clothing that is less subject to fashionable change, is heat- and cold-sensitive, and is electronically wired, but even here, the use of energy remains a concern. Certainly, while "performance" and practicality are likely to become an aspect of brand desirability, the quest for novelty always seems to win out over concern for resources.

On the face of it, the supposedly neutral style of world dress is attire that has diffused outward from the West, originating in Europe and the United States, ironically echoing Colonial dominance in attitudes to dress and civilizing imperatives. The globalization of dress is on one level informed by high fashion and its offshoots, right down to generic styles. E-linkages have allowed powerful brands to target consumers and track trends, delivering to customers in the fastest possible time. While fundamental similarities within everyday dress exist, common ideals of attractiveness and hairstyling are also countered by individualized ways of wearing clothes, ethnic differences, degrees of affluence, and customization of various kinds. Nowhere in the world does one see fully homogeneous clothing, for all societies, large or small, consist of people with different religions, ethnic beliefs, occupations, income levels, and class affiliations. Western dress is perhaps the most dominant style, but Muslim cultures, among others, offer a widespread and challenging counterpoint. Global dress is unquestionably an uneven conglomeration of differing tastes and imperatives.

Certainly, there is strong pressure from corporate brands to continue to produce generic clothing, in the twenty-first century seemingly dominating rural and urban attire. Yet the urge to retain individuality, prestige, and cultural affiliation remains strong as well, and whether one is concerned with stylish fashion or everyday dress, nothing remains static as cultures continue to develop and change. There is little doubt that brand loyalty is diminishing and that consumers are, to a large degree, pushing for more choice and personalized styles, while shopping is becoming increasingly destination-based, a form of entertainment in the event-based Western world. At the same time, millions globally live in desperate conditions where purchasing new clothing can only be a dream.

References

Hines Tony, and Margaret Bruce. Fashion Marketing: Contemporary Issues. Oxford: Butterworth-Heinemann, 2007.

Eicher Joanne, ed. (1995). Dress and Ethnicity: Change across Space and Time. Oxford: Berg.

Hines Tony, and Margaret Bruce. (2007). *Fashion Marketing: Contemporary Issues*. Oxford: Butterworth-Heinemann.

Lipovetsky Gilles. (1994). The Empire of Fashion: Dressing Modern Democracy. Princeton, NJ: Princeton University Press.

Tungate Mark. (2005). *Fashion Brands: Branding Style from Armani to Zara*. London: Kogan Page.

47

MILAN:
The city of prêt-à-porter in a world of fast fashion

Simona Segre Reinach[1]

FROM ITALIAN STYLE TO MADE IN MILAN

Italian prêt-à-porter, which reached the peak of its success in the 1980s, is not a phenomenon that appeared from nowhere, so to speak. As White suggests in an important text devoted to the renaissance of Italian fashion (2000: 1–7), it has its roots in the postwar period, especially between 1945 and 1964, when, also thanks to American funding, the textile-clothing industry started up again at full capacity. Yet while it is right to speak of continuity regarding the capacity to produce clothing (Italian ready-to-wear certainly did not appear out of the blue, but was the outcome of textile and industrial development), in terms of the significance which fashion was to assume in Italian culture and economics, it was a radically new phenomenon. In the early 1970s, a turning point took place in the history of modern fashion Milan was at the very centre of this process that gave rise to the prêt-à-porter of the fashion designers, a fashion system that was to enjoy international commercial and media success.

Milan's role in fashion should not be taken for granted. The fact is that between the 1970s and 1980s Milan did not become the capital of fashion, as is often claimed, but the capital of prêt-à-porter. It is commonly believed that what we do and think in one place could not be done or thought in another. We should then fully understand what kind of fashion ready-to-wear is, the cultural and geographic *humus* in which it sprang up and flourished, and the extent to which one depends on the other and what transformations for fashion and for the city lie on the horizon.

Economic, cultural and geographical factors, as well as a certain spirit of the times, make up the main ingredients for the success of both Italian ready-to-wear and Milan as a fashion city. Milanese fashion had in actual fact been the product of an atmosphere of an 'opening up' to cross-disciplinary influences and a sense of cosmopolitanism, which from the 1960s onwards many Milanese professional exponents of journalism, photography, art and culture had contributed to creating. The presence of design was an essential part of this atmosphere: Milan was the city of design long before it became the city of fashion. Milanese design was a forerunner of what was to become the fashion phenomenon on a wider scale. The concept combined the creative skills, experimentation with new materials and the industrial infrastructure necessary to start up the economy, and all of these preconditions joined together under the name and direction of the reinvigorated profession of the designer. It is no coincidence that today, in 2005, the endangered Milan fashion industry is looking again at design, as an example of a sector that has been able to evolve and shape its own destiny rather than simply react to events.

Swift to make its mark and appreciated by intellectuals (a new factor not wholly unconnected to its success, despite the negative period the city and the country were going through in the years of political terrorism (1969–81) and the oil and industrial crises),

---

[1] From Simona Segre Reinach, Milan: The City of Pret-Á-Porter in a World of Fast Fashion, in Christopher Breward and David Gilbert (eds), Fashion World Cities (Bloomsbury).

fashion in Milan metabolized and provided a new driving force for the economy (Foot 2001). Ahead of other Italian cities, Milan was also able to combine the strengths of the manufacturing industry and the service industry. On the one hand, the city stood at the centre of an archipelago of specialized areas, the industrial districts, of which it is to a certain extent the capital. The industrial districts, on which the Italian prêt-à-porter system rests, are highly specialized, often vertically organized production areas: for example, Como for silk, Biella for wool, Carpi for knitwear, Castelgoffredo for hosiery, and the Italian Marches for footwear. On the other hand, Milan was also the leading Italian centre for communications: commercial TV channels started up in Milan, the editorial staffs of the leading fashion press were in Milan, as were the numerous advertising agencies and PR studios.

MILAN IN THE 1980S

In the 1980s, once it had recovered from the recession, and also thanks to the spirit of the fashion industry (as Gastel wrote, 'Fashion is the most fashionable thing there is' (1995: 164)), Milan became 'Milano da bere' (literally, 'drunken Milan', from an advertising slogan for Ramazzotti), an affluent, dynamic city, rich in events to be consumed at will, all marked by fashion and the world revolving around it, from Versace's supermodels, to the fashion shows and celebrity events linked to them. Milanese ready-to-wear became a stable phenomenon conferring a specific physiognomy or the city. This was also visible in the real estate acquisitions made by the fashion designers. Many *palazzi* of the old Milanese families changed hands in a few years. For example: the building in Via Borgonuovo belonging to Franco Marinotti (Snia-Viscosa) and the Riva cotton manufacturers became Giorgio Armani's headquarters. Palazzo Rizzoli in Via Gesù was transformed with the contribution of the architect Renzo Mongiardino into Gianni Versace's headquarters. The Missoni family acquired a six-storey palazzo in Via Durini. And, after the historic palazzi in the city centre (which, with the store windows of the luxury stores, formed the by-then-celebrated 'Fashion District'), in the following decade it was to be the turn of the former industrial areas outside the city centre to become the focus of restyling by the fashion designers, when entire districts such as Porta Genova, the Bovisa and Porta Vittoria were upgraded thanks to the interest of fashion entrepreneurs in those areas.

In the 1980s the fashion show dominated the Milan stage. Trussardi transformed his catwalks into shows of great impact, taking place in unusual locations such as the La Scala opera house, Piazza del Duomo, the Brera Art Gallery, the Central Station and San Siro horse race track. Apart from their actual participation, the impression in the 1980s was that large parts of the city and its citizens were intimately involved in fashion culture, which was itself entwined with the worlds of advertising, the television studios and the Socialist Party. In that decade the relationship between design and fashion grew even closer: *Memphis* and radical architecture included fashion in their creative horizon. And, from the mid-1980s, with the ongoing economic growth, the financial aspect of fashion was also strengthened. Milan's role became international, thanks to the export of designer label garments and in general to the success Italian designers were enjoying in Europe and in the United States (in 1982 *Time Magazine* dedicated its cover to Armani, the first fashion designer after Christian Dior to be awarded the honour), especially in New York.

The Armani story is in many ways a parable of Milanese ready-to-wear with the contract with Gft (1978) sealing the new relationship between fashion design and industry, restraint and rigour as hallmarks of the designer, and the huge billboards in Via Dell'Orso for Emporio Armani as the symbol of the democratic spread of fashion. Armani, born in 1934, is part of the first generation of fashion creators who made their name in the new fashion city of Milan. Stefano Dolce and Domenico Gabbana are representatives of the second. It is singular that they are still described by journalists as the 'young designers', although they are now over forty and other, much younger creators are on the scene. The 'young' label is probably still applied to Dolce and Gabbana as the last followers of the original model of Milan prêt-à-porter, whose features we may sum up thus: a heroic debut with 'a summons to show' (in this specific case, a phone call from Beppe

Modenese, president of the Italian Chamber of Fashion); business skills (they financed the first show themselves and then immediately founded the firm); segmentation of their product into first lines, second lines, jeans, perfumes and licences; spectacular promotional strategies; and the use of endorsers from the star system. Their high-profile advertising presence at strategic points in the city, like the airport, has helped to lock their identity with the city.

MILAN IN THE 1990S

The New Yorker argued that if Armani could be considered the Volkswagen of Milan, Miuccia Prada was its Mercedes. The city of Milan in the 1990s – the decade when Prada reached success – was very different from the one that had generated the fashion designers and the 'young' fashion designers. It was difficult to see this at the time, but today it seems obvious. Miuccia Prada (whose story is similar to that of many former Milanese girls from a good middle-class background) had little in common with the biographies of the first fashion designers, such as Armani, Versace, Krizia, Missoni and Coveri. First, she was not a fashion designer, at least not in the sense of knowing how to cut, sew and make a dress. As the British newspaper *The Observer* commented recently:

> Miuccia Prada doesn't sew, embroider or knit. I never saw her sketch a skirt or a shoe, nor is she likely to pick up a pair of scissors and cut out a dress. . . . She is not that kind of designer. Instead she surrounds herself with talented people whose job is to translate her themes, concepts and especially her taste into clothes that bear the Prada name. (16 May 2004)

Second, her success as a designer did not start in Milan – a city that on the contrary opposed her, and where the leading fashion press deserted her first shows – but in New York. After her New York 'certification', she won over her home town. Only after having made their name in the United States, did Miuccia Prada and her husband Patrizio Bertelli also make their mark in Milan. And, in Foot's shrewd observation, the fact that the most celebrated luxury producer in the world needed to start with the New York shows to make her name may be seen 'as a symptom of a slow decline in the central role of Milan within the world fashion industry' (2001: 154). That said, Miuccia Prada has surfed the wave of the crisis in prêt-à-porter, which she had astutely anticipated, even though it was still in the distance. At the end of the age of the democratization of fashion and the heroic times of the 'summons to show', Prada presented herself as a producer of elite, cerebral luxury.

YEAR 2000: THE TRANSFORMATION OF PRÊT-À-PORTER

Since the close of the twentieth century, many things are changing in fashion. Italian ready-to-wear is struggling in the twists and turns of the de-location of production, Chinese competition, counterfeiting and the fluctuating meanings of the idea of 'Made in Italy'. The 'democratic' model on which ready-to-wear was based – namely, fashion accessible through the trickle down of brands (first lines, second lines, young lines, fragrances, licences, etc.) – is gradually being replaced by a polarized orientation: extreme luxury, the almost unique item, on the one hand, presented in stores of great style and, on the other, fast fashion, the fashion of Zara, Mango, H&M and many others. Fast fashion is not based on a vertical, integrated production system, as Italian prêt-à-porter originally was. The garments may be made anywhere, wherever convenient, in China or Eastern Europe. The expiry of the Multifibre Agreement, on 1 January 2005, which liberalized the entry of Chinese textile products into global markets, as I have said above, represents a further difficulty for the leadership of Italian fashion. The culture of appearances is being transformed, consumers are not content with complete, linear lifestyles, such as Armani's sobriety or Versace's glamour, presented at regular seasonal intervals. The provisional, changing identities of new consumers favour the fast, fragmented proposals of the new fashion. From research I am currently undertaking on the relationship between Italy and China and their textile and fashion industries (Segre 2005). I have learned that Italy still represents a model for China, at least as far as style and branding is concerned, but in many ways it is really China's vision of fashion that is at the vanguard. China is more attuned to fast fashion, just as Italy is by definition the home of prêt-à-porter.

BEYOND PRÊT-À-PORTER AND THE FUTURE OF MILAN

Milan is the capital of prêt-à-porter, one of several possible fashion systems that have dominated the modern history of Western clothing, its manufacture and consumption, so far. Ready-to-wear is a production and cultural model that reached its highest peak and success in business and communications in Milan. The evolution of the culture (and production) of clothing apparel, increasingly transnational, is however changing the privileged role of Milan in fashion's world order. The transformation of fashion cannot but leave its mark on Milan. The result is widely visible in its streets. The international luxury brands continue to open new stores in the prestige locations in the city centre, such as Louis Vuitton in Galleria Vittorio Emanuele and Ralph Lauren in Via Montenapoleone, the first monobrand store in Italy. At the same time, however, the same streets are dotted with new fast fashion stores, the Scandinavian H&M (taking the place of Fiorucci) and the Spanish Zara (in Corso Vittorio Emanuele).

Is Milan aware of this transformation? And how is it equipping itself to remain one of the capitals of style? Signs of change may be seen at the institutional level. The new Florence Fashion Centre is collaborating with Sistema Moda and Milan to deal with the crisis in the trade and set up a joint project for the relaunch of 'Made in Italy', with greater collaboration between the city of Rome, the home of high fashion, Florence, with its Pitti Uomo, Pitti Filati and Pitti Bimbo events, and Milan, where the prêt-à-porter fashion shows take place. The idea is to integrate the Italian know-how, which preceded the rise of Milan, and to enhance the whole image of 'Made in Italy', not just the ready-to-wear with which Milan is linked. On this subject Mario Boselli, President of the National Chamber of Fashion, states: 'In France, fashion is only Paris, but in Italy it is Milan, Florence and also Rome. It is an integrated process in which each part works together with the others and gives its contribution to the whole system' (quoted in *Women's Wear Daily,* 2 March 2001). Giovanni Bozzetti, Milan City Councillor for Fashion, shares this view: 'I see in our future a nation which plays a compact game, each with its own speciality – Milan for ready to wear, Rome for high fashion, Florence for menswear, Naples for tailoring' (*Milano è la Moda,* ClassEditori, 2004: 137.)

The traditional rivalry between Paris and Milan – which in the 1980s had led several fashion designers to 'choose' one or the other, seems to be fading, faced with Asian competition that is much closer to the new successful fast fashion system. Significantly Gft, Gruppo Finanaziario Tessile (one of the largest textile companies that had a primary role in the history of Italian ready-to-wear) has announced that by 2010 it will move completely to China. In response to such trends and to promote better European cooperation, a protocol agreement was signed (in Milan, since Lombardy with its 200,000 workers, is confirmed as the leading textile concentration in Europe) between Mario Boselli, president of the Italian Chamber of Fashion, and Didier Grumbach, president of the *Fédération Française de la Couture,* 'for a joint strategy regarding processes and changes to avoid being overwhelmed by [competition from the East]' (*Corriere Economia,* 13 December 2004: 26). In October 2005 a new textile association was also founded in Milan, with the aim of relaunching the Italian textile industry. The association, called *Milano Unica* is based in Milan and brings together in the city many different Italian textile exhibitions, IdeaBiella (wool), IdeaComo (silk), Moda In (textile and accessories) and Shirt Avenue. It is clear then that Milan aims at preserving its fashion leadership.

On 2 May 2005, at Palazzo Mezzanotte, in Piazza degli Affari, Milan, a two-day meeting was held, entitled '*Milano di moda:* First strategic conference on fashion' also described by the press as the 'Convocation of the States General of Fashion'. Guests were the historical protagonists of Milanese ready-to-wear – such as Ottavio and Rosita Missoni, Dolce and Gabbana, Mariuccia Mandelli, Laura Biagiotti, Roberto Cavalli, the forerunners of ready-to-wear, like Elio Fiorucci, the exponents of the National Chamber of Fashion, various major luxury companies, and the main universities in Milan. One message emerged loud and clear: 'only by changing everything can we win back our leadership', by which they admitted, perhaps officially for the first time, having lost it. That 'everything' to be changed merged in a criticism of the symbolic and structural centre of ready-to-wear, the fashion show, whose model goes back to 1951 and which appears, for many speakers, wholly inadequate to tackle the new market. The timing and presentation of models must change. No longer should shows last one week, but fewer concentrated days, four at most, to give journalists and buyers the time to travel between the increasingly numerous fashion weeks in the different cities throughout the world. And above all, the garments on the catwalks ought to be those of the current season, as happens in the 'design week', another significant event in the cultural and business life of Milan, and not those for the following season, so as not to give time for fast fashion protagonists (and the Chinese) to copy the models.

It is significant that no representative of systems other than ready-to-wear was present at the conference; there was no fast fashion company, no 'Chinese competitor' apart from an entrepreneur from Prato (the Italian city that hosts one of the largest Chinese communities in Europe and where there are a few very successful and entirely Chinese-owned fast fashion companies) invited more as an orientalist curiosity than as a witness of the new transnational phase of fashion. Moreover, among the 'rival' cities, only Paris and New York were mentioned, as if the geographical and cultural context had remained stationary since the 1980s. Milan still *means* fashion, argued Stefano Zecchi, Councillor for Fashion in the Milan City Council in his paper to the meeting, but the question we must ask is whether it is still *in* fashion.

In fact, despite the recent changes, Milan continues to be an ideal city for clothes shopping, due to the range, quality and variety of products on offer. Alongside boutiques, flagship stores, restored *palazzi* and the *maisons* of the great fashion designers – which still constitute the most visible part, but are probably destined to become future archaeological remains – we may glimpse a new network of shops and artistic-craft-business activities, which greatly remind us of the shape of Milan in the 1960s and 1970s, with its innovative stores such as Fiorucci, Gulp, Cose, La Drogheria Solferino and the creative atmosphere of the beginnings of prêt-à-porter.

Little tailors and dressmakers' shops, craft shops, new interpretations of luxury and commercial initiatives of various kinds are again flourishing in the city, standing apart from both the mass-production of the colossal flagship stores, and that of the new giants of fast fashion. As Gilbert writes, 'relatively small, independent designers and retailers may sustain a viable independent fashion culture, often within distinctive districts of the city' (2000: 13).

In the Isola district, to give an example of the new creativity, which seems to be once more arising in the city, there is the so-called *Stecca degli Artigiani*. This is built on a former industrial area (Siemens-Electra) abandoned in the 1960s and 1970s and then relaunched in the 1980s by the Milan City Council to host various artisan and artistic workshops. Another example is the former Braun Boveri factory – occupied by artists in the mid 1980s – now the official headquarters of a Centre for Contemporary Art. I like to think of this district – one of the many where this transformation is beginning to be seen – as a metaphor for a possible future for Milan. A future upgrading as a vital shopping city (and not just for tourists), in continuity with its history as a Hanseatic city, as Aldo Bonomi (2004). describes it, where the experience of fashion may live alongside the newly emerging expressions of creativity And perhaps it is no coincidence that the inhabitants of this neighbour-hood, bordering on the Garibaldi district where the colossal 'City of Fashion' will arise, have demonstrated against the enactment of the plan, fearing that the new initiative – seen by many inhabitants of the area as a barefaced colonization by a prêt-à-porter singing its swan song – will destroy the authentic substratum of this district. But what the inhabitants of the Isola perhaps do not see is that here Milan is already in the future, where boutiques like Agata Ruiz de la Prada's in Via Maroncelli stand alongside new dressmakers' and independent stores of various kinds.

Fashion is an important part of the show of urban life and its experiential aspect, as Gilbert (2000: 11) argues, is closely linked to the vitality and the quality of the place where purchases are made. As Diego Della Valle, Chief Executive of Tod's states, 'a brand must eschew look-alike stores across the world and offer products specific to various cities' (Michault 2004). But in Milan in particular, the designer fashion seems more intractable about transforming, about measuring up to the changed scenario, almost oppressed by the weight of its glorious past. The transition from a culture exclusively linked to prêt-à-porter to a more articulate, complex interaction of the global and the local is the key point on which the future of Milan as capital of style depends. For this reason, in Milan creativity currently no longer seems to exhaust itself in fashion, which in the last few years has been perceived as more than a significant experience, almost as an incursion on the life of the city.

Prêt-à-porter today is being criticized and deconsecrated. 'Fashion Weak' is the title of a recent happening made by an independent group of young Milanese activists during one of the last official fashion weeks, to protest against the imposition of fashion on reluctant Milanese citizens – the exact opposite of what happened in the 1980s. The 'Fashion Weak' happening, we must however point out, was organized in one of the most prestigious fashion schools in Milan. So, if it is true that fashion cannot be denied as an essential feature of the city, especially in Milan, where it is consubstantial, it is equally true that Milan must find a new role in the increasingly wider transnational network of fashion capitals, and start to offer experience and not just products: a shopping city able to communicate first of all the essence of itself and its continuing vitality.

References

Bonomi, A. (2004). "Milano, l'importanza di ridiventare leader." Corriere della Sera, 22 December.

Foot J. (2001) Milano dopo il miracolo, Milan: Feltrinelli.

Gastel M. (1995) 50 anni di moda italiana, Milan: Vallardi.

Gilbert D. (2000) 'Urban outfitting. The city and the spaces of fashion culture', in S. Bruzzi and P. Church Gibson (eds) Fashion Cultures: Theories, Explorations and Analysis, London: Routledge.

Michault J. (2004) "The road to China? A soft approach." International Herald Tribune on-line version, 7 December, www.iht.com/articles/2004/12/06/style/fhong.php

Segre S. (2005) '"China and Italy": Fashion Fashion versus Prêt à Porter. Towards a new culture of fashion', Fashion Theory, 9(1): 43–56.

White N. (2000) Reconstructing Italian Fashion: America and the Development of the Italian Fashion Industry, Oxford: Berg.

48

FROM SYMBOLS TO SPIRIT:
Changing conceptions of national identity in Chinese fashion

Christine Tsui[1]

In the years between 2004 and 2010 I interviewed thirteen top fashion designers for two books that I was writing on Chinese designers. During the discussions, I found these designers frequently highlighted their passion for revealing their Chinese "roots" and "heritage" or the "5,000 years of Chinese history and culture" in their clothing. The designers often claimed their intention to present the profundity of Chinese culture to spectators at fashion events (Leng 2005; Tsui 2009). "The national is the international" (*minzu de jiushi shijie de*) has been one of the most frequently used slogans by Chinese fashion media journalists and designers. In her book *Chinese Fashion from Mao to Now*, Wu Juanjuan also described the rising Chinese design stars with the phrase: "the more national, the more international" (Wu 2009: 141). Everywhere we look, from historical academic articles, interviews with designers themselves, and through to popular media sources, the spirit of "nationalism" is palpable in China's fashion scene.

Most of the literature written on Chinese fashion and national identity formation concentrates on dress before the end of the Mao era. In contrast, this chapter focuses on Chinese fashion in the globalized and market-oriented post-Mao era—that is, from the 1980s to the twenty-first century.

China proclaimed it had "opened-the-door" to the world in the 1980s when the post-Mao government of Deng Xiaoping led a program of economic liberalization and internationalization. Theoretically, we could claim that China started its globalization from the 1980s.

However, while China is an internationally engaged economy today, Chinese designers still explicitly manifest strong hallmarks of nationalism that actively essentialize "Chineseness." This paradox deserves greater attention. Accordingly, I set myself the task of exploring the evolution of Chinese fashion in the years of "opening and reform," to understand the evolution of Chinese fashion design in the age of market-oriented nationalism.

CHINESE FASHION SINCE THE POST-MAO ERA: FROM SYMBOLS TO SPIRIT

On October 1, 2006, Chinese designer Frankie Xie presented his brand Jefen at Paris Fashion Week. This was the first time a (mainland) Chinese designer had paraded a collection at the top four international fashion weeks. The show was regarded as "a historical day for the Chinese fashion industry, and the Chinese designer has won world reorganization" (Xinhua News Agency 2006).

From a spectator's point of view, Jefen has very few traces of any Chinese costume or symbols, but its founder and chief designer Xie still stressed that he drew his inspiration from Chinese culture: "For a Chinese designer, it is important to understand the essence of Chinese culture and spirit, which is its profundity, its broadness and its tolerance of foreign culture," he says. "Without this understanding, it will only be superficial to apply such Chinese elements as peonies and *qipao* to a costume" (Zhang 2011).

---

[1] From Christine Tsui, (2013) From Symbols to Spirit: Changing Conceptions of National Identity in Chinese Fashion, *Fashion Theory*, Volume 17, No. 5, Taylor & Francis.

Xie's statement depicts the unshakeable position of Chinese culture in his design. It simultaneously shows his intention to redefine Chinese culture in the minds of Western audiences. Xie also noted the once-omnipresence of the *qipao* and other traditional Chinese symbols, and instead of adopting the same strategy to penetrate the international market as his predecessors, he endeavored to remove the old images of Chinese fashion from the minds of Western spectators and replace them with a new form of Chinese culture—one that is more than merely *qipaos* and peonies.

In 2008, designer Ma Ke also moved from her invocation of tradition through the Tombs of Stone Warriors and exhibited another line, provocatively called Wuyong (*Useless*), at the Haute Couture Fashion Week in Paris. This was the debut of a (mainland) Chinese designer at the distinguished Haute Couture Fashion Week. Themed within the idea of "anti-fashion luxury," Wuyong invoked the feeling of naturalness and simplicity. The collection had no significant symbols of "Chineseness." However, the collection was still entitled "Ma Ke's Oriental Fashion Philosophy" by *Harper's Bazaar* (July 2008)—the absence of overt Chinese symbolism clearly did not prevent the spectators from feeling its Chinese flavor.

During my interviews with Ma Ke, she revealed her close affinity with her Chinese roots. She once talked about her rejection of a generous invitation to go to Italy for further study of fashion design from an Italian fashion journalist—one of the judges at the second Brother Cup contest at which Ma Ke won the first prize (Tsui 2009). Ma said because "her roots" were in China she feared she would lose her inspiration for design if she left her homeland. From her early work in 1994 invoking the Qin Warrior Tombs through to 1996 when she established her brand Exception and until her latest collection Wuyong, Ma's works demonstrated a transformation from one that highlighted Chinese culture in its traditional symbolic forms like the Qin warriors to one that emphasized a more amorphous Chineseness—its spirit. To Ma Ke, clothing carries "spiritual qualities" that help to convey the message from the designers to the wearers (www.wuyonguseless.com, official Wuyong website). To achieve this end, she opened a studio solely for Wuyong in the southern China city of Zhuhai, hired a team of craft workers, and directed that all aspects of the production be done by hand—from fabric weaving to the final assembly of the clothing. Her long-term objective for Wuyong is to preserve the traditional crafts of China.

The changes in interpretations of "Chineseness" in Ma Ke's designs mirrors Xie's journey. They both aim to deliver Chinese culture through their design, but at the same time, they are trying to remove the clichéd *qipao* and dragon symbols imprinted in 1980s and 1990s and establish a different "Chinese" culture in a modern way in the twenty-first century. The desire to redefine the conception of Chinese culture and deliver a "modern" image for China can also be traced to several emerging younger designers who recently paraded their collections in 2012 and 2013 during the London and Paris Fashion Weeks.

Zhang Huishan, born in the 1980s and trained at the elite Central Saint Martins College of Art and Design, paraded his eponymous label in February 2013 at London Fashion Week (www.londonfashion week.co.uk). When interviewed by *Vogue* in 2012, he stated, "I want to promote a contemporary angle of Chinese culture" (Adams 2012). Ji Cheng, another Chinese designer trained in an Italian fashion institute, also showed in London at the same time, and she also claims her objective to be the delivery of an "aesthetic of modern China" to the international audience (Chung 2012).

This new identity is no longer in the form of traditional Chinese symbols, instead, it is a conceptual theme that can be defined as "spirit," "philosophy," and/or "modern culture"; nevertheless, it is still about "Chineseness." To achieve this shift Chinese designers primarily use two different types of formats to reflect their translation to "the Chinese spirit."

THE CHINESE NATIONAL IDENTITY: NATIONALISM AND PATRIOTISM

Dittmer and Kim (1993: 13) define national identity as the relationship between nation and state that emerges when the people of that nation identify with the state; Whiting (1995: 296) argues that "national identity emerges in how the policy-making elite perceives and articulates the image of China in its relationship to the world"; Smith (1993: 15) states that national identity comprises both a cultural and political identity and is located in a political community as well as a cultural one. I argue that the national identity of Chinese fashion designers is a consequence of politics that is manipulated by both the state and the people (designers), in both active and passive ways. I articulate this argument by analyzing the aforementioned phenomenon from three angles: what exactly is "national identity"; how was it formed; and, in the mind of designers, why is "national identity" so important for their career?

Although nationalism is not something unique to China, the significance that Chinese designers attach to it in their clothes is very unusual among international designers. For instance, from what we can observe from the fashion magazines, catwalk shows, and television interviews, very few Western designers would restrict their design inspiration to their own ethnic cultures and/or traditions—their inspirations can be from anywhere and any part of the world—Europe, Asia, Africa, or even outer space. To a certain degree the ethnicity of Western designers remains vague to the general public—a British designer may work for a French fashion group or an American designer may have an Italian patronage. It would be weird to hear someone like John Galliano say, "As an English designer I feel it an honor to work for Dior." But it is highly likely that a Chinese designer would say, "As a Chinese designer I feel it an honor to work for Dior," if he or she were in the position to become the chief designer of a classic European or American brand. As Chinese scholar Zheng Yongnian defines it, "Nationalism is about us against them. It is important to sharpen the sentiments about we-ness versus they-ness when nationalism is constructed" (Zheng 1999: 46), which explains the attitude of Chinese designers to Western fashion when competing in the global fashion market. Chinese designers believe it is important to differentiate themselves through their ethnicity from "they-ness"—the Western designers.

Chinese nationalism has been influencing Chinese people's thinking since the impact of the Opium Wars in the mid-nineteenth century forced greater numbers of Chinese to think about their country in relation to other powerful nations. With the spread of Marxism from the 1920s onwards, nationalist thinking became increasingly influenced by notions of "anti-imperialism" (Schrecker 1971).

After the establishment of the People's Republic of China under Communist Party leadership in 1949, "anti-bourgeois" sentiments underscored the new communist-style "nationalism" (Guo 2004; Tao and Jin 2004; Zheng 1999). Theoretically this position ended at the close of the 1970s—after the Cultural Revolution, however, as an individual who was born at the beginning of the 1970s, I remember the textbooks I read during primary and high school—people living in capitalist countries only have pecuniary interests with each other; capitalists would rather pour milk into a river rather than share it with other people; capitalists make money by exploiting labor . . . In general, the impression that I had of "capitalist" countries was that they were a group of cruel people. They did not have any of the affections and emotions that normal human beings would have. When I started my first job in the early 1990s, translating for American expatriates who had come to China to build a Sino-US joint venture, I met a young American woman of a similar age to me. She told me it was her first time away from her family and that coming to such distant country left her mother and her in tears when she left home. I was quite surprised to know that capitalists also cried when a family member departed.

After the Cultural Revolution, at the end of the 1970s, the state started its "open-door" policy. Inviting Pierre Cardin was an indication of welcoming Western culture and technology—however, it was done in an extremely cautious manner and at an extremely limited pace. The leadership showed its capacity to use nationalism as a mechanism for achieving political goals after the June 4 crackdown in 1989. A new wave of "nationalism" was prompted in earnest with the 1992 Patriotic Education Campaign that was rolled out through the school system.

Hunt (1993) argued that patriotism is a better term for describing and explaining the particular characteristics of the Chinese search for national identity. Patriotism can be interpreted as "national interest," "national tradition," "national spirit," "national harmony," and "Chineseness" (Guo 2004: 1). Zheng made a similar statement that "China's modern nationalism has also built from a modern notion of Chinese tradition and ethnic unity" (1999: 68). This propaganda of loving the nation and national traditions conforms exactly to the cognition that is embedded in the minds of the designers (and myself) through the school system. "Patriotism" has always been a core theme filtering through the education system, starting from primary school and through to universities, since the establishment of the People's Republic. Although education to promote patriotism is compulsory in many countries, in China patriotism is equivalent to "loving the Communist Party"—as the Communist Party built the new China—without the Communist Party, there would be no new China (*meiyou Gongchandang jiu meiyou xin Zhogguo*). Loyalty to the party is equivalent to loyalty to the country—which imprints love of the country with a party political tone. To ensure the continuity of the convention, the Communist Party started to breed the "Young Pioneers (of the party)" (*shaonian-xianfengdui*) and "the Members of the Communist Youth League" (*Gongqing tuanyuan*) among school-aged children. Students who enthusiastically apply to join the groups are considered to be manifesting "advanced thought" (*sixiang xianjin*). Hence, Patriotism Education in China imposes much stronger political imprints on individuals.

Designer Liu Yang shared an anecdote with me during our interviews (Tsui 2009). He was invited to attend Leipzig Fashion Week in 1996 in Germany. Liu was shocked by the content of the many monochromatic pictures of "China" hanging around the stage when he entered the exhibition hall. The pictures displayed included one of a group of children in shabby clothing sitting in a dilapidated classroom; another of a crowd of men and women gathered around eating monkey's brain; a shriveled, hunchbacked old man hacking a goose with a cleaver in a dim, cramped shop . . . Liu was seriously offended—maybe the organizer did not intend to offend and just aimed to show the indigenous lifestyle of Chinese people, but they only exhibited the backwardness of China. To Liu this portrayal of China in such a negative light could have become a political issue on his return to China—and he wanted to ensure that he was properly honoring his homeland rather than participating in denigrating the image of his country. Eventually he forced the organizer to remove the pictures by threatening to cut into pieces all the clothing destined for the show.

To the state, nationalism is an active and conscious political operation; to Chinese fashion designers, nationalism becomes an idiosyncrasy imposed by the state but embraced in their work—so depicting "Chinese" identity is a result of such a patriotic campaign…At the same time, nationalism is also a mechanism used by Chinese designers, first, to distinguish them from the Western fashion and, second, to gain rapid recognition from the global market. The mechanism is playing a more evident role for the younger emerging designers. Wang Haizhen, who trained at the London College of Fashion for his undergraduate studies and Central Saint Martins College of Art and Design for his master's degree, received the Fashion Fringe Awards from Christopher Bailey, the Chief Creative Officer of Burberry, in 2012. Wang, despite his very international background, stated during an interview that:

> Even if you can't see any obvious Oriental influences, like dragons for example, across my pieces, the man who made this collection—me—is Chinese and that will always be there, even though I was trained in the West. (Attlee 2013)

Yang Du studied textile prints during her undergraduate studies and women's design for her master's degree in London. Her collection's signature is exaggerated, quirky, fun animal prints on giant T-shirts and/or cashmeres. Trained at Central Saint Martins College of Art and Design and working at Vivienne Westwood, Galliano, and Giles Deacon, Yang was reported to be "too crazy for a Chinese" by the celebrity professor Louise Wilson (*Jing Daily* 2012). Despite few traces of Chineseness in her collections, Yang also proclaimed that:

> I'm proud to be Chinese. I came over to study when I was 22. My culture is in my blood. So studying at Central Saint Martins taught me how to find myself and be who I am. (*Jing Daily* 2012)

These two young designers are demonstrating their connection with their Chinese identity but it could also be regarded as a highly effective tactic for establishing a unique market niche because their designs would not be recognizably "Chinese" to most observers. The ascending power of China as a nation internationally means that such expressions of national distinctiveness provide a comparative advantage for China's designers in their desire for prominence on the world stage, and currently the word "China" helps to gain quick international attention.

Nationalism plays a dual role in Chinese fashion. It is both a result of patriotic education as well as a mechanism manipulated for competition with the Western designers. Chinese fashion designers have long had the ambition to dominate the world fashion stage. In fact, the Chinese are ambitious. The often-repeated question in China is "when will Chinese win international awards (recognition)?," such as Academy Awards, a Nobel Prize, the World Cup, or have a billionaire and entrepreneur like Bill Gates, to name just a few. The desire "to be the best in the world" seems to be a particularly strong idiosyncrasy in many Chinese. The regular logic is: China has the largest population so we should be able to produce a few geniuses from such a big population; we have 5,000 years of cultural history so we should have many valuable things to share with the world. Nationalism is currently construed as a form of competition against other countries, rather than a collaboration and engagement with other countries.

THE EVOLUTION: SOCIALIST MODERNIZATION

Nationalism has evolved from "anti-imperialism" into "patriotism" over the past century. "Anti-imperialism" certainly agrees with "patriotism," but "patriotism" does not necessarily mean "anti-imperialism"; the two norms are not bound together any more. And most importantly of all, in the twenty-first century, "anti-imperialism" and "patriotism" no longer require being opposed to foreign influences.

This change is all to the good fortune of the younger generation of designers—they can be patriotic and learn Western fashion techniques at the same time. The increasing presence of Chinese designers in the international fashion weeks proves the more positive influence of Western culture on Chinese designers. The aforementioned Chinese designer Frankie Xie, who was the first designer representing (mainland) China to show at Paris Fashion Week, worked for Kenzo in Paris, Tokyo, and Hong Kong for nearly ten years. The several aforementioned emerging young Chinese designers like Zhang Huishan, Masha Ma, Wang Haizhen, Yang Du, and Uma Wang all trained at the elite fashion school Central Saint Martins College of Art and Design. Even those who grew up during Mao's era and had no opportunity to go overseas for education received certain influences from the Western fashion figures, of which, Pierre Cardin was widely regarded as the most impactful.

"Learning from the West" but at the same time still complying with the "patriotic" principle is a typical process in "socialist modernization." Chinese growing up in the post-Mao era have learned—during modernization under the framework of the socialist system—to absorb the parts that benefit the development of its socialist political regime and reject anything that may hurt the state. There has been a clear movement through the decades, from directly reproducing well-known Chinese symbols to imitating Western designers' work through to representing the Chinese spirit. On this path Chinese fashion designers eventually found a formula that fits comfortably with their nature and the trend towards modernization—a Western form replete with Chinese spirit. The spirit emerges from their daily life experiences, or from perceived traditional cultural virtues—such as the desire for peace, harmony, and balance, or their way of transforming the traditional symbols and/or costume forms to contemporary ones. Such an evolution is the result of modernization, hybridization, and competition between nationalism and globalization.

SUMMARY AND CONCLUSION

Chinese fashion carries an overt, salient national identity resulting from the nationalism that has spread through every aspect of society and the education system as a consequence of the current leadership's desire to legitimize their rule. However, expressions of national identity have evolved from the use of concrete traditional Chinese symbols to invocations of an abstract Chinese spirit. The spirit is manifest in two different styles: first, the works of the "Zen" designers that create oriental feelings of peace, calm, and harmony, by adopting the pale and/or neutral colors, natural fabrics, and naturally flowing shapes; and, second, the designers that invoke a "modern" China either by sourcing inspiration from contemporary daily life or rejuvenating traditional Chinese elements with a modern look. This article argues that evolution from traditional symbols to the spiritual form signifies a new form of the Chinese "nationalism": instead of delivering Chinese culture in an *explicit, direct,* and *exterior* form, Chinese designers switch to convey "Chineseness" in a *subtle, indirect,* and *hidden* form. The evolution is a result of modernization, hybridization, and competition between nationalism and globalization. The importation of Western culture and technology has helped rejuvenate local traditions and transform them into new forms that connect directly with contemporary Chinese lifestyles. At the same time, the dominance of the party-state on people's ideology makes it almost impossible for any Western culture and ideology to completely overtake the position of national culture, or to even dismantle local national tradition.

Although our current fashion systems originated in the West, it is worth noting that the monopoly of the Western fashion industries on the global fashion system is being dispersed by non-Western fashion. The emergence of Japanese fashion in the 1960s and 1970s, attracted Western audiences with "three key elements of Japanese aesthetic philosophy—irregularity, imperfection and asymmetry" (Steele 1991: 186), and now the younger generation of Chinese fashion designers seems poised to achieve another wave of diversification of the global fashion scene. It is possible that Chinese fashion will eventually impact on global fashion by sharing the Chinese spirit. As the largest luxury fashion goods consuming country, the growing scale of the Chinese market will entrench the West's burgeoning desire to learn about Chinese culture and values, and this trend will support the integration of Chinese fashion into the global fashion system. Over the last few decades, Chinese designers are gradually moving from the periphery of the global fashion system toward its center.

References

Adams, Esther. 2012. "Back to the Future: Huishan Zhang's Fall Collection Is Rooted in Traditionalism." *Vogue* February 18. http://www.vogue.com/vogue-daily/article/back-to-the-future-huishan-zhangs-fall-collection-is-rooted-in-traditionalism/#1 (accessed March 17, 2013).

Attlee, D. Florence. 2013. "Why China Is Sitting on Fashion's Front Row." *CNN* February 26. http://www.cnn.com/2013/02/26/world/asia/china-london-fashion-week/ (accessed March 17, 2013).

Chung, Waikit. 2012. "Ji Cheng at AW12." *China Design Hub* April 5. http://chinadesignhub.com/2012/04/ji-cheng-at-awl2/ (accessed April 15, 2013).

Dittmer, Lowell and Samuel Kim. 1993. "In Search of a Theory of National Identity." In Lowell Dittmer and Samuel Kim (eds) *China's Quest for National Identity*, pp. 1–31. Ithaca, NY, and London: Cornell University Press.

Guo, Yingjie. 2004. *Cultural Nationalism in Contemporary China: The Search for National Identity under Reform.* London and New York: RoutledgeCurzon.

Hunt, Michael H. 1993. "Chinese National Identity and the Strong State: The Late Qing-Republican Crisis." In Lowell Dittmer and Samuel Kim (eds) *Chinese Quest for National Identity*, pp. 62–79. Ithaca, NY, and New York: Cornell University Press.

Ji, Min. 1995. "Hu Xiaodan, 'Writing' Forbidden City on the Dress" (Hu Xiaodan, bazijincheng "xie" zaifushishang). *Wen Wei Po Daily News (Wenhuibao)* October 20: 10.

Jing Daily. 2012. "9 Questions for Fashion Designer Yang Du." *Jing Daily June 18.* http://www.jingdaily.com/9-questions-for-fashion-designer-yang-du/18992/ (accessed March 17, 2013).

Leng, Yun. 2005. *Dialogue, Three Generations of Chinese Fashion Designer* (Shanghai Designers only) (*Duihua Zhongguo sandai shizhuang shejishi*). Shanghai: Shanghai Bookstore Publisher.

Leng, Yun. 2013. *China Fashion: Conversations with Designers* (Chinese Edition, *Zhongguo shishang: Yu Zhonguo shejishi duihua*). Hong Kong: Hong Kong University Press.

Rhodes, Alexandra. 2012. "Newgen: Huishan Zhang." *Hunger TV* September 14. http://www.hungertv.com/

fashion/feature/newgen-huishan-zhang/ (accessed March 17, 2013).

Schrecker, John E. 1971. *Imperialism and Chinese Nationalism: Germany in Shantung.* Cambridge, MA: Harvard University Press.

Smith, Anthony. 1993. *National Identity.* Reno, Las Vegas, NV, and London: University of Nevada Press.

Steele, Valerie. 1991. *Women of Fashion.* New York: Rizzoli.

Tao, Dongfeng and Yuanpu Jin (eds). 2004. *Cultural Studies in China.* Singapore: Marshall Cavendish.

Tsui, Christine. 2009. *China Fashion: Conversations with Designers.* Oxford and New York: Berg.

Wang, Gungwu. 1995. *The Chinese Way: Chinese Position in International Relations.* Oslo: Scandinavian University Press.

Whiting, Allen. 1995. "Chinese Nationalism and Foreign Policy after Deng." *The China Quarterly* 142: pp. 295–316.

Wu, Juanjuan. 2009. *Chinese Fashion from Mao to Now.* Oxford: Berg.

Xinhua News Agency. 2006. "China Makes Historic Debut at Paris Fashion Week." *china.org.cn* October 2. http://www.china.org.cn/english/Life/182880.htm (accessed August 10, 2012).

Zhang, Jing. 2011. "Dressed for Success." *China Daily* March 11. http://europe.chinadaily.com.cn/epaper/2011-03/11/content_12155767.htm (accessed August 10, 2012).

Zheng, Yongnian. 1999. *Discovering Chinese Nationalism in China: Modernization, Identity, and International Relations.* Cambridge: Cambridge University Press.

FURTHER READING

Breward, Christopher and David Gilbert (eds). 2006. *Fashion's World Cities*. Berg.

Crewe, Louise. 2017. *The Geographies of Fashion: Consumption, Space, and Value*. Bloomsbury.

Kondo, Dorrine. 1997. *About Face: Performing Race in Fashion and Theater*. Routledge.

Ling, Wessie. Simone Segre-Reinach (eds.) (2018) *Fashion in Multiple Chinas: Chinese Styles in the Transglobal Landscape*, London: I.B. Tauris

Lipovetsky, Gilles. 2002. *The Empire of Fashion: Dressing Modern Democracy*. Princeton University Press.

Luvaas, Brent. 2012. *DIY Style: Fashion, Music, and Global Digital Cultures*. Berg.

Luvaas, Brent and Joanne B. Eicher. 2018. *The Anthropology of Dress and Fashion: A Reader*. Bloomsbury.

Paulicelli, Eugenia and Hazel Clark (eds). 2009. *The Fabric of Cultures: Fashion, Identity, and Globalization*. Routledge.

Peirson-Smith, A. and Hancock, J.H. (eds.) (2018). *Transglobal Fashion Narratives: clothing communication, style statements and brand storytelling*. Bristol: Intellect Books.

Tu, Thuy Linh Nguyen. 2011. *The Beautiful Generation: Asian Americans and the Cultural Economy of Fashion*. Duke University Press.

Zhao, Jianhua. 2013. *The Chinese Fashion Industry: An Ethnographic Approach*. Bloomsbury.

Figure 36 Belted Boy.
Source: Brent Luvaas

Part XI

Beauty and the Body

Figure 37 Hirakash, Photo Courtesy of Brent Luvaas.
Source: Brent Luvaas

INTRODUCTION

Myles Ethan Lascity

THE NEW FACE OF MAKEUP

"Today is a great day for lash equality," begins the CoverGirl commercial from November 2016. Introducing the brand's *So Lashy! Mascara*, the narrator continues to say that the product "works for all lash types." The advertisement flashes to CoverGirls including singer Katy Perry, actress Sofia Vagara, vlogger Nura Afia, actress Amy Pham, and R&B duo Chloe x Halle. However, the spokesperson who drew the most attention was the narrator, make-up artist and Internet celebrity James Charles.

Yes, CoverGirl had introduced its first Cover*Boy*. The campaign was the first by the make-up brand to include a male-identifying spokesperson. The advertisements also helped introduce Charles, a 17-year-old with a healthy YouTube and Instagram following, to a national audience.

The move by CoverGirl was celebrated across the pop culture landscape, as The New York Times and Seventeen interviewed Charles. This is not the first time an advertisement featured a male in makeup MAC Cosmetics began featuring drag queen RuPaul in their advertisements in the 1980s (see Hancock in this issue) and the J. Crew catalogue featured a young boy wearing pink nail polish in 2011. However, CoverGirl's move was perhaps the most prominent inclusion of men using a stereotypically feminine product. Still, some of these examples have provoked outrage from conservative elements of society. In the case of CoverGirl's inclusion of Charles, a mommy blogger wondered whether to tell her son what Charles was doing is "sinful and wrong" (Greenfield, 2016).

Despite the outcry, a glance at Charles' social media feeds shows that his videos are as much about art as gender and sexuality. His YouTube videos range from the simplistic application of face freckles and bleached brows to tutorials on using blue/green eye shadow and large pieces of glitter to create a "Chunky Glitter Festival" look and purple eye shadow design to resemble Snapchat's "galaxy filter." His YouTube videos constitute a version of aspirational labor (Duffy, 2016), which, for Charles, has paid off. However, Charles' videos help to remind us of the performativity of gender (Butler 2006) and the reaction to his work with CoverGirl highlight how understandings of sex, gender and sexuality are often "conflated" (Entwistle, 2015: 142).

Charles, for what it's worth, does not identify as transgender, just gay. During an interview on *Ellen*, Charles said, "When I first told my parents, I wanted to do makeup, … that was a big thing." His parents were supportive, but didn't fully understand his interest. "It just took a lot of explaining and a lot of kind of understanding because men in makeup obviously is a very new concept; it has not been widely accepted in the past, so it was definitely a learning process," he said (Charles, 2016).

Charles is correct, in a sense, because men in makeup are rarely discussed in contemporary western society. It is important to note that this, as with all uses of fashion and appearance, are highlight contextual and dependent upon temporal, geographic and cultural changes (Kaiser, 2013). What is accepted, and even lauded in one setting is often criticized, ridiculed or even prohibited in another. For example, men wearing makeup is common in certain situations, like during performances, and outside of contemporary western contexts, in places such as South Korea (see Miller, this volume). The spilt of male and female fashion and styling in the West can be traced to the 1400s, with the differences becoming more stark in the mid-to-late 1660s. By the 1800s, simple male styles were contrasted with more fanciful male appearance, and men then avoided the fanciful looks adopted by women (Hollander 1994, 63-78). This division between normative presentations of male and female appearance has proved remarkably durable in the centuries since. While the contrasts and waves and waned, and there had been some movement toward more unisex styles, ultimately these fashions proved to be more fads as opposed to lasting changes (Paoletti, 2015).

As such, fashion and concern for personal appearance remains largely in the feminine realm, and men involved in these areas are often considered not successfully masculine. "Effeminacy and effeminate styles of dressing have been associated with homosexuality for as long as homosexuality has had a name," writes Shaun Cole (2000, 31). This scenario, however, can also be attributed to the cultural classifications people are offered. Our bodies and our gender displays are always marked, but some classification systems are more inclusive than others; in the U.S. and in most Western cultures that has defaulted to a binary male-female classification (Bordo, 1999: 36-43).

However, Charles' use of makeup in the national advertising campaign helps challenge the gender binaries that are being increasingly questioned in contemporary Western society. Cross-dressing, in particular, has been understood as a practice that challenges the gender binary or normative gender performances (Kaiser, 2012: 165), and further illustrates the difficulty in separating sexuality and gender (Entwistle, 2015: 175). Still, given the long historical separation between gender performances and the assumption that masculinity does not include makeup, it is unsurprising that when Charles sells a stereotypical feminine product that he would receive some pushback.

Like the chapters in this section, Charles' rise from social media star to mainstream cosmetic spokesperson remind us of the power of the mass media to construct and define social expectations. Advertising, particularly, works on the myth of individual agency while reinforcing cultural norms that empower some individuals and oppress others (Purvis, 2013). However, the rise of the Internet and social media has challenged some of the mass media's power and influence by giving amateurs and fans an alternative place to influence cultural systems (Duffy, 2015: 87-113; Rocamora, 2013). Amateurs are able to promote their talents and suggest changing norms, but brands and media producers have also shown a willingness to accept a small, select number of newcomers into larger cultural system.

A BODY OF WORK

Charles' YouTube channel, along with some of his influencer friends and the chapters in this section, further remind us of the performative nature of gender and the power of social expectations. Two videos, for example, adhere more strictly to gender norms than some of Charles' makeup tips. These videos introduce Victor, a dark haired, facial-hair clad husband of Charles's best friend, as "Daddy." In "Daddy Does My Voiceover," Charles creates and entire look, while Vincent voices the instructions from a typical male point of view. This video includes Vincent describing makeup applicator as "this dirty sponge" and when Charles applies makeover over his foundation, Vincent muses that he is putting "baby powder" under his eyes to "basically cover up all the work we just did." The same formula is repeated in "Daddy Does My Makeup" where Vincent is tasked with applying makeup and, instead, using foundation to draws penises on Charles' face.

In comparison, there are several videos where Charles gives makeup tips to male YouTubers, playing with the performativity of gender across accounts and personalities. Charles helped Ben J. Pierce with a "pop of color" look that included a bit of blue eye shadow on the inner corner of the eye and fake lashes. In two other videos, Charles teaches social media stars Joey Graceffa and Ricky Dillion how to apply makeup; in both videos the "students remain stereotypically with masculine despite the use of foundation and lipstick and eye makeup. Two videos particularly play with the idea of drag and camp. One video is titled "Boy Glam Makeup with William" where Charles does make-up for the mononymous social media drag. The second is a video just of Charles, called the "Mrs. Claus Drag Makeup Tutorial." In the later video, Charles mentions that he does not do drag often, but that his followers requested the video. And, like a good social media star, he provided it.

Still, it would be a misrepresentation to ignore the artistry that goes into Charles' makeup techniques. Many of Charles' looks are well outside any gender dynamics and clearly done for artistic purposes; for example, Charles' videos show viewers how to look like a burn victim for Halloween. However, Charles' Instagram is even more experimental, showing looks where he applied purple crystals to his face and chest, including a look where he is made up to look like a Ouija board, and a third that resembles a second face being stretched over his own. These types of personal creations are far more carnivalesque and fantasy-driven — something fashion gives us the opportunity to engage in (Wilson, 2003: 246) — rather than simply transcending the gender norms. There is an act of fancifulness and play in Charles's work that is not generally on display in everyday life.

Much of what Charles produces could be characterized as camp — the elevation of the inauthentic and fake style over what is believed to be "real" (Sontag, 1966). Charles' makeup displays are elevated beyond gender performativity toward the artifice of the camp aesthetic being more artificial and outlandish. Noting that camp is often seen as a political statement (Padva, 2000), perhaps it is unsurprising that viewers read Charles' presence as a man wearing makeup outside of its artistry.

CONTESTING HEGEMONY IN ADVERTISING

Likewise, due to the prominence and frequency of contemporary advertising, it is hard to ignore its effects on how we understand gender and beauty standards. It has long been known that advertising has an adverse effect on women, often portraying women as in a variety of subordinate positions (Goffman, 1979). Perhaps, it has been Jean Kilbourne who has most prominently taken aim at the advertising as a standard bearer in the "Killing Us Softly" series (2010). The thrust of such criticism rests on the charge that consumers who attempt to act out the "idealizations" through extreme dieting or other body modifications internalize advertising messages. This is a process that has been developed over decades, and advertising has moved from selling us clothing and products to selling lifestyles and bodies (see Vincent, this volume).

Advertising's ability to create and solidify beauty standards is a reoccurring theme in this section's chapters. All mass media — advertising included — has the ability to solidify not only the standards of weight and appearance, but also of idealizations of race and skin tone (McClintock, 2013; O'Barr, 1994), hair (see Cheang and Biddle-Perry, this volume), and sexuality (see Rossi, this volume). Also, despite the difference in gender expectations, not even men are immune to advertising effects. The "athletic, muscular male body" has become the aesthetic standard even since Calvin Klein used naked men to sell jeans and underwear (Bordo, 1999:185).

It is for these reasons that popular culture — again, advertising included — is always a site of contention as certain meanings and images and given preference over others (Fiske, 2011: 17). While the culture industries once had totally control over what messages were created and offered to the public, the rise of Charles' and similar social media stars illustrates at least an illusion of the democratization of popular culture and social norms. Prior to the advent of social media, a male wearing makeup would have been unlikely to become the face of CoverGirl. However, now that Charles was able to develop a social media following, he was able to prove his viability to a wider audience. This, in turn, allowed the brand to take a chance on him.

Still, though, the hand of hegemony is at work with Charles' collaboration with CoverGirl. On his own YouTube channel, Charles had creative control and exercises it by playing with gender expectations, but also through artistic makeup displays. Many of his makeup techniques would turn heads at school or in the workplace. However, much of the subversive practices are removed from the videos releases on CoverGirl's YouTube channel. Of the four videos which Charles created for CoverGirl, the first video was a tutorial explaining how to create a "skull" for Halloween. The video — Charles' initial introduction to the CoverGirl line — was relatively safe since make-up *is* socially accepted for men during Halloween. Charles' "Pop of Color Holiday Makeup Tutorial" challenged norms a bit more as he showed viewers how to apply a gamut of makeup from foundation and concealer to mascara, eyeliner and lipstick. And, the third and fourth videos featured both Charles and singer Zendaya — one where Zendaya interviews Charles and another where the duo took a 10-minute eye makeup challenge. By the end of the makeup video, both Charles and Zendaya were wearing blue and purple eyeshadow in a commonly seen manner.

This transition seems to indicate two competing desires. First, there is a clear social implication for Charles' inclusion on the CoverGirl campaign. The brand seems willing to question, if not outright defy, normative understandings of gender by bringing the male Charles to promote makeup. However, while CoverGirl was willing to take a bit of risk, it did this so slowly. Firstly, this was done by introducing Charles for the socially acceptable Halloween makeup, and then for relatively traditional feminine uses of makeup. The brand did not push Charles' artistic creations, but rather attempted to remain relatively low-key. A cynic might argue that CoverGirl's move was a bit of tokenism to appeal to a diversifying audience, while a more generous viewer might say it the brand wants to take up a social cause without risking its bottom line. The popular culture landscape is littered with such tradeoffs when producers want to push the envelope enough, but not too far.

STANDARD SETTERS AND CHANGE MAKERS

As the chapters in this section remind us, advertising remains a highly contentious space that sets and contests cultural norms. However, as Charles' start and later inclusion into a CoverGirl's advertising campaign shows us, the social media platforms are giving users a space to exercise their voice and gain recognition. This often involves large amounts of unpaid labor and little chance of return on the investment (Duffy, 2015), however, cultural producers seem increasingly likely to adopt this growing set of cultural intermediaries into their own fold.

Largely, undertakings by bloggers and social media influences is done as a labor of love that is often highly gendered and linked to the "feminized" sites of production — like makeup (Duffy, 2016). The idea that bloggers get paid to do what they love obscures many of the issues about who has the access to economic and cultural capital to create viable social influencing channels. Often, those with expendable economic, social and cultural capital, who could have made it in traditional media spheres, are those now utilizing social media the most. Ultimately though, as Charles illustrates, Internet platforms have the potential to allow novel, creative voices into the process, but this potential remains somewhat unrealized since only certain producers get picked up into the mainstream culture. Further, those lucky few — like Charles — tend to become more conventional as they are accepted into the dominant culture.

Examining and challenging the embedded power dynamics is a reoccurring theme in the following chapters. Vincent explains how advertising offering set standards of beauty leads consumers to figuratively and literally internalize desired bodies. This promotion and understanding of idealized images, is reflected in different ways in chapters by Rossi, and Cheang and Biddle-Perry. Rossi points out that advertising's practice of sexualizing women helped to reinforce heteronormativity, even when highlighting same sex-pairing. While advertising campaigns have pushed acceptability standards of public nudity, they have done so by reinforcing traditional gender roles. Meanwhile, Cheang and Biddle-Perry turn to evolving ideals of hair care and styling to show the constructed and changing nature of what we collectively understand as "natural."

Miller's chapter reminds us that normative understandings are both in flux and culturally specific. While makeup and masculinity is still an emerging concept in Western cultures, Korea has long embraced men's use of such products. Hancock's chapter adds that it can be good business to be more socially aware and push the bounds for inclusion, even if it takes years for others to follow suit. Finally, Valentine notes some of the ways in which advertising can subvert hegemonic norms, by highlighting diversity and pushing non-normative bodies to the forefront of advertising. In this section on Beauty and The Body, we can see that change may not occur quickly, but that beauty standards are malleable and subject to evolution. As such, while we may have long road toward a more inclusive beauty industry, there should be some hope for a more diverse future.

References

Butler, Judith. (2006), *Gender Trouble: Feminism and the Subversion of Identity*. New York: Routledge.
Charles, James, (2016), Interviewed by Ellen DeGeneres on *Ellen*, November 14.
Cole, Shuan. (2000), *'Don We Now Our Gay Apparel': Gay Men's Dress in the Twentieth Century*. New York: Berg
Duffy, Brooke Erin (2012), *Remake, Remodel: Women's Magazines in the Digital Age*. Chicago: University of Illinois Press.
  2015. Amateur, Autonomous, and Collaborative: Myths of Aspiring Female Cultural Producers in Web 2.0. *Critical Studies in Media Communication* 32:1, pp. 48–64.
Entwistle, Joanne (2015), *The Fashioned Body: Fashion, Dress & Modern Social Theory*. Malden, MA: Polity.
Fiske, John, (2011), *Understanding Popular Culture*. New York: Routledge
Goffman, Erving., (1979), *Gender Advertisements*. Cambridge, MA: Harvard University Press.
Greenfield, Beth (2016), Christian Mom Can't Handle Seeing CoverGirl's James Charles on TV. *Yahoo! Beauty*. https://www.yahoo.com/beauty/christian-mom-cant-handle-seeing-covergirls-james-charles-on-tv-191911399.html
Hollander, Anne (1994), *Sex and Suits: The Evolution of Modern Dress*. New York: Kodansha.
Kaiser, Susan (2012), *Fashion and Cultural Studies*. New York: Berg.
Kilborne, Jean (2011), *Killing Us Softly 4*, Media Education Foundation.
McClintock, Anne (2013), Soft-soaping Empire: Commodity Racism and Imperial Advertising. Laurie Ouellette, *The Media Studies Reader*, edited by 227–240. New York: Routledge.
Padva, Gilad (2000), *Priscilla* Fights Back: The Politicization of Camp Subculture. *Journal of Communication Inquiry* 24:2, pp. 216–243.
Purvis, Tony (2013), Advertising — a way of life. Chris Wharton, *Advertising as Culture*, edited by 13–32. Chicago, IL: Intellect.
O'Barr, William. (1994), *Culture and the Ad: Exploring Otherness in the World of Advertising*. Boulder, CO: Westview Press.
Rocamora, Agnés. (2013), "How New are New Media? The Case of Fashion Blogs." In Djurdja Bartlett, Shaun Cole and Agnés Rocamora (eds.), *Fashion Media: Past and Present*, pp. 155–164. New York: Bloomsbury.
Sontag, Susan (1966) *Against Interpretation*. New York: Farrar, Straus & Giroux.
Wilson, Elizabeth, (2003) *Adorned in Dreams*. New York: I.B. Tauris.

Further reading

Klein, Naomi (1991), *The Beauty Myth*: How Images of Beauty Are Used Against Women. New York: Perennial/ Harper Collins.

49

EPILOGUE:
Fashioning the body today

Susan J. Vincent[1]

My first contention—and it is a big one—is that dress no longer really matters to us. Collectively, we are no longer upset, challenged, angered, inspired or captivated by clothes and their appearance on the body. When compared to any other time over the past 500 years, our emotional engagement with the matter of dress is slight, and our attention is found to be elsewhere. As with a dull conversation, we are only going through the motions, for our real interest has been caught by something different. This is not to say that clothes are of negligible importance to the individual—far from it. On a personal level, dress has as great a power as ever: impacting on how we feel about ourselves and how others judge us. As writer Kate Cann describes it, 'wearing the right stuff can make you feel great about yourself'. And we all know the profound emotional discomfort caused by wearing the 'wrong stuff'—the clothes that do not match our sense of self at the time—and the attendant sensation of temporarily being an unwilling inhabitant of this particular physical envelope. But on a societal level, judgements about what might constitute the right stuff and the wrong stuff, and why, are manifested only very rarely.

An exception might be found in the workplace, where usually there are rules—written or unwritten—about acceptability of appearance. In this case an employee is obliged to reflect his or her employer's values and culture, and most usually conform to expectations. This can work both ways on the formality continuum, however, as attested by one Cambridge graduate who, while working for Greenpeace, wore her hair in dreadlocks 'to match her boss'. And some companies like Sky, are now stepping back from enforcing a dress code: 'We want people to enjoy working here, and the freedom to choose how you look at work is part of that'; although it is fair to say that few employers are as permissive. Another aspect of dress practice that has definitely engendered debate is the wearing of religiously charged clothing. For example, Nadia Eweida recently sued her employer, British Airways, for banning her from wearing a necklace bearing a Christian cross. Disciplined by British Airways in the latter part of 2006 for refusing to comply with uniform regulations, Eweida responded by accusing the company of discrimination. In January 2008 she eventually lost the case. In a related vein, in 2006 the BBC discussed the implications of newsreader Fiona Bruce's decision to wear a cross, though it took no action. Again in 2006, Aishah Azmi, a Muslim teaching assistant, was suspended, and later dismissed, for refusing to remove her veil in the classroom. Like Eweida, Azmi took her case to an employment tribunal, and also lost. At the same time, Jack Straw, a former foreign secretary and Member of Parliament for Blackburn (a constituency with a high Muslim population) suggested that the wearing of full veils was detrimental to positive relations between Muslims and non-Muslims.

Outside these contexts there is little evidence that clothing systems any longer get under the cultural skin, irritating, niggling, demanding notice. Our attitude to

---

[1] From Susan J. Vincent (2009) Epilogue: Fashioning The Body Today. The Anatomy of Fashion: Dressing the Body From the Renaissance to the Present Day, Oxford: Berg, 158–74.

fashionable dress worn in day-to-day situations is blasé; concerns about who wears it when have all but evaporated in the powerful light of modernity. Of course there is interest in celebrity individuals and their celebrated individual outfits—Liz Hurley in *that* safety pin dress by Versace for example, or the awarding of the worst-dressed status that allows us lesser mortals the delightful but fleeting pleasures of *schadenfreude*. However, none of this really matters: it is a ripple on the surface of public attention rather than being a manifestation of fundamental interest, and it has, moreover, much more to do with the cult of fame than any kind of sartorial value system.

If we are no longer concerned with clothing, where then is our attention fixed? Simply put, culturally we have shed our garments, or at the least we look through them unseeingly. For now the locus of awareness, and the site of intervention and activity, is to be found in the body itself. The aesthetics, health, rights and ontological status of the body are the subject of vigorous scientific, legal and moral debate; a debate that pervades our lives daily, if not through personal experience, then through the ubiquity of media text and images. Whether the issue is stem cell research, fertility treatments, cloning, disability, obesity, pornography or eating disorders, the conversation is vocal and often impassioned. Even in certain sectors of the academic world, 'embodiment' is—to borrow a fashion metaphor—the new black.

If clothing has shrunk in a discursive sense, then it has certainly thinned and reduced its physical form. We cover ourselves only minimally, leaving large areas of the skin exposed to the elements and to the gaze. Some do this with a near disregard for climatic conditions, not protecting themselves very much against the sun, the rain or the cold. […] Furthermore, when we do envelop the flesh, our garments are generally close fitting and sewn from fine, lightweight fabrics that reveal, rather than hide, the body's contours. Little is suggested; much is declared. Indeed, there has been a collapse, or blurring, of the distinction between the public and private realms. The boundary between what is on show for all and what is private and intimate has been radically redrawn. This applies not just to the parts and amount of anatomy disclosed, but also to the revelation of undergarments, which layered with other items have a stylistic outer life of their own. This is democratization of dress indeed, where we all get a visual share of the body's secrets.

The foregrounding of the corporeal, the placing of the body in the starring role centre stage, argues, I think, that we have the sense of our physicality as something dependable. Our bodies have a robust durability upon which the environment has relatively little effect. We no longer recognize a potential risk in every burning hearth, in candles used for lighting, or in the seasons and the weather, for the dangers we fear come in a microscopic form. Against the invisible legion that corrupts a healthy organism from the inside and hijacks the body's functioning for its own purposes, clothing is no protection at all. Except for the surgical mask—which in our society is confined to medicalized contexts when the body's integrity is at its most precariously uncertain—we fight our fears with antibacterial soaps, vitamin supplements, medicines and disinfectants. The relationship that we picture for ourselves in the wider world is altogether more benign. We therefore pursue an immediacy of physical contact with our environment, and the mediating properties of dress are only dimly remembered as we pull on our gloves on a frosty morning.

Many of our contemporary attitudes to the body have their origin in the 1920s and 1930s. In this period between the wars a whole cluster of interconnected social changes set the foundations for our own particular looks and practices. For a start, modernity cut a swathe through the yards of cloth that previously formed the dressed figure. Hem lines went up, foundation garments became lighter, and sporting and leisure activities—increasingly popular from the latter part of Victoria's reign—encouraged the development of more informal styles. Women's clothes came to be typified by Chanel's simple, reduced designs and easy-to-wear, pliant fabrics. On holiday or at the beach, swimsuits, beach pyjamas, vests and shorts publicly revealed the physique of both sexes for the first time ever. Naturally, the fashionable sloughing off of clothes was a gradual affair, with the rich stripping faster and further and the middle and lower classes setting a more modest pace and morality. However, within a relatively short time, even the most conservative in the community became accustomed to the new norms of disclosure.

Accompanying the new revelation of the body was its radical new look: 'tan was the skin colour of modernism'. A number of developments conspired to overturn the centuries-old aesthetic of whiteness. Medical opinion had begun to champion the benefits of the sun, its therapeutic qualities being recognized as efficacious against certain skin conditions and diseases such as tuberculosis and rickets. Sunshine, it was argued, was 'the highest expression of preventive medicine'. According to this new conception of health, 'the wearing of unhygienic clothes' atrophied the skin, preventing 'the direct action of the air and sun' upon it. A revolution of medical thought, indeed. In 1924 Dr Saleeby established the influential Sunlight League, which aimed to spread the good news of heliotherapy, particularly when combined with the benefits of sea bathing. Local and national governments were soon persuaded that intervention along these lines could substantially improve the health of the urban poor, especially the young. Mr Lansbury, the First Commissioner of Works, was particularly keen on the provision of sunbathing sites in London parks; and in 1934 Tower Beach—created with the blessing of George V and over 1,500 barge loads of sand—was opened for the enjoyment of the capital's children.

This medical endorsement of judicious tanning only provided extra impetus to what was already a growing fashion for sunbathing. Following the example of the rich at play in the Riviera, millions of ordinary English began to take to the beach in sundresses, ever-diminishing swimsuits and the new invention of sunglasses. Also during this same period, cosmetics swept into widespread use. It was a contested progress, with the rich, the young and the daring leading the way, but nevertheless the triumph of makeup was swift and absolute. In 1931, for instance, the *Sunday Express* reported that for every 1 lipstick sold ten years previously, 1,500 were being sold today. Shadowing, or perhaps driving, demand, cosmetic advertising burgeoned. Starting in the early 1930s, the amount spent on face powder ads began to escalate in leaps and bounds, in one year rising by nearly 40 per cent. The number of advertisements for lipstick carried by women's magazines showed a similar expansion. For example, in 1936 there were 60 per cent more than in a corresponding period just one year before. As Robert Graves and Alan Hodge remembered it, looking back from less than a decade later: All hairdressers, beauty parlours, large stores, chemists and branches of Woolworth's now sold cosmetics and nail-enamel.'

If the decades following the First World War established the tanned, outdoors body as the physical ideal, they dictated that it must also be slim and young. In dramatic contrast to the full, mature contours of the Edwardian era—'magnificent, handsome, statuesquely beautiful'—modernity declared itself thin and youthful. 'Slimming was now a cult', wrote Graves and Hodges of the 19s, with a panoply of pills, diets, machines and exercises to help the willing lose weight. Lucy Duff Gordon also wrote of the 'slimming craze', contrasting the models she used to show her designs with the post-war ideal of womanhood. Her 'goddesses' were tall and heavy—several weighing considerably more than eleven stone—with 'generous curves' and 'a full bust'.

Maturity was the keynote of their attractions. The new fashion, however, completely reversed this. Clothes were now designed for the young or were designed to make older women look young.

For those who lived through these changes, the comparison between the old order and the new was often poignant, sometimes bewildering. Whether welcomed or not, a paradigm shift had occurred in the role and rights of the body. Sex began to be talked of openly; incessantly, some would say. Marie Stopes opened her first clinic in 1921; Freud entered the popular consciousness; Havelock Ellis's work began to be more widely known; and reformed laws saw a significant rise in the number of divorces.

Furthermore, in 1928 universal suffrage meant that, in theory at least, all adults had a say about this. While hindsight artificially smoothes the course of these developments, generalizing what was fragmented and initially a minority experience only, nonetheless, much of what we consider as ordinary had its origins in these extraordinary times.

The rise of the body as a focus of society's interest and energies has resulted in a corresponding diminution of the role of clothing in the staging of appearance. How people look remains as much a cultural preoccupation as ever, but garments now have less significance in the creation of that look, and the size, shape and characteristics of the body wearing them have more. Again, this is a trend whose origins can be discerned in the interwar years. In 1932 Lucy Duff Gordon speculated that dressing would never figure in social life as it had done at the turn of the century. 'It is regarded as of infinitely less importance nowadays.' The cult of beauty, she maintained, had actually increased—girls were 'far better groomed' and 'far more *soignée*' than their mothers—'but they think less of clothes'. These were sentiments echoed, or perhaps inspired, by Chanel. As a dress designer, she was virtually nihilistic, for behind her clothes was an implied but unexpressed philosophy: the clothes do not really matter at all, it is the way you look that counts.' The shift of focus onto the body's appearance— as opposed to the appearance of the body when dressed—helps explain the astounding rise of cosmetic surgery and techniques of body modification. Modern garments, form fitting and adaptive to the wearer's contours, have a reduced capacity to fashion our shape, and we ourselves have a reduced interest in their fashioning possibilities. Because of this, an increasing amount of the work of appearance has been displaced onto skin and flesh and bone.

Devoting time and energy to dressing, adapting to discomforts of constriction and bulk, learning to move gracefully in complicated garments, manipulating them for visual and aural effect: these disciplines and skills have given way to effort expended on diet, exercise, washing and the maintenance of health. We used to live through our clothes; now we just live. An increasingly large number eschew the decorative properties of fabric altogether, choosing instead the adornment of incisions made directly into their person. Tattoos and piercings have expanded their traditionally reduced range in our society, and are now found on more bodies and more body parts than a short time ago would have been imaginable. The skin of men and women is patterned with colour and shape; brows, nose, lips, tongue, bellies and genitals flash with the metallic glint of studs and rings. Then there is the explosion in the popularity of surgical interventions. Again, this can be traced to the 1920s, when a few people on the quest for aesthetic enhancement began to choose from plastic surgery techniques developed to patch and repair the maimed and wounded of the battlefields. Very recently, however, the small market for this elective surgery has burgeoned, as indeed has the range of interventions now possible. Working from the top down, a surgical menu of what's on offer gives us hair transplants for male-pattern baldness; eyelid surgery for a wider, more youthful gaze; nose, ear and chin reshapings; implants to fill out hollow cheeks; face and neck lifts; breast enlargements, reductions (both female and male) and uplifts; nipple correction for a perkier appearance; arm lifts to tighten sagging skin; tummy tucks, with liposuction for recalcitrant fat; buttock lifts to pull in drooping flesh and buttock implants to push it out; vaginal tightening, labial reduction and inserts for a shapelier calf. Cosmetic dental surgery, a specialism all its own, offers dental implants to fill the gaps; straightening and whitening procedures to correct the imperfections; and porcelain tooth veneers to just cover up. This list of interventions is by no means exhaustive, and new procedures are arriving on the market all the time.

Meanwhile, there are throngs of people, list metaphorically in hand, crowding to this particular marketplace to shop. For example, according to the British Association of Aesthetic Plastic Surgeons (BAAPS), in 2007 a total of 32,453 surgical procedures were performed by its members. When compared with the total UK population, this figure is not large, but it is nevertheless 12.2 per cent larger than the figure the year before. Breaking down this statistic, also between 2006 and 2007 the number of face lifts rose by 36 per cent; eyelid operations by 13 per cent; and nose reshapings by 13 per cent. These are examples of a pattern of consistent increase seen over the early years of our new millennium. Overall, from 2002 to 2007, there was a rise of 300 per cent in the number of people electing cosmetic surgery. In those same five years, breast augmentation—the most popular cosmetic surgery procedure in the UK—increased by 275 per cent. Although the huge majority of those presenting for surgery are female, the numbers of operations on men are showing a steady rise too, with some specific procedures greatly increasing in popularity. In 2007 rhinoplasty on men, or nose reshaping, increased by 36 per cent from the year before; liposuction increased by 18 per cent; and tummy tucks by 61 per cent. None of these statistics, furthermore, include either operations undertaken by surgeons who are not members of BAAPS or those performed on Britons abroad, who sign up for medical tourism to take advantage of cheaper rates overseas. Adding these would significantly increase the percentages. Furthermore, it is not just the number of operations that is rising; multiple procedures are becoming more common. One of these is the 'mummy tuck', a post-partum tummy tuck, breast lift and liposuction combined. According to one source, BAAPS identifies new mothers as the fastest growing group wanting surgery. To help with the all-over transformation that patients are beginning to request, 'Some surgeons have even taken to working in pairs, one taking on the face while the other handles the body.' Says a former BAAPS president, people have started to see cosmetic surgery as being little different from a trip to the salon. Certainly, in a poll commissioned by *The Observer* in September 2003, 46 per cent of women aged twenty-five to thirty have had, or would consider having, cosmetic surgery. Given the rise in the number of procedures undertaken since then, this figure can now only be higher.

Then there are the non-surgical cosmetic procedures, the injections of fillers and Botox that are designed to plump or smooth away the signs of aging, and microdermabrasion, which scours it away. The effects of these interventions last from a few months to a couple years, and then need to be performed again. Injected into the face to hide lines, furrows and thinness, dermal fillers do just what it says on the tin— or rather, on the syringe. Botox, a dilute solution of the botulinum toxin, works by paralysis, freezing the muscles so that wrinkles are flattened away. Injections to the face deaden the lines of age and expression; injections to the hands smooth away the batterings of life; application to the armpits and feet stop the body sweating. As Botox and fillers can be administered by beauticians, who are not obliged to keep records in the way hospitals are, it is impossible to know with any accuracy just how many people use these products, just how often. However, it is certain that they greatly exceed the numbers who opt for the more invasive surgical interventions. For Hadley Freeman, deputy fashion editor of *The Guardian,* Botox is 'the encroaching tide' that 'has tsunamied the country'.

Whatever the statistics that lie behind the industry's practice, in a very short time the idea of surgical and clinical aesthetic interventions has become a normalized one. Through media coverage, advertising, and the images of the famous for whom the results have been either successful or disastrous, the possibility of body modification is ever present. And this is without our own personal experiences, or the stories reported through our networks of acquaintances and friends of friends. The ubiquity of at least the concept of physical alteration hides from us a rather large historical irony. One common response to clothes worn by previous generations is a kind of bewildered amazement at their 'unnaturalness'. As we have seen, garments sometimes worked without particular reference to the body's shape beneath; they perhaps constricted or exaggerated a portion of the anatomy; and very often the properties of the cloth from which they were constructed intruded into the performance of wearing. Today clothing is made very differently. Our garments are put on and off easily, and form a flexible adaptive envelope that demands far less of its wearer. Nowadays dress does not markedly disguise, constrain or alter the body's contours; nowadays these contours are defined by the scalpel. The aesthetic work, the 'unnaturalness', has become embodied: eyes widened, fat removed, sagging tightened and wrinkles smoothed, we take our selves and we improve on nature. We may find the idea of false calves pushed down a pair of stockings amusing, but who laughs at calf implants inserted in the operating theatre?

It is probably pretty clear, however, that we need to scrutinize the idea of 'naturalness' more closely. It would be easy to set the purity of the body draped with cloth against the artificiality of a body altered by surgery, but it would be wrong. All adornment is a work of culture: tying a hair ribbon or wearing a pair of shoes is as much a cultural intervention as sucking out fat deposits under anaesthetic. Washed, fed and dressed, by the time the body reports ready for duty it is hopelessly compromised by 'unnaturalness'. For all that, however, a corset and a mummy tuck are not the same kind of thing. They may both be cultural interventions that affect the body, but to deny the palpable differences would be as misleading as to falsely range them on opposing sides of the nature—culture divide. How, then, does concentrating on the body as the site of fashioning differ from taking garments as the focus of the fashion project?

Most immediately noticeable is the degree to which the rise of the surgical industry has led to the body becoming commodified. It is marketed, sold and sliced up, just like any other object. Advertising techniques heavily reinforce the message. Images of ideal bodies with a price tag attached to every perfected part clearly spell out the message that you, too, can buy yourself a physique like the one pictured. Prospective shoppers are encouraged with 'buy now, pay later' deals, a range of finance options, and discount offers on featured procedures. Some providers hold out cash incentives if customers refer friends and family; and forget the book token—vouchers that can be redeemed against surgery are 'the perfect gift'. The words used by purchasers of cosmetic surgery suggest that they have internalized this objectification of their body bits. As excited by the pleasures of ownership as young children impatiently tearing the paper from presents, those newly emerged from under the knife are eager to draw attention to their new anatomy. 'I want to show the world my new body', boasted celebrity Kerry Katona in an interview given after her extensive surgery. Of her breasts, which had previously fitted implants removed, and then an uplift, she explained, 'I can't stop feeling them and showing them off! . . . I love showing my body off now and I'm whipping them out at every opportunity!' Highlighting the commercialized nature of her transformation, she answers possible critics bluntly: 'Sod them! Who wouldn't do it for free?' The sentiments of high-profile Katona are echoed by other, more ordinary people. After travelling abroad for surgery costing £7,500—a breast uplift, implants, tummy tuck and vaginal tightening—Linda was thrilled with 'the new-improved me', and reported wanting 'to flaunt my new body'. Surgery, she said, 'made me a whole new woman'. The words that Linda and Kerry chose to describe their experiences perfectly demonstrate what Alex Kuczynski, a journalist who has recently investigated the US cosmetic surgery industry, has found. In recent years, Kuczynski writes, 'women have begun to flaunt their surgery and revel in the artificiality'.

One result of identifying the authentic self with the post-operative one is that it binds an individual's identity closer to his or her physical looks. Whereas those who fashion themselves without clinical or surgical interventions in some degree assert the independence of character from body, believing the reshaped anatomy to be the real 'me' reduces the scope of that 'me' and ties it more firmly to appearance. Ironically, doing so leaves the subject of surgery more vulnerable to the insecurities or dissatisfactions that prompted the surgery in the first place. Given this, the growing number signing up for multiple procedures or ongoing treatments is unsurprising. According to one plastic surgery professional, 'There's an increasing realization that it's not just one aspect of your appearance that is inadequate. Unattractive teeth will still ruin your face even if you have a nose job.' Like sawing a wobbly table leg, an intervention here often shows up the 'need' for an intervention there. Added to this, the industry has now 'found more and more procedures a person can have, giving them complexes about parts of the body heretofore rarely considered' It is commonly accepted that body dysmorphia—acute dissatisfaction with one's body image that has no basis in observable reality—is on the rise. It is perfectly conceivable that this rise is linked to our emphasis on the body in general, and the influence of cosmetic surgery in particular.

The tendency of such body work to bind the subject more closely still to its enterprise, leads to recurrent and repeated interventions. Like the persistent touching of a sore spot, it proves very difficult to leave well alone. Little wonder then, the degree to which the language of addiction is used in connection with the quest for the authentic and deserved body. Scholarly critiques talk in terms of 'cosmetic surgery junkies' and the 'surgical fix', and Alex Kuczynski's whole investigative appraisal of the industry—*Beauty*

Junkies—is structured about this paradigm. When asked in an interview whether she was tempted by more surgery 'despite knowing you could die on the operating table', Kerry Katona replied unequivocally: 'Absolutely, I'd love liposuction on my legs—I'm addicted now!'

Although there is nothing intrinsic to the enterprise that dictates that this should be so, the appearance that aesthetic surgery and its related non-surgical procedures is currently committed to reproducing is a very particular one. Anything wrinkled, lumpy, too small or too big, is out. Only the 'right' breasts, noses, eyelids, vaginas—one can substitute virtually any body part here—are acceptable. More and more it is an aesthetic that reduces the variety of nature and herds us towards a loss of individual difference. This is 'eugenics-lite', where not conforming to the ideal has become something that has to be fixed. Whether it's the wrong sort of nipples, an insufficiently pert bottom, or—with a whole extra tangle of complex but unexamined moral issues—eyes that look too Asian or the distinctive features of Down's syndrome sufferers, the drive is to 'correct' the faulty. Moreover, not only is the norm being defined against increasingly narrow parameters, it is being defined in spite of what is naturally possible. Thus the ideal of large bouncing breasts attached to a slender torso and slim hips is, by natural standards, a bit of a freak. A woman without fat deposits on her belly and thighs is unlikely to have the subcutaneous wherewithal to manage a large bust, and it will certainly not remain pointing cheerily skywards when she lies down. Similarly impossible is a face that shows no lines or wrinkles, and has trouble registering the finer nuances of emotion. This is an insistent redefinition of the norm as something that in reality is only attainable by surgical or clinical intervention, and it results in such featureless uniformity that attempts to perceive distinguishing differences simply slide off its Teflon-coated surface.

In this respect it is not the invasiveness of surgery that marks its difference from dress, but its drive to homogeneity and, allied to that, its secretive nature. In fashion, clothes—and piercings and tattoos, incidentally—usually work to express individuality, albeit within conformity to a general look. No one wants to be dressed identically, and indeed, uniform is a sartorial shorthand for an individual's fascistic loss of autonomy. Moreover, the point of clothes is that they advertise themselves; they draw attention to what they are and how they interact with the body they adorn. As interventions, they clearly privilege the cultural over the relatively dull state of the natural, unadorned canvas. 'Clothing', to use art historian Anne Hollander's words, 'hides the commonness of nakedness; and so, by all its variable creative means, it produces the quality of individuality—all the mysteries of uncommonness, all the distinctions of quality and mode.' Cosmetic surgery, as we understand it, does nothing like this. It is the champion of naked uniformity. It works to reduce individuality and it aims as much as possible to hide the evidence of its own involvement. No matter how unlikely the anatomical end product, it must seem as though nature, unassisted, doled it out. Thus, while our desire to shape our appearance according to the dominant aesthetic is the same as it has ever been, our means of achieving this, and the ramifications of our interventions, have become very different. Thanks to cosmetic surgery that peels, pins, lifts and tucks, our skin, like cloth, is cut, sewn and tailored to perfection. But, as currently constituted, it is a dead-end aesthetic without the creativity, variety or outward-looking energy that characterizes the previous centuries of fashionable dress.

FACE VALUE:
Subversive beauty ideals in contemporary fashion marketing

Maria Mackinney-Valentin[1]

The perception of beauty in visual culture has been subject to constant negotiation as argued by Umberto Eco in *History of Beauty* (2004), informed as it is by the cultural norms of a given spatial and temporal context. However, at least since the 1920s, fashion communication with regard to the faces of fashion has been dominated by the current beauty standards, i.e., 'contemporary seductiveness' (Laver 1946: 203). Faces are considered here to be the personification of a specific brand. The question is what the subversive beauty ideals really communicate in fashion marketing. If fashion marketing is understood as 'the process by which companies create value for customers and build strong customer relationships, in order to capture value from customers in return' (Kotler and Armstrong 2010: 29), the cases will show how the exchange of values between companies and consumers seems at first glance to differ radically not only from conventional beauty ideals but also from the general norms for status representation within Euro-American markets.

Since the middle of the nineteenth century, fashion has been formally organized as cycles of sartorial expressions, and thereby fashion has also contributed to regulating the changing perceptions of corporeal beauty as personified by the fashion model. The history of the fashion model as a tool in marketing – a 'walking advertisement' (Craik 1994: 77) – can be traced back to fashion designer Charles Frederick Worth and The House of Worth in the 1860s when the wife of the designer Marie Vernet was sent out in public to parade her husband's designs. She has since been widely considered to be the 'blueprint fashion model' (Quick 1997: 24).

Showing the latest designs on attractive house models that mirrored contemporary beauty ideals was seen to increase the attractiveness of the looks to potential customers. In the late 1920s, designer Paul Poiret began bringing his models on tour and used models rather than aristocrats for a different effect. With the establishment of Lucy Clayton's model agency in 1928, modelling as an occupation gained a higher social standing (Craik 1994: 77). Since then, models have experienced a rise in status and are an important part of the contemporary fashion system (Quick 1997; Kawamura 2005).

While celebrity icons are seen in the early Hollywood days (e.g. Clara Bow in the 1920s), the symbiotic relationship between fashion designers and celebrities may be traced back to the 1950s with Audrey Hepburn and Hubert de Givenchy (Agins 1999: 137). This strategy of *guilt by association* between celebrities and fashion has increased as a way of making the face of a brand more three-dimensional because of the public persona an actress or singer may have. Especially since the rise of the supermodel in the 1990s, the distinction between model and celebrity has become less clear.

FACE VALUE

Fashion is organized according to a cadence of change seen in recurring seasonal collections and fashion

---

[1] From Maria Mackinney-Valentin, Face Value: Subversive Beauty Ideals in Contemporary Fashion Marketing, Fashion, Style & Popular Culture, Intellect, pp 13–27.

weeks. This institutionalization of change apparently for its own sake has invited satire such as: 'Fashion is a form of ugliness so intolerable that we have to alter it every six months' (Wilde [1887] 2004: 39). Fashion, including the faces in fashion, is to a certain extent driven by a certain level of what might be considered *ugly* as a means to break with current standards and thereby live up to the dogma of *newness* that characterizes fashion understood as 'the intoxication of sensation and novelty' (Lipovetsky 1994: 146). This notion of ugly is not the equivalent of beauty as a relative construction, but is rather an elusive aesthetic value that is collectively agreed upon as fashionable at a given time and place, as well as within a specific brand identity. The function of this ugliness is to express both social individualization and brand distinction. In that sense, ugly is an ambiguous quality, which is not limited to contemporary fashion ideals. In the exhibition 'Sciaparelli and Prada: Impossible Conversations' (2012) at the Metropolitan Museum in New York, one of the themes was 'Ugly Chic'. Each in their own way, the two featured designers challenged categories of good and bad taste. Elsa Schiaparelli achieved ugly chic by elevating objects such as insects, tree bark, cellophane and lobsters to high fashion (2007: 61) and Miuccia Prada challenged standards of beauty through unusual combinations of colour, print and materials.

Definitions of good and bad taste, what is beautiful or ugly, have, historically speaking, been determined by social, cultural and historical context (Eco 2007: 391). However, the rise of postmodernism in the 1980s entailed an increase in the sense of relativity concerning aesthetic values (Jameson [1981] 1998). The postmodern condition lacks any controlling idea also within the aesthetic domain, which in turn gives rise to the dogma that 'everything is equivalent and is mixed indiscriminately in the same morose and funeral exaltation' (Baudrillard [1981] 2000: 44). This understanding of relativity offers the potential 'to transform something ugly into an object of pleasure' (Eco 2007: 436). Recent developments in fashion campaigns and runway shows seem to confirm this tendency towards greater volatility in the representation of physical standards of beauty. The case studies are analysed within the framework of this transformative understanding of beauty in mainstream Euro-American fashion magazines that contain campaign ads, runway images, fashion spreads and editorial content referring to faces of fashion.

The fashion industry in general and the use of models in particular has been criticized for distorting perceptions of beauty by creating impossible ideals. Misshapen bodies are to be regarded as problems to be rectified or disguised within these constricted views of beauty. When a female celebrity endorses a cosmetic brand, her role is designed to be an ideal for the consumers implying that the product being promoted holds the promise of the user becoming a better version of herself. Any mistakes or flaws appear to be included in mainstream fashion magazines only for the sensation of having them fixed in order to return to the realm of perfection that the traditional magazine may be seen to represent. This process may be described as 'Body management as a means of "normalizing" the body' (Craik 1994: 66).

The fashion system in general and the model industry in particular is criticized for being concerned only with surfaces and models being viewed according to the 'perfection' of their bodies. This tendency has been prevalent in modelling since the beginning of the twentieth century 'Models sell commodities by using their bodies to produce commercialized affect in relationship to specific goods: glamour, elegance, cool' (Brown 2012: 37). This effect was often ensured contractually. An example is an exclusive contract between model Jose Borain and Calvin Klein from the late 1980s, according to which the model was required to maintain her weight, hairstyle and all other features of physiognomy and physical appearance. That is to say if she became disfigured, disabled, suffered illness or mental impairment, the contract could be annulled (Craik 1994: 90).

Though the fashion film is gaining in popularity, print advertisements in public space and in women's magazines have traditionally been the prime site for promoting and playing with standards of beauty at a given time. Since the first women's magazines appeared in the early seventeenth century, they have played a prescriptive role in guiding women in how to look, feel and behave through style guides, advice on life and love and fashion spreads but also indirectly with fashion ads 'The idea that clothes constitute a language and means of communication has been central to the proliferation of the fashion industry and its promotion through women's magazines and by sanctioning role models' (Craik 1994: 65). These role models (e.g. TV personalities, movie stars, singers, royalty) come to represent a standard of beauty for ordinary women (Craik 1994: 62) implicated as they are in the dissemination of body aesthetics (Entwistle 2009:16). The world of fashion modelling is often noted for its celebration of youth, 'beauty' and the 'thin' body (Entwistle 2009: 8). This perception has prevailed in the fashion industry through most of the twentieth century, and it is the departure from this practice specifically in regard to faces that is the objective when analysing the case studies.

FACE VALUE: CASE STUDIES

The question is whether this celebration of anomaly – the older, handicapped, gender bent, awkward or derelict model – is symptomatic of a move from fashion dictatorship of perfection towards a greater relativity in the perception and representation of beauty, or whether this recent visual turn in the faces of fashion is still just a two-dimensional image designed to create social distinction (Simmel 1971; McCracken 1990; Bourdieu 1999; Aldridge 2003; Rogers 2003). If the latter is the case, does the scrambled social message represent a return to the sentiments expressed by fashion model Naomi Campbell 'People only take models at face value?' (Craik 1994: 87). The following case studies will explore the apparent rise of the *imperfect* models that challenge perceptions of gender, class, age, body and sexuality as traditional parameters defining the faces in fashion. The aim of the case studies is to explore how these cases produce subversive commercialized effect and alternative glamour and elegance.

Case 1: Freak chic

As we have seen, fashion models are traditionally celebrated as ideals of physical perfection. However, in recent years there have been a number of models where the imperfect has played an ambiguous role. One example is seen with the performance artist Rick Genest, also known as *Zombie Boy,* who is famous for being tattooed as a skeleton over his entire body and face. After visiting Genest's Facebook page, Nicola Formicetti, creative director of Mugler, used Genest as the face of the Mugler Autumn/Winter (AW) 2011 'Anatomy of Change' collection both on the runway and in the advertising campaigns. Genest was also featured in Lady Gaga's video for 'Born This Way'. In an online interview, Genest refers to himself as a 'sideshow freak' (cranetv.com). A similar example from outside fashion is seen with the hit 'I Fink You Freeky' by the South African band Die Antwoord. The video for the song, which features a series of characters that might be considered freakish, reached more than 20 million hits in 2012 (http://www.youtube.com/watch?v=8Uee_mcxvrw). This promotion of *freak* chic both by Genest himself, by Mugler and Die Antwoort indicates a social appetite for the irregular, abnormal or even monstrous.

Historically speaking, the sideshow freak is specific to the circus or fairs where people who were unusual (e.g. size or appearance) were exhibited. In that sense, Genest represents a departure from the celebration of the perfect towards a more ambiguous aesthetic where what is generally considered wrong or ugly is rendered desirable at least within a specific context.

Another example of physical imperfection is seen with the use of models with genetic defects. In the Spring/Summer (SS) 2011 Givenchy campaign, creative director Riccardo Tisci chose albino model Stephen Thompson as the face. In addition to having a physical handicap, being an albino is also a social and cultural taboo in certain cultures where albinos are considered social outcasts (Brown 2008). The fact that Thompson is albino was not concealed in the campaign. On the contrary, the use of over-lighting of the images served to emphasize his whiteness, suggesting that his condition be a potential within the context of the campaign. So, rather than being a self-proclaimed freak as in the example of Genest, the notion of physical imperfection became not a choice but a condition in the example of Thompson.

A third example of physical imperfection is impairment, which is used to communicate messages of empowerment. This was seen when Bethany Hamilton, a professional surfer who survived a shark attack but lost an arm, took part in Volvo's 'Life on Board' campaign (2004). Another example is Shannon Murray who was featured in a window campaign for Debenhams in her wheelchair (2010). There are a number of examples of models with prosthetic legs. One is Aimee Mullins who is an accomplished athlete in track and field despite having had both her legs amputated. She walked for Alexander McQueen in carved prosthetic legs in 1999. She is currently an ambassador of beauty brand L'Oreal. Oscar Pistorius, the triple world record holder and triple Paralympic Champion in the 100-, 200- and 400-metre races, was the face of AMen, a scent by Mugler in 2011. In addition, German model Mario Galla walked the Michalsky show at Berlin fashion week in 2011 (michalsky.com) with an exposed prosthetic leg.

While this tendency to use disabled models may appear to be a move towards greater tolerance, there might also be an element of taking subversive images and using them in marketing on a more symbolic level where what is *foul* becomes fair because of the potential for distinction, regardless of the social reality of the images.

Case 2: Gender bending

From Marlene Dietrich and Diane Keaton to David Bowie and Boy George, gender bending in and through fashion within the framework of popular culture has taken place since at least the turn of the twentieth century. However, the recent development in fashion indicates a move beyond the play and negotiation of gender identities in fashion. Actress Tilda Swinton was the face of the Pringle of Scotland menswear line AW 2010. Andrej Pejic is a highly androgynous male model embracing his feminine side by walking runway shows for both men's and women's lines. Pushing the boundaries of gender conventions in fashion, he wore the symbolic wedding dress for the Jean Paul Gaultier SS 2011 show. In 2011, he was the face of Dutch company Hema's women's lingerie campaign for the Mega Push-Up Bra (hema.nl).

While the examples of Tilda Swinton and Andrej Pejic operate within the realm of cross-dressing, Brazilian model Leandro Cerezo, or T. Lea, takes gender bending a physical step further. Lea is a transgendered fashion model, male-to-female, who started her sexual reassignment process in 2008. She has been the face of Givenchy in 2010 and has been featured in magazines such as *Love*, *Interview* and French *Vogue*. Finally, the choice of actor Brad Pitt as the face for the iconic perfume Chanel No. 5 for the Fall 2012 campaign marks a gendered departure from the brand's previous faces that have included actresses Catherine Deneuve and Nicole Kidman.

These examples might challenge social and cultural restrictions regarding gender and sexuality as a positive side effect, but as a marketing strategy they appear to adopt contemporary consumer behaviour of communicating a confusing message as a deliberate strategy in status representation.

Case 3: Granny chic

There are two versions of the granny chic trend in fashion marketing:

1 Looking intentionally aged such as when designer Jean-Paul Gaultier dressed his models in grey wigs in his AW 2011; model Freja Beha wore a grey wig for the AW 2011 Chanel campaign; model Kristen McMenamy, 46, went naturally grey or when celebrity Pixie Geldof, teenage blogger Tavi Gevinson and model Kate Moss dyed their hair grey.
2 The fashion world's recent senior moment with the rising of the 60+ model. Among the examples are Valerie Pain, 66, for Debenhams campaign in 2010 (Debenhams.com); Carmen Dell'Orefice, 78, for Rolex SS 2009 (rolex.com); Daphne Selfe, 82, for the AW 2010 Wunderkind campaign (wunderkind.com); and Iris Apfel, 90, for MAC cosmetics in 2012 (maccosmetics.com). Older models have also been featured in fashion campaigns with family portraits as the visual theme. Examples are Missoni SS 2010; Tommy Hilfiger with the payoff 'Home with the Hilfigers' in 2011 (global. tommy.com); and Dolce & Gabbana SS 2010 featuring Madonna.

The foregrounding of granny chic may be seen as an effort to dismantle negative age stereotypes. However, historically speaking, the old in fashion has been synonymous with the outdated. Considering the obsession with youth in contemporary society, the paradox of celebrating the physically old seems too edgy to be only about combating ageism. It is more likely that the use of older models and the imitation of age markers such as grey hair may be an expression of fashion brands tapping into the social strategies among the fashion-forward consumers and therefore it may have little to do with actual, chronological age.

A different take on age as a subversive beauty ideal in fashion marketing is the demonstratively young faces. An example that caused a public stir was the fashion spread 'Cadeaux' featured in French *Vogue* 2011 with then-10-year-old Thylane Lena-Rose Blondeau posing provocatively. While this might be a conscious provocation of morals, it does not seem to tap into the social mechanisms in fashion the way the foregrounding of older age does. While looking intentionally old in a society obsessed with youth demonstrates social courage that works as social currency for distinction, the staging of a child as a sexy adult just pushes the boundaries of the accepted for the sake of provocation alone and ultimately to sell a product. While the social mechanism and commercially motivated sensationalism are surely linked, there is a distinct quality of the former that is not present in the latter.

Case 4: Geek chic

Geek chic is essentially about the paradoxical celebration of the socially awkward in an industry concerned with influential first movers, control and beautiful surfaces. Geek is a term stemming from American teenage slang in the early 1980s where it was used to refer to peers who lacked social graces. In recent years, geek chic has been associated with a casual and quirky aesthetic epitomized by wearing glasses and intentionally mismatched looks. One of the icons of geek chic is the young fashion blogger Tavi Gevinson, who in 2007 started her blog The Style Rookie (thestylerookie.com) at the age of 11 from her room in her parents' house in a Chicago suburb. Her trademark style is offbeat, and on her blog she describes herself as a 'tiny dork', suggesting a celebration of the intentionally unhip. She has since become a fashion darling and was the face of an ad campaign for the Japanese clothing retail chain Uniqlo (2012), disseminating the geek style on a global scale.

A slightly different conception of geek chic in fashion marketing was seen with the choice of Norwegian chess whiz Magnus Carlsen, the youngest person in history to earn a number-one chess ranking, as the face of Dutch fashion brand G-Star Raw in 2010. In addition to fashion and chess being odd bedfellows, Magnus Carlsen cannot be said to represent classic beauty again emphasizing a similar quirkiness to that of Tavi Gevinson as an ambiguous means of extracting the social potential for distinction from the foul rather than the fair.

Case 5: Slumming

Since the millennium, several designers have explicitly used visual references to the homeless as part of their marketing tools both in runway staging and in the design and styling of the garments. The AW 2000 menswear collection by British designer Vivienne Westwood was inspired by homelessness not in the symbolic sense of contemporary consumers being restless brand nomads roaming the streets in the search for new territories, but actual homeless people. In a press release, Westwood described how she was inspired by the 'roving vagrant whose daily get-up is a battle gear for the harsh weather conditions' (Anon. 2010).

Westwood is neither the first nor the only one celebrating slumming. In 2000, John Galliano presented his AW collection for Dior that was inspired by the homeless people he had seen along the Seine in Paris. The look was then described as 'hobo chic' with reference to the derelict look and random mismatching similar to Vivienne Westwood's collection a decade later. In both 2000 and 2004, Galliano used newspaper print as a reference to homelessness. The print featured articles about himself, an idea he may have lifted from Schiaparelli who did the same after seeing local fishwives wearing hats made from newspapers in Copenhagen in 1935.

Also in Denmark, fashion brand Han Kjøbenhavn has used older, haggard-looking barflies as models that were street-casted for their AW 2011 and SS 2012 promo films. Swedish fashion brand Resteröd took homeless chic literally when they sent their AW 2012 collection down the runway for Copenhagen Fashion Week in 2012. Contrary to the other example of slumming, Resteröd's choice of models had a social outreach purpose in collaborating with *Hus Forbi*, the Danish street paper sold on the streets by homeless vendors to heighten awareness of the conditions for homeless people.

A slightly different take on slumming is the tendency to glamorize attire associated with criminals also known as *thug wear*. An example of thug wear could be sagging pants, which according to popular lore have roots in American prisons. In 2012, the limit seemed to be reached when Adidas released sneakers designed by Jeremy Scott with plastic shackles. Though the design was supposedly inspired by a 1980s toy monster, the shoes were taken off the market after criticism that they were degrading to African Americans because the shackles looked like 'slave shoes' (Considine 2012).

Slumming is not new in fashion. Coco Chanel encouraged her clients to dress like their maids, and hippies expressed their anti-materialist convictions through inconspicuous dress practice. So what is really at play when homeless people are celebrated as style icons, designers aestheticize poverty, and consumers pay overprice to look like a vagrant? While part of the purpose might be social outreach, the hybrid of luxury and discount as seen in slumming may also be symptomatic of new strategies in fashion marketing.

SOCIAL CURRENCY

Subversive beauty ideals in fashion marketing may be a step towards greater diversity in relation to beauty ideals or it could be the very opposite. The latter might be the case when considering older runway models. While this might appear to be the fashion brands encouraging age diversity, statements from model Veruschka who walked the SS 2011 Giles show at the age of 71 points in a different direction. To the *Daily Mail*, she described how she felt she was being used as a 'gimmick' (Jones 2010) by the brand. In this light, the use of older models may be seen more as a strategy for creating attention in line with the perception of fashion as 'a space where industry articulates issues of identity and signification for the purposes of competitive advantage' (Briggs 2005: 81). In this case, the promotion of various versions of what might be considered foul is foregrounded to achieve commercial gain rather than furthering social or cultural tolerance.

So more than shock tactics, the question is how and why these subversive beauty ideals appeal to consumers. In order to understand this, it is important to distinguish between consumer profiling, determined by, for instance, demographics, lifestyle, opinions and fashion adoption level (Jackson and Shaw 2008: 10) on the one hand, and the notion of social *currency* as a tool in status representation on the other. While the former is used in the relatively stable process of segmentation, the latter is more volatile because it represents the shifting symbolic signals in creating individual differentiation. Fashion is defined here as a social practice governed in part by 'the social possibility of an endless dynamic of renewal and diversification' (Lipovetsky 1994: 153). Social currency is defined by the values or ideals that are effective in acquiring social status within a specific time and place.

The cases suggest a move towards increased complexity in terms of social currency. Viewed within the framework of the exchange of values between fashion brands and consumers, freak chic, gender bending, granny chic, geek chic and slumming are less concerned with dismantling stereotypes of body, gender, age, social standing and class. Rather, it is the transgressing of boundaries, as such, that constitute within a symbolic framework a social currency defined by the courage of 'doing something wrong' (Davis 1992: 66). This strategy of adopting what is socially, culturally or ethically undesirable for the purpose of creating distinction may be termed 'Logic of Wrong' (LOW) (Mackinney-Valentin 2013). The fashion cycle has to a large extent organized the fashion industry while also institutionalizing the social process of distinction and imitation since the middle of the nineteenth century

(Veblen 1970; Simmel 1971). The premise of LOW is the decentralization of the fashion system fashion, which is mainly a result of especially fast fashion, new media and digitalization that have disturbed the conventional fashion cycle. With LOW, social status is negotiated, achieved and maintained through mainstream hesitance – as opposed to financial ability – to copying. When consumers mix supermarket fashion with luxury, niche reference groups and fashion tribes are more likely to influence consumers than traditional signifiers of class (Jackson and Shaw 2008: 12). As a result, consumers have been forced to find alternative means for status representation to enable a time lag that can stall the inevitable process of emulation.

This tendency for fashion to be out of style (Agins 1999: 282) has challenged the fashion industry, and the absorption of LOW into fashion campaigns and runway shows may be seen as an attempt to accommodate this development in consumer behaviour. If exclusivity is that which the masses have no access to, LOW might be seen as a new, elusive and, to some, even a repulsive strategy for attaining exclusivity.

Contemporary consumers explore elements that may be considered 'anti-fashion' (Polhemus 1978) as a subversive way of obtaining and maintaining the fashion lead. However, while anti-fashion has generally been considered to be politically motivated as in the 1970s where the freedom of wearing what you wanted was rooted in deeper issues of cultural radicalism (Steele 1997), the anti-fashion elements reflected in the choice of faces in contemporary fashion marketing have only derivative relations to political or social issues. In other words, the elements that appear to be anti-fashionable fulfil a social potential when framed as consumer independence.

Each of the cases demonstrated how brands absorb this value of consumer independence where breaking the social or cultural rules seem to manifest the collective value of individualism. So while the cases were visually diverse, they shared the same subversive strategy to a certain extent. While LOW does not operate by flaunting wealth and power, the brands in the cases were generally from the luxury fashion industry. This paradox further highlights the ambiguity of scrambling the signals.

References

Agins, Teri (1999), *The End of Fashion: The Mass Marketing of the Clothing Business*, New York: William Morrow.

Aldridge, Alan (2003), *Consumption*, Cambridge: Polity.

Anon. (2010), BBC, 18 January, 'Magazine Monitor', http://www.bbc.co.uk/blogs/magazinemonitor/2010/01/mondays_quote_of_the_day_101.shtml. Accessed 20 October 2012.

Baudrillard, Jean ([1981] 2000), *Simulacra and Simulation*, Ann Arbor: The University of Michigan Press.

Baudrillard, Jean (1998), *The Consumer Society: Myths and Structures*, London: Sage.

Bourdieu, Pierre (1999), *Distinction: A Social Critique of the Judgment of Taste*, London: Routledge.

Briggs, Adam (2005), 'Response', in C. Breward and C. Evans (eds), *Fashion and Modernity*, London: Berg, pp..

Brown, Elspeth (2012), 'From artist's model to the "Natural Girl": Containing sexuality in early-twentieth-century modelling', in J. Entwistle and E. Wissinger (eds), *Fashioning Models: Image, Text and Industry*, pp. 37–55. London: Berg.

Brown, Matt (2008), 'Albinos are hunted for body parts in Tanzania', *The National*, 8 November, http://www.thenational.ae/news/world/africa/albinos-are-hunted-for-body-parts-in-tanzania. Accessed 12 January 2013.

Considine, Austin (2012), 'When sneakers and race collide', *New York Times*, June 20, http://www.nytimes.com/2012/06/21/fashion/adidas-cancels-release-of-shackle-sneakers.html?_r=0. Accessed 12 January 2013.

Craik, Jennifer (1994), *The Face of Fashion*, New York: Routledge.

Crane.tv (2011), 'A Powerful and Intimate Interview with Rico Zombie', 28 July, http://www.youtube.com/watch?v=ZmeELC5EGv4. Accessed 16 January 2013.

Davis, Fred (1992), *Fashion, Culture and Identity*, Chicago: The University of Chicago Press.

Eco, Umberto (2004), *History of Beauty*, New York: Rizzoli.

Eco, Umberto (2007), *On Ugliness*, New York: Rizzoli.

Entwistle, Joanne (2009), *The Aesthetic Economy of Fashion: Markets and Value in Clothing and Modelling*, London: Berg.

Jackson, Tim and David Shaw (2008), *Mastering Fashion Marketing*, Hampshire: Palgrave Macmillan.

Jameson, Fredric ([1981] 1998), 'Postmodernism and consumer society', in Hal Foster (ed.), *The Anti-Aesthetic: Essays on Postmodern Culture*, pp. 111–25 New York: The New Press.

Jones, Liz (2010), 'She's back on the catwalk at 71, but sixties icon Veruschka hates today's designers', *Daily Mail*, 1 November, http://www.dailymail.co.uk/femail/article-1325455/Veruschka-The-Sixties-icon-catwalk-

71-says-HATES-todays-designers.html. Accessed on 14 January 2013.

Kawamura, Yuniya (2005), *Fashion-ology: An Introduction to Fashion Studies*, London: Berg.

Kotler, Philip and Gary Armstrong (2010), *Principles of Marketing*, Upper Saddle River: Prentice Hall.

Laver, James (1946), *Taste and Fashion: From the French Revolution to the Present Day*, London: George G. Harrap and Co.

Lipovetsky, Gilles (1994), *The Empire of Fashion: Dressing Modern Democracy*, Princeton: Princeton University Press.

Mackinney-Valentin, Maria (2013), 'Trend mechanisms in contemporary fashion', *Design Issues*, 29: 1, pp. 67–78.

McCracken, Grant (1990), *Culture and Consumption: New Approaches to the Symbolic Character of Consumer Goods and Activities*, Bloomington: Indiana University Press.

Polhemus, Ted (1978), *Fashion & Anti-Fashion Anthropology of Clothing and Adornment*, London: Thames and Hudson.

Quick, Harriet (1997), *Catwalking: A History of the Fashion Model*, London: Hamlyn.

Rogers, Everett (2003), *Diffusion of Innovations*, Cambridge: Free Press.

Schiaparelli, Elsa (2007), *Shocking Life: The Autobiography of Elsa Schiaparelli*, London: V&A Publications.

Simmel, Georg (1971), *On Individuality and Social Forms*, Chicago: University of Chicago Press.

Steele, Valerie (1997), 'Anti-fashion: The 1970s', *Fashion Theory: The Journal of Dress, Body & Culture*, 1: 3, pp. 279–96.

Veblen, Thorstein (1970), *The Theory of the Leisure Class: An Economic Study of Institutions*, London: Unwin Books.

Wilde, Oscar ([1887] 2004), 'Literary and other notes', in R. Ross (ed.), *Reviews*, Gutenberg: e-Book, http://www.gutenberg.org/files/14240/14240.txt.

51

ALL AGES, ALL RACES, ALL SEXES

Joseph H. Hancock II[1]

The beauty industry is a large segment of the fashion industry. One of the main players, Estée Lauder, is the owner of over twenty-five leading beauty and retailing chains around the world. The company has earned over $11 billion in sales and profits of $8.81 billion. This chapter relates the story of Estée Lauder and one of its outstanding subsidiaries: Makeup Art Cosmetics, commonly known as M.A.C.

HISTORY OF ESTÉE LAUDER

In the 1930s, Estée Lauter (who eventually changed her name to Lauder) founded the company when she began formulating and selling skin care products. With the help of her Hungarian uncle John Schotz (who was the original expert), Lauder developed her own variations of his face creams and cleaning oils.

In 1944, with her husband Joseph Lauder, Estée was able to add lipsticks, eye shadows, and face powders. She was adamant about getting her products into department stores and did so by offering samples and handouts for customers and by doing so enculturated the cosmetic ideology of gift with purchase. She traveled all over the country and eventually got her products into luxury department stores across the globe. She also did training seminars and taught everyone how to use the products.

In 1953, Estée Lauder launched her first fragrance, Youth Dew, which included perfume and bath oil. Lauder's big break came during the late 1950s when American cosmetic companies decided they wanted to launch European skin care lines. The company developed Re-Nutriv cream, which sold for $115 per pound until 1960. The cream's advertising campaign "established the sophisticated Lauder look—an image that Estée Lauder herself cultivated."

In 1968, with the help of a Vogue editor, Lauder launched Clinique, a hypoallergenic skin care line. She continued to do makeup and skin care herself, always doing demonstrations and training everyone from store personnel to professional models and fashion designers on how to use her products. Estée named her son Leonard president of the company, but she remained CEO. In 1979, she developed Prescriptive skin care and makeup for young professional women. In 1990, Lauder launched Origins, in 1991 she launched All Skins cosmetics, and in 1994 she bought a controlling stake in the hip Makeup Art Cosmetics. In 1998 Estée Lauder bought the rest of M.A.C. and the rest is history. In 2004, Estée Lauder died of a heart attack at the age of ninety-seven.

ESTÉE LAUDER TODAY

Today, the Estée Lauder company holds the beauty licenses of or owns the following companies: Arein Beauty, Aramis, Aveda, Bobbi Brown, Bumble and Bumble, Clinique, Coach, Darphin Paris, Donna Karan Cosmetics, Editions De Parfums Frédéric Malle, Ermenegildo Zegna, Estée Lauder, Flirt!, GLAMglow, Goodskin Labs, Jo Malone London, Kiton, La Mer, Lab Series, Le Labo, Marni, Michael Kors, Ojon, Origins, Osiao, Prescriptives, Rodin Olio Lusso, Smashbox, Tom Ford Beauty, Tommy Hilfiger, Tory Burch, and finally

---

[1] From Joseph H. Hancock, II, (2016), All Races, All Sexes, All Genders: M.A.C., Brand/Story: Cases and Explorations in Fashion Branding, 2nd Edition, New York: Bloomsbury.

M.A.C. Fabrizio Freda, the CEO of Estée Lauder, has stated that over the last few years the company has seen a steady growth in revenue. Estée Lauder's plan for expansion is increasing its international markets and product portfolio; the company is trying to push brand awareness through its many divisions and is devoted to developing a better online presence to generate revenue. It is also increasing its product exposure in social media.

The company is expanding its makeup lines to differentiate itself from the competition and continues to expand in the hair care arena through various retail outlets. Unlike many competitors, who turn to celebrities to promote brand awareness, Estée Lauder turns to fashion and retail. The company is focusing on geographic growth into markets in China, the Middle East, Eastern Europe, Brazil, and South Africa and on customers who purchase through travel and retail channels such as duty-free stores in airports.

Because of this growth strategy, Estée Lauder is planning to incorporate its higher-priced goods in these international markets. The company will market its skin care lines because they are its most successful product category. In 2014 the company launched the Somaly Mam Beauty Salon in Cambodia and the Jo Malone London brand at the Mitsukoshi store in Beijing, China. The company currently sells its products in more than 150 countries, with the United States being the largest consumer market (over 40 percent of sales) and with Europe, the Middle East, and Africa accounting for only a little over 30 percent of sales.

MAKEUP ART COSMETICS: M.A.C.

What keeps the Estée Lauder company thriving and growing is its unique brands representing various markets and cultural groups. M.A.C. Cosmetics, one of its acquisitions, is a leader in this area. In the early 1970s, two artists from Ontario, Canada—Frank Toskan and Frank Angelo—along with chemist Vic Casale developed and sold their own line of makeup for fashion models. Their product line was revolutionary because it was designed to work with skin colors and to reflect well on camera. It was significantly better than products that were currently available for fashion photography and film. At the time, fashion professionals relied on heavy base cosmetics for stage, screen, and visual effects. The makeup was thick and quite harmful to a model or actor's complexion.

Toskan and Angelo created something unique and amazing. Their line became known for its extensive range of colors and for its individual pots of color, an innovation over the usual prepackaged combinations. Moreover, their makeup was not as heavy, nor did it have a pancaked feel. It was unique because it was easy to use. The makeup line grew in popularity, and the two decided they wanted to sell their products to the public. So in 1985, they created the company Makeup Art Cosmetics, or what is commonly called M.A.C. Cosmetics.

The company has grown, and today you can buy M.A.C. cosmetics in over seventy countries. It currently employs over twelve thousand makeup artists and is known for its mantra: "all ages, all races, all sexes." The company has fostered an environment in which everyone is free to be whoever they want to be and to express who they are, and what better way to do it than through makeup? In addition to being a makeup choice for people of color because of its assortment for skin tones, M.A.C. has become the brand synonymous with drag queens, gay men, lesbians, transgendered people, rock stars, the gothic, punks, freaks, and those who are not normatively targeted as a market niche. Each M.A.C. employee serves these clients with respect and dignity, treating them as special as the fashion models and movie stars the brand served in the 1970s—because in the world of M.A.C. the customer is a star.

PHILANTHROPIC BRANDING WITH A TWIST: VIVA GLAM

In the article "The Ringleader: M.A.C.: How a Weird Indie Startup Took Over the World of Makeup," writer Danielle Pergament begins with this:

> Imagine you're at a dinner party. And not just any dinner party. You're at a dinner party seated next to Catherine Deneuve, who, by the way, is ignoring you and talking to Raquel Welch. To your right is Nicki Minaj, telling off-color jokes with RuPaul. Just as the

salad is served, the door bursts open and Lady Gaga blows in, Elton John and Liza Minnelli right behind her. You look in the corner and see...wait. Is that? Yes, there's Wonder Woman, discreetly picking a piece of spinach out of her teeth, while Barbie giggles next to her. And just when things can't get any weirder, you look across the table and lock eyes with Hello Kitty. She tilts her cartoon head and gives you a knowing look—one that says, Yep, welcome to M.A.C.

"What kind of a company ignites its charity program by selling lipstick with RuPaul, a drag queen, as its spokesperson?" The answer is M.A.C. The Canadian brand, created in 1985, has always been fearless and outspoken, and when it comes to the VIVA GLAM message, it's always been loud and clear.

In the mid-1990s, when most companies were focusing on supermodels, the founders of M.A.C. were focusing on stopping the spread of HIV and AIDS. The VIVA GLAM was a way to reach out to the world through the world of cosmetics. The idea was to start with a lipstick that resembled and had a symbiotic representation of a bullet to be the "shot fired round the world" announcing that M.A.C. Cosmetics was there to help those infected with HIV and AIDS. This was the first philanthropic effort to give 100 percent of all proceeds to help the cause. There is nothing held back at the helm of M.A.C.

By using RuPaul Charles as its spokesmodel for VIVA GLAM, M.A.C. was making a statement. It was a return to gay rights and the notion that gays have a voice in the community, especially in the world of fashion and cosmetics. It was the drag queens who started the gay rights movement at Stonewall on June 28, 1969. It was the likes of famous drag queens such as Sylvia Rivera (1951–2002) and Marsha P. Johnson (1944–1992) who led the fight for equality during the Stonewall years. By using a drag queen and a prominent voice in the gay community such as RuPaul, who had just released his single, *Supermodel (You Better Work)*, M.A.C. was making a statement on not only gay rights but also on building awareness about HIV/AIDS. Many in the fashion world and makeup industry died from AIDS.

M.A.C. also wanted to support HIV/AIDS awareness because AIDS had been stigmatized as a "gay disease." M.A.C. wanted to say, "We support everyone with HIV/AIDS, and it's not just a 'gay disease'—it impacts everyone." By using RuPaul, a leading gay celebrity, the campaign addressed the gay issue of HIV/AIDS head on and also gained the admiration of the gay community by using one of its biggest icons—a drag queen.

It is important for today's readers, especially those in college and even perhaps in high school, to know that during the 1980s many young individuals became infected with HIV/AIDS. Gay men and those with AIDS were often outcasts among their families and friends. People thought you could catch AIDS just from hugging someone with the disease. This disease was devastating and controversial because it was happening in our own country in our own backyards and to our friends and family members. Many lives were lost, and most individuals, especially in the gay communities, knew one or two people who died. More importantly, there is no cure for HIV/AIDS, and infection still occurs.

With 100 percent of the proceeds of every VIVA GLAM product going directly to men, women and children affected by HIV/AIDS, it was an unparalleled move. The idea of VIVA GLAM was to celebrate life and the outspoken attitude of the company. It was a connective tissue that encompassed the diversity of M.A.C. and its mantra...all ages, all races, all sexes. It was, and continues to be, the signature and the heart and soul of the company.

It is interesting to note that Estée Lauder bought an interest in M.A.C. the same year that it launched the VIVA GLAM campaign. Perhaps she noted the importance of such a campaign and knew that M.A.C. was doing something revolutionary. Not only were its products phenomenal, but the company was blatantly supporting a consumer market that had been stigmatized and ostracized. Estée Lauder probably recognized that M.A.C. addressed many consumers and was filling niche markets that had been completely overlooked since the dawn of the cosmetics industry.

VIVA GLAM spokespeople are provocative, alternative, and influential and reflect diverse communities. They are heroes we look up to for their personal triumphs, people who have invented themselves, and people who have created movements. Over the years the list has included RuPaul, K.D. Lang, Mary J. Blige, Lil' Kim, Sir Elton John, Shirley Manson, Christina Aguilera, Missy Elliott, Linda Evangelista, Chloe Sevigny, Boy George, Pamela Anderson, Eve White, Lisa Marie Presley, Debbie Harry, Dita von Teese, Fergie, Lady Gaga, Cyndi Lauper, Ricky Martin, Nicki Minaj, Miley Cyrus, and Rihanna.

This campaign continues and reflects the future of fashion branding with its provocative way of addressing awareness. M.A.C. was the first to take a stance on HIV/AIDS awareness, and the consumers have voted through their purchases that this philanthropic action is just as important. Since its inception, this fund has raised over $270 million by selling tubes of lipstick for $16.

M.A.C.'s approach is phenomenal. The idea of giving 100 percent of all proceeds to charity is unique, with most companies giving a smaller percentage. As time has progressed, this approach has perhaps become less avante-garde and risqué because consumer markets are more accepting of the gay, lesbian, and transgender communities. But what is still unique about M.A.C. is its marketing directed toward minorities of color, and it is capturing their consumer dollars at all times. While more cosmetic companies are marketing toward people of color, such as with Queen Latifah's commercials for *CoverGirl*, it should be noted that M.A.C. did it first, and it continues to bank on women of color such as Rihanna and Nicki Minaj for drawing attention to its brand. While Miley Cyrus was deemed the most recent face of VIVA GLAM, we can all be assured that M.A.C. will continue its unique approach of reaching all consumers with a new celebrity that is out-of-the-box for the fashion industry in its next VIVA GLAM campaign.

MAKING UP IS MASCULINE:
The increasing cultural connections between masculinity and make-up

Janice Miller[1]

A great deal more work on make-up exists in disciplines that examine the relationship between consumer psychology, patterns of consumption and marketing. This work largely focuses on the behavioural aspects of make-up use. Fabricant and Gould (1993) are interested in what they term women's make-up 'careers'. They examine the way women from a variety of age groups navigate their use of make-up throughout the life-course alongside their perceptions of appropriate femininity. Gentina et al. (2012) take a similar approach, this time focusing on teenage girls and arguing that make-up is part of a 'rite of passage' into womanhood for these young women. In a similar vein, Rudd (1997) sees make-up as having a ritualistic role in the lives of women. Such work then, makes useful connections between gendered identities and practices of cosmetic use in relation to groups of women. However, its purpose is neither to question the broader cultural mechanisms that situate make-up so forcefully within the lives of these women in the first place, nor to understand how such practices are perpetuated through the products of popular culture. Consequently, a more sustained, interdisciplinary, Cultural Studies approach to the analysis of such practices would add a significant voice to this work and provide a fuller understanding of the distinct ways individuals make their identities through their body, what motivates such interventions and what the wider, cultural implications might be.

When make-up has been written about by writers taking such a critical and cultural approach, it is often not the discreet object of study. Instead it is discussed within work where the first concern is sexual difference. In such work, make-up is understandably situated with the feminine and seen as 'part of the process by which the ideal body of femininity – and hence the feminine body subject – is constructed' (Bartky 1990: 71). For writers like Bartky, make-up might be marketed to women with the possibility of individual expression, but it is ultimately the mechanism by which women's bodies are made '... "object and prey" for the man ...' (Bartky 1990: 72). It is through processes like making-up their faces that women aim to achieve 'a badge of acceptability in most social and professional contexts' (Bartky 1990). This is made clear by reactions to the unmade-up female face, which opens itself to a variety of negative comments and prohibitions (see Biddle-Perry and Miller 2009; Miller 2013). Bartky argues that 'the disciplinary project of femininity' – of which make-up is a part – 'is a "set-up": it requires such radical and extensive measures of bodily transformation that virtually every woman who gives herself to it is destined in some degree to fail' (Bartky 1990: 72).

THE MALE BODY AND GENDER IDENTITY

It is right that such work emphasizes the significantly punitive role of embodiment in the position of women historically. However, writing in 2004, Tim Edwards argued that 'If the sociology of the body is still in its

---

[1] From Janice Miller, Making Up is Masculine: The Increasing Cultural Connections Between Masculinity and Make-Up, Critical Studies in Men's Fashion, Volume 1, Issue 3, pp. 241–53, Intellect.

infancy and consequently underdeveloped, then the sociology of the body and its relationship to masculinity more specifically has yet to be born and is next to non-existent' (2004: 132–33). In the last fifteen years or so a variety of writers have responded to the need to better understand the relationship between men and their bodies within a range of disciplines. Some have looked at men's feelings about their bodies, what affects these feelings and thus their 'body image' (see e.g. Kimmel and Mahalik 2004; Morrison et al. 2004; Tager et al. 2006; Reardon and Govender 2011). Some writers have looked at gay men's feelings about their bodies and how this might contrast with straight men (see Tiggeman et al. 2007). Other work has focused on the relationship between muscularity and the idealized male body (see Leit et al. 2002; Hargreaves and Tiggeman 2009; Hunt et al. 2013) or more extreme incarnations of the muscular male body in body-building cultures (Broom and Tovey 2009; Locks and Richardson 2012). Many have also looked at the health implications of some of the activities men engage in to achieve such bodies: steroid use for example (Keane 2004).

Much of this work is underpinned by the need to understand how men's consumption patterns might have shifted in response to changing ideals of masculinity. The attempt to market what were previously understood to be 'feminine' products to men is part and parcel of the shifting codes of masculinity that have made it a focus for contestation and reformulation since the 1980s, as a response to the gains made by second wave feminism in the 1970s (See e.g. Edwards 2004). In particular the much vaunted metrosexual typified in global celebrity culture by David Beckham is both a manifestation of cultural shifts in masculinity and a marketing phenomenon: a man who delights 'in the consumerist heaven that is the modern-day metropolis. Sexually ambivalent, the "metrosexual" embraces gay culture but only as a product of late capitalism' (Genz and Brabon 2009: 139). Whilst in academic circles the dominance of metrosexuality as a description for contemporary, narcissistic and image driven masculinity is increasingly open to critique, it is certainly with this kind of masculine identity that the global boom in the marketing of a variety of what would previously have been deemed feminine products towards men is located. As Mary Talbot writes 'Men are clearly being caught up in the itemization of the body as a visible object requiring work, with education in discriminatory practices essential for that work. They are increasingly achieving the subject position of consumer masculinity when buying and using commodities' (2010: 156).

In response to this, further work has examined how the body might act as a site of expression for a variety of masculine identities via fashion and other forms of body modification like tattooing (Cole 2000; Negrin 2008). It is also unsurprising that research which considers how best to understand the male consumer in order to market products towards them has been interested in how they feel about products that are not traditionally seen to be masculine. Since men have been increasingly targeted with products that challenge stereotypical notions of masculine behaviour and interests, then examining what might make some men hold back from consuming them is important (see e.g. Mason 2002). McNeill and Douglas (2011) focus on the market for 'grooming' products in New Zealand. In this context they argue that very traditional notions of appropriate masculine behaviour prevail and result in some ambivalence about whether, and how, to appropriately consume such items whilst still retaining a sense of an appropriately gendered self on the part of the consumers they studied. One of their most significant findings is the identification of a tendency for male consumers to justify their grooming behaviours through the language of utility. Thus, any possibility that their masculinity might be undermined is offset with assertions of traditional, masculine, practical concerns around function and performance.

MEN AND MAKE-UP

Such concerns are echoed in the marketing of many contemporary make-up ranges to men. In the advertising for Tom Ford for men, the designer's 2013 collection of cosmetic products directed towards male consumers, the male model, frowning, pensive, strong and healthy, determinedly paints a strip of concealer under his eye like warpaint. He thus transforms himself into a warrior, spreading bronzer with an affirmative male hand onto his cheek – no delicate patting of the finger to apply the product as a woman might. The cleansing face mask is worn as just that, a mask, which evokes notions of super-heroic masculinity (see Miller 2013). Joan Riviere (2011) argued that gender was a masquerade and might be understood as an 'anxiety ridden compensatory gesture' (Doane 1991: 38). Such marketing campaigns and the attitudes of the men in McNeill and Douglas' study could be seen in similar terms. In both cases traditional masculinity is re-enforced. In the case of the marketing images, this might be seen as an attempt to assimilate some forms of making up into masculine cultures and to address the anxieties of male consumers who are still making decisions about how they should consume these products.

Cosmetics have been an integral part of the fashioning and refashioning of the female body for hundreds of years. But it is important to remember that, as Richard Corson (2003) has clearly demonstrated, the use of cosmetics has not always been unique to women. At different times men have worn make-up to assert their membership of certain subcultural groups like Punks or New Romantics in the 1970s and 1980s, for example. Of course, the wearing of make-up by men in various performance settings has long been appropriate. In music performances of various kinds for example, made-up male faces have come to be relatively commonplace. Historically in popular music this often signalled transgression by crossing the expected boundaries of behaviour in many historical and cultural contexts. This transgression was marked out in the visibility of make-up on the faces of some performers (Miller 2013). Obviously many others were wearing make-up that could not be seen and over time many of these originally transgressive inscriptions have become innocuous (black eyeliner on both male and female performers for example), mainstream expressions that arguably signal more about an individual's role as a music performer than their gendered identity (Miller 2013).

Beyond music, make-up on male performers, presenters or politicians most often functions to either characterize or correct rather than to transgress. In such contexts it seems natural and commonplace that make-up should be worn by men and it is accepted as a necessary part of preparing the body for the camera or stage. Importantly, most often it is not intended to be visible. As Place and Madry write in their manual of professional make-up aimed towards make-up artists working for the screen, 'Men's eyes can be lined, but the make-up must not become visible on the screen in closeups' (1989: 219). What the advice given in this manual clearly defines are the acceptable and distinct ways a make-up artist should constitute a masculine and a feminine face through the process of making-up. Place and Madry set out clear expectations of what should be worn and how, providing a clear demarcation between the genders: 'Cheek colours should be used sparingly for men, if at all' (1989) the manual states. The perceived 'problem' of performances that require an individual to be themselves onstage and to interact with their audience close-up afterwards or to wear their make-up in some other public setting are tackled too with the advice that 'the best solution for men is a natural tan cake or cream stick, but if that is impractical, a transparent liquid makeup or bronzing gel for streetwear works just as well' (1989: 213). The manual makes clear the belief that for a man to be recognized as wearing make-up, outside of a performance space would be a source of embarrassment. As a result, it impresses upon its reader the importance of maintaining the ideals of masculine identity. As with many texts the constructed-ness of masculinity and femininity (see e.g. Butler 1990; Riviere 2011; Holmlund 2012) is denied and naturalized and anything which threatens to destabilize or reveal such constructions is seen as a source of at best ambivalence, and at worst shame. Such sentiments seem to reflect a tendency for mainstream western culture to understand practices that do not hold with distinct gender categorizations as signalling something about sexual identity that is troubling to a 'gender system [that] is said to posit heterosexuality as a primary sign of gender normality' (Seidman 1993: 114).

Yet, as we move into the twenty-first century the possibility of including some form of 'making-up' of the face within the grooming routines of men is increasingly presented to consumers with ranges of make-up targeted at male consumers by global brands like Jean Paul Gaultier, Clinique and Tom Ford whose advertising has already been discussed here. When they do so, press coverage tends towards the sensationalist in two ways. First, such sensationalism fails to acknowledge the relatively conservative nature of many products on sale, which, in fact, echoes the kinds of appropriate masculine make-up use recounted by Place and Madry (1989). Here the emphasis is on concealers, bronzers and products to darken eyebrows and there is, therefore, a correlation between the perfected, male made-up face seen on-screen and what is increasingly offered to men via the make-up marketed towards them. The perhaps slight anomaly to this is in Jean Paul Gaultier's current range, Monsieur, which offers lip balm in stick form with three shades; clear, light and dark. The chocolate brown lipstick offered by the designer to male consumers in 2004 has disappeared

THE LANGUAGE OF GROOMING

Whilst global brands attempt to sell make-up as the next natural progression from skincare in men's grooming routine, whatever their sexuality, there is plenty of subtle resistance to the notion that men should care at all. It should also be remembered that many brands have failed to market such products successfully – Aramis or the United Kingdom High Street chemist Superdrug and its 'Taxi Man' range lay testament to this. Even those who have embraced skincare with aplomb seem to remain at best ambivalent about the idea of making up as a routine practice. In an article from September 2013 Lee Kynaston, a writer on men's grooming and beauty asks 'Makeup for men: We're not buying so why are companies still trying to sell it to us?' and acknowledges that 'as much as the grooming press – me included – has pretended cosmetics are very much part of the modern man's washbag, they're simply not' (2013). An article from Esquire magazine gives a wink of irony that does not reassure the reader of its jocularity and a 'cure' for the 'sissy stuff by providing advice on how to groom with 'no nonsense toiletries' instead of 'frilly potions' (Cury 2003).

Such statements, first, make clear that the language of cosmetics is important to a full understanding of how they are used, by whom and why. Otherwise, these semantic 'muddy waters' make room for many inflammatory statements about what a man's choice to use such products might signal in relation to sexuality. Of course, any suggestion that there is a natural correlation between gay men and cosmetics is an unsubstantiated stereotype. The complex semantics that pervade discourses of make-up and cosmetics is far from straightforward. Yet it is increasingly important to understanding contemporary gender ideals and technologies of the body more generally. As the possible ways in which bodies can be fashioned and refashioned are ever growing, it is no longer enough to use cosmetics or grooming as catch all terms to understand what individuals do to their bodies when they use such products, or how such use in turn makes individual or sociocultural expressions of identity. Much of the existing research referenced in this article does not make clear demarcation between different types of cosmetics and grooming products and yet, I would argue, there is a pressing need for future work to begin to do so. Second, they act as acute reminders of what societies will do when their ideological boundaries are threatened and serves to demonstrate how 'masculinity is held up as the "norm" in Western culture [and] any deviation from it is viewed with great unease' (Arnold 2001: 111). Male consumers are clearly affected by such concerns. Consequently in the hierarchy of normalized gendered behaviours, for men to moisturize their skin is a world away from the application of make-up and the boundary between the two is one that many men, like Kynaston – though happy to indulge in skincare routines – do not always seem happy to cross.

Understanding how different grooming and cosmetic products are both perceived by and sold to men is essential to understand both why some products are taken up by them and others rejected as well as what the implications of such products and marketing on men's body image and sense of identity might be. Steve Robertson (2007) reminds us that it is since the advent of modernity that bodies and appearance have increasingly become a currency for both men and women, since it is increasingly commodified and associated with the expression of identity. However, since gender is accepted to be a construct (see e.g. Butler 1990) framed by stereotypes and contrasting expected behaviours from the different genders, the ways identity was expressed by individuals was often bound by such expectations to varying degrees. Whilst it has been clearly and forcefully argued by many writers that we must remember that men do not fit common stereotypes and that masculinities are multiple (see e.g. Connell 2005), affected by a variety of factors including class (Horowitz 2013; Crane 2012) and culture (Gutman 2003; Bourdieu 2001; Morrell et al. 2012), men have traditionally focused more of their energies on the function of their bodies than their appearance (Robertson 2007). Contemporary masculinity has been proven by a number of researchers to be in a recurring negotiation between the two. For example, the work of Reardon and Govender (2011) has seen positive male body image to be an increasing concern amongst contemporary men. However, they note too, that the achievement of an idealized masculine body acts as a precursor to more conventional displays of masculine power and aggression, thanks to the confidence such a body provokes in the individual possessing it. Such work establishes the possibility then that a concern with appearance functions increasingly to give men the confidence to exert their masculine power in quite conventional ways.

MEN AND MAKE-UP IN SOUTH KOREA

Despite the myriad masculinities that circulate in culture in all their complexity, Tim Edwards clearly establishes the way the male body plays a significant role in 'forming and maintaining inequalities and social divisions between men' (2004: 135). In South Korea, make-up use has increasingly become the norm amongst young, professional men and functions to mark out the kinds of social divisions between men of which Tim Edwards speaks. In 2011/2012 Korean men spent over £300,000,000 on cosmetic products (Anon. 2012). While some of these male consumers locate their use of cosmetics within the negotiation of their romantic lives, the prevailing concern seems to be the importance of an idealized and refined bodily presentation to their professional roles. As one man states 'My bosses always emphasized the importance of giving a good first impression to clients . . . So, to take extra care of my skin and look, I began using cosmetics' (Kwon et al. 2012). Much media coverage of this 'phenomenon' therefore, largely attributes it to increased competition for jobs and romantic partners in a culture that is significantly appearance oriented (see Anon. 2012).

Thus, where Edwards sees classed masculinities played out in professional contexts via the 'development of particular skills, from perfecting handshakes to playing golf' (2004: 127) in this more contemporary context 'physical capital' – as Pierre Bourdieu (1984) might term such bodily statements of social position – is the new currency. Increasingly in this context, the male body and its technologies have become a site for what Pierre Bourdieu would understand as 'aesthetic stances . . . opportunities to assert one's position in social space, as a rank to be upheld or a distance to be kept' (1984: 57). In South Korea then, make-up and what it can achieve in terms of the refinement of the male body has come to equate to personal and professional success, as it is assimilated into masculine corporate culture. For men in this context paying attention to their appearance becomes the mechanism through which they access what Connell (2005) would describe as the 'patriarchal dividend'.

Whilst make-up might seem ostensibly too feminine to be part of the masculine, professional identity game, in South Korea men's use of make-up is less about expressive inscriptions or the use of colour – which are so often a part of a woman's make-up routine – and a great deal more about producing a refined notion of a healthy, male face. Concealers are used to mask under eye circles and to remove signs of tiredness. Any colour is largely restricted to mimicking or improving on 'nature'; black or brown pencils that thicken and enhance eyebrows for example. Colour Correcting (CC) creams (so called 'multi-tasking' products that provide skin care, sun protection and colour) are used to even out the skin, to cover blemishes and to work against sallowness or redness. These creams often contain light-reflecting particles to give an illusion of luminous and thus 'healthy' skin. In creating a declaration of health on the surface of the body, it can be argued that make-up functions here to produce a man 'fit for work'; one who looks healthy, professional and able. Such stances can be argued to be conventionally masculine since as Joan Williams argues, industrial societies emphasize that 'a man's social position . . . [is] determined by his own success. And the key to success was work' (1999: 26) (see also Christiansen and Palkovitz 2001). Thus we might argue that any bodily practice which assists men in navigating the workplace and its hierarchies can always be somewhat understood as a masculine practice whatever its form.

References

Arnold, Rebecca (2001), *Fashion, Desire and Anxiety: Image and Morality in the Twentieth Century*, London: IB Tauris.

Bartky, Sandra (1990), *Femininity and Domination: Studies in the Phenomenology of Oppression*, New York: Routledge.

Biddle-Perry, Geraldine and Sarah Cheang (2009), *Hair: Styling, Culture and Fashion*, Oxford: Berg.

Biddle-Perry, Gerladine and Janice Miller (2009), "... and If Looks Could Kill: Making up the Face of Evil." In C. Balmain and L. Drawmer (eds.), *Something Wicked This Way Comes: Essay on Evil and Human Wickedness*, 7–25. New York, NY: Rodopi.

Bourdieu, Pierre (1984), *Distinction: A Social Critique of the Judgement of Taste*, New York: Routledge and Kegan Paul Ltd.

Bourdieu, Pierre (2001), *Masculine Domination*, Redwood City, CA: Stanford University Press.

Broom, Alex and Phillip Tovey (2009), *Men's Health: Body, Identity and Social Context*. Chichester: John Wiley & Sons.

Butler, Judith (1990), *Gender Trouble: Feminism and the Subversion of Identity*. London: Taylor and Francis.

Christiansen, Shawn L. and Rob Palkovitz (2001), "Why the "Good Provider" role still matters providing as a form of paternal involvement', *Journal of Family Issues*, 22: 1, pp. 84–106.

Cole, Shaun (2000), *Don we now Our Gay Apparel: Gay Men's Dress in the Twentieth Century*, Oxford: Berg.

Connell, Raewyn (2005), *Masculinities*, 2nd ed., Cambridge: Polity Press.

Corson, Richard (2003), *Fashions in Makeup: From Ancient to Modern Times*, 3rd rev. ed., London: P. Owen.

Crane, Diana (2012), *Fashion and its Social Agendas: Class, Gender, and Identity in Clothing*, Chicago: University of Chicago Press.

Cury, James Oliver (2003), 'The cure: How not to be a metrosexual', *Esquire*, 1 December, http://www.esquire.com/features/man-at-his-best/ESQ1203-DEC_MANLY+&cd=1&hl=en&ct=clnk&gl=uk. Accessed 26 November 2013.

Doane, Mary Ann (1991), *Femme Fatales: Feminism, Film Theory, Psychoanalysis*, New York: Routledge.

Edwards, Tim (2004), *Cultures of Masculinity*, London: Routledge.

Fabricant, Stacey M. and Stephen J. Gould (1993), "Women's makeup careers: An interpretive study of color cosmetic use and "face value"', *Psychology & Marketing*, 10: 6, pp. 531–48.

Gentina, Elodie, Kay M. Palan and Marie-Helene Fosse-Gomez (2012), 'The practice of using makeup: A consumption ritual of adolescent girls', *Journal of Consumer Behaviour*, 11: 2, pp. 115–23.

Genz, Stephanie and Benjamin A. Brabon. (2009), *Postfeminism: Cultural Texts and Theories*, Edinburgh: Edinburgh University Press.

Gutmann, Matthew C. (ed.) (2003), *Changing Men and Masculinities in Latin America*, Durham, NC: Duke University Press.

Hargreaves, D. A. and M. Tiggemann. (2009), 'Muscular ideal media images and men's body image: Social comparison processing and individuals vulnerability', *Psychology of Men and Masculinity*, 10: 2, pp. 109–19.

Holmlund, Chris (2012), 'Masculinity as multiple masquerade: The "mature" Stallone and the Stallone clone', in C. Cohan and I. R. Vark (eds), *Screening the Male: Exploring Masculinities in Hollywood Cinema*, 213–229. Oxford: Routledge.

Horowitz, Roger (ed.) (2013), *Boys and Their Toys: Masculinity, Class and Technology in America*, New York: Routledge.

Hunt, Christopher John, Karen Gonsalkorale and Stuart B. Murray. (2013), 'Threatened masculinity and muscularity: An experimental examination of multiple aspects of muscularity in men', *Body Image*, 10: 3, pp. 290–99.

Keane, Helen (2005), 'Diagnosing the male steroid user: Drug use, body image and disordered masculinity', *Health*, 9: 2, pp. 189–208.

Kimmel, S. B. and J. R. Mahalik. (2004), 'Measuring masculine body ideal distress: Development of a measure', *International Journal of Men's Health*, 3: 1, pp. 1–10.

Kwon Ji-youn, Yoon Sung-won and Park Jin-hai (2012), 'More men wear makeup', *Korean Times*, n.d., http://www.koreatimes.co.kr/www/common/printpreview.asp?categoryCode=399&newsIdx=140586. Accessed 18 July 2013.

Kynaston, Lee (2013), 'Make-up for men: We're not buying so why are companies still trying to sell it to us?', *Telegraph*, 25 September, http://www.telegraph.co.uk/men/fashion-and-style/10330132/Make-up-for-men-were-not-buying-so-why-are-companies-still-trying-to-sell-it-to-us.html. Accessed 12 November 2013.

Leit, R. A., J. J. Gray and H. G. Pope (2002), 'The media's representation of the ideal male body: A cause for muscle dysmorphia?', *International Journal of Eating Disorders*, 31: 3, pp. 334–38.

Locks, Adam and Niall Richardson (eds) (2012), *Critical Readings in Bodybuilding*, vol. 9, London: Routledge.

Mason, S. (2002), 'Marketing to men', *Global Cosmetic Industry*, 170: 3, pp. 26–29.

McNeill, Lisa S. and Katie Douglas (2011), 'Retailing masculinity: Gender expectations and social image of male grooming products in New Zealand', *Journal of Retailing and Consumer Services*, 18: 5, pp. 448–54.

Miller, Janice (2013), 'Heroes and villains: When men wear makeup', in S. Bruzzi and P. Church Gibson (eds), *Fashion Cultures Revisited: Theories, Explorations and Analysis*, 341–51. Oxford: Routledge.pp.

Morrell, Robert, Rachel Jewkes and Graham Lindegger (2012), 'Hegemonic masculinity/masculinities in South Africa culture, power, and gender politics', *Men and Masculinities*, 15: 1, pp. 11–30.

Morrison, T. G., R. Kalin and M. A. Morrison. (2004), 'Body image evaluation and body image among adolescents: A test of sociocultural and social comparison theories', *Adolescence*, 39: 155, pp. 571–92.

Negrin, Llewellyn (2008), *Appearance and Identity: Fashioning the Body in Postmodernity*, London: Palgrave.

Place, Stan and Bobbi Ray Madry (1989), *The Art and Science of Professional Makeup*, London: Cengage Learning.

Reardon, Candice A. and Kaymarlin Govender (2011), 'Shaping Up': The Relationship between Traditional Masculinity, Conflict Resolution and Body Image among Adolescent Boys in South Africa', *Vulnerable Children and Youth Studies*, 6: 1, pp. 78–87.

Riviere, Joan (2011), 'Womanliness as Masquerade', in Athol Hughes (ed.), *The Inner World and Joan Riviere: Collected Papers, 1929–1958*. London: Karnac, pp. 89–101.

Robertson, Steve (2007), *Understanding Men and Health: Masculinities, Identity and Well-Being*, Maidenhead: Open University Press.

Rudd, Nancy A. (1997), 'Cosmetics consumption and use among women: Ritualized activities that construct and transform the self', *Journal of Ritual Studies*, 11: 2, pp. 59–77.

Seidman, Steven (1993), 'Identity and politics in "postmodern" gay culture', in Michael Warner (ed.), *Fear of a Queer Planet: Queer Politics and Social Theory*, 105–142. Minneapolis: University of Minnesota Press.

Tager, D., G. E. Good and J. Morrison. (2006), 'Our bodies, ourselves revisited: Male body image and psychological well-being', *International Journal of Men's Health*, 5: 3, pp. 228–37.

Talbot, Mary (2010), *Language and Gender*, 2nd ed., Cambridge: Polity Press.

Tiggemann, Marika, Yolanda Martins, and Alana Kirkbride (2007), 'Oh to be lean and muscular: Body image ideals in gay and heterosexual men', *Psychology of Men & Masculinity*, 8: 1, pp. 15–24.

Williams, Joan (1999), *Unbending Gender: Why Family and Work Conflict and What to do About it*, Oxford: Oxford University Press.

Williamson, Lucy (2012), 'South Korean men get the makeup habit', *BBC News Magazine*, 3 December, http://www.bbc.co.uk/news/magazine-20522028. Accessed 12 May 2014.

53

HAIR AND HUMAN IDENTITY

Sarah Cheang and Geraldine Biddle-Perry[1]

Hair grows all over the human body, interestingly, at the same rate of about one to one-and-a-half centimetres a month, although hairs on different parts of the body have different life-spans before they drop out: 'Leg hairs, for example, last around two months, armpit hairs left to their own devices make it to six months, but head hairs grow non-stop for six years or more' (Barnett 2006: 39). It is this capacity for our head hair, whatever its colour or curl, to carry on growing continuously, that makes it distinctive, and differentiates us from all other mammals who—with the exception of the musk ox—merely grow and shed with the seasons (Barnett 2006).

Our closest mammalian relatives, the monkeys and apes, possess beards, moustaches, coloured caps and even hairless rear ends that serve as a form of social identification; in our primeval condition it was the sheer volume of our head hair in relation to our relatively scant body hair that labelled us as human (Morris 1987: 21). Head hair that could grow to a considerable length provided a highly visible and unique species signal. Human technological advance provided the means to overcome the physical restrictions of long and weighty hair through cutting and shaving it with blades, knives and eventually scissors, or curtailing it with combs, pins and ties, hats and various head coverings (Morris 1987: 22) Function and form came together in the distinctively human capacity to modify, shape and reshape our hairy heads with endless stylistic innovation. This separated 'us' from 'them': the humans from the animals, and one human grouping from another. The musk ox might grow its hair long, but it has not yet evolved a salon culture.

Forms of hair management established hair as an early performative element in social enterprise and cultural organization, along with other forms of body adornment such as tattooing, ornaments and clothing (Turner 1991: 5–6; Wilson 1985: 3). Ancient tribal divisions were articulated through a system of distinctions between cut and uncut hair. Ancient Hittite men, for example, shaved off their beards, moustaches and even eyebrows, as well as a spot above the ear, but left their head hair and side whiskers to grow long; Moabite men shaved their foreheads back to the crown, combing the long remaining hair back to fall to the shoulders; ancient Egyptians shaved their heads, but large and intricate wigs were worn by high-class women and their servants (Corson 1965: 26–8). The relationship between growth and restraint offers a hairy equation that is constantly exploited and reworked in different formulations to signal shifting understandings of social status and identity across time and across cultures.

Marina Warner's (1995) classic exposition on hair in fairy tale and legend details how hair is a consistent theme in fairy stories, folk tales and traditional songs: enchanted or disguised, both sexes are metamorphosed into hairier and furrier, wilder and/or more domesticated versions of themselves. The meanings and values of such changes, she argues, shift according to gender, but are equally essentially grounded in sexuality. Wolves, bears, donkeys and goats offer a fantasy of bestial hairiness that operates to reveal men's

---

[1] From Sarah Cheang and Geraldine Biddle-Perry (2008), Hair and Human Identity, *Hair: Styling, Culture and Fashion*, pp. 243–253.

baser animal instincts (and sometimes dumb stupidity); cats provide the female metamorphic alternative—the witch's familiar of choice—but other animal skins are also worn by the wronged woman or the fugitive as evidence, one way or another, of male contamination (Warner 1995: 354–60). Hair's presentation and representation reveals the nature of the fears and anxieties that disturb and define the human condition by being allied to a spectrum of animal-like qualities.

Warner's work offers an insight into how humans, though emphasizing their difference and distinction from animals, nevertheless continually build on this physiology of hair as something shared with all creatures of 'pelt, fur and hide' (1995: 354). Hair reminds us how close and how distant we are from the animal within. Occupying the middle ground, fauns, satyrs and mermaids offer an imaginative half-way house, and their head hair and hairy bodies function as a metaphorical device to explore and emphasize this liminal status. In tales of mermaids their hair becomes analogous with both sexual maturity and the very act of feminine expression. Long golden locks are spun and woven like the threads of narrative and the singing of songs, the movement of the brush and comb matching the backwards and forwards motion of the shuttle in the loom (Gitter 1984: 938, 941). But spinning and weaving have other connotations—of webs of deceit and of entrapment. Hair's magical powers are manifested in this generative capacity for symbolic uncertainty. Powell and Roach argue,

> hair is a performance, one that happens at the boundaries of self-expression and social identity, of creativity and conformity, and of production and consumption. Hair lends itself particularly well to self-fashioning performance because it is liminal, on the threshold, 'betwixt and between', not only of nature and culture, but also of life and death. (Powell and Roach 2004: 79)

Hairy and hairless, dressed and undressed, visible and hidden, human hair and its practices become part of a whole connotative moral universe of complex meanings attached to the human body, and the habitual modes of vision through which it is produced and consumed. All human bodies are created hairy and some bodies, regardless of gender, are created hairier than others. The discourses that surround hair's removal, trimming and shaping operate as ideological mechanisms, culturally regulating the display and management of the individual and collective social body. Hair's management and modification operate not just as an adjunct to the social body but rather, like dress and ornamentation, come to constitute the social body itself.

HAIR STEREOTYPES AND 'NATURAL' QUALITIES

As highly visible social markers, different hair colours and textures have particular physical and behavioural characteristics attached to them, creating stereotypes that are highly pervasive. In white people, dark hair and light hair tend to be diametrically opposed, the former being connected to seriousness, and the latter to fun (Synnott 1993: 103–27). Red hair is viewed as unusual, and pejoratively as 'weird', so that *ginger* can be a term of abuse.

Historically, red hair has had negative connotations of witchcraft, and of Judas's betrayal of Jesus (Roach 2005: 9–87). In contemporary Western society, more common associations are with a 'hot' temperament, clowns and Irish and Scottish identity. Studies show that redheads feel that they are treated differently from others, especially during their school years, and men are particularly affected by negative stereotyping. Ginger males are singled out for derision and classed as weak and sexually unattractive. Such discrimination on the grounds of hair colour appears to be quite socially acceptable, and women with light-red hair may prefer to describe themselves as 'strawberry blonde' to capitalize on the more positive feminine attributes of blondeness (Anderson 2001).

Blondeness is also a particular type of whiteness, predominantly associated with the snowy north of the Scandinavian countries or northern Europe (Dyer 1997: 20–1; Young 1997). During the early-twentieth century, racial prejudice against people of Jewish, Celtic and non-white descent in Europe, America and the Soviet Union produced a new interest in blondeness. This reached its apotheosis in the Nazi project to engineer a racially 'pure' and 'perfect' German race by encouraging the breeding of Nordic-looking blonde-haired, blue-eyed children and exterminating the darker, 'undesirable' elements from the gene pool (Pitman 2003: 167–201; Weitz 2004: 19–20). At its most reductive, the dichotomy of black/blonde identities is encapsulated by the central premise of the film *King Kong* (1930, with remakes), in which a savage black gorilla of enormous proportions is so entranced by a white blonde woman that he cannot harm her.

People of European descent have long exploited blonde hair's positive associations with light, goodness and beauty. Edwardian explorer Mrs French Sheldon claimed to have dazzled natives of East Africa in 1906 with a white gown and long blonde wig that apparently rendered her all-powerful and untouchable (Boisseau 2000: 33–35). Almost a century later, journalist Joanna Pitman (2003: 1–3). relates how in northern Kenya she was treated as possessing almost miraculous powers of healing because of her blonde hair, in a conflation of blondeness and Western medicine. Blondeness is also linked with certain stereotypes of femininity: infantilism, stupidity, glamour and sexual attraction (Synnott 1993: 108–9; Cox 1999: 159–60). However, hair that has been obviously bleached and dyed has the negative overtones of artificiality, sometimes provoking a crisis of 'natural' identity. Bleached hair, as opposed to the healthy 'natural' goodness of sun-kissed blonde hair, has had a brassy, self-destructive, lower-class vulgarity (Cox 1999: 161). In contrast, more natural-looking dyes can be used by medium and dark-haired women who had been blonde as children to regain that former blondeness. This is conceptualized as a return to the 'real' genetically blonde self, so that a synthetic process is used to maintain the identity of 'natural' blonde (Ilyin 2000: 23).

There are two kinds of signification and identity formation at work here. On the one hand, hair colour is treated as just one manifestation of a particular genetic make-up that is imagined to affect the individual in a number of other ways. On the other hand, people can adopt a particular colour to change their persona as participants in a postmodern consumer culture that encourages body modification and maintenance as an essential part of self-expression (Featherstone 1991). Marion Roach's book, *The Roots of Desire* (2005), explores her own identity as a redhead through both the myths and stereotypes of red-headed femininity, but is framed around a personal journey to establish the exact genetic markers of her hair, creating a final sense of her own identity as a 'true', biologically determined redhead. Similarly, Pitman makes it very clear in the opening paragraph of her book that it was the natural action of the sun and not a packet of bleach that had produced her arresting head of blonde hair in Kenya, demanding that she too should be understood as a genetic blonde, free from artifice. Thus, hair is part of the more general question of where our sense of self resides in the body—in the brain, in the flesh, in the senses, in our DNA or in the parts of the body that can consciously be used to signal to others (Merleau-Ponty 1962; Goffman 1971). The answer to this question is loaded with value judgements and negative assumptions about any claims to identity that are not 'natural'.

Here we encounter a nature/nurture paradox. In human identity, biological and cultural factors are blended, so that what is 'natural' must be questioned. Furthermore, the social articulation of race, class, gender and sexuality is intertwined, and each discourse has its own set of corporeal scientific proofs that tend to reify culturally constructed classifications At the same time, the social conditions experienced by members of a particular race, class, gender or sexuality will affect the way in which the body is nourished, shaped, used and presented. Anthropologist Mary Douglas proposes that: 'The social body constrains the way the physical body is perceived' (Douglas 1970: 65). The values, customs and restrictions that society places upon the human body affect the way in which the body is experienced and understood. Thus, the lived experience of having a particular hair type (the 'natural'), and the daily dressing processes to which that hair is subjected (the 'unnatural'), affects and restricts a person's understanding of himself or herself. In the struggle for self-determination under racial discrimination and/or imperialism, the symbolic and biological connections between hair and notions of race and breeding have accorded a heavily loaded significance to 'natural' hair.

This is most powerfully the case with the Afro, a hairstyle that exploits the kinky texture of black people's hair in the creation of a soft, dense halo of long, tightly curling hair. African Americans have straightened their hair since the days of slavery, using chemicals, hot combs and grease, allowing women to achieve the 'femininity' of long, flowing locks, and men to feel well-groomed and sophisticated (Craig 1997; Kelley 1997). Thus, whilst straightened hairstyles might not qualify as an effective challenge to racial hierarchies (Weitz 2001), hair straightening should not be seen as a straightforward emulation of white hair textures, but as a styling strategy in a society dominated by white ideals of beauty (Craig 1997, 2002; Banks 2000). In the context of the American Black Power movement and of African nationalism, the Afro of the 1960s and 1970s was a style that demonstrated a self-asserted, anti-white-culture stance, which along with clothing such as the dashiki, looked to Africa for inspiration (Kelley 1997). As Kobena Mercer (1994: 100) writes, black hairstyling can be 'evaluated as a popular art form articulating a variety of aesthetic "solutions" to a range of "problems" created by ideologies of race and racism'.

It is highly significant that the Afro was also termed the *natural,* for notions of 'Africa' and 'nature' operated together as a counter to Western culture as artificial and oppressive (Mercer 1994: 105–13; Soper 1995: 71–81). In the Afro, a 'woolly' or 'nappy' head of hair was not stigmatized, but was teased out into eye-catching proportions and paraded as a revalorized component of self-asserted, liberated and truly 'authentic' black identity—a way for black Americans to 'be themselves'. It should also be noted that the Afro was a contested style within black communities. For many women, notably of an older generation, unstraightened hair signalled a lack of self-respect, so that hair that had been allowed to revert to its natural state would seem like a social nightmare (Cleage 1993; Byrd and Tharps 2001: 132–64). Very tightly curled hair is still 'bad' hair (Banks 2000: 107), and the existence of books such as *Nappyisms: Affirmations for Nappy-Headed People and Wannabes* (Jones 2003) attests to the continuing need for wearers of the 'natural' to defend their choice against a dominant culture which finds natural hair unattractive.

However, the Afro is a cultivated style—long hair combed and cut into a rounded shape. It is not a totally natural style, and neither is it quintessentially African (Mercer 1994: 111). Where slaves wore their hair long and bushy, this was the result of being denied access to hair care; styling the hair through a combination of shaving and bunching, cutting and growing, combing and braiding was an important part of collective and individual identification, and one of the few areas of free expression (White and White 1995: 56). The 'naturalness' of the Afro is thus very loaded as 'natural' hair was being used by black Americans to construct 'African-American' rather than 'negro' identity (Mercer 1994: 107). As a Nigerian living in New York puts it: 'In Africa the hair is purely to decorate. It's different here because of the race issue' (Ifoema Ibo cited in Byrd and Tharps 2001: 164).

Black hair's symbolic and physical antithesis—blonde hair—is no less totemic in terms of racial identity, yet has a very different relationship to concepts of nature. For Caucasian blonde hair, the high racial status of Nordic looks combines with the styling, make-up and body modifications of female beauty regimes that produce 'normal' femininity (Bordo 2003), to create blonde hair as a product of nature that is improved by culture, within certain limits. Cultural constructions of race and gender are thus naturalized in the body, and blondeness projected as a 'natural' asset worth striving for.

CONCLUSION: CONTESTING NATURAL IDENTITY

Clearly, it is hair's malleability and hair's relationship to the body that gives it great power and multivalence within the systems of representation and identity, whether the dominant social ideologies are challenged or confirmed. To be an Asian with naturally curly hair creates a disquieting lack of racial belonging and a concomitant loss of cultural identity. A recent Internet discussion hosted by the Chinese History Forum reveals that without the straight hair that is the badge of Asian genes, one Chinese woman had always felt 'talked about and treated like an outsider' (Spikeyli 2007). By contrast, Rose Weitz's study of women, hairstyling and social power gives the example of an Asian American who feels compelled to perm her naturally straight hair every few months to avoid looking 'too Asian' (Weitz 2001: 676). Such strategies undertaken to resist racial stereotyping whilst submitting to a dominant white-identified ideology of beauty can be related to debates around plastic surgery, such as the remodelling of Asian eye shape to create a more 'desirable', rounded eye (Kaw 1993; Gilman 1999: 98–111; Zane 2003). To perm Asian hair is also to transcend the flesh in a postmodern corporeality rooted in consumer culture. However, unlike plastic surgery, hair keeps growing, forcing us to deal with our biological roots on a regular basis, continually converting identity from an innate 'natural' genetic inheritance to a daily, performative act (Gilroy 1998).

If the human body is an image of society, then hair's malleability makes it a doubly valuable asset in social expression by exploiting an antithetical clash between the 'corporeal/natural' and the 'cultural/unnatural'. The word *nature* is often used to mean the very 'essence' of human identity, but 'nature' also figures as something that is corrected by culture (straightening 'bad' hair) *and* something that offers an escape from culture (growing 'natural' hair to contest social norms such as racial oppression) (Soper 1995: 28–9, 33–5). A crucial factor in hair's power as a social symbol is that, unlike clothing, hair is an intrinsic part of the body. It is manufactured according to the dictates of our genes, springing forth from our follicles to display physical characteristics that span the generations. Handed down to us by our parents, and their parents before them, the colour and texture of our hair is thus intimately connected to the notion of biologically inherited, essentially 'given' and therefore 'natural' qualities. Hair practices can communicate a desire to embrace, deny or contest the culturally constituted meanings of that lineage.

The key issue here is the near impossibility of natural human hair. In nearly all situations, head and body hair must be managed as an essential part of human social existence. As a result, hair in its totally natural state is rarely met with in society (Watson 1998), whilst concepts of natural hair become yet another representational tool to be used in the cultural construction of human identity. It is the centrality of the nature/culture opposition in Western thought that gives 'natural' hair its significant role in the symbolic definition of human identity, in addition to its role in biological designations. Whatever we do with our hair, we are constantly grappling with a 'natural' and a constructed self in our daily hair practices.

References

Anderson E. (2001), '"There Are Some Things in Life You Can't Choose… An Investigation into Discrimination against People with Red Hair"', *Manchester Sociology Working Papers*, 28.

Banks I. (2000), *Hair Matters: Beauty, Power and Black Women's Consciousness.* New York: New York University Press.

Barnett A. (2006), '"Tressed to Impress"', *New Scientist*, 4 November: 39–41.

Boisseau T. J. (2000), '"White Queens at the Chicago World's Fair": New Womanhood in the Service of Class, Race and Nation', *Gender and History*, 12 (1): 33–81.

Bordo S. (2003), *Unbearable Weight: Feminism, Western Culture and the Body* (10th anniversary edn), Berkeley: University of California Press.

Byrd A. D. and Tharps L. L. (2001), *Hair Story: Untangling the Roots of Black Hair in America*, New York: St Martin's Griffin.

Cleage P. (1993), '"Hairpeace"', *African-American Review*, 27 (1) (Spring): 37–41.

Corson R. (1965), *Fashions in Hair: The First 5000 Years*, London: Peter Owen.

Cox C. (1999), *Good Hair Days: A History of British Hairstyling.* London: Quartet Books.

Craig M. (1997), '"The Decline and Fall of the Conk; or, How to Read a Process"', *Fashion Theory*, 1 (4): 399–420.

Craig M. (2002), *Ain't I a Beauty Queen: Black Women, Beauty and the Politics of Race*, Oxford: Oxford University Press.

Douglas M. (1970), *Natural Symbols: Explorations in Cosmology*, London: Barrie and Rockliff: The Cresset Press.

Dyer R. (1997), *White*, London: Routledge.

Featherstone M. (1991), 'The Body in Consumer Culture', in M. Featherstone et al. (ed), *The Body: Social Process and Cultural Theory*, London: Sage Publications.

Gilman S. (1999), *Making the Body Beautiful: A Cultural History of Aesthetic Surgery*, Princeton, NJ: Princeton University Press.

Gilroy P. (1998), '"Race Ends Here"', *Ethnic and Racial Studies*, 21 (5): 838–47.

Gitter E. (1984), '"The Power of Women's Hair in the Victorian Imagination"', *PMLA*, 99 (5): 936–54.

Goffman E. (1971), *The Presentation of Self in Everyday Life*, Harmondsworth: Penguin.

Ilyin N. (2000), *Blonde Like Me*, New York: Touchstone.

Jones L. (2003), *Nappyisms: Affirmations for Nappy-Headed People and Wannabes*, Dallas: Manelock.

Kaw E. (1993), '"Medicalization of Racial Features": Asian-American Women and Cosmetic Surgery', *Medical Anthropology Quarterly*, 7 (1) (March): 74–89.

Kelley R.D.G. (1997), '"Nap Time": Historicizing the Afro', *Fashion Theory*, 1 (4) (December): 339–51.

Mercer K. (1994), *Welcome to the Jungle*, New York: Routledge.

Merleau-Ponty M. (1962), *The Phenomenology of Perception*, London: Routledge.

Morris D. (1987), *Bodywatching: A Field Guide to the Human Species*, London: Grafton Books.

Pitman J. (2003), *On Blondes*, London: Bloomsbury.

Powell M. K. and J. Roach. (2004), 'Big Hair', *Eighteenth Century Studies*, 38 (1): 79–99.

Roach, M. (2005), *The Roots of Desire: The Myth, Meaning and Sexual Power of Red Hair*. New York: Bloomsbury.

Soper K. (1995), *What Is Nature?* Oxford: Blackwell.

Spikeyli. (2007), 'Chinese People with Curly Hair', 14 September, http://www.chinahistoryforum.com/index.php?showtopic=19017, accessed 11 March 2008.

Synnott A. (1993), *The Body Social: Symbolism, Self and Society*, London and New York: Routledge.

Turner B. S (1991), 'Recent Developments in the Theory of the Body', in M. Featherstone, M Hepworth and B. S. Turner (eds.), *The Body: Social Process and Cultural Theory*, London: Sage Publications.

Warner M. (1995), *From the Beast to the Blonde: On Fairy Tales and Their Tellers*, New York: Farrar, Straus & Giroux.

Watson J. L. (1998), *'Living Ghosts*: Long-haired Destitutes in Colonial Hong Kong', in A. Hiltebeitel and B. D. Miller (eds.), *Hair: Its Power and Meaning in Asian Cultures*, Albany: State University of New York Press.

Weitz R. (2001), '"Women and Their Hair": Seeking Power through Resistance and Accommodation', *Gender and Society*, 15 (5): 667–86.

White S. and G. White. (1995), 'Slave Hair and African-American Culture in the Eighteenth and Nineteenth Centuries', *The Journal of Southern History*, 61(1): 45–76.

Wilson, E. (1985), *Adorned in Dreams: Fashion and Modernity*. London: Virago.

Young, R. J. C. (1997), *'Hybridism and the Ethnicity of the English'*, in K. Ansell Pearson, B. Parry and J. Squires (eds.), *Cultural Readings of Imperialism: Edward Said and the Gravity of History*. London: Lawrence and Wishart.

Zane, K. (2003), *'Reflections on a Yellow Eye*: Asian i(\eye/)cons and Cosmetic Surgery', in A. Jones (ed), *The Feminist and Visual Culture Reader*. London: Routledge.

54

OUTDOOR PORNIFICATION:
Advertising heterosexuality in the streets

Leena-Maija Rossi[1]

Advertising imagery plays a definite role in the sexualization of urban space. Contemporary advertising and soft-core porn are connected through several representative means: exposing the body; fragmenting it by cropping and foregrounding the culturally eroticized parts of it; and using stereotypically gendering, eroticizing and racializing sets of images. But how is it exactly that a pose for the camera becomes 'softly' pornographic? What kinds of poses am I, as a viewer, ready and willing to categorize and describe as soft-core in advertising? To rephrase my question using the terms launched to feminist discourse by Judith Butler (1999; 1993), what kinds of *performatives* of gender and sexuality are *reiterated* and *cited* over and over again in these poses? How are gender and sexuality *done* in advertising?

And what about the issue of context? Linda Williams (2004: 3) has coined the term 'on-scenity' to describe the 'insistent appearing' of representations once deemed obscene in the public arena. How do pornified images – for instance, the mainstream images of advertising, which cite and repeat the codes of pornography – function in the public space? And how is streetscape, the urban landscape formed by streets and city dwellers, affected by these images? In this chapter, I discuss these questions from two perspectives: first pondering how advertising imagery in general operates in the streetscape, and then looking at some specific images.

To make it clear from the start, my intention is not to oppose pornography as a monolithic, solely oppressive phenomenon (on porn's multifariousness, see, for example, Snitow 1983; Attwood 2002), but to analyse specific modes of representation and their public presentation. My aim is to bring together a queer-feminist viewpoint – criticizing the heteronormativity (Berlant and Warner 2000: 312) and heterosexism of mainstream advertising imagery – and a politically sensitive approach which que(e)ries whether people have the right not to be exposed to stiffly stereotypical representations of sexuality or eroticism in the public space. When close-reading my case study, one of the clothing company Hennes & Mauritz's ad campaigns, I also try to bring forth the possibilities and challenges of representing 'nonstandard intimacies' in public (see Berlant and Warner 2000: 322–3; also Clarke 2000).

Images do not function as a 'mere' reflection of the world. They play an essential part in the societal production of meaning, knowledge and power, thereby shaping the realities we live in. As an example of this, advertising constantly produces knowledge on both sexuality and the gendered idea of beauty, fixed as a presupposition on to women and female femininity. Furthermore, the knowledge thereby produced does not concern just any kind of sexuality, but more precisely heterosexuality. The power constituting, being constituted by and entangled in that knowledge

---

[1] From Rossi Leena-Maija (2007), Outdoor Pornification: Advertising Heterosexuality in the Streets, in Pornification: Sex and Sexuality in Media Culture, pp. 127-138, Oxford: Berg.

(Foucault 1990) is the normative power of the position of heterosexuality as the 'dominant fiction' (Silverman 1996: 178) of Western societies. The heterosexual regime supports, maintains and naturalizes a notion of two internally unified, 'opposite but complementary' genders that are supposed to be hierarchically and essentially different from each other. This normative, norm-producing scene – or a kind of *screen* through which we look at things (Silverman 1996: 135, 195–227) – is constantly being performed, brought in front of us by advertising in the urban environment.

'ON-SCENE': PORNIFICATION IN THE STREETSCAPE

Media may be thought of as a key factor in the constitution of the public sphere where people 'make sense' of the world, receive information, argue about information and (ideally) participate in rational decisions concerning political and public issues (McGuigan 1996; see also Clarke 2000: 2–3). For instance Brian McNair has used the concept of the public sphere to refer to the mediation of knowledge/information on sexuality to the 'society as a whole' (1996: 23). The queer critic Eric Clarke, again, has emphasized that the public sphere may also be conceptualized as signifying a qualitative relation instead of distinct material things (such as media), or a spatial ensemble of places; thus, he writes, 'those disenfranchised from the venues that claim publicness can ask more insistently whether they actually embody this quality' (2000: 2–3). I shall, nevertheless, focus here on a particular set of spaces and images: the advertising imagery presented to the public in the street. Even from this angle, Clarke's question concerning the qualities embodied by the disenfranchised is still highly valid.

Street constitutes a space in which people move around every day, where they have their routine-bound, but also wandering and exploratory routes. Street can also be thought of as an urban landscape, the streetscape. The varying meanings of streetscape are constructed in reciprocal action, in interactive relationships for which visibility, acts of seeing and being seen, are crucial (Saarikangas 1996: 306). Mediated encounters with pornified heteronormative imagery on the street differ radically from domestic ones. At home, we do have at our disposal various filters between the images and ourselves (Poynor 2006: 44). A sticker politely telling 'No ads, please' partly blocks the flow of commercial imagery into our homes. One does not have to subscribe newspapers or magazines, own a television or even have an Internet connection. Remote control enables us to be selective in terms of incoming audiovisuality: we may switch the channels and switch off the television at will. However, home may of course also offer a space for consuming porn through television, Internet and magazines (Juffer 1998). Pornified imagery forms only a part of the knowledge that constantly obfuscates the border between the public and the private, and connects the private sphere to public networks of power. One example of the latter phenomenon would, of course, be the vast deployment, accessibility and production of amateur porn.

Home and street thus offer very different spaces for sexual encounters – even if one would take a stranger home to have sex with. One should, nevertheless, challenge the idea of a total freedom of choice prevailing in the privacy of homes in relation to watching pornified imagery. It is rather a question of relative freedom, and a different control over the space than the one we have on the street. The remote control and compulsory switching of television channels hardly remove the sexual tinge permeating the repertoire of TV programming. However, they offer the possibility of temporarily removing the unwanted visual representations from sight. On the streetscape such removal is not possible. The images are there and they stay there (even though changing into other images at a regular interval): hung along the streets, at the bus stops, inside the vehicles of public transportation, in the store windows. It is difficult for a sighted person to move around on the streetscape without looking at advertising. Jim McGuigan (1996: 26) has even argued in a Habermasian vein that the 'sophisticated communicational techniques' of advertising have 'hijacked' the public sphere.

In the public space of the streetscape, people gendered as women and men are both exposed to the multiplicity of images and at display themselves. They stand not only as looking subjects but also as objects for the looks of strangers, and potentially also objects for sexual assessment and desire. The images in the streetscape obviously do not interfere with the bodily integrity of people in the same way as the comments and suggestions presented by fellow men (possibly also women) on the street, not to mention outright physical harassment. Yet we should not underestimate the effective position of the images in the network of power formed by the streetscape. Advertising, which nowadays seems to be so central to the meaning of the streetscape (Poynor 2006: 44), does participate in the formation of sexual encounters and their conditions. Men and women are looked at in relation to the imagery of advertising and the discourses constructed by it. These repetitive images present themselves as a source of knowledge concerning beauty and desirability. On the streetscape those images, colourful, glowing sources of gendering and sexualizing knowledge-power, loci of ideals, provide an instant surface for reflection and comparison in relation to the bodily contours and surfaces of the people moving on the streets.

Jean Gagnon, who has analysed heterosexual pornography from the angle of male viewers and consumers, describes the cityscape as a 'cultural reservoir where individuals draw the representations that they more or less consciously incorporate into their lives and value-systems' (1988: 25). He categorizes pornography as a specifically urban phenomenon, part of the network of images in the cities and a quintessential part of the realm of advertising and consumerism. He also writes about the *rhetoric of the city*, which largely derives from the rhetoric of advertising images and is constituted in the interaction between the knowledges of individual consumers and the knowledges of the producers of advertising (both advertisers of the products and the people planning and realizing the ads). This rhetoric is, according to Gagnon, stereotypical and overpowered by consumer myths: a 'reservoir of stereotyped attitudes' (1988: 25–7). It is also thoroughly gendered, and continuously naturalizes and foregrounds heterosexuality. This rhetoric is in use when people move around in the streets, 'accompanied by a running commentary' (Cauquelin cited by Gagnon 1988: 220–7) consisting of the images and texts attached to them. The comments and outright imperatives presented by advertisements illustrate the idea (1) of perfection: they participate both in the production of feelings of bodily inadequacy and dissatisfaction (Grogan 1999: 94–116), and in processes through which people on the streets are urged to strive for 'picture-perfect' ideals without being able to settle for a 'good enough' (Silverman 1996: 220–7; also Poynor 2006: 37) body-image.

Gagnon also connects advertising, pornography and the cityscape to the ideology of permanent relationships – the ideology central to heteronormativity. He writes:

> In the city, solitude is never greater than when one lives in close proximity to the crowd and the possibilities of contact it offers. We should also note in passing that solitude has a pejorative connotation . . . If I remain solitary, I feel that I am lacking and that I have failed to obey the imperative of the urban enterprise . . . This pattern is maintained by some ramifications of the pornography industry. (Gagnon 1988: 32)

The urban fantasy is thus permeated by the ideology of encounter, which connects images, texts and public places to each other (Gagnon 1988: 33; see also Ahmed 2000: 32). In the urban fantasy, encounters with the gendered and sexualized characters represented by advertising become amalgamated in our reality. Nevertheless, these images and the viewers' relationship to them may also be read through the problematic of non-encountering.

LOOKING BACK FROM THE IMAGE

Pornography, both soft and hardcore, has been criticized for objectifying women, or at least not subjectifying them enough – for not 'taking others seriously' (Snitow 1983). One essential guarantee for agency, claimed for by the feminist critics of visual culture, has been the right to look, and even to gaze intently, instead of just being the object or the bearer of the look (see e.g. Linker 1983; hooks 1992). Arguably it may be said that even though (hetero *and* homo) sexualizing representations of the male body have become more and more common in advertising imagery, women are still more often placed in front of the camera, to be scrutinized by the gaze it represents. But what does it mean that not only do we look at the images, but they also look back at us (Gagnon 1988: 26)? Would the intense looks directed at the viewers by the models of the ads be signifiers of a potent agency, a strong subjectivity? Or could the looks, and the often soft-pornified and heterosexualized agency they represent, be rethought and made more complex through the subjectifying notion of interpellation?

The French philosopher Louis Althusser shed light on the workings of ideology by using the example of the representative of the law, a cop, hailing a man in the street (1971: 170–86). In the Althusserian interpretation the man, through this interpellation, becomes a subject in the twofold meaning of the word: not only is he *subjected to* the act of hailing, he also becomes recognized *as a subject with agency*. Judith Butler (1997: 24–5) has emphasized that the power of interpellation, or subjectification, not only resides in the law but just equally in the conventionality and the ritualistic dimension of the act. Could we, then, think that the soft-pornified public images, and their often heteronormative ideology, get to formulate, gender and sexualize our subjectivities as the images repeatedly look at us, addressing, inviting, interpelling us, over and over again? What are these images subjecting us to?

Looks or gazes directed at viewers from advertising images effectively arrest our looks. It is interesting that the authorities assessing the codes of advertising repeatedly appeal to this eye-catching ability – and this appeal also gives a twist to the problematics of arresting images. The ethical bodies of advertising may emphasize that the images of women should not be used *solely* for catching the eye of the viewers, nor should the ads represent 'sexual promises or cues which do not have any connection to the advertised product'. Do the products advertised by images emphasizing the conventionally eroticized parts of female bodies always and necessarily have a direct connection to sexuality and sex? Does this apply, for instance, to women's underwear advertised in the public space? Is the main function and purpose of women's fashion, and the repetitious and citational acts of 'feminine' dressing up in general, to represent, or 'do', sexuality in public? And not just any kind of sexuality, but normative eroticism, which supposedly attracts representatives of the 'opposite sex'.

FLIRT BETWEEN WOMEN: ONE SOFT-CORE METHOD

Late in 2003, before Christmas, the Swedish-originating but multinationally operating clothing company Hennes & Mauritz was advertising women's underwear on outdoor billboards in the streets of Helsinki, as in many other bigger towns and cities in its vast marketing area. The advertising campaign is analysed here as an example, both typical and slightly exceptional, of the visual techniques used for selling the product *and* titillating the viewers by producing and repeating certain forms of knowledge concerning female sexuality. Close reading these images, I sketch some features in the visual grammar of the signifiers habitually used in soft-pornified advertising in public spaces, the streetscape included. The atypicality of these images, again, connects to their ways of representing inter-female relationships. Nevertheless, I suggest that even their atypicality, or non-normativity, is rather ostensible since the representations of intimacy in the campaign quite easily fall into the representational category of female friendship.

The H&M campaign in question consisted of images showing three female models in several different poses and groupings: all three together, in a 'twosome' and posing alone. One of the models was black and easily recognizable as the supermodel Naomi Campbell. The other two were white and anonymous: the campaign used Campbell's status as the main attraction and she also performed alone in video clips on the company's website. The lighting and dramatic colours – the combination of 'Christmassy' red and black – used in the photos emphasized the fair skin of the white models, one of which was a blonde and the other a reddish brunette. All the models were slim (the blonde one even remarkably thin), longhaired and conventionally 'good-looking' and thus performed the dominant heteronormative idea of feminine female beauty. The deliberate choice of models representing different skin colours situated H&M as a company within the popular advertising rhetoric of tolerance, which Benetton had already launched in the 1980s. This kind of rhetorical choice could be read as a self-rehabilitating move from H&M, which had been heavily criticized on ethical grounds: both for using extremely thin and young-looking models, and for benefiting from circumventing the terms of ethical trade. On the other hand, the representational use of Campbell's body – especially in the website video clips – can be seen as echoing the Western tradition of stereotypical eroticization of black female bodies (see e.g. Hall 1999: 264–9). Neither did her status as a supermodel diminish the accent of overt sexualization. The configuration in which the black model was the famous one and the white models anonymous might of course even be read as turning the tables on racialized hierarchy – but in the end the 'equality' thus achieved merely concerned the stereotypically eroticizing display of the represented bodies.

Besides 'multi-ethnicity', the other obvious theme of the H&M campaign was intimate bodily closeness between women. This was most evident in the images presenting the 'black-and-white couple', but also in the photos showing all three women together: they had been directed to stand close to each other, bare bodies touching, arms on each others' shoulders or around each others' waists. Some of the compositions blatantly called for a reference to the traditional girl-on-girl subgenre of heteroporn in which female-to-female intimacy is frequently used for titillation of the (male) viewer: 'lesbian' scenes may serve as a metaphoric foreplay or warm-up before the 'actual' heterosexual penetration takes place, but they may also be used for arousing the viewers 'as such'. Heather Butler has aptly called these woman-to-woman porn scenes 'the lesbo-jelly in the heterodonut' (Butler 2004: 168, 173). The poses of the female models in the H&M campaign were easy to interpret flirting with this genre of 'lesbo-jelly': horny and malleable, ready for sex. This was secured by the several signifiers conventionally referring to, and emphasizing, sex and sexuality. Sartorial codes (black, red and lacy underwear drawing attention to the breasts, the buttocks and the pubic area) formed even clichéd porn-citations. The downcast eyes or the furtive looks were used to signify seductiveness combined with submissiveness while the moist-looking red lips were either invitingly parted, imitated a kiss or framed a dashing laughter. The red background of the images constituted, together with the black underwear, a colour combination which media imageries have taught us to associate with environments of sexual consumption: brothels and striptease-joints, or more mundane but 'naughty' bedroom scenes.

The women in the ads were either cuddling or looked like they had stopped in the middle of playing and frolicking with each other. One of the scenes *might have* been interpreted as representing the white woman *almost* kissing the black woman's ear. In many of the images, women not only actively foregrounded their breasts but also curved their backs in order to focus the viewers' attention to their bottom and pelvis. Was this imagery meant to be arousing while not 'revealing everything', in other words, soft-core (Williams 1989: 30)? I would say, at least close to it.

As explicitly sexualized, and not representing a male-female couple, the images might have been interpreted as representing moments of lesbian intimacy, moments of 'nonstandard intimacy in public' (Berlant and Warner 2000: 322–3). This interpretation, however, requires a quite conscious reading against the grain – which has certainly historically been a standard viewing practice among the lesbian and gay identified audiences of films, television, advertising and art (see e.g. Dyer 1985). Instead of looking *at each* other in a clearly desiring way, the models either looked seductively towards the gaze of camera/the alleged viewer, or away from the image towards its edges, or they had closed their eyes. There was no eye contact between the models. This way they, at most, invited the potential viewer – not each other – into an erotic exchange. And even though one might think that this invitation was addressed to the female viewers as well, one might just as well assume that the erotically coded address was intended *mainly* towards a male audience.

The female audience may have been supposed to remain safely in the realm of identification and not to experience desire. Or it may have been thought that the 'desire' of female consumers could be channelled towards the fetishized underwear and acquiring them in order to repeat the advertised, idealized gender performance as closely as possible. This understanding of a heteronormative structure of looking, identifying and desiring corresponds to a highly conventional account of the directions of desire and identification. Even though the relationship between desire and identification tends to be much more complicated, and the border between them quite blurred (Lewis and Rolley 1997; Stacey 1994: 138–70), it is generally thought that women watch images of women as models for ideal appearance, whereas men have been thought of as getting sexual pleasure out of watching images of women, 'naturally' desiring them as objects of their 'male gaze' (cf. Mulvey 1989). Scenes of female-to-female intimacy, as represented in the H&M campaign, are conventionally read as representations of friendship, non-romantic and non-erotic intimacy – and thus as non-threatening towards the heterosexual regime. The lack of intensity between the models in the campaign can be thought of signifying exactly the non-erotic, almost platonic closeness, and thus actually forming an effective obstacle for queer reading. A poignant signifier for this lack of intimacy could be found in one of the images in which the hand of the black woman rests inertly on the shoulder of the blonde. The gesture is not caressing, but plain passive.

It may have been the intention of the designers of the campaign, and even of the advertiser, to produce a set of sexually ambivalent, multiracialized images enhancing tolerance, or even promoting diversity beyond tolerance in the public sphere (Clarke 2000: 171–2), but ultimately the codes chosen made it difficult – at least for me as a viewer – to foreground this interpretation. And, gloomily enough, almost alloutdoor advertising repeats the same pattern of heterosexualizing female bodies, quite often through poses citing the codes of soft-core porn. This imagery, explicitly addressing heterosexual men and women, seems to convey generalized knowledge on women's constant wish to be desired by men, and to become partners in heterosexual exchange. The codes utilized in this knowledge production are not only heteronormative: they also normatively restrict the ways heterosexuality and hetero-eroticism may be performed (see e.g. Berlant and Warner 2000: 316, 318–20). Only certain types of bodies are represented as desirable, only certain conventions of poses as 'sexy' or erotic.

References

Althusser, L. (1971), *Lenin and Philosophy and Other Essays*. Translated by Ben Brewster. New York, NY & London: Routledge.

Attwood, F. (2002). 'Reading Porn: The Paradigm Shift in Pornography Research', *Sexualities* 5 (1): 91–105.

Berlant, L. and M. Warner. (2000), 'Sex in Public', in L. Berlant (ed), *Intimacy*, Chicago, IL: The University of Chicago Press.

Butler, J. (1993), *Bodies that Matter. On the Discursive Limits of 'Sex'*, London & New York, NY: Routledge.

Butler, J. (1977), *Excitable Speech, a Politics of the Performative*. London & New York, NY: Routledge

Butler, J. (1999), *Gender Trouble. Feminism and the Subversion of Identity*. London & New York, NY: Routledge.

Clarke, E. O. (2000), *Virtuous Vice. Homoerotics, and the Public Sphere*. Dunham, NC and London: Duke University Press.

Foucault, M. (1990), *The History of Sexuality, Introduction*. Trans. Robert Hurley. New York: Vintage.

Gagnon, J. (1988), *Pornography in the Urban World. (La pornographie et le monde urbain, 1984)*, transl. James Boake and Jeanluc Svoboda. Toronto: Art Metropole.

Grogan, S. (1981), *Body Image. Understanding Body Dissatisfaction in Men, Women and Children*. London & New York: Routledge.

Hall, S. (1999), 'The Spectacle of the 'Other,' in S. Hall (ed.), *Representation. Cultural Representations and Signifying Practices*. London: Sage.

hooks, b. (1992), *Yearning: Race, Gender, and Cultural Politics*. Boston, MA: South End Press.

Juffer, J. (1998), *At Home with Pornography. Women, Sexuality, and Everyday Life*. New York, NY: New York University Press.

Lewis, R. and Rolley, K. (1997), '(Ad)dressing the Dyke. Lesbian Looks and Lesbian Lesbians Looking', in M. Nava, A. Blake, I. MacRury and B. Richards (eds.), *Buy This Book, Studies in Advertising and Consumption*. London & New York, NY: Routledge.

Linker, K. (1983), 'Representation and Sexuality', *Parachute*. No. 32.

McGuigan, J. (1996), *Culture and the Public Sphere*. London and New York, NY: Routledge.

McNair, B. (1996), *Mediated Sex. Pornography and the Postmodern Culture*. London and New York, NY: Arnold.

Mulvey, L. (1988), *Visual and Other Pleasures*. Bloomington & Indianapolis, IN: Indiana University Press.

Poynor, R. (2006), *Designing Pornotopia: Travels in Visual Culture*. New York: Princeton Architectural Press.

Saarikangas, K. (1996), 'Katseita, kohtaamisia, kosketuksia. Tilassa muodostuvat merkitykset', *Tiede ja edistys* 4/96, 306–18.

Silverman, K. (1996), *The Threshold of the Visible World*. London & New York, NY: Routledge.

Snitow, A. (1983), 'Mass Market Romance: Pornography for Women is Different', In A. Snitow, C. Stansell and S. Thompson (eds), *Desire. The Politics of Sexuality*. London: Virago.

Stacey, J. (1994), *Star Gazing, Hollywood Cinema and Female Spectatorship*. London & New York, NY: Routledge.

Williams, L. (1989), *Hard Core: Power, Pleasure, and the 'Frenzy of the Visible'*, Berkeley, CA: University of California Press.

Williams, L. (2004), 'Introduction', in L. Williams (ed.), *Porn Studies*. Durham, NC and London: Duke University Press.

FURTHER READING

Biddle-Perry, Geraldine and Sarah Cheang, (2008), *Hair: Styling, Culture and Fashion*, Oxford, Berg.

Calefato, Patrizia (2004), *The Clothed Body*, Oxford: Berg.

Hancock, Joseph, (2016), *Brand/Story: Cases and Explorations in Fashion Branding*, Fairchild: New York.

Hancock II, Joseph H., Toni Johnson-Woods and Vicki Karaminas, (2013), *Fashion in Popular Culture*, Bristol: Intellect.

Lynch, Annette and Katalin Medvedev (2018), *Fashion, Agencey and Empowerment, Performing Agency, Following Script*, London: Bloomsbury.

Paasonen, Susana, Kaarina Nikunen and Laura Saarenmaa (2007), *Pornification: Sex and Sexuality in Media Culture*, Oxford: Berg.

Vincent, Susan (2009), *The Anatomy of Fashion: Dressing the Body From the Renaissance to the Present Day*, Oxford: Berg.

Figure 38 Natural Hair-Girl, Photo Courtesy of Brent Luvaas.
Source: Brent Luvaas

INDEX

abangan 176
Abbott, Susan 186
Abercrombie & Fitch 93, 96–7
access, co-creation 187–8, 189–90
accessories 63
acrylics 224
adaptive customization 179
adidas 223, 228, 410, 460
advertising 67
    for BVD 322–4
    creative direction of 95
    creativity for 67
    fashion 319
    fashion propaganda through 355
    hegemony in 445–6
    imagery 480–5
    men's underwear 322–6, 336–41
    pornification in streetscape 481–2
    rhetoric of tolerance 484
Aeropostale 150
Aertex 338
aesthetic fashion 27
aesthetics of poverty 34–6
Afia, Nura 443
African Americans 27–8, 31–2
African secondhand clothing markets 417–18
Afro hairstyles 477
Aglaia (Jaeger) 338
Agreement on Textiles and Clothing (ATC) 68, 134
AI *see* Artificial Intelligence (AI)
Aitken, Robert 149
Alexa 167
Al Fayed, Mohammed 273
Alipay app 169
Allport, G. W. 362
Aloha floral shirts 406
Althusser, Louis 483
altruism, moral-norm activation theory of 101

Amazon 54, 169
Amazon Eco 167
Amelan, Bjorn 30–1
American Apparel (AA) 87, 118, 258, 278
    characteristics 279
    culture 281
    culture in firm 282
    leadership style 282
    marketing 282–3
    master narratives 279
    mission 281–2
    vision 281
American fashion
    American apparel brand
        characteristics 279
        culture 281
        culture in firm 282
        leadership style 282
        marketing 282–3
        master narratives 279
        mission 281–2
        vision 281
    marketing culture in 278
    mythologies 279–83
        connection to branding 279
        creation 279
    national identity in 278
    Polo Ralph Lauren brand
        characteristics 279
        culture 279–80
        culture in firm 280
        leadership style 280
        marketing 280
        master narratives 279
        mission 280
        vision 279–80
    Tommy Hilfiger brand
        characteristics 279
        culture 280
        culture in firm 281

        leadership style 281
        marketing 281
        master narratives 279
        mission 280–1
        vision 280
American Museum of Natural History 9
American National Textile Center 78
Anal Delinquents 283
Andrade, Rita 214, 217–22
Angeleno magazine 273
anthropometrics 196
anti-consumerism 100–1
anti-imperialism 435
anti-Muslim rhetoric 254
anxiety 100
Apache women 12
Apeagyeri, P. R. 196
apparel co-design 179–80
apparel industry, Canada 132–9
    boutiques 137–8
    chain stores 137–8
    department stores 136–7
    dominant retail chains 138
    early development 132–3
    garment manufacturers 134–5
    garment retail in 136–7
    mail order 136
    manufacturer-retailers chain 138
    T. Eaton Co. 135–6
    transition 138–9
    twentieth-century development 133–4
apparel mass customization 180–2
Apple, Inc. 54, 58
AR *see* augmented reality (AR)
Architectonics 20
Archives of Psychology (Barr) 369–71
Arden, Elizabeth 17
Ardley, Barry 386
Argyleculture brand 264, 265

Arianne Lingerie, Montreal   135
Aritzia   138
Armani, Giorgio   119, 426
Arquette, Patricia   156
art   103
art-architecture complex   285
art deco style   9
Artificial Intelligence (AI)   171–2, 257
The Art of the Trench web campaign   257
aspiration in fashion   93
  assumption   93–4
  criteria   94–6
  empowering criteria
    advertisement, creative direction of   95
    model's physical traits   95
    model's visual cues   96
  honest criteria
    advertisement, creative direction of   95
    model's physical traits   94–5
    model's visual cues   95
  industry implications   96–7
  socially responsible criteria
    advertisement, creative direction of   96
    model's physical traits   96
  targets   94
  taxonomy   94–6
  women's evaluations of   94
ATC *see* Agreement on Textiles and Clothing (ATC)
athleisure   215–16
Atlas Corporation   140, 141
atmospherics   197, 213
attaché cases   393
A.T. Stewart and Co.   140
Attala, A.   103
Auburn, Rachel   27
augmented reality (AR)   167
"Aussie digger" (military) uniforms   409
Austin Powers   268
Australianness of fashion   406–8
  aesthetic dimension   407
  Australiana imagery   406
  bodies, clothes, identities, mapping relationship between   408–9
  bush wear   406
  clothing history   407
  cultural articulation   407–8
  cultural practice   407

dressing up body-space relations   409–10
essence   408
fabrics   407
garments   407
national dress, revelation and concealment in   410–11
sense of dress   407, 410
style, sense of   408–9, 410
swimming culture in   410–11
swimwear and surfwear   406
and un-Australianness,   411–12
version   406
Australian Textile, Clothing, Footwear and Leather (TCFL) Forum   75
auto-ethnographies   6–7
Autograph   60
automation, in fashion industry   165–6
Azmi, Aishah   448

BAAPS *see* British Association of Aesthetic Plastic Surgeons (BAAPS)
Bainbridge   219
Baker, Avery   257
Baker, Josephine   27
Baker, Pamela C.   5, 10, 11, 12
Baldwin, James   27
Balenciaga, Cristóbal   293
Ballin, Montreal   135
Banana Republic   422
Bangladesh   52–3
Barber, N.   375
Barnard, Malcolm   316
Barr, Estelle De Young   364
Barrie, Scott   27
Barron, Lee   258, 267–76
Barry, Ben   89–90, 93–7
Barthes, Roland   279, 281, 315
Bartky, Sandra   467
Bastien, Vincent   231, 232
batik shirts   406
Baudelaire, Charles   394
Baudrillard, Jean   272, 292
Baulch, Emma   176
Baumann, Z.   100
The Bay   129, 136
Beard, N.   99, 101
Beaton, Cecil   334
beauty   103
beauty industry   463–6
  Estée Lauder company   463–4

M.A.C.   463, 464–6
VIVA GLAM   464–6
Beauvais, Tammy   10
Beaver, Bobby   182
Beaver, Jeff   182
Becker, Harold   301
Beckham, David   228, 255, 274, 468
Bedell, Geraldine   78
Beijing   300, 302
Belk, R. W.   361, 362
Benenson, Fira   142
Berendt, John   322
Berenson, Marisa   294
berets   406
Berkshire Hathaway Corporation   166
Bertelli, Patrizio   427
bespoke suit   194
bespoke tailoring   193–4
  data analysis
    social media/blogs   197–8
    3D technology   196–7
    web atmospherics   197
  historiography of   194–5
  industry perspective   198
  literature discussion   195–6
  survey   194
'Be the Buyer' programme   190
Better view designed (BVD)   322–4, 338
  advertisements for   322–4
  battles among brands   324–5
  and boys in brands played on   326
  focus shifts   325–6
  homoerotic/"gay" *trompe l'oeil*   326
Betts, Kate   36
Bhabba, Homi   219
BID *see* Business Improvement District (BID)
Biddle-Perry, Geraldine   474–8
big data management   168–9
Billabong   223
Binkley, S.   100
Birkin, Jane   154
Birkin bag   127–8, 154
Birtwistle, G.   232
Bishop, Kelly   158
Black, Kate   88
Black Book (Kitwana)   261
black fashion   26–32
black hair   477
black memorabilia   30
blanket coats   9
Blass, Bill   13, 18

Blaszczyk, Regina Lee 3
bleached hair 476
Bledel, Alexis 158
blockchain technology 171
bloggers 346–7
blondeness 475–6
blue-collar labour 388–9
Blumer, Herbert 364, 367–71
Boardman, Serena 394
Boateng, Oswald 193
Bodnar, Elena 119
body
    maintenance 271
    modification 451–2
    technologies 227–8
Boffo 20
Bohan, Marc 13
Boijmans Van Beuningen Museum, Rotterdam 42
Bon Marché 219
Bonomi, Aldo 429
Bonwit, Paul 140
Bonwit's liaison 142
Bonwit Teller 128–9, 140–5
Boorstin, Danie 268
Borrelli, L. 158
Boselli, Mario 428
Boston 151
Botox 452
Boucicaut, Aristide 219
Bourdieu, Pierre 269, 270, 302, 471
Boutiques San Francisco 130, 138
Bowie, David 287, 288, 458
Boyd, Anita 128, 154–60
Bozzetti, Giovanni 428
Bracewell, Michael 290
BRAD *see* British Rate and Data (BRAD)
Braddock, Sarah 224, 225
branding, fashion 186, 253–9, 272, 355
    communication 253–4
    communities 201
    definition 253
    differential 253
    ethos 241
    fashion 253–9
    identity 231, 232, 241, 242, 253–4
    management 241, 254
    in new unstable world order 254–9
    personality 241
    social media 256
    values 231, 241

Branquinho, Veronique 287
Braun Boveri factory 429
Brazil 217–22
Breward, Christopher 13
Brexit 254
Brick and Mortar Retailing and Shopping 127, 213
    growth 129–30
    identity 127–8
    image 130
    leadership 128–9
    location 128
British Association of Aesthetic Plastic Surgeons (BAAPS) 451
British Celanese 338, 339
British Rate and Data (BRAD) 328, 329
Brooker, Daphne 56
Brooker, Hylan 27
Brooks, Ethel 111
Brooks Brothers 180, 181, 195
Bruce, Fiona 448
Buckley, Reka 268
Budman, Michael 138
Buenos Aires 219–20
Buffett, Warren 166
Burberry brand 256, 257, 420
Burlington Industries 77
Burns, L. D. 372
Burroughs, William 288
Burrows, Stephen 13, 27
Burton, Montague 194
Bush, Kate 287
Business Improvement District (BID) 18
Business Insider (BI) 167
Business of Fashion (BoF) 165
Busteed, Kimberley 408, 409
Butler, Heather 484
Butler, Judith 480, 483
button blankets 11, 12
buyer-supplier relationship 69
BVD *see* better view designed (BVD)

CAD *see* computer-aided design (CAD)
Calder, Alexander 285
California 224
Calvin Klein brand 18, 51, 57, 256, 293, 324
Campbell, John L. 120
Campbell, Naomi 345, 457, 483
camp dress 12
Campelo, Adriana 149

Canada 101, 129–30, 406–7
    boutiques in 137–8
    chain stores in 137–8
    department stores in 136–7
    dominant retail chains in 138
    garment industry
        early development 132–3
        manufacturers 134–5
        retailers 136–7
        transition 138–9
        twentieth-century development 133–4
    mail order in 136
    manufacturer-retailers chain in 138
    The T. Eaton Co. 135–6
Canada Goose 130
Canadelle 129, 135
Canadian Apparel and Textile Industries Program (CATIP) 139
Canadian Light 218
Candy, Lorraine 274
Cann, Kate 448
Cannarozzi, Antonella 294
Canterbury 223
Cardin, Pierre 13
Carlsen, Magnus 459
Carnegie Hall, New York 16
Carrigan, M. 103
Carter, M. 375
Cary-Williams, Robert 274
Casa Alemã 220
Casa Mappin 218
case studies 6–7
    American apparel brand 281–3
    in co-creative branding strategies 186–91
    faces value 457–60
    of lululemon 200–6
    Missoni for Target, co-branding strategies 234–7
    ModCloth 188–91
    Polo Ralph Lauren brand 279–80
    Tommy Hilfiger brand 280–1
catalog sales 136
CATIP *see* Canadian Apparel and Textile Industries Program (CATIP)
Catrall, Kim 155
catwalk 27
cause-related fashion merchandise 118, 120

Cavalli, Roberto   244
celebrities   268, 275
celebrity brand narrative framing   242
Céline   13
Cerezo, Leandro   458
CFDA see China Fashion Designers Association (CFDA); Council of Fashion Designers of America (CFDA)
Chaiken, Julie   9
chain store challenge   56–61
   age profile   57
   products   59–61
   retail environments   59
   shopping   58–9
Chalayan, Hussein   117, 118
Chambost, Pol   292
Chan, Ricky   89, 99–103
Chanel   63, 64, 169
Chang, W.-L.   233
Charles, James   443–5
   makeup techniques   444–5
   makeup videos   444–5
Charney, Dove   87, 281–3
Chase, Edna Woolman   17
Cheang, Sarah   474–8
Chevalier, M.   233
Chicago   151
child laborers   86–7, 111–15
chilkat blankets   12
China Fashion Designers Association (CFDA)   302
Chinese fashion   300, 402, 431, 435–6
   brands   303–4
   cities   303
   creative centers   302
   designers   300, 302, 431
   designs   431
   fables   304–5
      brand communications process   307
      brand ethos/brand mission   305–6
      future   307–8
      stylistic brand identity   306–7
   global recognition   307
   national identity and   432–5
   post-Mao era   431–2
   socialist modernization   435
   from symbols to spirit   431–2
   system   302–3
Chouinard, Yvon   105–9
Chouinard Equipment   105–6

Christabel   268
Christel, Deborah   130
Christina America   135
Chung, Alexa   256
circular fashion system   87
Claeys, Franky   289
Clarke, Eric   481
Clarke A.   330
climbing hardware   105
Cline, Elizabeth   88
Clinique   463, 470
Clinton, Hillary   255
clogs   406
Clooney, George   154
clothes   5, 63
721 Club   143–4
clutch bags   391–5
Coats   74
co-branding, for luxury fashion brands   231, 233–4
   aims   233
   Missoni for Target, case study   234
      evaluation and analysis   235–6
      implications of co-branding   234–5
      recommendations   236–7
Coco Chanel   223, 253, 275, 460
co-creation   186
   access   187–8, 189–90
   building blocks   187–8
   dialogue   187, 189–91
   risk assessment   188, 190
   transparency   188, 190
CODA brands   151–2
Coddington, Grace   345
co-designers   183–4
co-design process   179–82
Coelho, P. R. P   374
Cohen, A. A.   218
Cole, Shaun   444
collaborative commerce   76–7, 79
collaborative customization   179
Collaborative Product Management software   77
collective behavior theories   373–4
Collective Survival Sac   118
College Girls Department   143
colour
   and age   379–80
   in dress   380
Colour Correcting (CC) creams   471–2
Combs, Sean "Diddy"   261, 264
Comme des Garçons   416

communications   350
Communist Party, China   433–4
companies   74–5
Companies with a Conscience (Scott and Rothman)   107
computer-aided design (CAD)   51, 77, 79
Cone Communications   120
Conley, Chip   107
Conran, Terence   59
conspicuous consumption   35
consumption, fashion   361–2
convenience driven partnership   72
Cooper, Cynthia   129, 132–9
Coopers Inc. of Kenosha   339
Cornejo, Maria   27
Cornellani, Italian menswear company   195
corporate social responsibility (CSR)
   commitment to   121
   and disaster   120–1
   in fashion industry   90–1
Corson, Richard   469
cosmetic customization   179
cosmetics   469
cosmetic surgery   451–5
Cosmopolitan magazine   344
cost analysis   66
Costume Institute   16
Council of Fashion Designers of America (CFDA)   18
Courtaulds   224
CoverBoy   443
CoverGirls   443, 445–6
cowboy   387–8
"cradle to grave" approach   87
Craik, Jennifer   64, 215, 223–9, 269–71, 273, 362, 364
Crane, Diana   351, 395
creative customers   187
creative person   62–3
creative production   301
creativity   62–3
   for advertising   67
   as behaviour   62
   connecting   65
   for cost analysis   66
   data processing for   65–6
   definition   62
   designs   66
   and disaster   119–20
   and fashion   63–5
   importance of   62

for marketing   66–7
market research for   65
for production opportunities   66
for promotion   67
technological and technical innovation for   66
The Crisis of the Negro Intellectual   29
critical scholarship   6–7
CRM *see* customer relationship management (CRM)
Crompton Corset Co.   133
crowd-sourcing   188
Cruse, Harold   29
CSR *see* corporate social responsibility (CSR)
Cunningham, Cotter   170
CustomCoutureBridal   181
customer relationship management (CRM)   201
customization   80
CutOnYourBias.com   188
Czajkowski, Caroline   172, 200–6
Czuchry, Matt   158

Damhorst, M. L.   94
DaSila, Alison   120
data analytics   168–9
data breaches   172
data processing   65–6
Davis, Fred   63, 120, 394
Davis, Glyn   289
Davis, Miles   27
Daydream Nation   258, 300, 302, 303, 304, 305–8
Dazed and Confused   342
Deacon, Giles   274
De Bord, Matthew   58
de Castelbajac, Jean-Charles   28
decision-making   168–9
de Givenchy, Hubert   13, 455
deHart, Jacob   183
de La Renta, Oscar   13
Deleuze, Gilles   288
de-materialization   402
demi-bespoke tailoring   195
DeMontigny, Angela   10
Dene Fur Clouds   10
Deneuve, Catherine   458
denim jeans   423
Denver   151
de Perthuis, Karen   294
de Potter, Peter   286, 289
Designbyhumans website   181

designer collaborations   215–16
designer decade   26
Design Group   57
designs   8, 66
    creativity   52
    First Nation   8–11
    Indian   8–9
    Japanese textile   37–8
    North American Indians   8–11
desires   102
dialogue   187, 189
Dickinson, S. J.   233
Die Antwoort   457
Dietrich, Marlene   458
diffusion of fashion   349
    aesthetic judgments   351–2
    agents   349
    fashion journalists   352
    fashion magazine editors   352–3
    fashion propaganda through advertising   355
    influential leaders of   350
    institutional   350–1
    sociological theories of   351
    strategies
        fashion dolls   353
        fashion shows   353–4
    technological influences on   354–5
    theories of   349–50
diffusion of innovation   373
digital landscape   165
Dillards   77
Dillion, Ricky   444
Dior   129, 285
Dior, Christian   285, 291, 292
Direct Marketing Association   58
disasters   117–18
    cause-related consumption   120
    corporate social responsibility and   120–1
    creativity and   119–20
    fashion industry responses to   117–19
    weatherproof clothing for   118
disposability   101
Dittmer, Lowell   432
Division, Joy   288
DIY Style (Luvaas)   174
Doherty, Maureen   59
Dolce, Stefano   426
Dolce & Gabbana   256, 416
Dominion Corset Co.   133
Donahue, Mary   9

Donna Karan brand   18, 293
Dore, Garance   257
double greenness, Patagonia clothing   108
Double RRL brand   214
Douglas, Katie   468, 469
Douglas, Mary   476
downward comparisons   94
dreams   102
dress
    age and   450
    body and   449–50
    camp   12
    choice of   369–70
    colour in   380
    democratization of   449
    as expression of pecuniary culture   368–9
    globalization and   419–24
    health and   450
    history   3–5
    materials   8–9
    national   406–8
    power of   448–9
    practices   448
    in social life   451
    societal level   448
    style   372
    totem pole   9
    Victorian   12
    women   368–70
Dress History: New Directions in Theory and Practice (Pollen)   4
3D tailoring   195–6
Du, Yang   434, 435
Dumas, Jean Louis   154, 155, 159
Dundovic, Laura   408
Dunst, Kirsten   415
Duofold   324
DuPont   74, 224
Dupuis Frères   136
Dylex   137

earrings   10
1 East Fifty-fourth Street   144
Ecko, Mark   261, 263
Ecko Unlimited brand   261
Eco, Umberto   455
eco-fashion   102, 105
e-commerce   58, 77, 79
"The Economic Theory of Women's Dress"   367–8
editors, fashion magazine   352–3

Edwards, Tim   467, 471
Eicher, Joanne   419
Eileen Fisher   88–9
Elbaz, Alber   285
elegance   103
Element S(urvival) Coat   119–20
Elizabeth Arden   144
Elizabeth Hurley Beach   267, 269, 271–3, 275–6
Elle Décor   58
Ellis, Havelock   450
e-marketplaces   79
Emergency Bra (Bodnar)   119
Emporio Armani   426
Empowerment Plan (Scott)   119
English, Bonnie   6
enterprise branding   186
Enterprise Resource Planning (ERP)   166
Entman, Robert M.   242
Environmental Illness   289
ERP *see* Enterprise Resource Planning (ERP)
Estée Lauder company
　history of   463
　today   463–4
e-tailoring   196
Ethical Trading Initiative (ETI)   86
Ethiopia   53
ETI *see* Ethical Trading Initiative (ETI)
Ettelgui, Joseph   59
Euro-American fashion   29
Europe   5
Evans, Jessica   268
Everest, Timothy   194
Everett, Ronald   10
Eweida, Nadia   448
Exhibition of Industrial Art in Textiles and Costumes   9
exhibitions, fashion   4
experiential retailing   213–14
Experiential Retailing: Concepts and Strategies That Sell (Kim, Sullivan & Forney)   213
exploitation   112
　see also labor exploitation
extended self   361
Extreme Measures   269

Fabrican   227
Fabricant, Stacey M.   467
fabric hand   37
fabric research   66
Facebook   196, 197–8, 200, 201–2
The Face magazine   56
faces   455
　of fashion   455–60
　value   455–7
　　case studies   457–60
　　freak chic   457–8
　　geek chic   459
　　gender bending   458
　　granny chic   458–9
　　slumming   459–60
　　social currency   460–1
Faiers, Jonathan   4
Fair Labor Standards Act (FLSA)   113–14
Fairman, Agnes Rowe   142
Faking It: Originals, Copies, and Counterfeits   4
Farfetch   169
fashion   3, 26, 369
　advertising   319
　AI and   171–2
　apps, growth of   170
　aspiration in   93–7
　blogging   346–7
　branding   253–9
　business
　　global   5
　　history of   3–4
　　material culture of   5–6
　capitals   5
　and celebrity   346–7
　as collective behavior   367–71
　communication   315–20
　as consumer behavior   367–71
　and creativity   63–5
　and custom   369
　cycles   364–5, 372–6
　　long-term   375
　　short-term   372–5
　democracy   26
　diffusion   349–55
　disciplines   4–5
　dolls   353
　eco   102
　fast   99–100, 101
　as game   63–4
　as global force   255
　history of   3–4
　as identity   362–5
　imagery   93–4
　immediacy   257
　Japanese   34–9
　journalists   352
　labor practices in industry   86–7
　as language   63, 78, 316
　luxury   102
　methods   4–5
　movements   367
　national identity in   278
　New York   13–19
　official   26
　older customer markets
　　adjusting cut   378–9
　　colour and age, adjustment based on   379–80
　　conceptualization   378
　　culture   278
　　framing   377–8
　　move younger   378
　　women   377–8
　older woman in   317
　Patagonia clothing   105–9
　producers   349
　propaganda through advertising   355
　shows   353–4
　as social and cultural mirror   255
　social responsibility and   85–6
　sports clothing as   223–5
　street   26
　sustainability and   85–6
　system, changes in   377
　technocracy *versus* consumerism and   77–8
　writing *versus* image   317–20
　written   317
Fashion and Textile Museum, London   4
Fashion Canada agency   134
Fashion Delivers Charitable Foundation   120
fashion designers
　China   302
　Hong Kong   302
　Im, Siki   20–5
　Kelly, Patrick   26–32
　North American Indians   8–9
　see also specific designers
Fashion Group International   17
Fashion Institute of Technology   17
fashion magazines   317, 318
　by age and socio-economic status   329
　ageism and   331
　age slippage and   331

change shape   343–5
and constitution of identity   328
editors   352–3
lifestyle   329
models, makeovers and celebrities   330
negotiating age   330–1
older market and   329
in visual culture   329–30
Vogue   331–4
women's   328–9
see also specific magazines
fashion motivation, psychological analysis of
general problem, overview of   369–70
group attitudes   370
Fashion Movements (Blumer)   367
fashion retail mobility   169–70
fashions' great black hope
black Paris   27–8
context   26–7
Kelly, Patrick   26–32
selling blackness   30–1
time and travel   29–30
fashion star system   300–2
Fashion Studies: Research Methods, Sites, and Practices (Jenss)   3
The Fashion System (Barthes)   315, 317
fast fashion   99–102, 421, 427
Fast Retailing Co.   52
Fastskin   410
Feasey, Rebecca   344
feggy jaay garments   418
The Female Gaze (Gamman and Marshment)   343
female-to-female intimacy   483–5
femininity   270
Ferragni, Chiara   257
Ferretti, Dante   288
Field, Marshall   140
Fifth Avenue Merchants Association   15
Fillon, François   254
Fionda, A. M.   231, 232
First Nation   8–9
accessories designs   10–11
fashionable garments design   10–11
fashion designers   8–9
jewelry-making and design   9–10
local materials, use of   12
objectives of designers   11–12
sources of inspiration   12

Fisher, Walter R.   242
FitBit, sports watch   167
FLSA *see* Fair Labor Standards Act (FLSA)
Flugel, J. C.   338, 375
Forever 21   52
Formicetti, Nicola   457
Forney, Judith Cardona   213
Foster, Hal   285
Four Weddings and a Funeral (Newell)   267, 269–70
Fraley, Keith A.   6
frame theory   241–2
freak chic   457–8
Freda, Fabrizio   464
Free People   187
Free Trade Agreement (FTA)   134
Freidenwald-Fishman, Eric   107
Freud, Sigmund   62, 159
Frijters, Paul   374
fripes   416
Frith, Mark   344
Fruit of the Loom (FOL)   166
FTA *see* Free Trade Agreement (FTA)
functionality driven partnership   72
Funny Face film   345
fur products   10
Fury, Alexander   288

Gabbana, Domenico   426
Gad, T.   257–8
Gagnon, Jean   482
Gale, Colin   74–80
Galla, Mario   458
Gallagher, Mary   410
Galliano, John   291, 297
Gap   52, 60, 77, 422
Garment District, New York   14–16, 18
garments   63
Australian   407
fashionable designs   10–11
feggy jaay   418
polypropylene   106
see also specific garments
GATT *see* General Agreement on Tariffs and Trade (GATT)
Gaultier, Jean-Paul   38, 286, 470
GEC *see* Guest Education Centre (GEC)
geek chic   459
gender
ambiguity   296
bending   458
identity   467–8

General Agreement on Tariffs and Trade (GATT)   134
Genest, Rick   457
Genet, Jean   29
geo-location based software   165
George, Boy   458
George Smith & Co.   340
Gevinson, Tavi   459
Ghesquière, Nicolas   285
Gianakopoulos, Spilios   20
Gibson, Pamela Church   316, 342–7
Gifford, Kathie Lee   86
Gilbert, David   402, 429
Gildan, Montreal   135
Gilmore, J. H.   179
Gilmore Girls   158–9
Gimbel, Sophie   142
Gitlin, Todd   242
Gladys Tilden   142
global crisis   254
global expansions   214
global fashion
business   5
clothing staples   403
on national costume   403
reinvention in   402–4
Global Flagship store   147
global items of clothing   406
globalization of dress   419–24
consumption   423–4
environment and   423–4
materials   423–4
styles   421–3
Global Positioning System (GPS)   170
global retailing   54–5
global sourcing   54–5
Gobé, Marc   201
Godbold, Brian   51, 56–61
Goffman, Erving   241–2, 393
golden mean   375
Golding, William   20
Goodman, Bergdorf   15
Goodwin, M. E.   155–6
Google Glass   167
Gordon, Lucy Duff   450, 451
gossip magazines   344
Gould, Stephen J.   467
Govender, Kaymarlin   471
GPS *see* Global Positioning System (GPS)
Graceffa, Joey   444
granny chic   458–9
Grant, Dorothy   10

Graves, Robert   450
Gray, John   275
Gray, Natalie   258, 261–6
Grazia magazine   343, 344, 346
Great Western Garment
    Company   133
Green, Denise Nicole   6
Green, Don   138
Green, Racing   58
Green, Ronald   10
'Green Eileen' program   88
greenwash   88, 107, 108
Gregory, Paul   375
Grieg, Geordie   271, 276
grooming, language of   470–1
Groupe Dynamite   138
Grumbach, Didier   428
Gruppo Finanziario Tessile   428
Gu, Zhaohui   365, 383–9
Gucci brand   18
Guest Education Centre (GEC)   201
Guggenheim Museum, New York   16
Guiltinan, J.   100
Gundle, Stephen C.V.   268

Habitent   118
habitus   269, 275
Hack, Jefferson   342
Hadid, Gigi   256, 257
Haida art   10
Hair   474
    function and form   474
    and human identity   474–8
    management   474
    natural qualities   475–7
    powers   475
    presentation and
        representation   475
    stereotypes   475–7
    styles   477
Haiti   88, 90
Haizhen, Wang   434, 435
Hall, Stuart   26
Halls, Z.   334
Halston, Roy   13, 224–5
Hamilton, Bethany   458
Hamnett, Katherine   60
Hancock, Joseph H.   6, 213–16, 278, 386
Hancock II, Joseph H.   365, 383–9, 463–6
The Handbook of Fashion Studies (Black et al.)   3

handicapping   392
Hanes   324, 326
Han Kjøbenhavn brand   460
Hanoi   150
Hansen, Karen Tranberg   413–18
Harper's Bazaar magazine   15, 16, 159, 344
Hatch   324
Hatch, Mary Jo   186
Haynes, Todd   289
HBC *see* Hudson's Bay
    Company (HBC)
Heath, T.   233
Heat magazine   344
Hedley, Lauren   215, 231–7
Heiliger, Evangeline M.   120
Hello magazine   344
Helmut Lang brand   20
Hennes & Mauritz (H&M)   52, 87, 214, 215, 240, 421, 480, 483
    co-branding campaigns   242
    fashion branding   241
        celebrity brand narrative
            framing   242
        frame theory   241–2
        narrative theory   241–2
        research methodology   242–3
            affordable luxury and
                fantasy   244
            design principle   246
            fashion heritage   245–6
            glamour   244
            lifestyle aspirations   244
            limited edition   243–4
            quality lines   244–5
            reciprocity, gift giving   246
            uniqueness   245
        streetscene   240–1
Henry Morgan's stores   136
Hepburn, Audrey   345, 455
Hepburn, Sharon J.   89, 105–9
heritage   102–3
Hermes, Joke   344
Hermès company   127–8, 154, 257
    bags   154–9
    brand   155–6
    Gilmore Girls   158–9
    Le Divorce (Ivory)   156–7
    Medium   156
    Sex and the City   154–5
heterosexuality   480–1
heterosexual pornography   482
Heydenreich, Daniel   220

hifu   35–6
high-quality segment (HQS)   76
hijabers   176, 177
Hijab Street Style (Pelangi)   176
Hill, David T.   176
Hiorns, Roger   293
hip-hop consumers   262–4
hip-hop fashion   261–2
hip-hop menswear brands   261–2
    consumers   262–3
    decline   264–5
    equity   264–5
    future   265–6
    urban consumer   263–4
hip-hop music   261–2
hippies   9
Hishinuma, Yoshiki   225
History of Beauty (Eco)   455
The History of Underclothes   336
HKTDC *see* Hong Kong
    Trade Development
    Council (HKTDC)
H&M *see* Hennes & Mauritz (H&M)
Hodge, Alan   450
Hodges, Nancy   68–72
Hollander, Anne   120, 454
Holmes, William   144
Holt, Douglas   279
Holt Renfrew   129, 137
home shopping   58
Home Shopping Network   58
homosocial grooming behaviour   343
Hong Kong, fashion   101, 300
    brands   303–4
    cities   303
    creative centers   302
    designers   302
    fables   304–5
        brand communications
            process   307
        brand ethos/brand
            mission   305–6
        future   307–8
        stylistic brand identity   306–7
        global recognition   307
        system   302–3
Hong Kong Trade Development
    Council (HKTDC)   302
Horton, C.   189
Hot Tuna   223
Hourani, Rad   296
Howard, John   408
HQS *see* high-quality segment (HQS)

Hudson's Bay Company (HBC)   136, 137
Huishan, Zhang   432, 435
humanitarian crises   254
Hunt, Michael H.   433
Hurley, Elizabeth   258, 267–76
   actress becomes model   267–9
   as fashion figure   270
   model becomes designer   269–74
   as theory and fashion fusion   274–6
hypermasculinity   386

I Am Love   294
IC3-D   181
ICI   224
identity   100
   clothing and   362–3
   fashion and   362–5
   search for   362–3
i-D magazine   288
Im, Siki   6, 20–5
   awards   20
   collections   20–3
   designs   20–1
   education   20
   Fall/Winter 2010 collections   21
   interview with Hancock   22–5
   menswear designs   20–1
   Spring/Summer Spring 2009 collections   23
   works   20
image clothing   317
Indian Craft Shop   10
Indian suppliers   68–9
   in apparel exports to USA   68
   benefits of sourcing from   71
   buyer-supplier relationships   69
   challenges of sourcing from   71
   convenience   70
   expertise   69–70
   functionality   70
   interpretation   69
   method   69
   partnership   71
      focus on   71–2
      types   72
   prices   70–1
   quality   70
   service   71
   sourcing in global context   68
   and United States, relationship-building between   68–72
indiDenim   181

Indonesia   174, 401–2
   fashion industries in   174
      hijaber style   175–6
      photographers   175
      street style   174–5
      street-style photos   174–7
      subculture, import of   176–7
   streets in   174–5
industrial policies   75–6
information and technology   79–80
institutional diffusion   350–1
In Style magazine   344
International Garment Workers Union   15
Internet   346
Internet of Things (IoT)   167
Intolerable Cruelty (Cohen)   154
IoT *see* Internet of Things (IoT)
I-Pad   168
I-Phone   167, 168
Irving Samuel   135
Islam   176
Isle of Man   387
Issey Miyake: Photographs by Irving Penn   38
Italian fashion   425–6
Italy   5
item shopping   60

Jaarsma, Mella   117, 118
Jackson, Betty   60
Jacobs, Marc   13, 27, 102, 255, 291
Jacob stores   138
Jaeger   379
Jaeger, Gustav   338
Jakarta Fashion Week (JFW)   401–2
Jakarta Street Journal   174
Jantzen   223
Japanese fashion   34–9
   aesthetics of poverty   34–6
   conceptualization   38–9
   cultural heritage   36–7
   designers   34
   textile design   37–8
Jardin, Walter   324
Javanese Islam   176
Jay-Z   261, 262–3, 275
J. Crew brand   58, 77, 214, 256, 443
Jefen brand   431
Jenss, Heike   3
Jewish Museum, London   4
JFW *see* Jakarta Fashion Week (JFW)
Jil Sander boutique   293, 294

João IV, Dom   217
Jobling, Paul   319, 336–41
Jockey International   340
Jocks and Nerds (Martin, Koda)   386
Joe College   388
Joffe, Bruce H.   319, 322–6
joggers   216
Johanssen, Scarlett   274
Johnson, Marsha P.   464
Jo Malone London brand   464
Jones, Carla   176
Jones, Leslie   90
Jones, Terry   288
Jonsson, Fredrik U.   196, 197
Jordan, Michael   226
Joseph Ribkoff International   135
journalists, fashion   352
Jovi   56
Jovovich, Milla   275
Joy, Annamma   89, 99–103
Juanjuan, Wu   431
Julian, C. C.   361
Jung, C. G.   62, 63

Kaiser, Susan B.   6
Kapferer, Jean-Noel   231, 232
Kardashian, Kim   256
Karl Lagerfeld brand   20
Kates, Mitch   78
Katona, Kerry   453
Katz, Elihu   350
Kaur, Jasbir   74–80
Kawakubo, Rei   6, 34–8, 225, 403, 416
Kawamura, Yuniya   317, 318, 349–55
Ke, Ma   432
Keaton, Diane   458
Keller, K. L.   233
Kellwood   263
Kelly, Grace   154
Kelly, Patrick   6, 26–32
   as allegory   28
   fashion for   28
   importance   30
   as influential designer   28
   legacy   28
   in Paris fashion industry   27, 29–30
   traveller   29–30
   works   27–32
Kenya   53
khaki shorts   407, 409
Khan, Naeem   404
Kidman, Nicole   274, 415, 458
Kilbourne, Jean   445

Killian, Scott   181
Kim, Samuel   432
Kim, Youn-Kyung   213
kimono   36, 37
kimonos   406
King Kong film   476
Kingston School of Art   56
Kitching, John   220
kitsch   27
KKK (Kenosha Klosed Krotch) brand   339, 341
Klein, Anne   13, 262
Klein, Calvin   274
Klein, Steven   345
Klein, Yves   292
Klin, Elin   256
Kmart store   215
Knight, Nick   38
Knightley, Keira   275
Knit-to-Fit   133
Knowles, Beyonce   275
Knudsen   77
Koda, Harold   34–5, 386
Koger, Eric   188
Koger, Susan   188, 190
Kondo, Dorine   403
Konheim, Bud   113
Korgaonkar, Pradeep   201
Kors, Michael   13
Kouyaté, Lamine   416
Kozar, J. M.   94
Kroeber, Alfred   375
Kruip, Germaine   293
Küchler, Susanne   5
Kuczynski, Alex   453
Kurniawan, S. H.   196, 197
Kvadrat   291
Kynaston, Lee   470

labor abuse   111, 114–15
labor exploitation   111–14
labor practices, in fashion industry   86–7
labor rights   89
Lacroix, Christian   31
Lagerfeld, Karl   93
La Haine   23–4
Lambert, Eleanor   13, 17
Land's End   181, 422
Landsend and Tiffany & Co.   58
Lang, Helmut   286
Langenwater, G.   99
language, fashion as   63, 78

Lanvin and Chanel   142
Lapolla, Kendra   172, 186–91
Larry Gagosian art gallery   285
Lascity, Myles Ethan   128, 443–6
La Senza   138
Latour, Henri Fantin   290
Lau, Peter   303
Lau, Susie   256, 342
Lauder, Estée   270, 274, 275, 463–4
Lauder, Joseph   463
Laudi Vidni, online retailer   188
Laura   138
Laurent, Yves Saint   13
Laver, J.   364
Lavergne, Michael   87
Lazarsfeld, Paul   350
Lazuardy, Olivia   404
Lea, T.   458
LeBlanc, Susanne   155
Le Château boutique   137, 138
Le Divorce (Ivory)   156–7
Leena-Maija, Rossi   480–5
leggings   227
legwarmers   227
Le Mercure Gallant   318
le Pen, Marine   254
Let My People Go Surfing (Chouinard)   105
Levine, Martin   386
Levi Strauss & Co.   77, 180
Lewin, Lawrence   138
Lewis, Tasha L.   172, 200–6, 261–6
Lewis, Van Dyk   6
Leyendecker, J. C.   340
Life magazines   51
lifestyle magazines   329
lifestyle retailing   59
Li & Fung   101
Linard, Stephen   27
Lincoln Center for Performing Arts, New York   16
Liu, Lucy   155
Liz Claiborne   51, 77
L Bean retailer   58
'Logic of Wrong' (LOW)   460–1
London   5, 402
long-term fashion cycles   372, 375
Lopez, Jennifer   275
The Lord of the Flies (Golding)   20
Lord & Taylor   140, 256
Los Angeles   149, 150, 151
Louis Vuitton brand   13, 18, 102

LOW *see* 'Logic of Wrong' (LOW)
Low, David   337
Lowe, E. D.   375
Lowe, J. W. G.   375
Luck, Edwina   215, 231–7
Luiz, Washington   220
Lululemon Athletica   130, 131, 138, 172, 200, 216
 brand-building   200–1
 brand communities   201
 brand love   201
 consumers emotional attachments to   201
 consumers relationship with   201
 customer-centric approach   200–1
 Facebook page   201–6
  analysis findings   202–3
  content analysis   202
  customer loyalty via   203–4
  data   201–2
  fandom   205–6
 role in encouraging customer loyalty   204–5
 social media and   201
Lurie, Alison   120
Lusch, R. F.   186
Luvaas, Brent   172, 174–7
luxury fashion   102
luxury fashion branding
 ethos   231–3
 success factors of   232
lycra revolution   225–7
Lyle   339
Lynch, Annette   372–6
Lynch, Kevin   148

Ma, Joyce   59
Ma, Masha   435
M.A.C. *see* Makeup Art Cosmetics (M.A.C.)
McCardell, Claire   17, 224
McCartney, Stella   244–5
McClure, J. E.   374
MacDonald, Julien   60, 274
McDonaldization   100
McFashion *see* fast fashion
McGregor Hosiery, Toronto   135
McGuigan, Jim   481
Mackinney-Valentin, Maria   455–61
McNair, Brian   481
McNaught, Erin   409
McNeill, Lisa S.   468, 469
McQuarrie, Ella   141

McQuarrie, Hector   141
McQueen, Alexander   38, 458
McQuire, Scott   148, 149
Macron, Emmanuel   254
Macys   56
Made in Britain: Walsh Trainers   4
Made in Italy   427–8
made-to-measure suit   194
Madewell   324
Madry, Bobbi Ray   469, 470
magazines, fashion   317–18, 328
　by age and socio-economic
　　　status   329
　ageism and   331
　age slippage and   331
　change shape   343–5
　and constitution of identity   328
　lifestyle   329
　models, makeovers and
　　　celebrities   330
　negotiating age   330–1
　older market and   329, 330
　in visual culture   329–30
　Vogue   331–4
　women's   328–9
Magnifeco (Black)   88
Mahlke, Sascha   196, 197
Mahshie, Jeff   9
mail order business   58, 136
Mainbocher   142
makeup, new face of   443–4
Makeup Art Cosmetics
　　　(M.A.C.)   463, 464–6
make-up brand   443
male accessory   391–4
male luggage   392–3
Mamp, Michael   128, 140–5
MAN and his Clothes   337, 338, 339
Manchiraju, Srikant   361–5
Manhattan   14–15, 18, 150
Manlow, Veronica   253–9, 258,
　　　278–83
mannekins   41
The Man Who Fell to Earth
　　　(Roeg)   288
Mao jackets   406
Map, Body   27
Mappin, Herbert Joseph   220
Mappin, Walter John   220
Mappin fashion   220–2
Mappin stores   219–20
Mappin & Webb   219–20
Mapplethorpe, Robert   38

Maramotti, Achille   65
Maramotti, Luigi   51, 62–7
Marcketti, Sara   128, 140–5
Margiela, Martin   6, 286, 416
　art   42
　clothes   41–4
　designs   40–5
　fashion   40–5
　jacket   42–4
　rag clothes   41
　shows   40
　works   40–5
Marie Claire magazine   273
marketing   66–7, 169
　culture in fashion   278
　older customer   377–81
Marketing That Matters (Conley and
　　　Freidenwald-Fishman)   107
market research   65
Marks & Spencer   56–61
Marlboro Man   386, 387–8
Martin, Richard   386
masculinity   386, 467–8, 471
Mason, David   197
mass customization   179, 188
massification of fashion   364
materialism   361–2
materials
　culture studies, in fashion
　　　business   5–6
　dress   8–9
Matsushita, Hiroshi   37
Matthews, Kevin   365, 383–9
MaxMara group   62
Maynard, Margaret   407, 419–24
Mazzalovo, G.   233
Medium   156
Meisel, Steven   117
men
　body   467–8
　language of grooming   470–1
　and make-up   468–70
　and make-up in South
　　　Korea   471–2
　masculinity   467–8
Menkes, Suzy   293
men's fashion retailers   383–4
　culture and fashion
　　　branding   384–5
　visual merchandising
　　　branding   384–5
　definition   385
　memetics   385–9

men's underwear advertising   322–6,
　　　336
　ambiguities of pleasure   340–1
　health and   337–9
　pleasure, fetishism and
　　　sexuality   339–40
　spectatorship, ambiguities
　　　of   340–1
　sport and   337–9
　style   336–7
menswear   20–5, 133
Mercer, Kobena   477
Metropolitan Museum of Art   34
metrosexuality   468
MFA *see* Multi-Fibre
　　　Arrangement (MFA)
Michaels, Patricia   11
Mickey Blue Eyes   269
microfibre technology   227
Milan   5, 402, 404
　as fashion city   425
　fashion design   425
　future   428–30
　Italian style   425–6
　made in   425–6
　prêt-à-porter system   425–6,
　　　427–8
　in 1980s   426–7
　in 1990s   427
　in 2000   427–8
Milano Unica   428
military   388–9
Miller, Daniel   5, 330
Miller, Janice   467–72
Miller, Sandra   318
Miller, Sienna   275, 346
Millerson, S.   355
Milne & Faulkner   219
Minogue, Kylie   275
Mirren, Helen   159
Missoni   215
　for Target, co-branding
　　　strategies   234–7
Missoni, Angela   234
Missoni Art Colour   4
Miyake, Issey   6, 34, 36–8, 225
Miyake Modern (Simon)   37
Mizrahi, Issac   9, 262
MMM collection   245–6
mobility, fashion retail   169–70
ModCloth
　'Be the Buyer' programme   190
　case study   188–91

co-creative framework for
 branding   189
 dialogue   189
 dialogue + access   189–90
 dialogue + risk assessment   190
 dialogue + transparency   190
 entry point into   190–1
 profile   188–9
 'Social Butterflies' team   190
models   93–4, 455–7
Molloy, John T.   393
MoMu Fashion Museum, Antwerp   286
Monarch Wear of Manitoba   135
Montreal   132–5
Montroy Coat   135
Moore, C. M.   231, 232
Moore, Julianne   289
moral-norm activation theory of altruism   101
Morley Theta campaign   339
Moses   63
Moses, D'Arcy   10
Moses, Mods and Mr Fish: The Menswear Revolution   4
Moskowitz, David   214
Moss, Kate   276
Moss Brothers   133
Mother Hubbard dresses   406
Mrs Exeter phenomenon   334
Mugler   457
Mugler, Thierry   306
Mullins, Aimee   458
Multi-Fibre Arrangement (MFA)   53
Mundi-Wesport   216
Muniz, A. M.   186
Munsingwear   324
Murakami, Takashi   291
Muratovski, Gjoko   215, 231–7
Murray, Shannon   458
museums, fashion   4, 9
Mutiara, Irna   176
mutilated hosiery   417
MyCustomTailor   181
MyTailor   181

NAFTA *see* North American Free Trade Agreement (NAFTA)
Nakashima, George   292
Naked Lunch (Burroughs)   288
Nappyisms: Affirmations for Nappy-Headed People and Wannabes (Jones)   477

narrative theory   241–2
national dress
 defining   406–8
 forms   406
national identity   278, 432–5
nationalism   433, 434–5
Native American Tradition (Wood)   11
Nautica   51
Navajo art   9, 10
Navajo designers   12
Navicloth   324
Neimark, Ira   145
Nelson, Jim   384
Newell, Mike   267
New Tailors   193
New Travel Weekly magazine   119
New York   5, 140, 149, 402
 art-commerce balance   18–19
 as arts centre   16
 Canadian fashion in   134
 as centre of fashion   13–14
 designer branding   17–18
 fashion   13–19
 Garment District   14–16, 18
 institutionalization of fashion   16–17
 versus Paris   16, 18
 ready-to-wear in   15–16, 17
 Uniqlo in   149–51
New York Times Style magazine   20
New Zealand   406–7
Nguyen, Han   196
Nichols, Harvey   59
Nickell, Jake   183
Nicklas, Charlotte   4
Nicole Miller, Inc.   113
Niederland, W. G.   362
Nigeria   53, 418
Niinimaki, Kirsi   101
Nike   52, 77, 78, 86, 114, 223, 226
NikeiD website   181, 182
Niketown   229
Noguchi, Isamu   292
Nolin, Marie-Paule   137
non-surgical cosmetic procedures   452
Norell, Norman   16
North America   5, 51
North American Free Trade Agreement (NAFTA)   134
North American Indians   8
 accessories designs   10–11
 designs   8–9

 fashionable garments design   10–11
 fashion designers   8–9
 jewelry-making and design   9–10
 local materials, use of   12
 objectives of designers   11–12
 sources of inspiration   12
Nouvel, Jean   285
Nuh, Evita   174
Nutter, Tommy   197
Nygård International   135
Nystrom, P. H.   372, 373

Obama, Barack   254
Obama, Michelle   90
O'Cass, A.   361
O'Connor, Andrew   255
Odlum, Floyd   140–1
Odlum, Hortense   128–9, 140–5
 beauty salon   143
 beginnings   141
 721 Club   143–4
 College Girls Department   143
 Consumer Advisory Committee   144
 cooler and bigger   141–2
 hiring decisions   144
 milestones   144–5
 Rendezvous and Debutante   142–3
 Salon de Couture and   142
official fashion   26
O'Guinn, T.   186
Okonkwo, Uche   232
older customer fashion markets
 age/lifestyle   378
 colour and age, adjustment based on   379–80
 conceptualization   378
 culture   278
 cut adjustment   378–9
 framing   377–8
 move younger   378
 to older women   377–8
older woman, in fashion   317
O'Mahony, Marie   224, 225
O'Neal, Gwendolyn   261
online platforms   54
online retail environments   196
online retailers   187–8
Ontario   132
oral histories   6–7
Orta, Jorge   117

Orta, Lucy   117–18
Ossendrijver, Lucas   285, 296
Otieno, R.   196
Overdressed (Cline)   88
Ozbek, Rifat   9

Pagel, Mark   392
Pakistan   53
Palerma, Olivia   256
Paltrow, Gwenyneth   256
Parachute   138
Parasuco, Montreal   135
Paris   5, 27–8, 402
Paris Hilton   275
Parisian fashion system   26–7, 29–30
Paris is Burning   27
Parker, Sarah Jessica   155
Parnass, Harry   138
Parsons School of Design   15, 17
Pascale, B.   62
Patagonia   89
    business, beginnings of   105
    Chouinard Equipment   105–6
    dreams, desire, and demand, dilemmas of   107–9
    environmental policies and practices   107
    four decades   105–7
    othermade clothing   105
    sportswear
        production of   106
        today   107
        for uncommon-not fashionable-people   106–7
patriotism   433–5
Paulicelli, Eugenia   278
paulistanos   218
paulistas   218
Payaoni   171
PDM *see* product data management (PDM)
Pearson   77
Peck, K.   187
Pedro, Dom   217
Peerless Clothing, Montreal   129, 134–5
Pei, Guo   258, 300, 303, 305–8
Peirson-Smith, Anne   215, 240–7, 258, 300–9, 315–20
Pejic, Andrej   458
Pelangi, Dian   176, 401
Pelly, Nicola   138
Penn, Irving   38, 93

Penney, James Cash   140
Penn Railroad Station   14
Pergament, Danielle   464
Perry, Katy   443
Pesco underwear   337
Pesendorfer, Wolfgang   373–4
Petrescu, Maria   201
Pham, Amy   443
Phat Farm   258, 261, 262, 263
Phau, I.   232
Philadelphia   149, 151
Philippe, Patek   102
Philo, Phoebe   285
Pierce, Ben J.   444
piercings   451
Pilcher, Nancy   409
Piller, Frank   181, 184
Pine, II, B. J.   179
Piore, Michael   112–13
Pistorius, Oscar   458
Pitt, Brad   458
Place, Stan   469, 470
Plains Indians   9
Playa, Cassette   28
Playtex brand   129, 135
pleating   37
PLM *see* Product Lifecycle Management (PLM)
"plus fours"   406
Poiret, Paul   354, 403, 455
Pollen, Annabella   4
Polo Ralph Lauren (PRL)   51, 258, 278
    characteristics   279
    culture   279–80
    culture in firm   280
    leadership style   280
    marketing   280
    master narratives   279
    mission   280
    vision   279–80
polyester (capilene) underwear   106
polypropylene (diaper liner) garments   106
ponchos   406
Poole, Henry   193
pornification in streetscape   481–2
pornography   482–3
Portlock, Henry   220
Potter, Dennis   268
Poupée Rouge boutique   137
Powerhouse Museum, Sydney   37
Prada, Miuccia   427, 456
Prada store   78, 226

Prahalad, C. K.   186, 187, 188, 191
Pratt Institute   15
Prendergast, G.   232
prêt-à-porter   425
    in 1980s   425–7
    transformation of   427–8
price sensitive partnership   72
Primark   52
The Princess of Wales Fashion Handbook   271–2
PRL *see* Polo Ralph Lauren (PRL)
Proctor and Gamble   170
product data management (PDM)   77, 166
production-consumption cycle   85
production opportunities   66
Product Launch Planning (PLP) software   167
Product Lifecycle Management (PLM)   77, 166
products, fashioning
    cheap   52–4
    development   51–2
    fast delivery   52–4
    global retailing   54–5
    sourcing   54–5
Project Catwalk   274
proletarianization   402
promotion   67
Prouvé, Jean   285
Provenance   171
public sphere   481
Pueblan   9
Puma   223
purposeful obsolescence   375

qipaos   432
quality   102–3
Quality, Value and Convenience (QVC)   58, 170
Quebec   129, 132
The Queen (Frears)   159
Quigley, C.   29
Quiksilver   223
Quillin, J.   187
Quinn, Bradley   229, 292
QVC *see* Quality, Value and Convenience (QVC)
QVC Fashion Channel   58

racism   29
Radford, Robert   292
radio frequency identification   78

Raf Simons Redux (Frisa)   288
Ralph Lauren brand   9, 18, 93, 214, 265, 383, 384
Ramaswamy, Venkat   186, 187, 188, 191
Ramroop, Andrew   198
Rana Plaza factory, Bangladesh   86
Rancière, Jacques   292
Rangel, Valerie   89–90, 117–21
Rantisi, Norma   5
ready-to-wear   15–16, 17, 133, 195, 425, 428
Reardon, Candice A.   471
rebel   387
Red Nations Art   10
Reebok   223
Rees-Roberts, Nick   258, 285–97
Reformasi   176
Refuge Wear series (Orta)   118
Reinach, Simona Segre   404, 425–30
Reitman's   138
relational space, Uniqlo and   147–9
Rendezvous and Debutante   142–3
Re-Nutriv cream   463
research, fashion businesses   6–7
responses to disaster   117–19
The Responsible Company: What We've Learned from Patagonia's First 40 Years (Chouinard)   108
Resteröd brand   460
retail innovation   78
RetailMeNot, Inc.   170
retail systems   53, 77, 78
retailtainment   213–14
Rexroth, Marilyn   154
Richardson, Terry   282, 295
Richmond, John   27
Rikasari, Diana   174, 401
Rio de Janeiro   217, 218, 219–20
Ripcurl   223
risk assessment, co-creation   188, 190
Ritzer, G   100, 151
Rivera, Sylvia   464
Riviera Inc.   135
Riviere, Joan   469
Rivoli, Pietra   87
Rizzo, Olivier   286
Roach, Marion   476
Roberts, Julia   415
Robertson, Steve   470
Rocamora, Agnes   320
Rocawear   258, 261, 262

Rockwell, Norman   280
Roebuck   136
Rogers, Everett   373
Rogers, Millicent   9, 12
Rojek, Chris   268, 270
Roosevelt, Franklin   115
Roots   138
The Roots of Desire (Roach)   476
Rose Studio   258, 300, 303, 304, 305, 307–8
Rosin, Hanna   394
Ross, Frances   193–9
Rossellini, Isabella   275
Rothman, Howard   107
Rothstein, Richard   114–15
Rough Guide to Hip-Hop (Shapiro)   265
Row, Savile   20
Royal College of Art   56
Rozario, Kevin   119, 121
Rubinstein, Helena   17
Ruby, Sterling   291
Rudd, Nancy A.   467
Ruggerone, L.   332
Russian Vogue magazine   273
Rykiel, Sonia   245–6
Ryle, Gilbert   41

Sabrina, Raja Nadia   401
SAC *see* Sustainable Apparel Coalition (SAC)
Safe (Haynes)   289
SAGA magazine   328–31
Saks   77
Saks Fifth Avenue's Salon Moderne   142
Salgado, Felix   40
Salisbury, Peter   57
Salon de Couture   142
Salon Marie-Paule   137
Same, Tanya   60
Sander, Jil   286
Sanders, Elizabeth B.-N.   186, 187
San Francisco   151
Sanft, Auckie   135
São Paulo   217
   department store   219
   english influences in   217–18
   fashion   218–19
   Mappin fashion   220–2
   Mappin stores   219–20
   as modern city   218–19
   modernization   218

modern life   219
   origins   218
Sarabhai, Asha   59
saris   406
Saturday Night Fever (Badham)   225
Savage, Jon   287
Savile Row   193, 195
Saville, Peter   290
Schames, Cynthia Lane   156
Schenkman, B. O. N.   196, 197
Schiaparelli   142
Schiaparelli, Elsa   456
Schlegel, Valentine   292
Schneider, Hans   56
Schotz, John   463
Schultz, Majken   186
Schwartz, S.   101
Scott, Jeremy   28, 460
Scott, Mary   107
Scott, Veronika   119
Scott brand   337
Scroggies   136
Scuole Maramotti   65
Sean Jean   258
Sean John   261, 264
Sears store   136, 215
Seattle   151
secondhand clothing
   African markets   417–18
   charity   413–15
   commerce   413–15
   global contexts   416–17
   recycling   418
   from thrift to fashion   415–16
   trade   416–17
   from waste to recycling   415–16
Second Skin Swimwear   180
self   361–2
self-expression   369, 370
self-formation   269
self-presentation   269
Selfridge, Harry   140
Selfridges   59
semi-bespoke tailoring   195
Sen, Krishna   176
Senegal   418
Sennett, Richard   221
service-driven partnership   72
Seurat, Georges   295
Sex and the City: The Movie   154–5, 346
Shanghai   302
Shape magazine   273

Shapiro, Peter   265
Shaver, Dorothy   17, 140
Shelter Me series (Jaarsma)   118
Sherman, Cindy   38
Sherman, Lauren   257
Sherry, Jr, John F.   89, 99–103
Shirmax Organization   138
Shirtcreations.com   181
Sholevar, B.   362
shopping   58
short-term fashion cycles   372–5
   innovation, diffusion of   373
   by purposeful obsolescence   374–5
   status-driven models of   373–4
Siantar, Anastasia   404
Simian Films   269
Simmel, Georg   275, 362, 364
Simmons, Roland   416
Simmons, Russell   258, 261, 262, 263–4
Simons, Raf   52, 258, 404
   collaborations   286, 290–4
   collections   285, 287–97
   designs   286–7, 292
   fashion show   285
   hanging garden   294–6
   intermission   290–3
   man-machine   289–90
   menswear designs   286–8, 291, 292–3
   minimum-maximum   293–4
   modernist design heritage, re-evaluation of   292
   movement   296–7
   retail outlets   293
   subculture   286–9
Sims, David   38
Singapore Fashion Week   403–4
Singer, Sally   113
Singh, Kamlesh   68–72
Siriano, Christian   90
Skov, Lise   318
SKU plans *see* stock keeping unit (SKU) plans
Slimane, Hedi   52, 285
slumming   459–60
small and medium-sized enterprises (SMEs)   193
   fashion companies   193–4
smart tags   78
SMEs *see* small and medium-sized enterprises (SMEs)
Smestad, Liat   87, 111–15

Smith, Anthony   267–8, 364, 367–71, 433
Smith, Paul   57
Smith, Todd   262
Smith, Willi   27
Snow, Carmel   345
social comparison theory   94
social groups   316–17
social media   201
social-networking websites   182, 196
social responsibility, in fashion industry   85, 117
   commitment to   121
   community engagement   121
   cross-disciplinary collaboration   121
   CSR   89–91
   ethical fashion responses   89–91
   labor practices   86–7
   production, design and consumption challenges   87–9
social shopping via intelligent systems   169
sociological models of diffusion   351
Somaly Mam Beauty Salon   464
sombreros   406
Song, Aimee   256
sophistication   221
South Korea   471–2
Speedo   223, 227, 410
Spiegler, Marc   261
sports clothing
   as fashion   223–5
   from stylish to sporty style   228–9
sports watch   167
sportswear   17, 56, 60, 66, 106–7, 200, 215, 223–9, 263, 265, 293, 297, 383, 410
Sproles, G. B.   372
squash-blossom necklaces   10
Sri Lanka   53
Stag Club   144
'stag' party   143
Stanfield   133
St Anne   63
status-signaling degradation   374
status-signaling theory   373–4
Stecca degli Artigiani   429
Steele, V.   158, 292
Stefani, Gwen   275
Stella McCartney   87
Stengg, Werner   76

Stepanova, Varvara   41
Stitch Fix, San Francisco   168–9
stock keeping unit (SKU) plans   51
Stopes, Marie   450
Strauss, Levi   389
Strauss, Michael D.   372–6
Straw, Jack   448
street bloggers   347
street fashion   26
streetwear   226
style   372
subconscious values   101
Sui, Anna   9
Sullivan, Pauline   213
Superior Underwear   324
supply chain management   74, 76, 77, 79–80
sustainability, in fashion industry
   context   85–6
   CSR   89–91
   eco-fashion   102
   ethical fashion responses   89–91
   labor practices   86–7
   production, design and consumption challenges   87–9
   as social contract   99
Sustainable Apparel Coalition (SAC)   86
sweatshop   112–13
Swinton, Tilda   294, 458
Sydney Morning Herald Good Weekend Magazine   408
symbolic communication   316
Synchilla   106, 107
synthetic fibres   224
System D economies   170

Talbot, Mary   468
Talking to Myself (Yamamoto)   35
Tang, William   303
Target Corp.   53, 215
   for Missoni, co-branding strategies   234–7
Tatler magazine   270, 273
tattoos   451
taxonomies, aspiration in fashion   94
Taylor, Lou   3, 5
TCSG *see* Textile and Clothing Strategy Group (TCSG)
Tea Room, Mappin's   221
T. Eaton, Co.   129, 135–6
technical innovation   66

technocracy *versus* consumerism, fashion and   77–8
technological innovation   66
technology   54, 78
   in fashion industry   165–6
      Artificial Intelligence (AI)   171–2
      for big data management   168–9
      challenges and opportunities for future   172–3
      for decision-making   168–9
      for directive distribution and supply   166–7
      for e-commerce purchasing solutions   169
      ERP systems   166
      fashion apps, growth of   170
      for marketing   169
      PLM systems   166
      for product innovation and design   167–8
      retail mobility in developed and developing markets   169–70
      social shopping via intelligent systems   169
      WeChat   170–1
   updates   167
   wearable   165
television shopping channels   58
Tencent Holdings, Ltd.   171
Tesla, Nikola   290
Testino, Mario   346
Textile and Clothing Board   134
textile and clothing industry
   collaborative commerce   76–7
   companies and countries   74–5
   government strategies for   75–6
   industrial policies   75–6
   information and technology   79–80
   stores   78
   technocracy *versus* consumerism and fashion   77–8
Textile and Clothing Strategy Group (TCSG)   75
textile-recycling industry   413–14
themes   69
The Theory of Moral Sentiments (Smith)   367
The Theory of the Leisure Class (Veblen)   35, 368–9
Thomas, Sue   107

Thompson, Kaye   345
Threadless, T-shirt co-design website   181, 183–4, 187
Threadless brand   172
thug wear   460
Thurman, Uma   256
Timberland   258
Time magazine   36
Todor, John I.   108
Tom Ford   468, 470
Tommy Hilfiger   51, 169, 257, 258, 265, 278
   characteristics   279
   culture   280
   culture in firm   281
   leadership style   281
   marketing   281
   master narratives   279
   mission   280–1
   vision   280
Tommy Nutter - Rebel on the Row   4
Tommy Pier   257
top-handle bags   394–5
Topinka, Robert J.   258
Topkis   324, 325
Toronto   132–3, 151
Tortora, Phyllis G.   5
Tory Burch   167
totem pole dress   9
tracksuits   228
tradition   127
transparency, co-creation   188, 190
transparent customization   179
Trend-ology   4
Triangle Shirtwaist Company   52, 86
trickle-down, theory of fashion leadership   262
trickle-up, theory of fashion leadership   262
Tristan   138
Trump, Donald   254
Tuan, Yi-Fu   361
TUKA3D   166
Tungate, Mark   421
Tuplex   338
Turing, Alan   290
Turner, Graeme   268
turquoise   10
Twigg, Julia   317, 318, 328–35, 365, 377–81
Twitter   196, 197–8
Tyler, Liv   274

un-Australianness   408
underwears (mens), advertisements for   322–6, 336
   ambiguities of pleasure   340–1
   health and   337–9
   pleasure, fetishism and sexuality   339–40
   spectatorship, ambiguities of   340–1
   sport and   337–9
   style   336–7
Ungaro, Emanuel   13
Unicorn boutique   137
Union of Needletrades, Industrial and Textile Employees (UNITE)   113
Uniqlo   52, 54, 128, 147, 214
   brands and city   150–1
   CODA   151–2
   framing   148
   promotions   148–9
   and relational space   147–9
   shoppers building brand image   149–50
   social media outreach   148–9
   in United States   147–52
UNITE *see* Union of Needletrades, Industrial and Textile Employees (UNITE)
United Kingdom   59
United States   56–9, 68
   and India, relationship-building between   68–72
   Uniqlo in   147–52
Unknown Pleasures (Division)   288
upcycling process   88
upward comparisons   94
urban fantasy   482
Urban Fieldnotes   174
Utex Fashion Group   129, 135

Vagara, Sofia   443
Valle, Diego Della   430
Van Beirendonck, Walter   286, 296
Vanidades magazine   273
Vanity Fair Corporation (VFC)   166
Van Lamsweerde, Inez   38
Vargo, V. L.   186
Veblen, T.   35, 364, 367–71, 392
Vegas magazine   273
velvet   12
Venkatesh, Alladi   89, 99–103

Vernet, Marie   455
Versace   243, 244, 267–8
Versace, Donatella   271
VF Corp.   53
Victorian dress   12
Vincent, Susan J.   335, 448–54
Vinken, Barbara   6, 297
vintage   415
Vintageskivvies.com   322
virtual reality (VR)   167
virtual retail   58
visual merchandising   383–4
   definition   385
   as fashion branding   384–5
   memetics   385
      blue-collar worker   388–9
      cowboy   387–8
      Joe College   388
      military   388–9
      rebel   387
   in retail branding schemes   385–7
   retail space   385
VIVA GLAM   464–6
Vogue Italia   93
Vogue magazine   15, 117, 255, 273, 328, 331–2, 344–5
   dilution strategies   333
   localization strategies   333
   Mrs Exeter phenomenon   334
   negotiating age   332–3
   personalization strategies   333–4
   readership by age and socio-economic status   332
voluntary export restraints   134
von Samsonow, Elisabeth   278
VR *see* virtual reality (VR)
Vreeland, Caroline   256
Vreeland, Diana   345

Walker, Harriet   293
Wallach, Jeremy   176
Wallis, Jeffrey   56
Wall Street Journal   58
Walmart   52, 53, 422
Walthamstow School of Art   56
Wanamaker, John   140
Wang, Alexander   52
Wang, Jeff   89, 99–103
Wang, Uma   435
Ward, John   334

Warhol, Andy   31, 290
Warner, Marina   474, 475
Washington   151
Watanabe, Junya   225
Water and Oil   117
wearable art   8
wearable technology   165
weatherproof clothing   118
WebPDM software   166
Web 2.0 tool   196
Web 3.0 tool   196
WeChat China   169, 170–1
Weiss, Catharine   127–31
Weisser, Selma   59
Weitz, Rose   477–8
Welcome Stranger, menswear boutique in San Francisco   388
West, Kanye   265
Western Glove Works Ltd., Winnipeg   135
Westwood, Vivienne   38, 459
wetsuits   224
#whereUniqlo social campaign   148
White, Nicola   5, 425
whitewear   133
Whiting, Allen   432
Whitman, Kathy   10
Wild, Benjamin L.   365, 391–5
Willhelm, Bernhard   28
William, C. T.   186
Williams, Joan   472
Williams, Linda   480
Williams, Russell   385
Williamson, Matthew   244–5
Wilson, Louise   434
Winnipeg Shirt and Overall Company   133
Wintour, Anna   345–6
Witherspoon, Reese   415
Wolsey underwear   337
Wolstein, Laura   138
Woman & Home magazine   328–31, 343
woman's dress, economic theory of   367–8
women   41
   aspiration in fashion, evaluations of   94–7
   empowerment   95–6
   honesty, perceptions of   94–5

identities   328
magazines   328–9
Muslim   176
older, fashion marketing to   377–8
social responsibility   96
Women's Wear Daily (WWD)   15
WonderBra brand   129, 135
Wong, Jing   300, 305
Wong, Kay   300, 305
Wood, Margaret   11
world dress   419
'Worn Wear' program   89
Worth, Charles Frederick   30, 353–4, 455
Wouch-Wilker, Bianca   216
written clothing   317
Wu, Juanjuan   172, 179–84, 187
Wu, Yufan   386
Wyatt, Nioka   165–73

xenophobia   254
Xie, Frankie   431–2, 435

Yamamoto, Yohji   6, 34–8, 403
Yanai, Tadashi   52
Yang, Liu   434
Yazzie-Ballenger, Virginia   10
Y-front briefs   339
Yongnian, Zheng   433
Young, Lester   27
Yours magazine   328–31
Youth Dew   463
youthquake   17
You Tube   196, 197–8
Yunique PLM   166

Zahavi, Amotz   392
Zalando   169
Zambia   418
Zappos, online retailer   187
Zara   52, 54, 87, 99, 214, 420
Zazzle, mass customization website   172, 182–3, 187
ZDHC *see* Zero Discharge of Hazardous Chemicals (ZDHC)
Zecchi, Stefano   429
Zero Discharge of Hazardous Chemicals (ZDHC)   86
zero-waste model   88
Zeta-Jones, Catherine   154